NANCY
WEARS HATS

NANCY
WEARS HATS

ERNIE BUSHMILLER

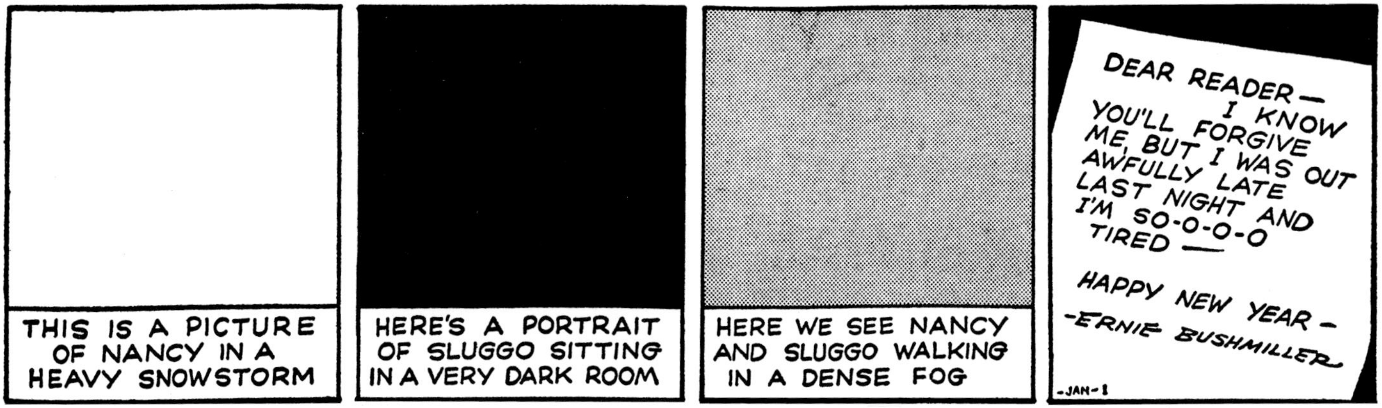
THIS IS A PICTURE OF NANCY IN A HEAVY SNOWSTORM
HERE'S A PORTRAIT OF SLUGGO SITTING IN A VERY DARK ROOM
HERE WE SEE NANCY AND SLUGGO WALKING IN A DENSE FOG
DEAR READER— I KNOW YOU'LL FORGIVE ME, BUT I WAS OUT AWFULLY LATE LAST NIGHT AND I'M SO-O-O-O TIRED —
HAPPY NEW YEAR -
-ERNIE BUSHMILLER
-JAN-1

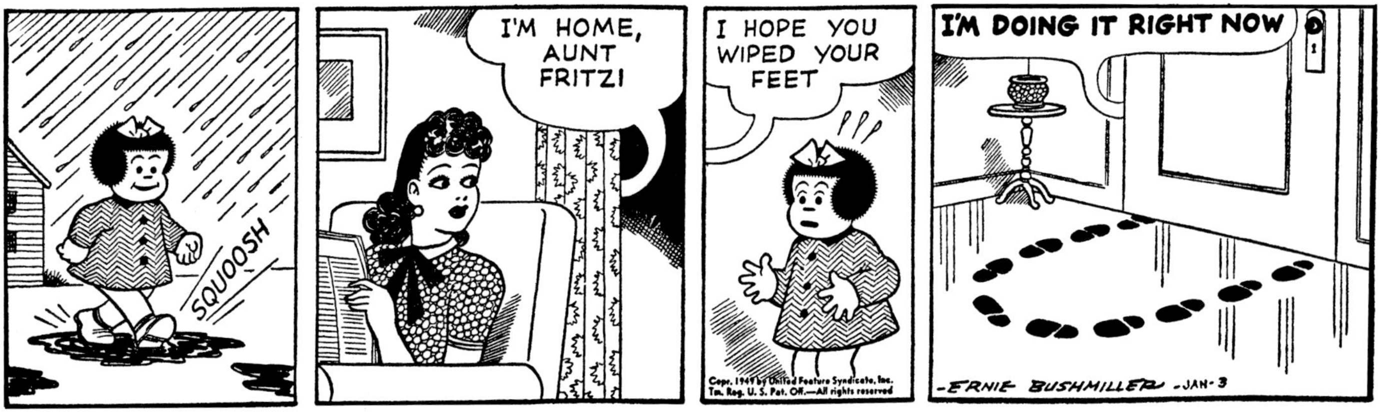
SQUOOSH
I'M HOME, AUNT FRITZI
I HOPE YOU WIPED YOUR FEET
Copr. 1949 by United Feature Syndicate, Inc. Tm. Reg. U. S. Pat. Off.—All rights reserved
I'M DOING IT RIGHT NOW
-ERNIE BUSHMILLER -JAN-3

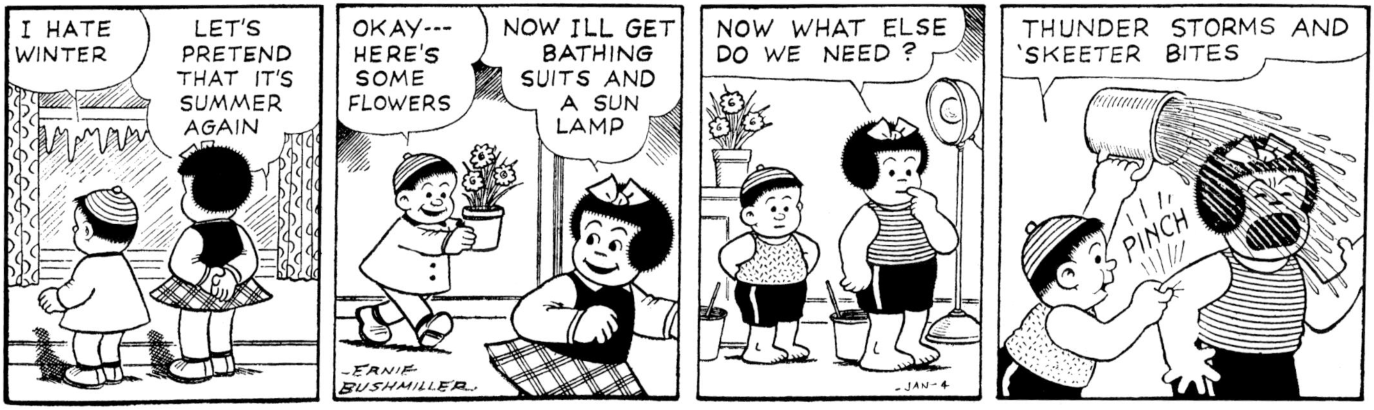
I HATE WINTER
LET'S PRETEND THAT IT'S SUMMER AGAIN
OKAY--- HERE'S SOME FLOWERS
NOW I'LL GET BATHING SUITS AND A SUN LAMP
-ERNIE BUSHMILLER
NOW WHAT ELSE DO WE NEED ?
-JAN-4
THUNDER STORMS AND 'SKEETER BITES
PINCH

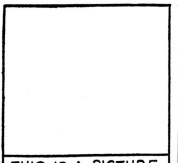

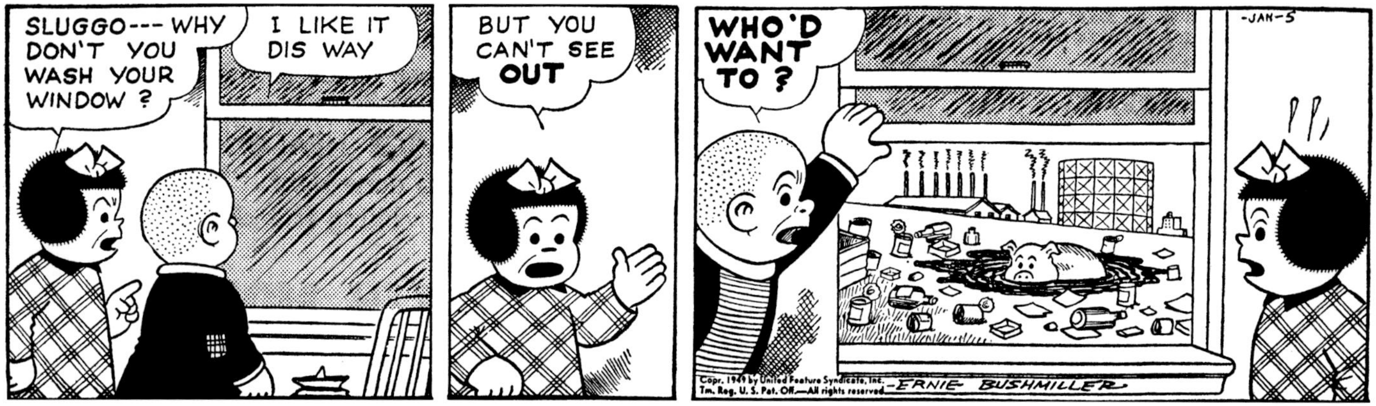
-JAN-5
SLUGGO--- WHY DON'T YOU WASH YOUR WINDOW ?
I LIKE IT DIS WAY
BUT YOU CAN'T SEE **OUT**
WHO'D WANT TO ?
Copr. 1949 by United Feature Syndicate, Inc. Tm. Reg. U. S. Pat. Off.—All rights reserved
-ERNIE BUSHMILLER

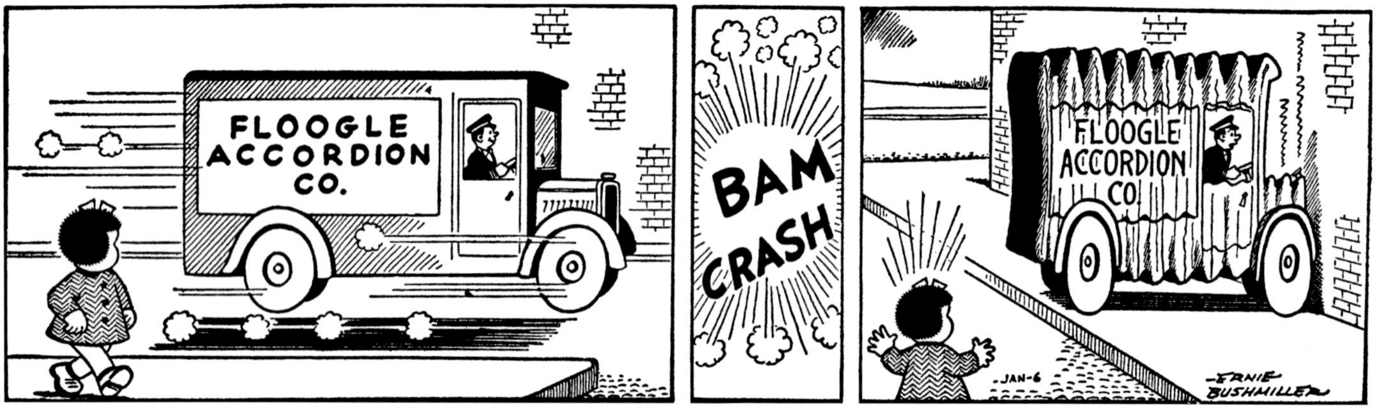
FLOOGLE ACCORDION CO.
BAM
CRASH
FLOOGLE ACCORDION CO.
-JAN-6
-ERNIE BUSHMILLER

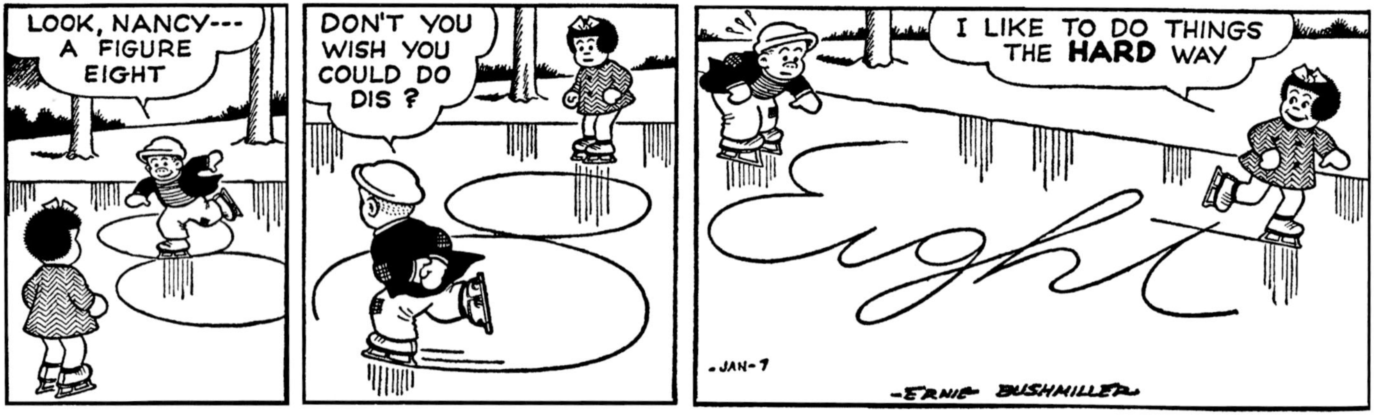
LOOK, NANCY--- A FIGURE EIGHT
DON'T YOU WISH YOU COULD DO DIS ?
I LIKE TO DO THINGS THE **HARD** WAY
eight
-JAN-7
-ERNIE BUSHMILLER

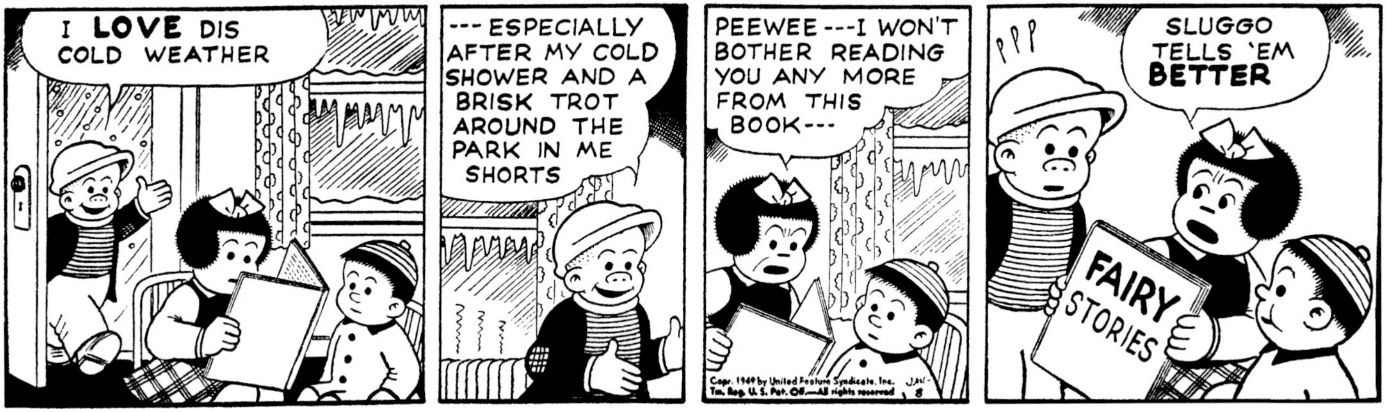
I LOVE DIS COLD WEATHER
--- ESPECIALLY AFTER MY COLD SHOWER AND A BRISK TROT AROUND THE PARK IN ME SHORTS
PEEWEE --- I WON'T BOTHER READING YOU ANY MORE FROM THIS BOOK---
Copr. 1949 by United Feature Syndicate, Inc. Tm. Reg. U. S. Pat. Off.—All rights reserved
JAN- 8
SLUGGO TELLS 'EM BETTER
FAIRY STORIES

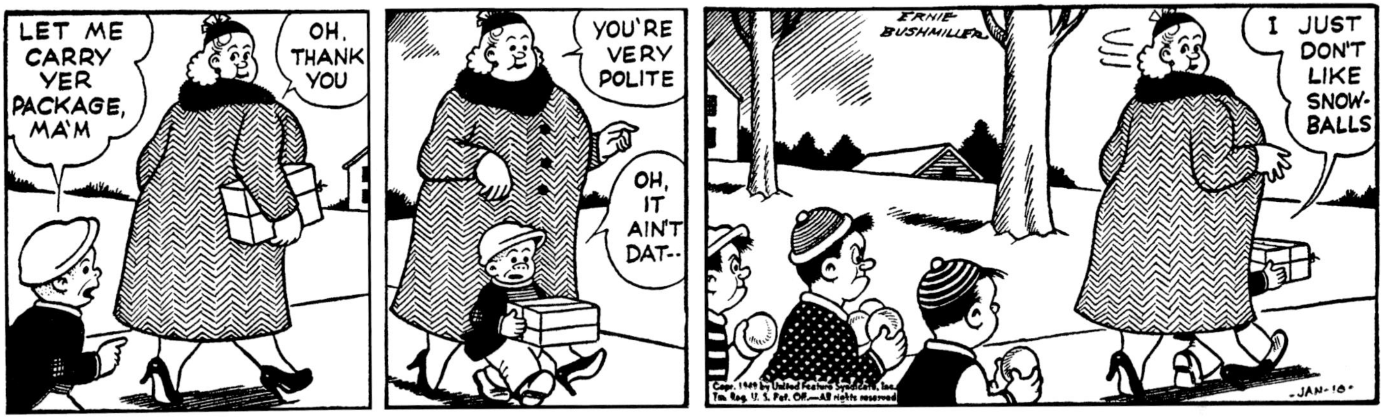
LET ME CARRY YER PACKAGE, MA'M
OH, THANK YOU
YOU'RE VERY POLITE
OH, IT AIN'T DAT--
ERNIE BUSHMILLER
I JUST DON'T LIKE SNOW-BALLS
Copr. 1949 by United Feature Syndicate, Inc. Tm. Reg. U. S. Pat. Off.—All rights reserved
JAN-10

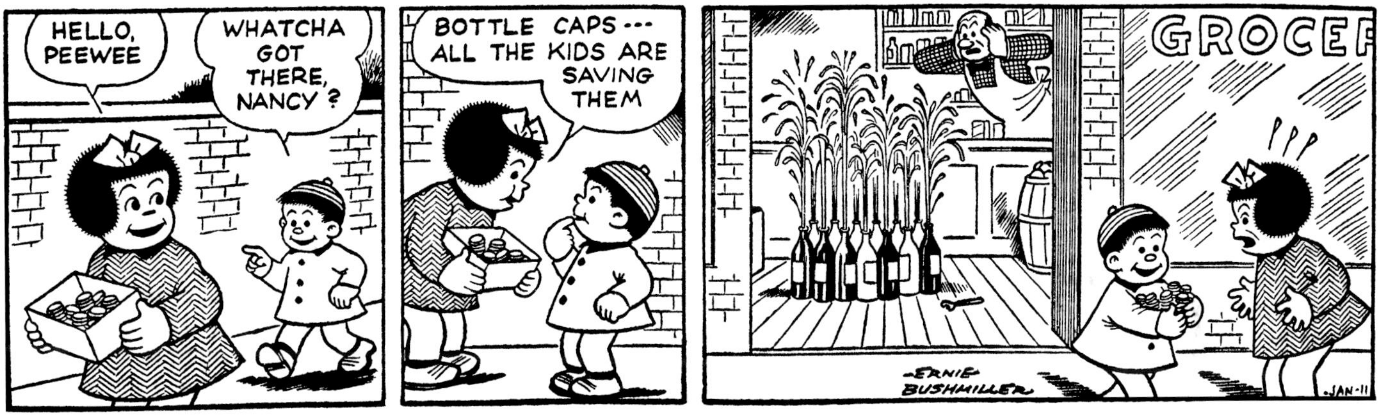
HELLO, PEEWEE
WHATCHA GOT THERE, NANCY ?
BOTTLE CAPS --- ALL THE KIDS ARE SAVING THEM
GROCEF
ERNIE BUSHMILLER
JAN-11

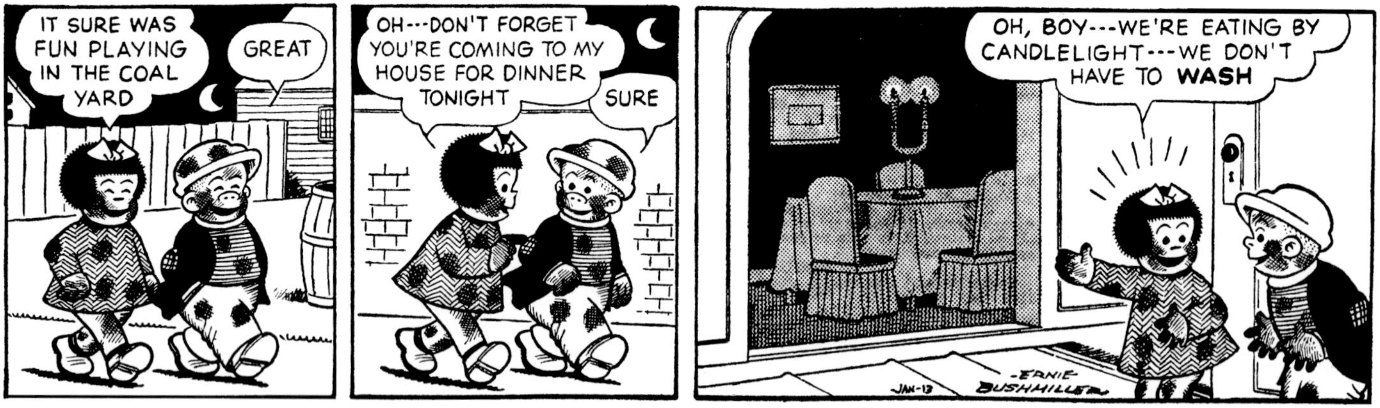

IT SURE WAS FUN PLAYING IN THE COAL YARD
GREAT
OH---DON'T FORGET YOU'RE COMING TO MY HOUSE FOR DINNER TONIGHT
SURE
OH, BOY---WE'RE EATING BY CANDLELIGHT---WE DON'T HAVE TO **WASH**
JAN-13
-ERNIE BUSHMILLER

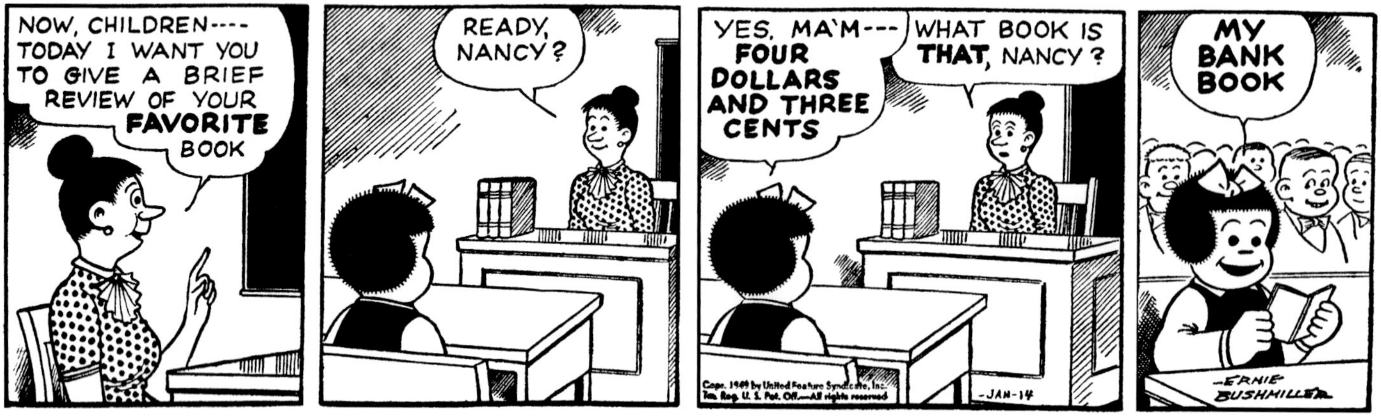

NOW, CHILDREN---- TODAY I WANT YOU TO GIVE A BRIEF REVIEW OF YOUR **FAVORITE** BOOK
READY, NANCY?
YES, MA'M--- **FOUR DOLLARS AND THREE CENTS**
WHAT BOOK IS **THAT**, NANCY?
Copr. 1949 by United Feature Syndicate, Inc. Tm. Reg. U. S. Pat. Off.—All rights reserved
-JAN-14
MY BANK BOOK
-ERNIE BUSHMILLER

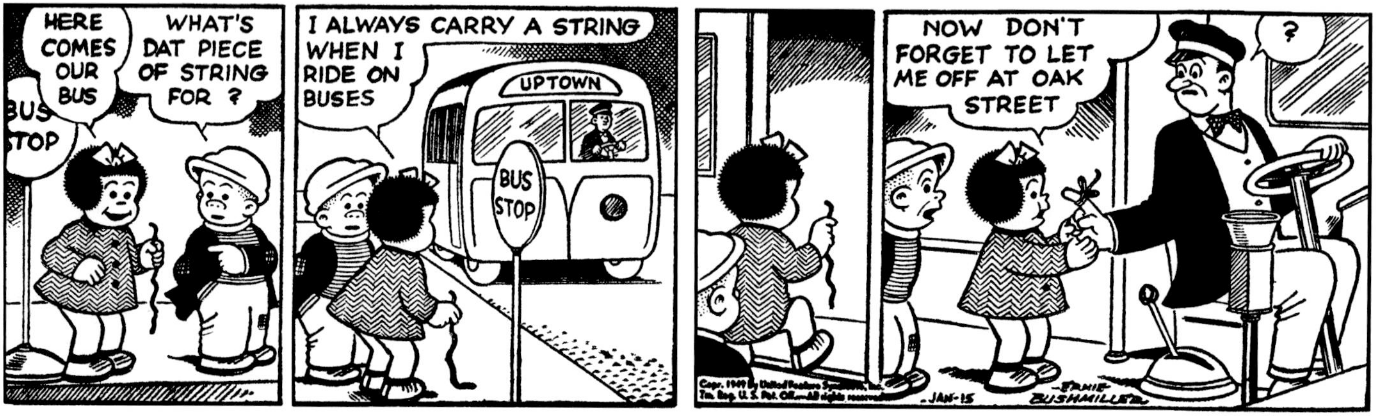

HERE COMES OUR BUS
WHAT'S DAT PIECE OF STRING FOR ?
BUS STOP
I ALWAYS CARRY A STRING WHEN I RIDE ON BUSES
UPTOWN
BUS STOP
NOW DON'T FORGET TO LET ME OFF AT OAK STREET
?
-JAN-15
-ERNIE BUSHMILLER

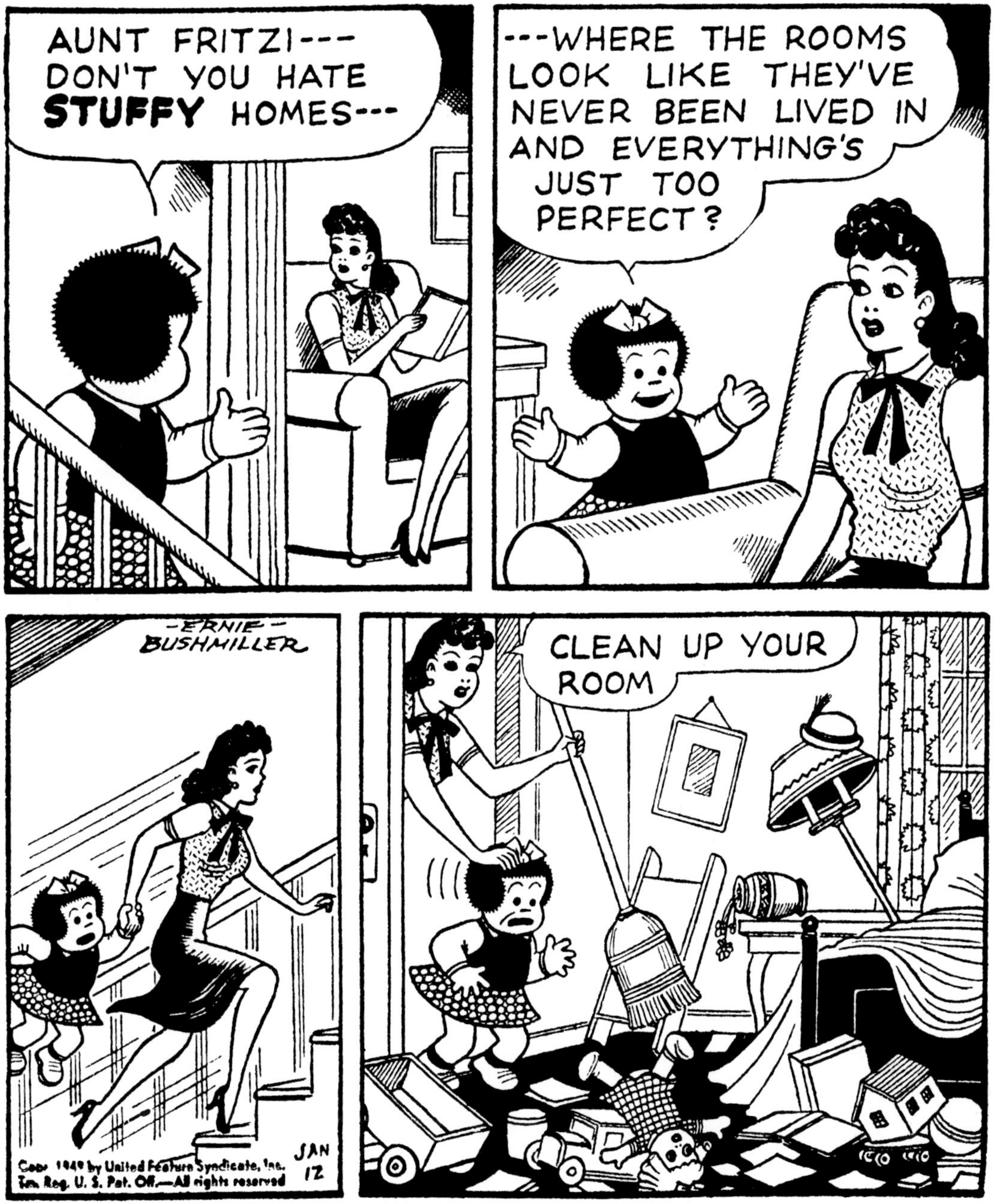
AUNT FRITZI--- DON'T YOU HATE **STUFFY** HOMES---
---WHERE THE ROOMS LOOK LIKE THEY'VE NEVER BEEN LIVED IN AND EVERYTHING'S JUST TOO PERFECT?
-ERNIE- BUSHMILLER
Copr. 1949 by United Feature Syndicate, Inc. Tm. Reg. U. S. Pat. Off.—All rights reserved
JAN 12
CLEAN UP YOUR ROOM

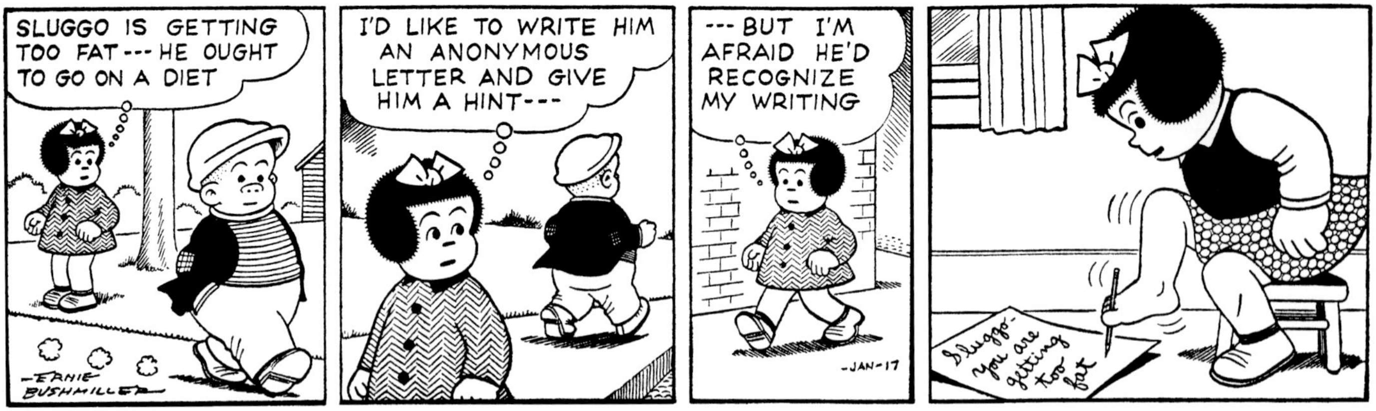
SLUGGO IS GETTING TOO FAT --- HE OUGHT TO GO ON A DIET
-ERNIE BUSHMILLER
I'D LIKE TO WRITE HIM AN ANONYMOUS LETTER AND GIVE HIM A HINT---
--- BUT I'M AFRAID HE'D RECOGNIZE MY WRITING
-JAN-17
Sluggo- you are getting too fat

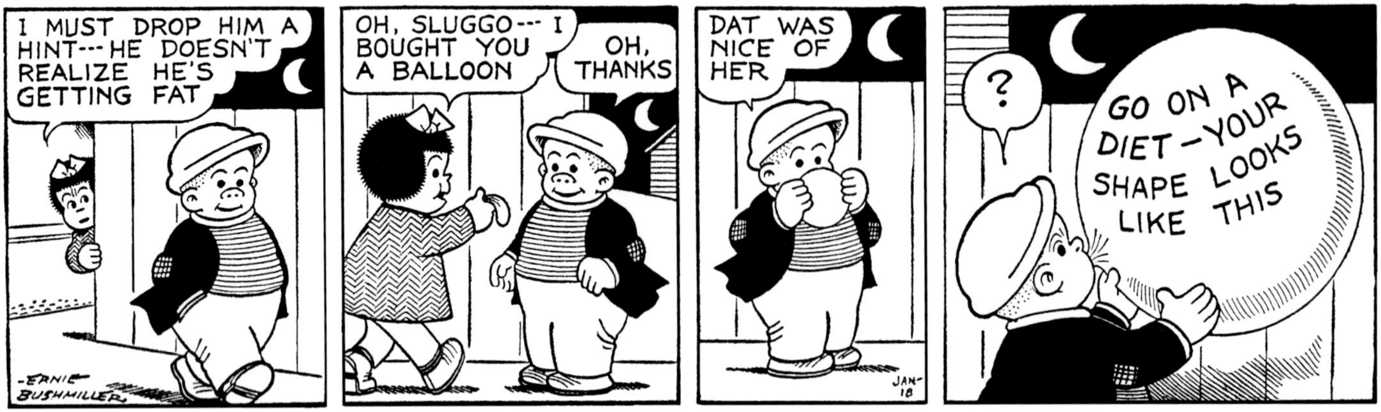
I MUST DROP HIM A HINT---HE DOESN'T REALIZE HE'S GETTING FAT
-ERNIE BUSHMILLER
OH, SLUGGO--- I BOUGHT YOU A BALLOON
OH, THANKS
DAT WAS NICE OF HER
JAN-18
?
GO ON A DIET - YOUR SHAPE LOOKS LIKE THIS

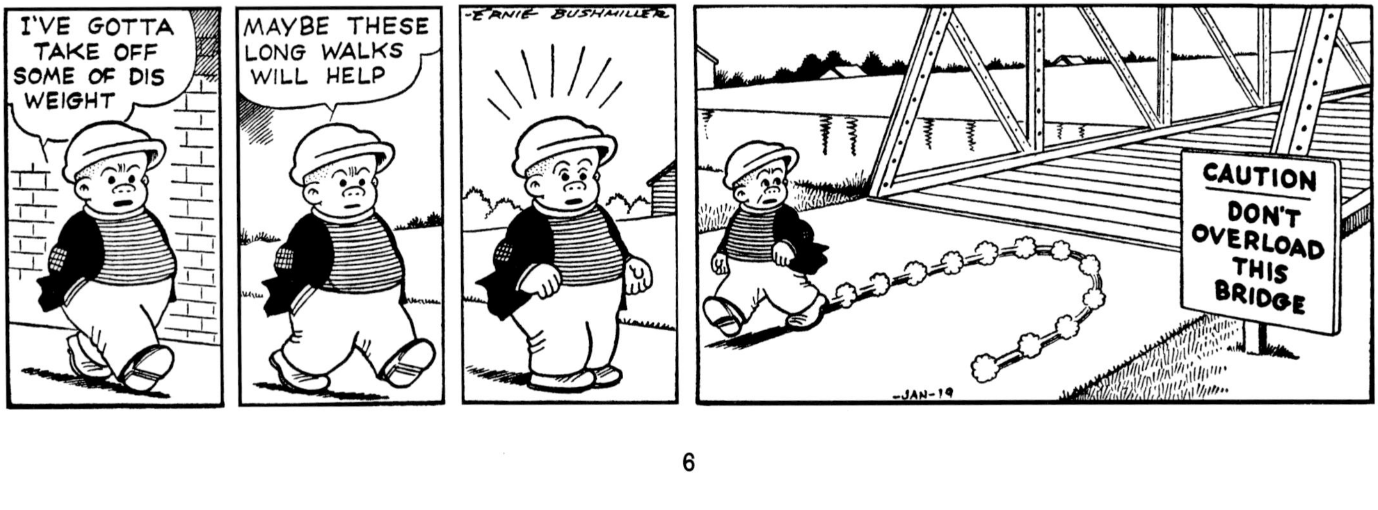
I'VE GOTTA TAKE OFF SOME OF DIS WEIGHT
MAYBE THESE LONG WALKS WILL HELP
-ERNIE BUSHMILLER
CAUTION
DON'T OVERLOAD THIS BRIDGE
-JAN-19

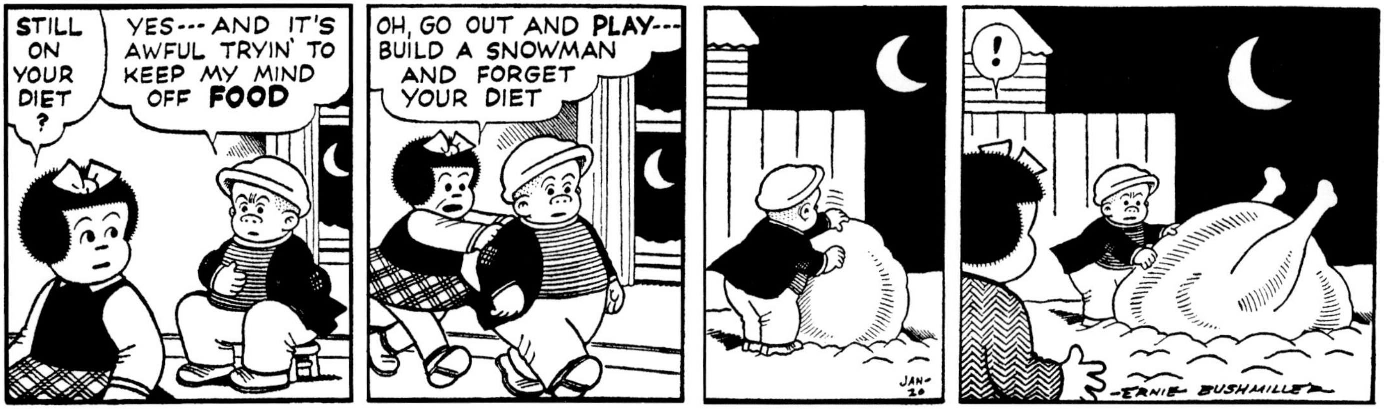
STILL ON YOUR DIET ?
YES--- AND IT'S AWFUL TRYIN' TO KEEP MY MIND OFF **FOOD**
OH, GO OUT AND **PLAY**--- BUILD A SNOWMAN AND FORGET YOUR DIET
JAN-20
!
-ERNIE BUSHMILLER

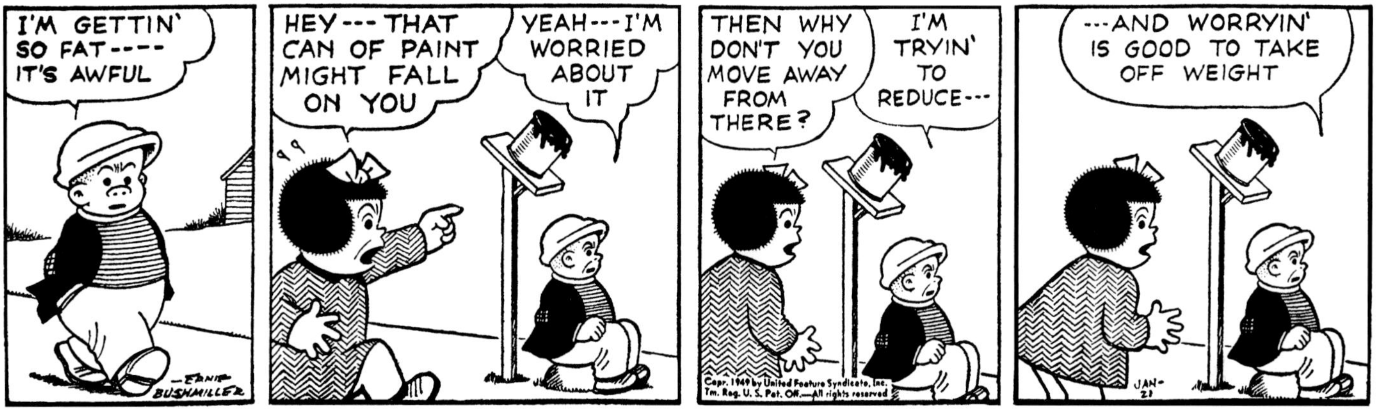
I'M GETTIN' SO FAT---- IT'S AWFUL
-ERNIE BUSHMILLER
HEY--- THAT CAN OF PAINT MIGHT FALL ON YOU
YEAH--- I'M WORRIED ABOUT IT
THEN WHY DON'T YOU MOVE AWAY FROM THERE?
I'M TRYIN' TO REDUCE---
Copr. 1949 by United Feature Syndicate, Inc.
Tm. Reg. U. S. Pat. Off.—All rights reserved
---AND WORRYIN' IS GOOD TO TAKE OFF WEIGHT
JAN-21

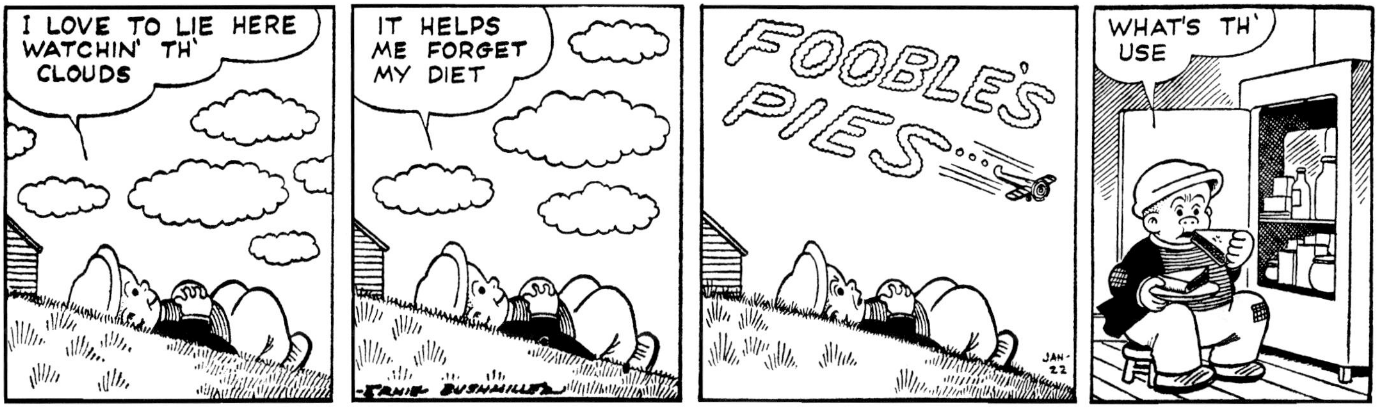
I LOVE TO LIE HERE WATCHIN' TH' CLOUDS
IT HELPS ME FORGET MY DIET
-ERNIE BUSHMILLER
FOOBLE'S PIES
JAN-22
WHAT'S TH' USE

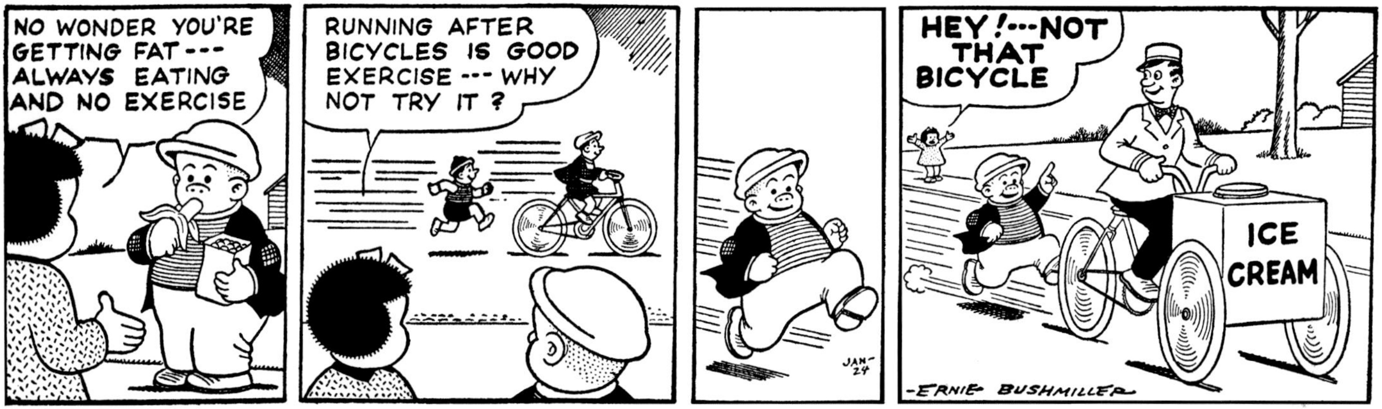
NO WONDER YOU'RE GETTING FAT --- ALWAYS EATING AND NO EXERCISE
RUNNING AFTER BICYCLES IS GOOD EXERCISE --- WHY NOT TRY IT ?
JAN-24
HEY !---NOT THAT BICYCLE
ICE CREAM
-ERNIE BUSHMILLER

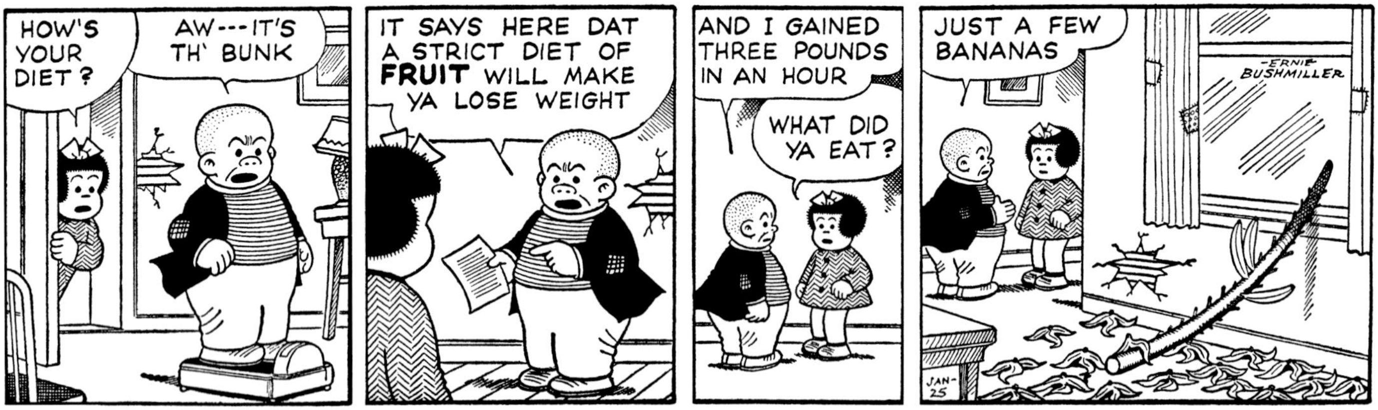
HOW'S YOUR DIET ?
AW---IT'S TH' BUNK
IT SAYS HERE DAT A STRICT DIET OF FRUIT WILL MAKE YA LOSE WEIGHT
AND I GAINED THREE POUNDS IN AN HOUR
WHAT DID YA EAT ?
JUST A FEW BANANAS
-ERNIE BUSHMILLER
JAN-25

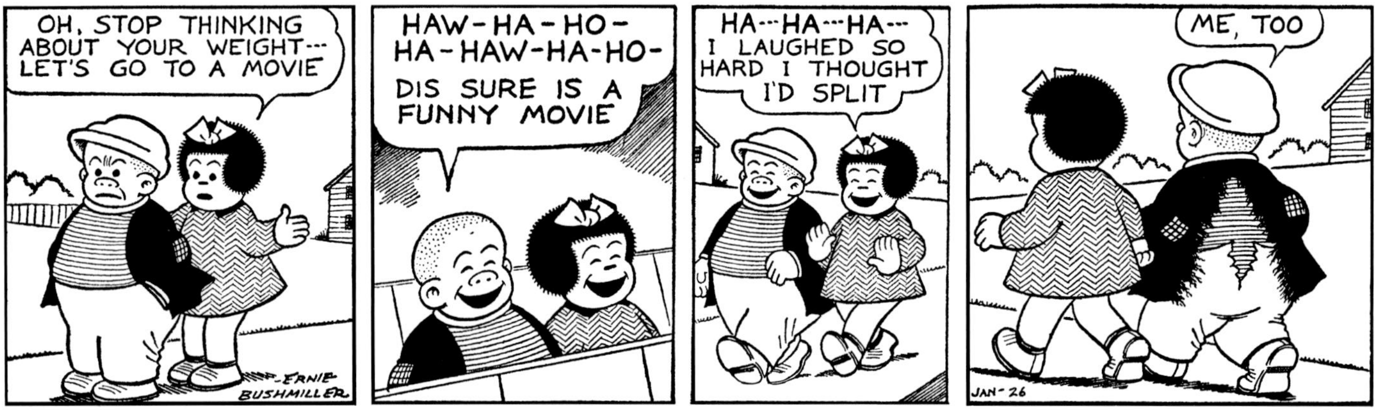
OH, STOP THINKING ABOUT YOUR WEIGHT--- LET'S GO TO A MOVIE
-ERNIE BUSHMILLER
HAW-HA-HO-HA-HAW-HA-HO-
DIS SURE IS A FUNNY MOVIE
HA---HA---HA--- I LAUGHED SO HARD I THOUGHT I'D SPLIT
ME, TOO
JAN-26

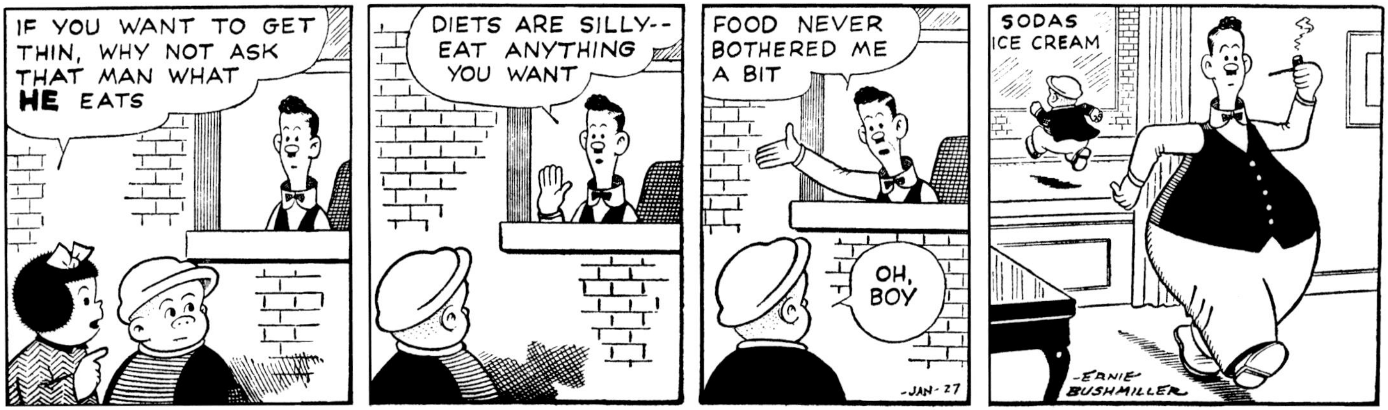
IF YOU WANT TO GET THIN, WHY NOT ASK THAT MAN WHAT HE EATS
DIETS ARE SILLY-- EAT ANYTHING YOU WANT
FOOD NEVER BOTHERED ME A BIT
OH, BOY
JAN-27
SODAS
ICE CREAM
-ERNIE BUSHMILLER

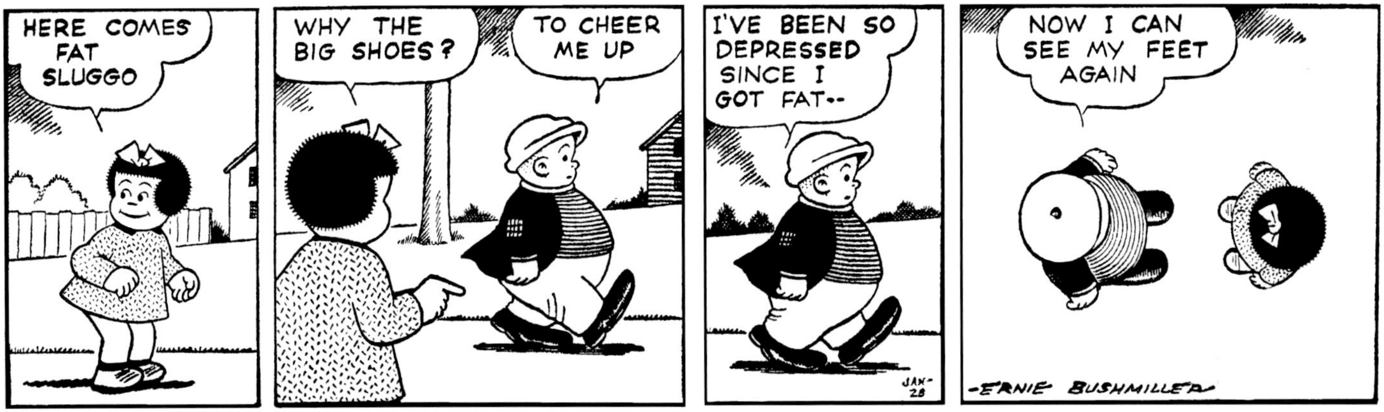
HERE COMES FAT SLUGGO
WHY THE BIG SHOES?
TO CHEER ME UP
I'VE BEEN SO DEPRESSED SINCE I GOT FAT--
JAN-28
NOW I CAN SEE MY FEET AGAIN
-ERNIE BUSHMILLER

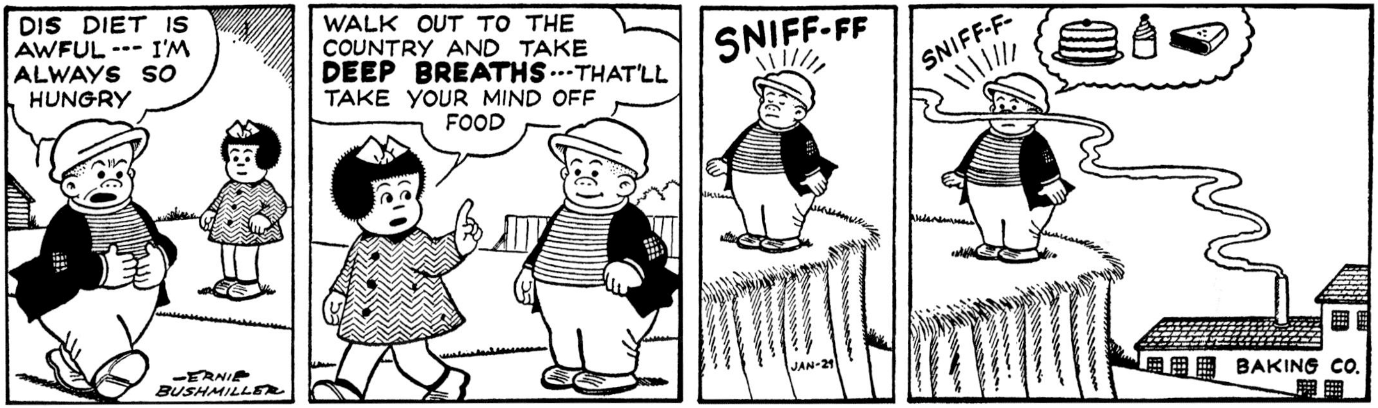
DIS DIET IS AWFUL--- I'M ALWAYS SO HUNGRY
-ERNIE BUSHMILLER
WALK OUT TO THE COUNTRY AND TAKE DEEP BREATHS---THAT'LL TAKE YOUR MIND OFF FOOD
SNIFF-FF
JAN-21
SNIFF-F-
BAKING CO.

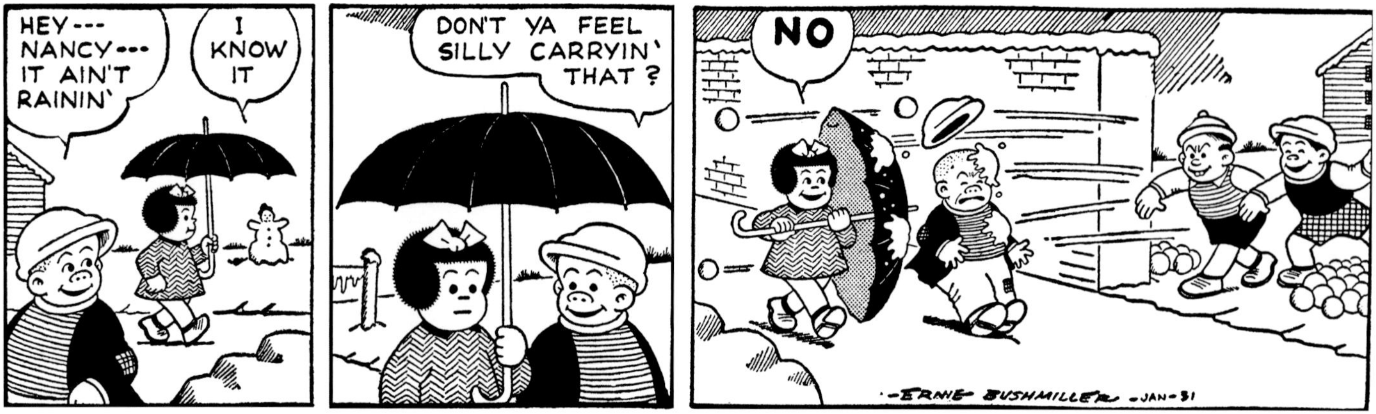
HEY--- NANCY--- IT AIN'T RAININ'
I KNOW IT
DON'T YA FEEL SILLY CARRYIN' THAT ?
NO
-ERNIE BUSHMILLER -JAN-31

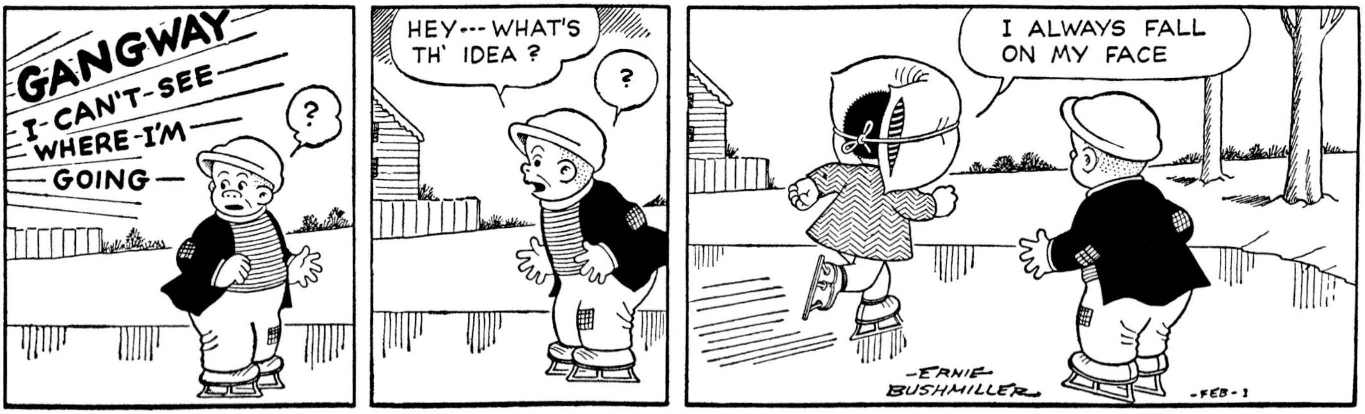
GANGWAY I-CAN'T-SEE WHERE-I'M GOING
?
HEY--- WHAT'S TH' IDEA ?
?
I ALWAYS FALL ON MY FACE
-ERNIE BUSHMILLER
-FEB-1

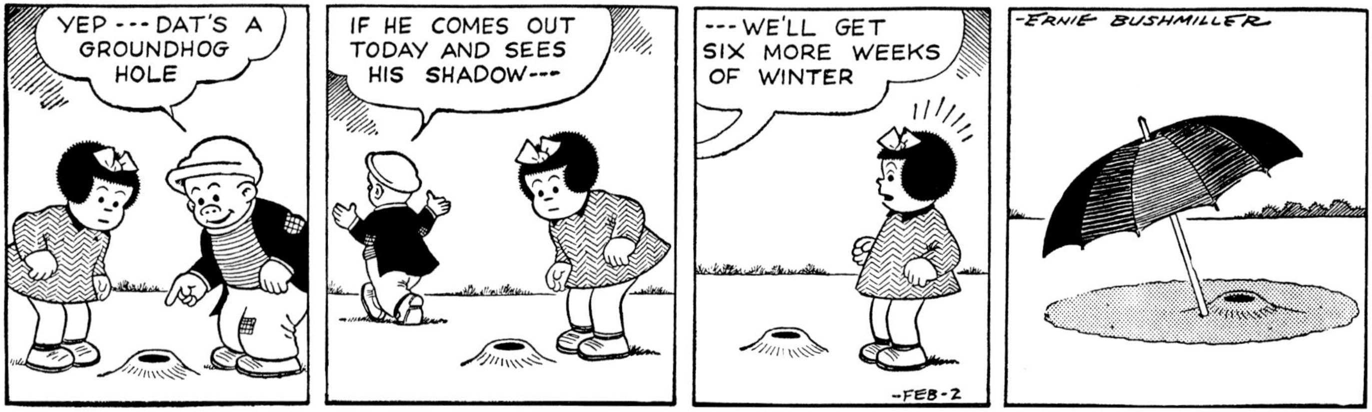
YEP--- DAT'S A GROUNDHOG HOLE
IF HE COMES OUT TODAY AND SEES HIS SHADOW---
---WE'LL GET SIX MORE WEEKS OF WINTER
-FEB-2
-ERNIE BUSHMILLER

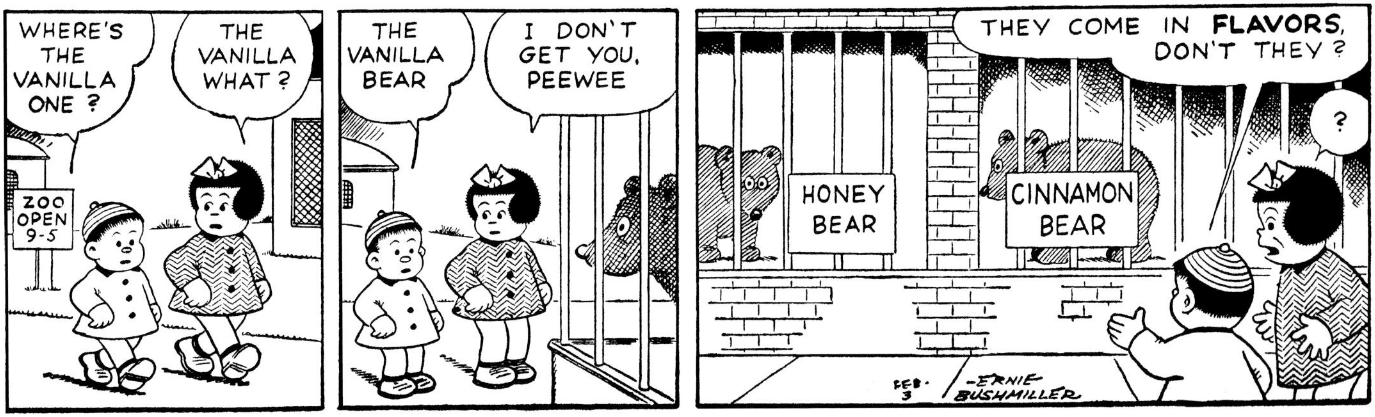
WHERE'S THE VANILLA ONE ?
THE VANILLA WHAT ?
ZOO OPEN 9-5
THE VANILLA BEAR
I DON'T GET YOU, PEEWEE
THEY COME IN **FLAVORS**, DON'T THEY ?
HONEY BEAR
CINNAMON BEAR
?
FEB. 3
ERNIE BUSHMILLER

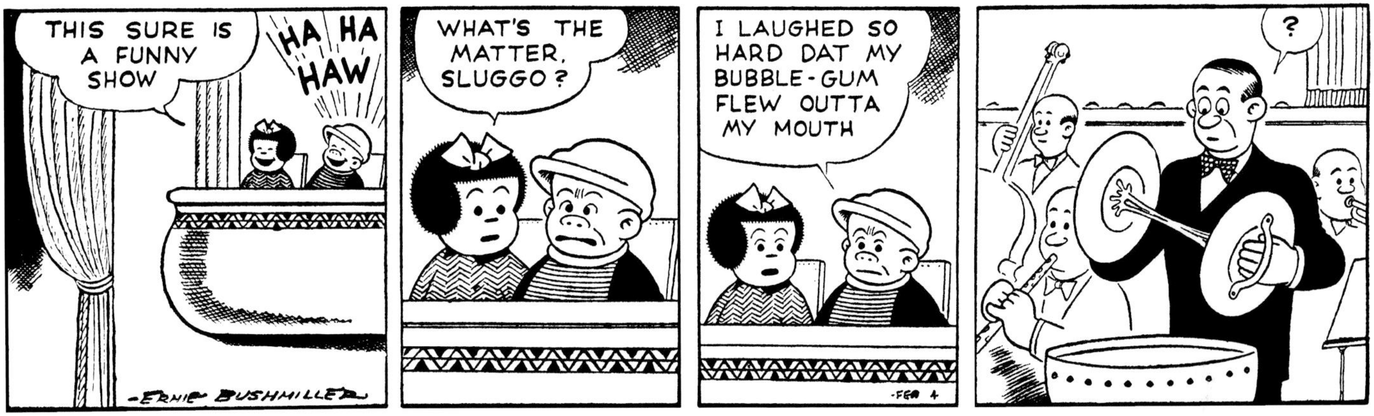
THIS SURE IS A FUNNY SHOW
HA HA HAW
ERNIE BUSHMILLER
WHAT'S THE MATTER, SLUGGO ?
I LAUGHED SO HARD DAT MY BUBBLE-GUM FLEW OUTTA MY MOUTH
FEB 4
?

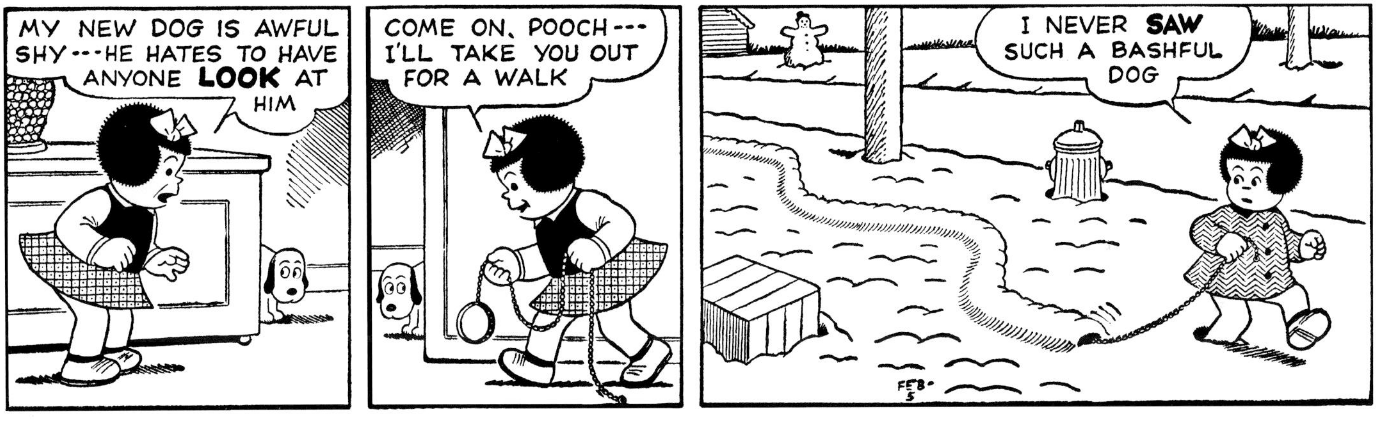
MY NEW DOG IS AWFUL SHY---HE HATES TO HAVE ANYONE **LOOK** AT HIM
COME ON, POOCH--- I'LL TAKE YOU OUT FOR A WALK
I NEVER **SAW** SUCH A BASHFUL DOG
FEB. 5

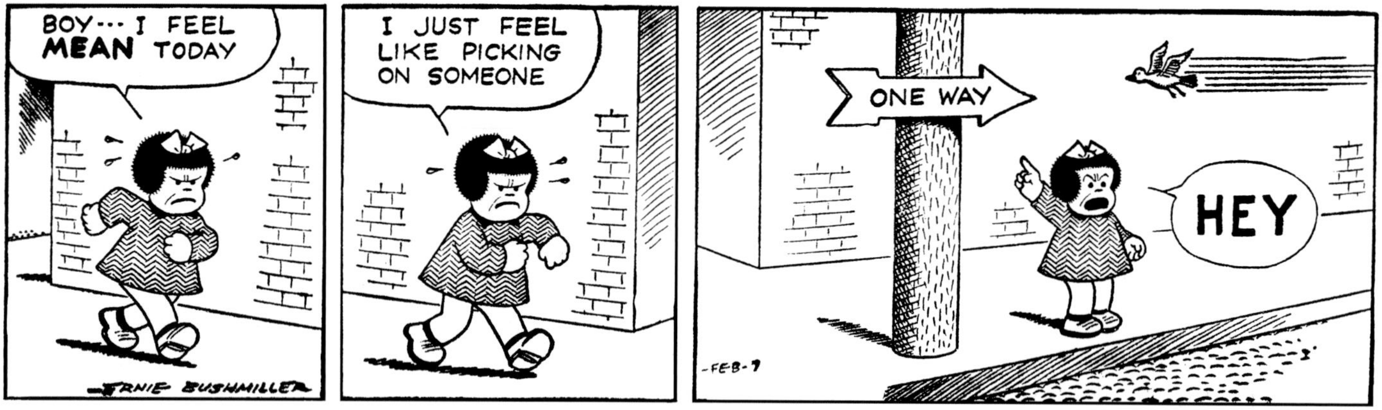
BOY--- I FEEL **MEAN** TODAY
ERNIE BUSHMILLER
I JUST FEEL LIKE PICKING ON SOMEONE
ONE WAY
HEY
FEB-7

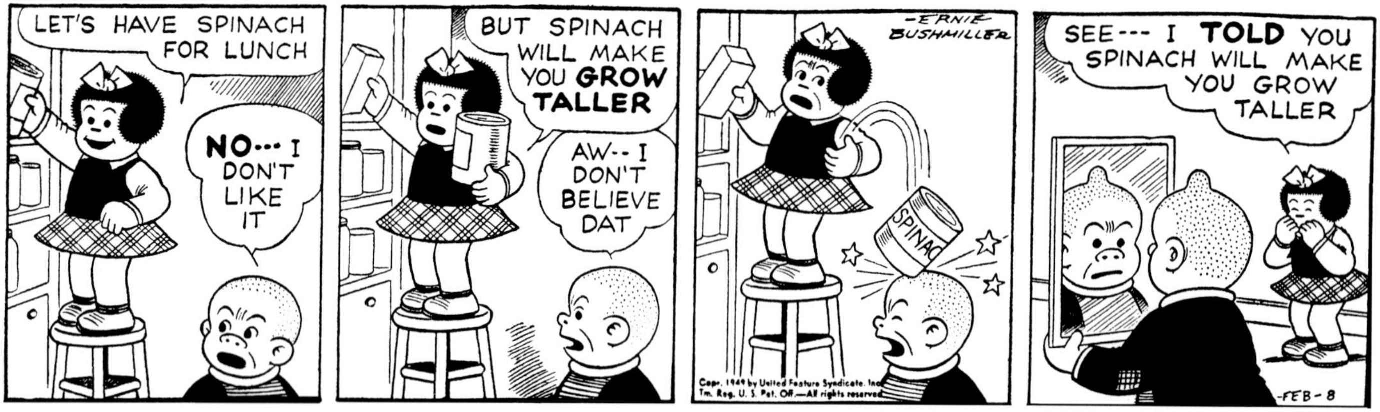
LET'S HAVE SPINACH FOR LUNCH
NO--- I DON'T LIKE IT
BUT SPINACH WILL MAKE YOU **GROW TALLER**
AW-- I DON'T BELIEVE DAT
ERNIE BUSHMILLER
SPINAC
Copr. 1949 by United Feature Syndicate, Inc.
Tm. Reg. U. S. Pat. Off.—All rights reserved
SEE--- I **TOLD** YOU SPINACH WILL MAKE YOU GROW TALLER
FEB-8

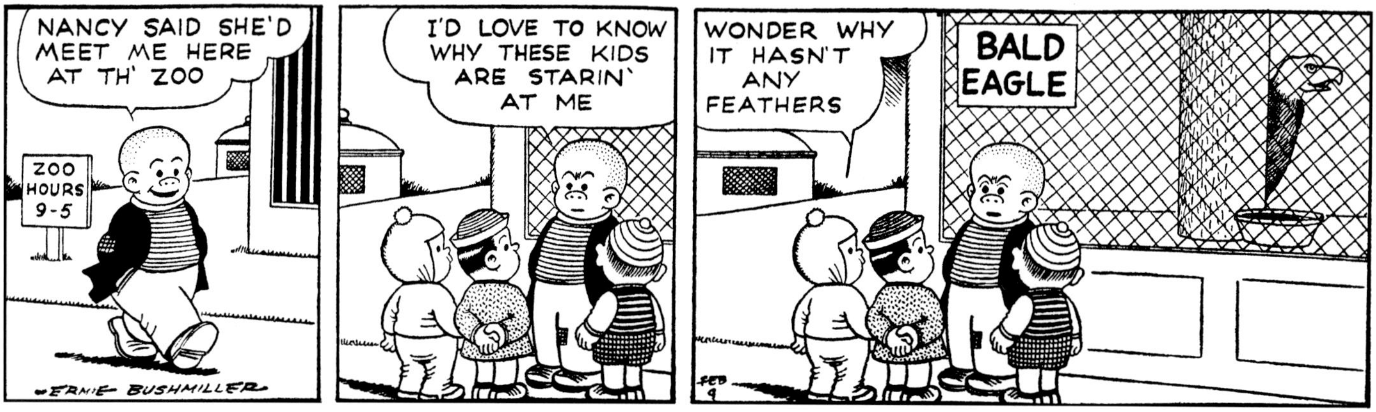
NANCY SAID SHE'D MEET ME HERE AT TH' ZOO
ZOO HOURS 9-5
ERNIE BUSHMILLER
I'D LOVE TO KNOW WHY THESE KIDS ARE STARIN' AT ME
WONDER WHY IT HASN'T ANY FEATHERS
BALD EAGLE
FEB 9

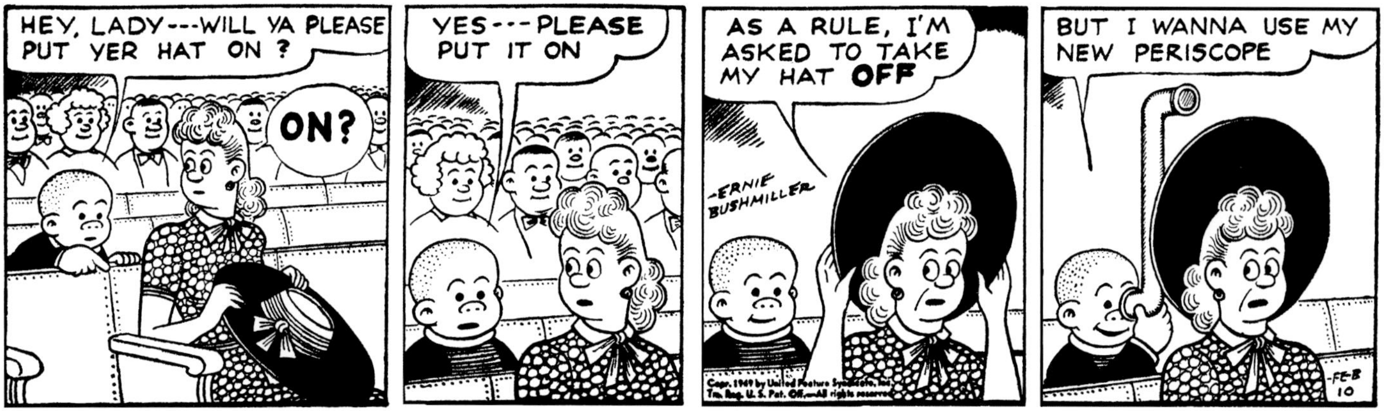
HEY, LADY---WILL YA PLEASE PUT YER HAT ON ?
ON?
YES---PLEASE PUT IT ON
AS A RULE, I'M ASKED TO TAKE MY HAT OFF
-ERNIE BUSHMILLER
Copr. 1949 by United Feature Syndicate, Inc. Tm. Reg. U. S. Pat. Off.—All rights reserved
BUT I WANNA USE MY NEW PERISCOPE
-FE-B 10

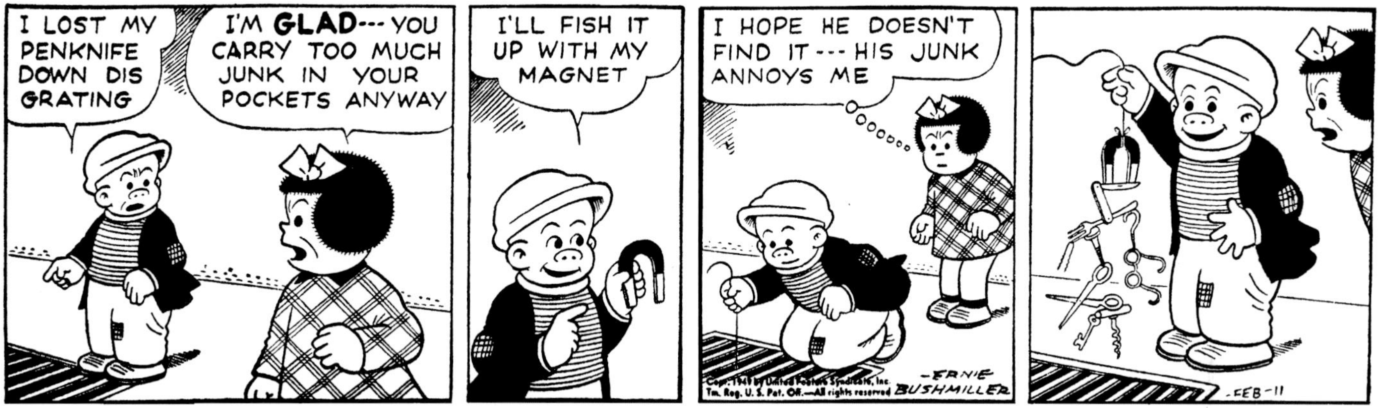
I LOST MY PENKNIFE DOWN DIS GRATING
I'M GLAD--- YOU CARRY TOO MUCH JUNK IN YOUR POCKETS ANYWAY
I'LL FISH IT UP WITH MY MAGNET
I HOPE HE DOESN'T FIND IT---HIS JUNK ANNOYS ME
Copr. 1949 by United Feature Syndicate, Inc. Tm. Reg. U. S. Pat. Off.—All rights reserved
-ERNIE BUSHMILLER
-FEB-11

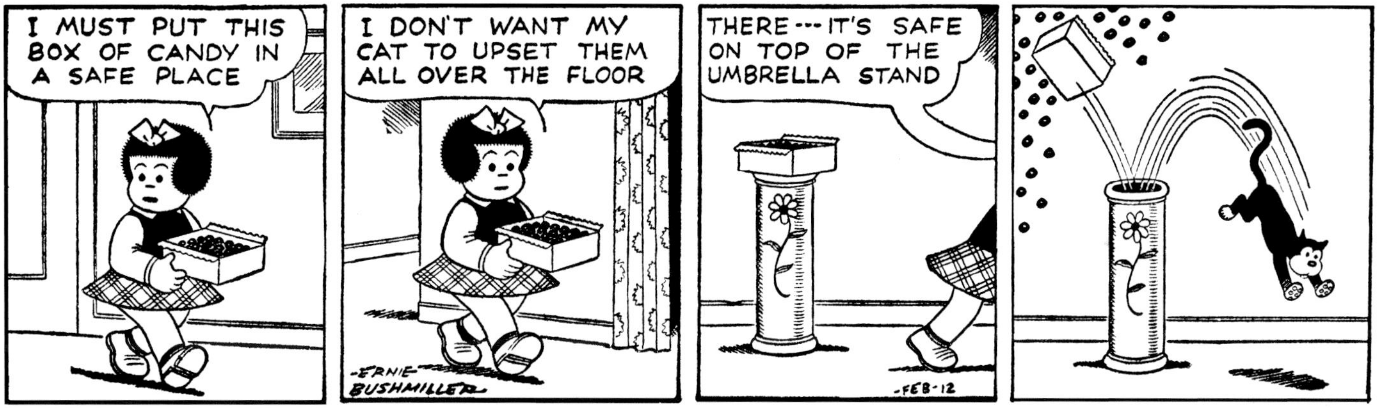
I MUST PUT THIS BOX OF CANDY IN A SAFE PLACE
I DON'T WANT MY CAT TO UPSET THEM ALL OVER THE FLOOR
-ERNIE BUSHMILLER
THERE---IT'S SAFE ON TOP OF THE UMBRELLA STAND
-FEB-12

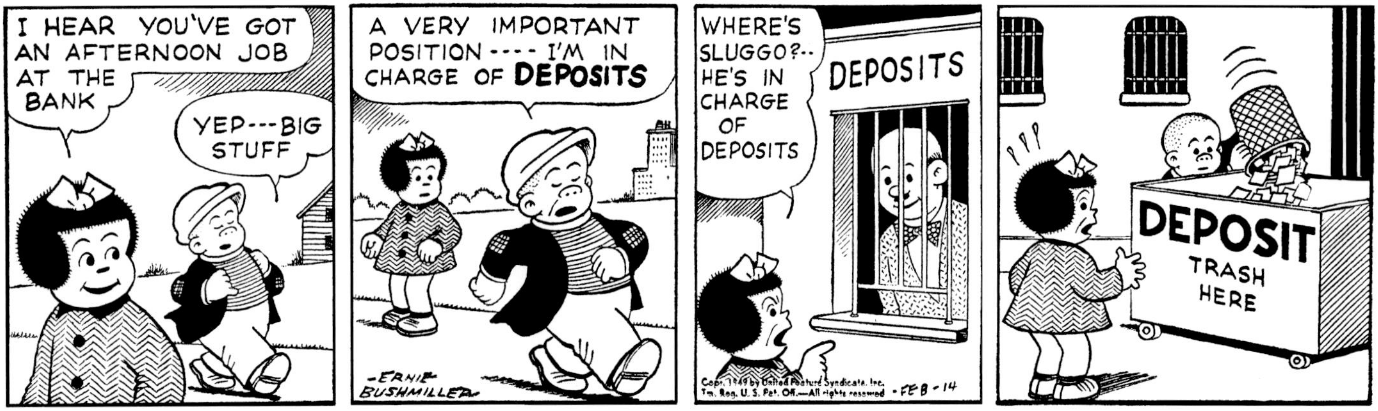
I HEAR YOU'VE GOT AN AFTERNOON JOB AT THE BANK
YEP---BIG STUFF
A VERY IMPORTANT POSITION ---- I'M IN CHARGE OF **DEPOSITS**
-ERNIE BUSHMILLER
WHERE'S SLUGGO?-- HE'S IN CHARGE OF DEPOSITS
DEPOSITS
Copr. 1949 by United Feature Syndicate, Inc. Tm. Reg. U. S. Pat. Off.—All rights reserved
-FEB-14
DEPOSIT
TRASH HERE

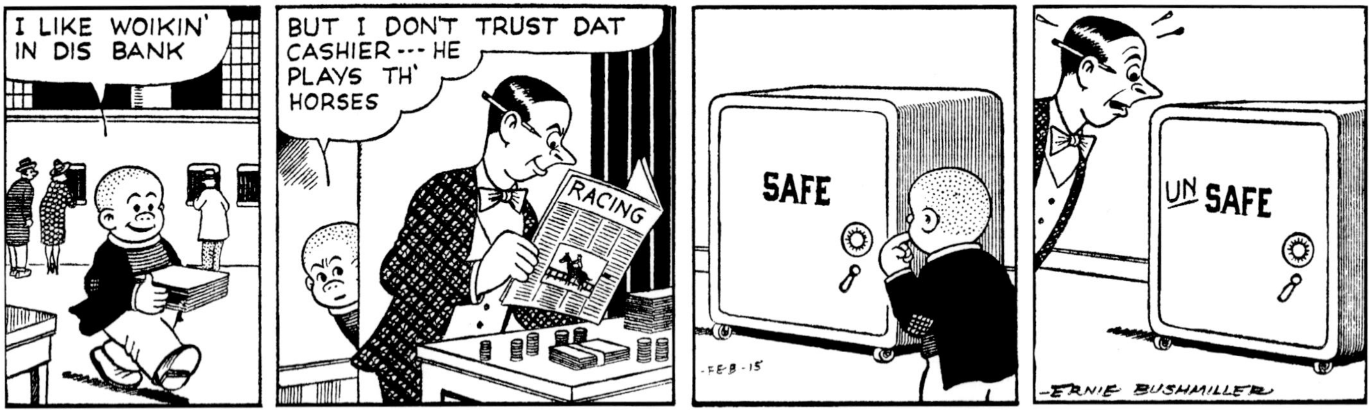
I LIKE WOIKIN' IN DIS BANK
BUT I DON'T TRUST DAT CASHIER --- HE PLAYS TH' HORSES
RACING
SAFE
-FEB-15
UN SAFE
-ERNIE BUSHMILLER

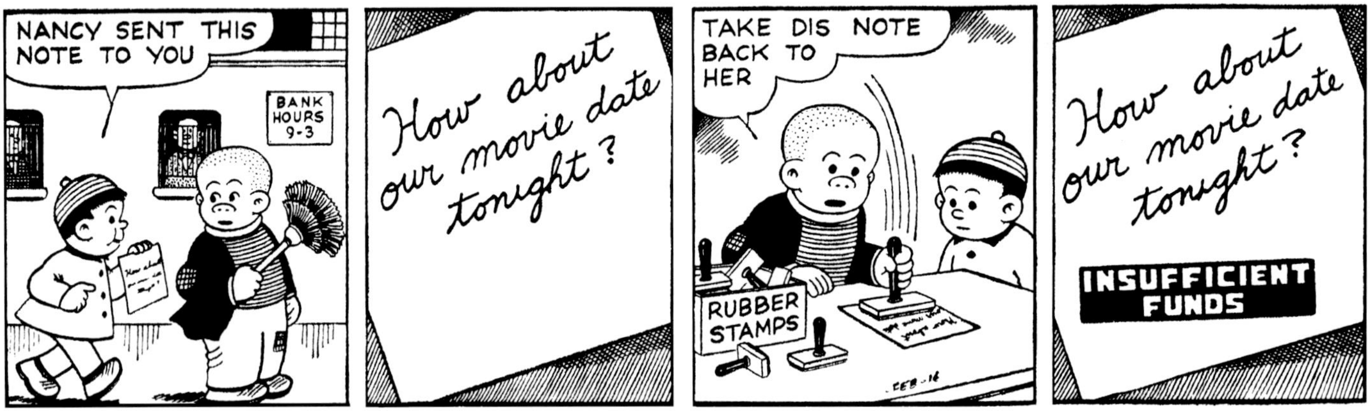
NANCY SENT THIS NOTE TO YOU
BANK HOURS 9-3
How about our movie date tonight?
TAKE DIS NOTE BACK TO HER
RUBBER STAMPS
-FEB-16
How about our movie date tonight?
INSUFFICIENT FUNDS

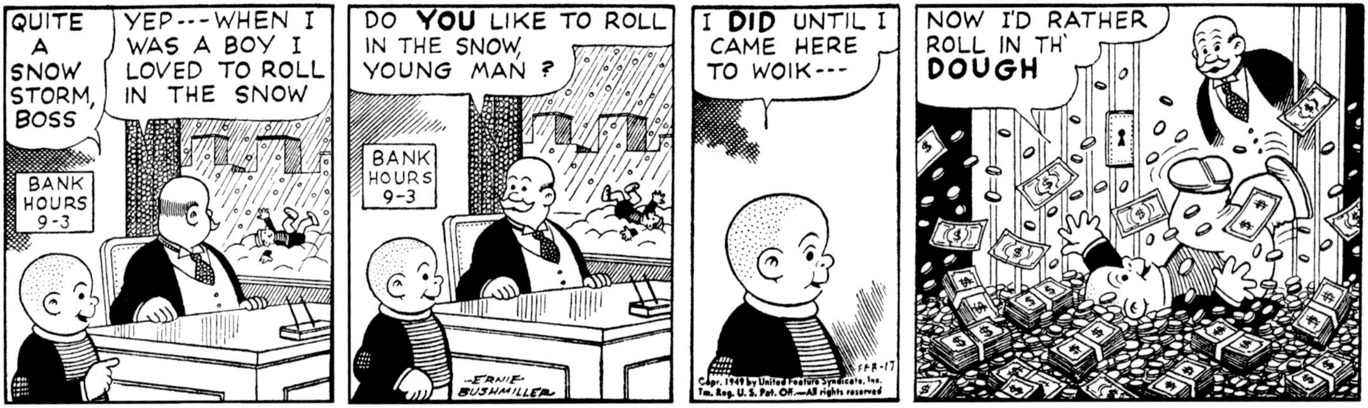
QUITE A SNOW STORM, BOSS
YEP---WHEN I WAS A BOY I LOVED TO ROLL IN THE SNOW
BANK HOURS 9-3
DO YOU LIKE TO ROLL IN THE SNOW, YOUNG MAN ?
BANK HOURS 9-3
-ERNIE BUSHMILLER
I DID UNTIL I CAME HERE TO WOIK---
FEB-17
Copr. 1949 by United Feature Syndicate, Inc. Tm. Reg. U. S. Pat. Off.—All rights reserved
NOW I'D RATHER ROLL IN TH' DOUGH

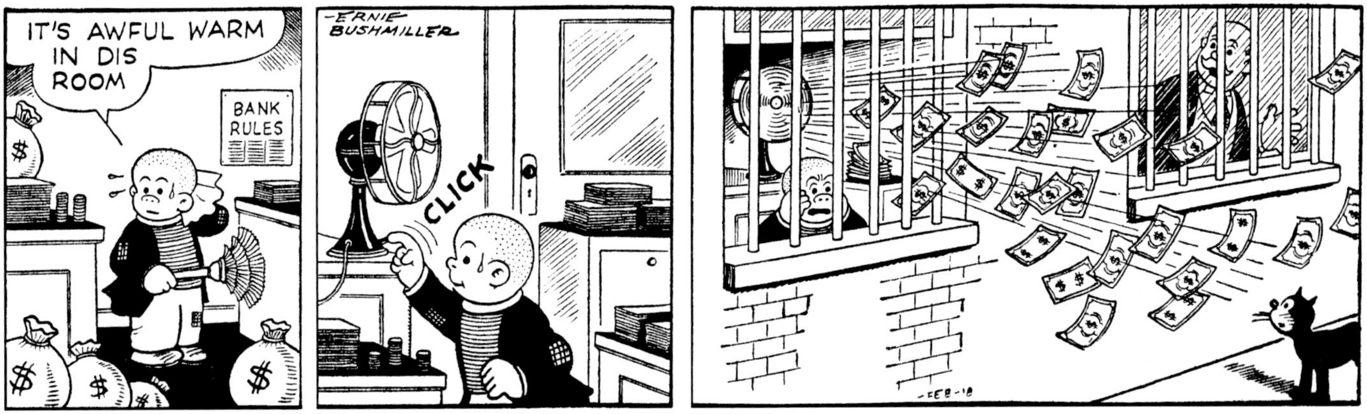
IT'S AWFUL WARM IN DIS ROOM
BANK RULES
-ERNIE BUSHMILLER
CLICK
FEB-18

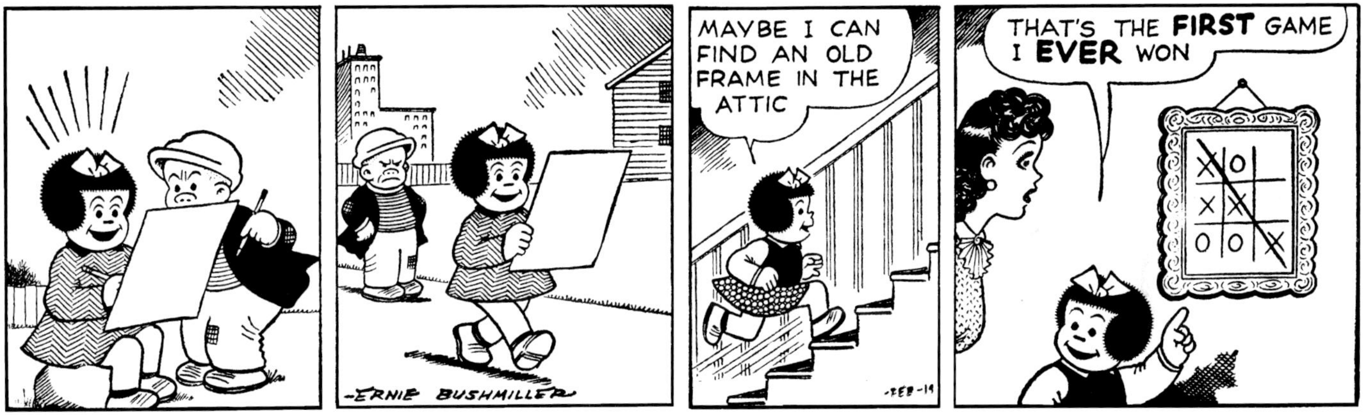
-ERNIE BUSHMILLER
MAYBE I CAN FIND AN OLD FRAME IN THE ATTIC
FEB-19
THAT'S THE FIRST GAME I EVER WON

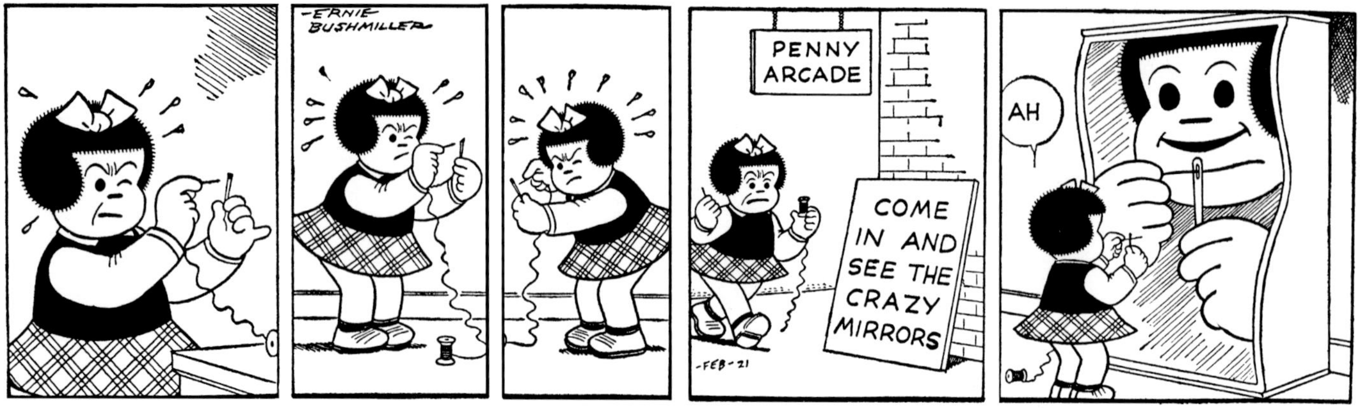
-ERNIE BUSHMILLER
PENNY ARCADE
COME IN AND SEE THE CRAZY MIRRORS
-FEB-21
AH

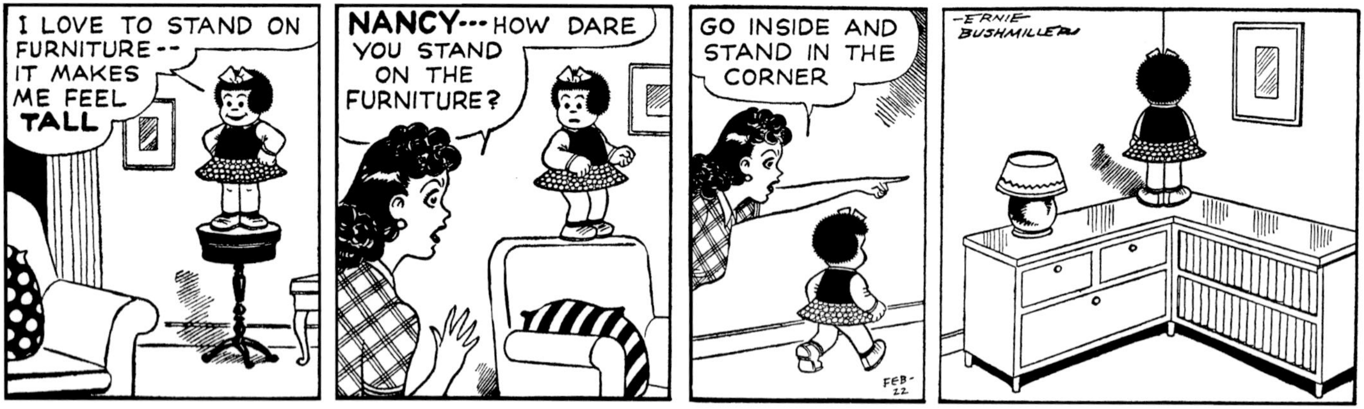
I LOVE TO STAND ON FURNITURE-- IT MAKES ME FEEL TALL
NANCY--- HOW DARE YOU STAND ON THE FURNITURE?
GO INSIDE AND STAND IN THE CORNER
FEB-22
-ERNIE BUSHMILLER

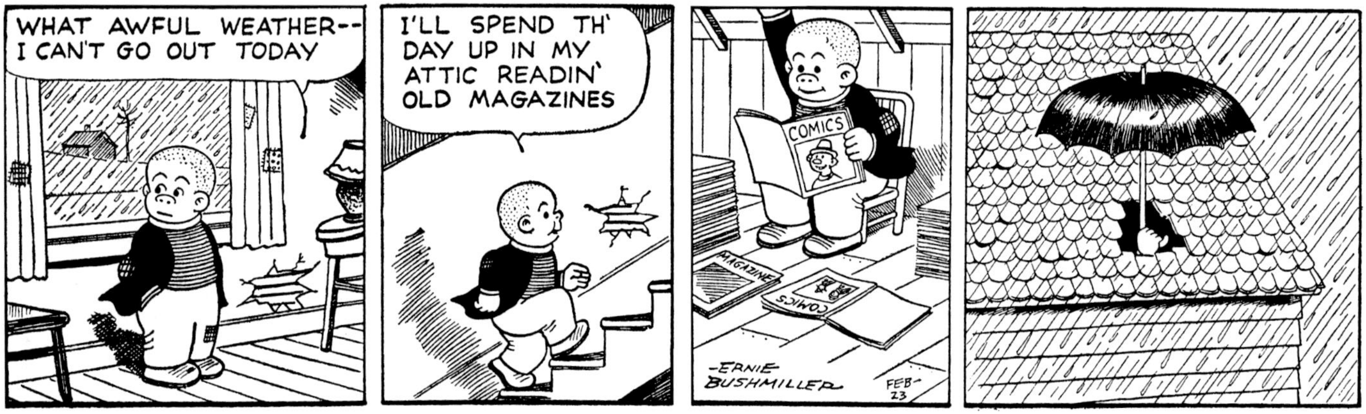
WHAT AWFUL WEATHER-- I CAN'T GO OUT TODAY
I'LL SPEND TH' DAY UP IN MY ATTIC READIN' OLD MAGAZINES
COMICS
MAGAZINE
COMICS
-ERNIE BUSHMILLER
FEB-23

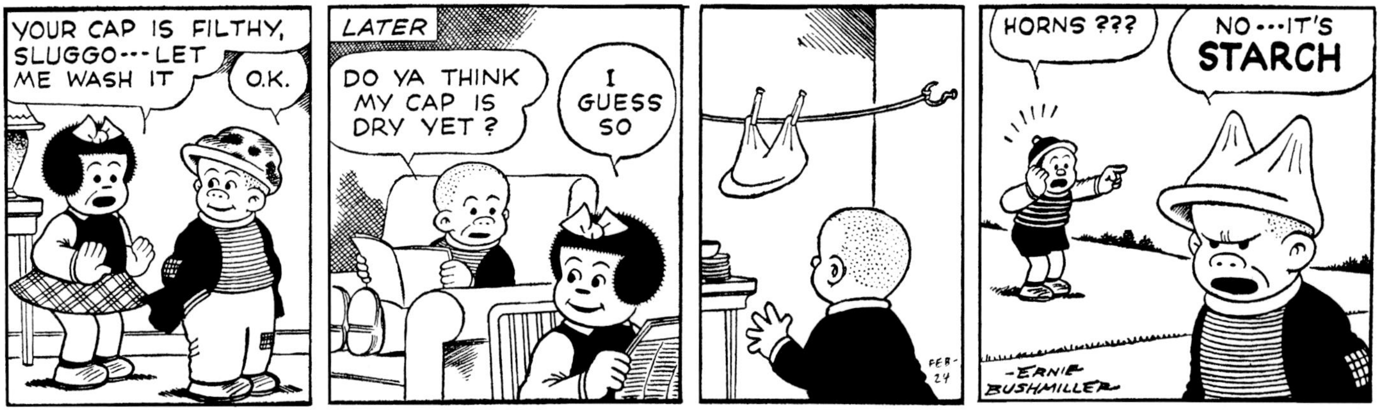

YOUR CAP IS FILTHY, SLUGGO---LET ME WASH IT
O.K.
LATER
DO YA THINK MY CAP IS DRY YET ?
I GUESS SO
FEB-24
HORNS ???
NO---IT'S STARCH
-ERNIE BUSHMILLER

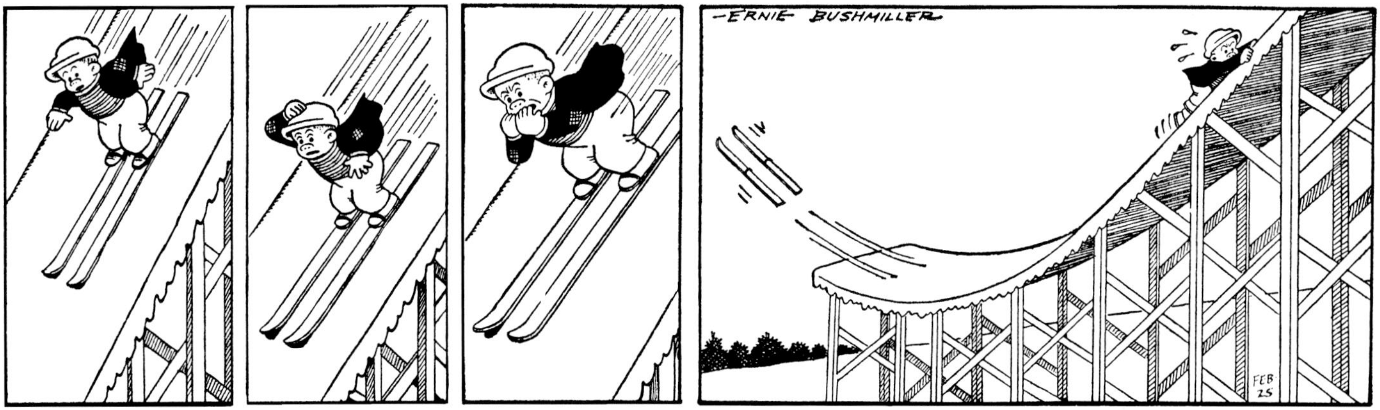

-ERNIE BUSHMILLER
FEB 25

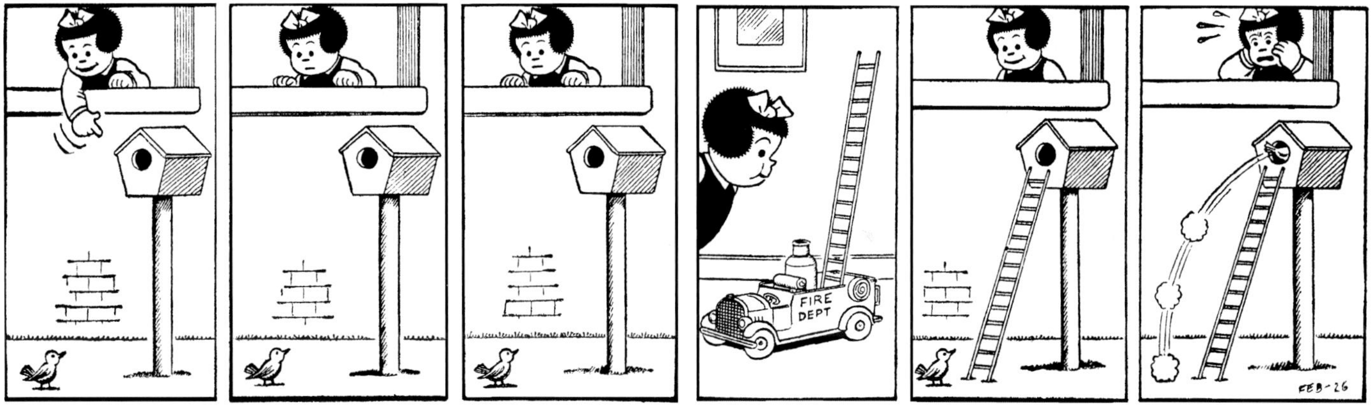

FIRE DEPT
FEB-26

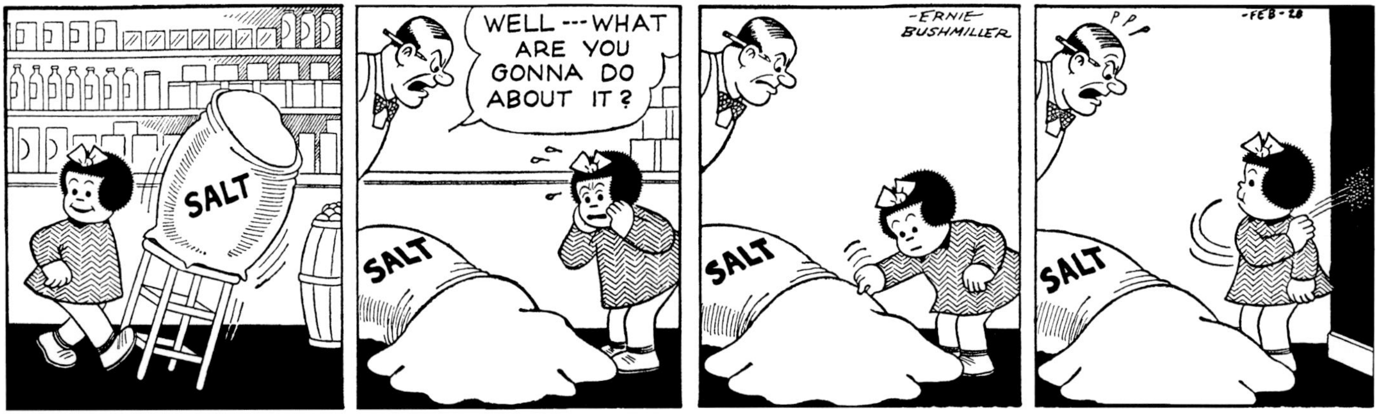
SALT
WELL --- WHAT ARE YOU GONNA DO ABOUT IT ?
SALT
-ERNIE BUSHMILLER
SALT
-FEB-28
SALT

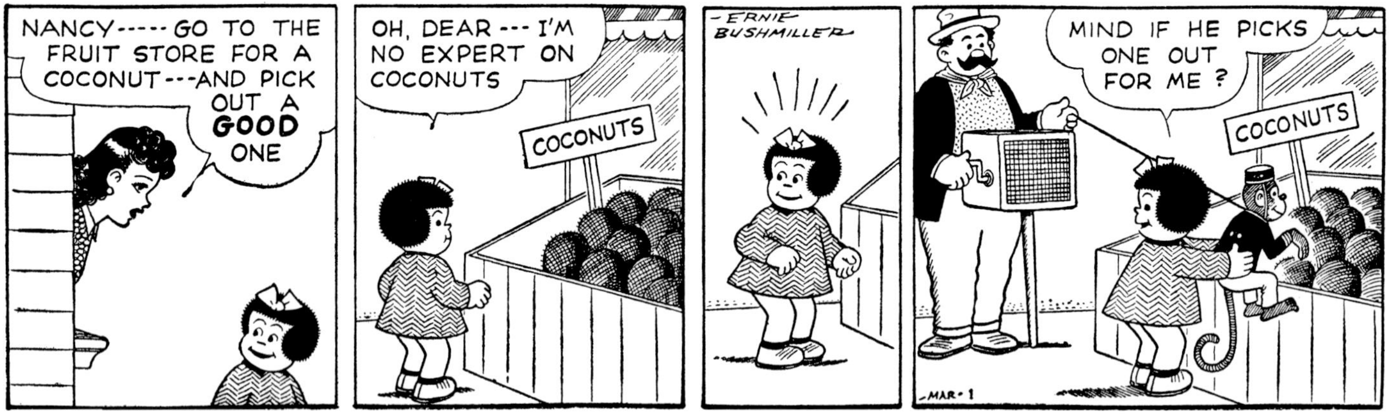
NANCY----- GO TO THE FRUIT STORE FOR A COCONUT --- AND PICK OUT A GOOD ONE
OH, DEAR --- I'M NO EXPERT ON COCONUTS
COCONUTS
-ERNIE BUSHMILLER
MIND IF HE PICKS ONE OUT FOR ME ?
COCONUTS
-MAR-1

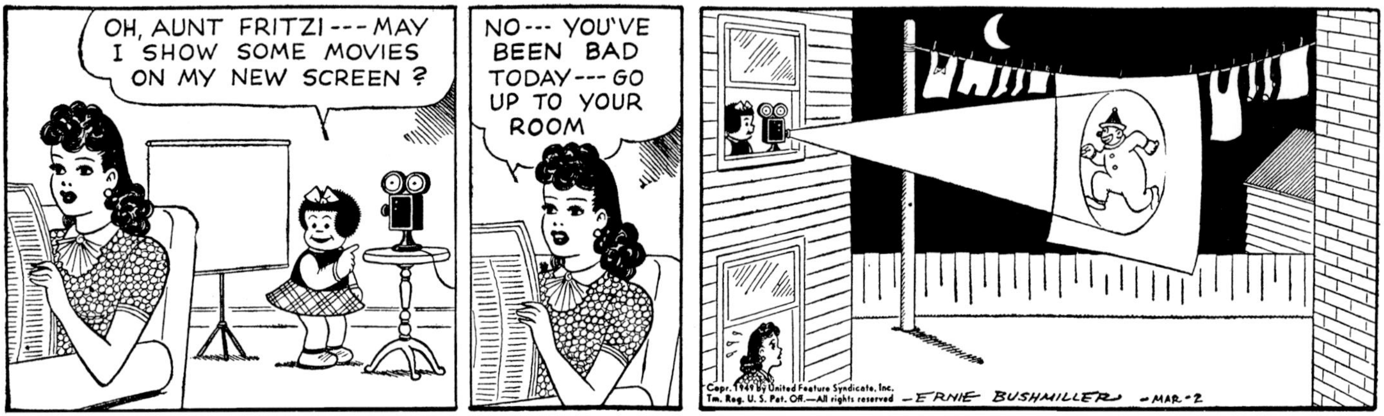
OH, AUNT FRITZI --- MAY I SHOW SOME MOVIES ON MY NEW SCREEN ?
NO--- YOU'VE BEEN BAD TODAY --- GO UP TO YOUR ROOM
Copr. 1949 by United Feature Syndicate, Inc. Tm. Reg. U. S. Pat. Off.—All rights reserved
-ERNIE BUSHMILLER
-MAR-2

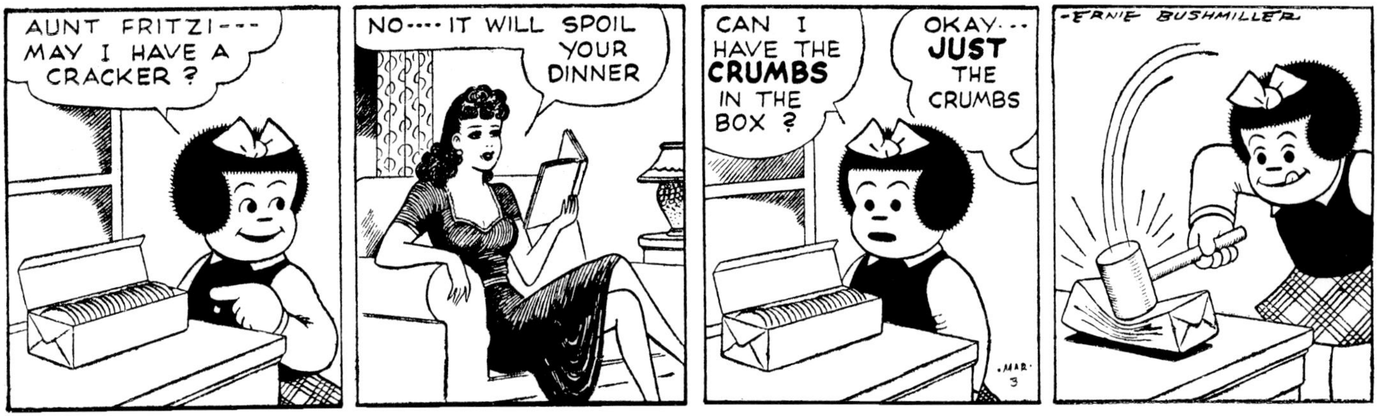
AUNT FRITZI--- MAY I HAVE A CRACKER ?
NO---- IT WILL SPOIL YOUR DINNER
CAN I HAVE THE **CRUMBS** IN THE BOX ?
OKAY--- **JUST** THE CRUMBS
·MAR· 3
-ERNIE BUSHMILLER

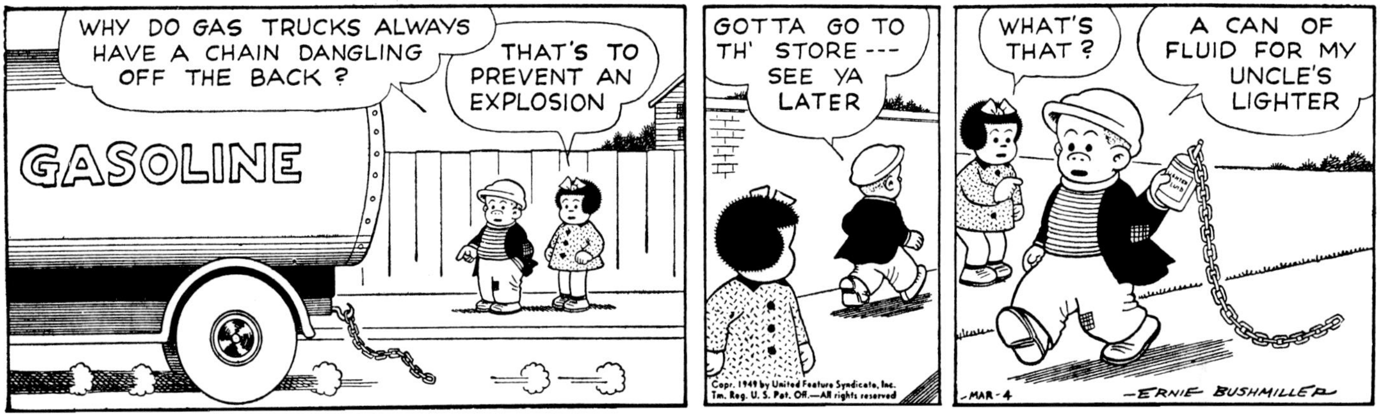
WHY DO GAS TRUCKS ALWAYS HAVE A CHAIN DANGLING OFF THE BACK ?
THAT'S TO PREVENT AN EXPLOSION
GASOLINE
GOTTA GO TO TH' STORE--- SEE YA LATER
Copr. 1949 by United Feature Syndicate, Inc.
Tm. Reg. U. S. Pat. Off.—All rights reserved
WHAT'S THAT ?
A CAN OF FLUID FOR MY UNCLE'S LIGHTER
-MAR-4
-ERNIE BUSHMILLER

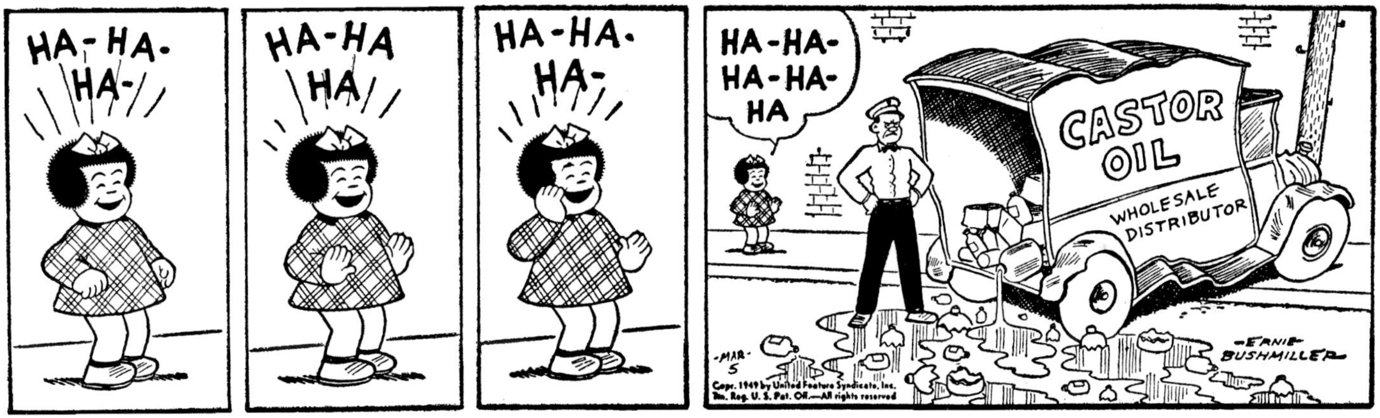
HA-HA-HA-
HA-HA HA
HA-HA-HA-
HA-HA-HA-HA-HA
CASTOR OIL
WHOLESALE DISTRIBUTOR
-MAR-5
-ERNIE BUSHMILLER
Copr. 1949 by United Feature Syndicate, Inc.
Tm. Reg. U. S. Pat. Off.—All rights reserved

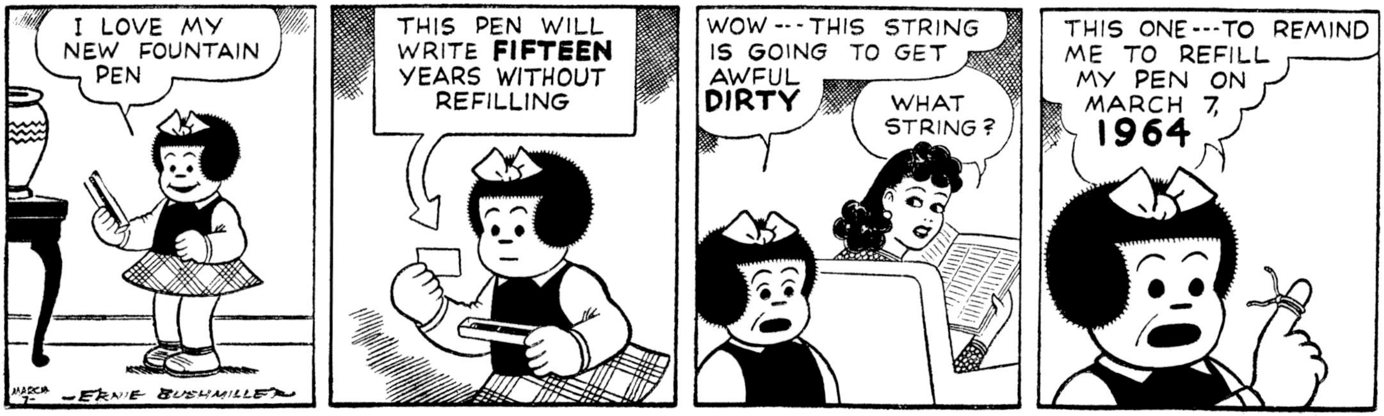
I LOVE MY NEW FOUNTAIN PEN
MARCH 7
ERNIE BUSHMILLER
THIS PEN WILL WRITE FIFTEEN YEARS WITHOUT REFILLING
WOW --- THIS STRING IS GOING TO GET AWFUL DIRTY
WHAT STRING?
THIS ONE --- TO REMIND ME TO REFILL MY PEN ON MARCH 7, 1964

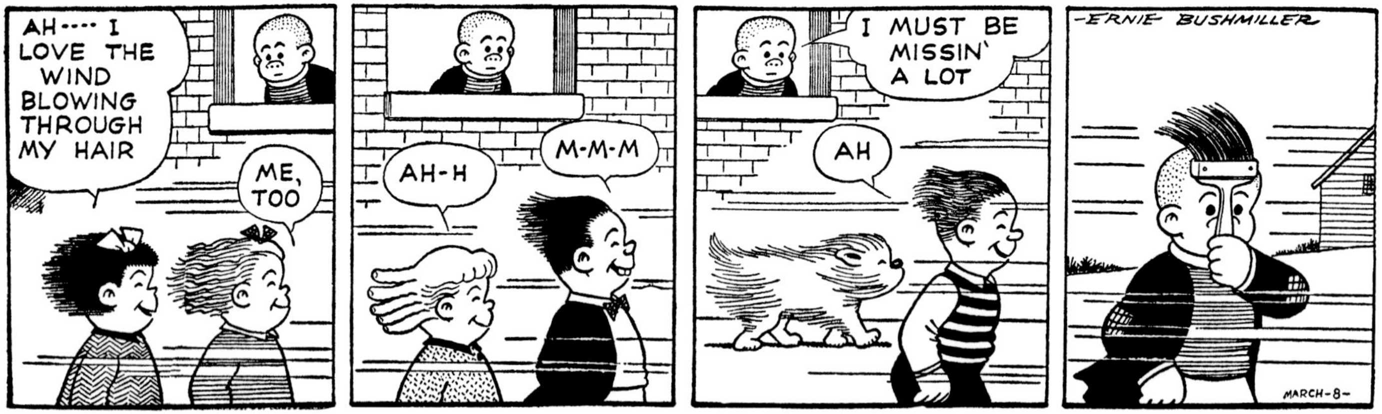
AH ---- I LOVE THE WIND BLOWING THROUGH MY HAIR
ME, TOO
AH-H
M-M-M
I MUST BE MISSIN' A LOT
AH
ERNIE BUSHMILLER
MARCH-8-

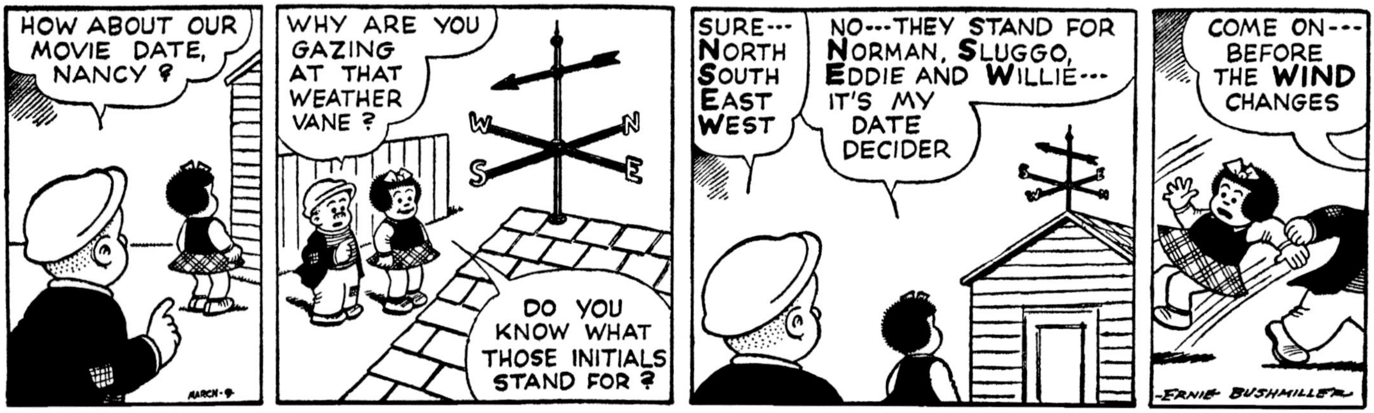
HOW ABOUT OUR MOVIE DATE, NANCY?
MARCH-9
WHY ARE YOU GAZING AT THAT WEATHER VANE?
W
N
S
E
DO YOU KNOW WHAT THOSE INITIALS STAND FOR?
SURE --- NORTH SOUTH EAST WEST
NO --- THEY STAND FOR NORMAN, SLUGGO, EDDIE AND WILLIE --- IT'S MY DATE DECIDER
COME ON --- BEFORE THE WIND CHANGES
ERNIE BUSHMILLER

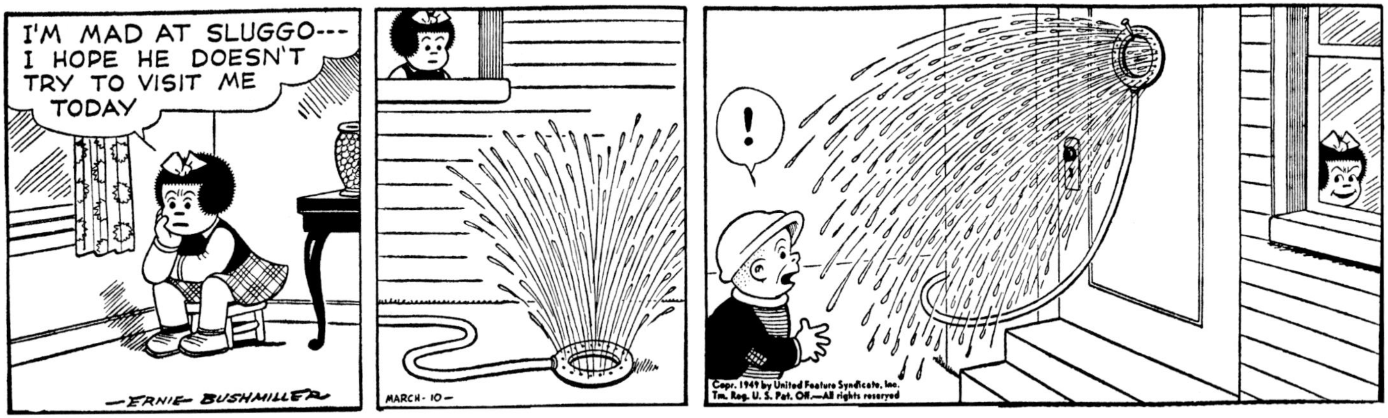
I'M MAD AT SLUGGO--- I HOPE HE DOESN'T TRY TO VISIT ME TODAY
ERNIE BUSHMILLER
MARCH-10-
!
Copr. 1949 by United Feature Syndicate, Inc.
Tm. Reg. U. S. Pat. Off.—All rights reserved

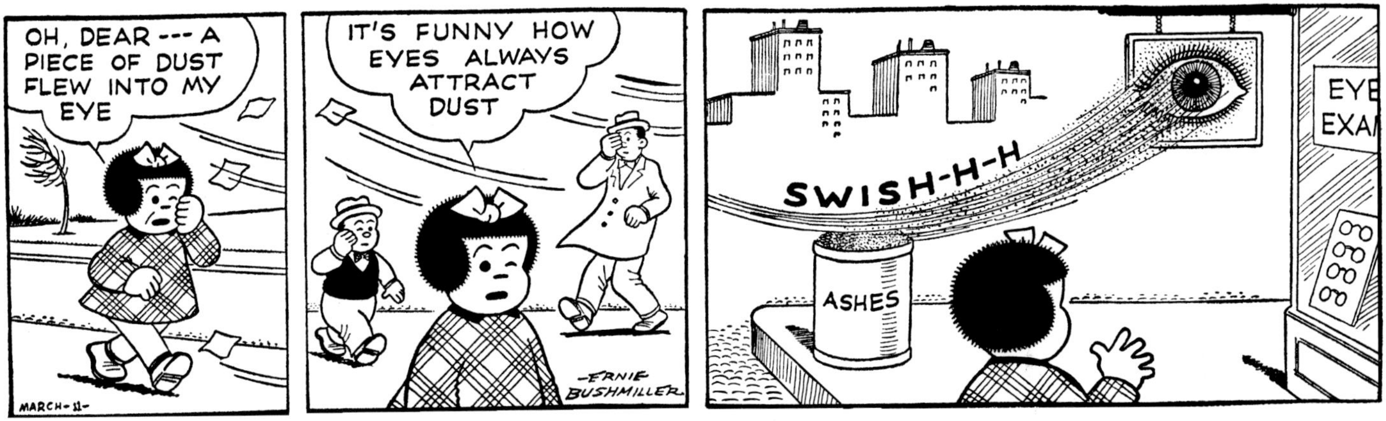
OH, DEAR --- A PIECE OF DUST FLEW INTO MY EYE
MARCH-11-
IT'S FUNNY HOW EYES ALWAYS ATTRACT DUST
ERNIE BUSHMILLER
SWISH-H-H
ASHES

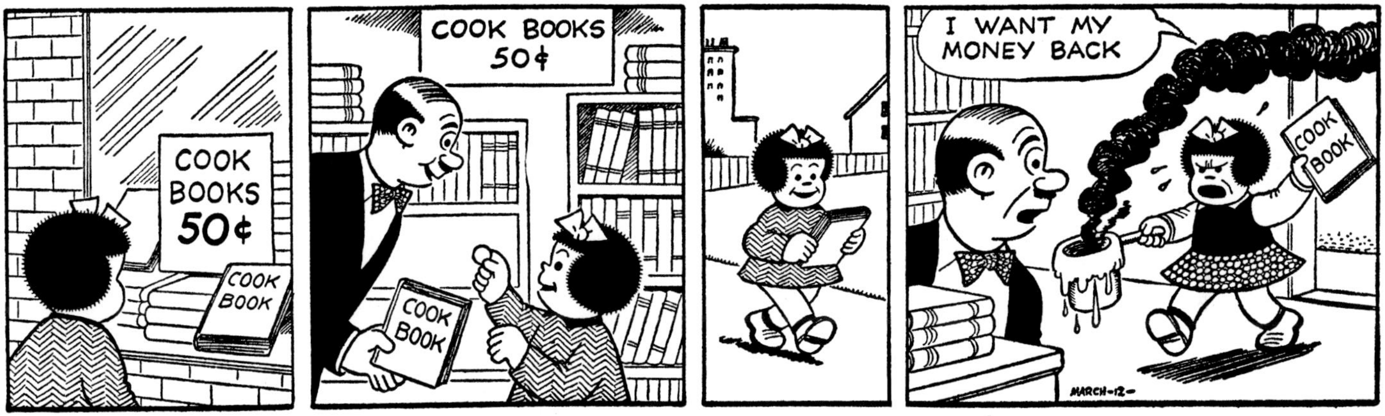
COOK BOOKS 50¢
COOK BOOK
COOK BOOKS 50¢
COOK BOOK
I WANT MY MONEY BACK
COOK BOOK
MARCH-12-

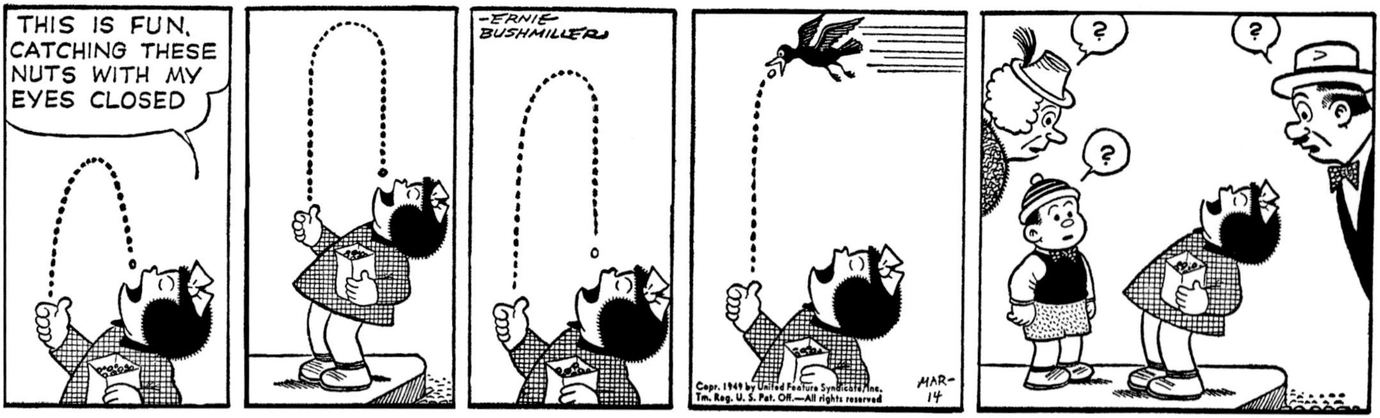
THIS IS FUN, CATCHING THESE NUTS WITH MY EYES CLOSED
-ERNIE BUSHMILLER
Copr. 1949 by United Feature Syndicate, Inc. Tm. Reg. U. S. Pat. Off.—All rights reserved
MAR-14
?
?
?

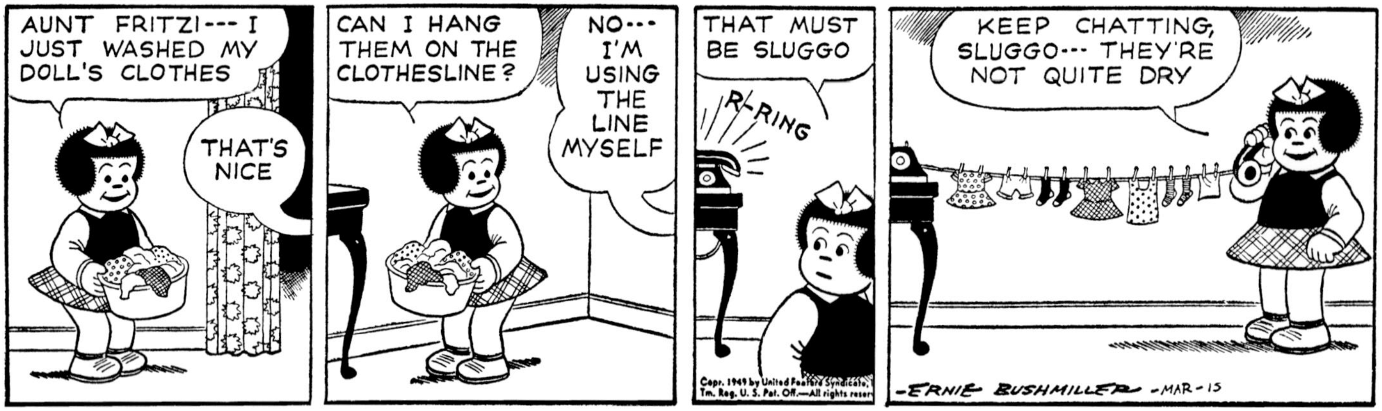
AUNT FRITZI--- I JUST WASHED MY DOLL'S CLOTHES
THAT'S NICE
CAN I HANG THEM ON THE CLOTHESLINE?
NO--- I'M USING THE LINE MYSELF
THAT MUST BE SLUGGO
R-RING
Copr. 1949 by United Feature Syndicate, Inc. Tm. Reg. U. S. Pat. Off.—All rights reserved
KEEP CHATTING, SLUGGO--- THEY'RE NOT QUITE DRY
-ERNIE BUSHMILLER -MAR-15

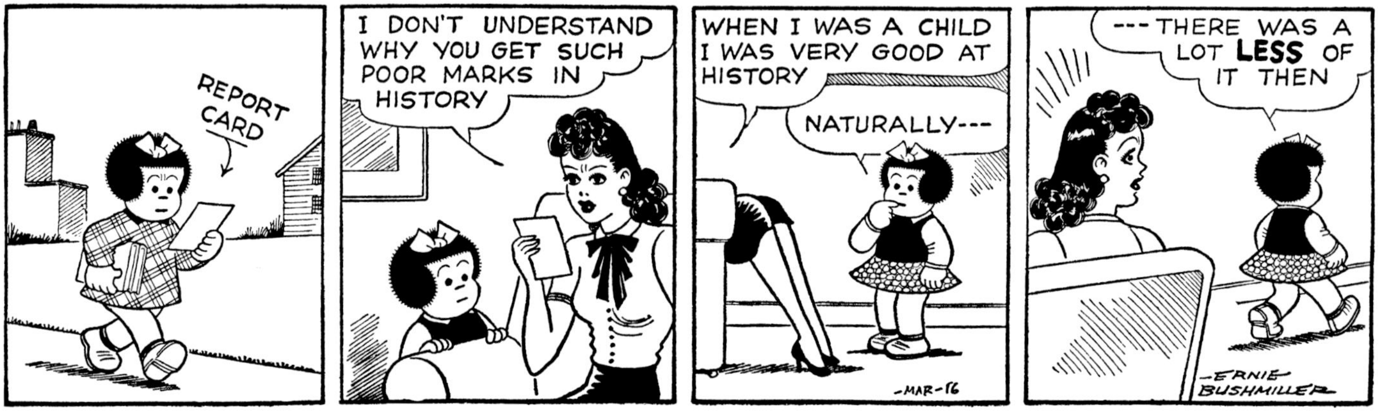
REPORT CARD
I DON'T UNDERSTAND WHY YOU GET SUCH POOR MARKS IN HISTORY
WHEN I WAS A CHILD I WAS VERY GOOD AT HISTORY
NATURALLY---
-MAR-16
---THERE WAS A LOT LESS OF IT THEN
-ERNIE BUSHMILLER

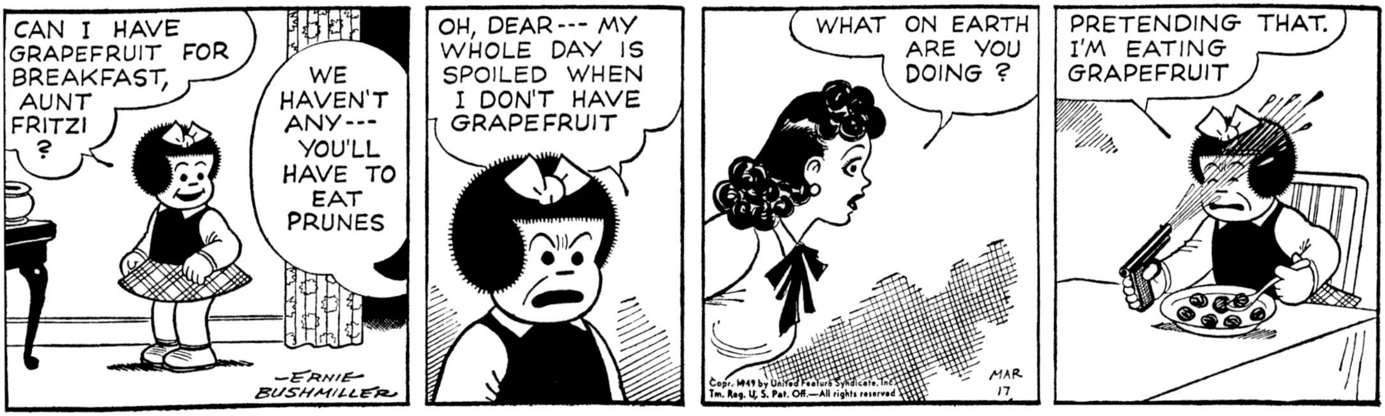
CAN I HAVE GRAPEFRUIT FOR BREAKFAST, AUNT FRITZI ?
WE HAVEN'T ANY--- YOU'LL HAVE TO EAT PRUNES
ERNIE BUSHMILLER
OH, DEAR--- MY WHOLE DAY IS SPOILED WHEN I DON'T HAVE GRAPEFRUIT
WHAT ON EARTH ARE YOU DOING ?
Copr. 1949 by United Feature Syndicate, Inc. Tm. Reg. U. S. Pat. Off.—All rights reserved
MAR 17
PRETENDING THAT. I'M EATING GRAPEFRUIT

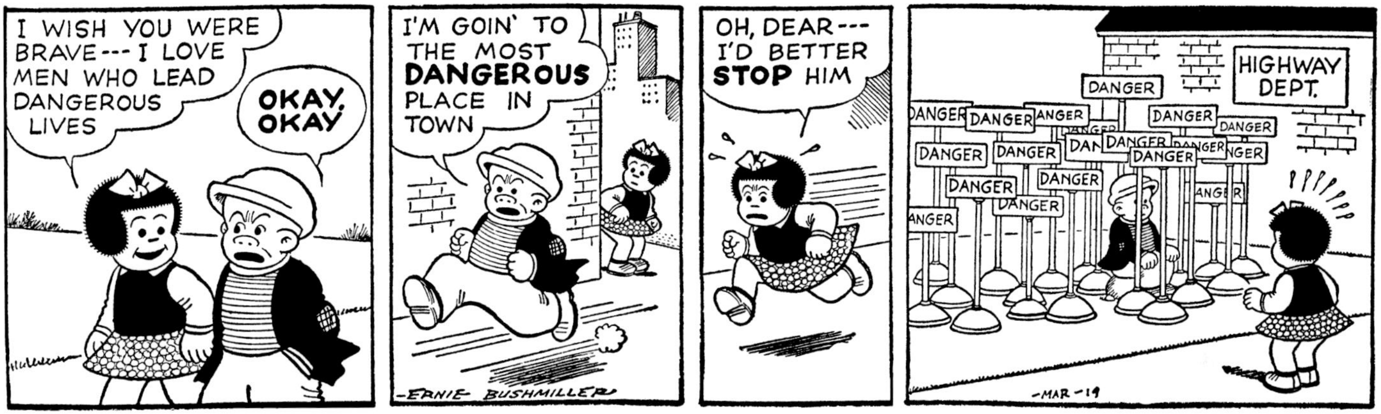
I WISH YOU WERE BRAVE--- I LOVE MEN WHO LEAD DANGEROUS LIVES
OKAY, OKAY
I'M GOIN' TO THE MOST DANGEROUS PLACE IN TOWN
ERNIE BUSHMILLER
OH, DEAR--- I'D BETTER STOP HIM
HIGHWAY DEPT.
DANGER
MAR-19

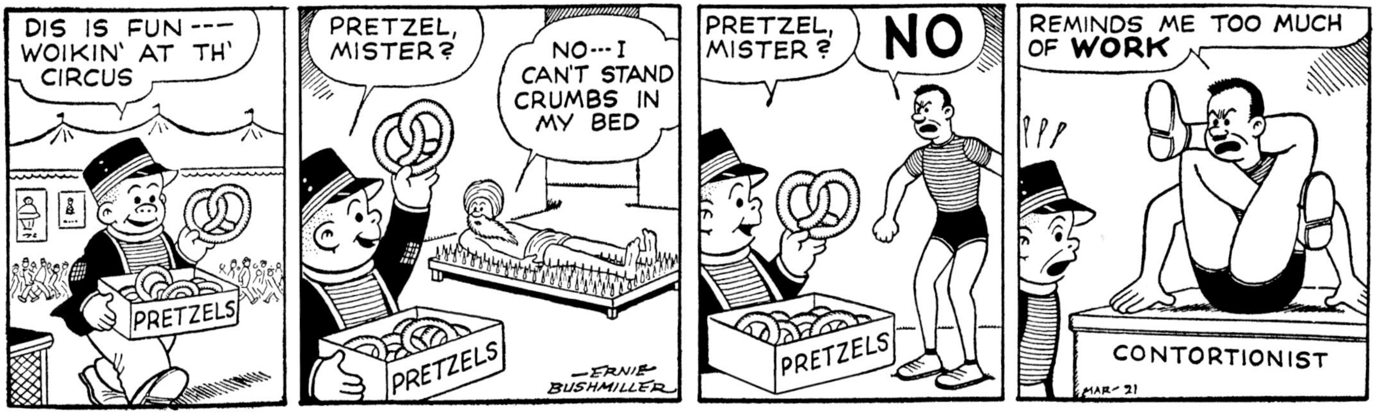
DIS IS FUN--- WOIKIN' AT TH' CIRCUS
PRETZELS
PRETZEL, MISTER ?
NO--- I CAN'T STAND CRUMBS IN MY BED
PRETZELS
ERNIE BUSHMILLER
PRETZEL, MISTER ?
NO
PRETZELS
REMINDS ME TOO MUCH OF WORK
CONTORTIONIST
MAR-21

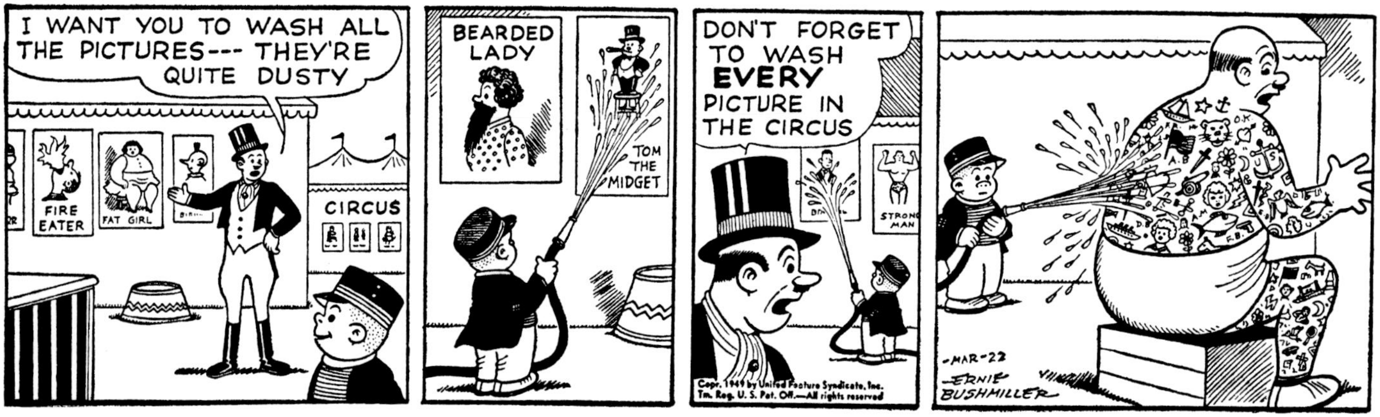
I WANT YOU TO WASH ALL THE PICTURES--- THEY'RE QUITE DUSTY
FIRE EATER
FAT GIRL
CIRCUS
BEARDED LADY
TOM THE MIDGET
DON'T FORGET TO WASH **EVERY** PICTURE IN THE CIRCUS
STRONG MAN
Copr. 1949 by United Feature Syndicate, Inc. Tm. Reg. U. S. Pat. Off.—All rights reserved
MAR-22
ERNIE BUSHMILLER

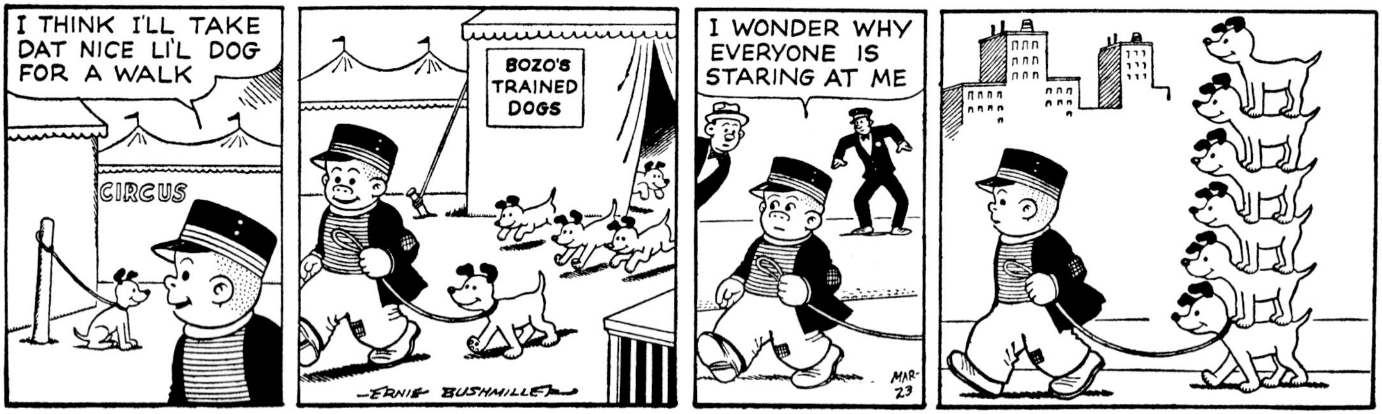
I THINK I'LL TAKE DAT NICE LI'L DOG FOR A WALK
CIRCUS
BOZO'S TRAINED DOGS
ERNIE BUSHMILLER
I WONDER WHY EVERYONE IS STARING AT ME
MAR-23

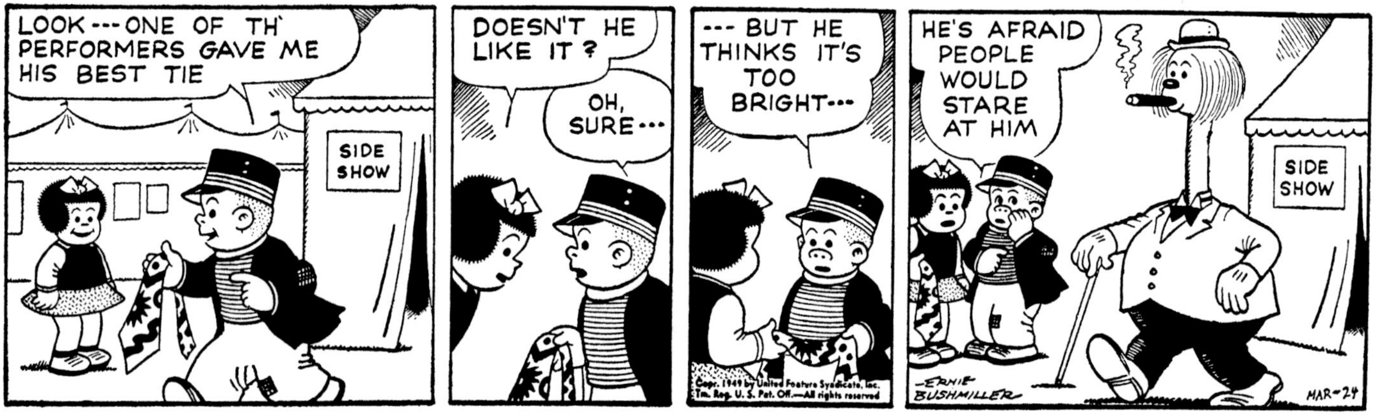
LOOK---ONE OF TH' PERFORMERS GAVE ME HIS BEST TIE
SIDE SHOW
DOESN'T HE LIKE IT ?
OH, SURE---
--- BUT HE THINKS IT'S TOO BRIGHT---
Copr. 1949 by United Feature Syndicate, Inc. Tm. Reg. U. S. Pat. Off.—All rights reserved
HE'S AFRAID PEOPLE WOULD STARE AT HIM
SIDE SHOW
ERNIE BUSHMILLER
MAR-24

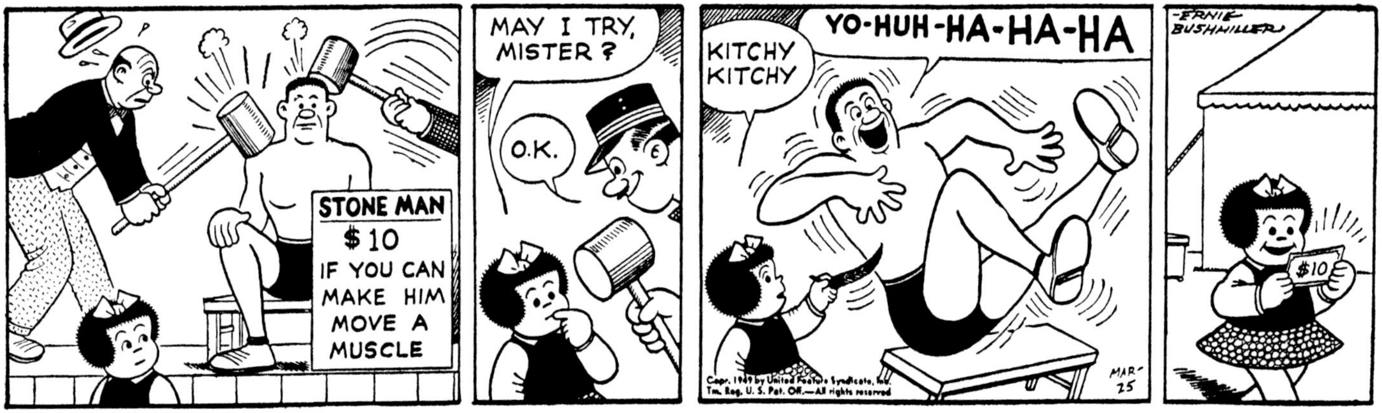
STONE MAN
$10
IF YOU CAN MAKE HIM MOVE A MUSCLE
MAY I TRY, MISTER?
O.K.
KITCHY KITCHY
YO-HUH-HA-HA-HA
Copr. 1949 by United Feature Syndicate, Inc. Tm. Reg. U. S. Pat. Off.—All rights reserved
MAR- 25
-ERNIE BUSHMILLER
$10

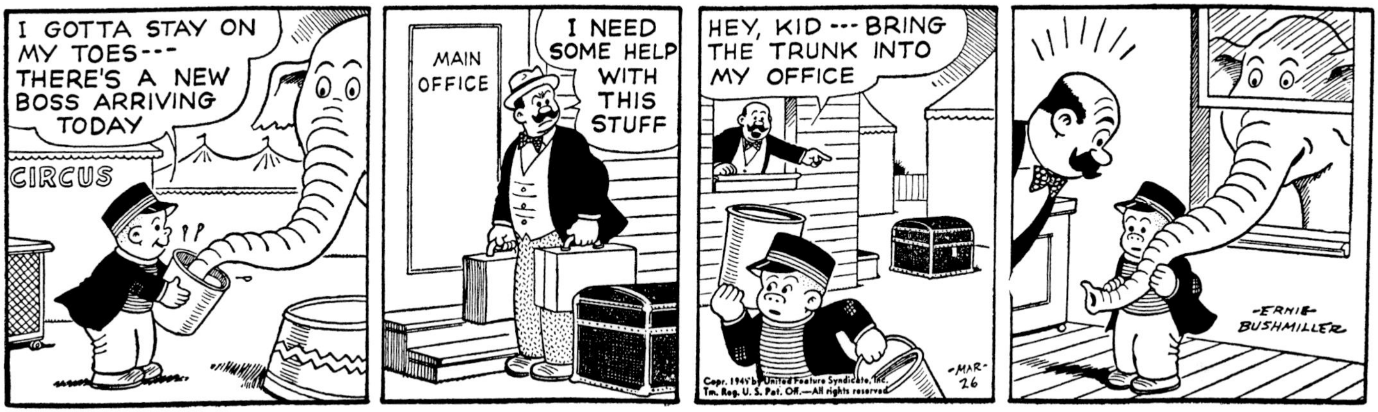
I GOTTA STAY ON MY TOES--- THERE'S A NEW BOSS ARRIVING TODAY
CIRCUS
MAIN OFFICE
I NEED SOME HELP WITH THIS STUFF
HEY, KID --- BRING THE TRUNK INTO MY OFFICE
Copr. 1949 by United Feature Syndicate, Inc. Tm. Reg. U. S. Pat. Off.—All rights reserved
-MAR- 26
-ERNIE BUSHMILLER

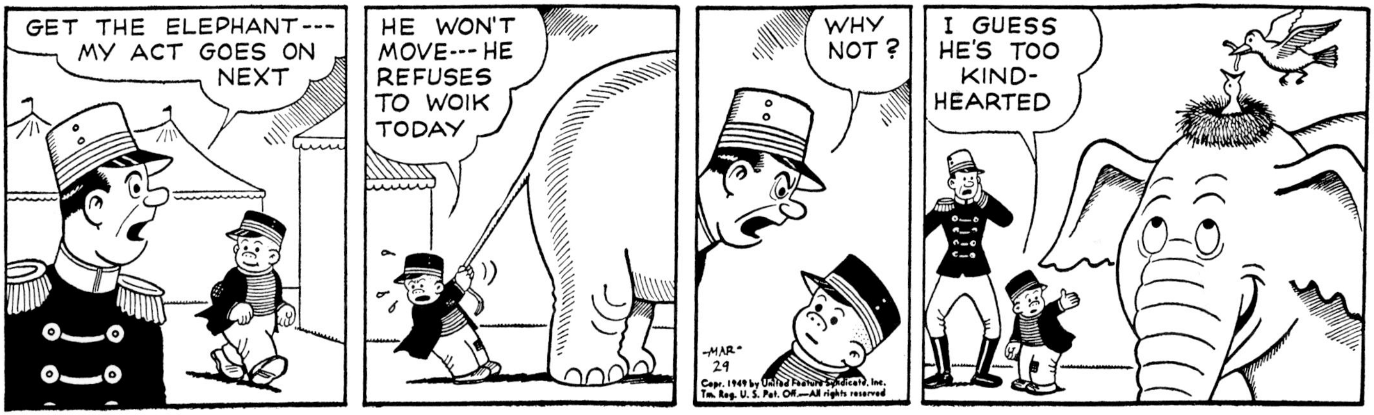
GET THE ELEPHANT--- MY ACT GOES ON NEXT
HE WON'T MOVE--- HE REFUSES TO WOIK TODAY
WHY NOT?
-MAR- 29
Copr. 1949 by United Feature Syndicate, Inc. Tm. Reg. U. S. Pat. Off.—All rights reserved
I GUESS HE'S TOO KIND-HEARTED

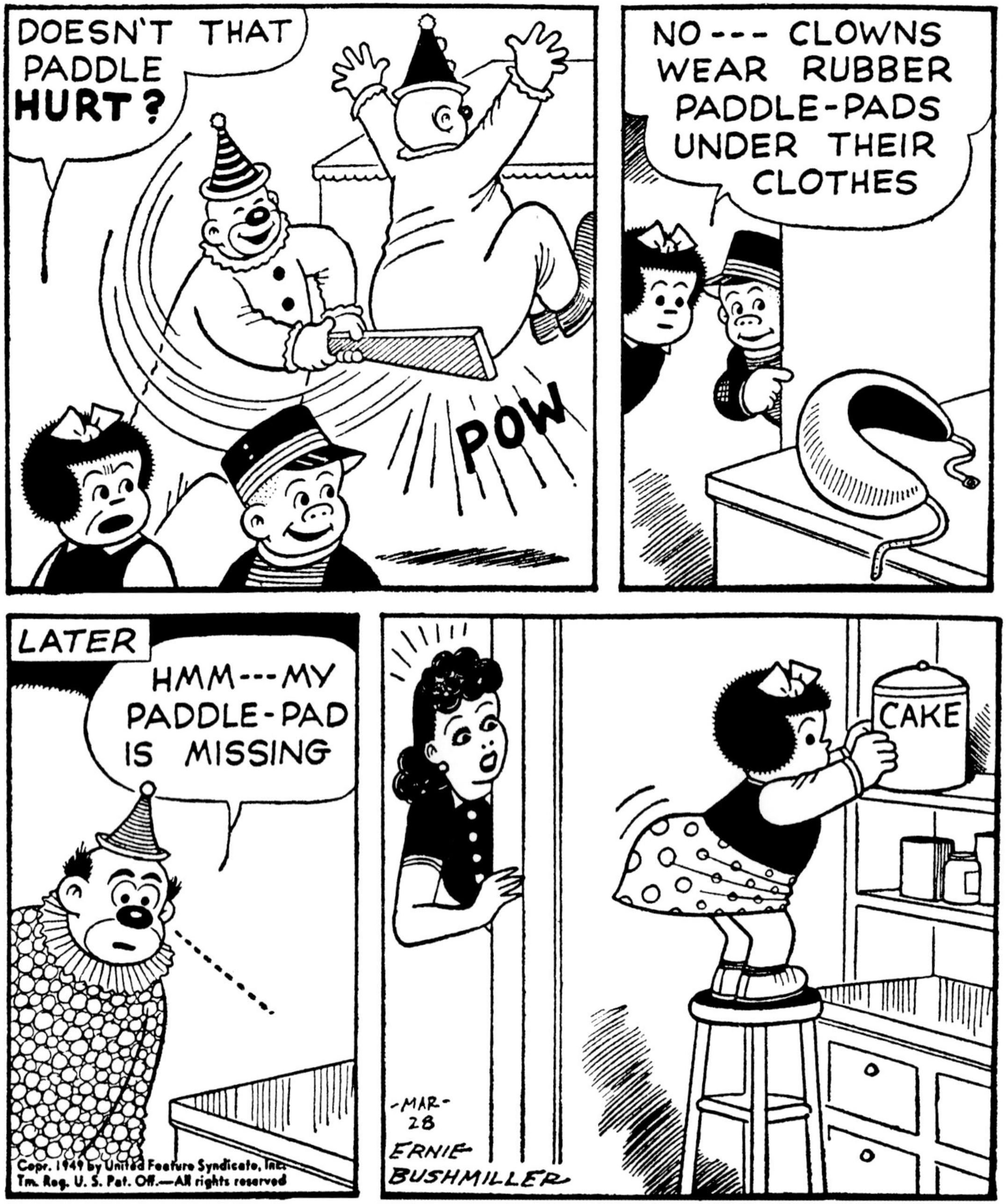
DOESN'T THAT PADDLE HURT?
POW
NO --- CLOWNS WEAR RUBBER PADDLE-PADS UNDER THEIR CLOTHES
LATER
HMM---MY PADDLE-PAD IS MISSING
Copr. 1949 by United Feature Syndicate, Inc.
Tm. Reg. U. S. Pat. Off.—All rights reserved
CAKE
-MAR- 28
ERNIE BUSHMILLER

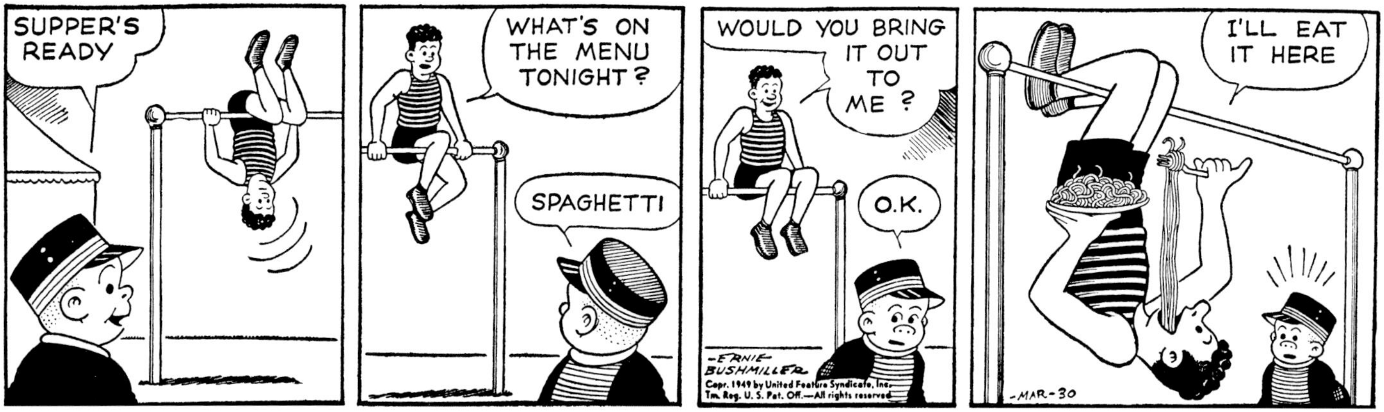
SUPPER'S READY
WHAT'S ON THE MENU TONIGHT?
SPAGHETTI
WOULD YOU BRING IT OUT TO ME?
O.K.
-ERNIE BUSHMILLER
Copr. 1949 by United Feature Syndicate, Inc. Tm. Reg. U. S. Pat. Off.—All rights reserved
I'LL EAT IT HERE
-MAR-30

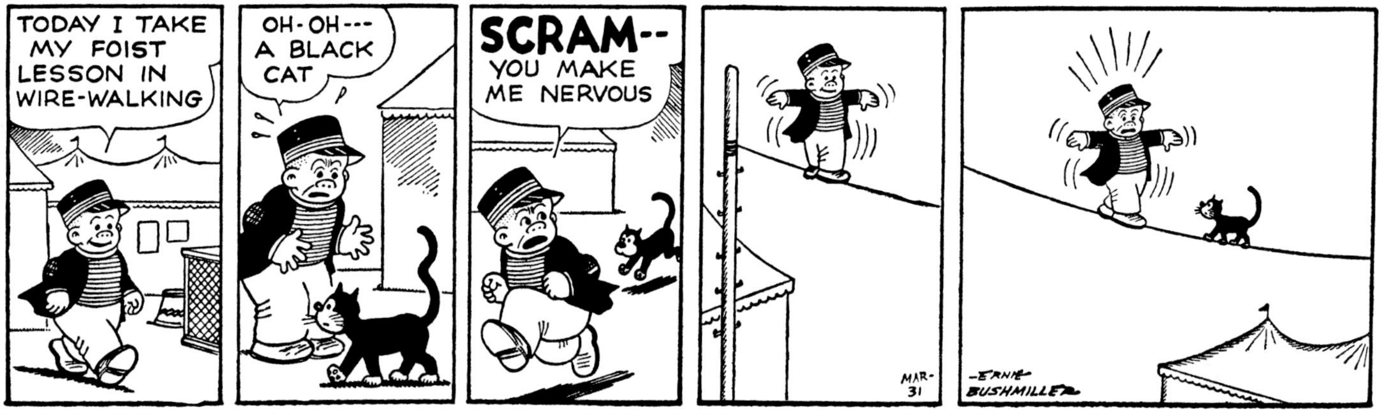
TODAY I TAKE MY FOIST LESSON IN WIRE-WALKING
OH-OH--- A BLACK CAT
SCRAM-- YOU MAKE ME NERVOUS
MAR-31
-ERNIE BUSHMILLER

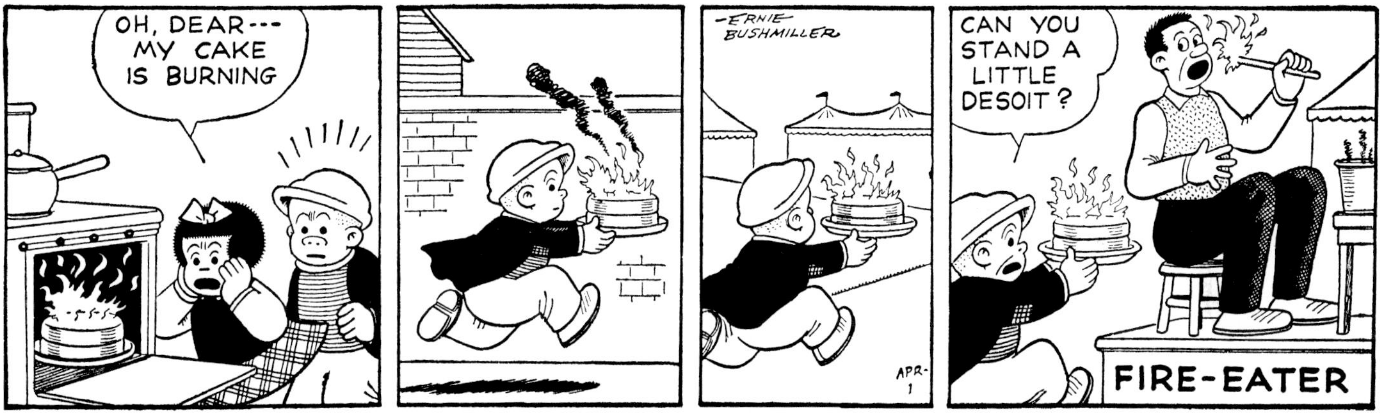
OH, DEAR--- MY CAKE IS BURNING
-ERNIE BUSHMILLER
APR-1
CAN YOU STAND A LITTLE DESOIT?
FIRE-EATER

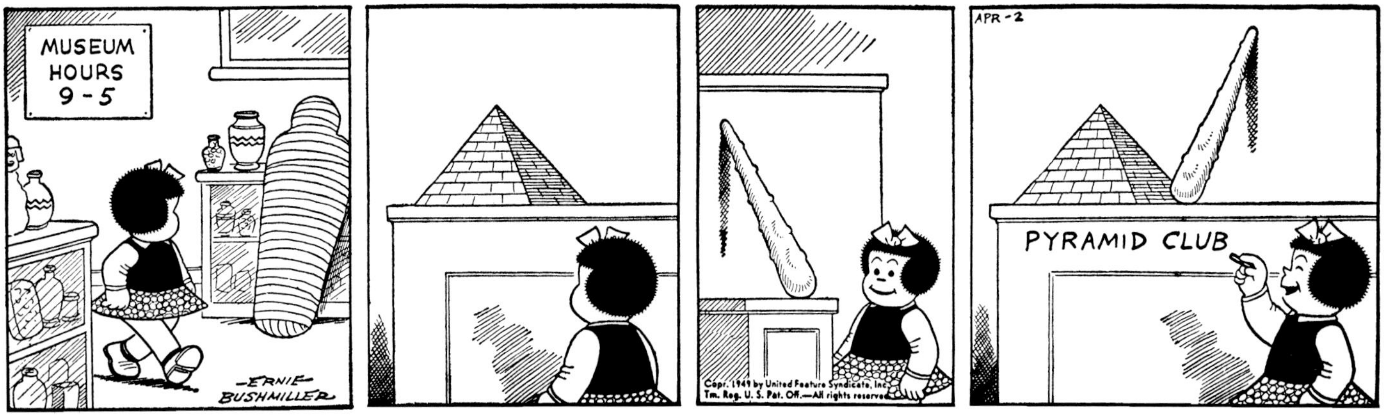
MUSEUM HOURS 9-5
ERNIE BUSHMILLER
Copr. 1949 by United Feature Syndicate, Inc. Tm. Reg. U. S. Pat. Off.—All rights reserved
APR-2
PYRAMID CLUB

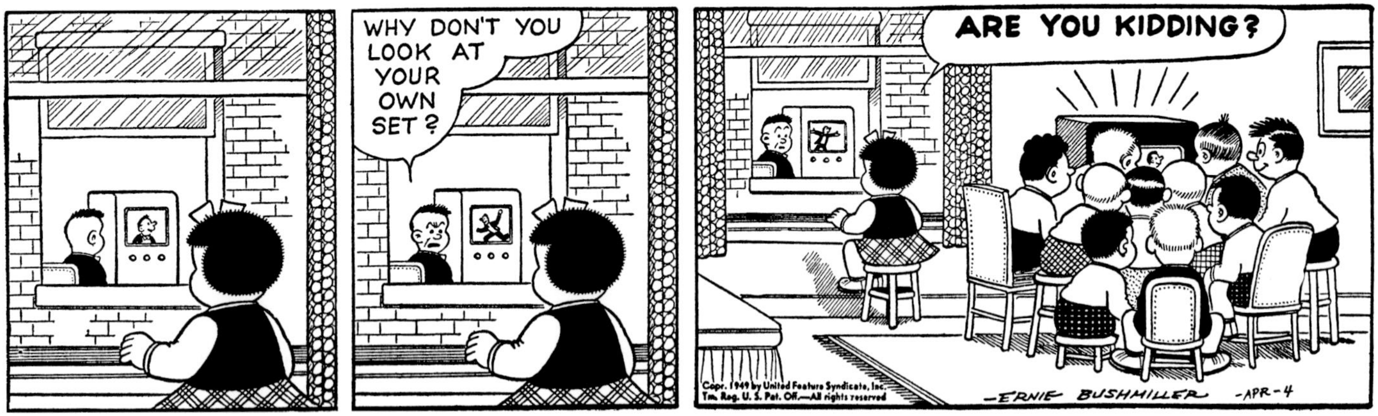
WHY DON'T YOU LOOK AT YOUR OWN SET?
ARE YOU KIDDING?
Copr. 1949 by United Feature Syndicate, Inc. Tm. Reg. U. S. Pat. Off.—All rights reserved
ERNIE BUSHMILLER
APR-4

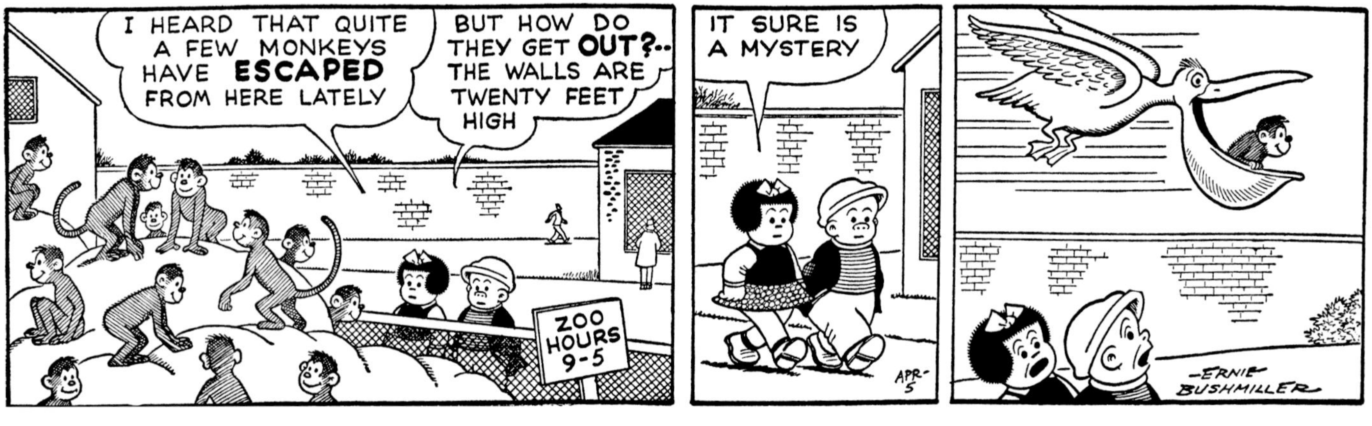
I HEARD THAT QUITE A FEW MONKEYS HAVE **ESCAPED** FROM HERE LATELY
BUT HOW DO THEY GET **OUT?**.. THE WALLS ARE TWENTY FEET HIGH
ZOO HOURS 9-5
IT SURE IS A MYSTERY
APR-5
ERNIE BUSHMILLER

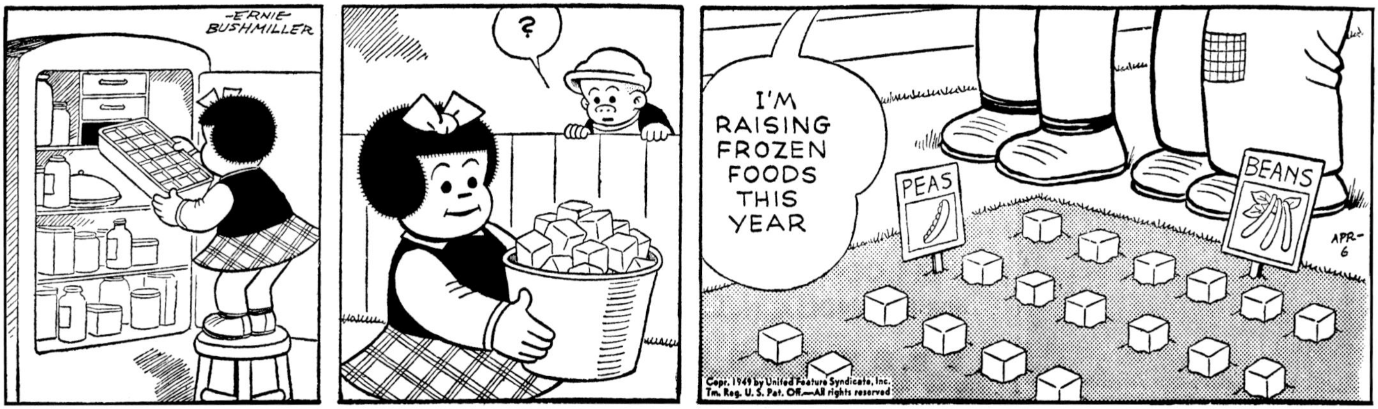
-ERNIE-
BUSHMILLER
?
I'M RAISING FROZEN FOODS THIS YEAR
PEAS
BEANS
APR-6
Copr. 1949 by United Feature Syndicate, Inc.
Tm. Reg. U. S. Pat. Off.—All rights reserved

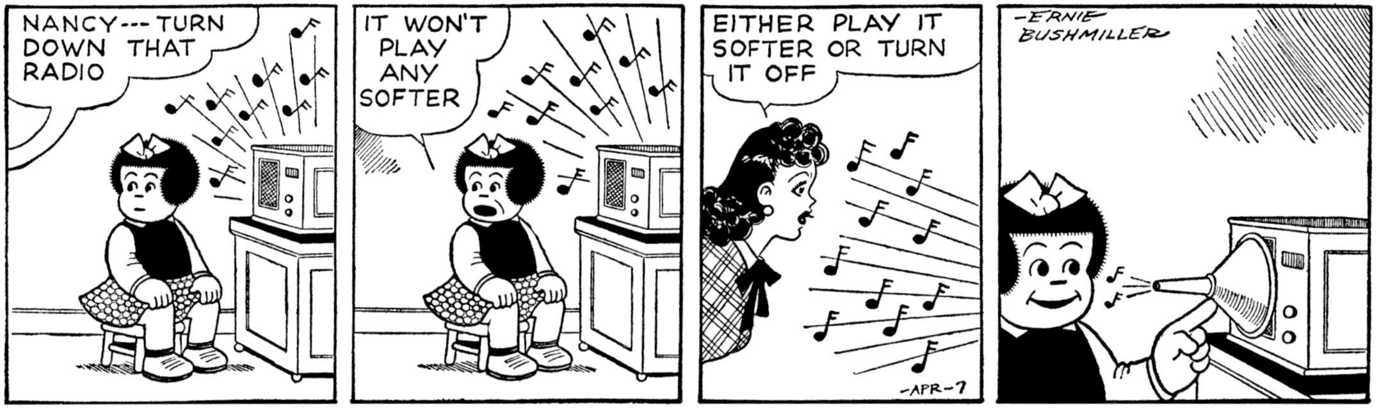
NANCY--- TURN DOWN THAT RADIO
IT WON'T PLAY ANY SOFTER
EITHER PLAY IT SOFTER OR TURN IT OFF
-APR-7
-ERNIE-
BUSHMILLER

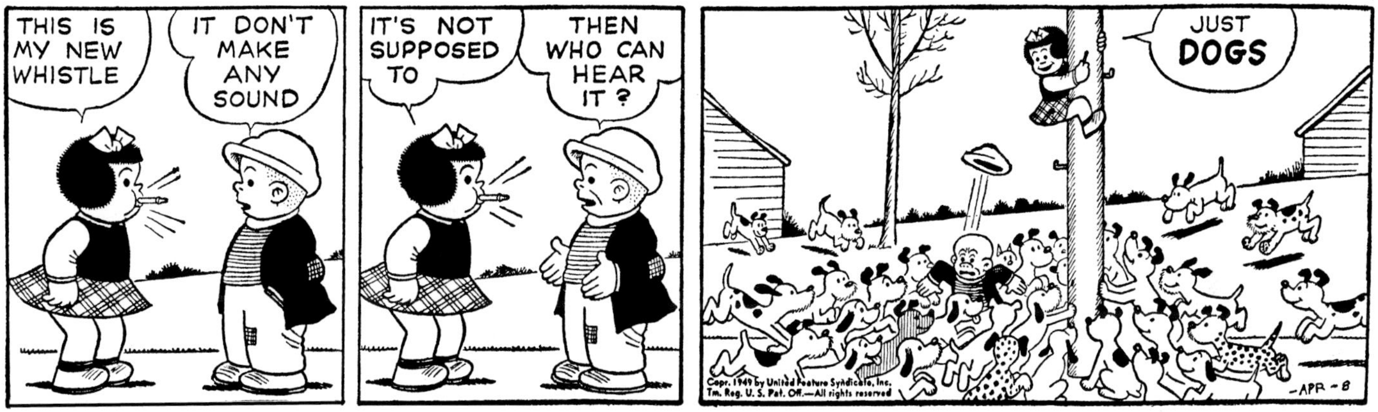
THIS IS MY NEW WHISTLE
IT DON'T MAKE ANY SOUND
IT'S NOT SUPPOSED TO
THEN WHO CAN HEAR IT ?
JUST DOGS
Copr. 1949 by United Feature Syndicate, Inc.
Tm. Reg. U. S. Pat. Off.—All rights reserved
-APR-8

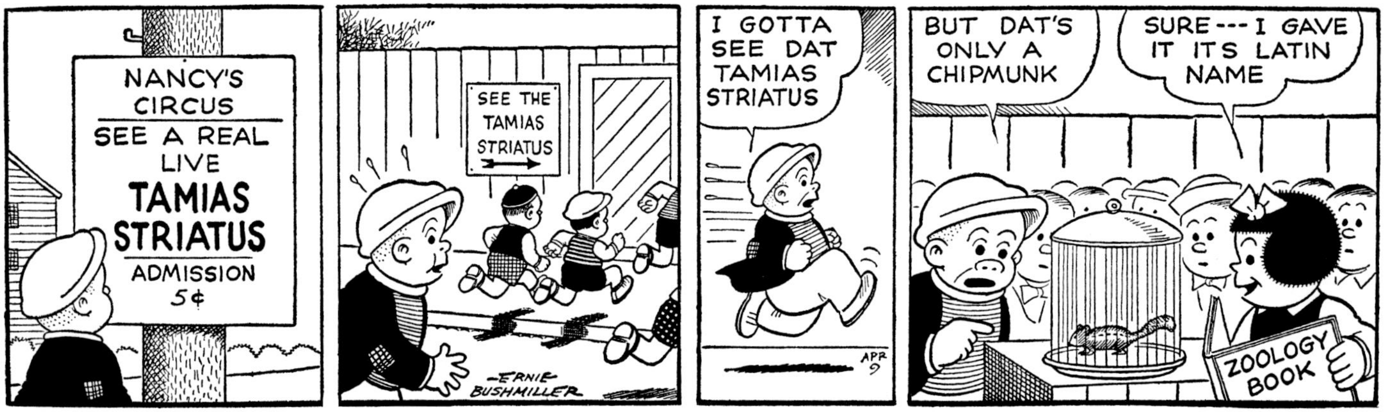
NANCY'S CIRCUS
SEE A REAL LIVE
TAMIAS STRIATUS
ADMISSION 5¢
SEE THE TAMIAS STRIATUS
ERNIE BUSHMILLER
I GOTTA SEE DAT TAMIAS STRIATUS
APR 9
BUT DAT'S ONLY A CHIPMUNK
SURE --- I GAVE IT ITS LATIN NAME
ZOOLOGY BOOK

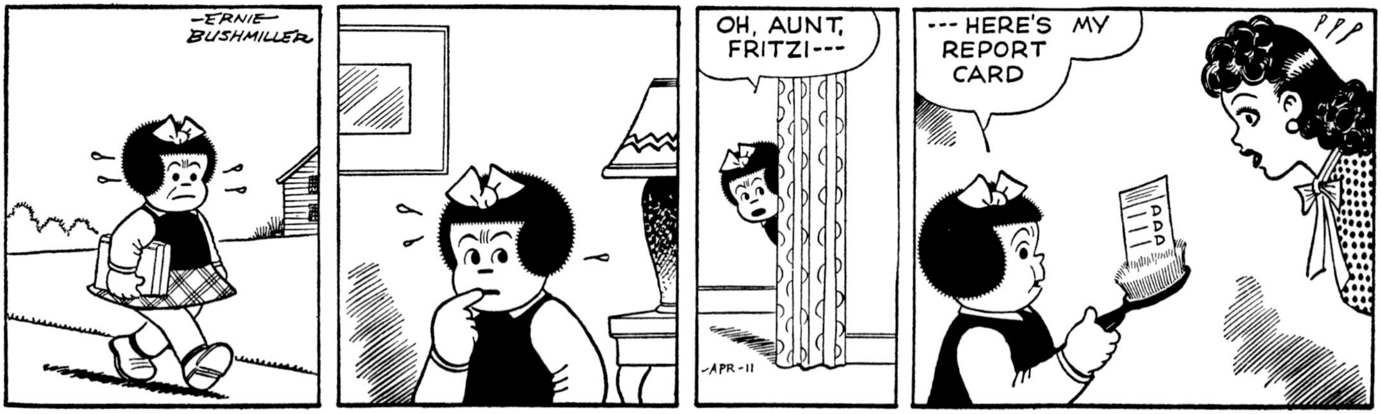
ERNIE BUSHMILLER
OH, AUNT FRITZI---
APR-11
--- HERE'S MY REPORT CARD
D
D
D

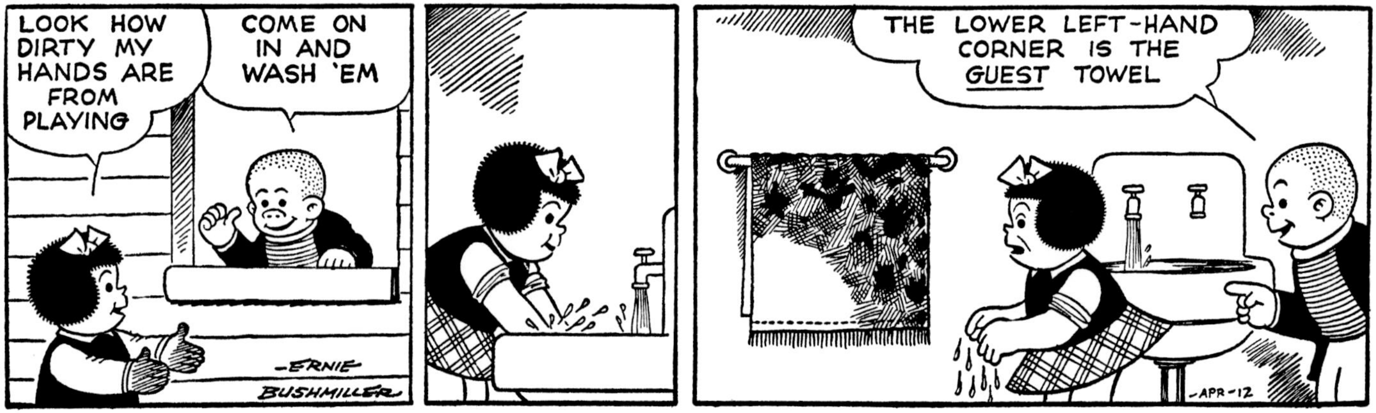
LOOK HOW DIRTY MY HANDS ARE FROM PLAYING
COME ON IN AND WASH 'EM
ERNIE BUSHMILLER
THE LOWER LEFT-HAND CORNER IS THE GUEST TOWEL
APR-12

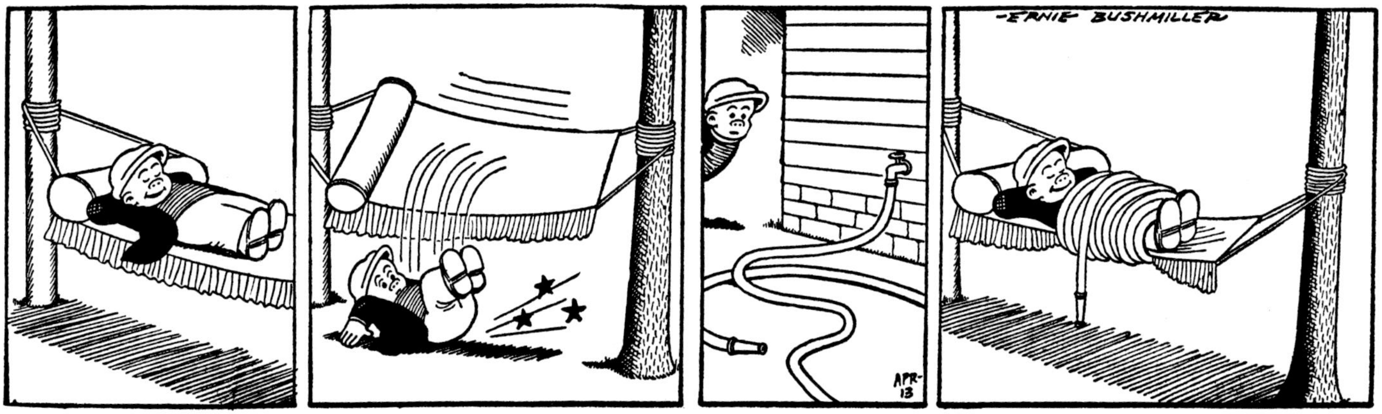
-ERNIE BUSHMILLER
APR-13

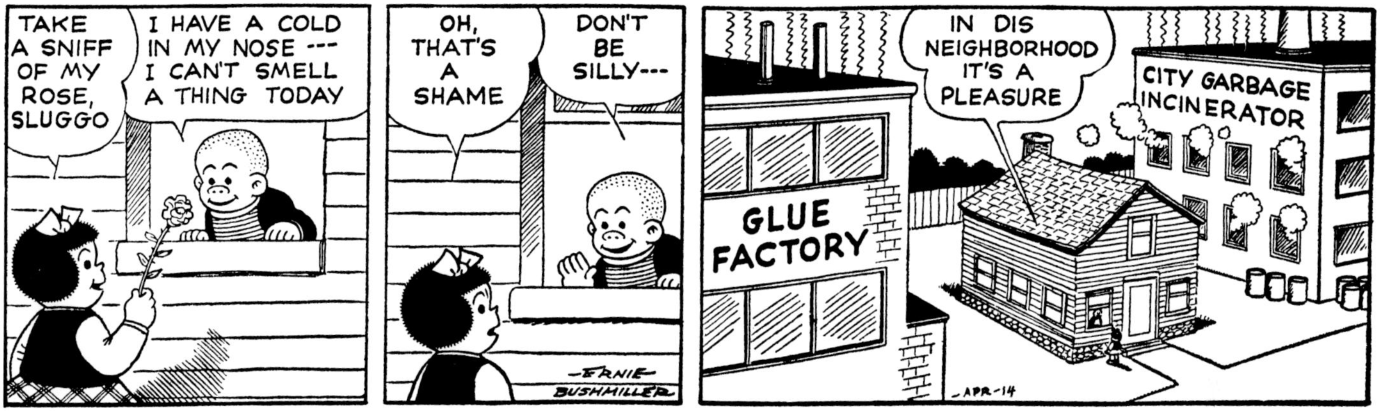
TAKE A SNIFF OF MY ROSE, SLUGGO
I HAVE A COLD IN MY NOSE --- I CAN'T SMELL A THING TODAY
OH, THAT'S A SHAME
DON'T BE SILLY---
-ERNIE BUSHMILLER
GLUE FACTORY
IN DIS NEIGHBORHOOD IT'S A PLEASURE
CITY GARBAGE INCINERATOR
APR-14

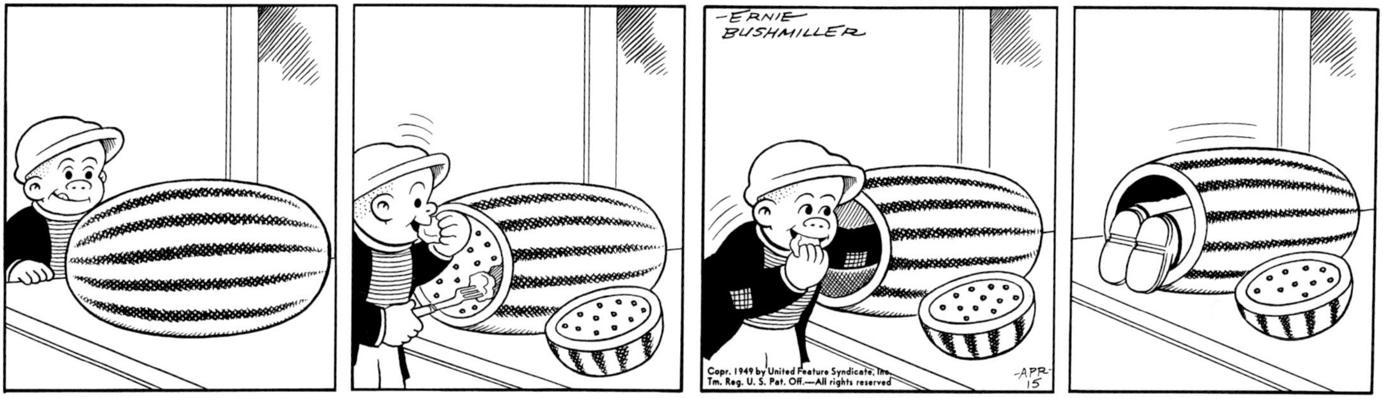
-ERNIE BUSHMILLER
Copr. 1949 by United Feature Syndicate, Inc.
Tm. Reg. U. S. Pat. Off.—All rights reserved
APR-15

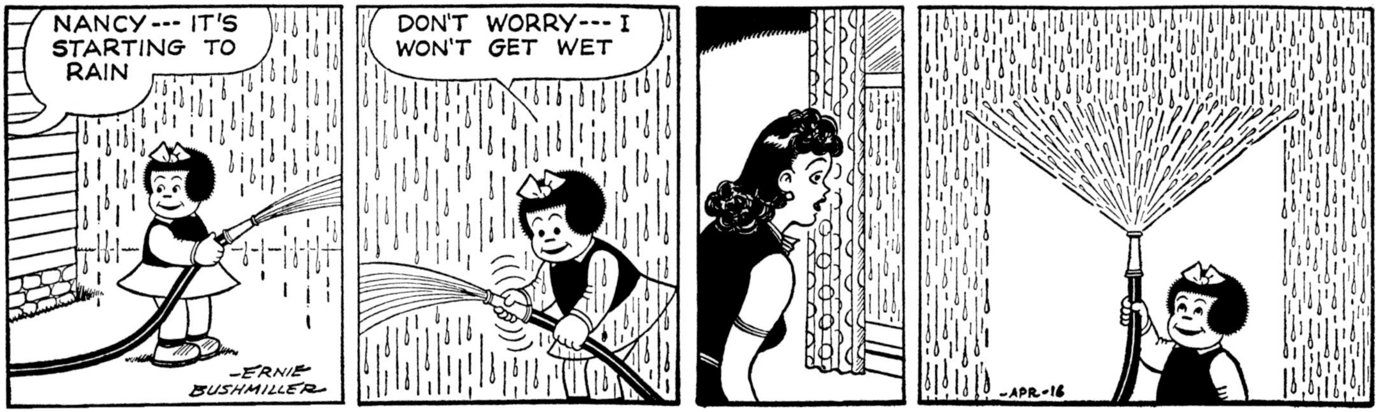
NANCY--- IT'S STARTING TO RAIN
-ERNIE BUSHMILLER
DON'T WORRY--- I WON'T GET WET
-APR-16

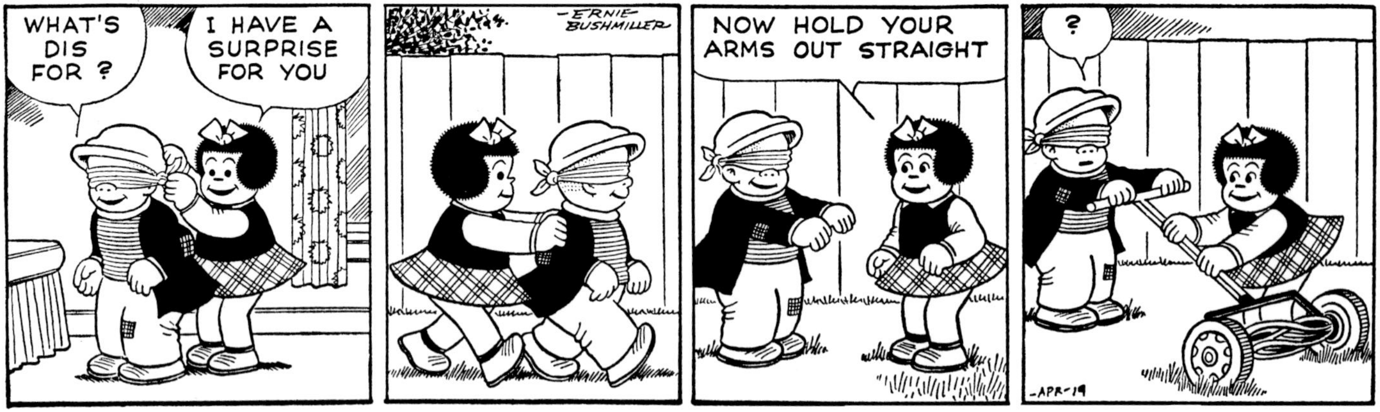
WHAT'S DIS FOR ?
I HAVE A SURPRISE FOR YOU
-ERNIE BUSHMILLER
NOW HOLD YOUR ARMS OUT STRAIGHT
?
-APR-19

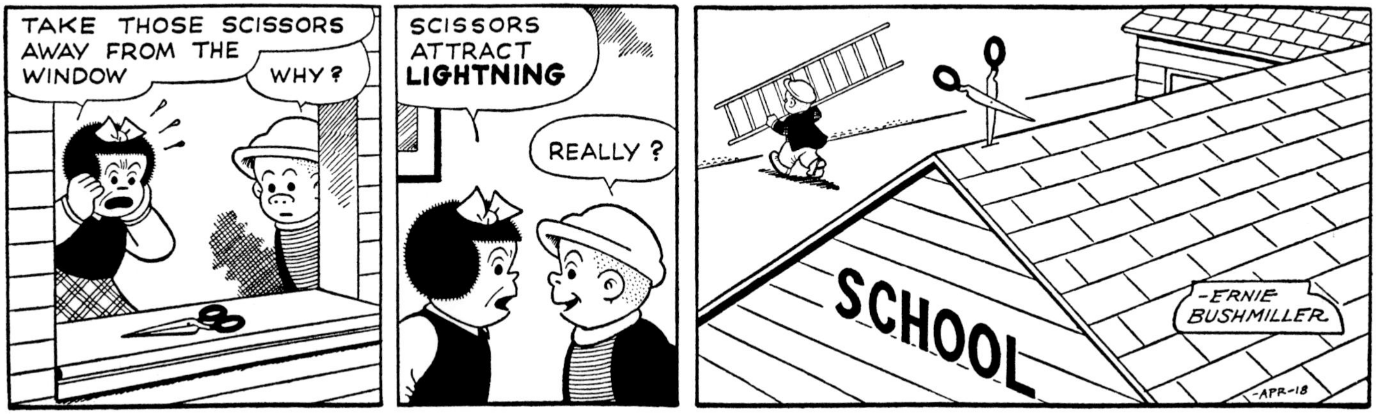
TAKE THOSE SCISSORS AWAY FROM THE WINDOW
WHY ?
SCISSORS ATTRACT LIGHTNING
REALLY ?
SCHOOL
-ERNIE BUSHMILLER
-APR-18

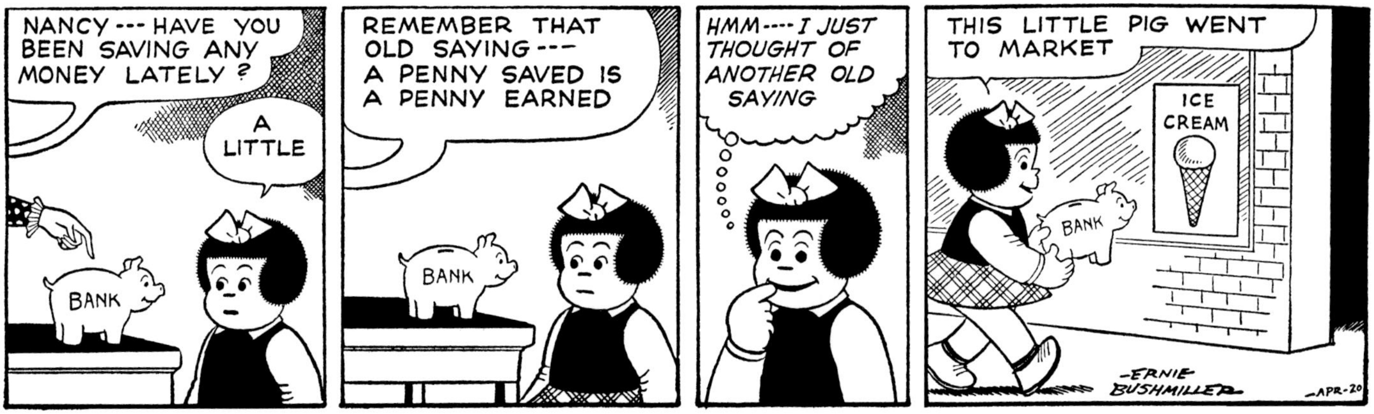
NANCY --- HAVE YOU BEEN SAVING ANY MONEY LATELY?
A LITTLE
BANK
REMEMBER THAT OLD SAYING --- A PENNY SAVED IS A PENNY EARNED
BANK
HMM ---- I JUST THOUGHT OF ANOTHER OLD SAYING
THIS LITTLE PIG WENT TO MARKET
ICE CREAM
BANK
-ERNIE BUSHMILLER
-APR-20

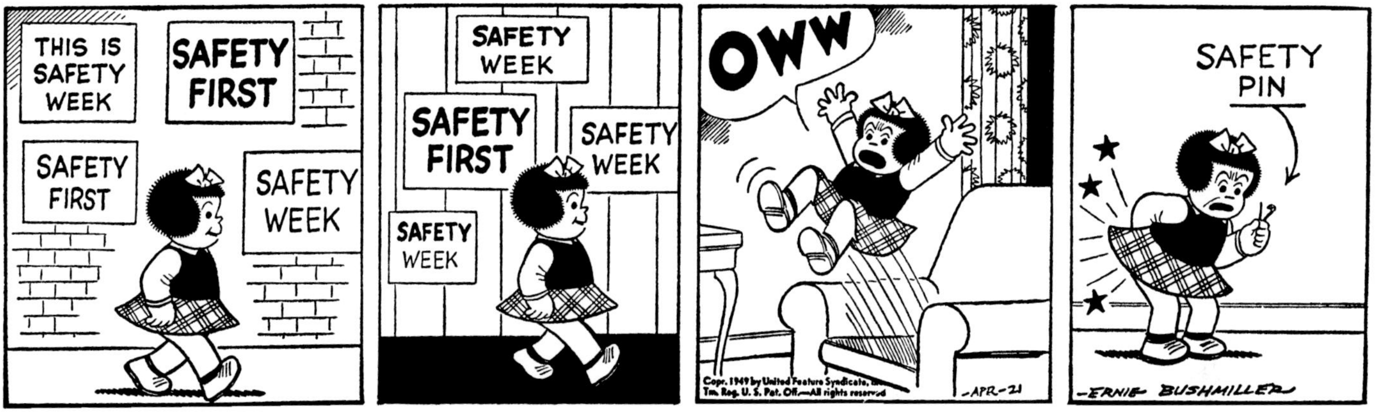
THIS IS SAFETY WEEK
SAFETY FIRST
SAFETY FIRST
SAFETY WEEK
SAFETY WEEK
SAFETY FIRST
SAFETY WEEK
SAFETY WEEK
OWW
Copr. 1949 by United Feature Syndicate,
Tm. Reg. U. S. Pat. Off.—All rights reserved
-APR-21
SAFETY PIN
-ERNIE BUSHMILLER

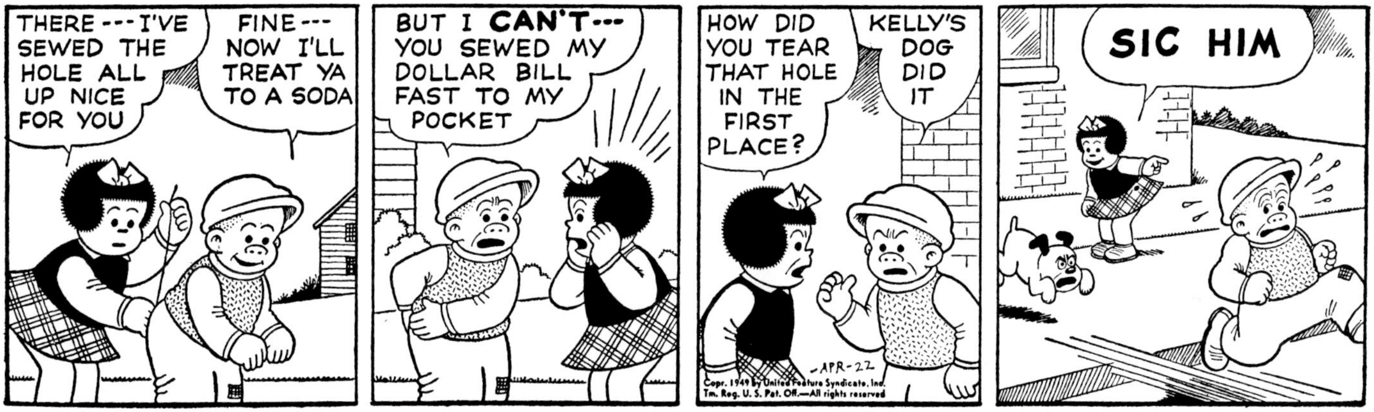
THERE --- I'VE SEWED THE HOLE ALL UP NICE FOR YOU
FINE --- NOW I'LL TREAT YA TO A SODA
BUT I CAN'T --- YOU SEWED MY DOLLAR BILL FAST TO MY POCKET
HOW DID YOU TEAR THAT HOLE IN THE FIRST PLACE?
KELLY'S DOG DID IT
-APR-22
Copr. 1949 by United Feature Syndicate, Inc.
Tm. Reg. U. S. Pat. Off.—All rights reserved
SIC HIM

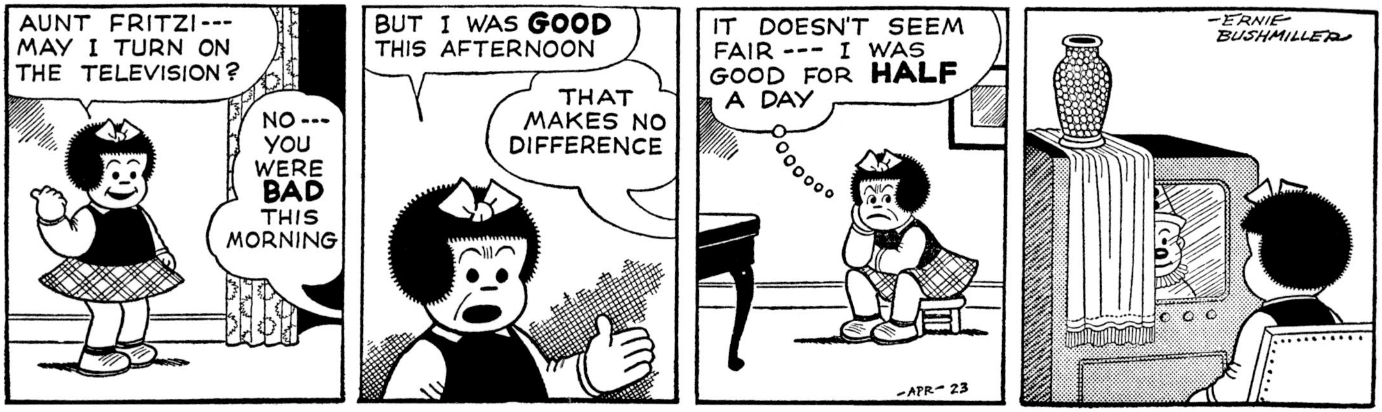
AUNT FRITZI--- MAY I TURN ON THE TELEVISION?
NO--- YOU WERE **BAD** THIS MORNING
BUT I WAS **GOOD** THIS AFTERNOON
THAT MAKES NO DIFFERENCE
IT DOESN'T SEEM FAIR --- I WAS GOOD FOR **HALF** A DAY
-APR- 23
-ERNIE BUSHMILLER

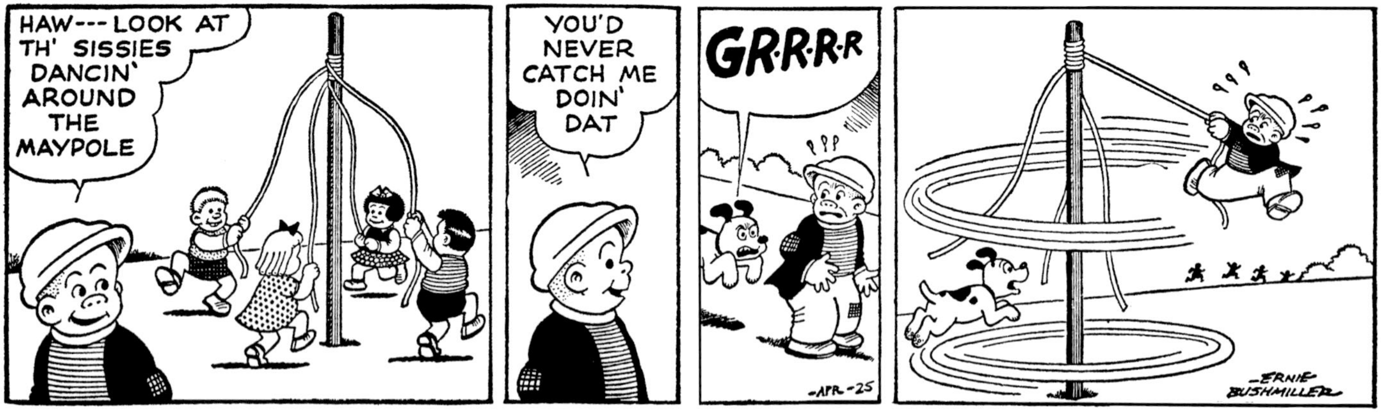
HAW---LOOK AT TH' SISSIES DANCIN' AROUND THE MAYPOLE
YOU'D NEVER CATCH ME DOIN' DAT
GR-R-R-R
-APR.-25
-ERNIE BUSHMILLER

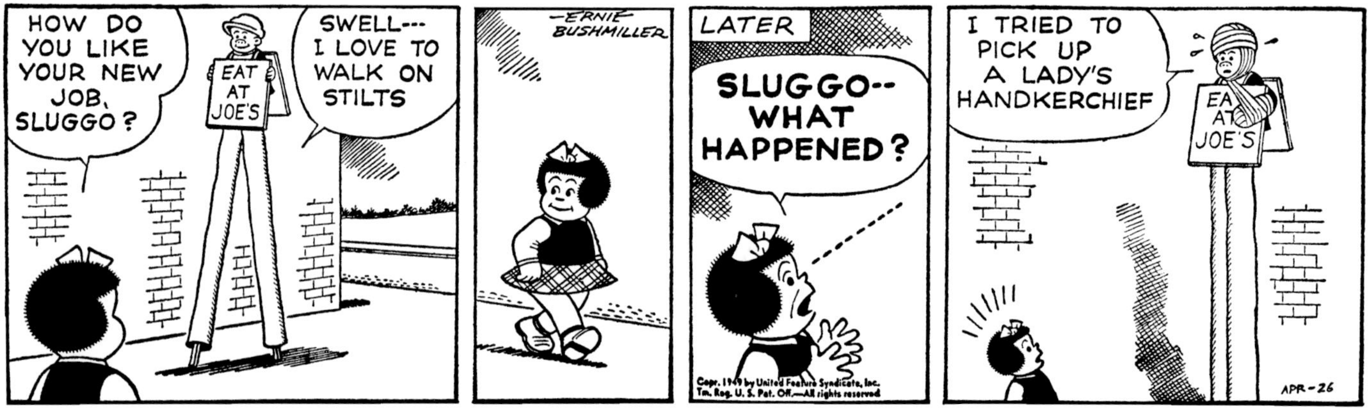
HOW DO YOU LIKE YOUR NEW JOB, SLUGGO?
EAT AT JOE'S
SWELL--- I LOVE TO WALK ON STILTS
-ERNIE BUSHMILLER
LATER
SLUGGO-- WHAT HAPPENED?
Copr. 1949 by United Feature Syndicate, Inc. Tm. Reg. U. S. Pat. Off.—All rights reserved
I TRIED TO PICK UP A LADY'S HANDKERCHIEF
EA AT JOE'S
APR-26

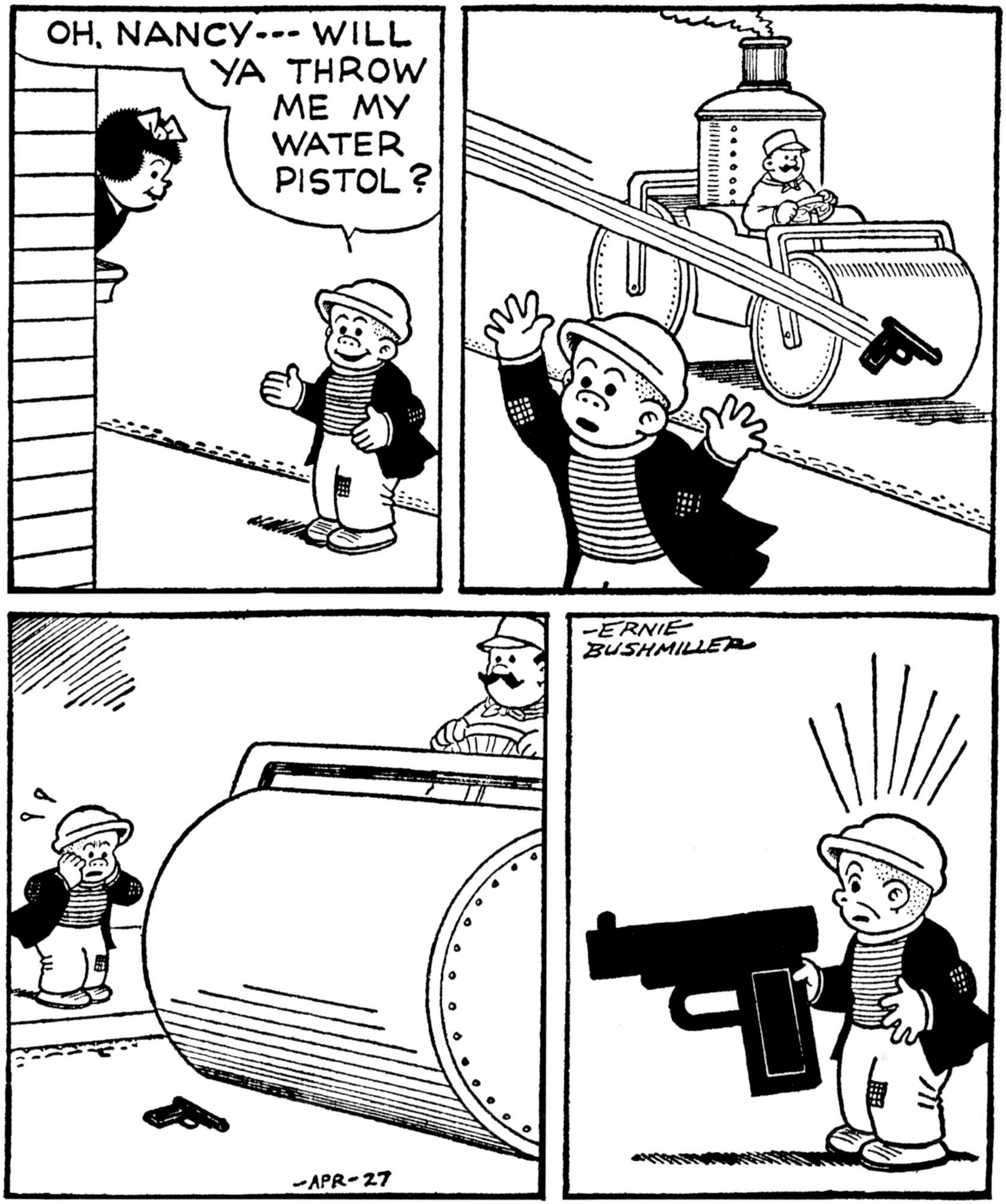
OH, NANCY--- WILL YA THROW ME MY WATER PISTOL?
-ERNIE BUSHMILLER
-APR-27

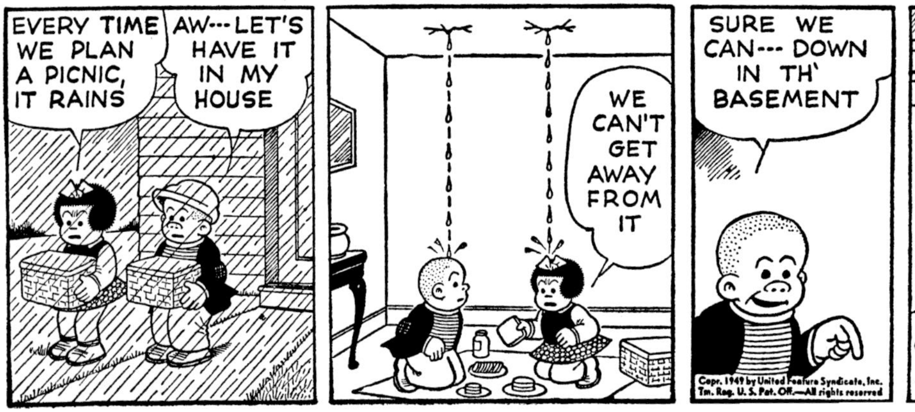
EVERY TIME WE PLAN A PICNIC, IT RAINS
AW--- LET'S HAVE IT IN MY HOUSE
WE CAN'T GET AWAY FROM IT
SURE WE CAN--- DOWN IN TH' BASEMENT
Copr. 1949 by United Feature Syndicate, Inc. Tm. Reg. U. S. Pat. Off.—All rights reserved
ERNIE BUSHMILLER
APR-28

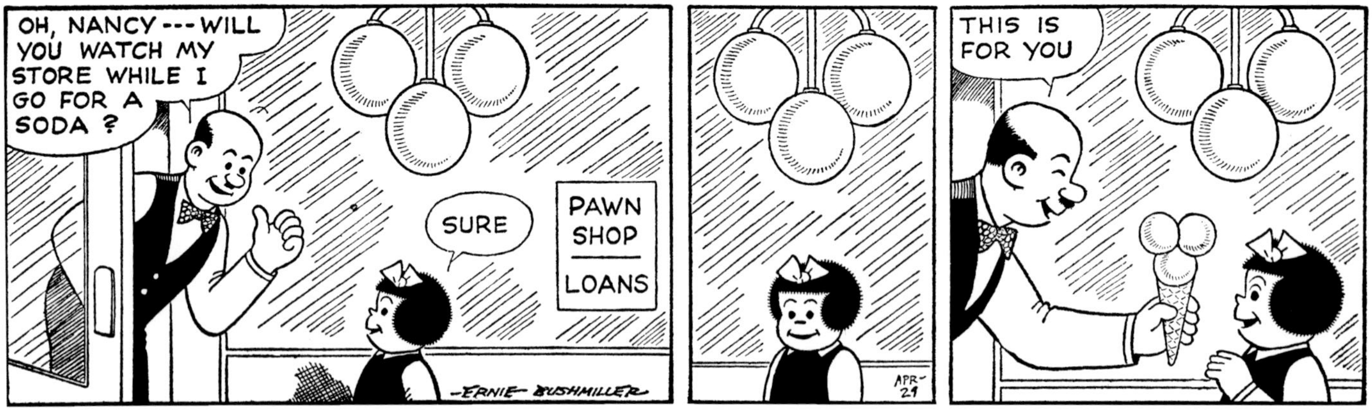
OH, NANCY --- WILL YOU WATCH MY STORE WHILE I GO FOR A SODA ?
SURE
PAWN SHOP
LOANS
ERNIE BUSHMILLER
APR-29
THIS IS FOR YOU

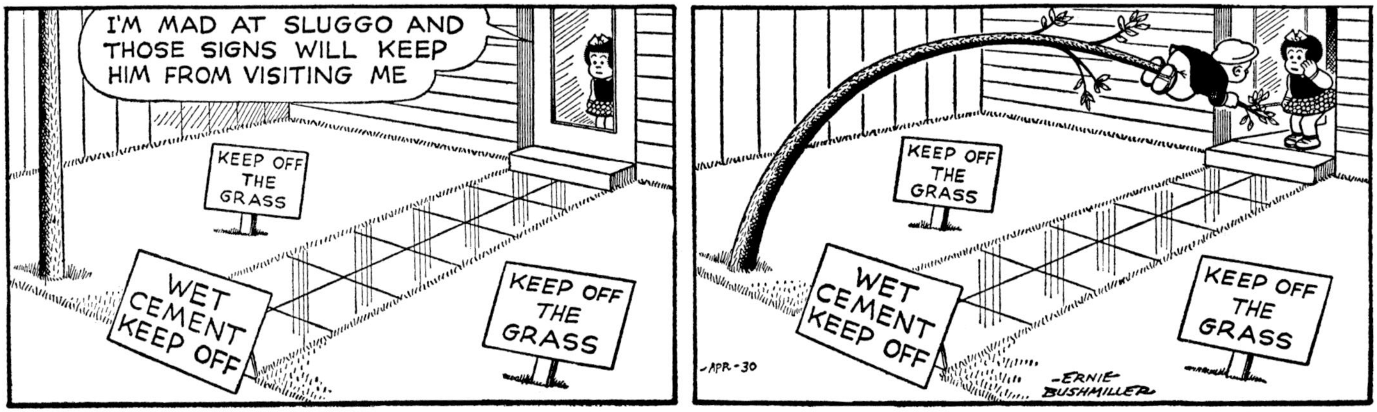
I'M MAD AT SLUGGO AND THOSE SIGNS WILL KEEP HIM FROM VISITING ME
KEEP OFF THE GRASS
WET CEMENT KEEP OFF
KEEP OFF THE GRASS
KEEP OFF THE GRASS
WET CEMENT KEEP OFF
KEEP OFF THE GRASS
APR-30
ERNIE BUSHMILLER

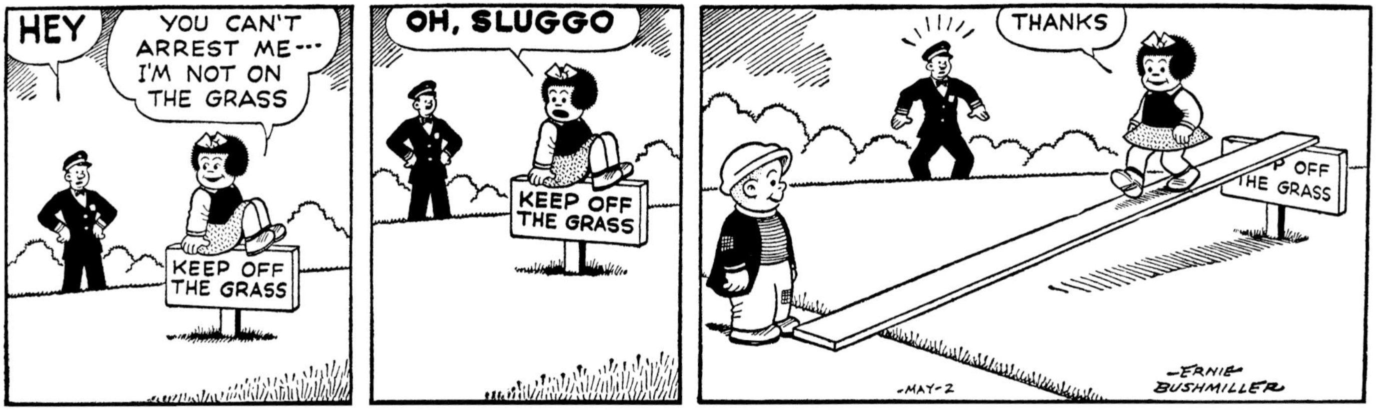
HEY
YOU CAN'T ARREST ME--- I'M NOT ON THE GRASS
KEEP OFF THE GRASS
OH, SLUGGO
KEEP OFF THE GRASS
THANKS
P OFF THE GRASS
-MAY-2
-ERNIE BUSHMILLER

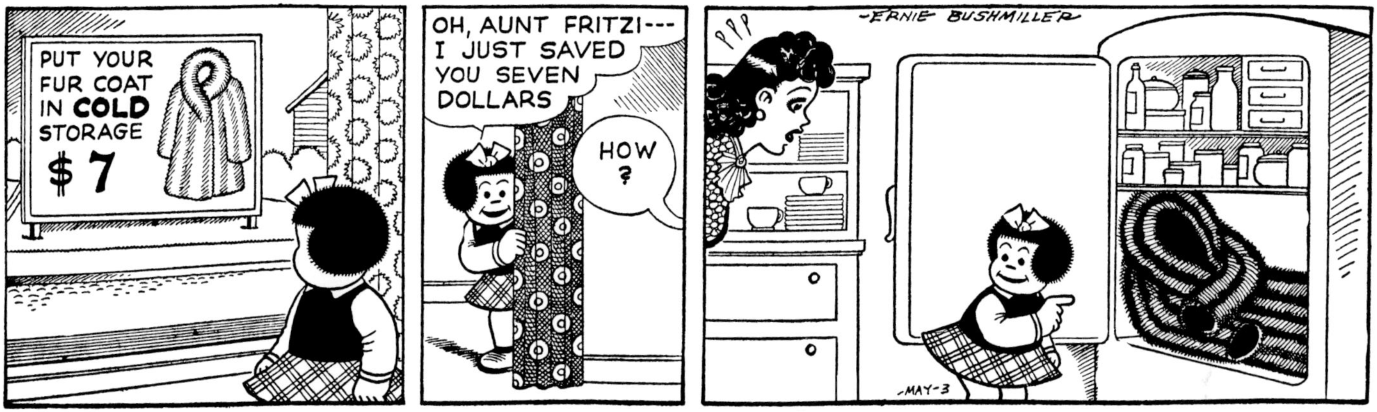
PUT YOUR FUR COAT IN COLD STORAGE $7
OH, AUNT FRITZI--- I JUST SAVED YOU SEVEN DOLLARS
HOW?
-ERNIE BUSHMILLER
-MAY-3

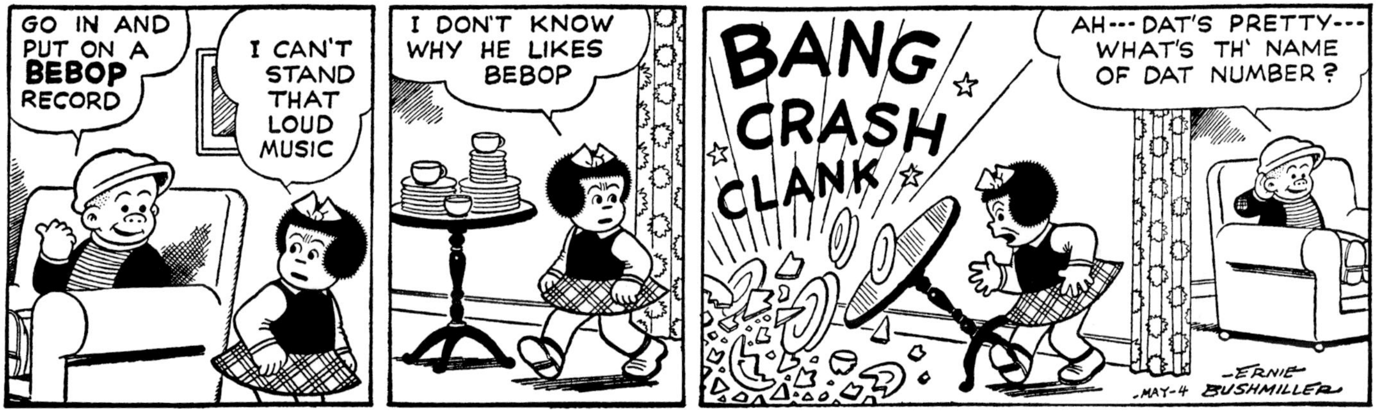
GO IN AND PUT ON A BEBOP RECORD
I CAN'T STAND THAT LOUD MUSIC
I DON'T KNOW WHY HE LIKES BEBOP
BANG
CRASH
CLANK
AH--- DAT'S PRETTY--- WHAT'S TH' NAME OF DAT NUMBER?
-MAY-4
-ERNIE BUSHMILLER

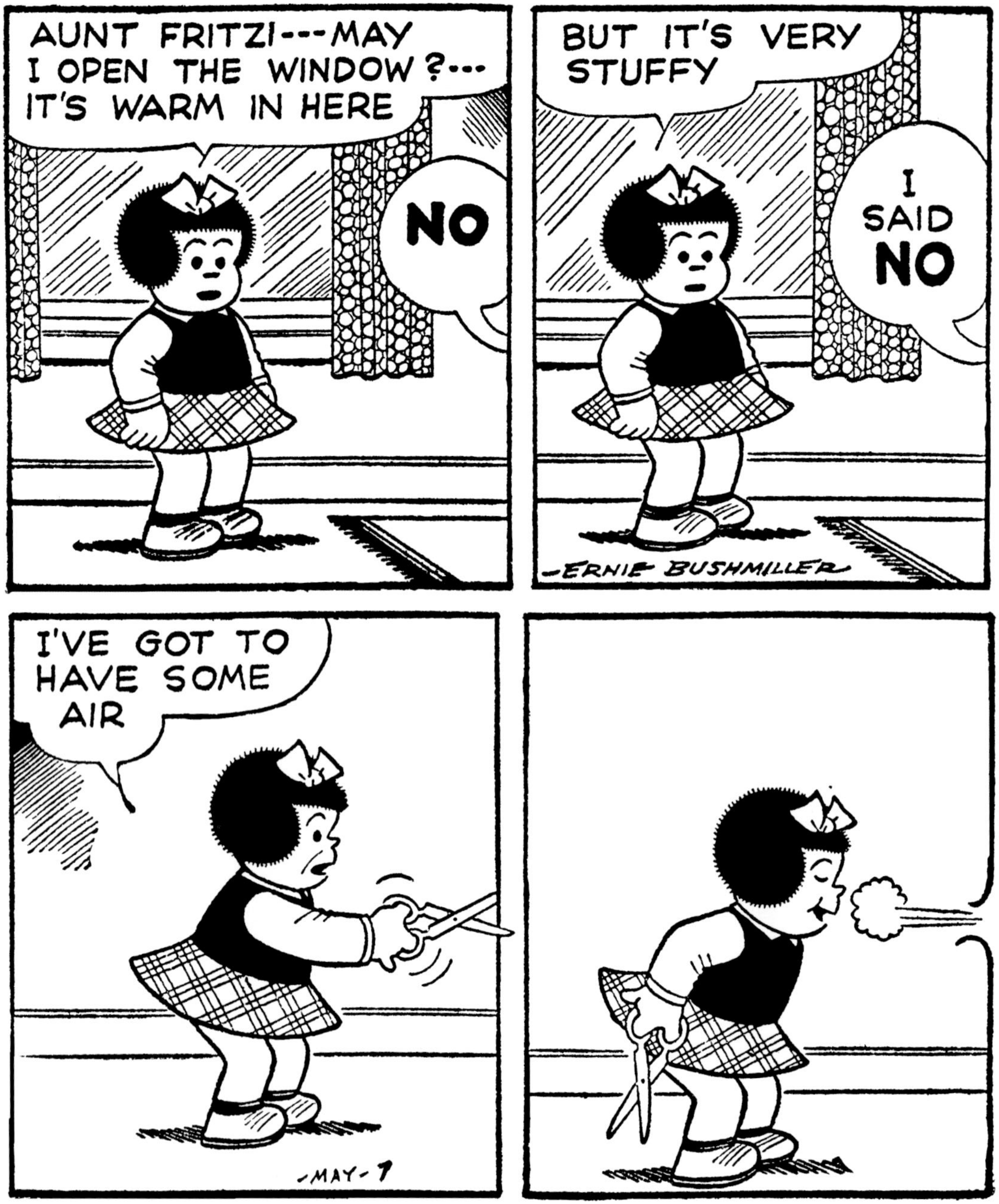
AUNT FRITZI---MAY I OPEN THE WINDOW?--- IT'S WARM IN HERE
NO
BUT IT'S VERY STUFFY
I SAID NO
ERNIE BUSHMILLER
I'VE GOT TO HAVE SOME AIR
MAY-7

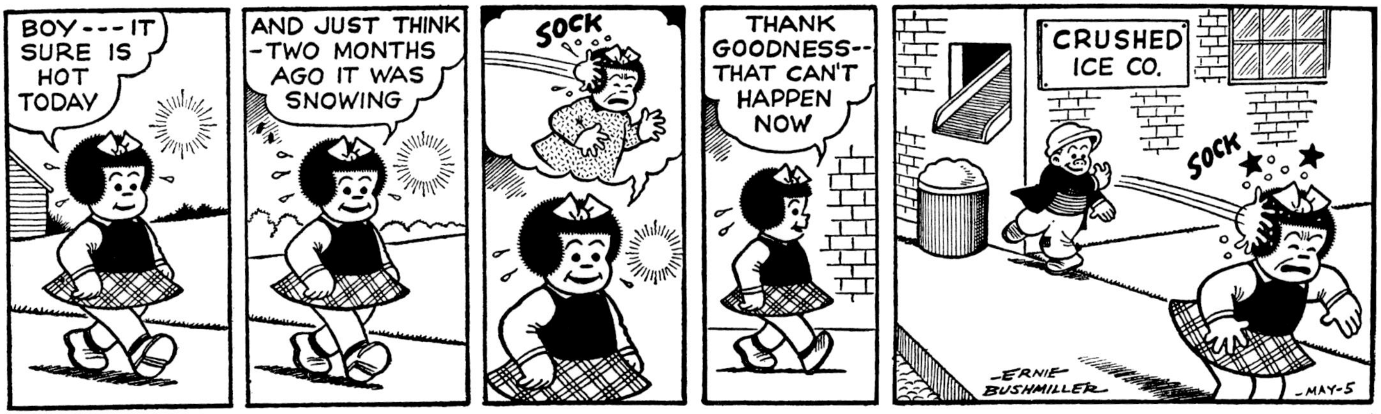
BOY---IT SURE IS HOT TODAY
AND JUST THINK -TWO MONTHS AGO IT WAS SNOWING
SOCK
THANK GOODNESS--THAT CAN'T HAPPEN NOW
CRUSHED ICE CO.
SOCK
-ERNIE BUSHMILLER
-MAY-5

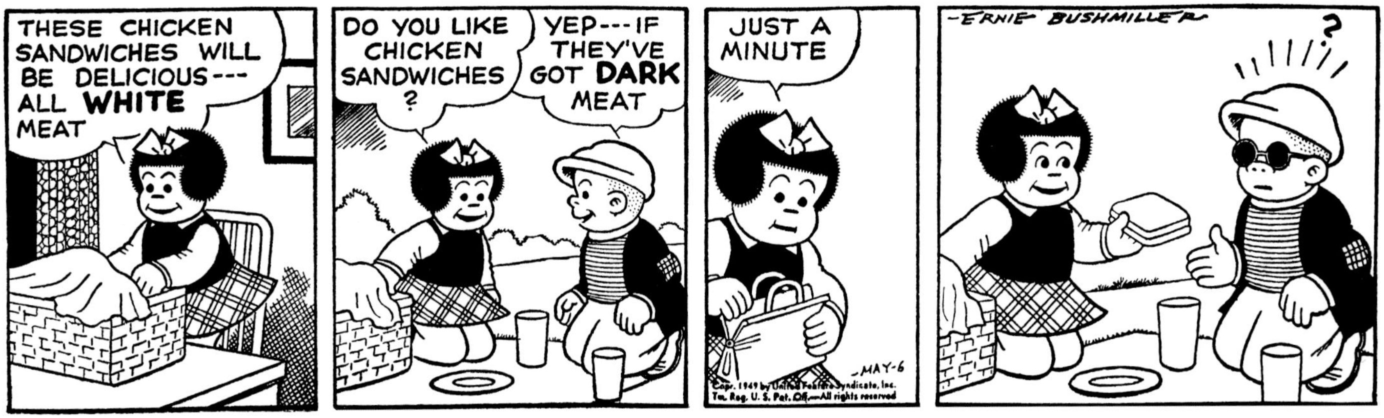
THESE CHICKEN SANDWICHES WILL BE DELICIOUS---ALL WHITE MEAT
DO YOU LIKE CHICKEN SANDWICHES ?
YEP---IF THEY'VE GOT DARK MEAT
JUST A MINUTE
-MAY-6
Copr. 1949 by United Feature Syndicate, Inc.
Tm. Reg. U. S. Pat. Off.—All rights reserved
-ERNIE BUSHMILLER
?

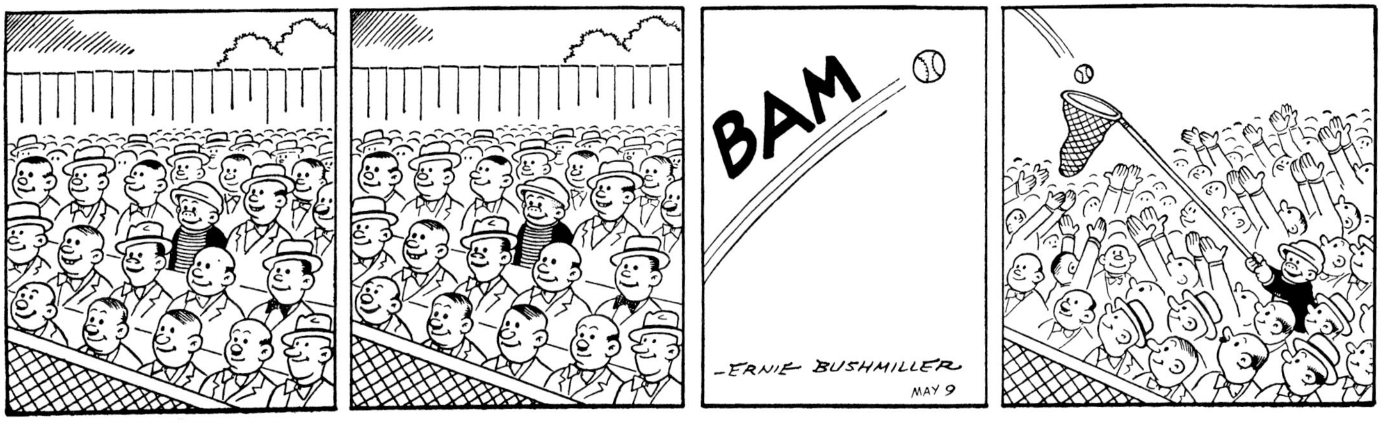
BAM
-ERNIE BUSHMILLER
MAY 9

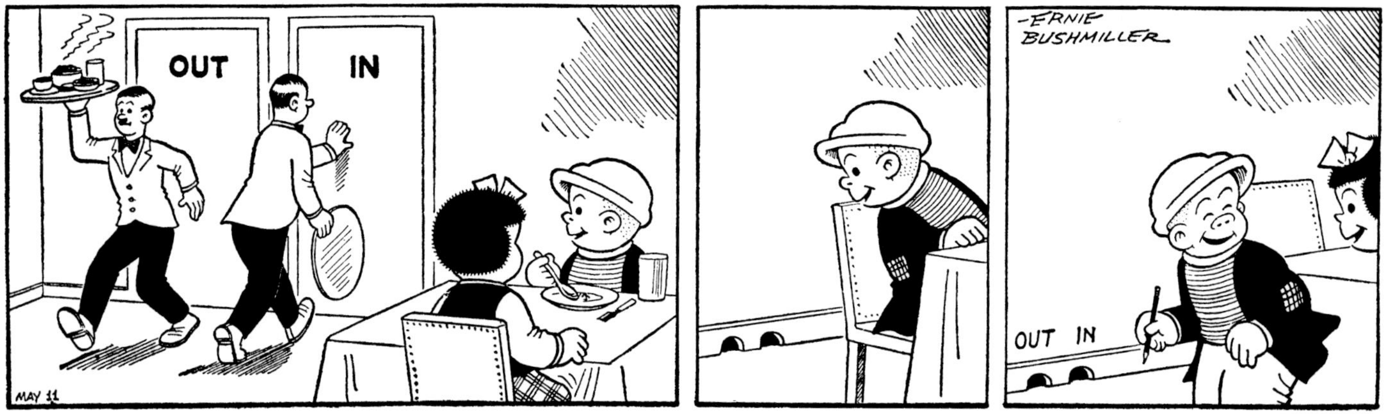
OUT
IN
MAY 11
-ERNIE BUSHMILLER
OUT IN

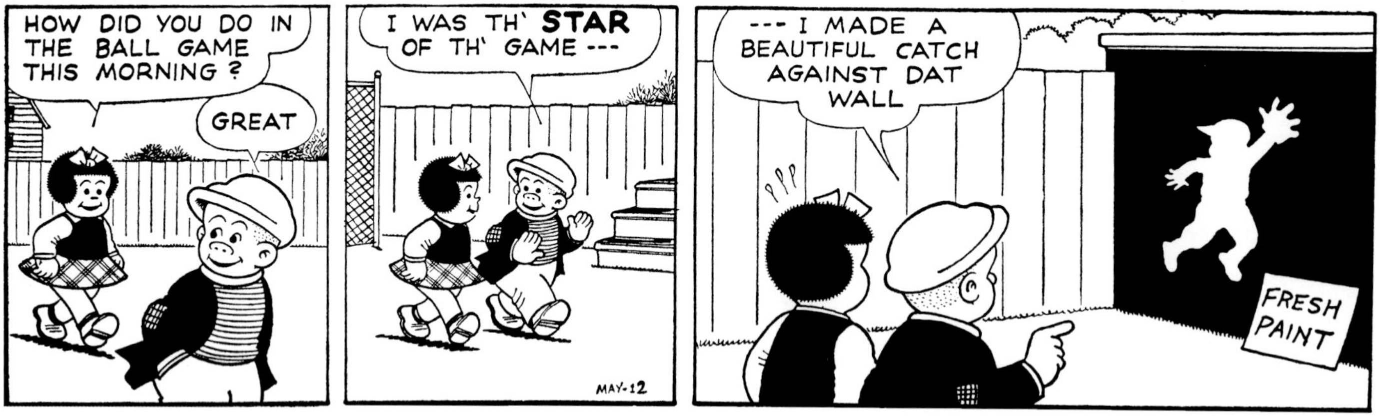
HOW DID YOU DO IN THE BALL GAME THIS MORNING ?
GREAT
I WAS TH' STAR OF TH' GAME ---
MAY-12
--- I MADE A BEAUTIFUL CATCH AGAINST DAT WALL
FRESH PAINT

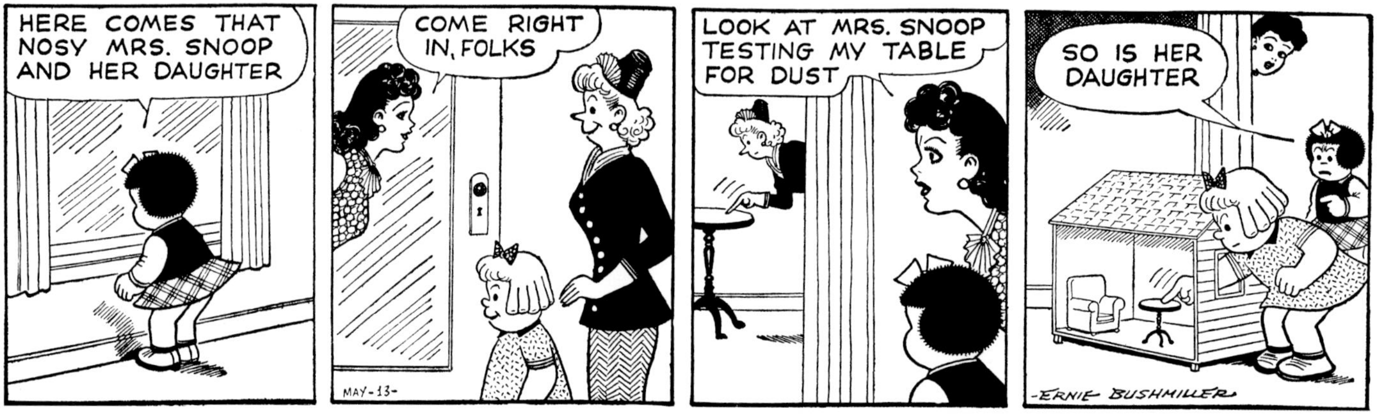
HERE COMES THAT NOSY MRS. SNOOP AND HER DAUGHTER
COME RIGHT IN, FOLKS
MAY-13-
LOOK AT MRS. SNOOP TESTING MY TABLE FOR DUST
SO IS HER DAUGHTER
-ERNIE BUSHMILLER

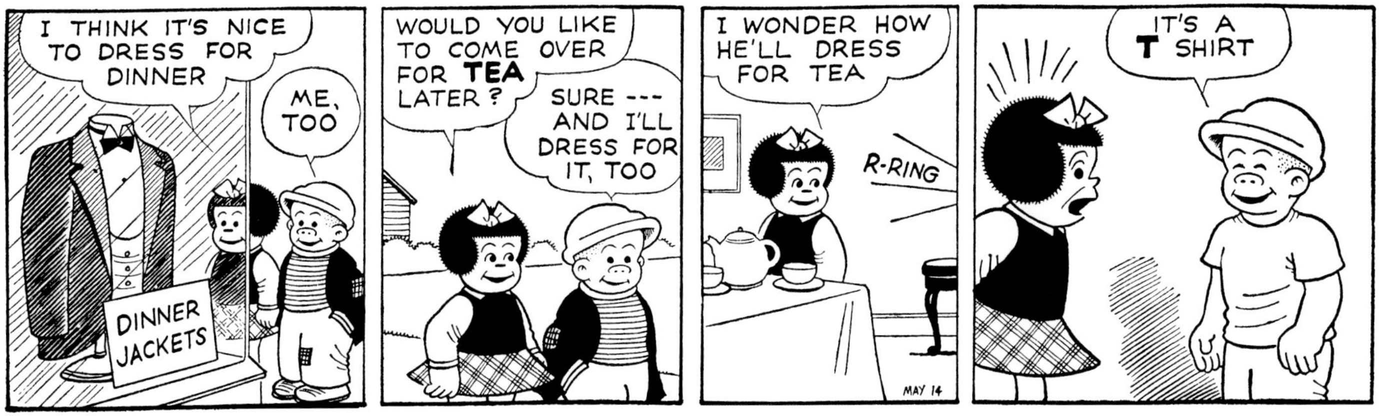
I THINK IT'S NICE TO DRESS FOR DINNER
DINNER JACKETS
ME, TOO
WOULD YOU LIKE TO COME OVER FOR **TEA** LATER ?
SURE --- AND I'LL DRESS FOR IT, TOO
I WONDER HOW HE'LL DRESS FOR TEA
R-RING
MAY 14
IT'S A **T** SHIRT

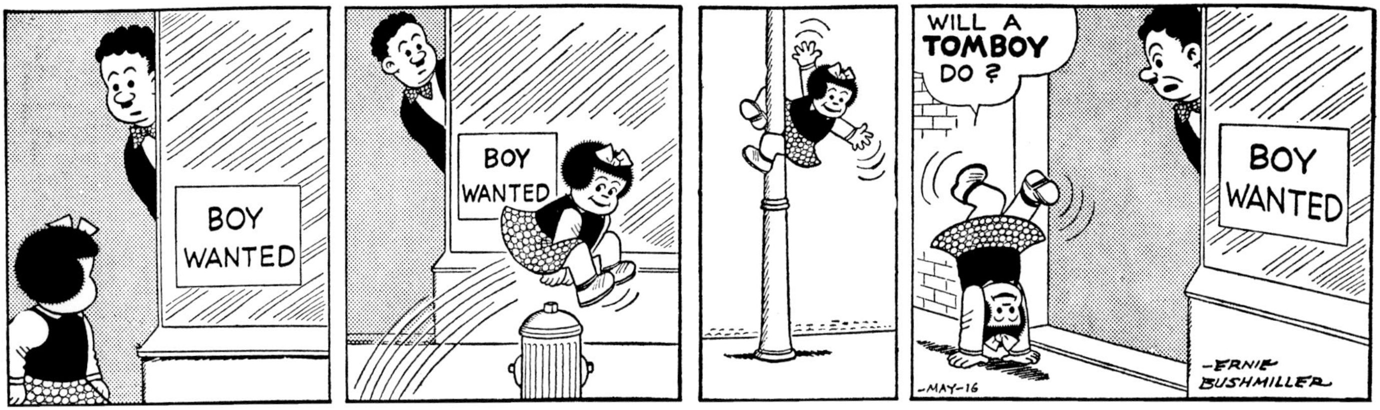
BOY WANTED
BOY WANTED
WILL A **TOMBOY** DO ?
BOY WANTED
-MAY-16
-ERNIE BUSHMILLER

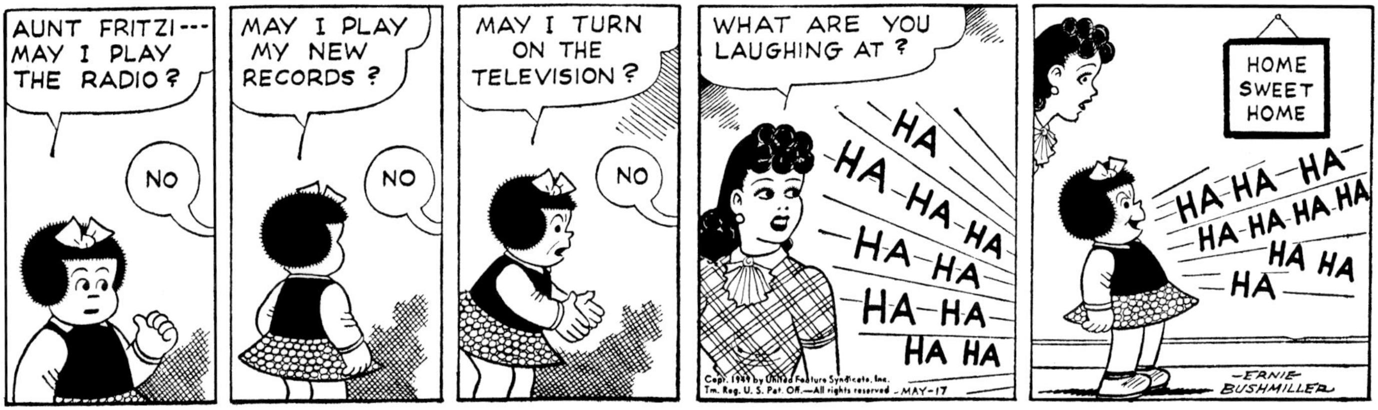
AUNT FRITZI--- MAY I PLAY THE RADIO ?
NO
MAY I PLAY MY NEW RECORDS ?
NO
MAY I TURN ON THE TELEVISION ?
NO
WHAT ARE YOU LAUGHING AT ?
HA HA-HA-HA-HA HA-HA HA-HA HA HA
Copr. 1949 by United Feature Syndicate, Inc.
Tm. Reg. U. S. Pat. Off.—All rights reserved
-MAY-17
HOME SWEET HOME
HA-HA-HA HA-HA-HA-HA HA-HA HA HA HA
-ERNIE BUSHMILLER

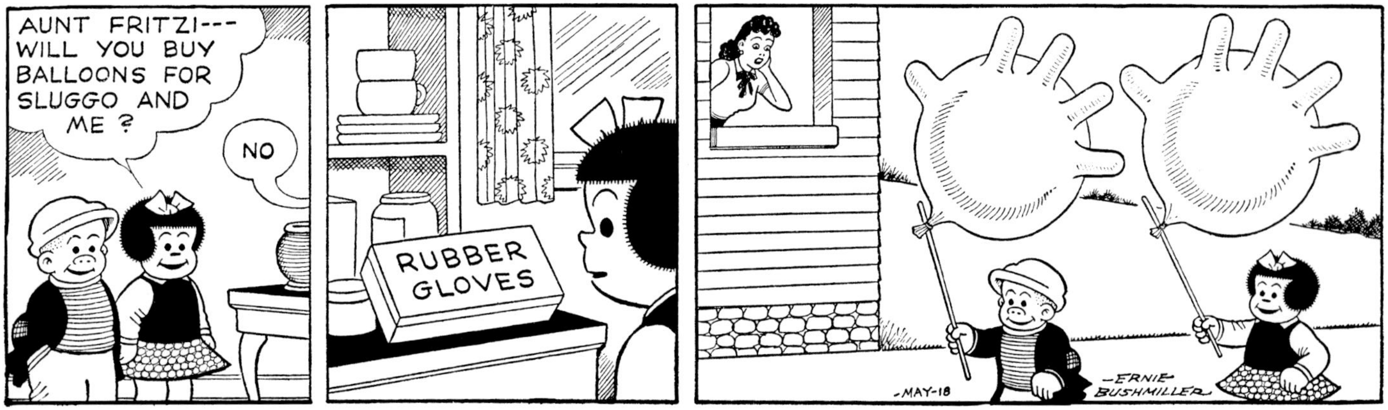
AUNT FRITZI--- WILL YOU BUY BALLOONS FOR SLUGGO AND ME ?
NO
RUBBER GLOVES
-MAY-18
-ERNIE BUSHMILLER

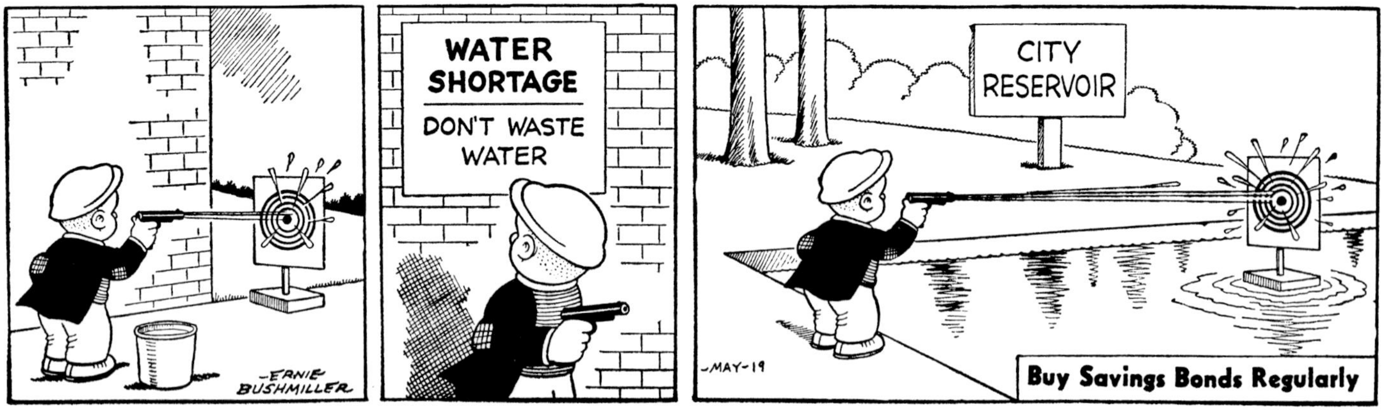
-ERNIE BUSHMILLER
WATER SHORTAGE
DON'T WASTE WATER
CITY RESERVOIR
-MAY-19
Buy Savings Bonds Regularly

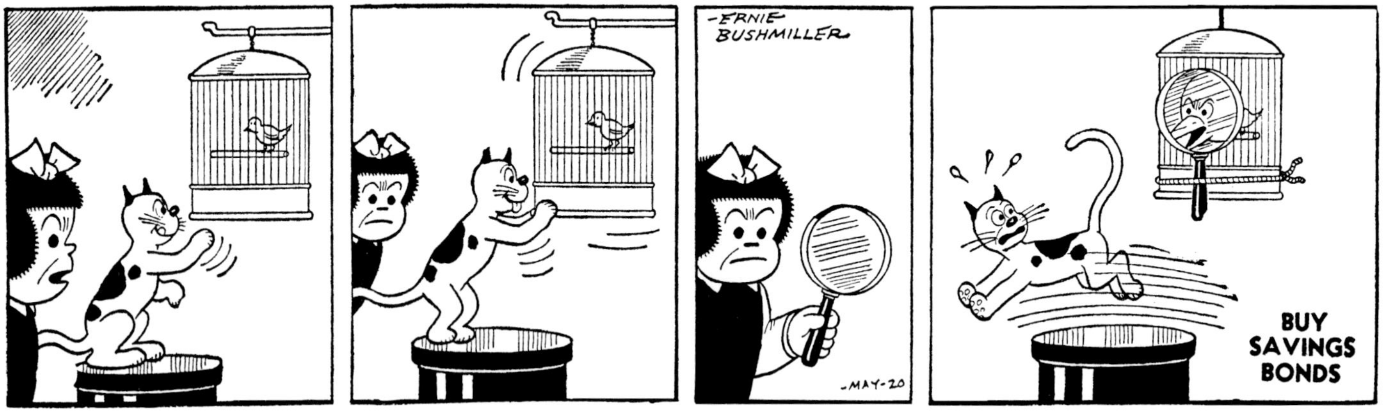
-ERNIE BUSHMILLER
-MAY-20
BUY SAVINGS BONDS

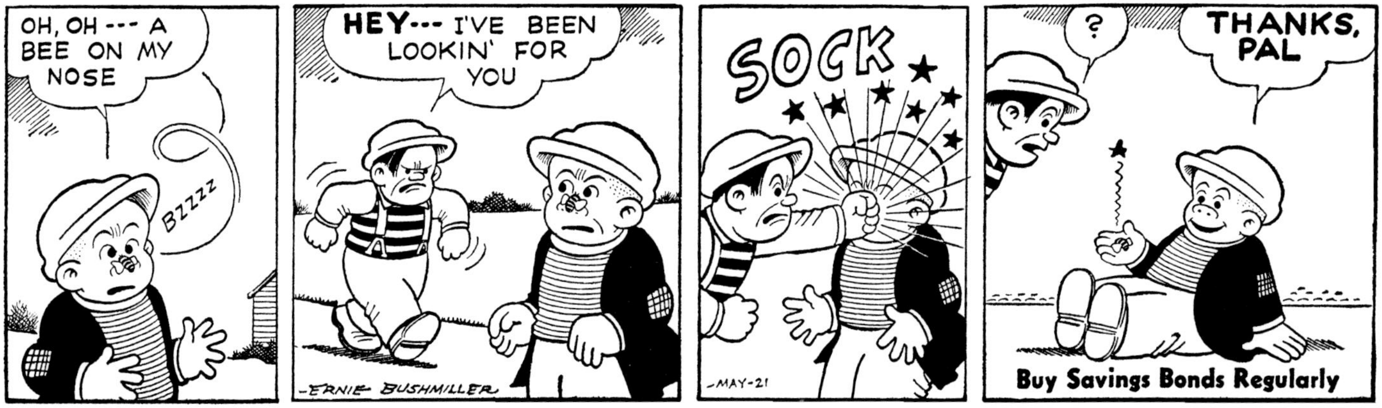
OH, OH --- A BEE ON MY NOSE
BZZZZ
HEY--- I'VE BEEN LOOKIN' FOR YOU
-ERNIE BUSHMILLER
SOCK
-MAY-21
?
THANKS, PAL
Buy Savings Bonds Regularly

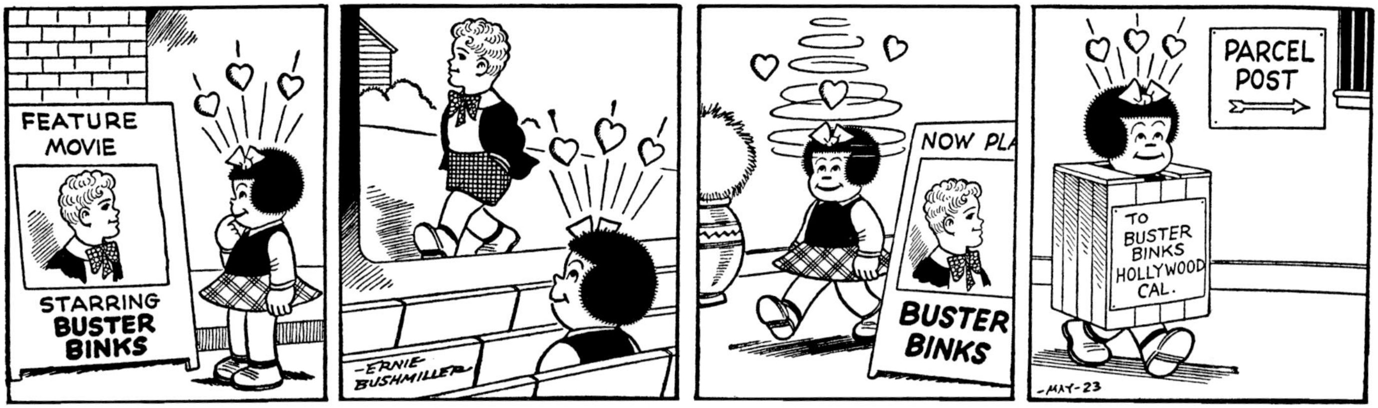
FEATURE MOVIE
STARRING BUSTER BINKS
-ERNIE BUSHMILLER
NOW PL
BUSTER BINKS
PARCEL POST
TO BUSTER BINKS HOLLYWOOD CAL.
-MAY-23

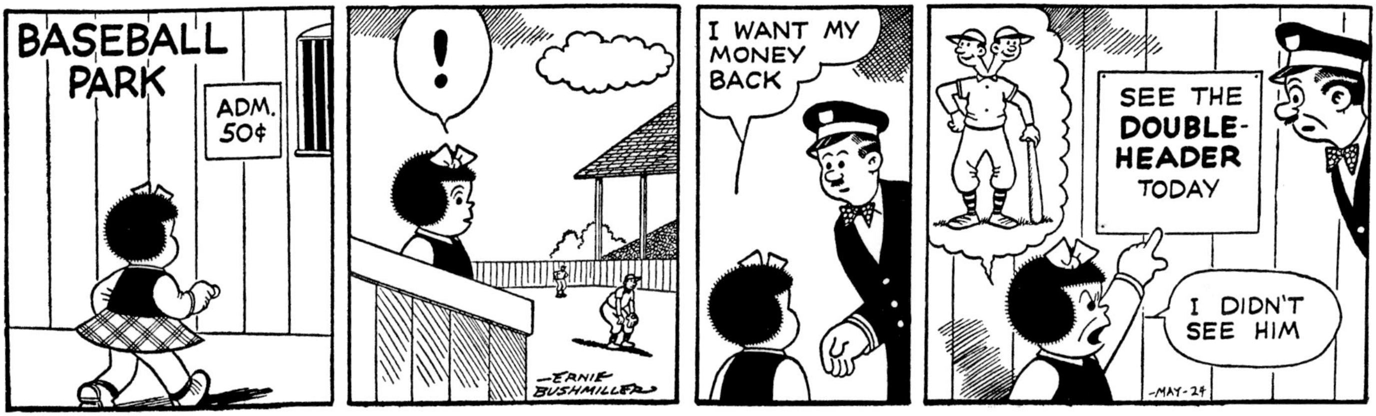
BASEBALL PARK
ADM. 50¢
!
-ERNIE BUSHMILLER
I WANT MY MONEY BACK
SEE THE DOUBLE-HEADER TODAY
I DIDN'T SEE HIM
-MAY-24

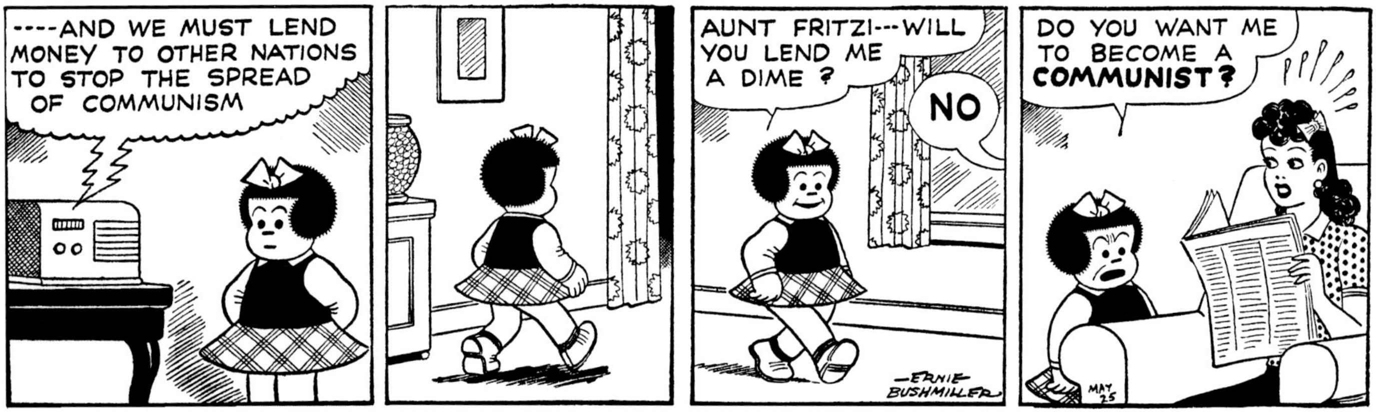
----AND WE MUST LEND MONEY TO OTHER NATIONS TO STOP THE SPREAD OF COMMUNISM
AUNT FRITZI---WILL YOU LEND ME A DIME ?
NO
DO YOU WANT ME TO BECOME A **COMMUNIST ?**
ERNIE BUSHMILLER
MAY 25

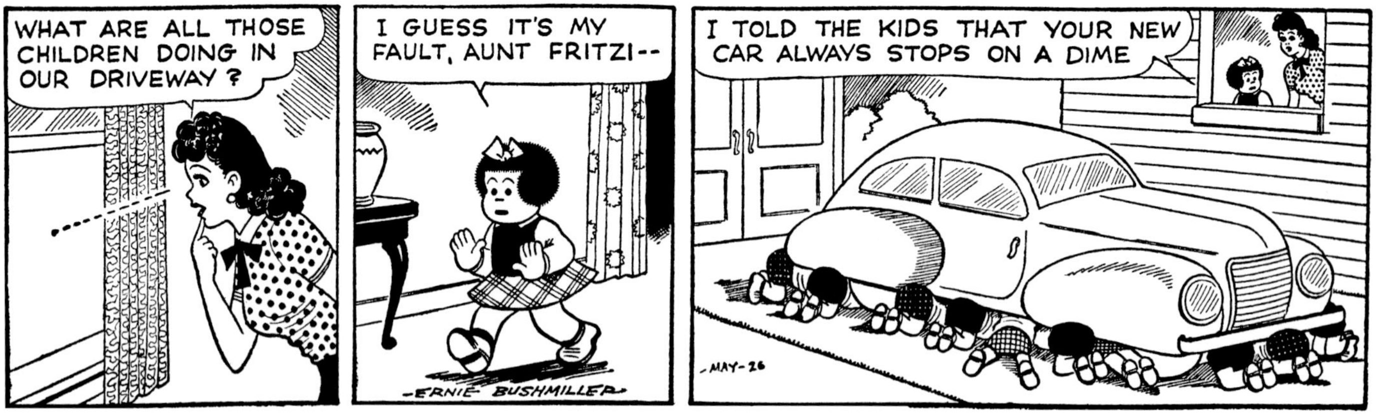
WHAT ARE ALL THOSE CHILDREN DOING IN OUR DRIVEWAY ?
I GUESS IT'S MY FAULT, AUNT FRITZI--
ERNIE BUSHMILLER
I TOLD THE KIDS THAT YOUR NEW CAR ALWAYS STOPS ON A DIME
MAY-26

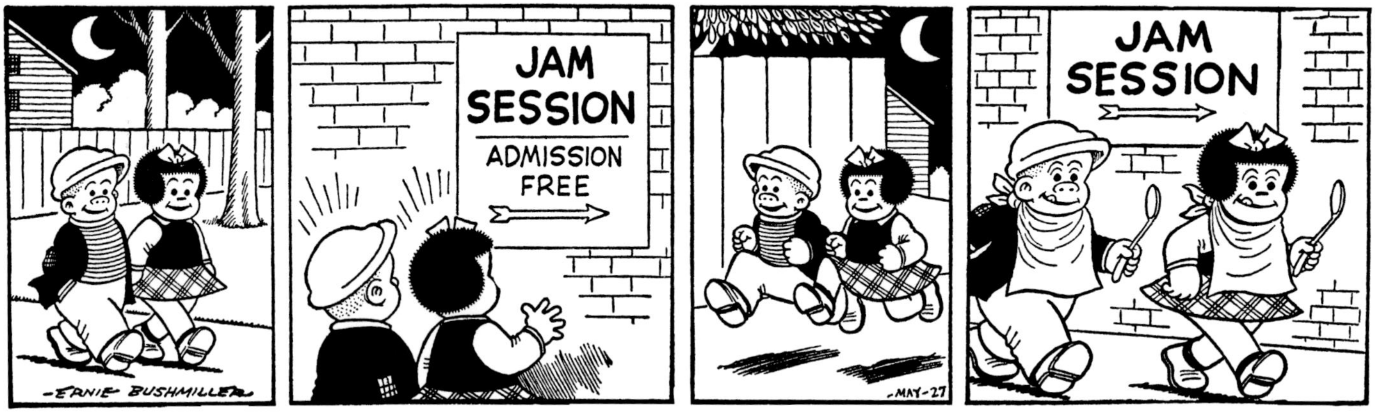
ERNIE BUSHMILLER
JAM SESSION
ADMISSION FREE
MAY-27
JAM SESSION

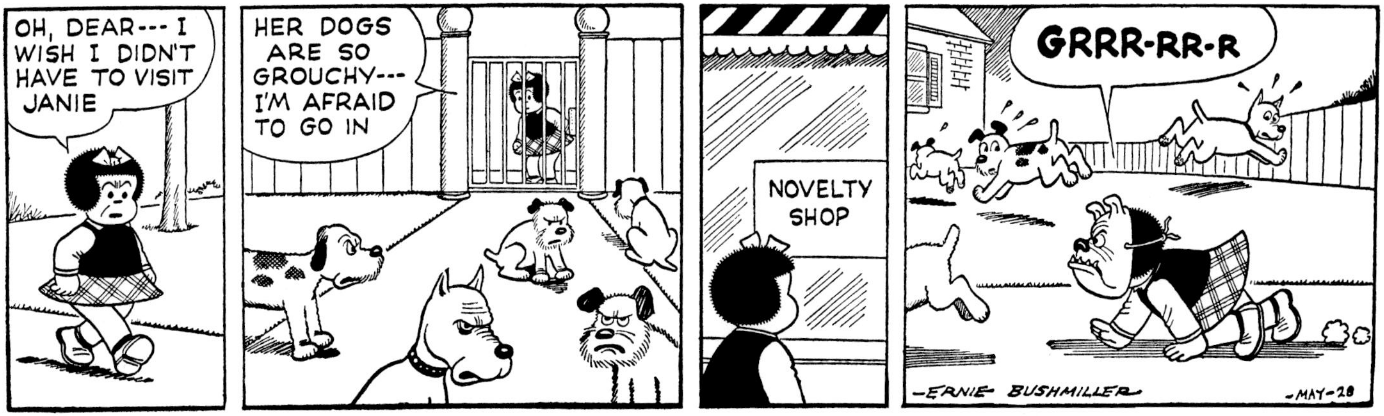
OH, DEAR--- I WISH I DIDN'T HAVE TO VISIT JANIE
HER DOGS ARE SO GROUCHY--- I'M AFRAID TO GO IN
NOVELTY SHOP
GRRR-RR-R
-ERNIE BUSHMILLER
-MAY-28

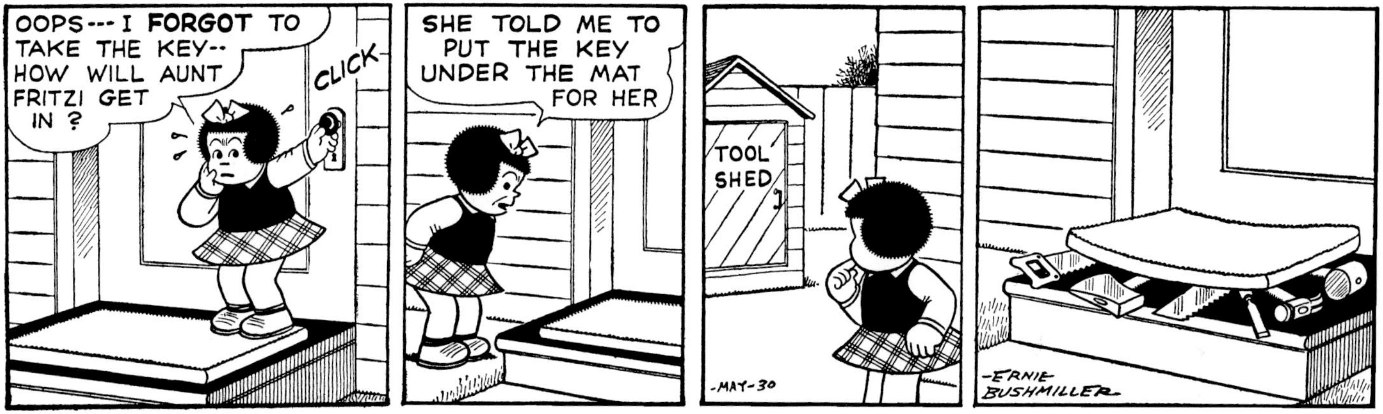
OOPS--- I FORGOT TO TAKE THE KEY-- HOW WILL AUNT FRITZI GET IN ?
CLICK
SHE TOLD ME TO PUT THE KEY UNDER THE MAT FOR HER
TOOL SHED
-MAY-30
-ERNIE BUSHMILLER

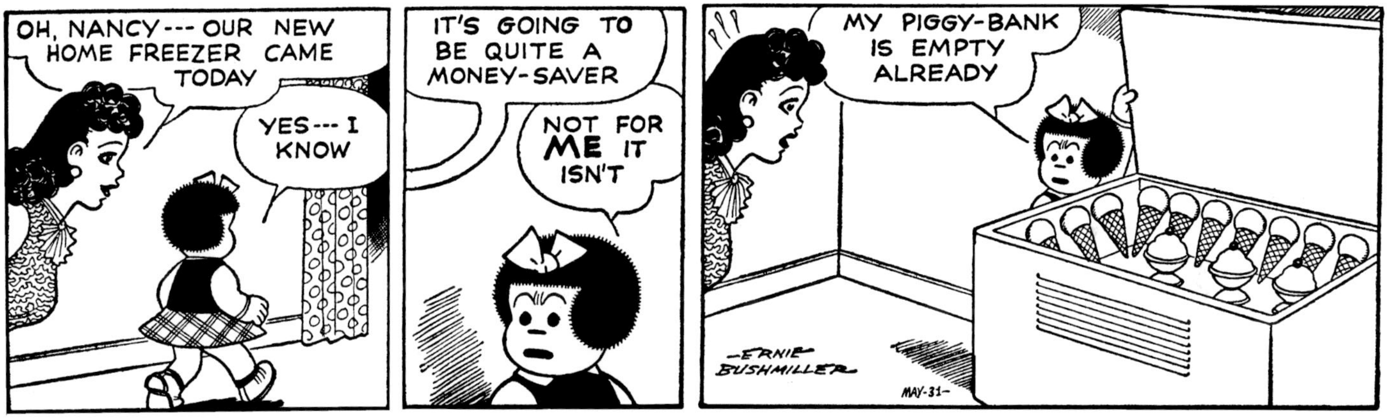
OH, NANCY--- OUR NEW HOME FREEZER CAME TODAY
YES--- I KNOW
IT'S GOING TO BE QUITE A MONEY-SAVER
NOT FOR ME IT ISN'T
MY PIGGY-BANK IS EMPTY ALREADY
-ERNIE BUSHMILLER
MAY-31-

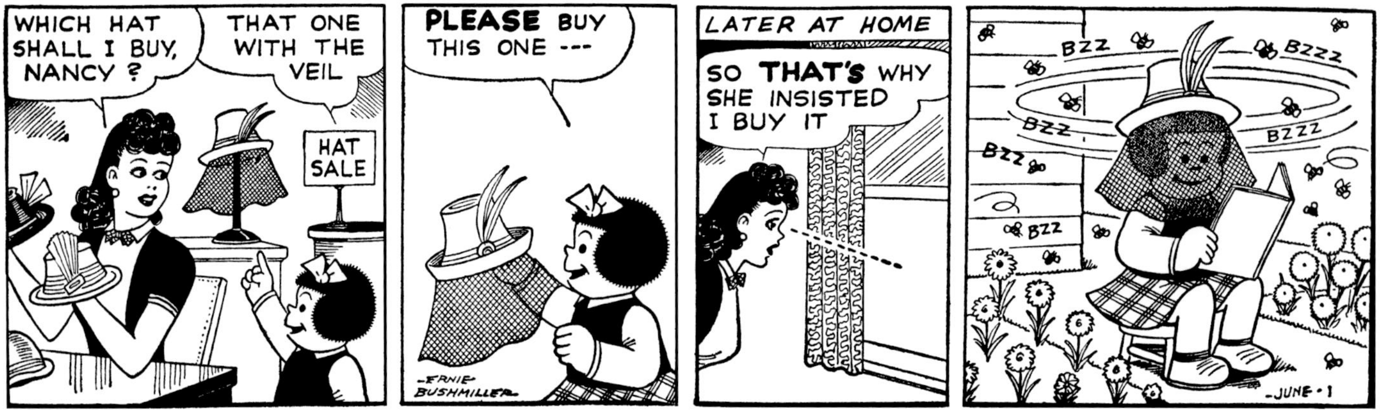
WHICH HAT SHALL I BUY, NANCY ?
THAT ONE WITH THE VEIL
HAT SALE
PLEASE BUY THIS ONE ---
-ERNIE BUSHMILLER
LATER AT HOME
SO THAT'S WHY SHE INSISTED I BUY IT
BZZ
BZZZ
BZZ
BZZZ
BZZ
BZZ
-JUNE-1

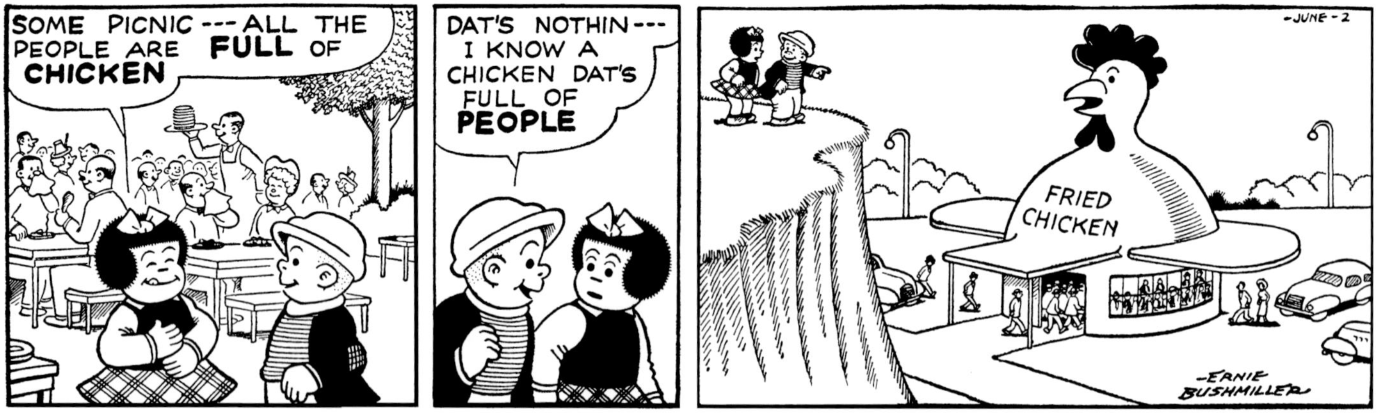
SOME PICNIC --- ALL THE PEOPLE ARE FULL OF CHICKEN
DAT'S NOTHIN --- I KNOW A CHICKEN DAT'S FULL OF PEOPLE
-JUNE-2
FRIED CHICKEN
-ERNIE BUSHMILLER

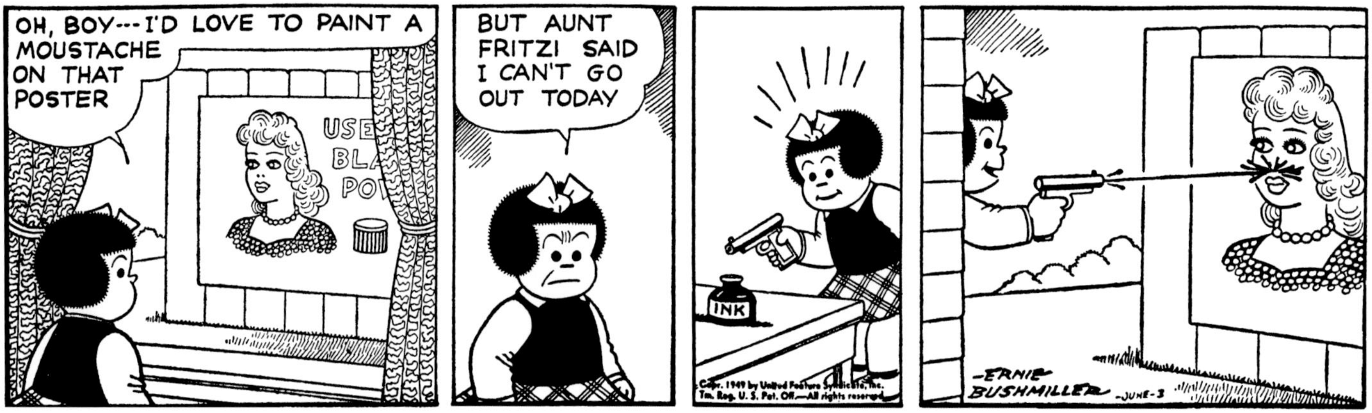
OH, BOY --- I'D LOVE TO PAINT A MOUSTACHE ON THAT POSTER
BUT AUNT FRITZI SAID I CAN'T GO OUT TODAY
INK
Copr. 1949 by United Feature Syndicate, Inc. Tm. Reg. U. S. Pat. Off.—All rights reserved
-ERNIE BUSHMILLER
-JUNE-3

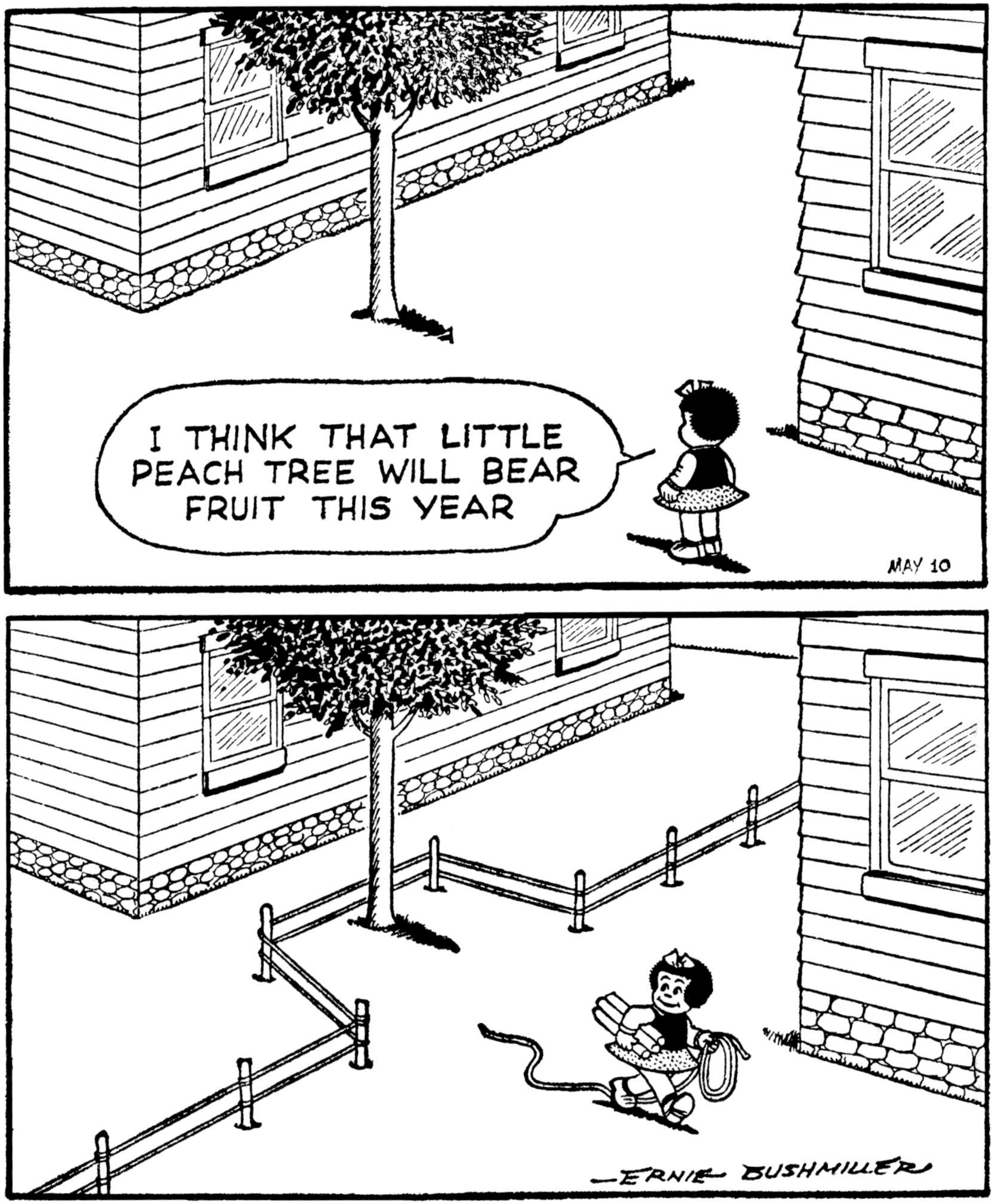
I THINK THAT LITTLE PEACH TREE WILL BEAR FRUIT THIS YEAR
MAY 10
ERNIE BUSHMILLER

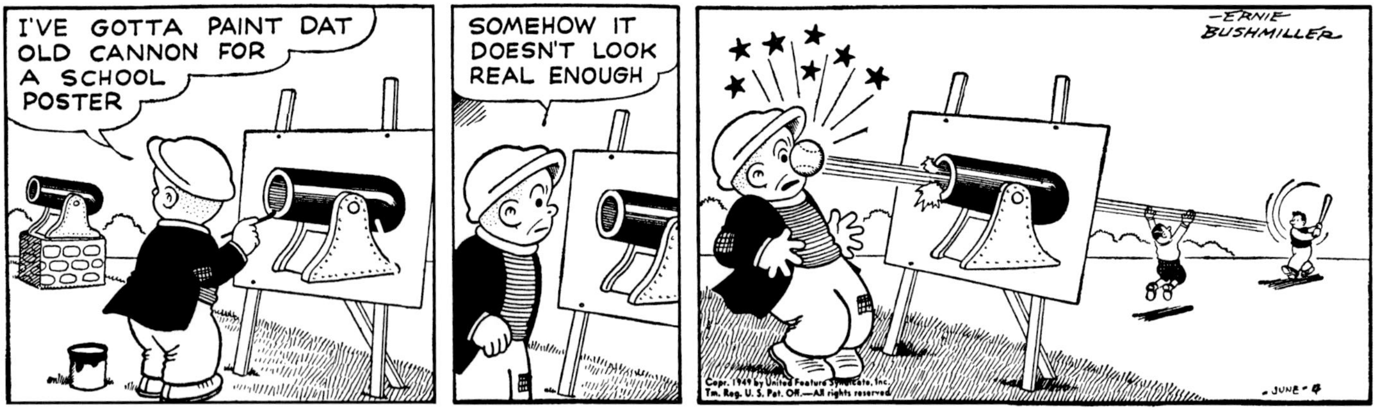
I'VE GOTTA PAINT DAT OLD CANNON FOR A SCHOOL POSTER
SOMEHOW IT DOESN'T LOOK REAL ENOUGH
-ERNIE BUSHMILLER
Copr. 1949 by United Feature Syndicate, Inc. Tm. Reg. U. S. Pat. Off.—All rights reserved
-JUNE-4

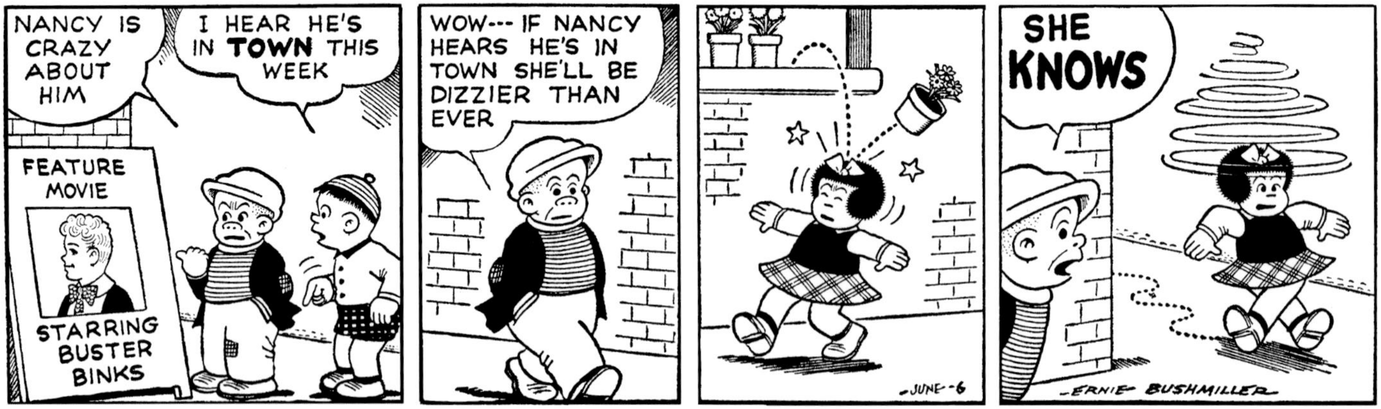
NANCY IS CRAZY ABOUT HIM
I HEAR HE'S IN **TOWN** THIS WEEK
FEATURE MOVIE
STARRING BUSTER BINKS
WOW--- IF NANCY HEARS HE'S IN TOWN SHE'LL BE DIZZIER THAN EVER
-JUNE-6
SHE KNOWS
-ERNIE BUSHMILLER

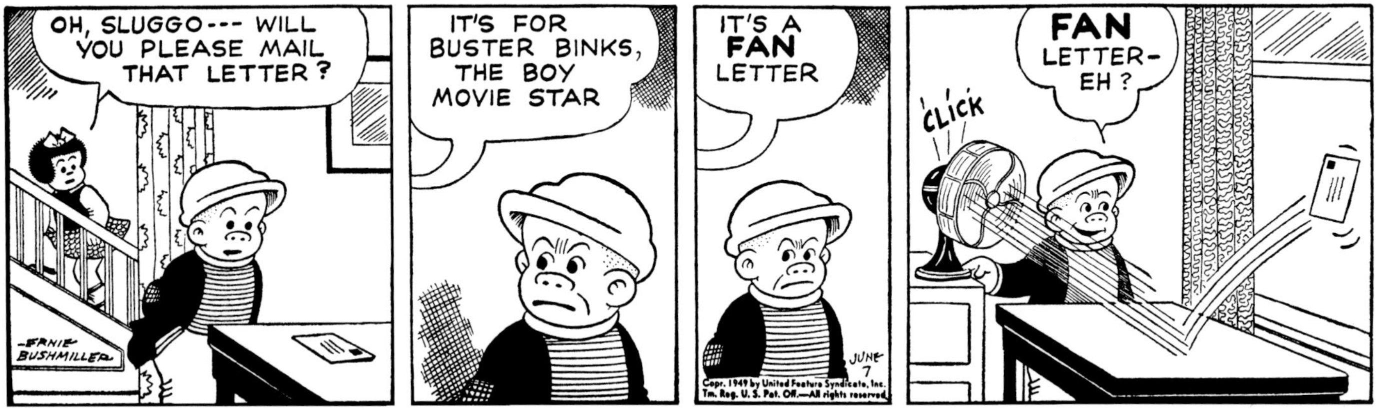
OH, SLUGGO--- WILL YOU PLEASE MAIL THAT LETTER?
-ERNIE BUSHMILLER
IT'S FOR BUSTER BINKS, THE BOY MOVIE STAR
IT'S A **FAN** LETTER
JUNE 7
Copr. 1949 by United Feature Syndicate, Inc. Tm. Reg. U. S. Pat. Off.—All rights reserved
CLICK
FAN LETTER-EH?

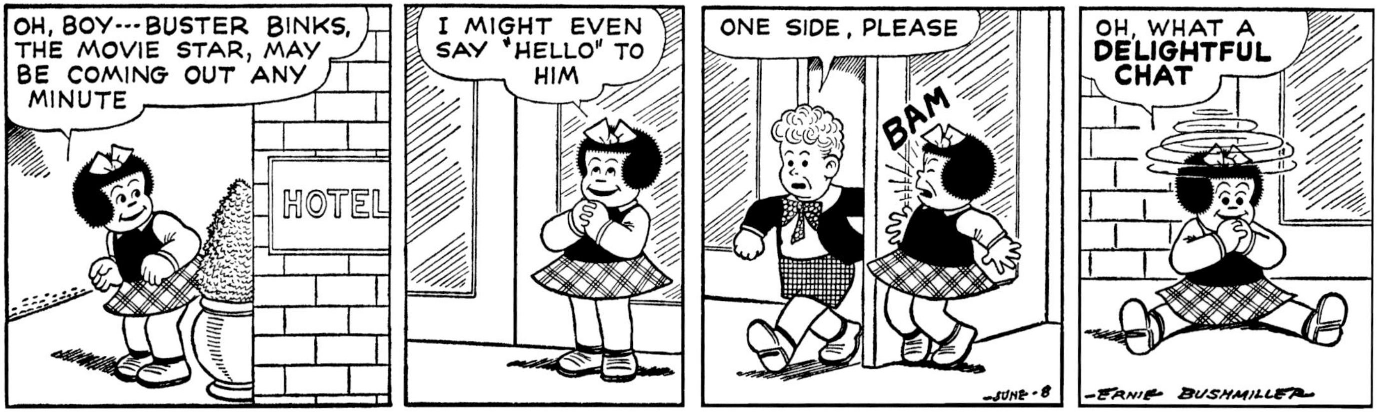
OH, BOY---BUSTER BINKS, THE MOVIE STAR, MAY BE COMING OUT ANY MINUTE
HOTEL
I MIGHT EVEN SAY "HELLO" TO HIM
ONE SIDE, PLEASE
BAM
JUNE-8
OH, WHAT A **DELIGHTFUL CHAT**
-ERNIE BUSHMILLER

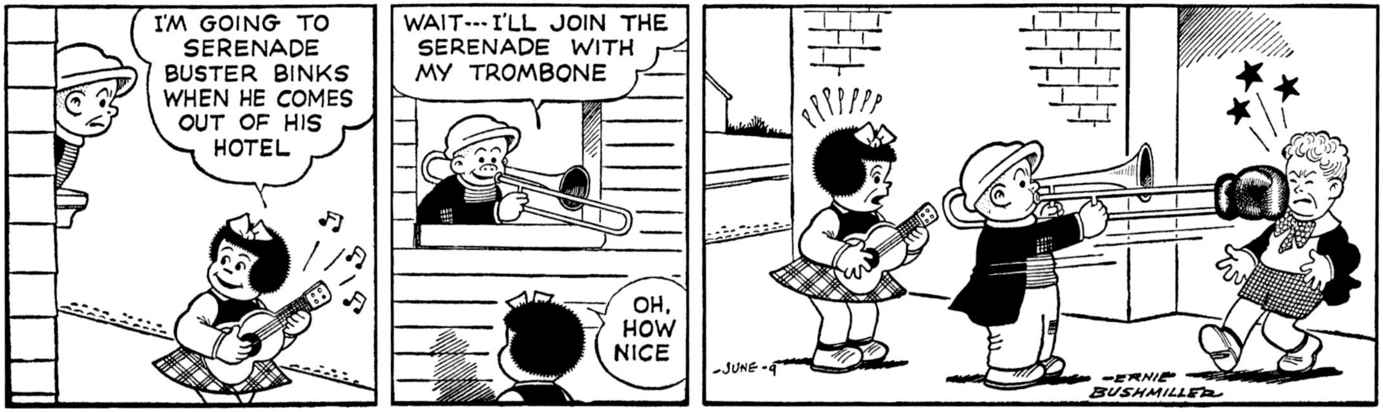
I'M GOING TO SERENADE BUSTER BINKS WHEN HE COMES OUT OF HIS HOTEL
WAIT---I'LL JOIN THE SERENADE WITH MY TROMBONE
OH, HOW NICE
-JUNE-9
-ERNIE BUSHMILLER

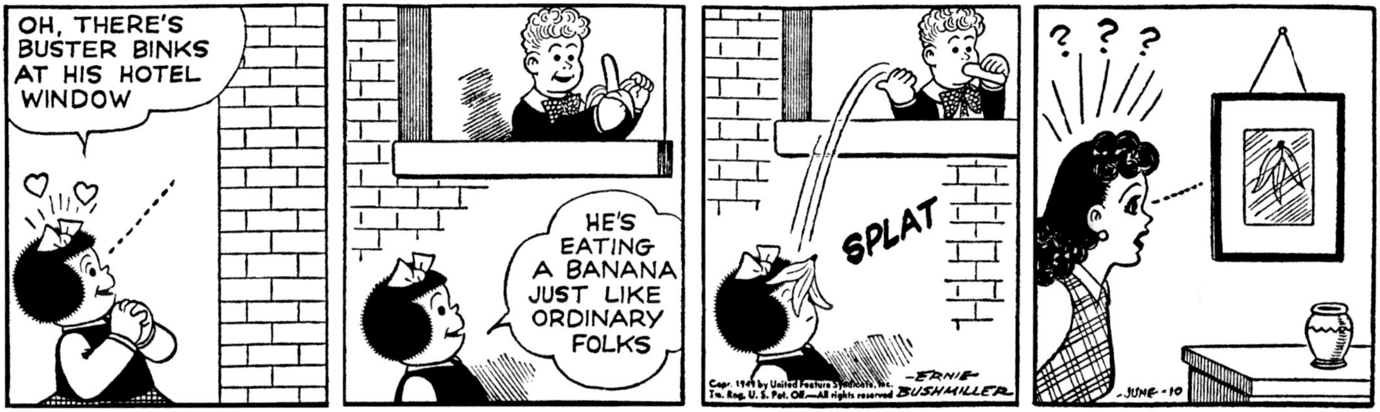
OH, THERE'S BUSTER BINKS AT HIS HOTEL WINDOW
HE'S EATING A BANANA JUST LIKE ORDINARY FOLKS
SPLAT
Copr. 1949 by United Feature Syndicate, Inc.
Tm. Reg. U. S. Pat. Off.—All rights reserved
-ERNIE BUSHMILLER
? ? ?
-JUNE-10

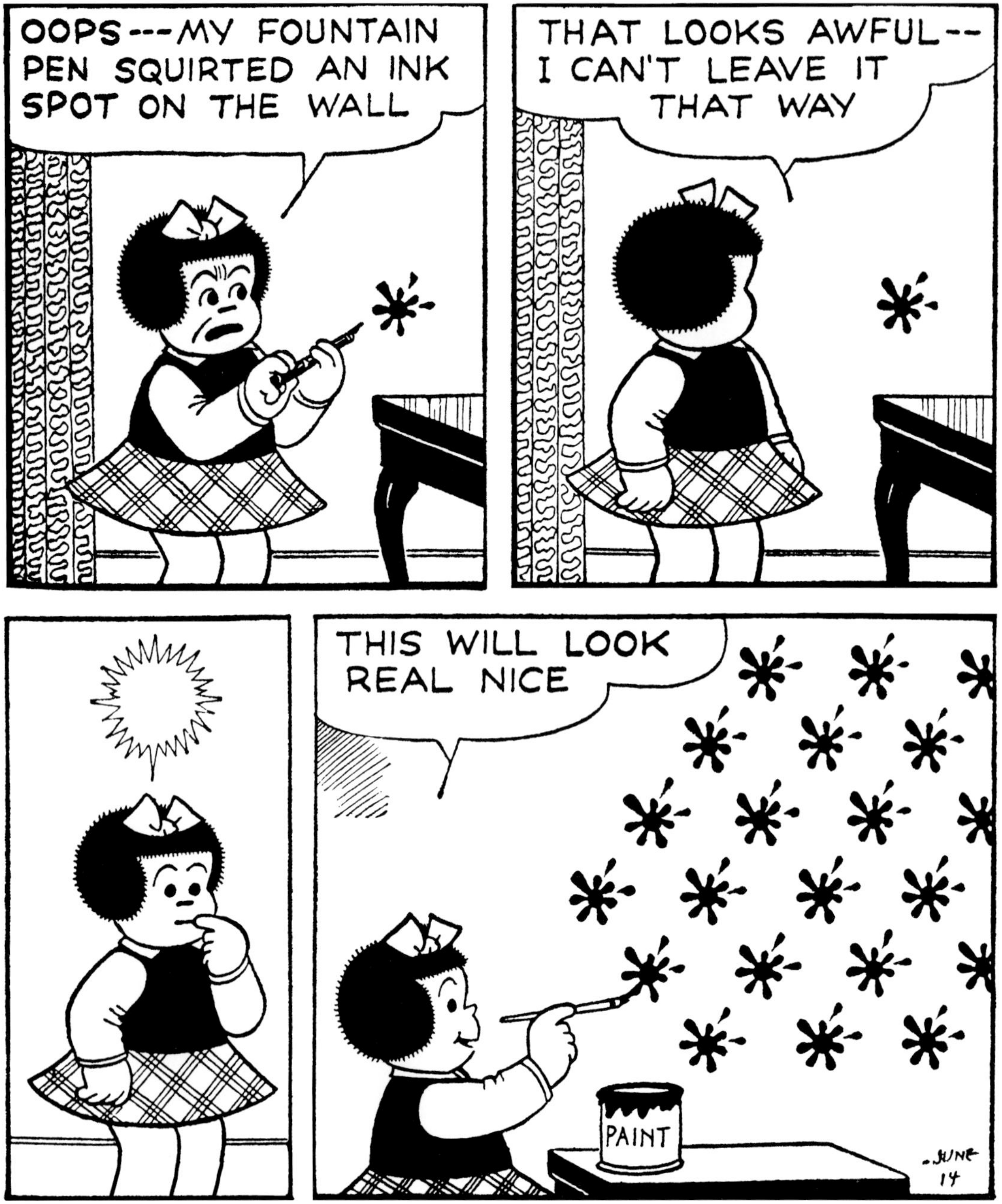
OOPS---MY FOUNTAIN PEN SQUIRTED AN INK SPOT ON THE WALL
THAT LOOKS AWFUL-- I CAN'T LEAVE IT THAT WAY
THIS WILL LOOK REAL NICE
PAINT
JUNE 14

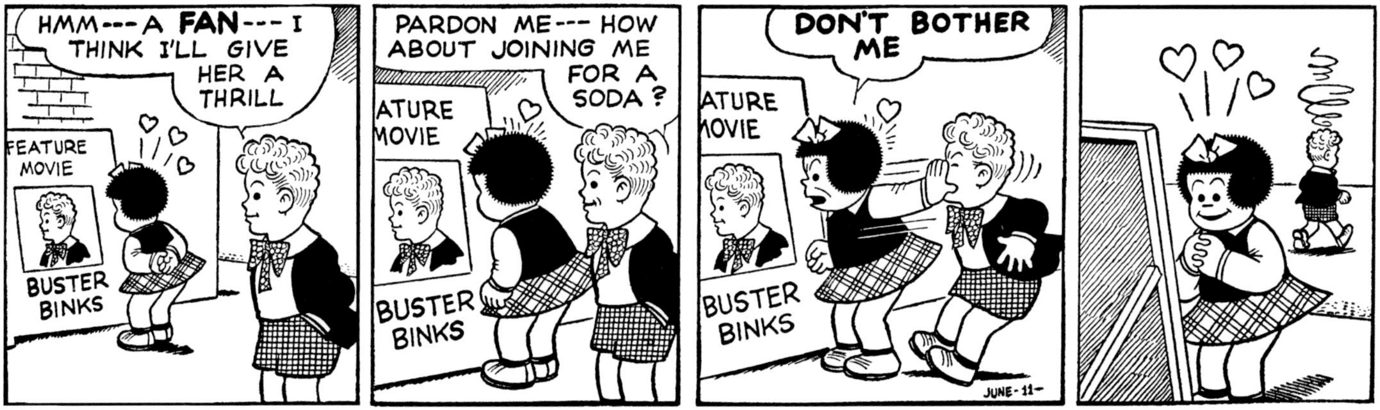

HMM---A **FAN**--- I THINK I'LL GIVE HER A THRILL
FEATURE MOVIE
BUSTER BINKS
PARDON ME--- HOW ABOUT JOINING ME FOR A SODA ?
ATURE MOVIE
BUSTER BINKS
DON'T BOTHER ME
ATURE MOVIE
BUSTER BINKS
JUNE-11-

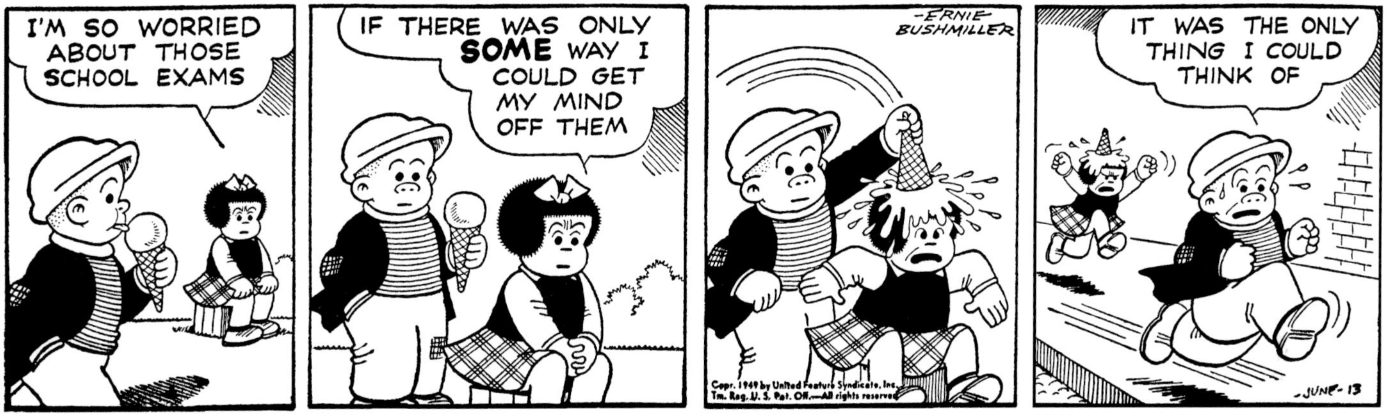

I'M SO WORRIED ABOUT THOSE SCHOOL EXAMS
IF THERE WAS ONLY **SOME** WAY I COULD GET MY MIND OFF THEM
-ERNIE BUSHMILLER
Copr. 1949 by United Feature Syndicate, Inc. Tm. Reg. U. S. Pat. Off.—All rights reserved
IT WAS THE ONLY THING I COULD THINK OF
-JUNE-13

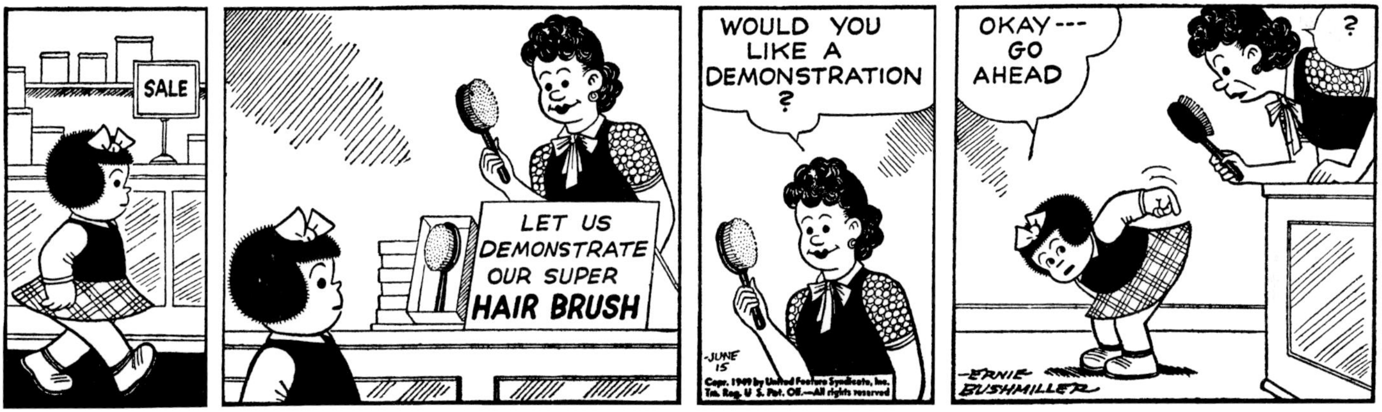

SALE
LET US DEMONSTRATE OUR SUPER **HAIR BRUSH**
WOULD YOU LIKE A DEMONSTRATION ?
-JUNE 15
Copr. 1949 by United Feature Syndicate, Inc. Tm. Reg. U. S. Pat. Off.—All rights reserved
OKAY--- GO AHEAD
?
-ERNIE BUSHMILLER

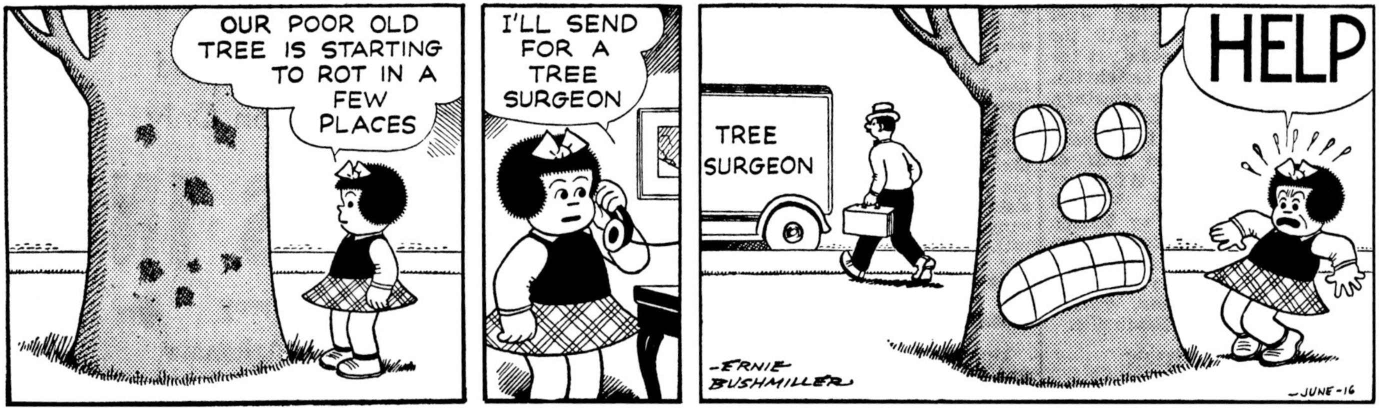
OUR POOR OLD TREE IS STARTING TO ROT IN A FEW PLACES
I'LL SEND FOR A TREE SURGEON
TREE SURGEON
HELP
-ERNIE BUSHMILLER
-JUNE-16

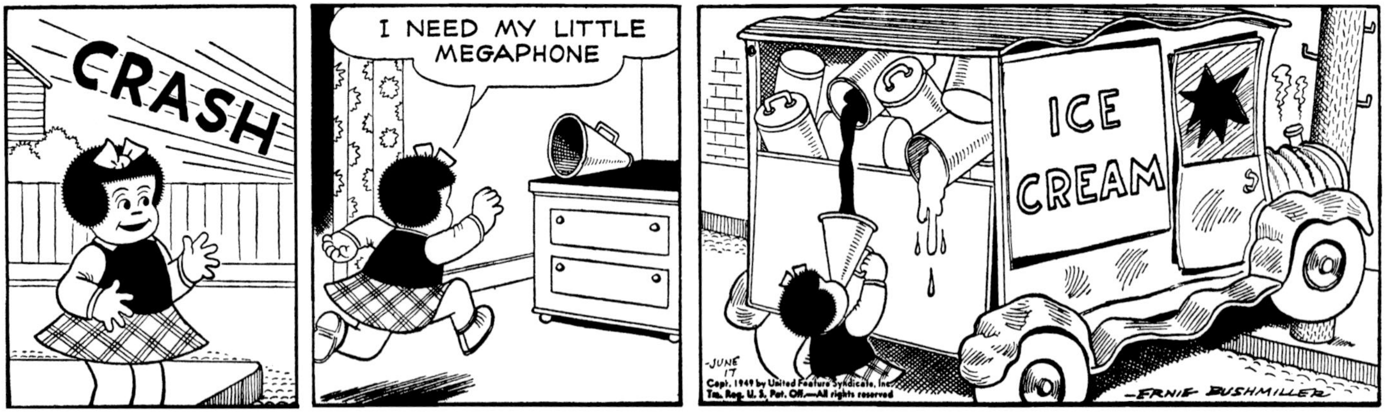
CRASH
I NEED MY LITTLE MEGAPHONE
ICE CREAM
-JUNE 17
Copr. 1949 by United Feature Syndicate, Inc.
Tm. Reg. U. S. Pat. Off.—All rights reserved
-ERNIE BUSHMILLER

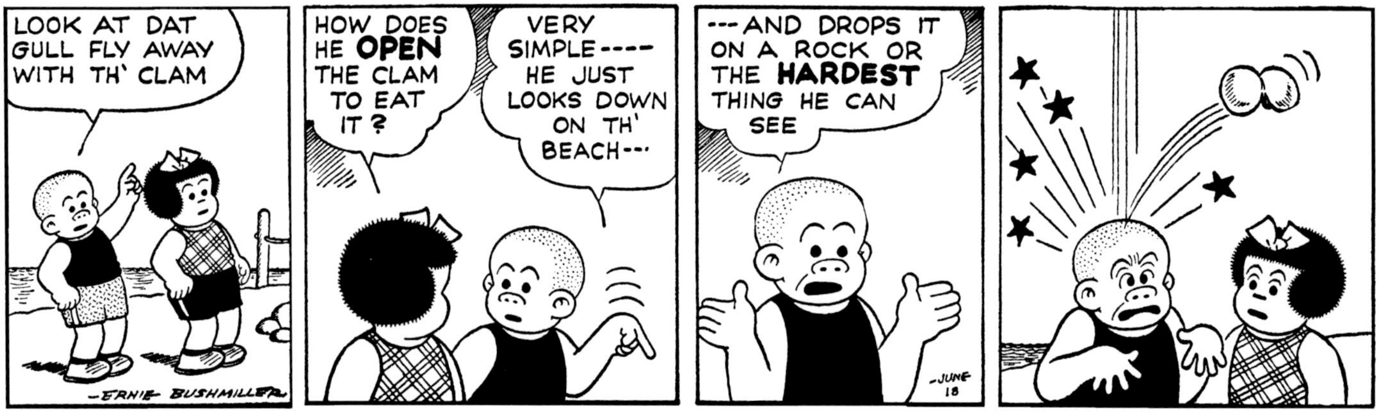
LOOK AT DAT GULL FLY AWAY WITH TH' CLAM
-ERNIE BUSHMILLER
HOW DOES HE **OPEN** THE CLAM TO EAT IT ?
VERY SIMPLE---- HE JUST LOOKS DOWN ON TH' BEACH---
---AND DROPS IT ON A ROCK OR THE **HARDEST** THING HE CAN SEE
-JUNE 18

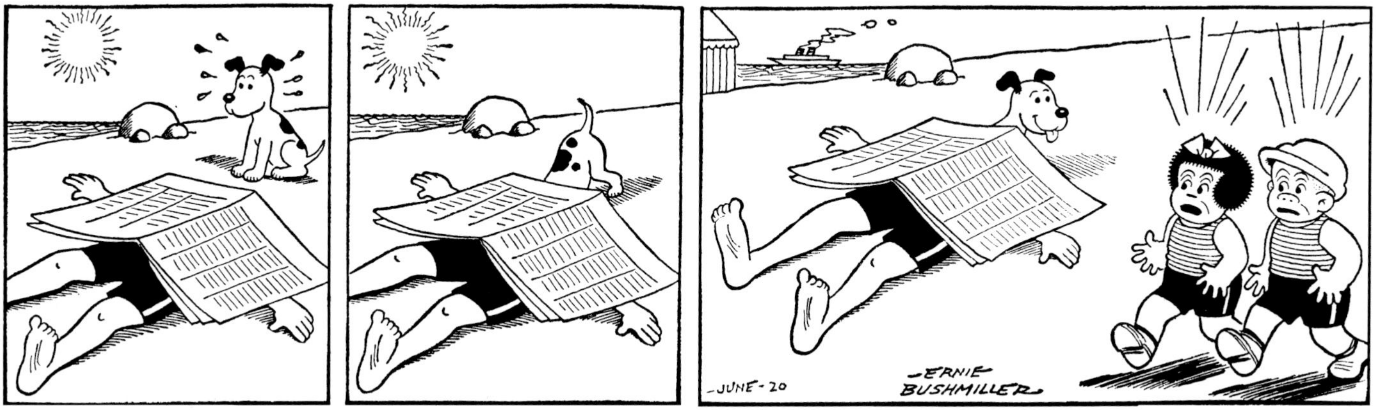
-JUNE-20
-ERNIE BUSHMILLER

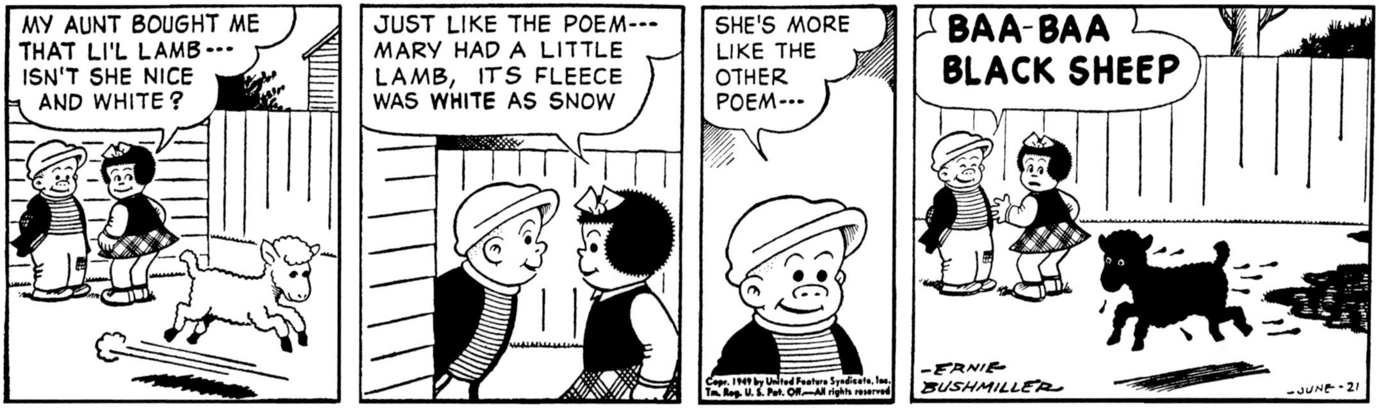
MY AUNT BOUGHT ME THAT LI'L LAMB--- ISN'T SHE NICE AND WHITE?
JUST LIKE THE POEM--- MARY HAD A LITTLE LAMB, ITS FLEECE WAS WHITE AS SNOW
SHE'S MORE LIKE THE OTHER POEM---
Copr. 1949 by United Feature Syndicate, Inc. Tm. Reg. U. S. Pat. Off.—All rights reserved
BAA-BAA BLACK SHEEP
-ERNIE BUSHMILLER
-JUNE-21

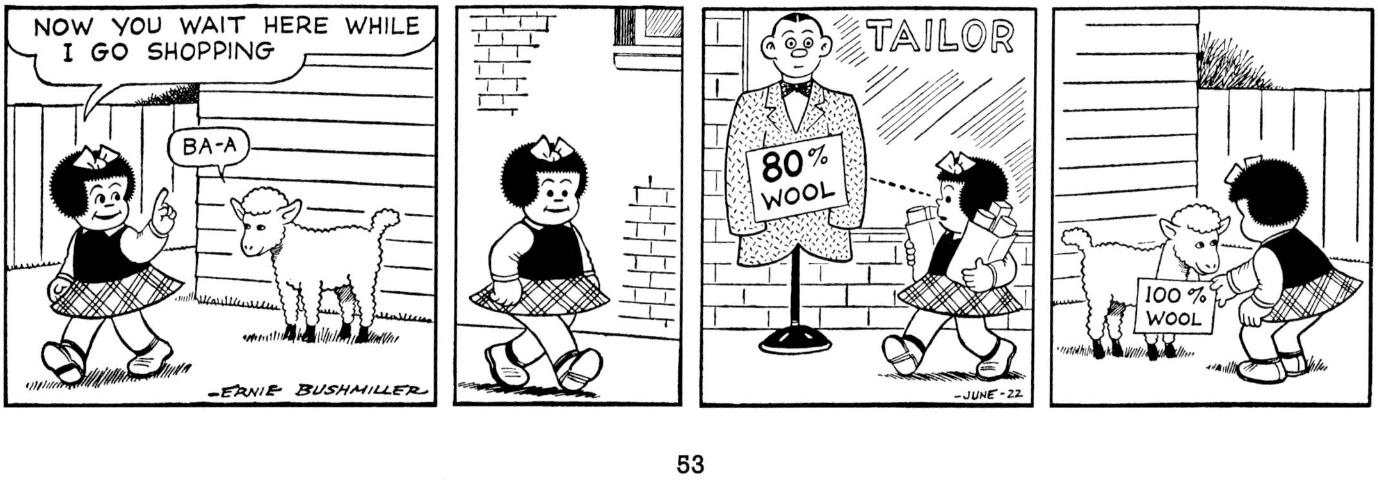
NOW YOU WAIT HERE WHILE I GO SHOPPING
BA-A
-ERNIE BUSHMILLER
TAILOR
80% WOOL
-JUNE-22
100% WOOL

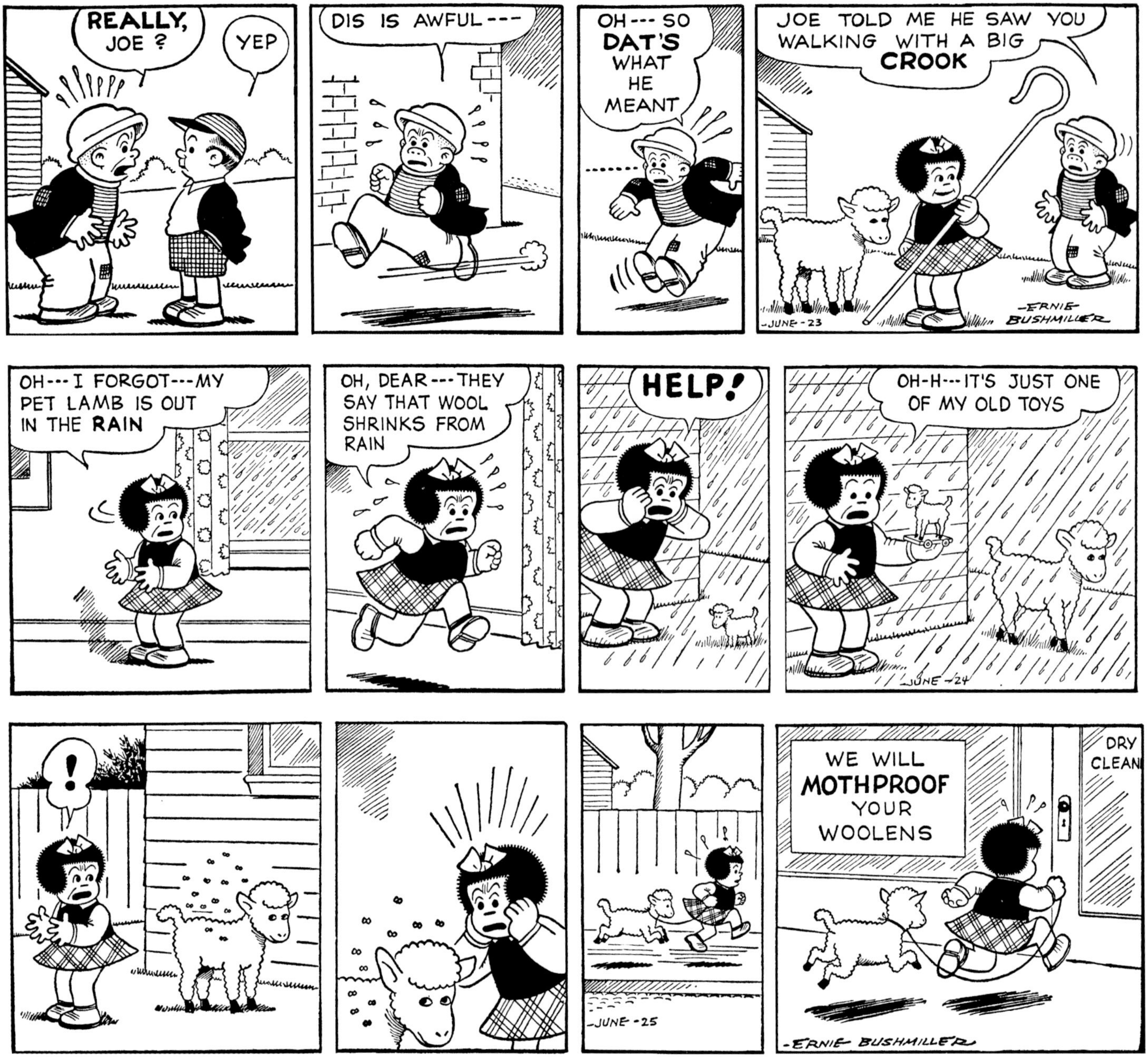
REALLY, JOE ?
YEP
DIS IS AWFUL ---
OH --- SO DAT'S WHAT HE MEANT
JOE TOLD ME HE SAW YOU WALKING WITH A BIG CROOK
-JUNE-23
-ERNIE BUSHMILLER
OH --- I FORGOT --- MY PET LAMB IS OUT IN THE RAIN
OH, DEAR --- THEY SAY THAT WOOL SHRINKS FROM RAIN
HELP!
OH-H --- IT'S JUST ONE OF MY OLD TOYS
-JUNE-24
!
-JUNE-25
WE WILL MOTHPROOF YOUR WOOLENS
DRY CLEAN
-ERNIE BUSHMILLER

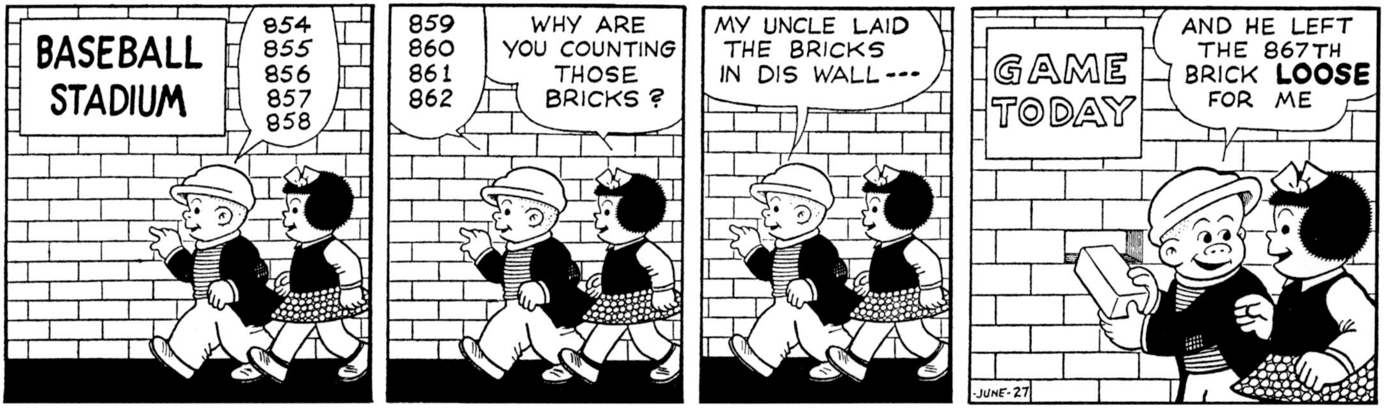
BASEBALL STADIUM
854 855 856 857 858
859 860 861 862
WHY ARE YOU COUNTING THOSE BRICKS?
MY UNCLE LAID THE BRICKS IN DIS WALL---
GAME TODAY
AND HE LEFT THE 867TH BRICK **LOOSE** FOR ME
-JUNE-27

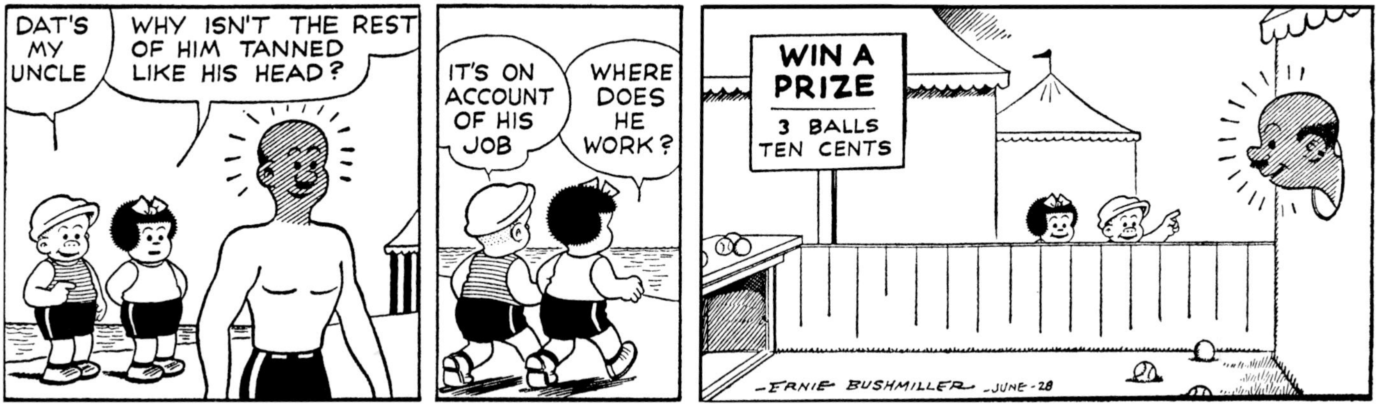
DAT'S MY UNCLE
WHY ISN'T THE REST OF HIM TANNED LIKE HIS HEAD?
IT'S ON ACCOUNT OF HIS JOB
WHERE DOES HE WORK?
WIN A PRIZE
3 BALLS TEN CENTS
-ERNIE BUSHMILLER- -JUNE-28

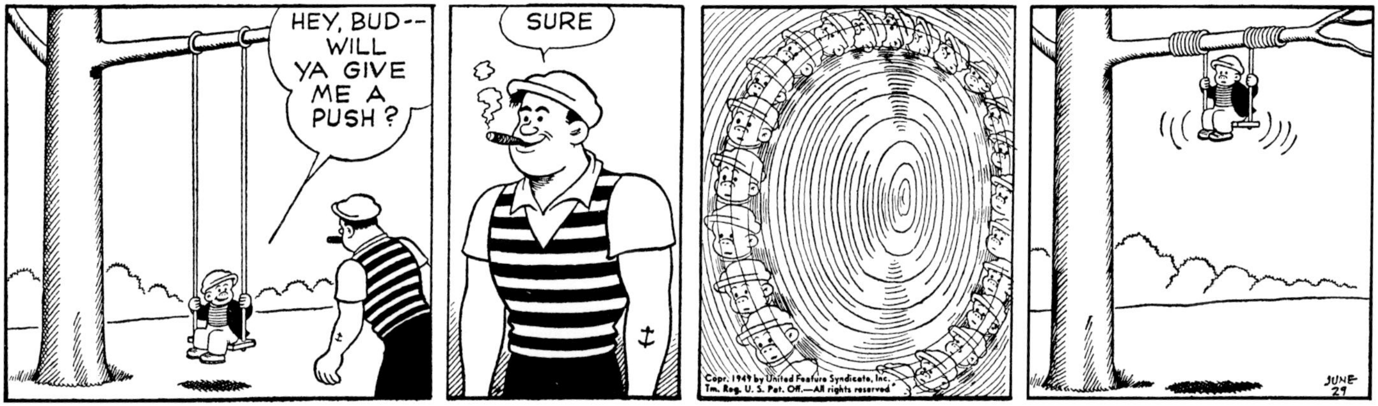
HEY, BUD-- WILL YA GIVE ME A PUSH?
SURE
Copr. 1949 by United Feature Syndicate, Inc. Tm. Reg. U. S. Pat. Off.—All rights reserved
JUNE 29

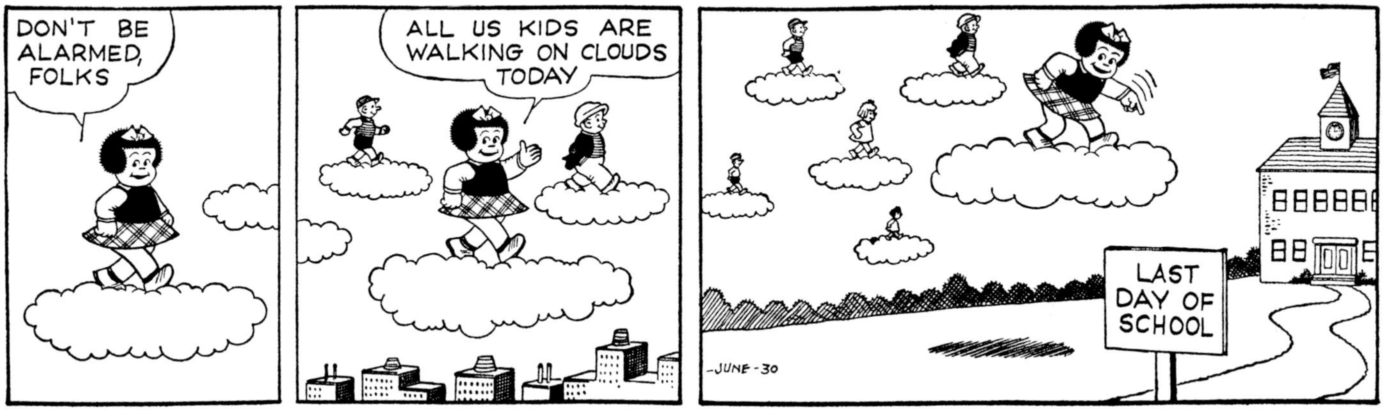
DON'T BE ALARMED, FOLKS
ALL US KIDS ARE WALKING ON CLOUDS TODAY
LAST DAY OF SCHOOL
JUNE-30

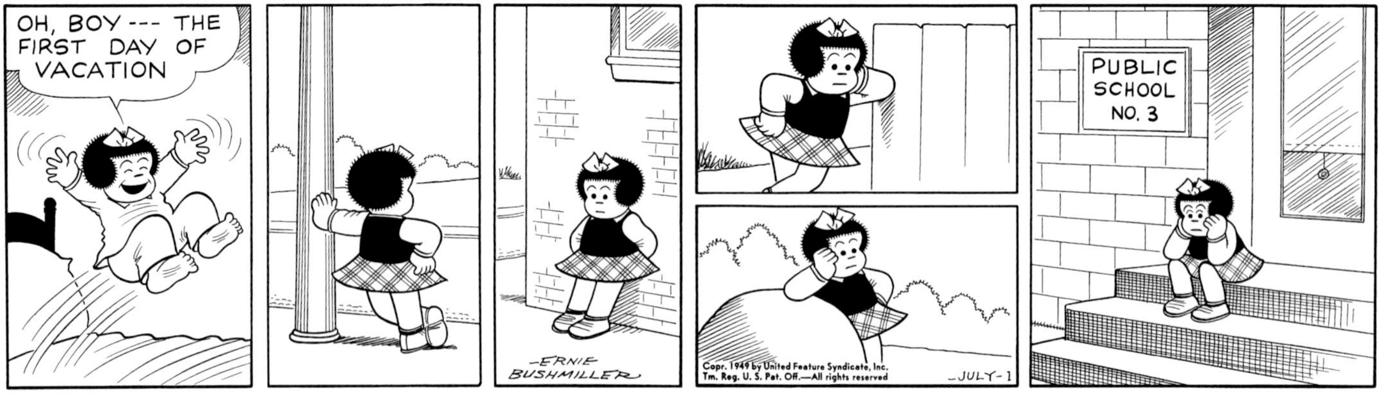
OH, BOY --- THE FIRST DAY OF VACATION
ERNIE BUSHMILLER
PUBLIC SCHOOL NO. 3
Copr. 1949 by United Feature Syndicate, Inc. Tm. Reg. U. S. Pat. Off.—All rights reserved
JULY-1

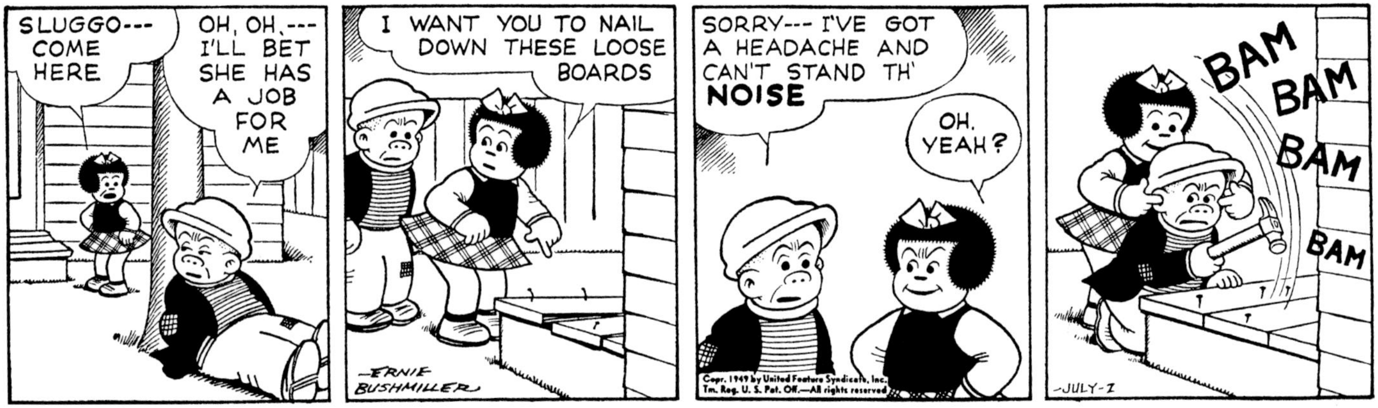
SLUGGO--- COME HERE
OH, OH,--- I'LL BET SHE HAS A JOB FOR ME
I WANT YOU TO NAIL DOWN THESE LOOSE BOARDS
ERNIE BUSHMILLER
SORRY--- I'VE GOT A HEADACHE AND CAN'T STAND TH' **NOISE**
OH. YEAH?
Copr. 1949 by United Feature Syndicate, Inc. Tm. Reg. U. S. Pat. Off.—All rights reserved
BAM
BAM
BAM
BAM
JULY-2

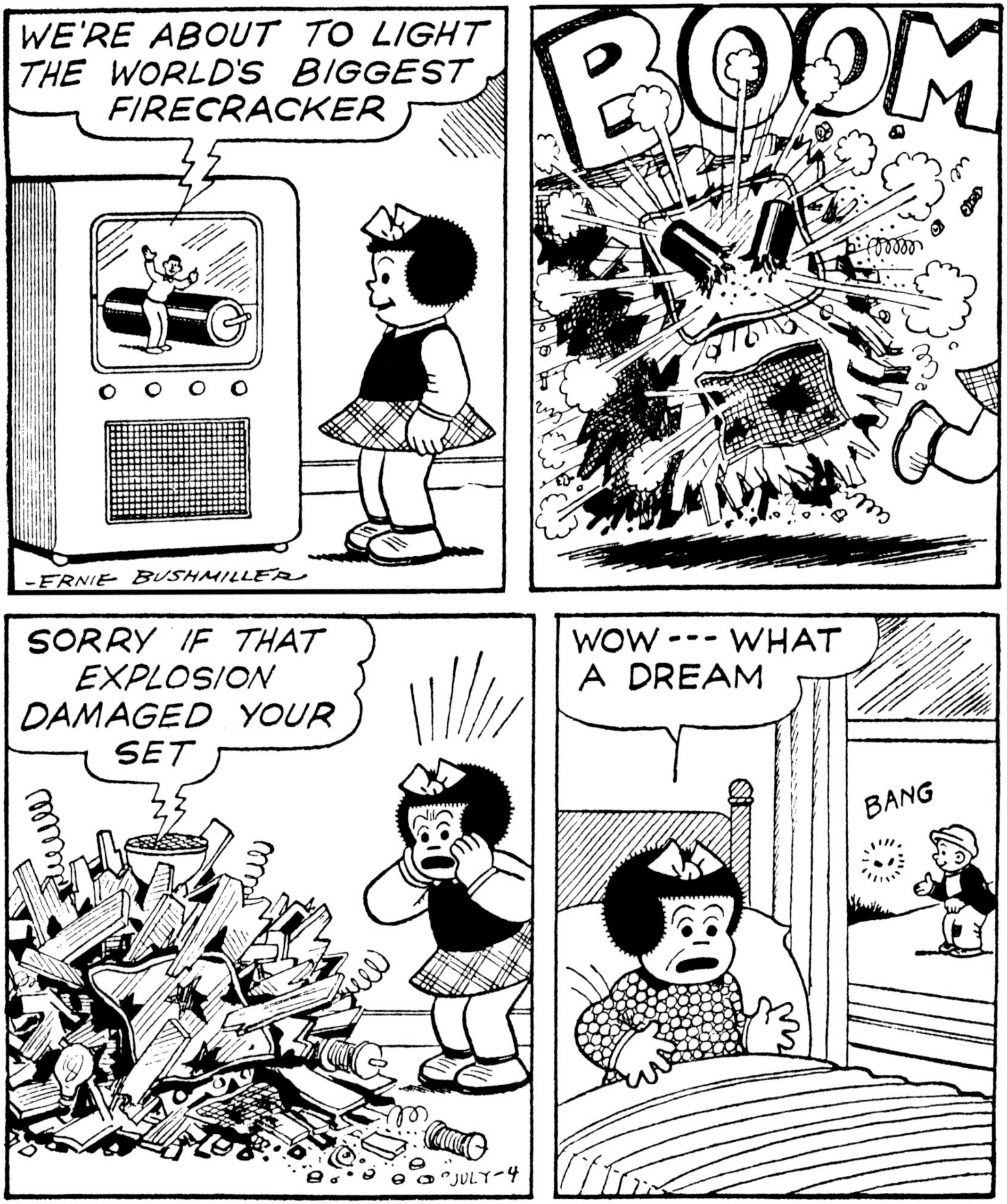
WE'RE ABOUT TO LIGHT THE WORLD'S BIGGEST FIRECRACKER
-ERNIE BUSHMILLER
BOOM
SORRY IF THAT EXPLOSION DAMAGED YOUR SET
JULY-4
WOW --- WHAT A DREAM
BANG

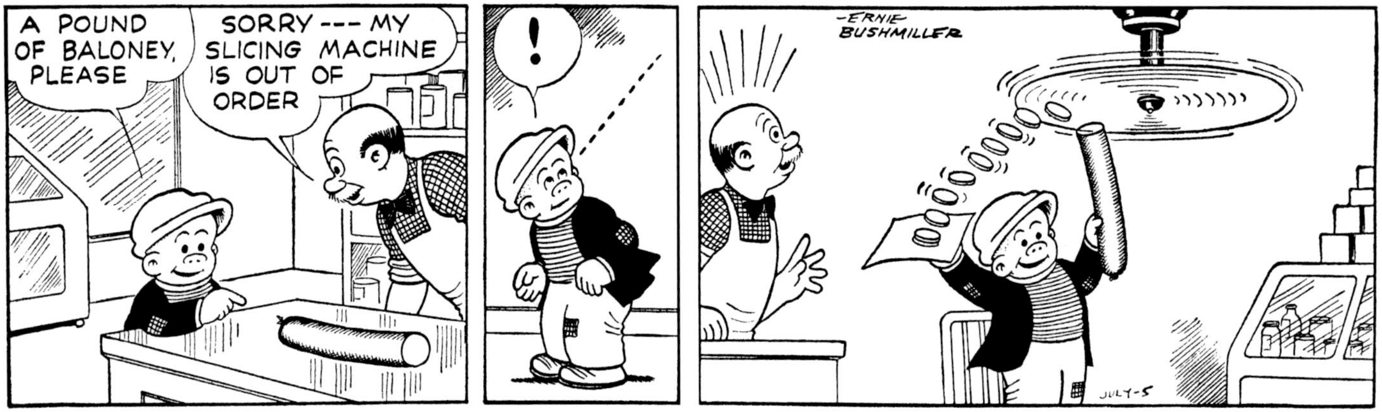
A POUND OF BALONEY, PLEASE
SORRY --- MY SLICING MACHINE IS OUT OF ORDER
!
-ERNIE BUSHMILLER
JULY-5

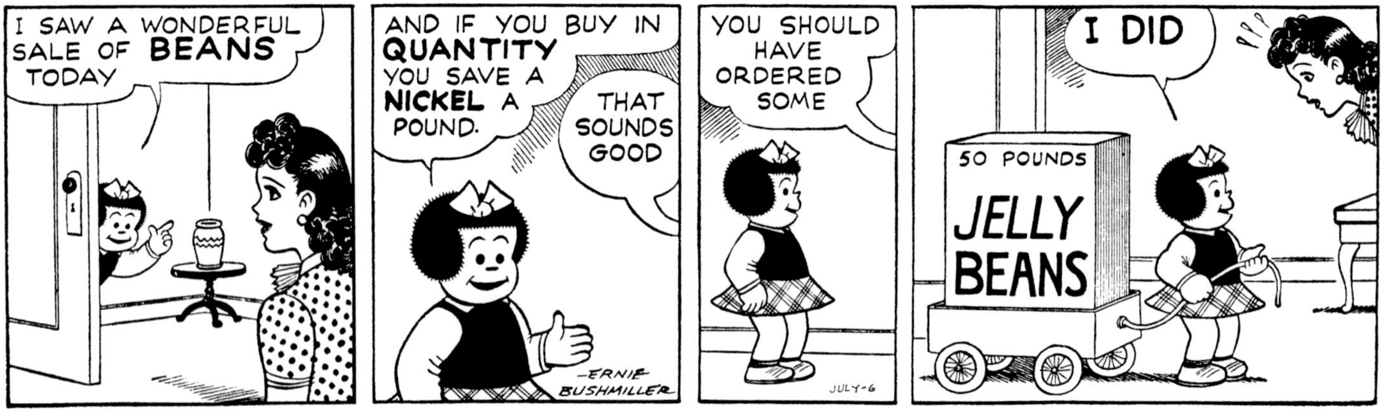
I SAW A WONDERFUL SALE OF **BEANS** TODAY
AND IF YOU BUY IN **QUANTITY** YOU SAVE A **NICKEL** A POUND.
THAT SOUNDS GOOD
-ERNIE BUSHMILLER
YOU SHOULD HAVE ORDERED SOME
JULY-6
I DID
50 POUNDS
JELLY BEANS

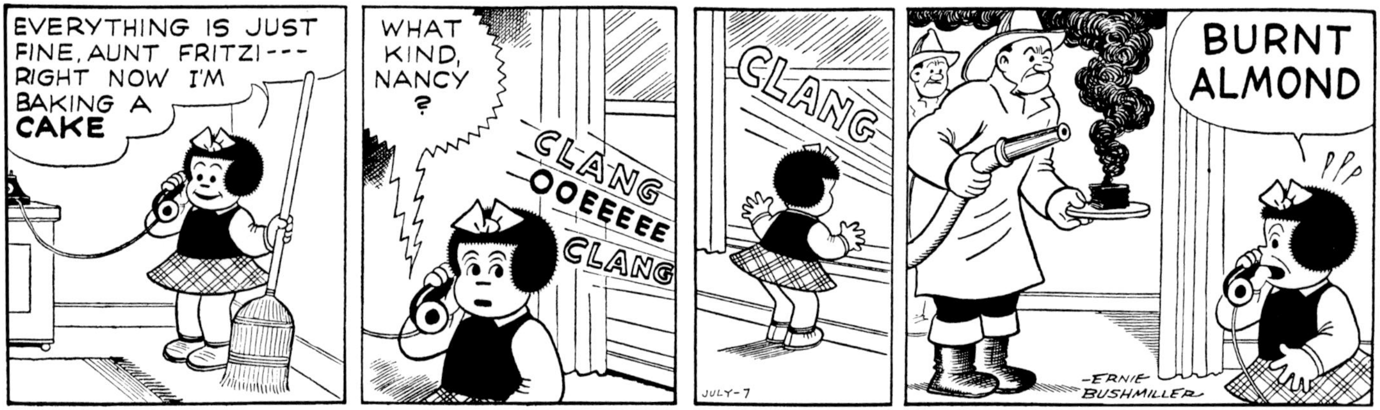
EVERYTHING IS JUST FINE, AUNT FRITZI--- RIGHT NOW I'M BAKING A **CAKE**
WHAT KIND, NANCY ?
CLANG
OOEEEEEE
CLANG
CLANG
JULY-7
BURNT ALMOND
-ERNIE BUSHMILLER

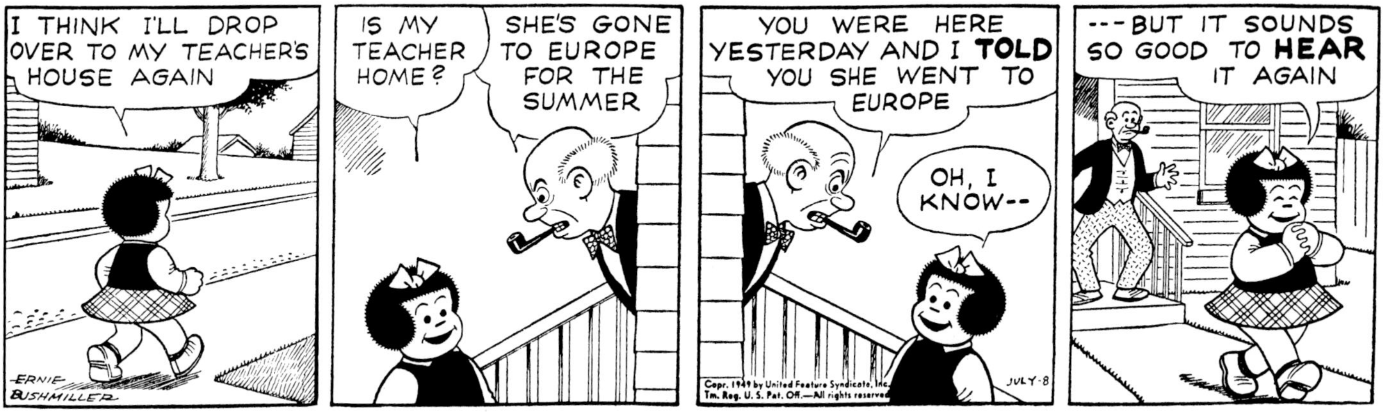
I THINK I'LL DROP OVER TO MY TEACHER'S HOUSE AGAIN
ERNIE BUSHMILLER
IS MY TEACHER HOME?
SHE'S GONE TO EUROPE FOR THE SUMMER
YOU WERE HERE YESTERDAY AND I **TOLD** YOU SHE WENT TO EUROPE
OH, I KNOW--
Copr. 1949 by United Feature Syndicate, Inc. Tm. Reg. U. S. Pat. Off.—All rights reserved
JULY-8
---BUT IT SOUNDS SO GOOD TO **HEAR** IT AGAIN

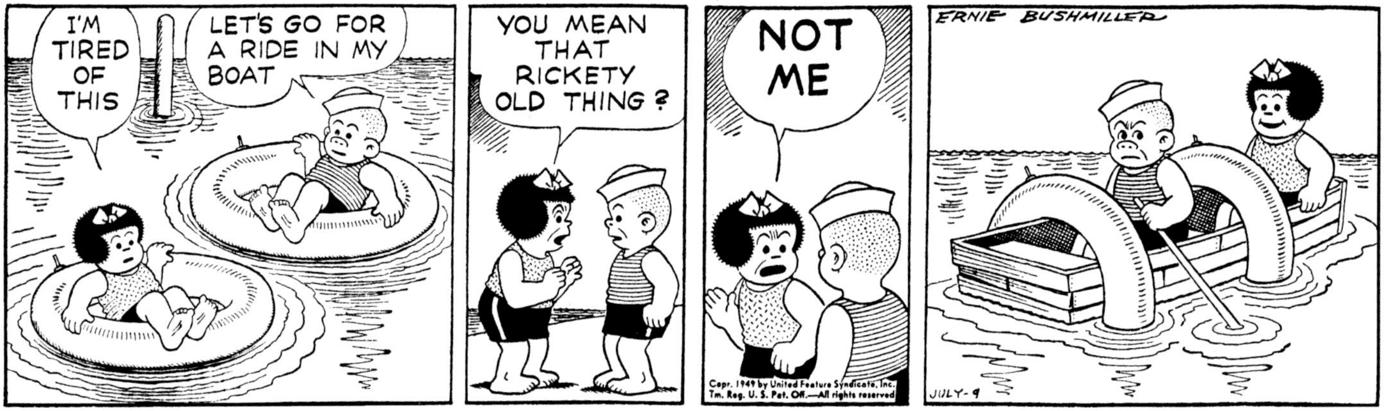
I'M TIRED OF THIS
LET'S GO FOR A RIDE IN MY BOAT
YOU MEAN THAT RICKETY OLD THING?
NOT ME
Copr. 1949 by United Feature Syndicate, Inc. Tm. Reg. U. S. Pat. Off.—All rights reserved
ERNIE BUSHMILLER
JULY-9

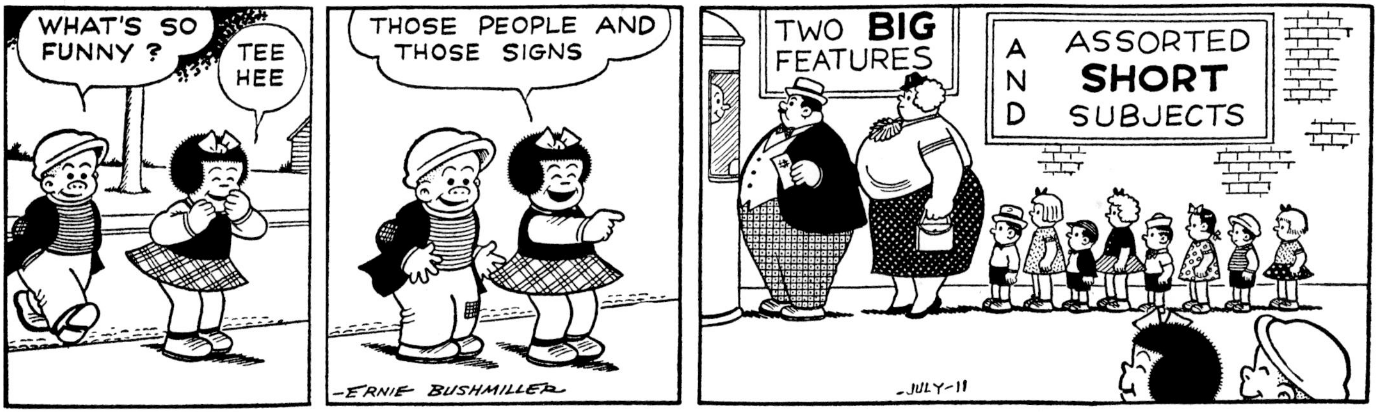
WHAT'S SO FUNNY?
TEE HEE
THOSE PEOPLE AND THOSE SIGNS
ERNIE BUSHMILLER
TWO **BIG** FEATURES
AND
ASSORTED **SHORT** SUBJECTS
JULY-11

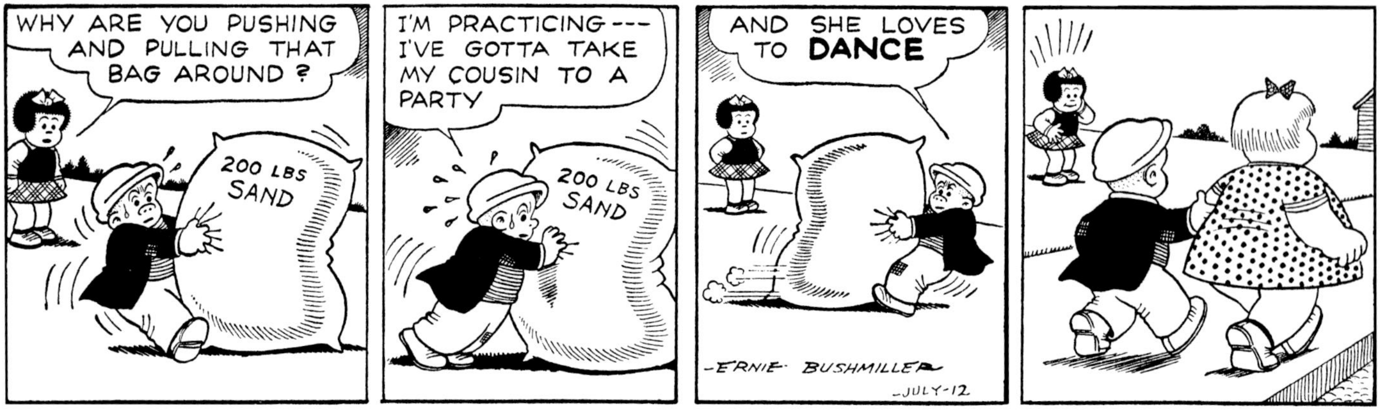
WHY ARE YOU PUSHING AND PULLING THAT BAG AROUND ?
200 LBS SAND
I'M PRACTICING--- I'VE GOTTA TAKE MY COUSIN TO A PARTY
200 LBS SAND
AND SHE LOVES TO **DANCE**
-ERNIE BUSHMILLER
-JULY-12

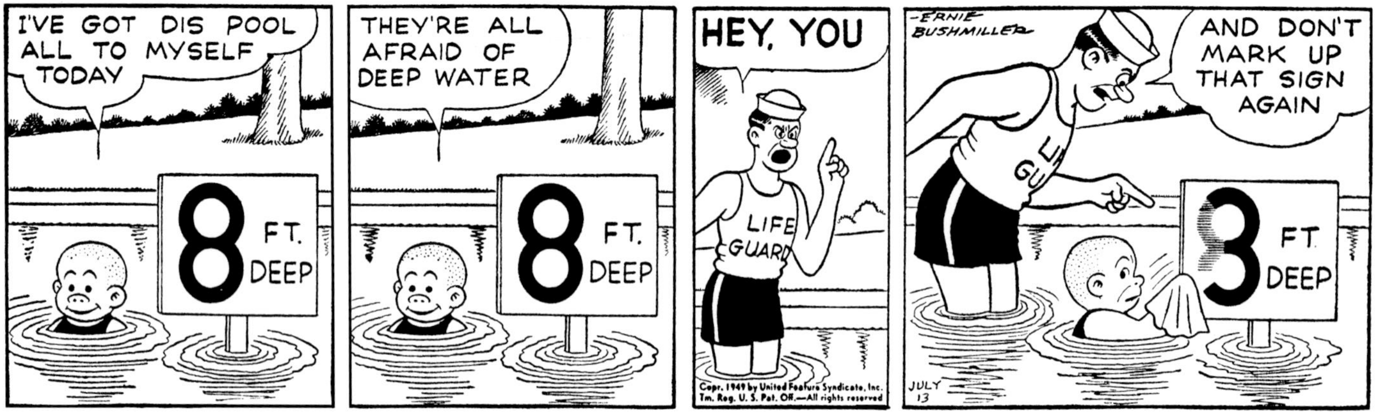
I'VE GOT DIS POOL ALL TO MYSELF TODAY
8 FT. DEEP
THEY'RE ALL AFRAID OF DEEP WATER
8 FT. DEEP
HEY, YOU
LIFE GUARD
Copr. 1949 by United Feature Syndicate, Inc.
Tm. Reg. U. S. Pat. Off.—All rights reserved
-ERNIE BUSHMILLER
AND DON'T MARK UP THAT SIGN AGAIN
3 FT. DEEP
JULY 13

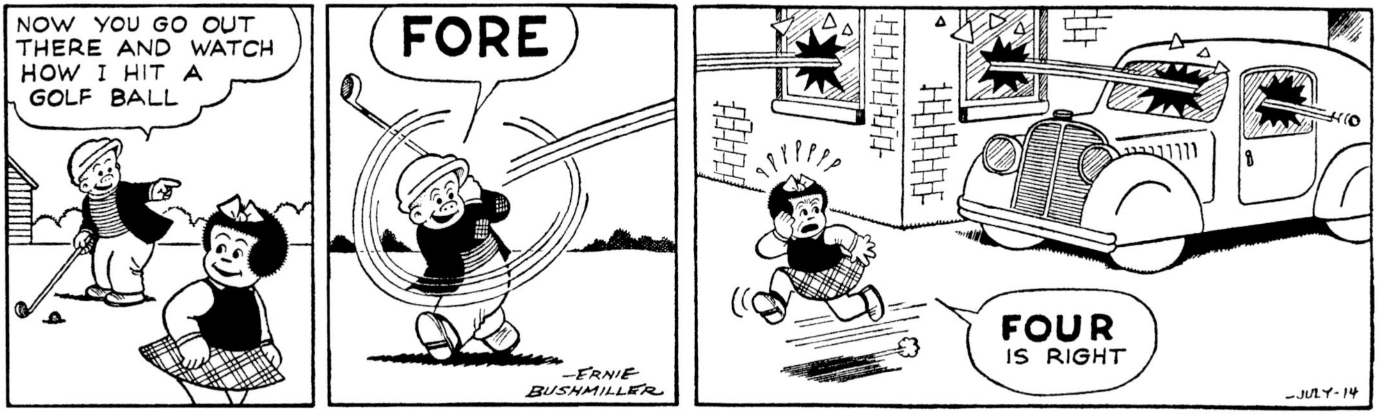
NOW YOU GO OUT THERE AND WATCH HOW I HIT A GOLF BALL
FORE
-ERNIE BUSHMILLER
FOUR IS RIGHT
-JULY-14

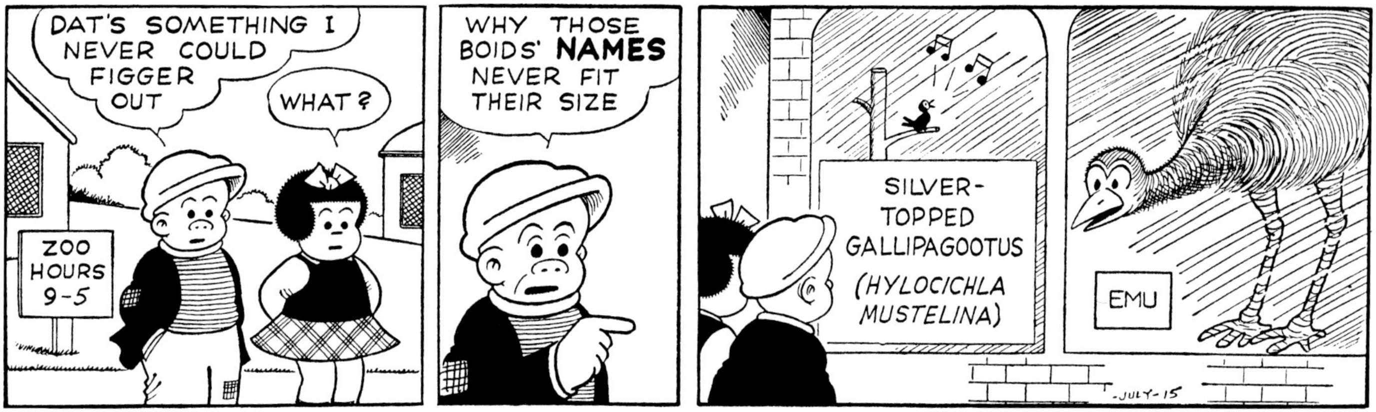
DAT'S SOMETHING I NEVER COULD FIGGER OUT
WHAT?
ZOO HOURS 9-5
WHY THOSE BOIDS' **NAMES** NEVER FIT THEIR SIZE
SILVER-TOPPED GALLIPAGOOTUS
(HYLOCICHLA MUSTELINA)
EMU
-JULY-15

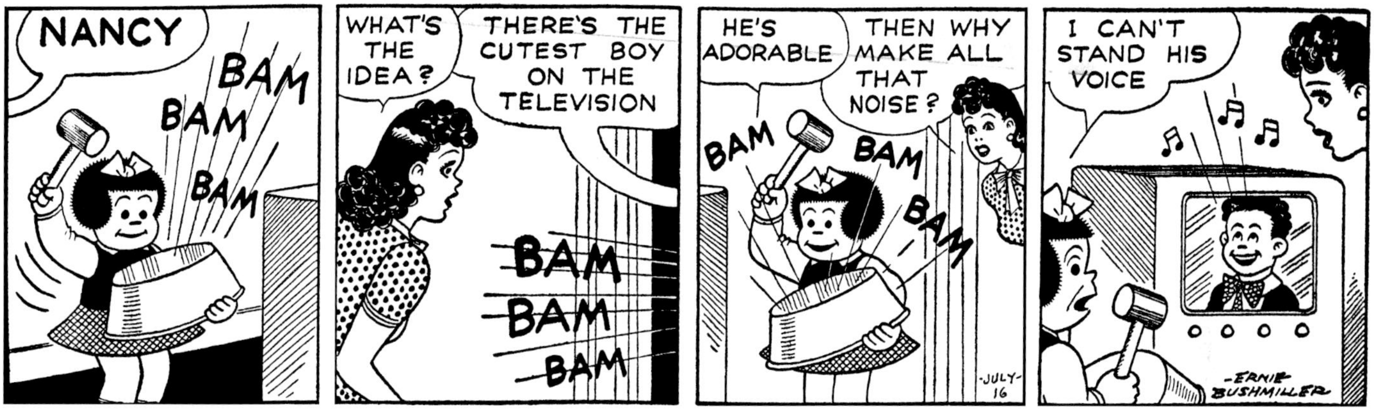
NANCY
BAM
BAM
BAM
WHAT'S THE IDEA?
THERE'S THE CUTEST BOY ON THE TELEVISION
BAM
BAM
BAM
HE'S ADORABLE
THEN WHY MAKE ALL THAT NOISE?
BAM
BAM
BAM
-JULY-16
I CAN'T STAND HIS VOICE
-ERNIE BUSHMILLER

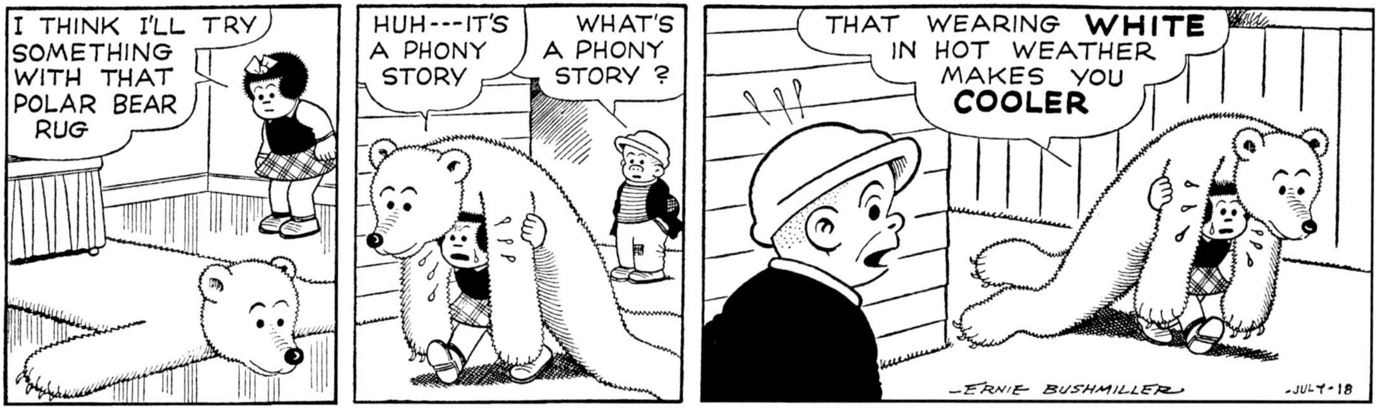
I THINK I'LL TRY SOMETHING WITH THAT POLAR BEAR RUG
HUH---IT'S A PHONY STORY
WHAT'S A PHONY STORY?
THAT WEARING **WHITE** IN HOT WEATHER MAKES YOU **COOLER**
-ERNIE BUSHMILLER
-JULY-18

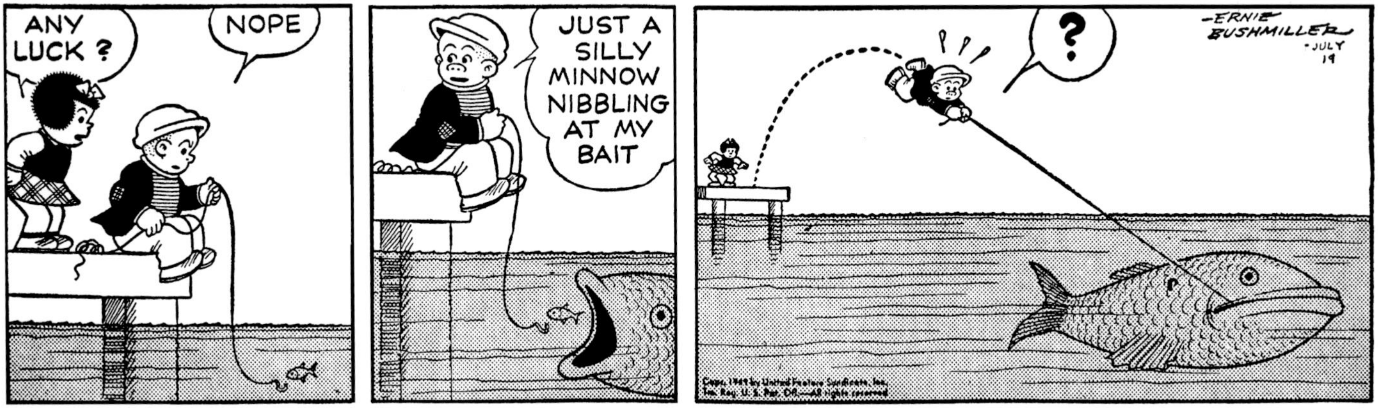
ANY LUCK ?
NOPE
JUST A SILLY MINNOW NIBBLING AT MY BAIT
?
ERNIE BUSHMILLER
JULY 19
Copr. 1949 by United Feature Syndicate, Inc. Tm. Reg. U. S. Pat. Off.—All rights reserved

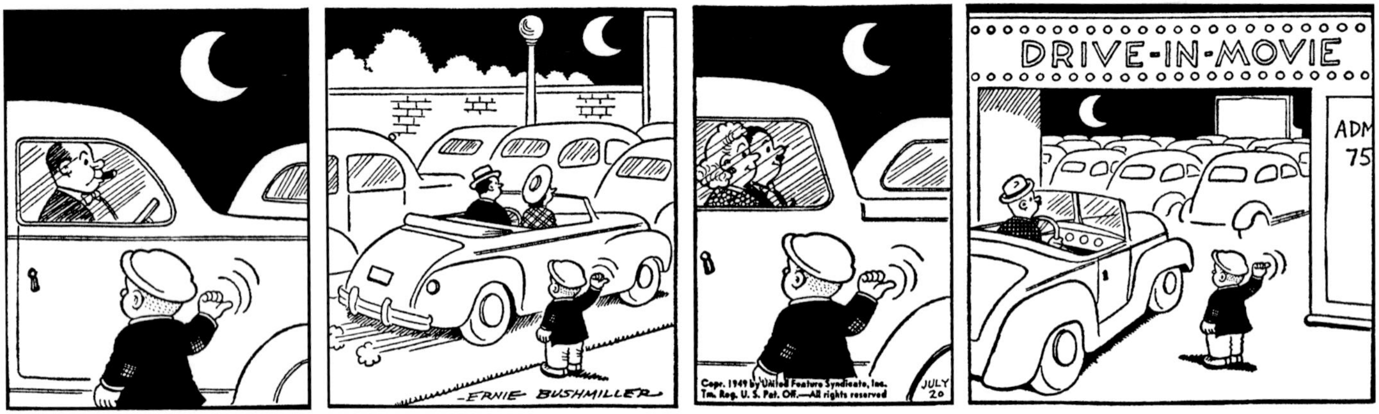
ERNIE BUSHMILLER
Copr. 1949 by United Feature Syndicate, Inc. Tm. Reg. U. S. Pat. Off.—All rights reserved
JULY 20
DRIVE-IN-MOVIE
ADM
75

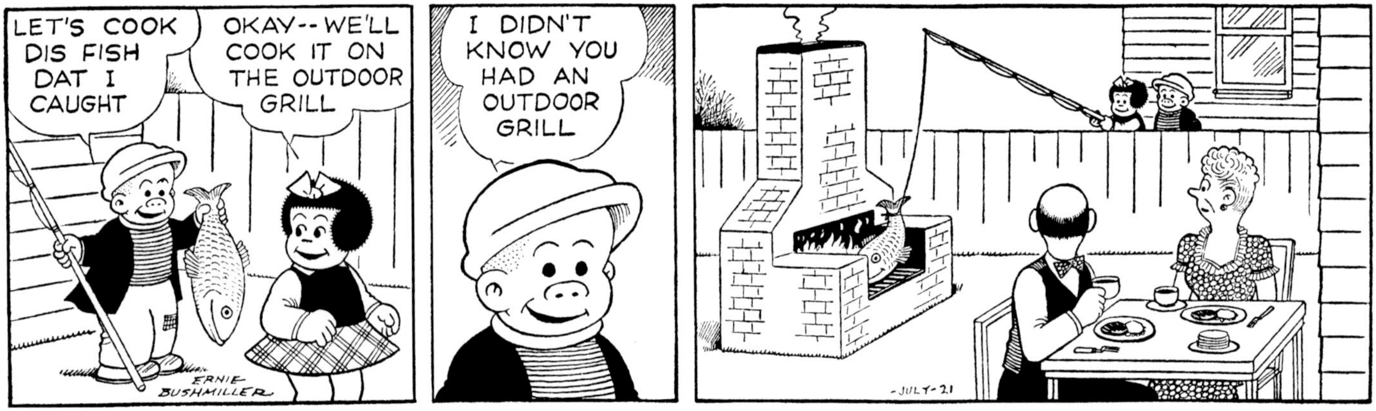
LET'S COOK DIS FISH DAT I CAUGHT
OKAY--WE'LL COOK IT ON THE OUTDOOR GRILL
ERNIE BUSHMILLER
I DIDN'T KNOW YOU HAD AN OUTDOOR GRILL
JULY-21

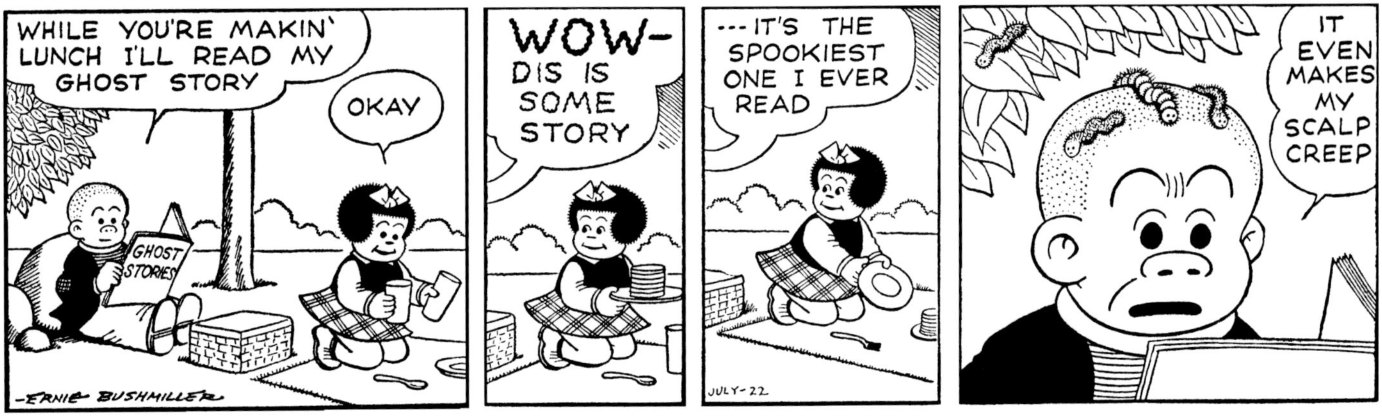
WHILE YOU'RE MAKIN' LUNCH I'LL READ MY GHOST STORY
OKAY
GHOST STORIES
ERNIE BUSHMILLER
WOW- DIS IS SOME STORY
---IT'S THE SPOOKIEST ONE I EVER READ
JULY-22
IT EVEN MAKES MY SCALP CREEP

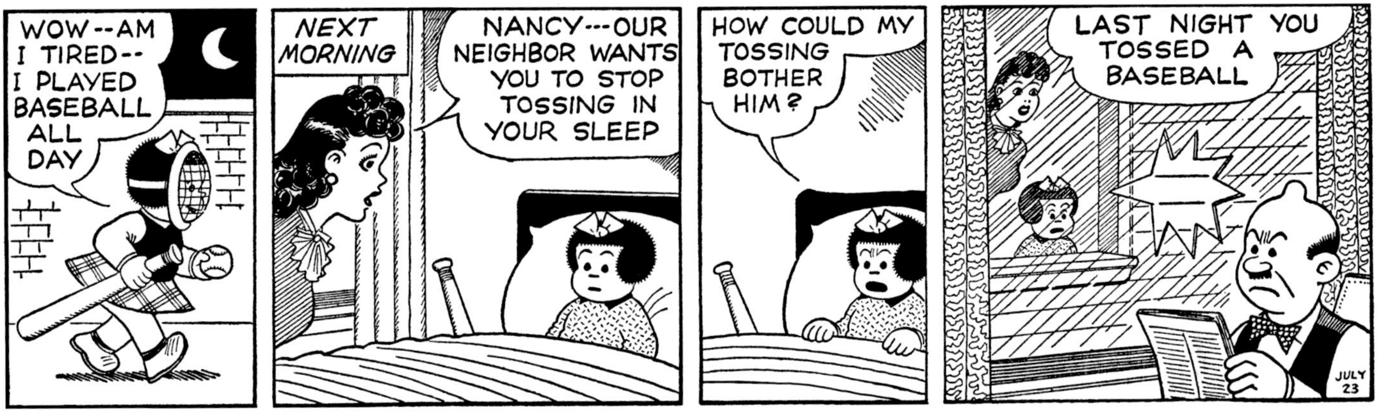
WOW--AM I TIRED-- I PLAYED BASEBALL ALL DAY
NEXT MORNING
NANCY---OUR NEIGHBOR WANTS YOU TO STOP TOSSING IN YOUR SLEEP
HOW COULD MY TOSSING BOTHER HIM?
LAST NIGHT YOU TOSSED A BASEBALL
JULY 23

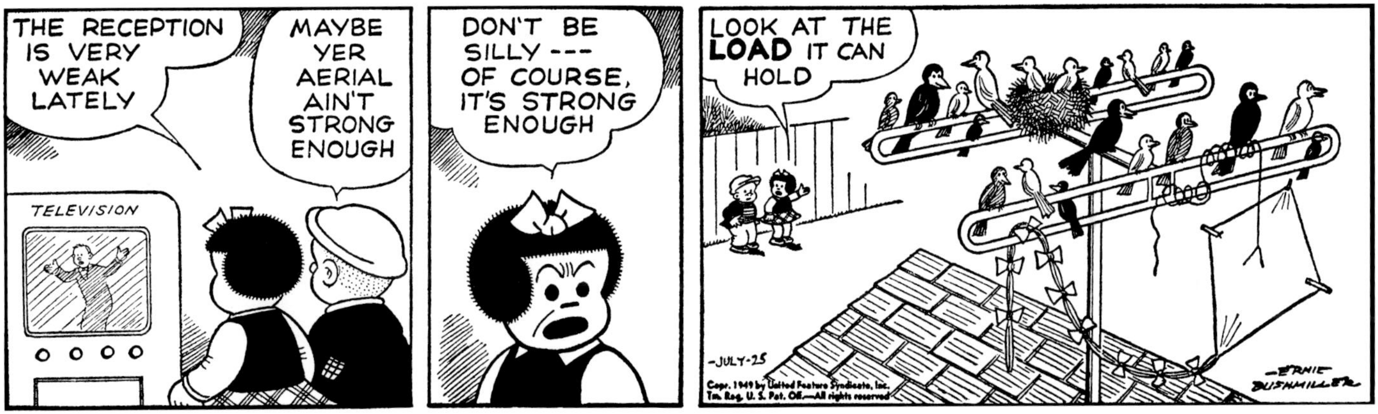
THE RECEPTION IS VERY WEAK LATELY
MAYBE YER AERIAL AIN'T STRONG ENOUGH
TELEVISION
DON'T BE SILLY --- OF COURSE, IT'S STRONG ENOUGH
LOOK AT THE **LOAD** IT CAN HOLD
JULY-25
Copr. 1949 by United Feature Syndicate, Inc.
Tm. Reg. U. S. Pat. Off.—All rights reserved
ERNIE BUSHMILLER

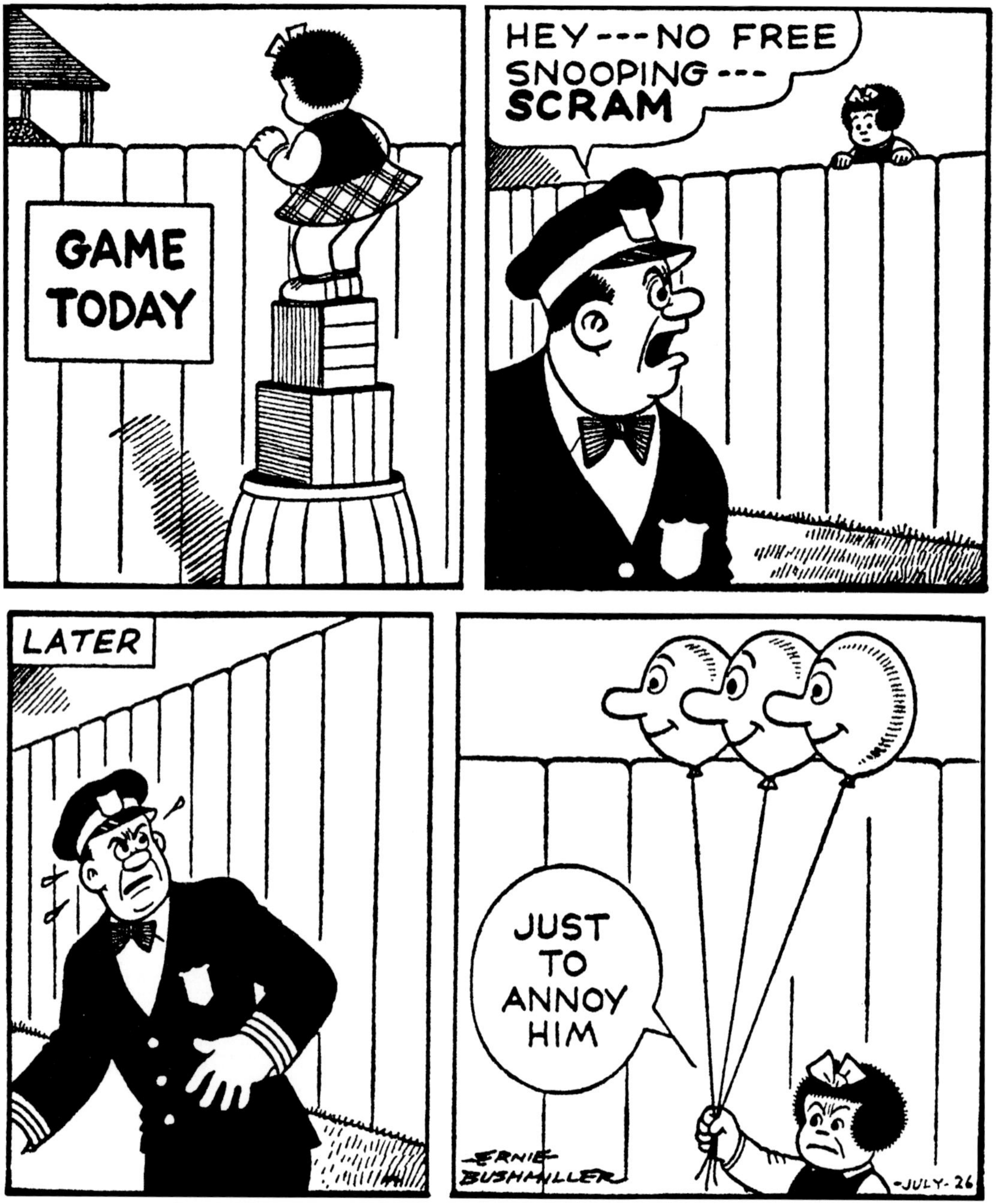
GAME TODAY
HEY---NO FREE SNOOPING--- SCRAM
LATER
JUST TO ANNOY HIM
ERNIE BUSHMILLER
JULY-26

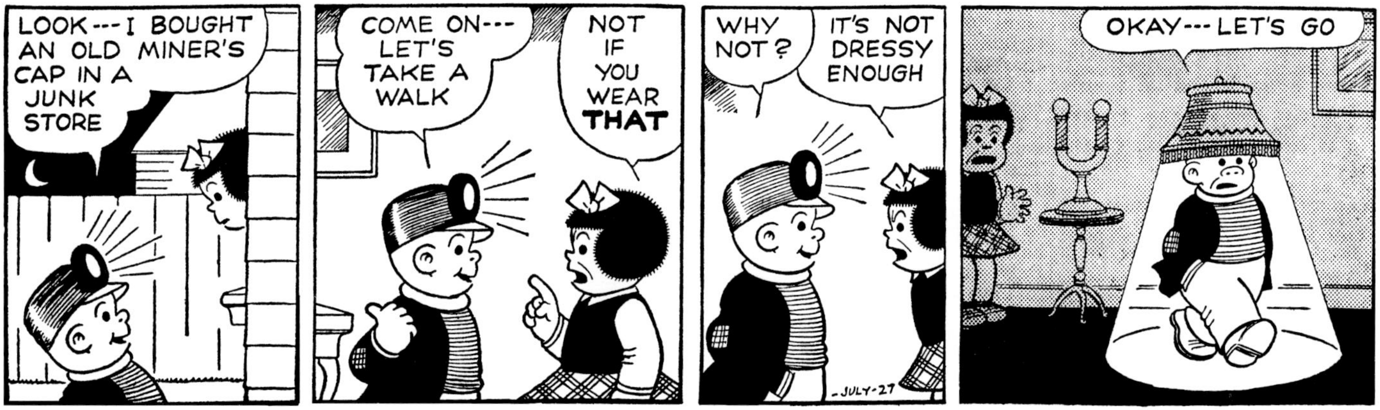
LOOK---I BOUGHT AN OLD MINER'S CAP IN A JUNK STORE
COME ON--- LET'S TAKE A WALK
NOT IF YOU WEAR **THAT**
WHY NOT?
IT'S NOT DRESSY ENOUGH
-JULY-27
OKAY---LET'S GO

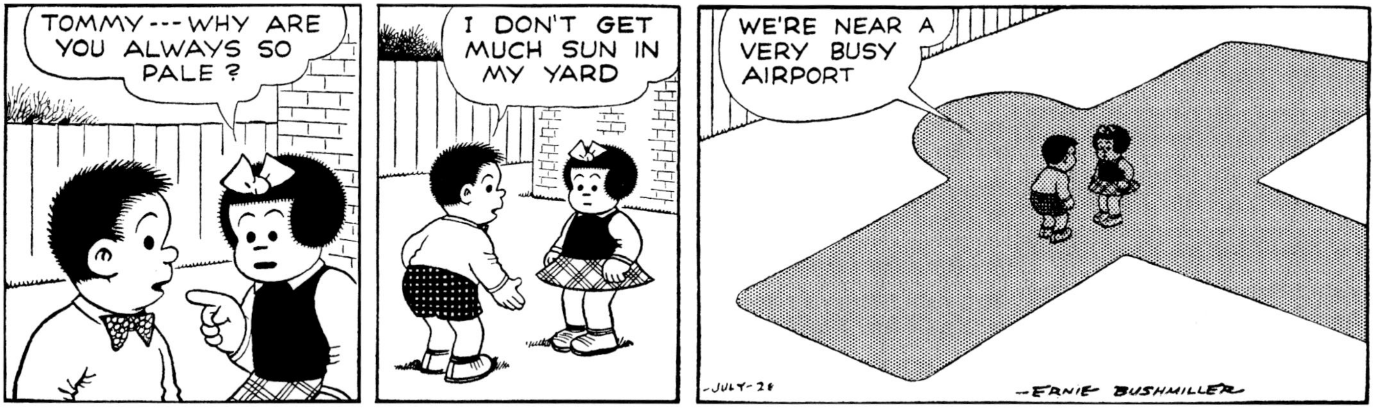
TOMMY---WHY ARE YOU ALWAYS SO PALE?
I DON'T GET MUCH SUN IN MY YARD
WE'RE NEAR A VERY BUSY AIRPORT
-JULY-28
-ERNIE BUSHMILLER

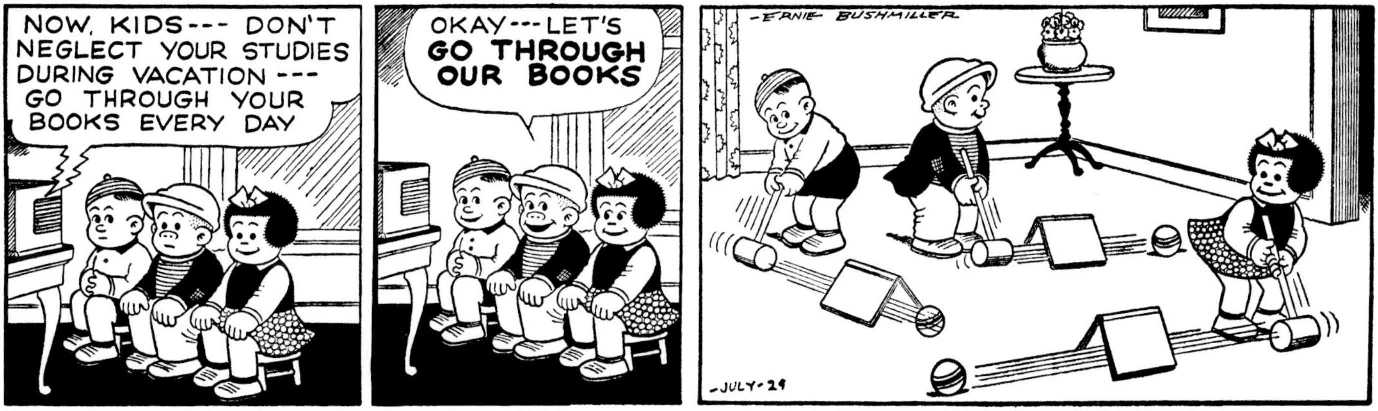
NOW, KIDS--- DON'T NEGLECT YOUR STUDIES DURING VACATION--- GO THROUGH YOUR BOOKS EVERY DAY
OKAY---LET'S **GO THROUGH OUR BOOKS**
-ERNIE BUSHMILLER
-JULY-29

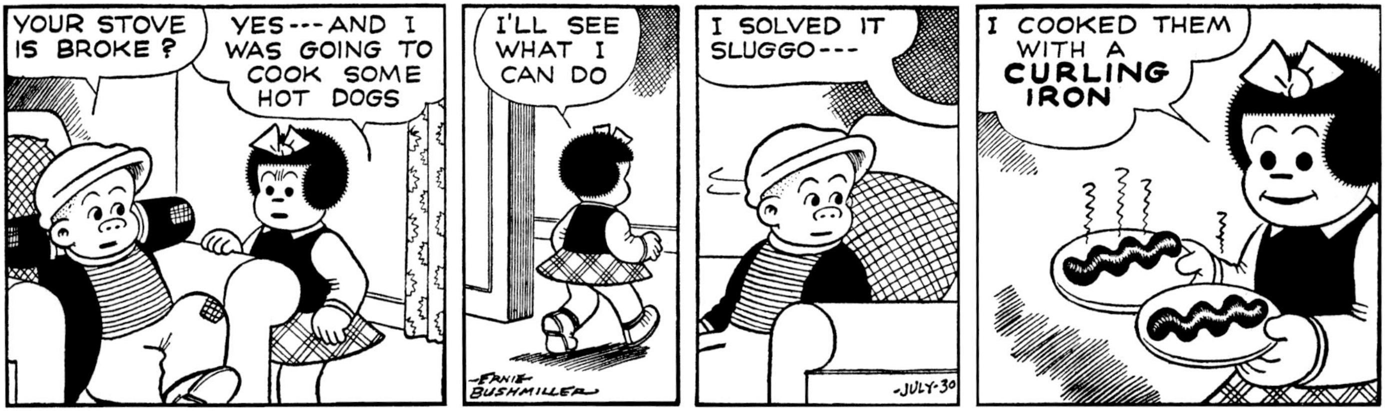
YOUR STOVE IS BROKE?
YES---AND I WAS GOING TO COOK SOME HOT DOGS
I'LL SEE WHAT I CAN DO
ERNIE BUSHMILLER
I SOLVED IT SLUGGO---
JULY-30
I COOKED THEM WITH A **CURLING IRON**

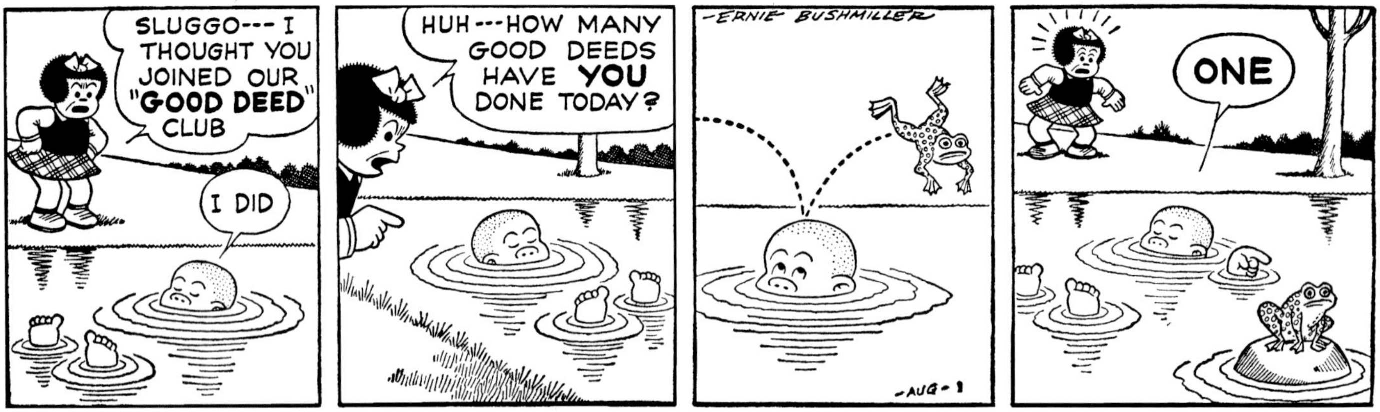
SLUGGO--- I THOUGHT YOU JOINED OUR "**GOOD DEED**" CLUB
I DID
HUH---HOW MANY GOOD DEEDS HAVE **YOU** DONE TODAY?
ERNIE BUSHMILLER
AUG-1
ONE

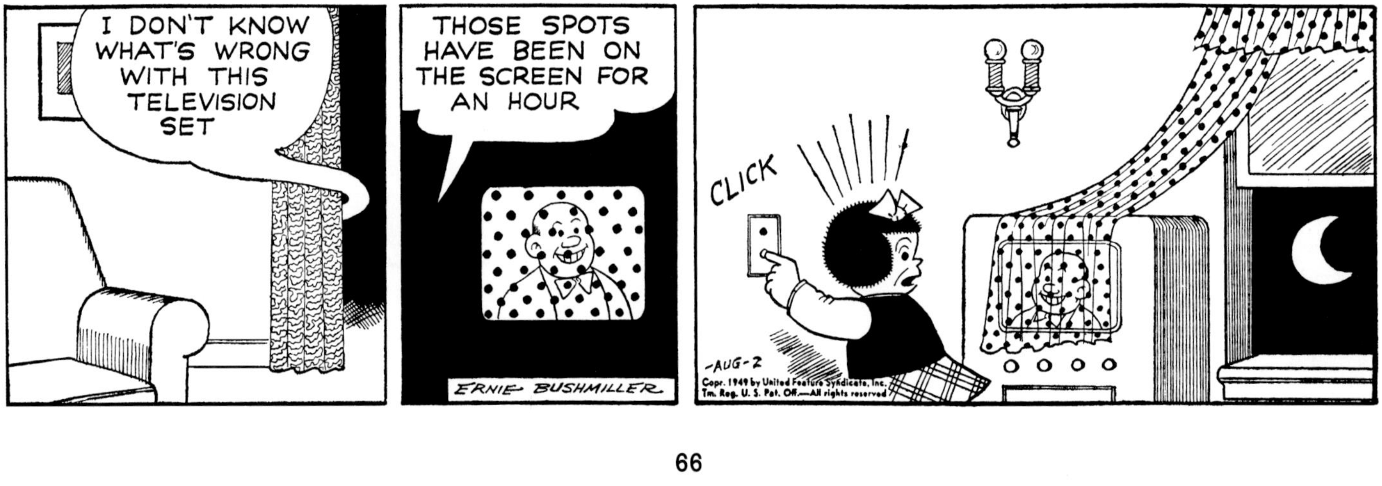
I DON'T KNOW WHAT'S WRONG WITH THIS TELEVISION SET
THOSE SPOTS HAVE BEEN ON THE SCREEN FOR AN HOUR
ERNIE BUSHMILLER
CLICK
AUG-2
Copr. 1949 by United Feature Syndicate, Inc. Tm. Reg. U. S. Pat. Off.—All rights reserved

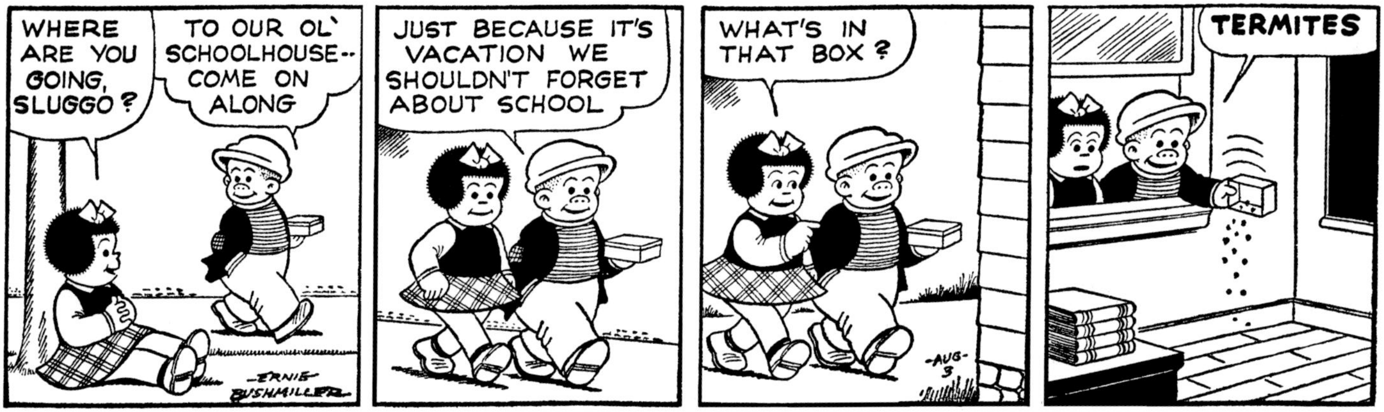
WHERE ARE YOU GOING, SLUGGO ?
TO OUR OL` SCHOOLHOUSE-- COME ON ALONG
ERNIE BUSHMILLER
JUST BECAUSE IT'S VACATION WE SHOULDN'T FORGET ABOUT SCHOOL
WHAT'S IN THAT BOX ?
AUG- 3
TERMITES

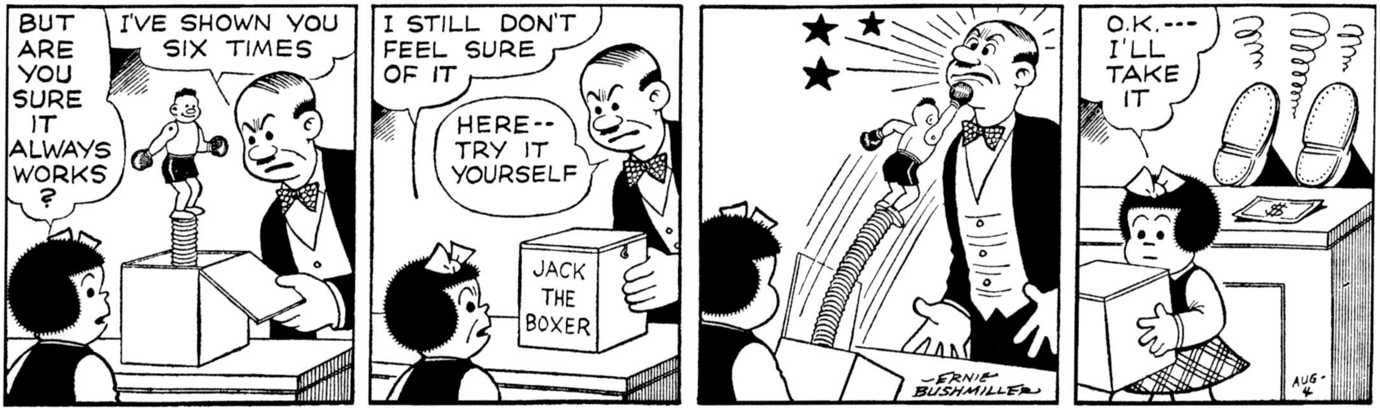
BUT ARE YOU SURE IT ALWAYS WORKS ?
I'VE SHOWN YOU SIX TIMES
I STILL DON'T FEEL SURE OF IT
HERE-- TRY IT YOURSELF
JACK THE BOXER
ERNIE BUSHMILLER
O.K.--- I'LL TAKE IT
AUG- 4

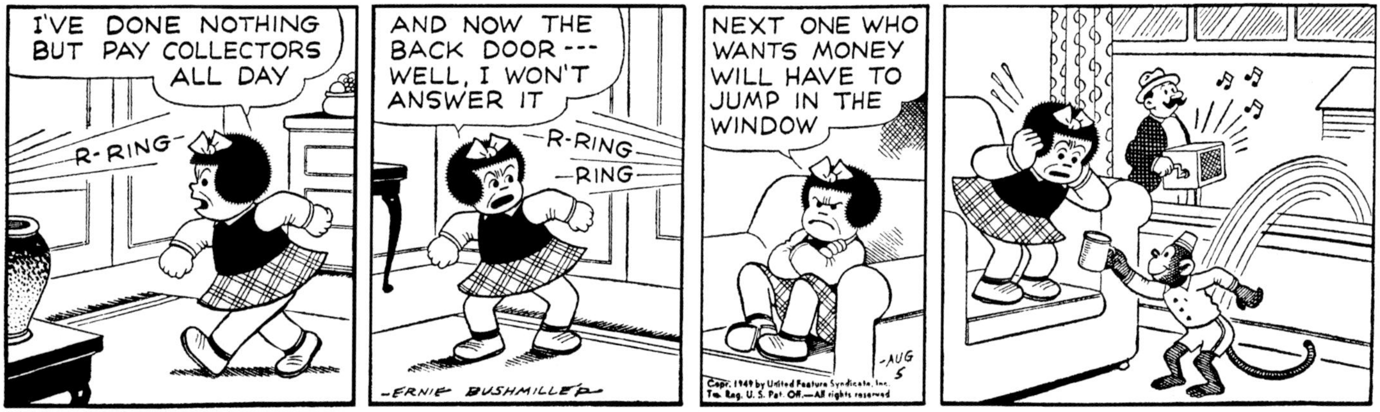
I'VE DONE NOTHING BUT PAY COLLECTORS ALL DAY
R-RING
ERNIE BUSHMILLER
AND NOW THE BACK DOOR--- WELL, I WON'T ANSWER IT
R-RING
RING
NEXT ONE WHO WANTS MONEY WILL HAVE TO JUMP IN THE WINDOW
AUG 5
Copr. 1949 by United Feature Syndicate, Inc.
Tm. Reg. U. S. Pat. Off.—All rights reserved

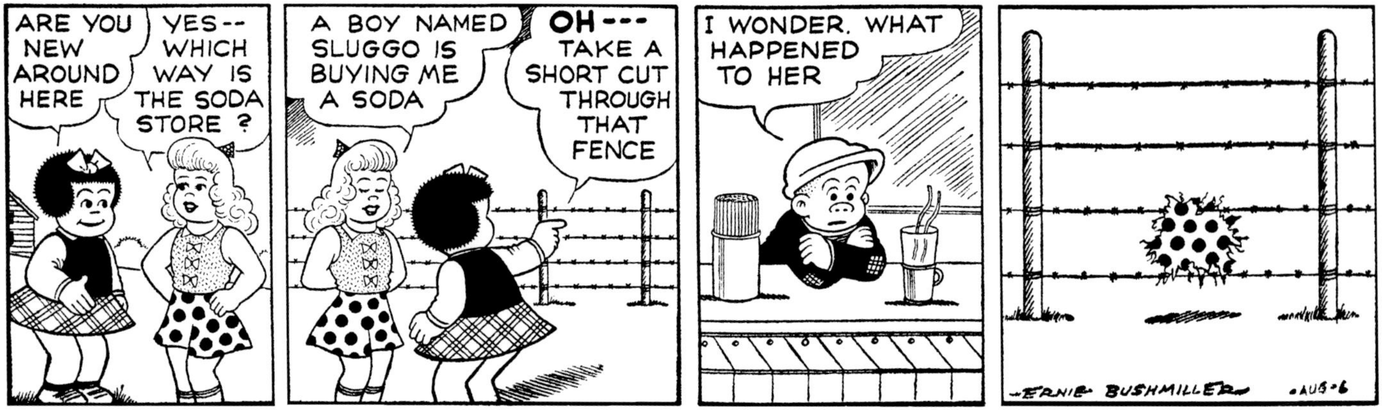
ARE YOU NEW AROUND HERE
YES-- WHICH WAY IS THE SODA STORE ?
A BOY NAMED SLUGGO IS BUYING ME A SODA
OH--- TAKE A SHORT CUT THROUGH THAT FENCE
I WONDER. WHAT HAPPENED TO HER
ERNIE BUSHMILLER
AUG-6

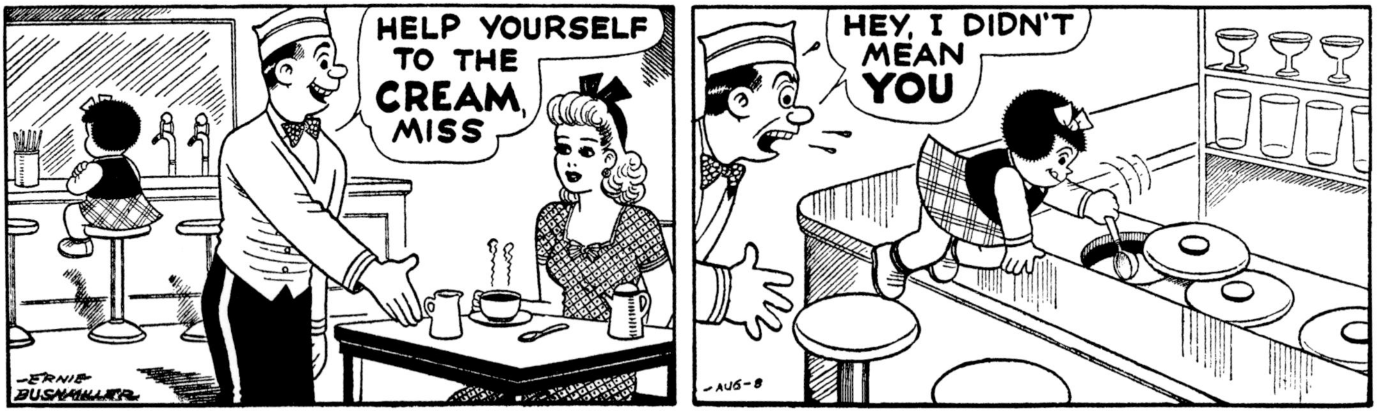
HELP YOURSELF TO THE CREAM, MISS
ERNIE BUSHMILLER
HEY, I DIDN'T MEAN YOU
AUG-8

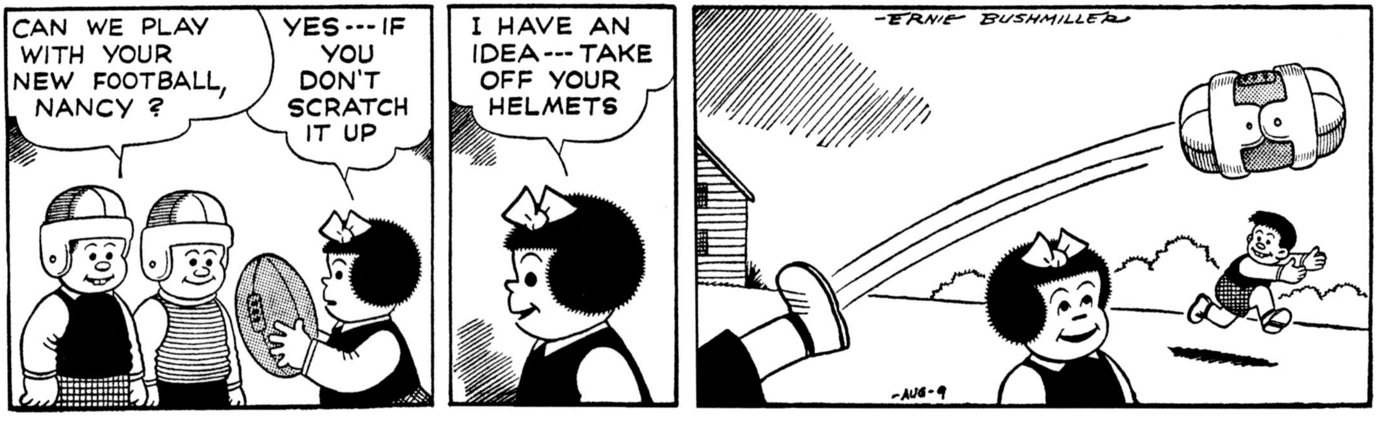
CAN WE PLAY WITH YOUR NEW FOOTBALL, NANCY ?
YES---IF YOU DON'T SCRATCH IT UP
I HAVE AN IDEA---TAKE OFF YOUR HELMETS
ERNIE BUSHMILLER
AUG-9

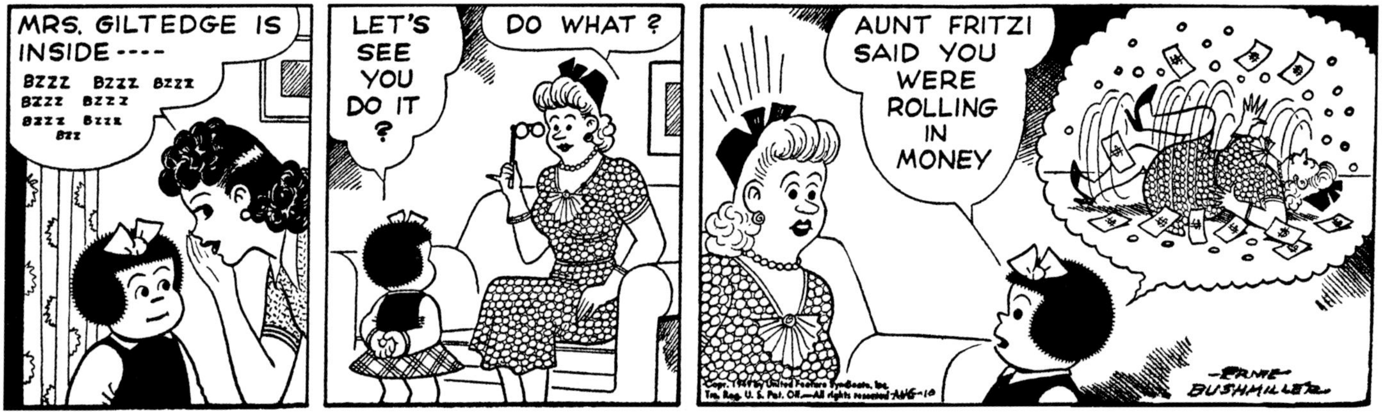
MRS. GILTEDGE IS INSIDE----
BZZZ BZZZ BZZZ BZZZ BZZZ BZZZ BZZZ BZZ
LET'S SEE YOU DO IT ?
DO WHAT ?
AUNT FRITZI SAID YOU WERE ROLLING IN MONEY
Copr. 1949 by United Feature Syndicate, Inc. Tm. Reg. U. S. Pat. Off.—All rights reserved AUG-10
ERNIE BUSHMILLER

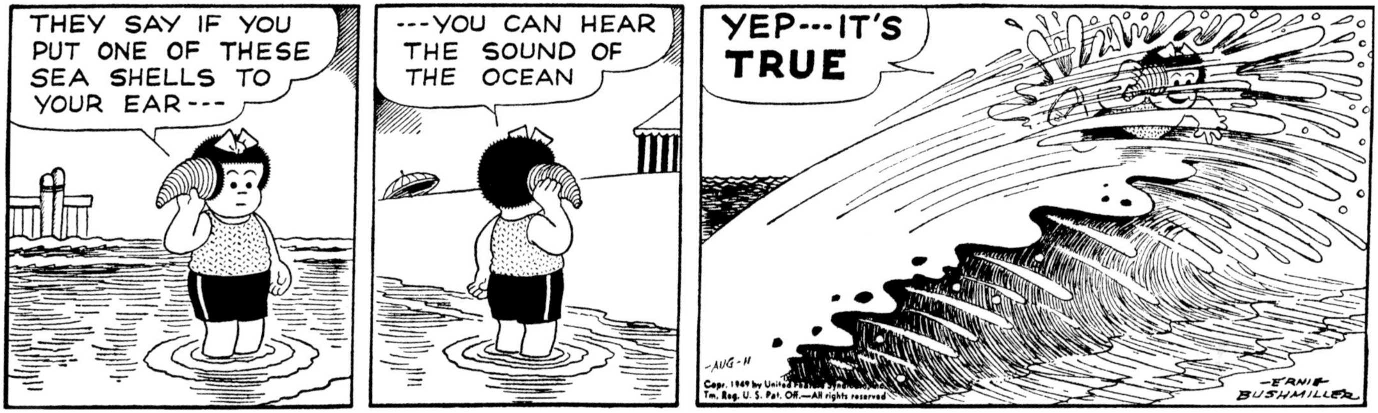
THEY SAY IF YOU PUT ONE OF THESE SEA SHELLS TO YOUR EAR---
---YOU CAN HEAR THE SOUND OF THE OCEAN
YEP---IT'S TRUE
AUG-11
Copr. 1949 by United Feature Syndicate, Inc. Tm. Reg. U. S. Pat. Off.—All rights reserved
ERNIE BUSHMILLER

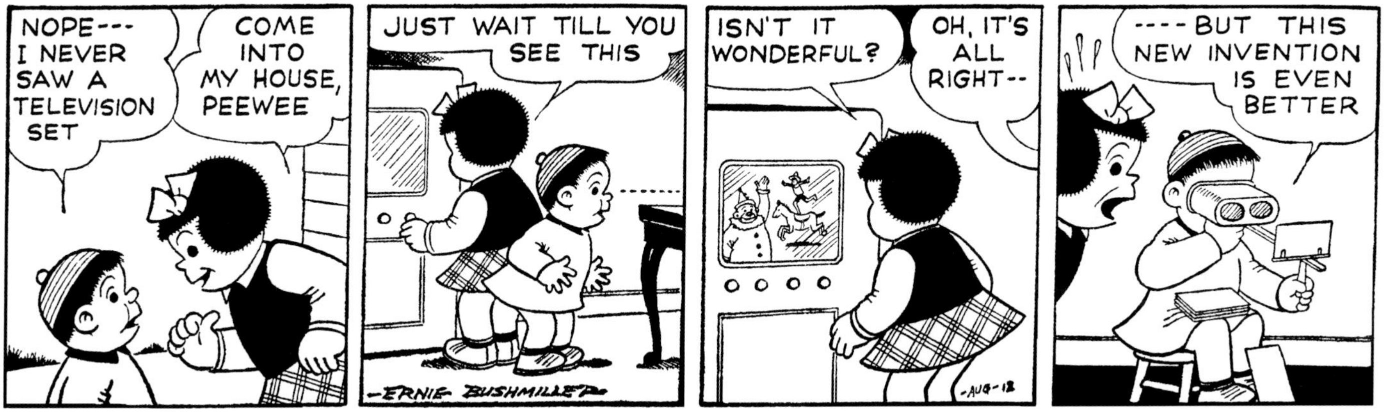
NOPE--- I NEVER SAW A TELEVISION SET
COME INTO MY HOUSE, PEEWEE
JUST WAIT TILL YOU SEE THIS
ERNIE BUSHMILLER
ISN'T IT WONDERFUL?
OH, IT'S ALL RIGHT--
AUG-12
----BUT THIS NEW INVENTION IS EVEN BETTER

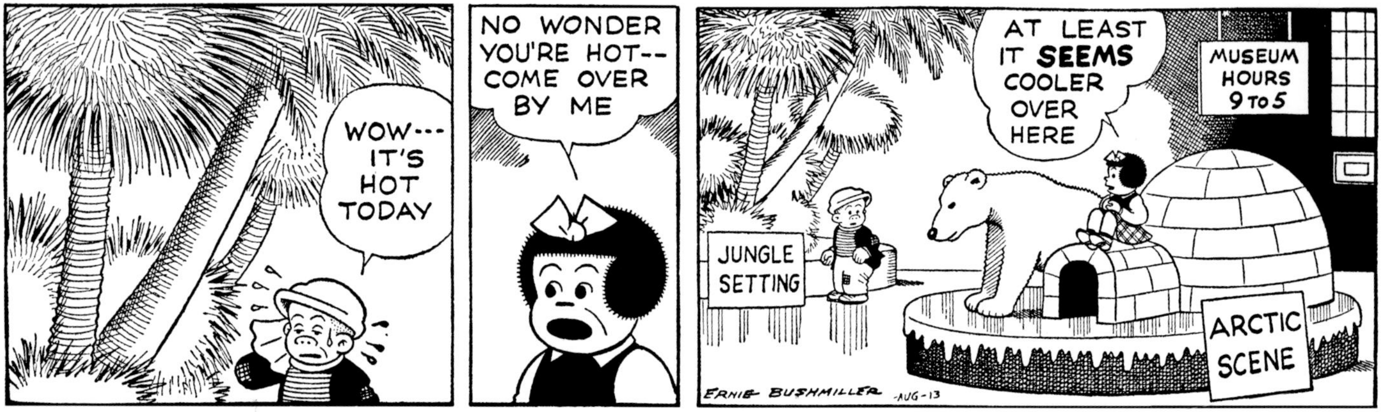
WOW--- IT'S HOT TODAY
NO WONDER YOU'RE HOT-- COME OVER BY ME
AT LEAST IT **SEEMS** COOLER OVER HERE
MUSEUM HOURS 9 TO 5
JUNGLE SETTING
ARCTIC SCENE
ERNIE BUSHMILLER
AUG-13

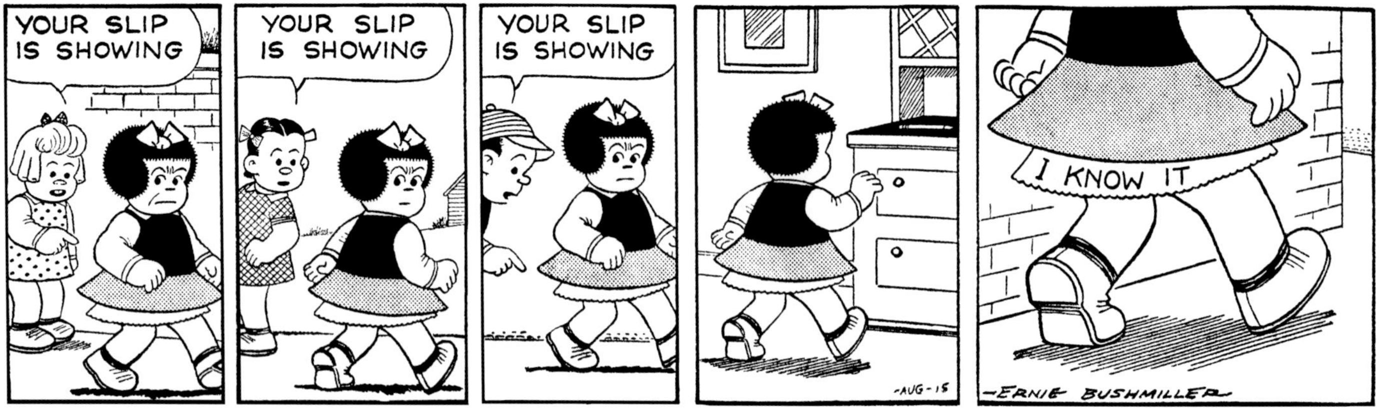
YOUR SLIP IS SHOWING
YOUR SLIP IS SHOWING
YOUR SLIP IS SHOWING
AUG-15
I KNOW IT
ERNIE BUSHMILLER

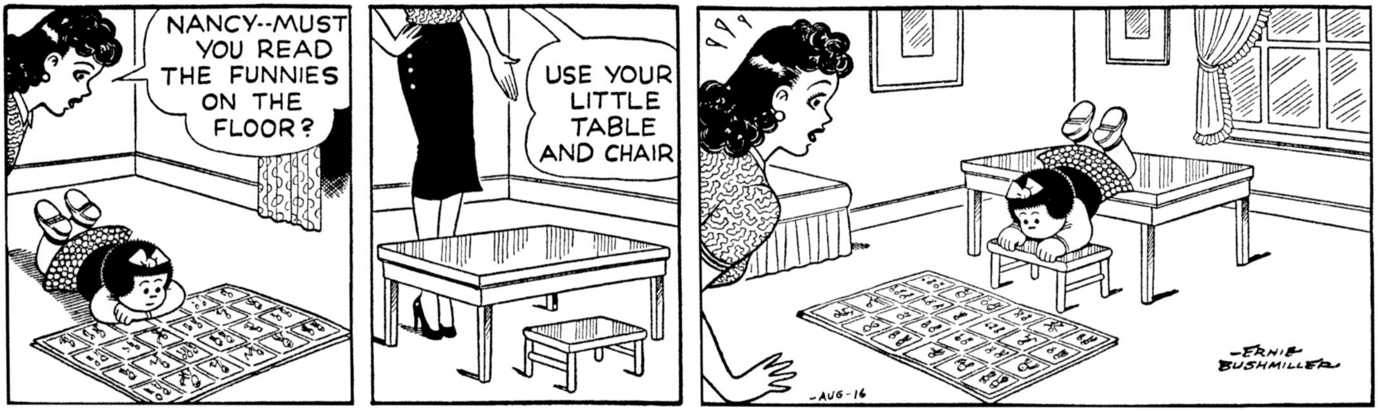
NANCY--MUST YOU READ THE FUNNIES ON THE FLOOR?
USE YOUR LITTLE TABLE AND CHAIR
AUG-16
ERNIE BUSHMILLER

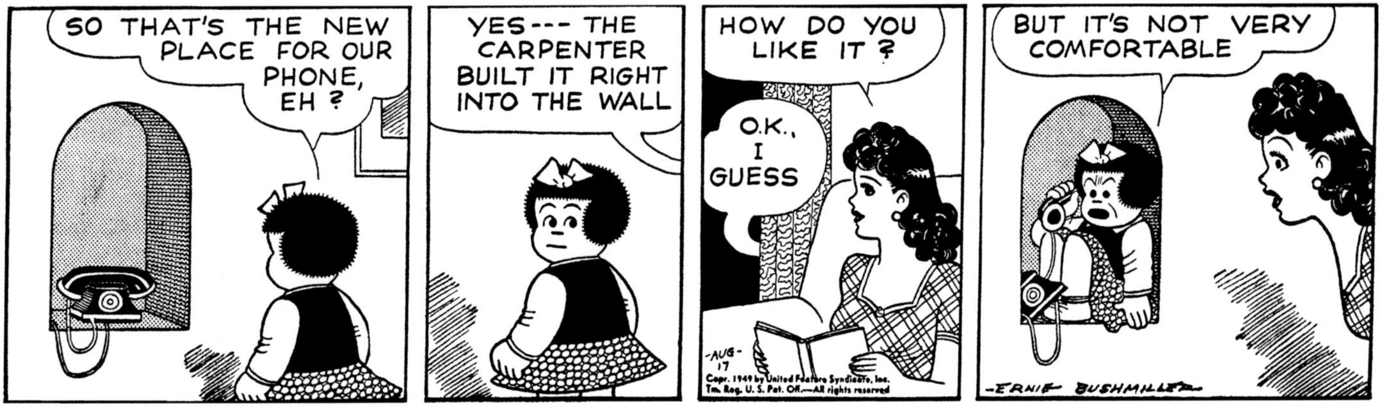
SO THAT'S THE NEW PLACE FOR OUR PHONE, EH ?
YES--- THE CARPENTER BUILT IT RIGHT INTO THE WALL
HOW DO YOU LIKE IT ?
O.K., I GUESS
-AUG-17
Copr. 1949 by United Feature Syndicate, Inc.
Tm. Reg. U. S. Pat. Off.—All rights reserved
BUT IT'S NOT VERY COMFORTABLE
-ERNIE BUSHMILLER

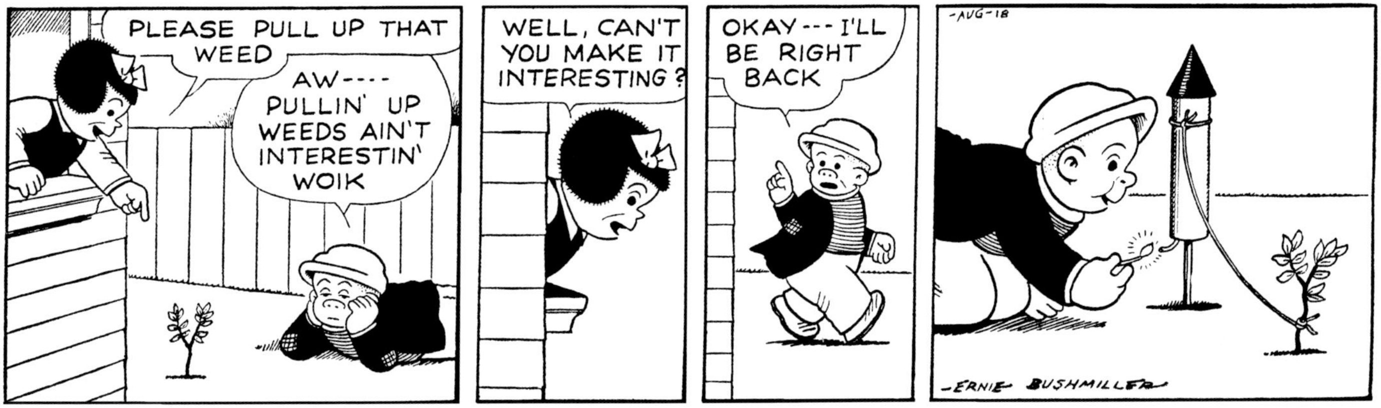
PLEASE PULL UP THAT WEED
AW---- PULLIN' UP WEEDS AIN'T INTERESTIN' WOIK
WELL, CAN'T YOU MAKE IT INTERESTING ?
OKAY--- I'LL BE RIGHT BACK
-AUG-18
-ERNIE BUSHMILLER

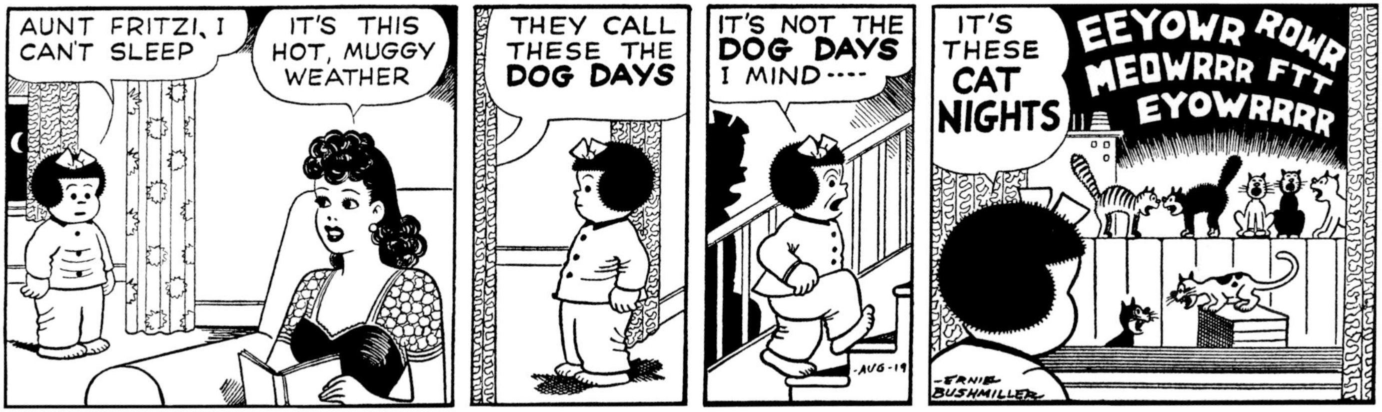
AUNT FRITZI, I CAN'T SLEEP
IT'S THIS HOT, MUGGY WEATHER
THEY CALL THESE THE DOG DAYS
IT'S NOT THE DOG DAYS I MIND----
-AUG-19
IT'S THESE CAT NIGHTS
EEYOWR ROWR MEOWRRR FTT EYOWRRRR
-ERNIE BUSHMILLER

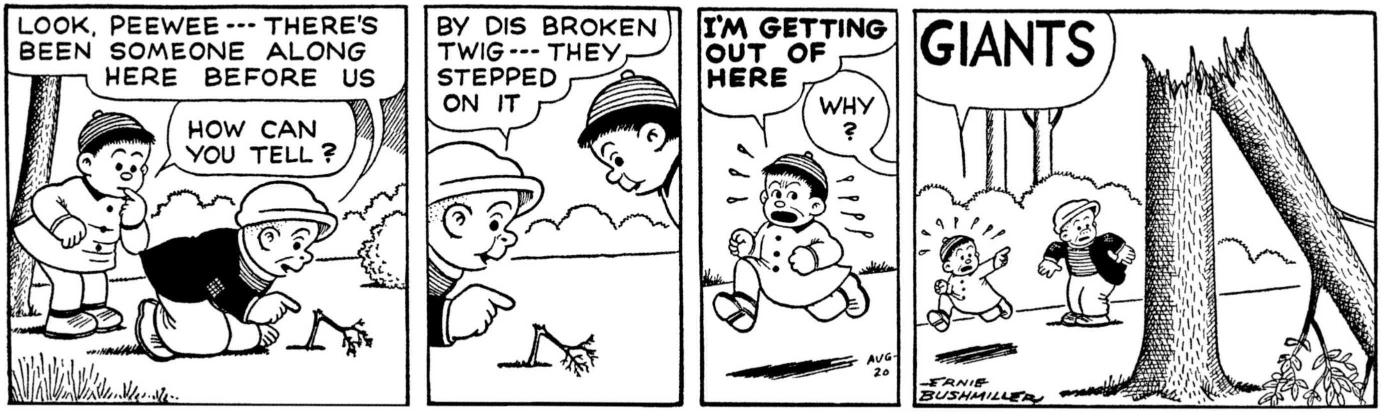
LOOK, PEEWEE --- THERE'S BEEN SOMEONE ALONG HERE BEFORE US
HOW CAN YOU TELL ?
BY DIS BROKEN TWIG --- THEY STEPPED ON IT
I'M GETTING OUT OF HERE
WHY ?
AUG-20
GIANTS
-ERNIE-
BUSHMILLER

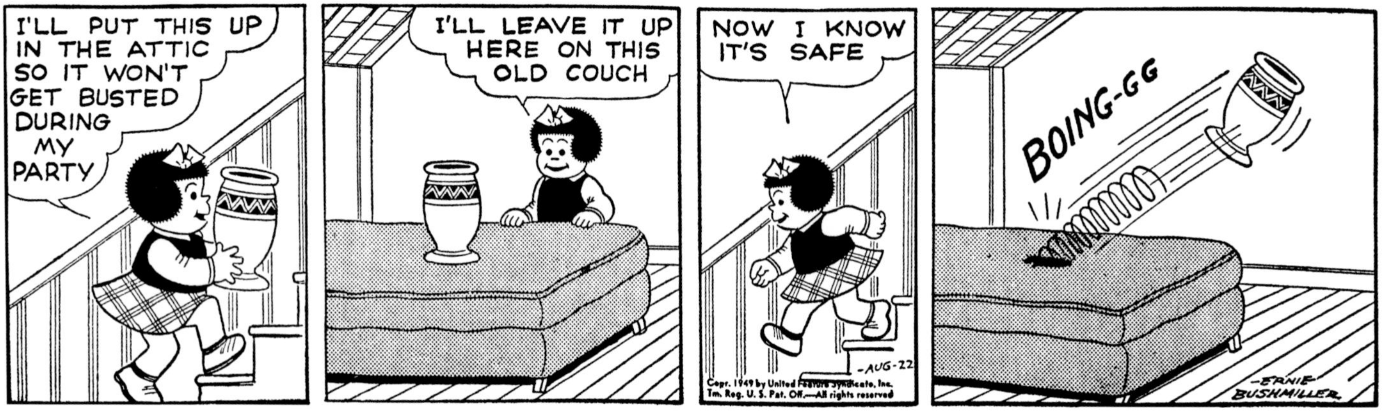
I'LL PUT THIS UP IN THE ATTIC SO IT WON'T GET BUSTED DURING MY PARTY
I'LL LEAVE IT UP HERE ON THIS OLD COUCH
NOW I KNOW IT'S SAFE
-AUG-22
Copr. 1949 by United Feature Syndicate, Inc.
Tm. Reg. U. S. Pat. Off.—All rights reserved
BOING-GG
-ERNIE-
BUSHMILLER

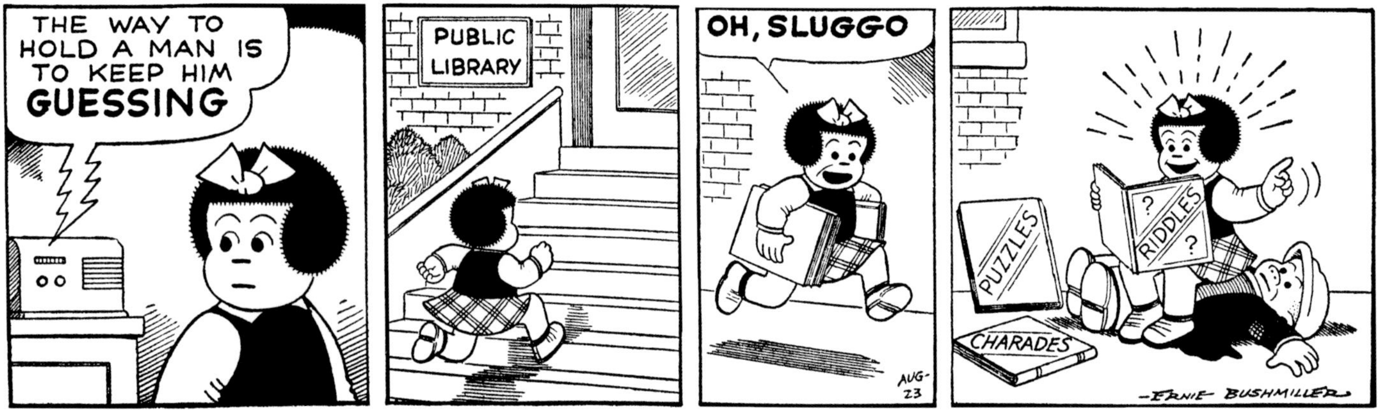
THE WAY TO HOLD A MAN IS TO KEEP HIM GUESSING
PUBLIC LIBRARY
OH, SLUGGO
AUG-23
PUZZLES
RIDDLES
CHARADES
-ERNIE- BUSHMILLER

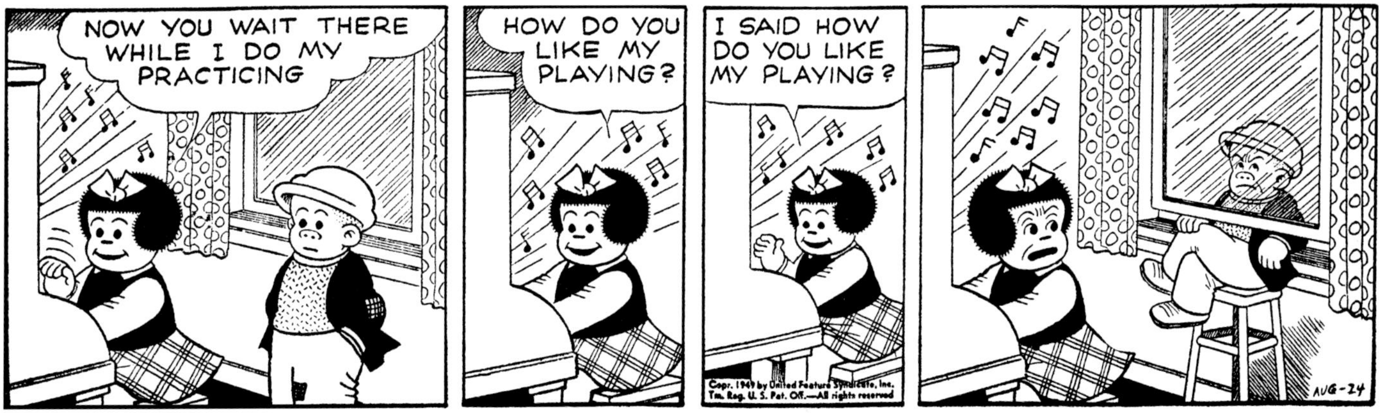
NOW YOU WAIT THERE WHILE I DO MY PRACTICING
HOW DO YOU LIKE MY PLAYING?
I SAID HOW DO YOU LIKE MY PLAYING?
Copr. 1949 by United Feature Syndicate, Inc. Tm. Reg. U. S. Pat. Off.—All rights reserved
AUG-24

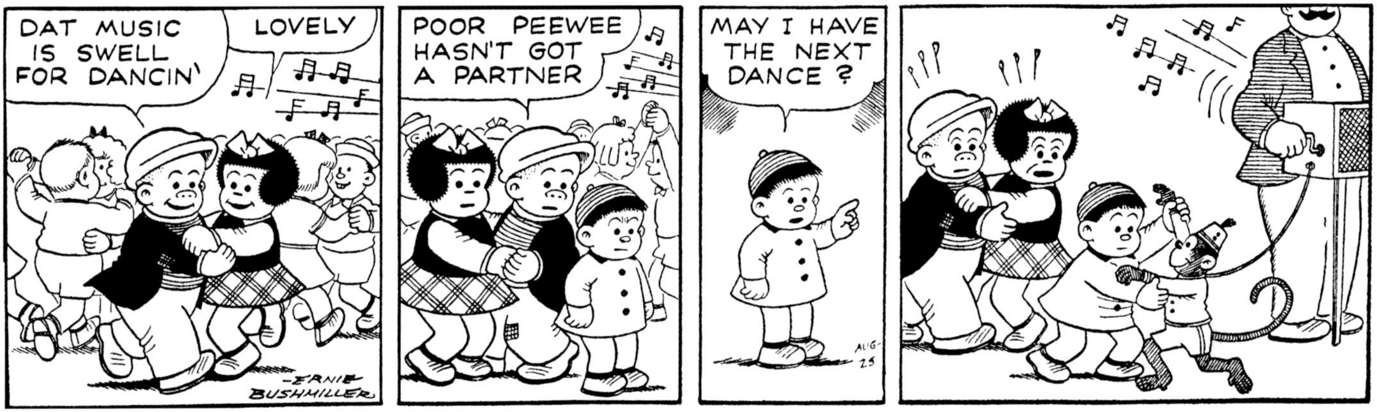
DAT MUSIC IS SWELL FOR DANCIN'
LOVELY
-ERNIE BUSHMILLER
POOR PEEWEE HASN'T GOT A PARTNER
MAY I HAVE THE NEXT DANCE?
AUG-25

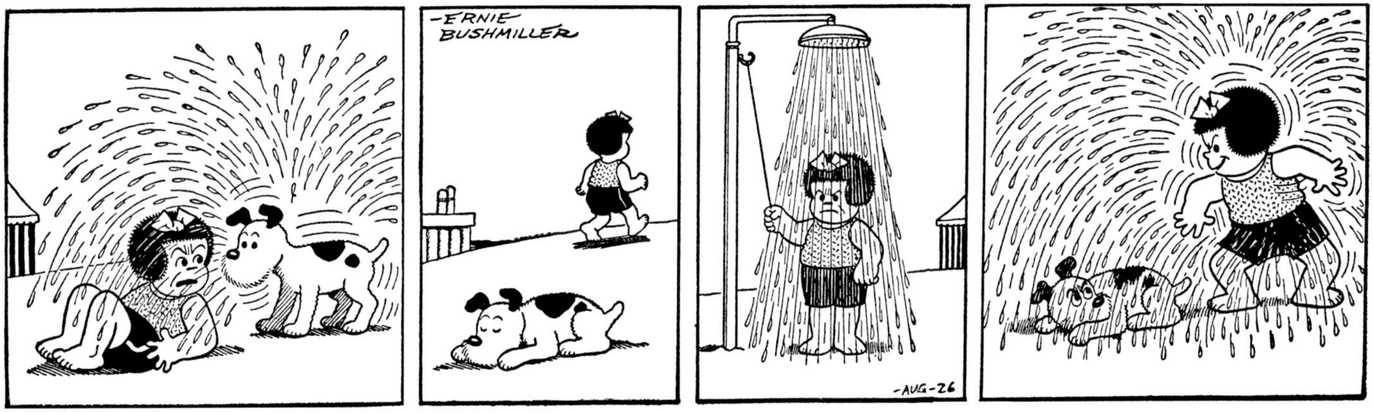
-ERNIE BUSHMILLER
-AUG-26

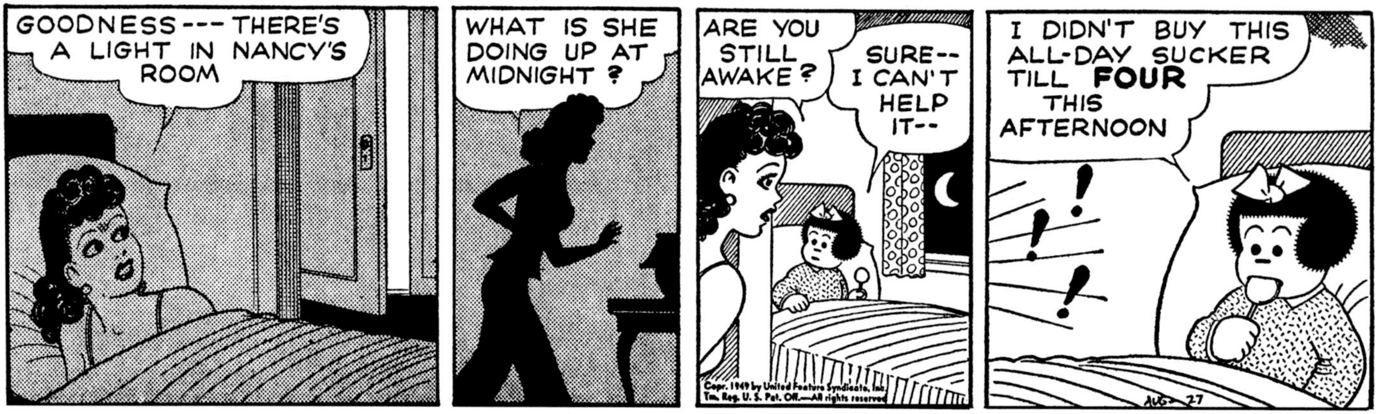
GOODNESS --- THERE'S A LIGHT IN NANCY'S ROOM
WHAT IS SHE DOING UP AT MIDNIGHT ?
ARE YOU STILL AWAKE ?
SURE-- I CAN'T HELP IT--
Copr. 1949 by United Feature Syndicate, Inc. Tm. Reg. U. S. Pat. Off.—All rights reserved
I DIDN'T BUY THIS ALL-DAY SUCKER TILL FOUR THIS AFTERNOON
AUG-27

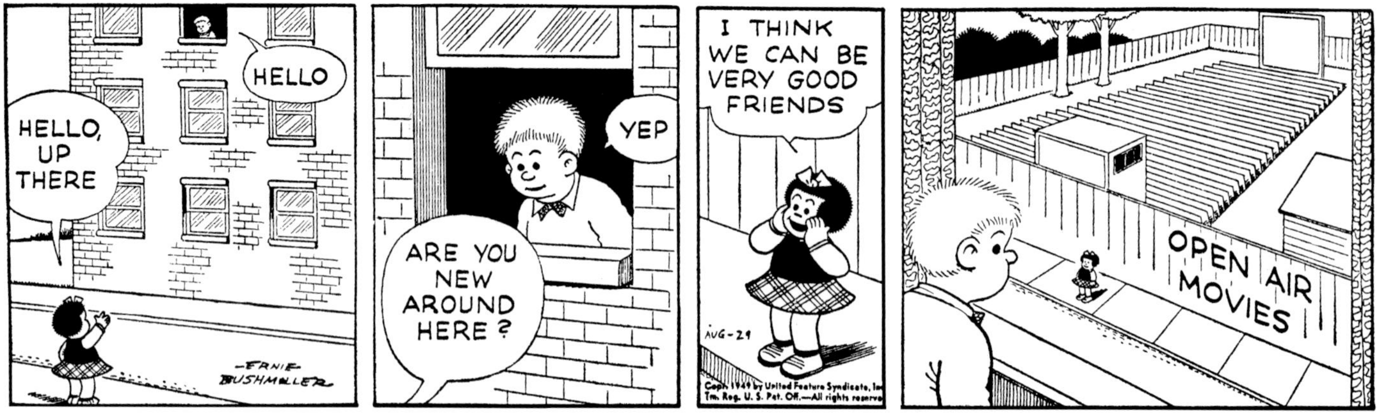
HELLO, UP THERE
HELLO
-ERNIE BUSHMILLER
YEP
ARE YOU NEW AROUND HERE ?
I THINK WE CAN BE VERY GOOD FRIENDS
AUG-29
Copr. 1949 by United Feature Syndicate, Inc. Tm. Reg. U. S. Pat. Off.—All rights reserved
OPEN AIR MOVIES

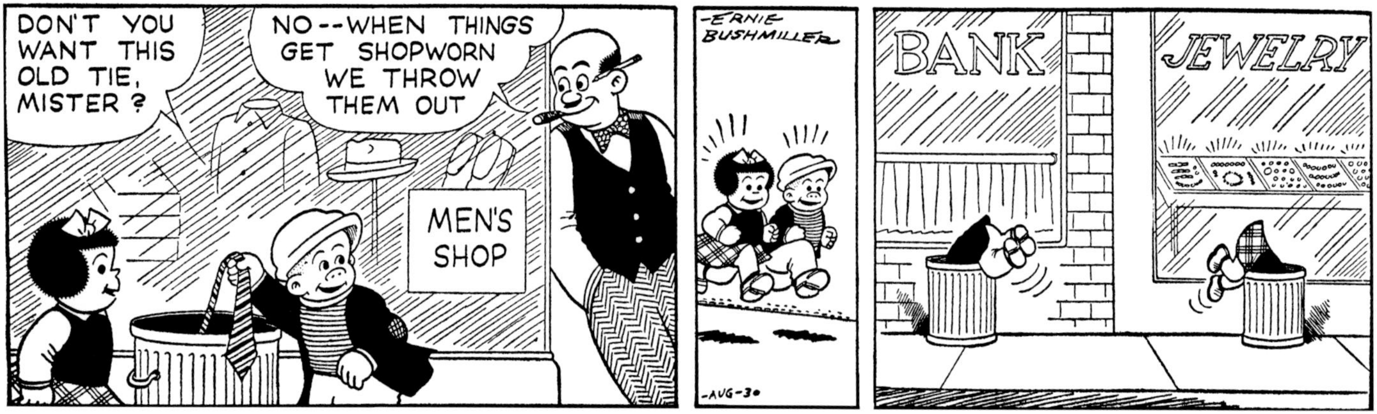
DON'T YOU WANT THIS OLD TIE, MISTER ?
NO--WHEN THINGS GET SHOPWORN WE THROW THEM OUT
MEN'S SHOP
-ERNIE BUSHMILLER
-AUG-30
BANK
JEWELRY

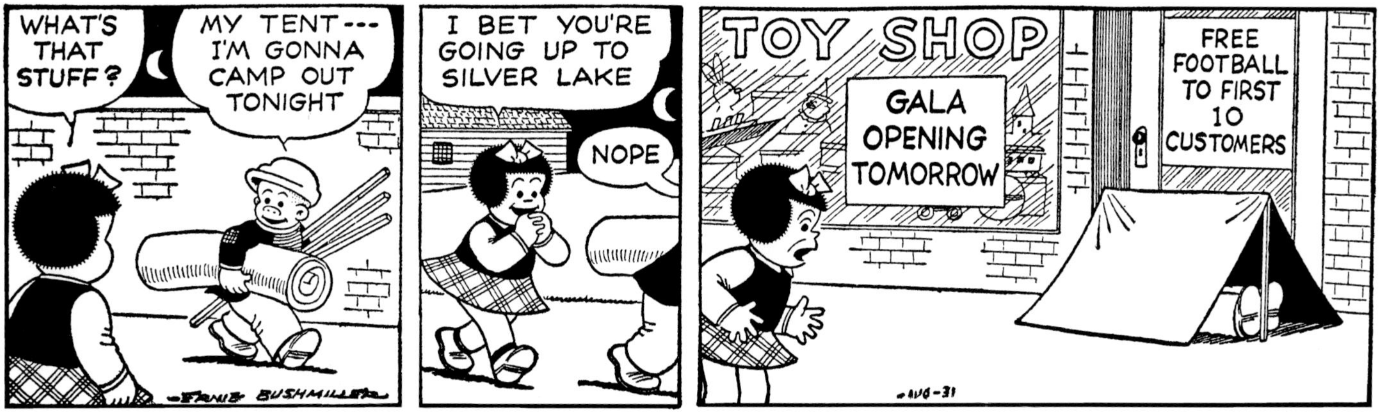
WHAT'S THAT STUFF?
MY TENT--- I'M GONNA CAMP OUT TONIGHT
ERNIE BUSHMILLER
I BET YOU'RE GOING UP TO SILVER LAKE
NOPE
TOY SHOP
GALA OPENING TOMORROW
FREE FOOTBALL TO FIRST 10 CUSTOMERS
AUG-31

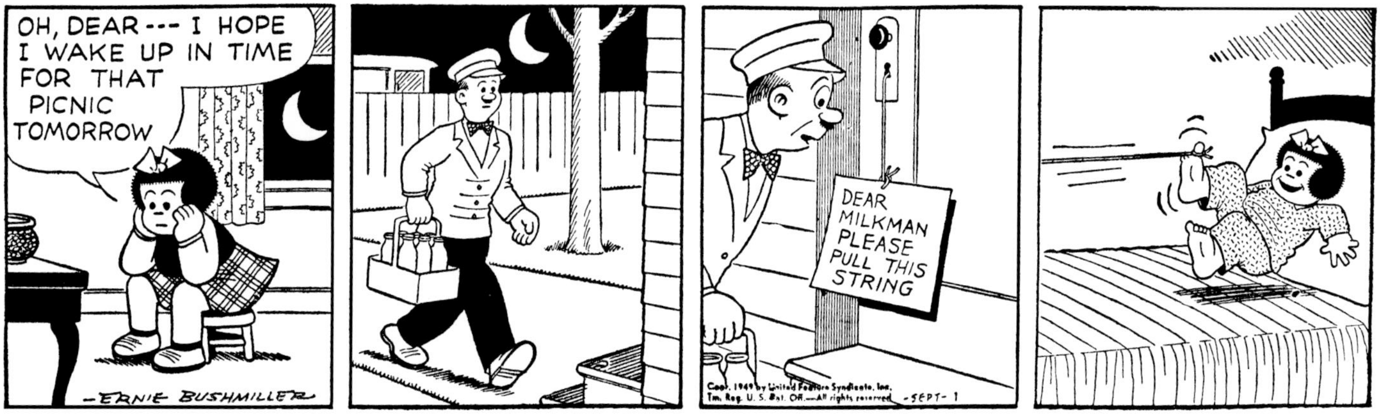
OH, DEAR--- I HOPE I WAKE UP IN TIME FOR THAT PICNIC TOMORROW
ERNIE BUSHMILLER
DEAR MILKMAN PLEASE PULL THIS STRING
Copr. 1949 by United Feature Syndicate, Inc.
Tm. Reg. U. S. Pat. Off.—All rights reserved
SEPT-1

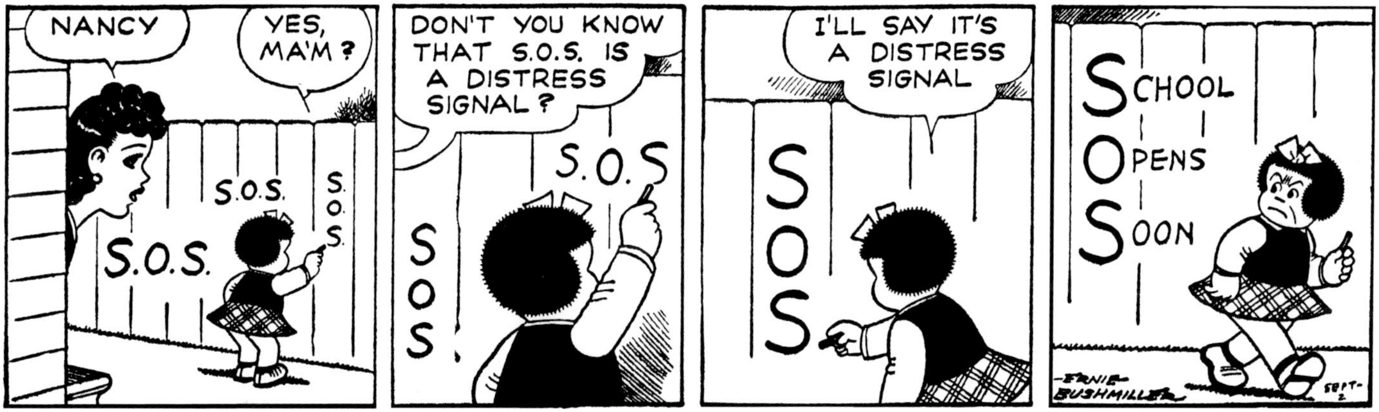
NANCY
YES, MA'M?
S.O.S.
S.O.S.
S.O.S.
S.O.S.
DON'T YOU KNOW THAT S.O.S. IS A DISTRESS SIGNAL?
S.O.S
SOS
I'LL SAY IT'S A DISTRESS SIGNAL
SOS
SCHOOL OPENS SOON
ERNIE BUSHMILLER
SEPT-2

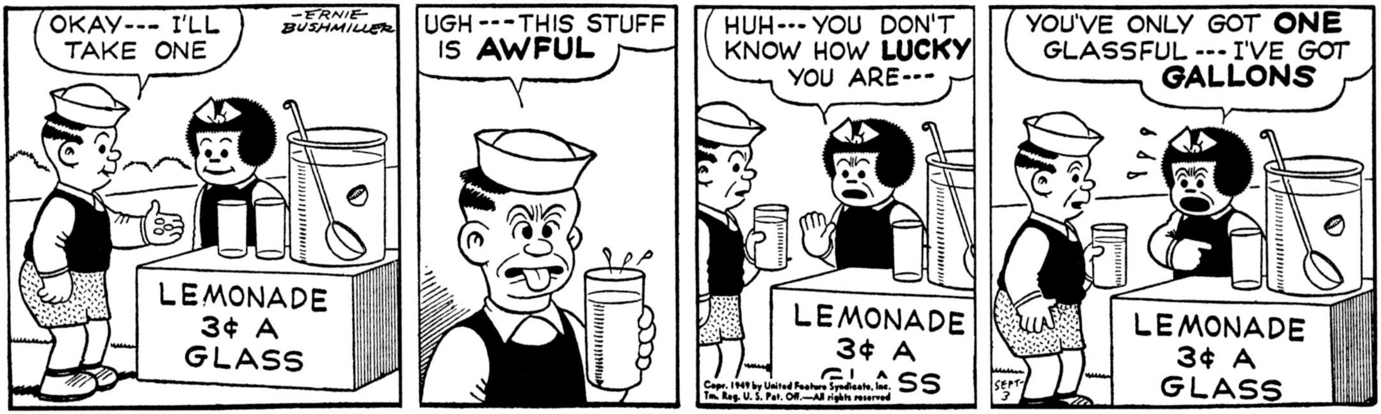
OKAY--- I'LL TAKE ONE
-ERNIE BUSHMILLER
LEMONADE 3¢ A GLASS
UGH---THIS STUFF IS **AWFUL**
HUH--- YOU DON'T KNOW HOW **LUCKY** YOU ARE---
LEMONADE 3¢ A GLASS
Copr. 1949 by United Feature Syndicate, Inc. Tm. Reg. U. S. Pat. Off.—All rights reserved
YOU'VE ONLY GOT **ONE** GLASSFUL --- I'VE GOT **GALLONS**
LEMONADE 3¢ A GLASS
SEPT-3

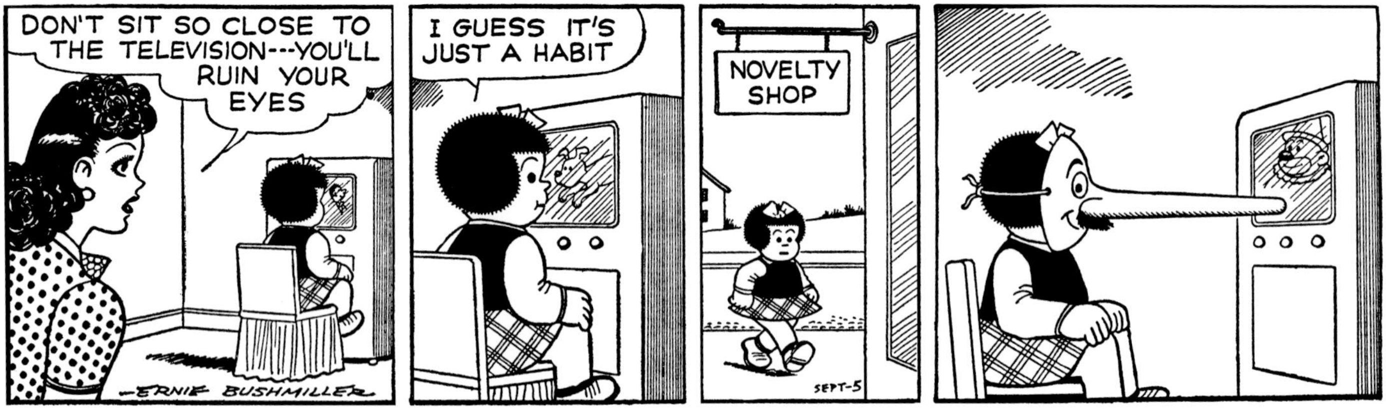
DON'T SIT SO CLOSE TO THE TELEVISION---YOU'LL RUIN YOUR EYES
-ERNIE BUSHMILLER
I GUESS IT'S JUST A HABIT
NOVELTY SHOP
SEPT-5

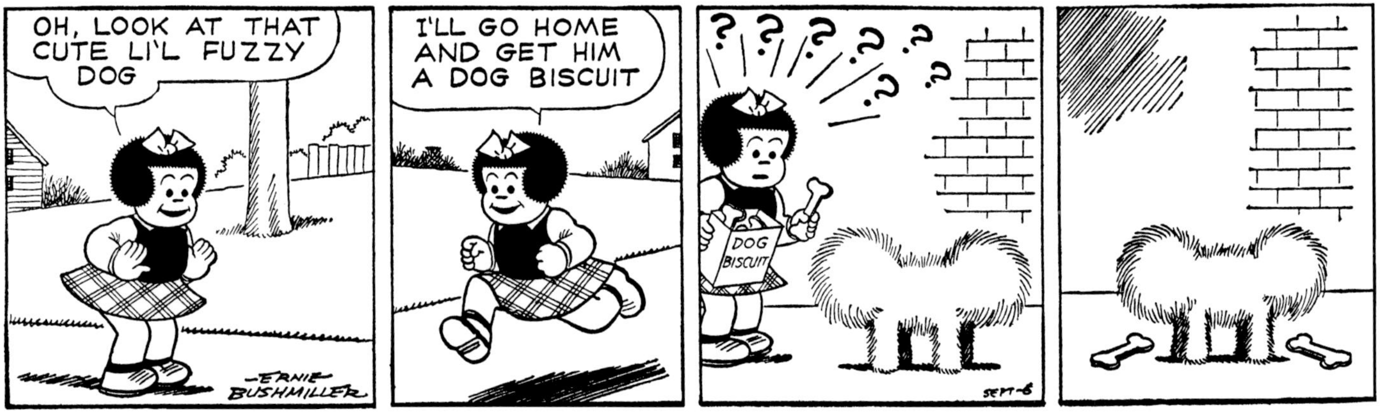
OH, LOOK AT THAT CUTE LI'L FUZZY DOG
-ERNIE BUSHMILLER
I'LL GO HOME AND GET HIM A DOG BISCUIT
DOG BISCUIT
SEPT-6

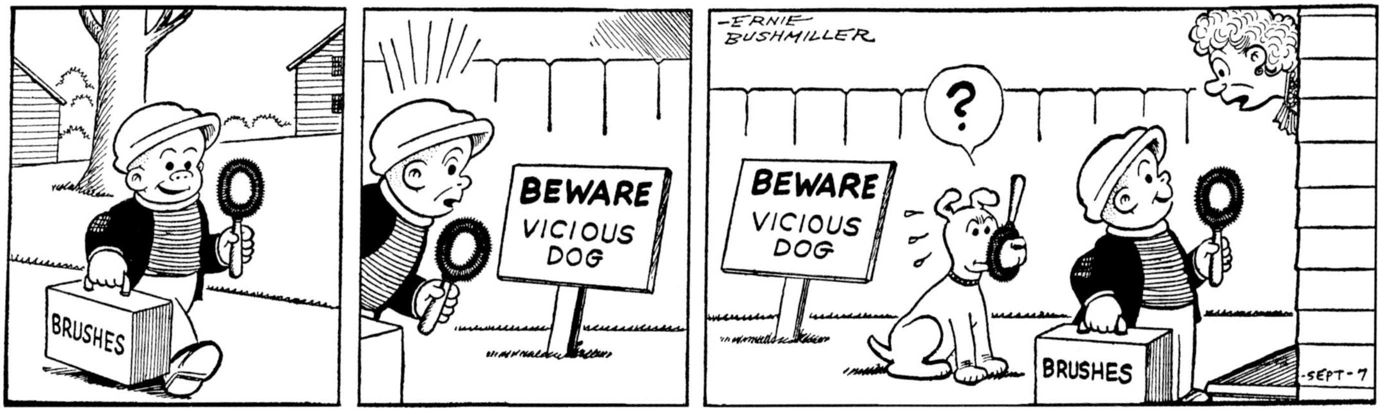
BRUSHES
BEWARE
VICIOUS DOG
-ERNIE BUSHMILLER
?
BEWARE
VICIOUS DOG
BRUSHES
-SEPT-7

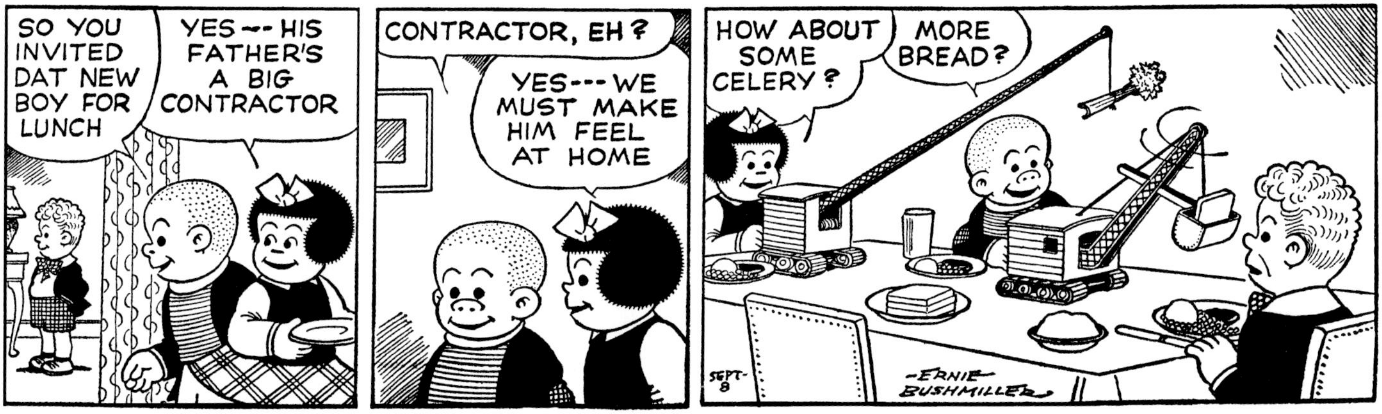
SO YOU INVITED DAT NEW BOY FOR LUNCH
YES -- HIS FATHER'S A BIG CONTRACTOR
CONTRACTOR, EH ?
YES--- WE MUST MAKE HIM FEEL AT HOME
HOW ABOUT SOME CELERY ?
MORE BREAD ?
SEPT-8
-ERNIE BUSHMILLER

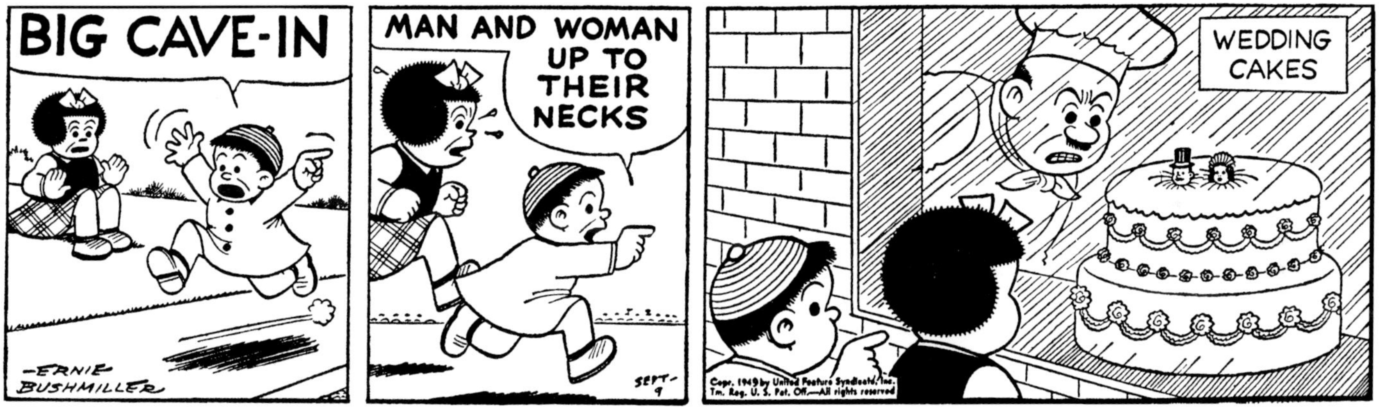
BIG CAVE-IN
-ERNIE BUSHMILLER
MAN AND WOMAN UP TO THEIR NECKS
SEPT-9
WEDDING CAKES
Copr. 1949 by United Feature Syndicate, Inc.
Tm. Reg. U. S. Pat. Off.—All rights reserved

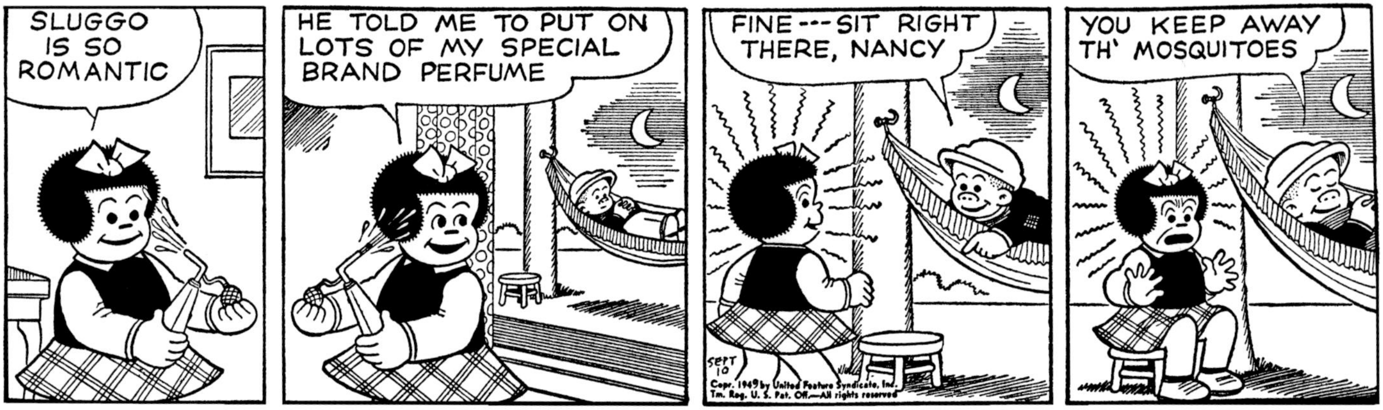
SLUGGO IS SO ROMANTIC
HE TOLD ME TO PUT ON LOTS OF MY SPECIAL BRAND PERFUME
FINE --- SIT RIGHT THERE, NANCY
SEPT 10
Copr. 1949 by United Feature Syndicate, Inc.
Tm. Reg. U. S. Pat. Off.—All rights reserved
YOU KEEP AWAY TH' MOSQUITOES

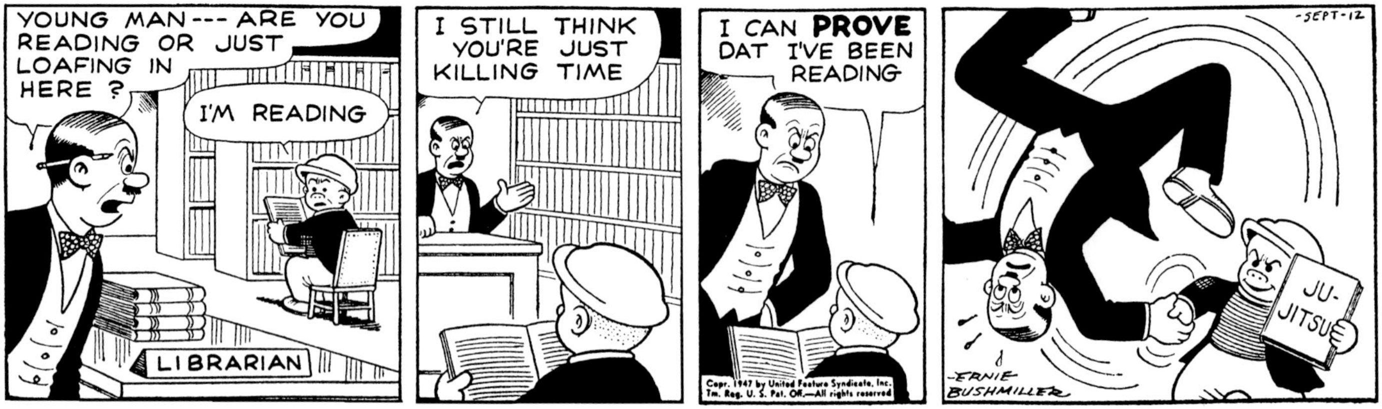
YOUNG MAN --- ARE YOU READING OR JUST LOAFING IN HERE ?
I'M READING
LIBRARIAN
I STILL THINK YOU'RE JUST KILLING TIME
I CAN **PROVE** DAT I'VE BEEN READING
Copr. 1947 by United Feature Syndicate, Inc.
Tm. Reg. U. S. Pat. Off.—All rights reserved
-SEPT-12
JU-JITSU
-ERNIE BUSHMILLER

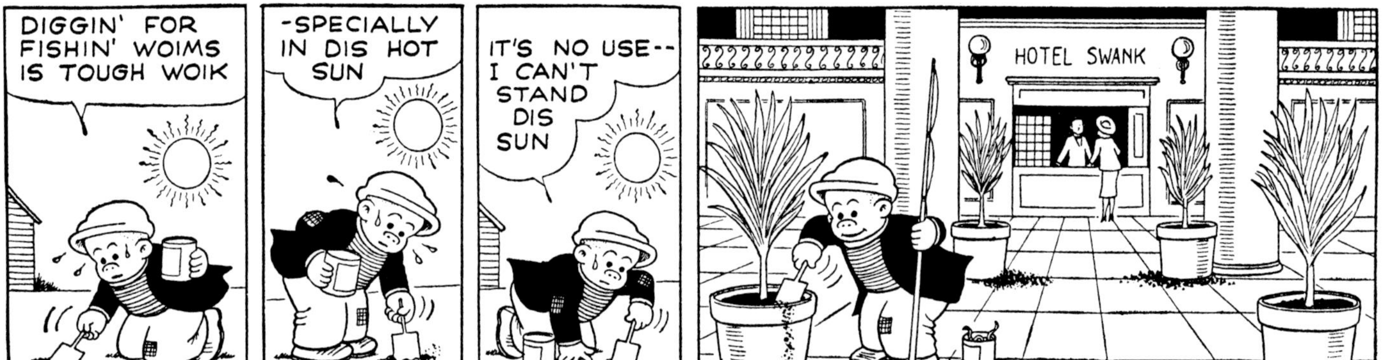
DIGGIN' FOR FISHIN' WOIMS IS TOUGH WOIK
-ERNIE BUSHMILLER
-SPECIALLY IN DIS HOT SUN
IT'S NO USE -- I CAN'T STAND DIS SUN
HOTEL SWANK
-SEPT-13

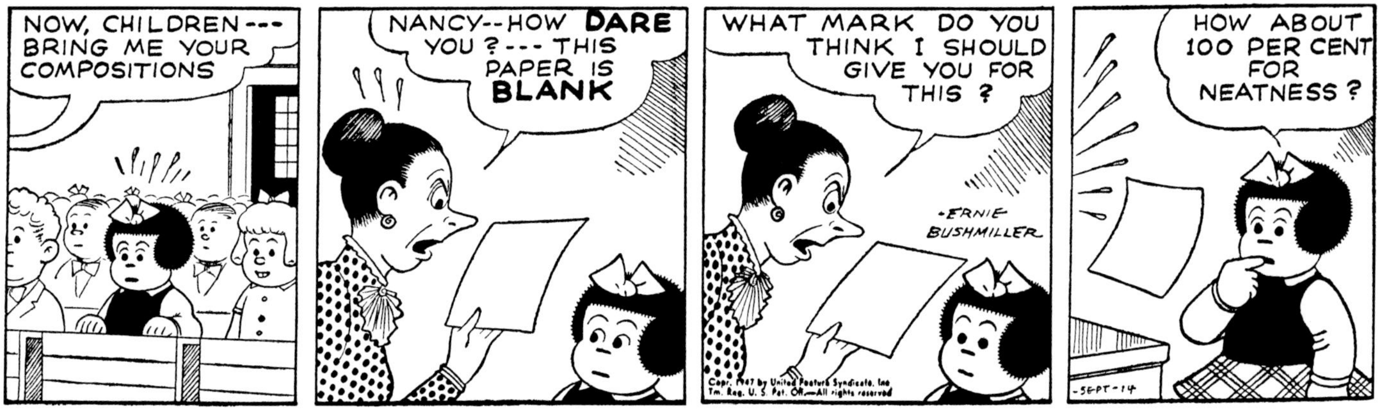
NOW, CHILDREN--- BRING ME YOUR COMPOSITIONS
NANCY--HOW DARE YOU ?--- THIS PAPER IS BLANK
WHAT MARK DO YOU THINK I SHOULD GIVE YOU FOR THIS ?
-ERNIE BUSHMILLER
Copr. 1947 by United Feature Syndicate, Inc. Tm. Reg. U. S. Pat. Off.—All rights reserved
HOW ABOUT 100 PER CENT FOR NEATNESS ?
-SEPT-14

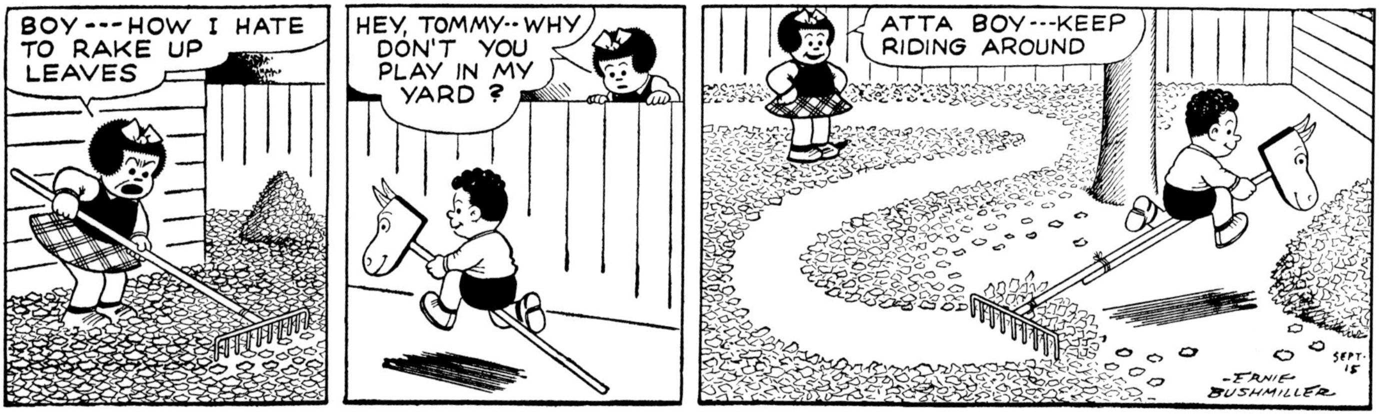
BOY---HOW I HATE TO RAKE UP LEAVES
HEY, TOMMY--WHY DON'T YOU PLAY IN MY YARD ?
ATTA BOY---KEEP RIDING AROUND
SEPT-15
-ERNIE BUSHMILLER

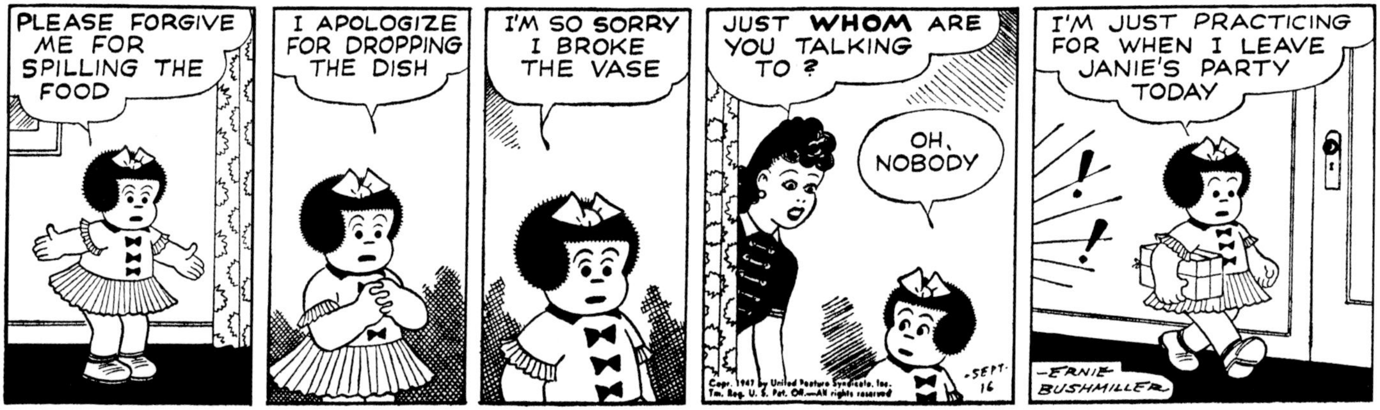
PLEASE FORGIVE ME FOR SPILLING THE FOOD
I APOLOGIZE FOR DROPPING THE DISH
I'M SO SORRY I BROKE THE VASE
JUST WHOM ARE YOU TALKING TO ?
OH, NOBODY
Copr. 1947 by United Feature Syndicate, Inc. Tm. Reg. U. S. Pat. Off.—All rights reserved
-SEPT-16
I'M JUST PRACTICING FOR WHEN I LEAVE JANIE'S PARTY TODAY
-ERNIE BUSHMILLER

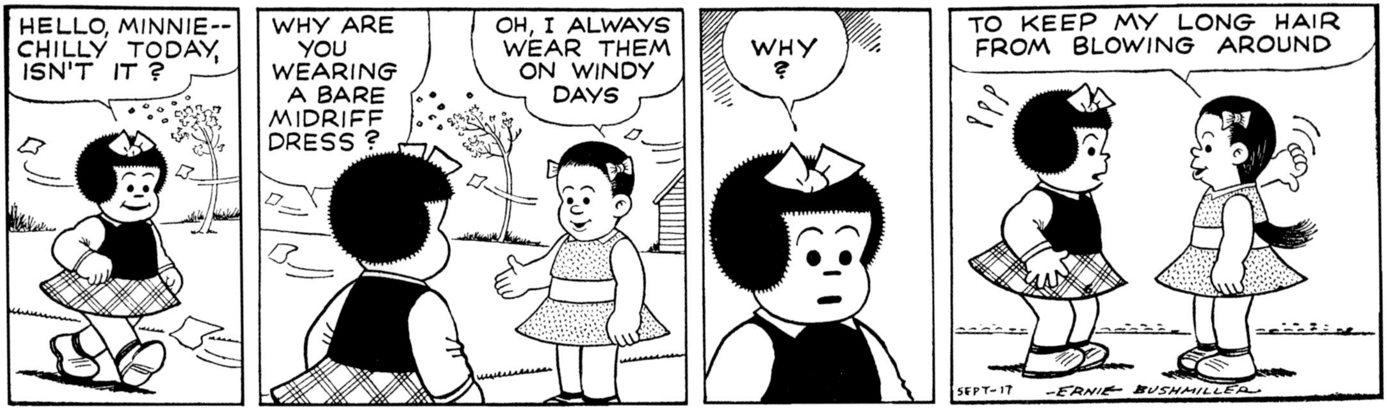
HELLO, MINNIE-- CHILLY TODAY, ISN'T IT ?
WHY ARE YOU WEARING A BARE MIDRIFF DRESS ?
OH, I ALWAYS WEAR THEM ON WINDY DAYS
WHY ?
TO KEEP MY LONG HAIR FROM BLOWING AROUND
SEPT-17
-ERNIE BUSHMILLER

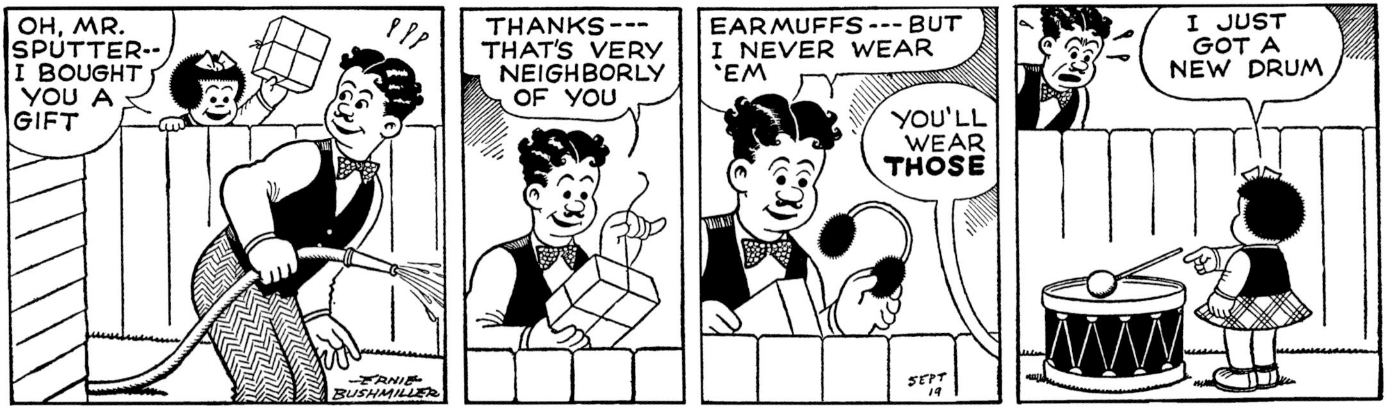
OH, MR. SPUTTER-- I BOUGHT YOU A GIFT
-ERNIE BUSHMILLER
THANKS--- THAT'S VERY NEIGHBORLY OF YOU
EARMUFFS---BUT I NEVER WEAR 'EM
YOU'LL WEAR **THOSE**
SEPT 19
I JUST GOT A NEW DRUM

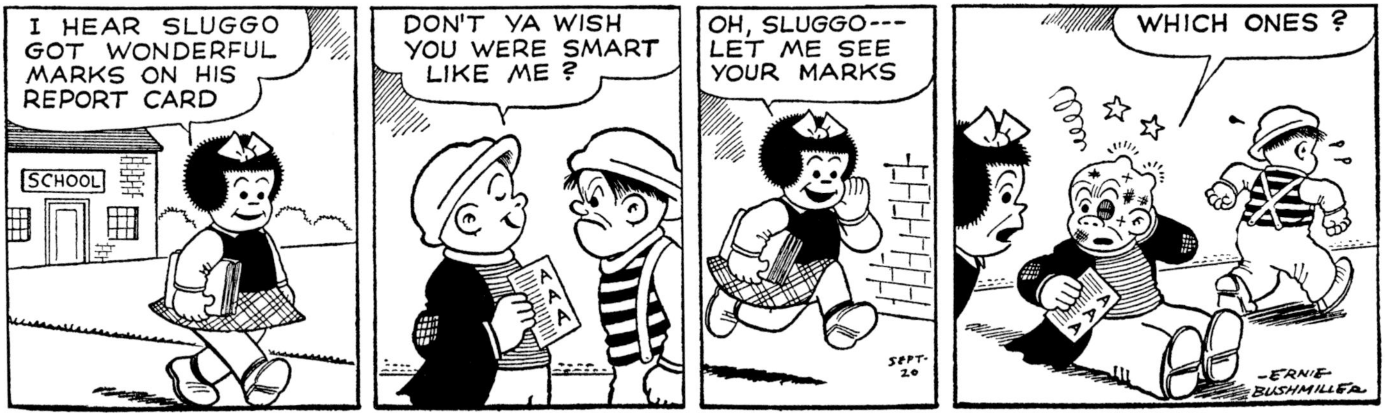
I HEAR SLUGGO GOT WONDERFUL MARKS ON HIS REPORT CARD
SCHOOL
DON'T YA WISH YOU WERE SMART LIKE ME ?
AAA
OH, SLUGGO--- LET ME SEE YOUR MARKS
SEPT-20
WHICH ONES ?
AAA
-ERNIE BUSHMILLER

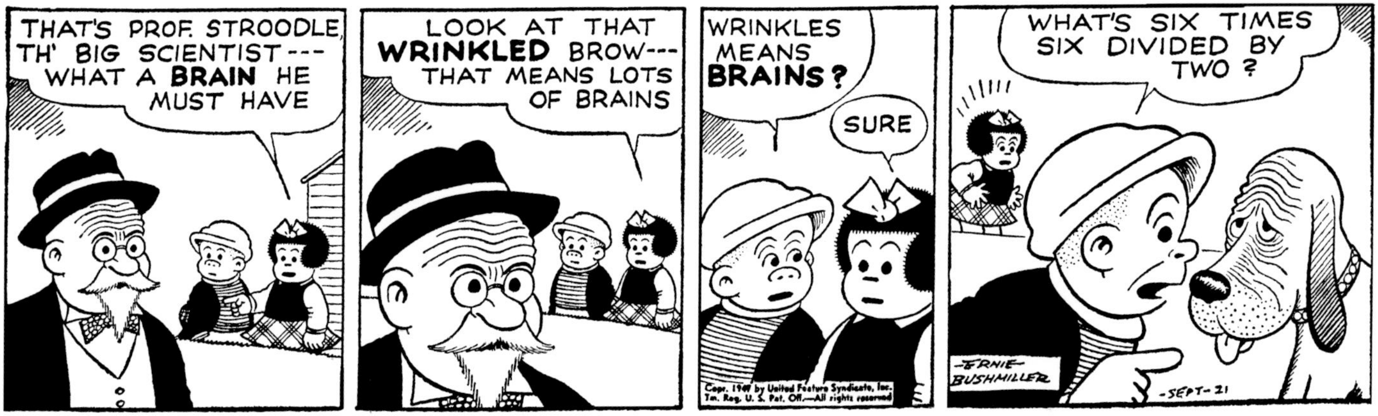
THAT'S PROF. STROODLE, TH' BIG SCIENTIST--- WHAT A **BRAIN** HE MUST HAVE
LOOK AT THAT **WRINKLED** BROW--- THAT MEANS LOTS OF BRAINS
WRINKLES MEANS **BRAINS**?
SURE
WHAT'S SIX TIMES SIX DIVIDED BY TWO ?
Copr. 1949 by United Feature Syndicate, Inc. Tm. Reg. U. S. Pat. Off.—All rights reserved
ERNIE BUSHMILLER
SEPT-21

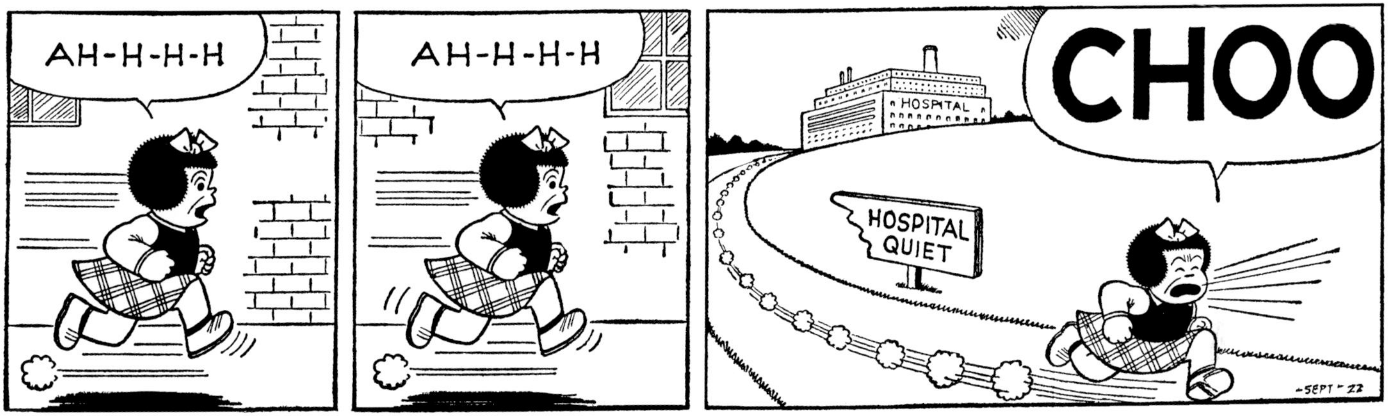
AH-H-H-H
AH-H-H-H
HOSPITAL
HOSPITAL QUIET
CHOO
SEPT-22

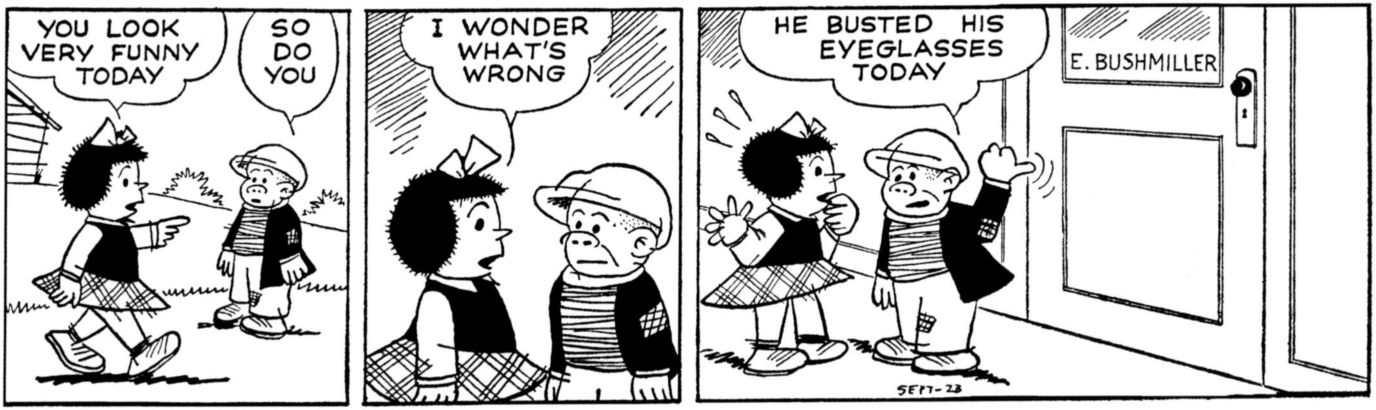
YOU LOOK VERY FUNNY TODAY
SO DO YOU
I WONDER WHAT'S WRONG
HE BUSTED HIS EYEGLASSES TODAY
E. BUSHMILLER
SEPT-23

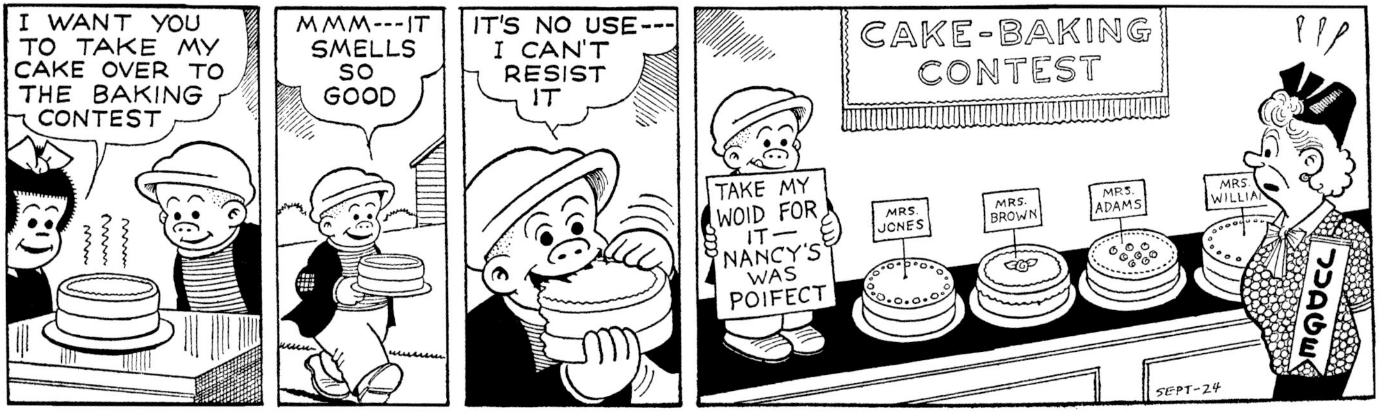
I WANT YOU TO TAKE MY CAKE OVER TO THE BAKING CONTEST
MMM---IT SMELLS SO GOOD
IT'S NO USE--- I CAN'T RESIST IT
CAKE-BAKING CONTEST
TAKE MY WOID FOR IT— NANCY'S WAS POIFECT
MRS. JONES
MRS. BROWN
MRS. ADAMS
MRS. WILLIA
JUDGE
SEPT-24

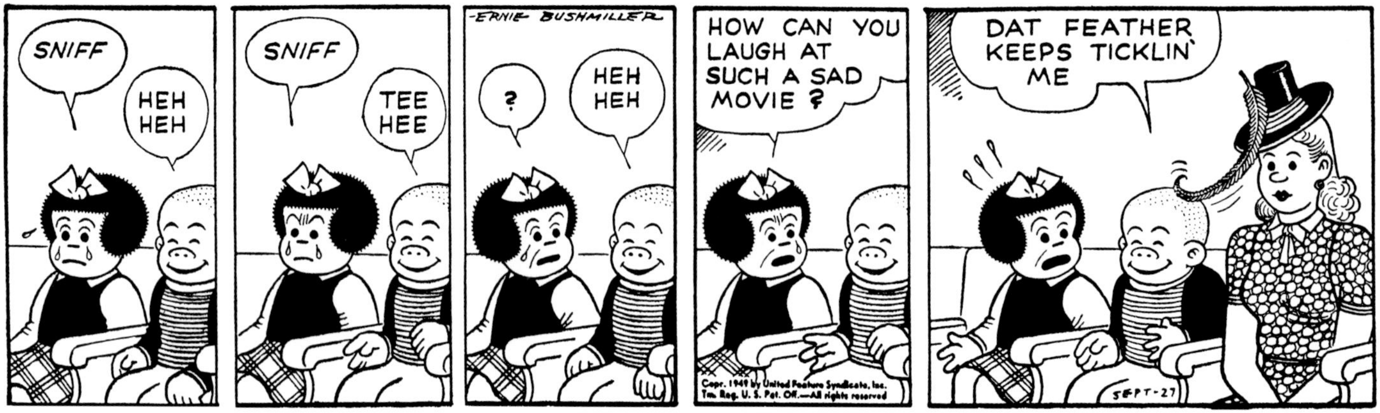
SNIFF
HEH HEH
SNIFF
TEE HEE
-ERNIE BUSHMILLER
?
HEH HEH
HOW CAN YOU LAUGH AT SUCH A SAD MOVIE ?
Copr. 1949 by United Feature Syndicate, Inc.
Tm. Reg. U. S. Pat. Off.—All rights reserved
DAT FEATHER KEEPS TICKLIN` ME
SEPT-27

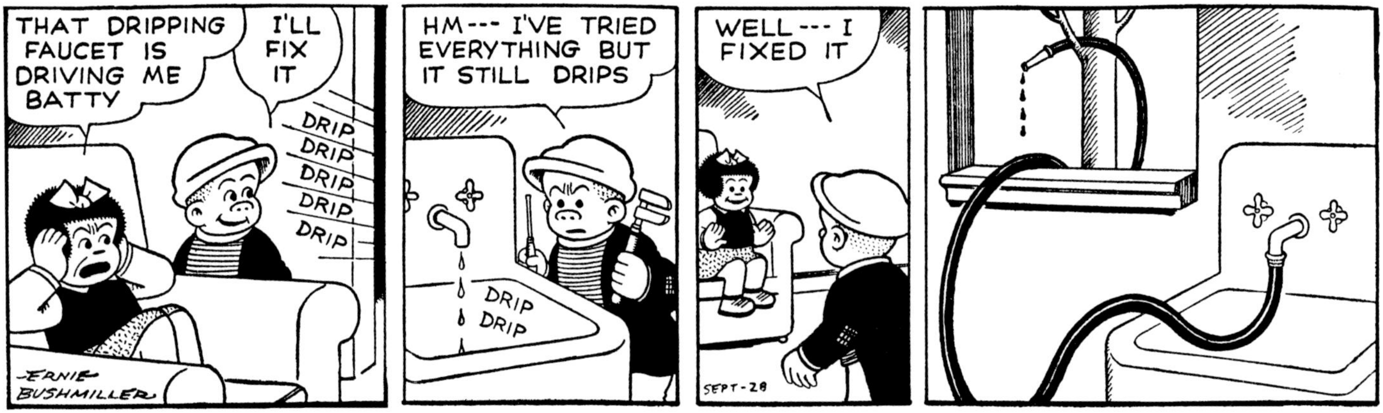
THAT DRIPPING FAUCET IS DRIVING ME BATTY
I'LL FIX IT
DRIP DRIP DRIP DRIP DRIP
-ERNIE BUSHMILLER
HM--- I'VE TRIED EVERYTHING BUT IT STILL DRIPS
DRIP DRIP
WELL--- I FIXED IT
SEPT-28

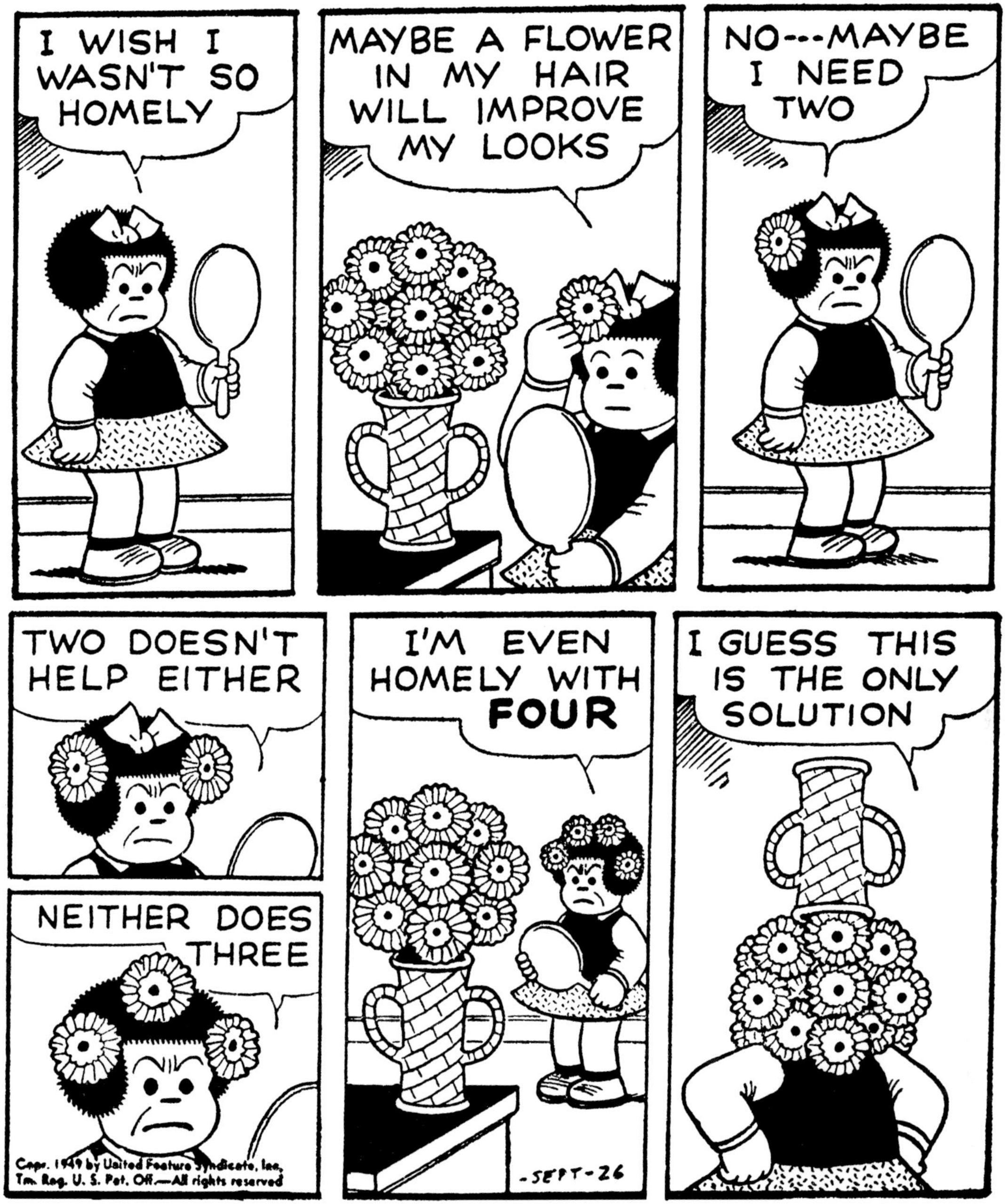
I WISH I WASN'T SO HOMELY
MAYBE A FLOWER IN MY HAIR WILL IMPROVE MY LOOKS
NO---MAYBE I NEED TWO
TWO DOESN'T HELP EITHER
NEITHER DOES THREE
Copr. 1949 by United Feature Syndicate, Inc., Tm. Reg. U. S. Pat. Off.—All rights reserved
I'M EVEN HOMELY WITH **FOUR**
-SEPT-26
I GUESS THIS IS THE ONLY SOLUTION

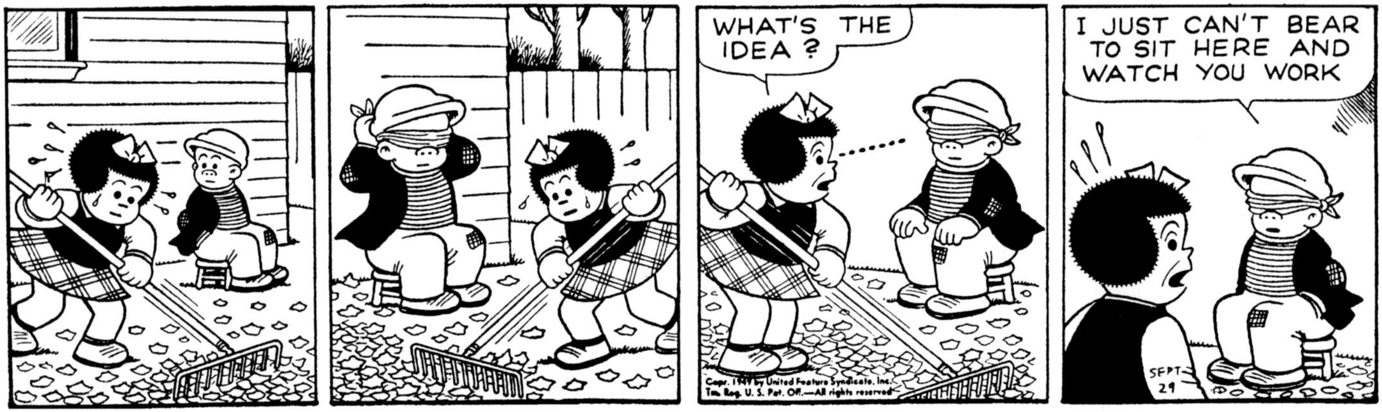
WHAT'S THE IDEA ?
Copr. 1949 by United Feature Syndicate, Inc.
Tm. Reg. U. S. Pat. Off.—All rights reserved
I JUST CAN'T BEAR TO SIT HERE AND WATCH YOU WORK
SEPT-29

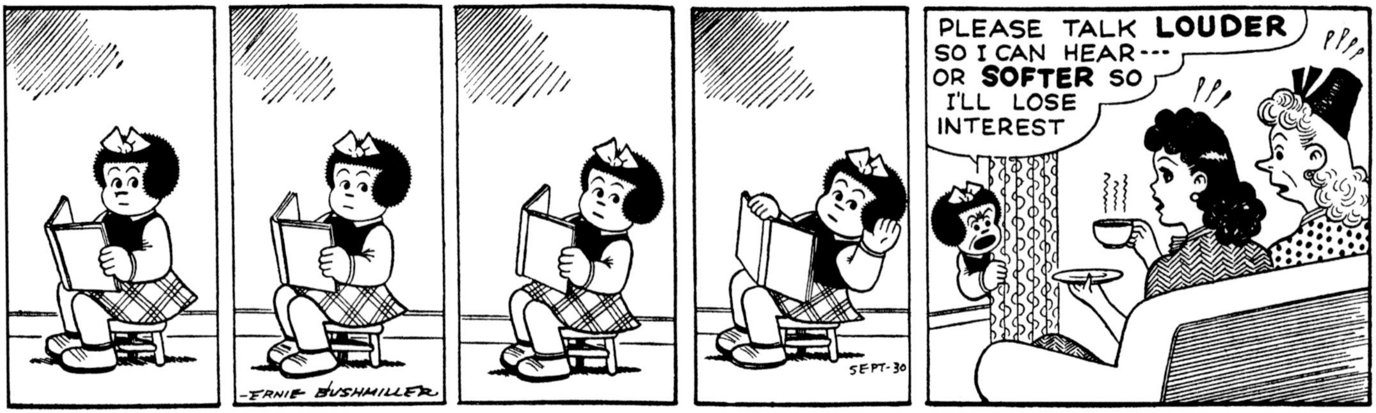
ERNIE BUSHMILLER
SEPT-30
PLEASE TALK LOUDER SO I CAN HEAR--- OR SOFTER SO I'LL LOSE INTEREST

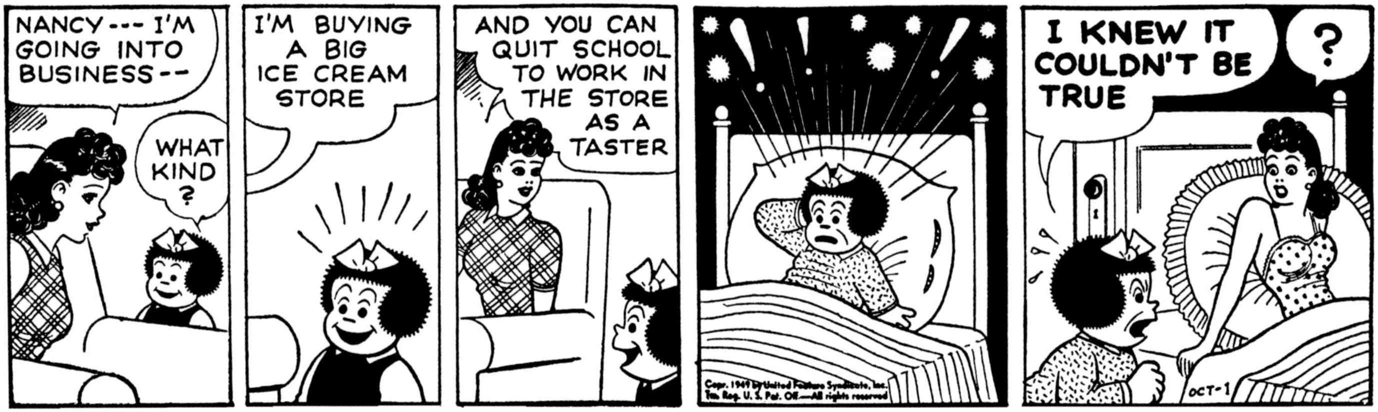
NANCY--- I'M GOING INTO BUSINESS--
WHAT KIND ?
I'M BUYING A BIG ICE CREAM STORE
AND YOU CAN QUIT SCHOOL TO WORK IN THE STORE AS A TASTER
Copr. 1949 by United Feature Syndicate, Inc.
Tm. Reg. U. S. Pat. Off.—All rights reserved
I KNEW IT COULDN'T BE TRUE
?
OCT-1

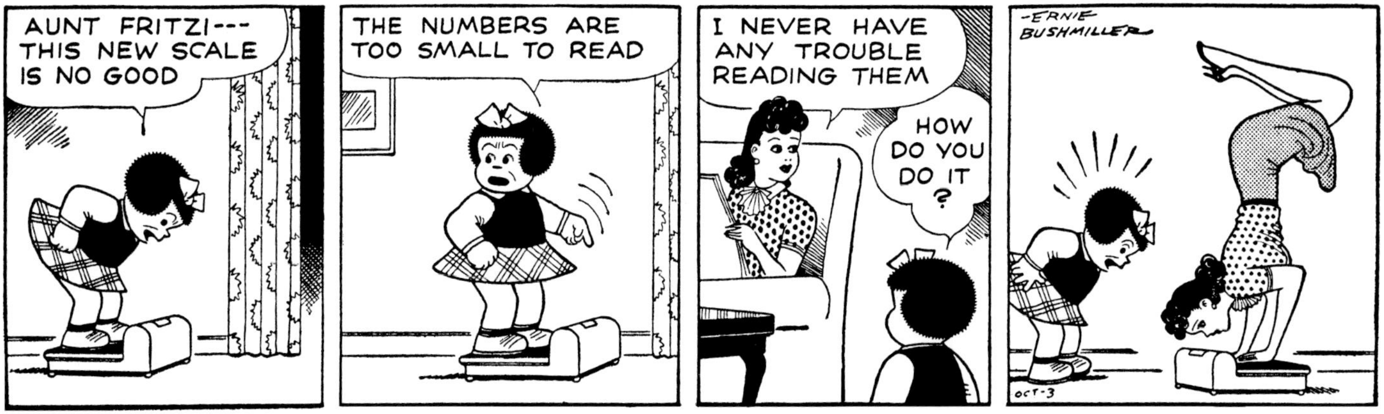
AUNT FRITZI--- THIS NEW SCALE IS NO GOOD
THE NUMBERS ARE TOO SMALL TO READ
I NEVER HAVE ANY TROUBLE READING THEM
HOW DO YOU DO IT ?
-ERNIE BUSHMILLER
OCT-3

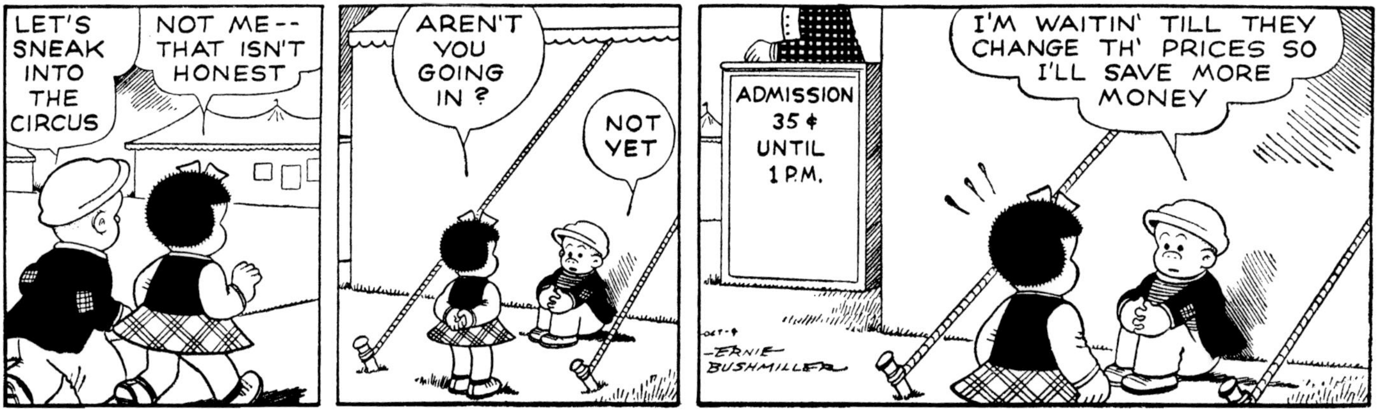
LET'S SNEAK INTO THE CIRCUS
NOT ME-- THAT ISN'T HONEST
AREN'T YOU GOING IN ?
NOT YET
ADMISSION 35 ¢ UNTIL 1 P.M.
I'M WAITIN' TILL THEY CHANGE TH' PRICES SO I'LL SAVE MORE MONEY
OCT-4
-ERNIE BUSHMILLER

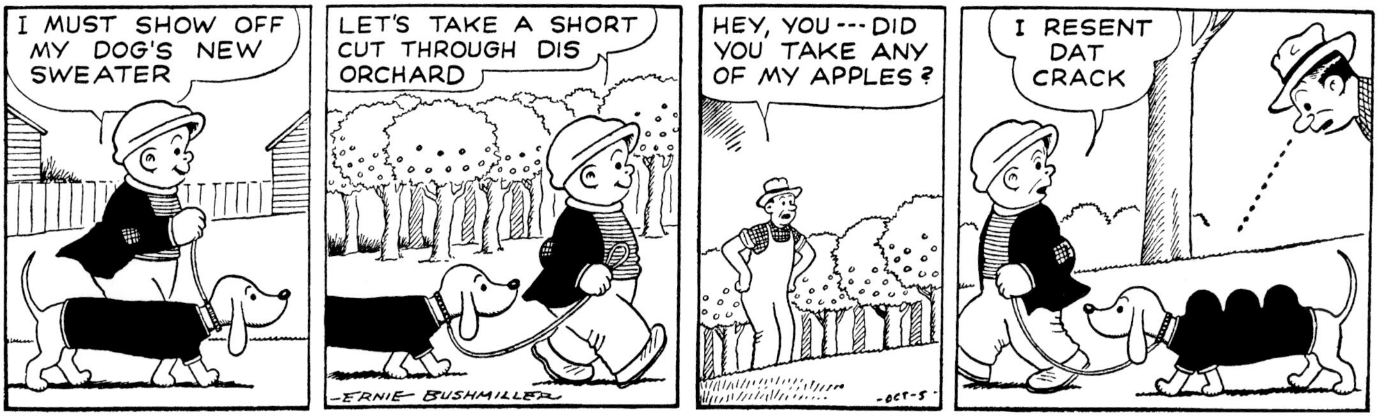
I MUST SHOW OFF MY DOG'S NEW SWEATER
LET'S TAKE A SHORT CUT THROUGH DIS ORCHARD
-ERNIE BUSHMILLER
HEY, YOU --- DID YOU TAKE ANY OF MY APPLES ?
OCT-5
I RESENT DAT CRACK

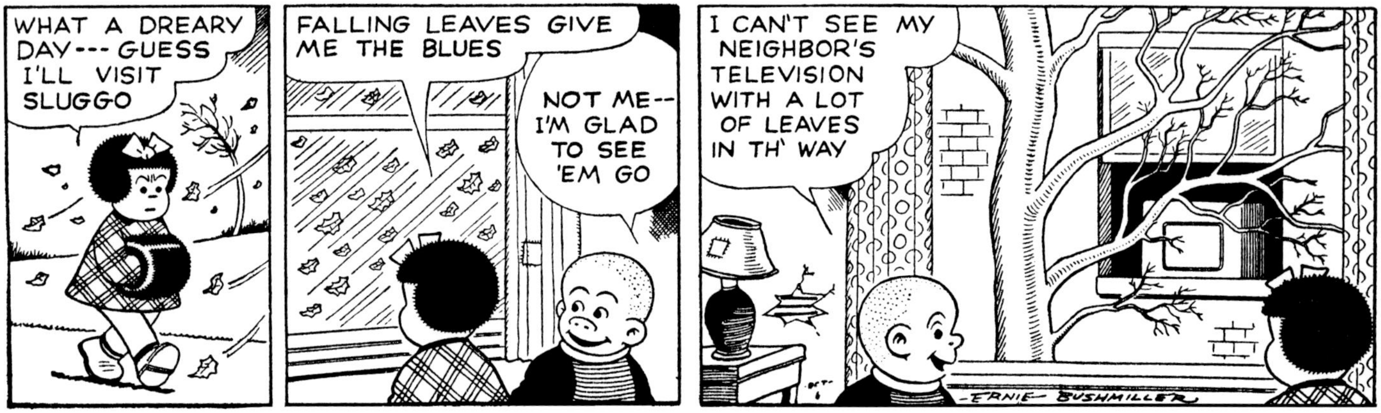
WHAT A DREARY DAY--- GUESS I'LL VISIT SLUGGO
FALLING LEAVES GIVE ME THE BLUES
NOT ME-- I'M GLAD TO SEE 'EM GO
I CAN'T SEE MY NEIGHBOR'S TELEVISION WITH A LOT OF LEAVES IN TH' WAY
-ERNIE BUSHMILLER

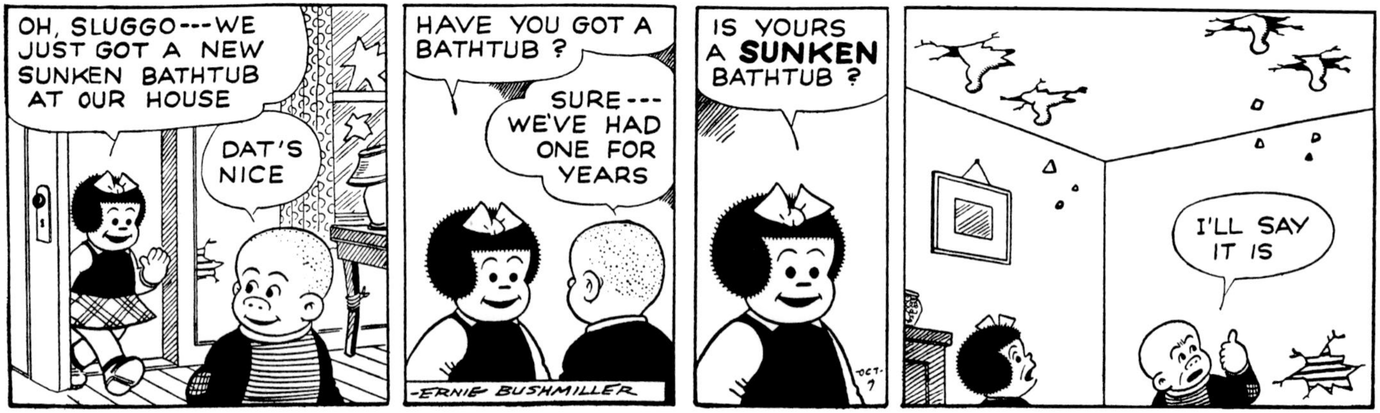
OH, SLUGGO---WE JUST GOT A NEW SUNKEN BATHTUB AT OUR HOUSE
DAT'S NICE
HAVE YOU GOT A BATHTUB ?
SURE--- WE'VE HAD ONE FOR YEARS
-ERNIE BUSHMILLER
IS YOURS A **SUNKEN** BATHTUB ?
I'LL SAY IT IS

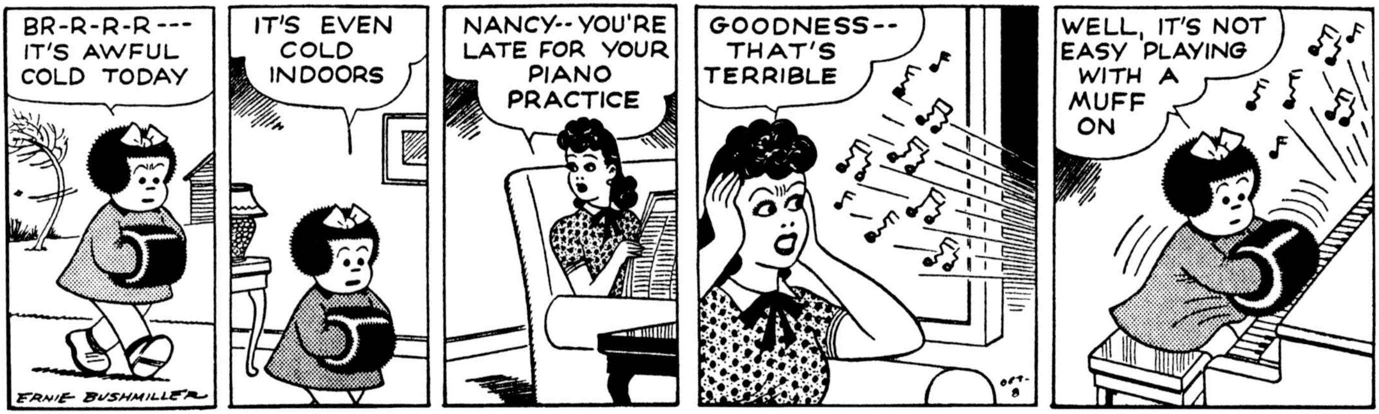
BR-R-R-R--- IT'S AWFUL COLD TODAY
ERNIE BUSHMILLER
IT'S EVEN COLD INDOORS
NANCY-- YOU'RE LATE FOR YOUR PIANO PRACTICE
GOODNESS-- THAT'S TERRIBLE
WELL, IT'S NOT EASY PLAYING WITH A MUFF ON

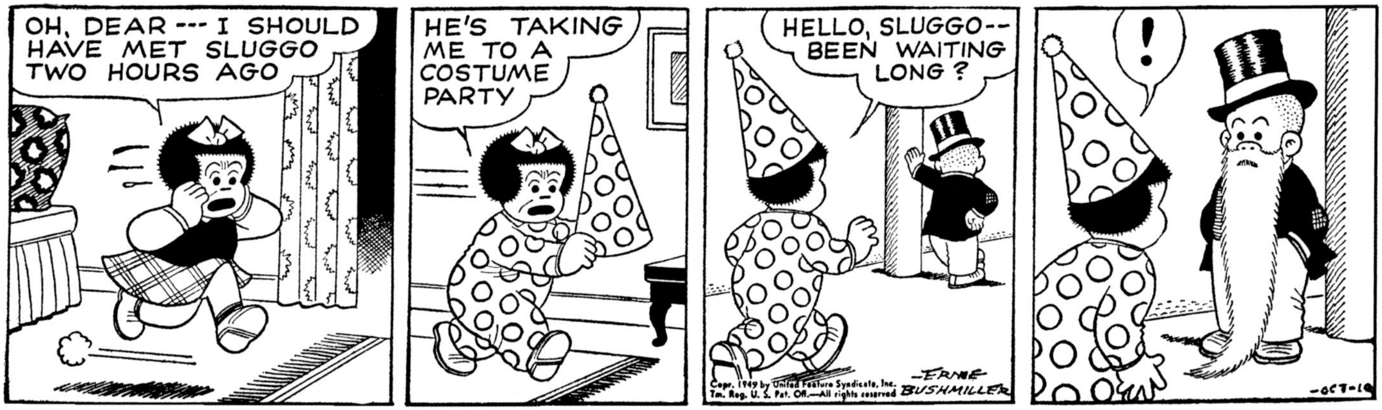
OH, DEAR --- I SHOULD HAVE MET SLUGGO TWO HOURS AGO
HE'S TAKING ME TO A COSTUME PARTY
HELLO, SLUGGO-- BEEN WAITING LONG ?
Copr. 1949 by United Feature Syndicate, Inc. Tm. Reg. U. S. Pat. Off.—All rights reserved
-ERNIE BUSHMILLER
!
-OCT-10

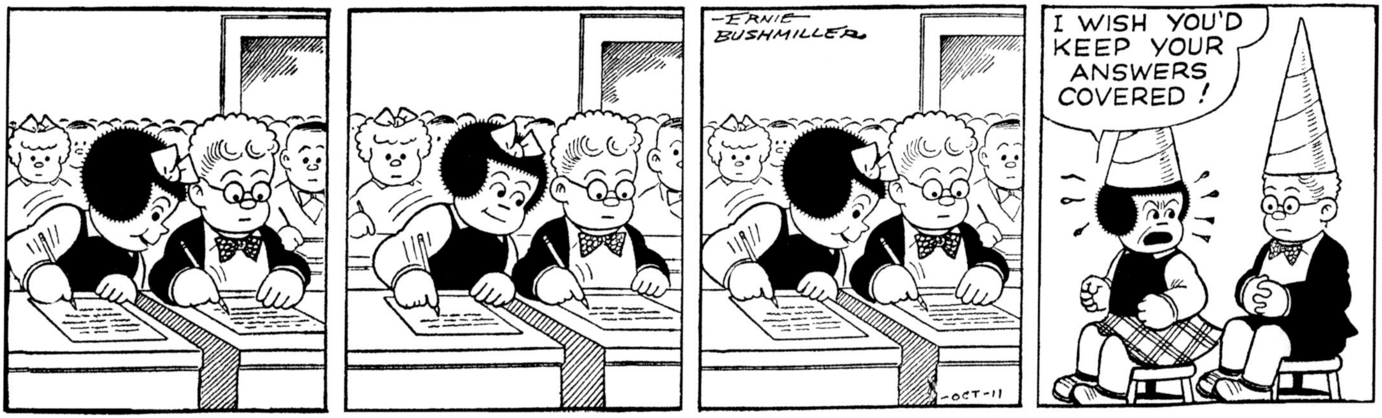
-ERNIE BUSHMILLER
-OCT-11
I WISH YOU'D KEEP YOUR ANSWERS COVERED !

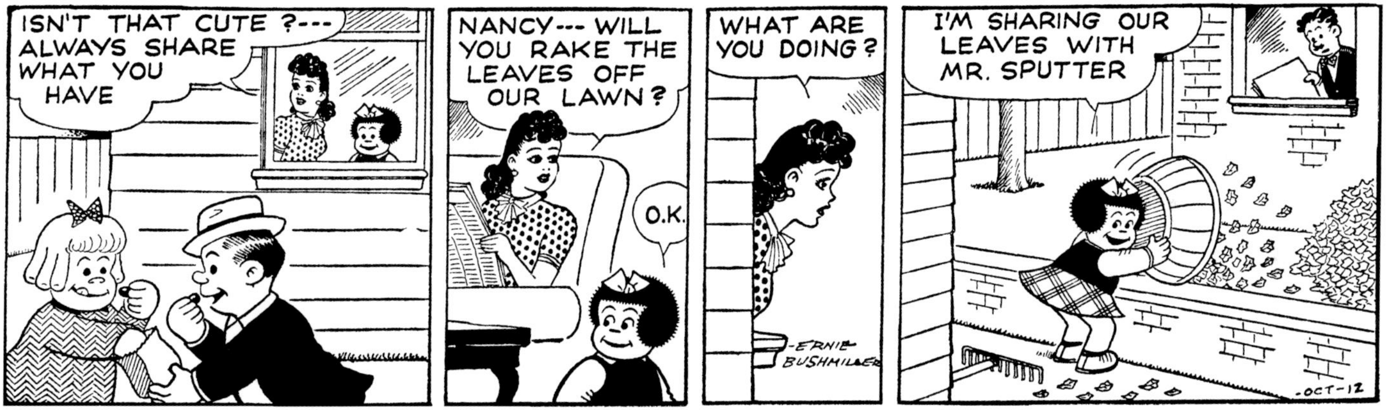
ISN'T THAT CUTE ?--- ALWAYS SHARE WHAT YOU HAVE
NANCY--- WILL YOU RAKE THE LEAVES OFF OUR LAWN ?
O.K.
WHAT ARE YOU DOING ?
-ERNIE BUSHMILLER
I'M SHARING OUR LEAVES WITH MR. SPUTTER
-OCT-12

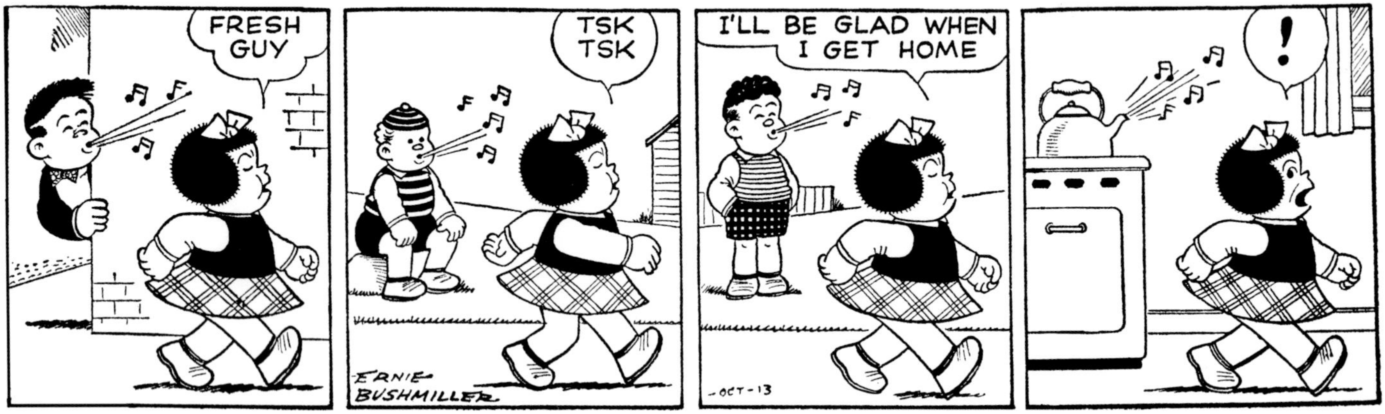
FRESH GUY
TSK TSK
ERNIE BUSHMILLER
I'LL BE GLAD WHEN I GET HOME
OCT-13
!

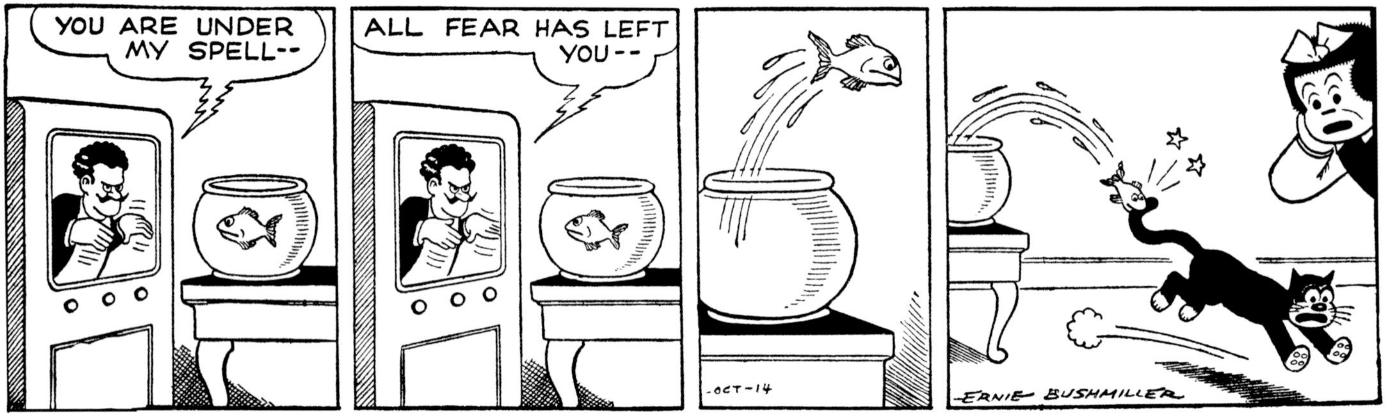
YOU ARE UNDER MY SPELL--
ALL FEAR HAS LEFT YOU--
OCT-14
ERNIE BUSHMILLER

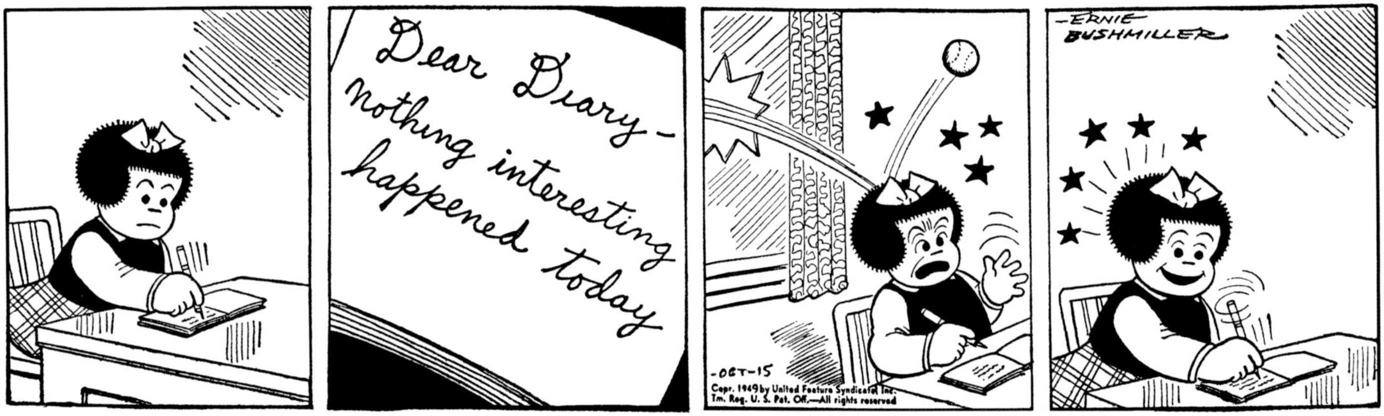
Dear Diary-
nothing interesting
happened today
OCT-15
Copr. 1949 by United Feature Syndicate, Inc.
Tm. Reg. U. S. Pat. Off.—All rights reserved
ERNIE BUSHMILLER

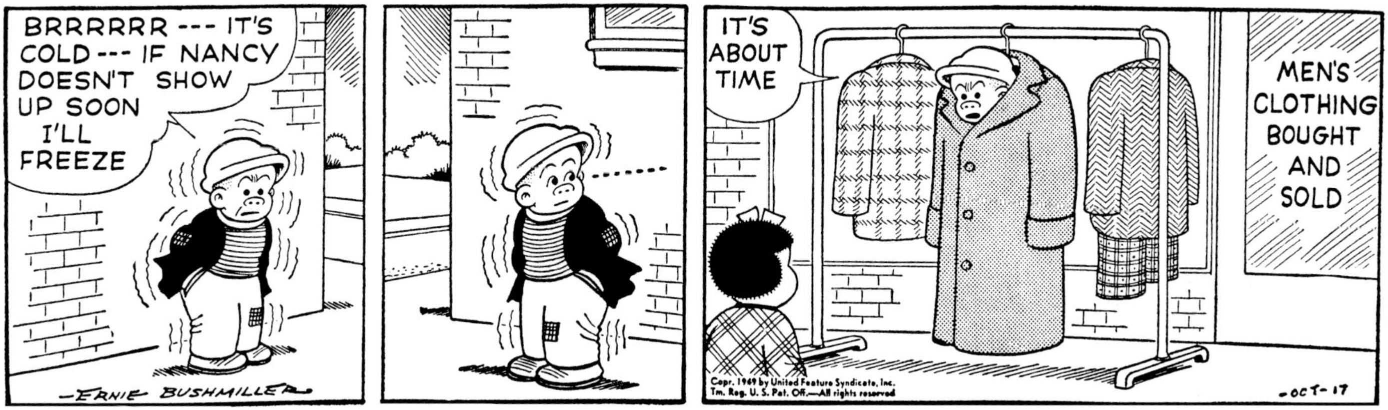
BRRRRRR --- IT'S COLD --- IF NANCY DOESN'T SHOW UP SOON I'LL FREEZE
-ERNIE BUSHMILLER
IT'S ABOUT TIME
MEN'S CLOTHING BOUGHT AND SOLD
Copr. 1949 by United Feature Syndicate, Inc.
Tm. Reg. U. S. Pat. Off.—All rights reserved
OCT-17

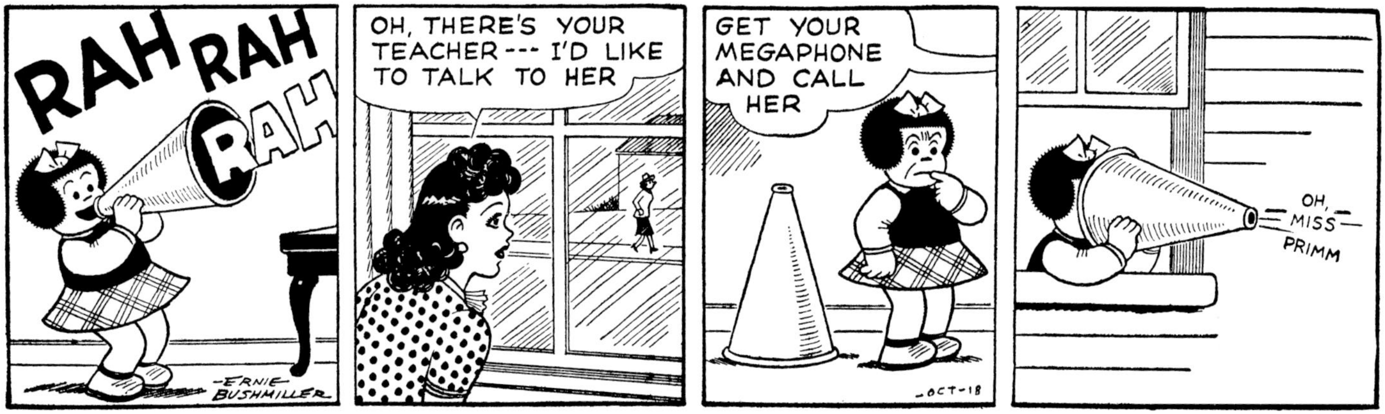
RAH RAH RAH
-ERNIE BUSHMILLER
OH, THERE'S YOUR TEACHER --- I'D LIKE TO TALK TO HER
GET YOUR MEGAPHONE AND CALL HER
OCT-18
OH, MISS PRIMM

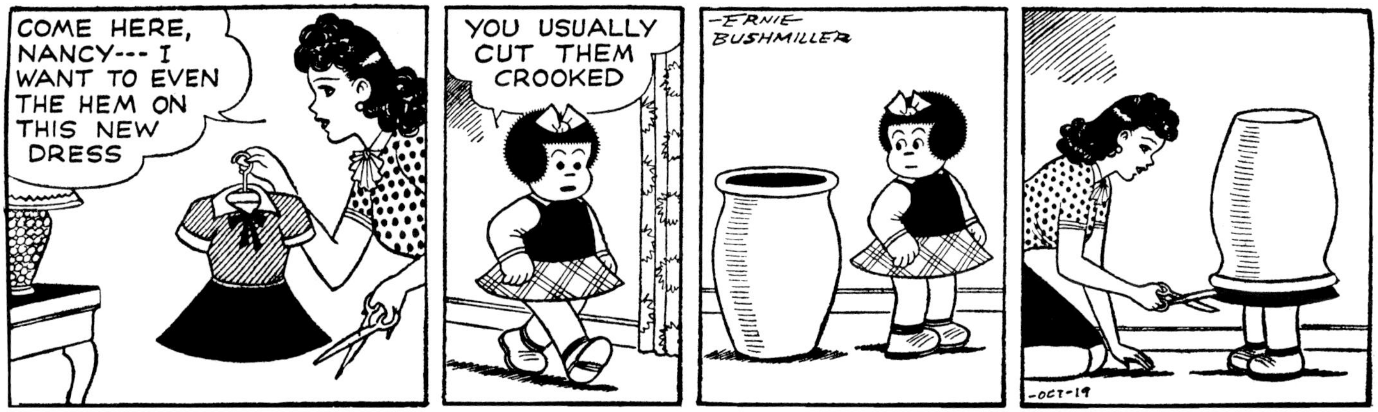
COME HERE, NANCY--- I WANT TO EVEN THE HEM ON THIS NEW DRESS
YOU USUALLY CUT THEM CROOKED
-ERNIE BUSHMILLER
OCT-19

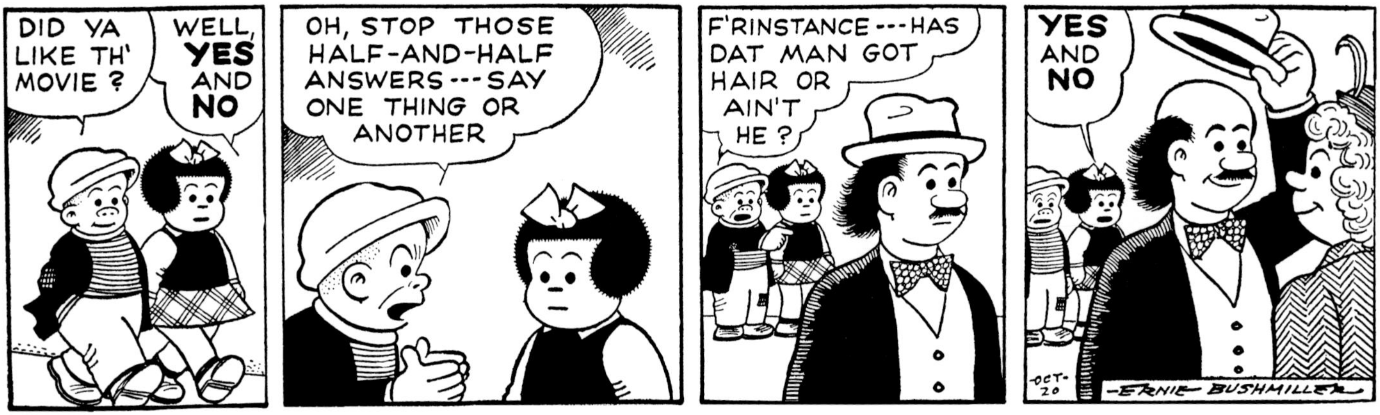
DID YA LIKE TH' MOVIE ?
WELL, **YES** AND **NO**
OH, STOP THOSE HALF-AND-HALF ANSWERS---SAY ONE THING OR ANOTHER
F'RINSTANCE---HAS DAT MAN GOT HAIR OR AIN'T HE ?
YES AND **NO**
OCT-20
ERNIE BUSHMILLER

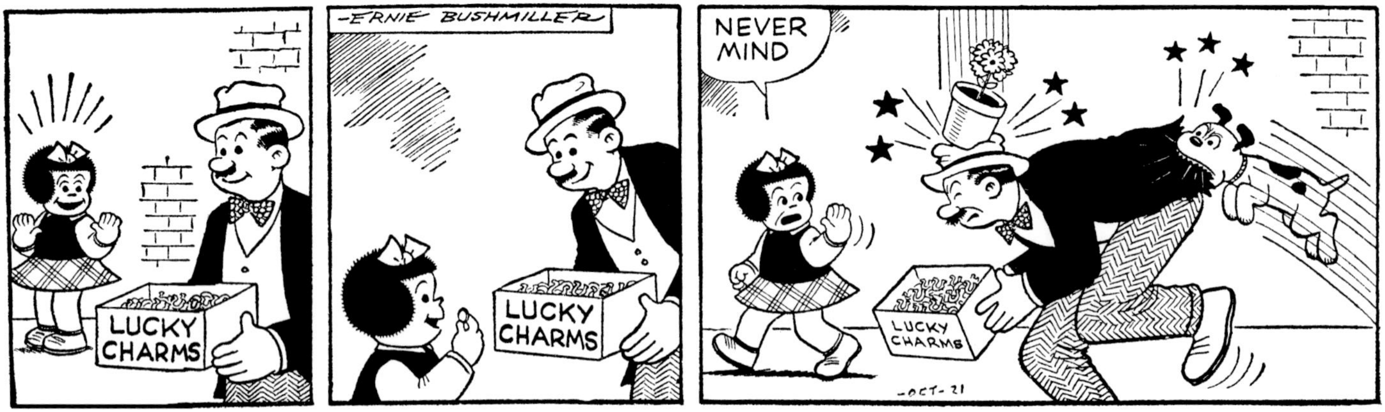
LUCKY CHARMS
ERNIE BUSHMILLER
LUCKY CHARMS
NEVER MIND
LUCKY CHARMS
OCT-21

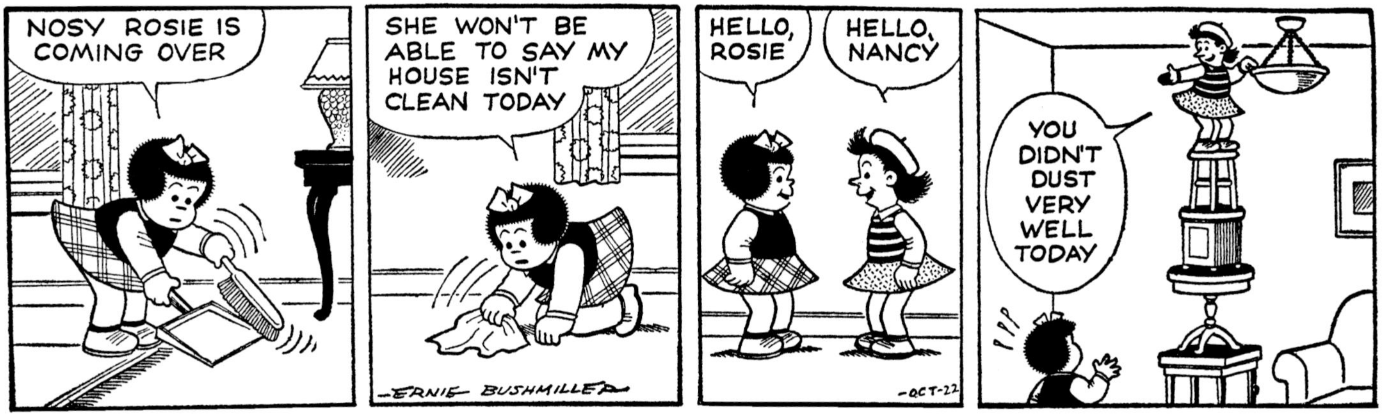
NOSY ROSIE IS COMING OVER
SHE WON'T BE ABLE TO SAY MY HOUSE ISN'T CLEAN TODAY
ERNIE BUSHMILLER
HELLO, ROSIE
HELLO, NANCY
OCT-22
YOU DIDN'T DUST VERY WELL TODAY

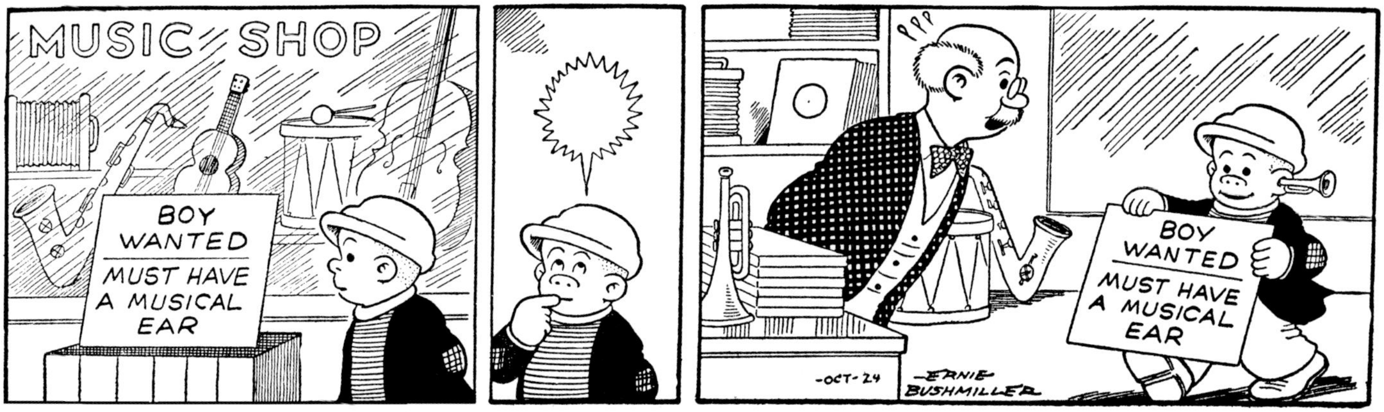
MUSIC SHOP
BOY WANTED
MUST HAVE A MUSICAL EAR
BOY WANTED
MUST HAVE A MUSICAL EAR
-OCT-24
-ERNIE BUSHMILLER

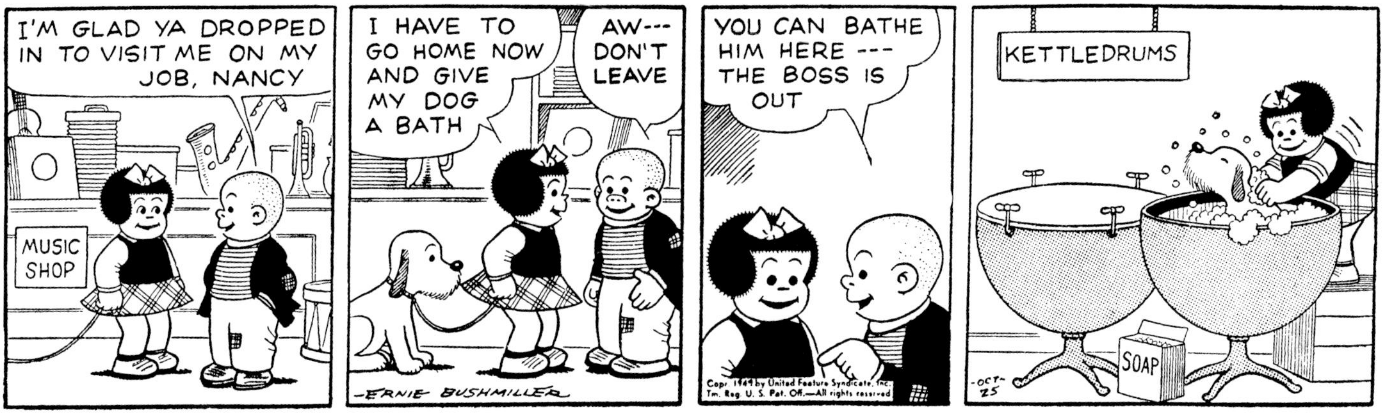
I'M GLAD YA DROPPED IN TO VISIT ME ON MY JOB, NANCY
MUSIC SHOP
I HAVE TO GO HOME NOW AND GIVE MY DOG A BATH
AW--- DON'T LEAVE
-ERNIE BUSHMILLER
YOU CAN BATHE HIM HERE --- THE BOSS IS OUT
Copr. 1944 by United Feature Syndicate, Inc.
Tm. Reg. U. S. Pat. Off.—All rights reserved
KETTLEDRUMS
SOAP
-OCT-25

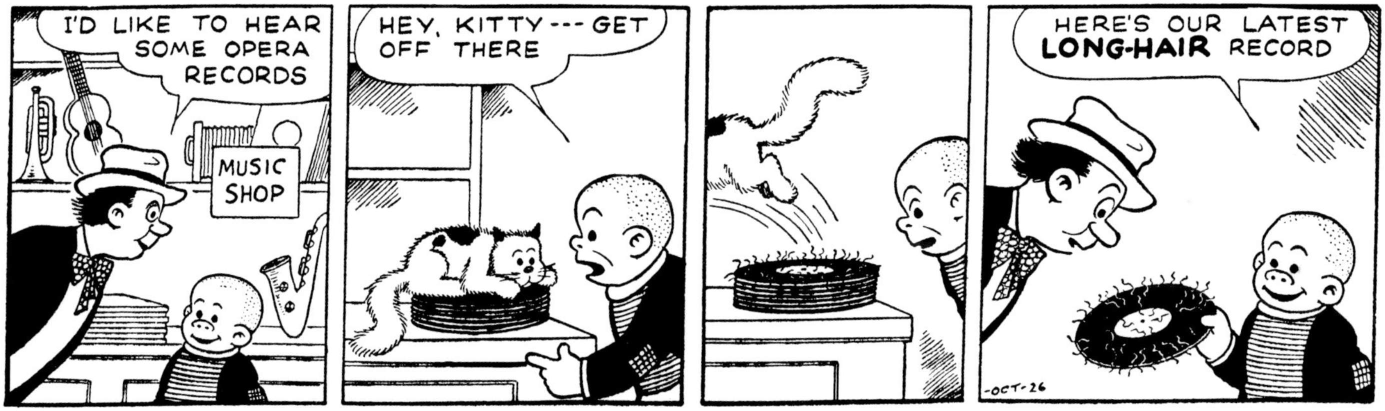
I'D LIKE TO HEAR SOME OPERA RECORDS
MUSIC SHOP
HEY, KITTY --- GET OFF THERE
HERE'S OUR LATEST **LONG-HAIR** RECORD
-OCT-26

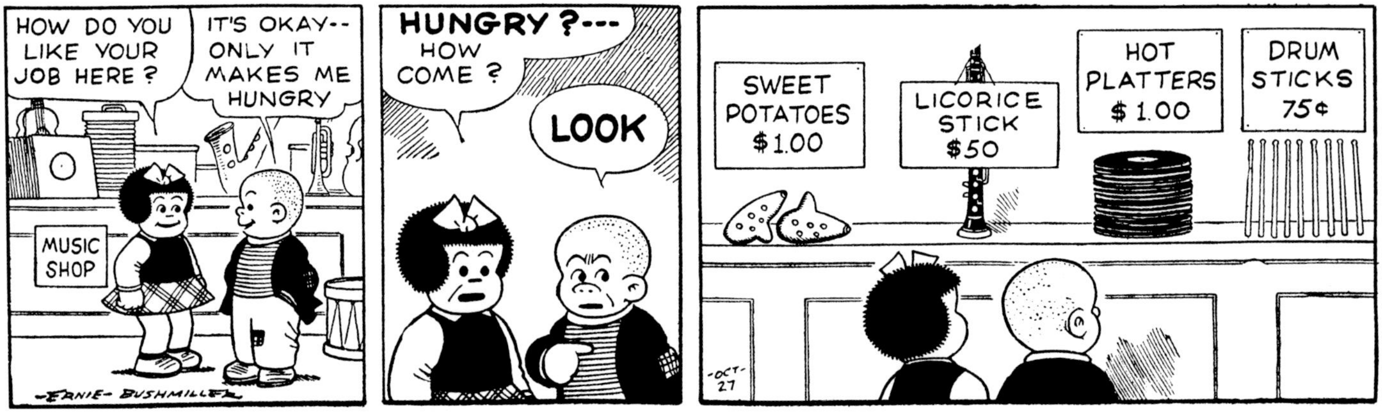
HOW DO YOU LIKE YOUR JOB HERE ?
IT'S OKAY-- ONLY IT MAKES ME HUNGRY
MUSIC SHOP
-ERNIE- BUSHMILLER
HUNGRY ?--- HOW COME ?
LOOK
SWEET POTATOES $1.00
LICORICE STICK $50
HOT PLATTERS $1.00
DRUM STICKS 75¢
-OCT- 27

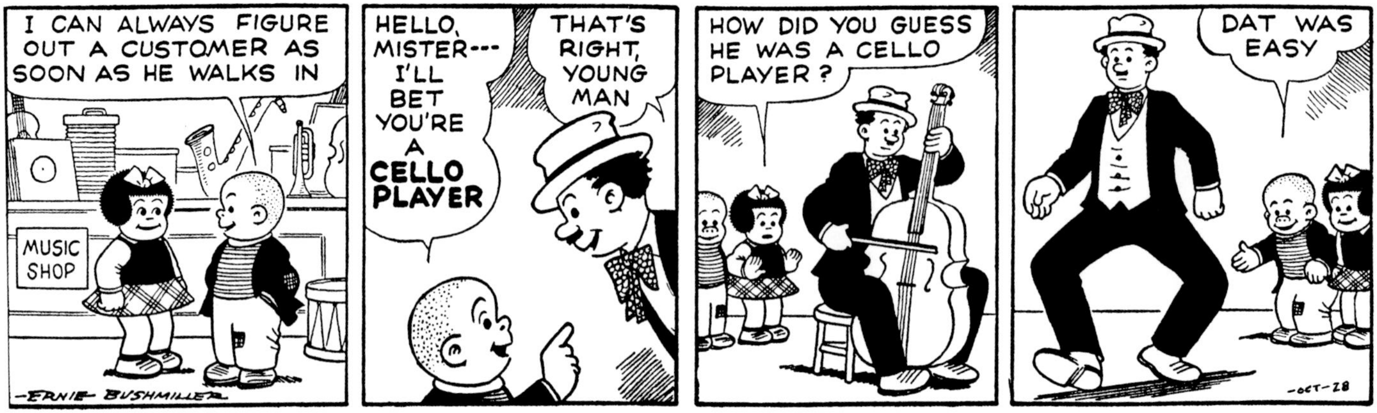
I CAN ALWAYS FIGURE OUT A CUSTOMER AS SOON AS HE WALKS IN
MUSIC SHOP
-ERNIE- BUSHMILLER
HELLO, MISTER--- I'LL BET YOU'RE A CELLO PLAYER
THAT'S RIGHT, YOUNG MAN
HOW DID YOU GUESS HE WAS A CELLO PLAYER ?
DAT WAS EASY
-OCT-28

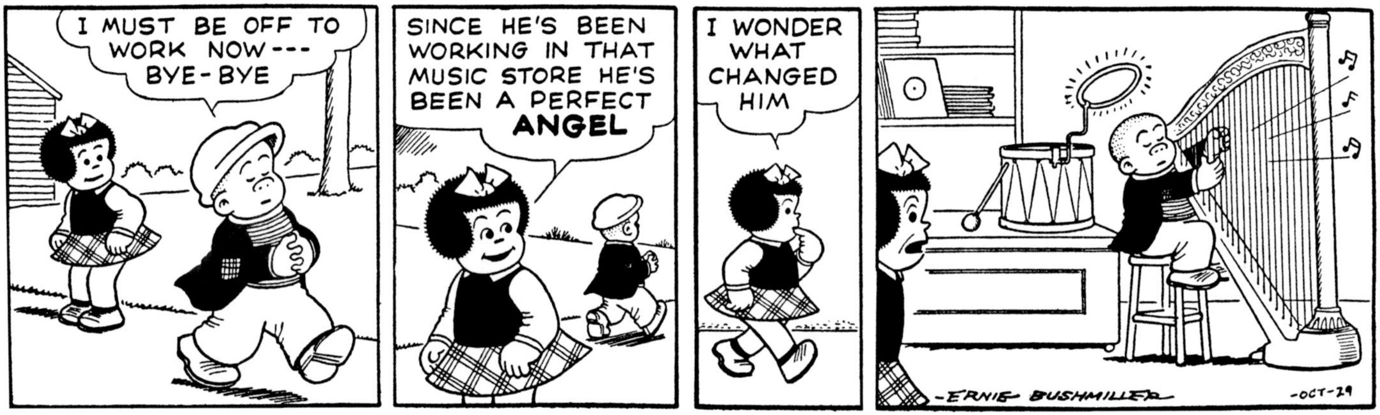
I MUST BE OFF TO WORK NOW--- BYE-BYE
SINCE HE'S BEEN WORKING IN THAT MUSIC STORE HE'S BEEN A PERFECT ANGEL
I WONDER WHAT CHANGED HIM
-ERNIE- BUSHMILLER
-OCT-29

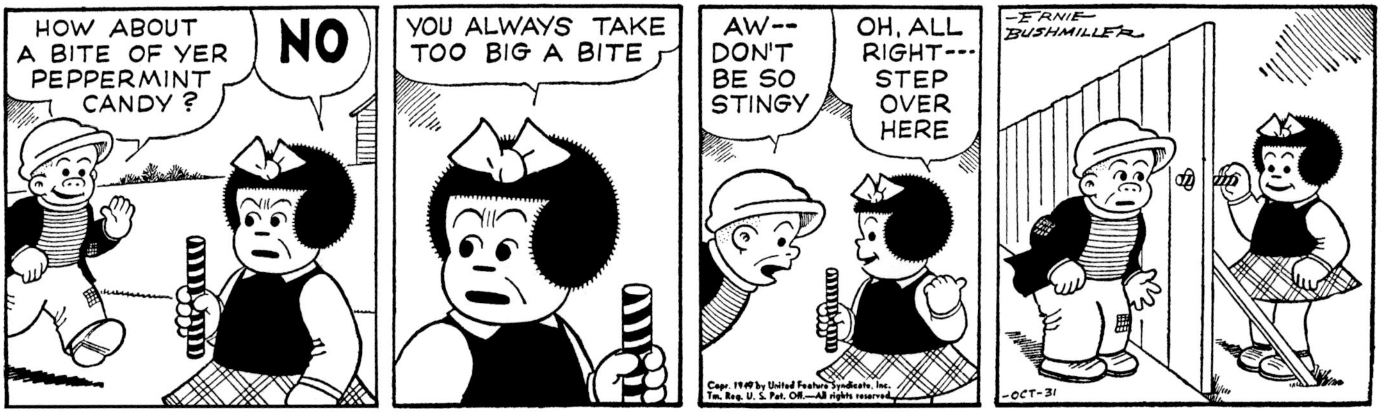
HOW ABOUT A BITE OF YER PEPPERMINT CANDY ?
NO
YOU ALWAYS TAKE TOO BIG A BITE
AW-- DON'T BE SO STINGY
OH, ALL RIGHT--- STEP OVER HERE
Copr. 1949 by United Feature Syndicate, Inc. Tm. Reg. U. S. Pat. Off.—All rights reserved.
-ERNIE BUSHMILLER
-OCT-31

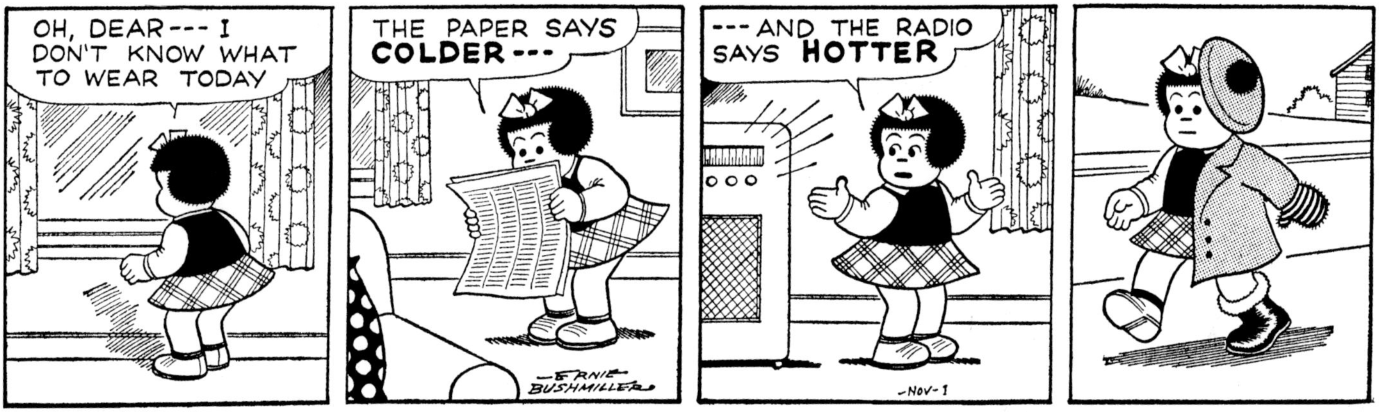
OH, DEAR--- I DON'T KNOW WHAT TO WEAR TODAY
THE PAPER SAYS **COLDER**---
-ERNIE BUSHMILLER
---AND THE RADIO SAYS **HOTTER**
-NOV-1

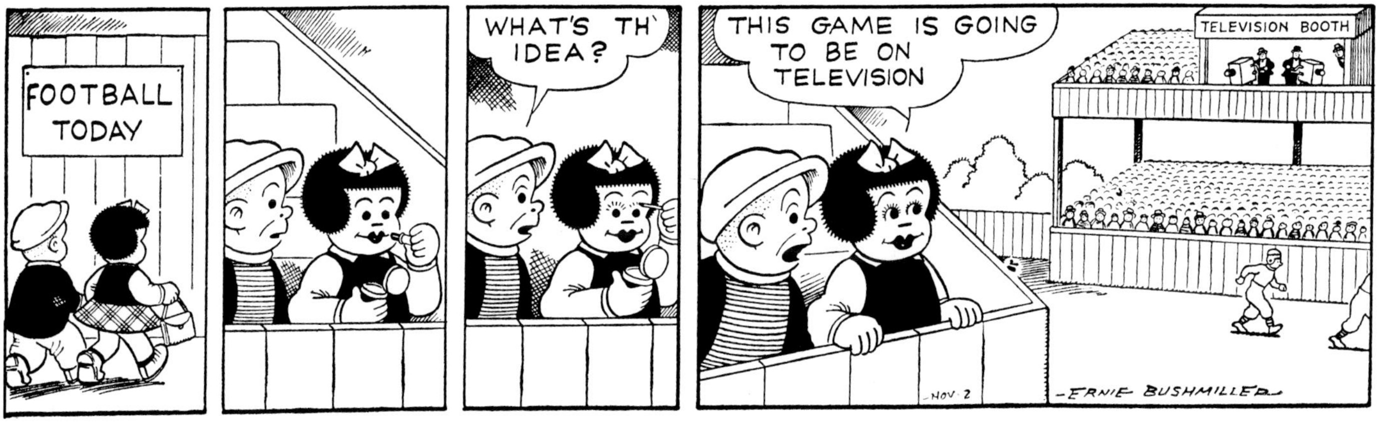
FOOTBALL TODAY
WHAT'S TH' IDEA?
THIS GAME IS GOING TO BE ON TELEVISION
TELEVISION BOOTH
-NOV-2
-ERNIE BUSHMILLER

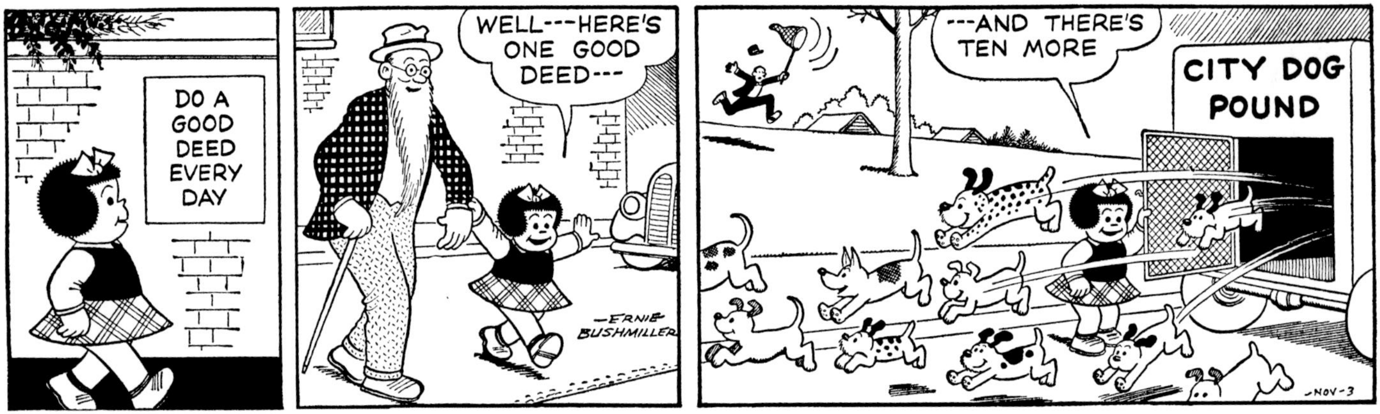
DO A GOOD DEED EVERY DAY
WELL---HERE'S ONE GOOD DEED---
-ERNIE BUSHMILLER
---AND THERE'S TEN MORE
CITY DOG POUND
-NOV-3

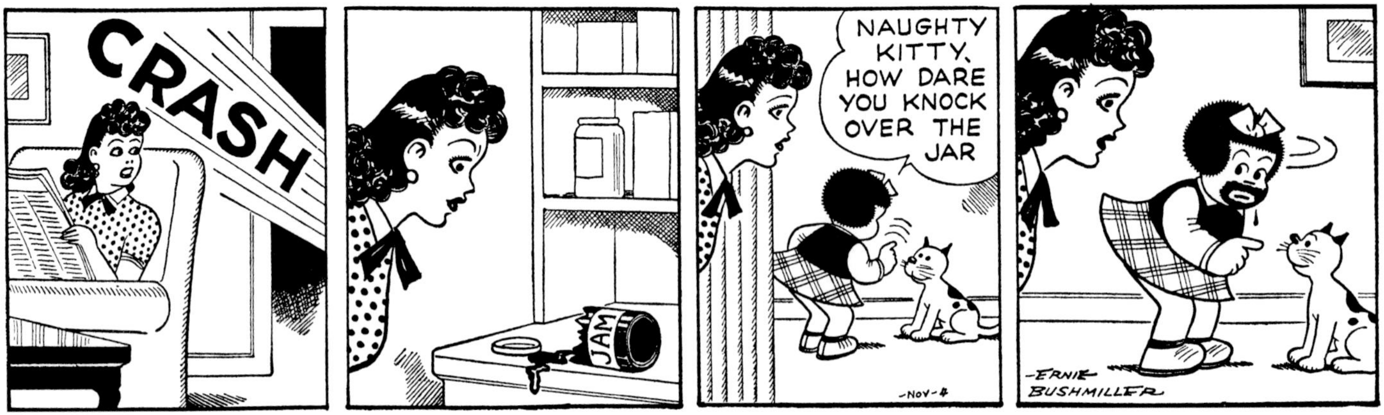
CRASH
JAM
NAUGHTY KITTY, HOW DARE YOU KNOCK OVER THE JAR
-NOV-4
-ERNIE BUSHMILLER

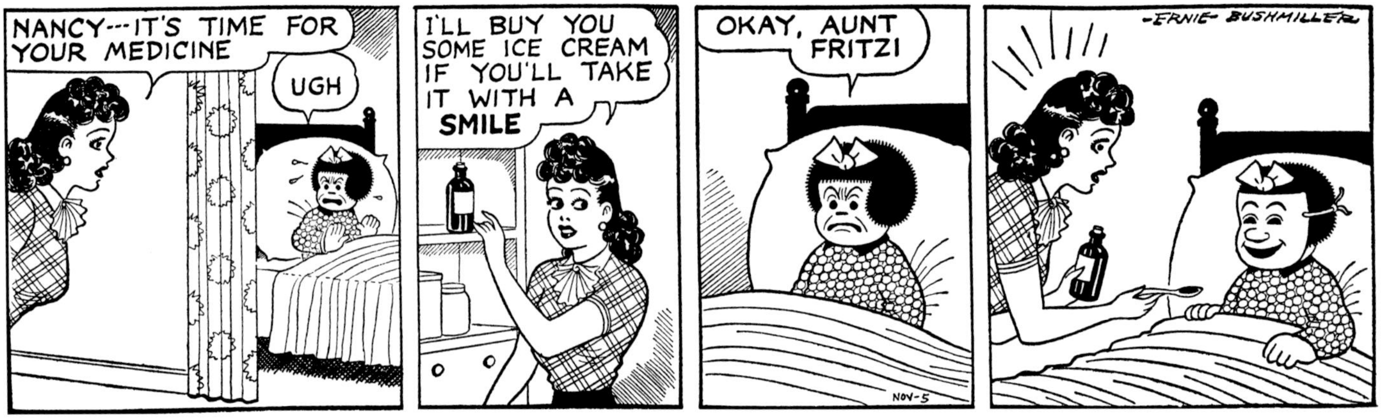
NANCY---IT'S TIME FOR YOUR MEDICINE
UGH
I'LL BUY YOU SOME ICE CREAM IF YOU'LL TAKE IT WITH A **SMILE**
OKAY, AUNT FRITZI
NOV-5
-ERNIE BUSHMILLER

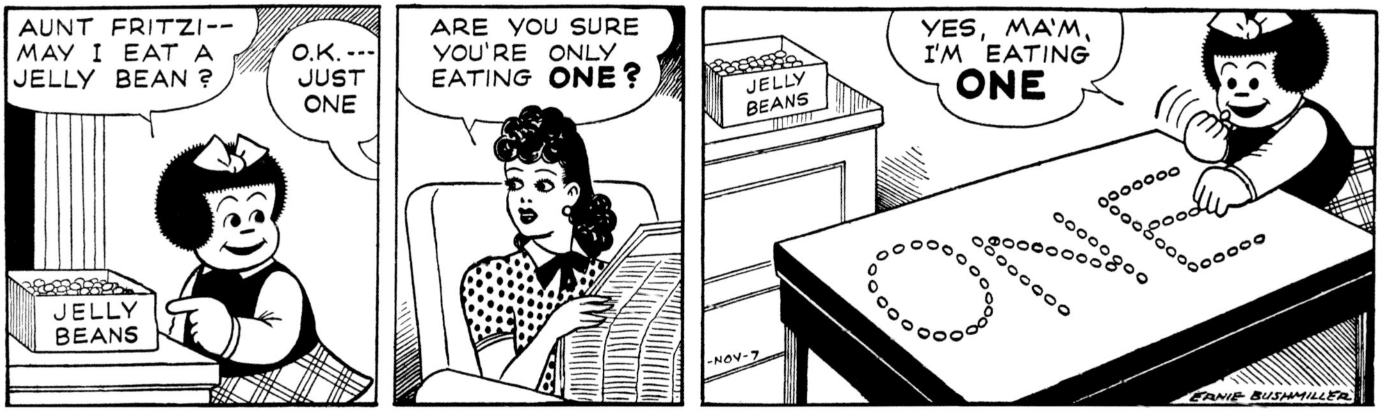
AUNT FRITZI-- MAY I EAT A JELLY BEAN ?
JELLY BEANS
O.K.--- JUST ONE
ARE YOU SURE YOU'RE ONLY EATING **ONE?**
JELLY BEANS
YES, MA'M, I'M EATING **ONE**
ONE
-NOV-7
ERNIE BUSHMILLER

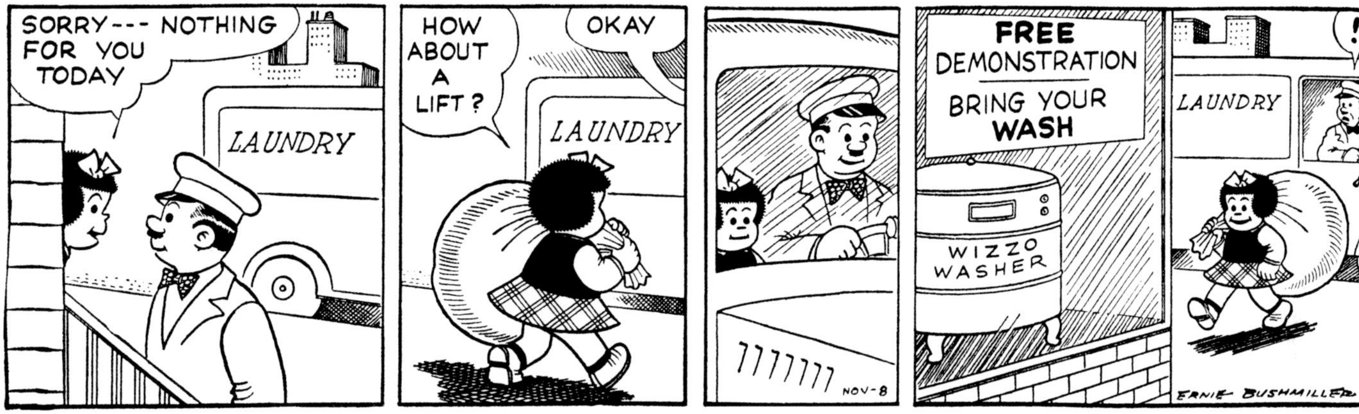
SORRY--- NOTHING FOR YOU TODAY
LAUNDRY
HOW ABOUT A LIFT ?
OKAY
LAUNDRY
NOV-8
FREE DEMONSTRATION
BRING YOUR **WASH**
WIZZO WASHER
LAUNDRY
!
ERNIE BUSHMILLER

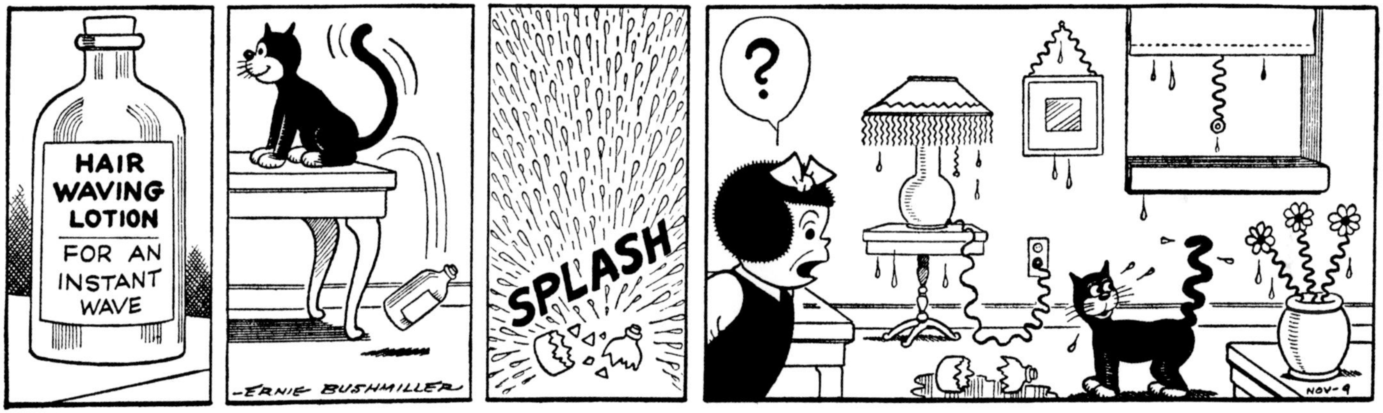
HAIR WAVING LOTION
FOR AN INSTANT WAVE
-ERNIE BUSHMILLER
SPLASH
?
NOV-9

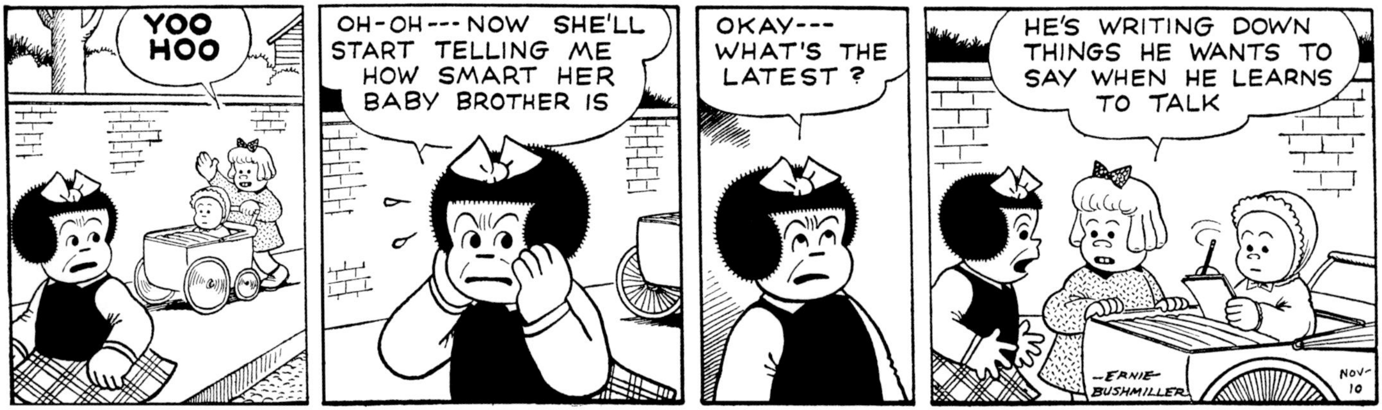
YOO HOO
OH-OH --- NOW SHE'LL START TELLING ME HOW SMART HER BABY BROTHER IS
OKAY--- WHAT'S THE LATEST ?
HE'S WRITING DOWN THINGS HE WANTS TO SAY WHEN HE LEARNS TO TALK
-ERNIE- BUSHMILLER
NOV- 10

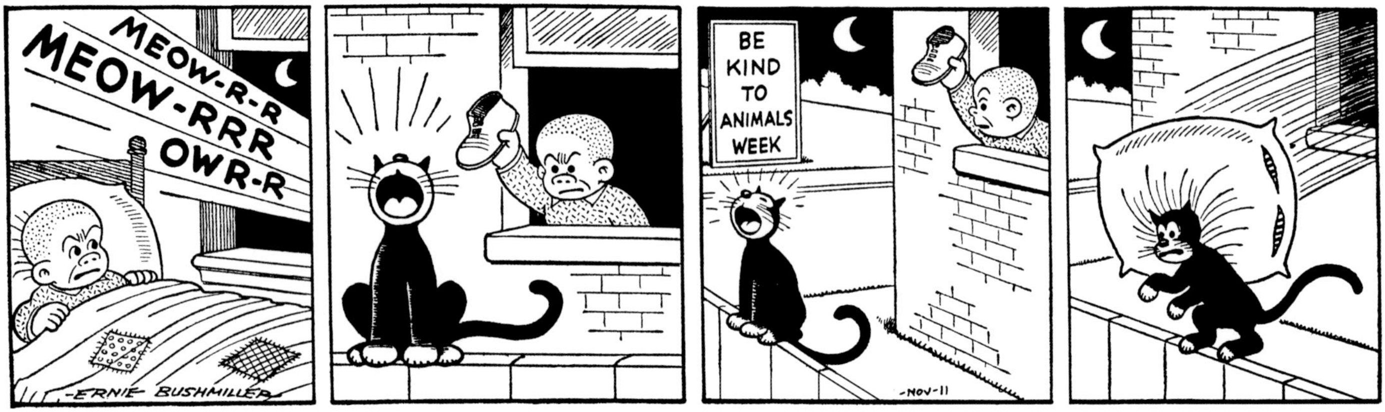
MEOW-R-R
MEOW-RRR
OWR-R
-ERNIE- BUSHMILLER
BE KIND TO ANIMALS WEEK
-NOV-11

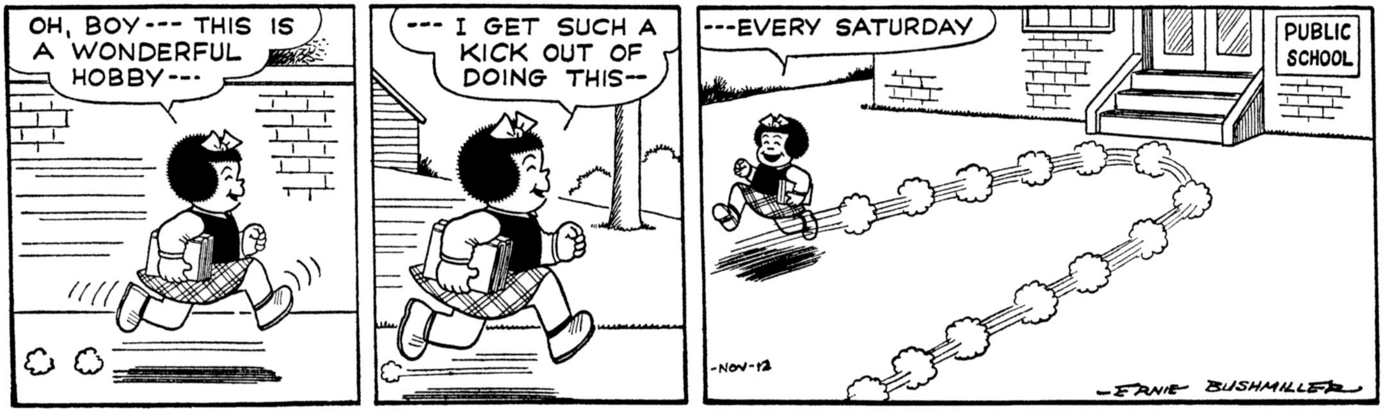
OH, BOY --- THIS IS A WONDERFUL HOBBY ---
--- I GET SUCH A KICK OUT OF DOING THIS--
---EVERY SATURDAY
PUBLIC SCHOOL
-NOV-12
-ERNIE- BUSHMILLER

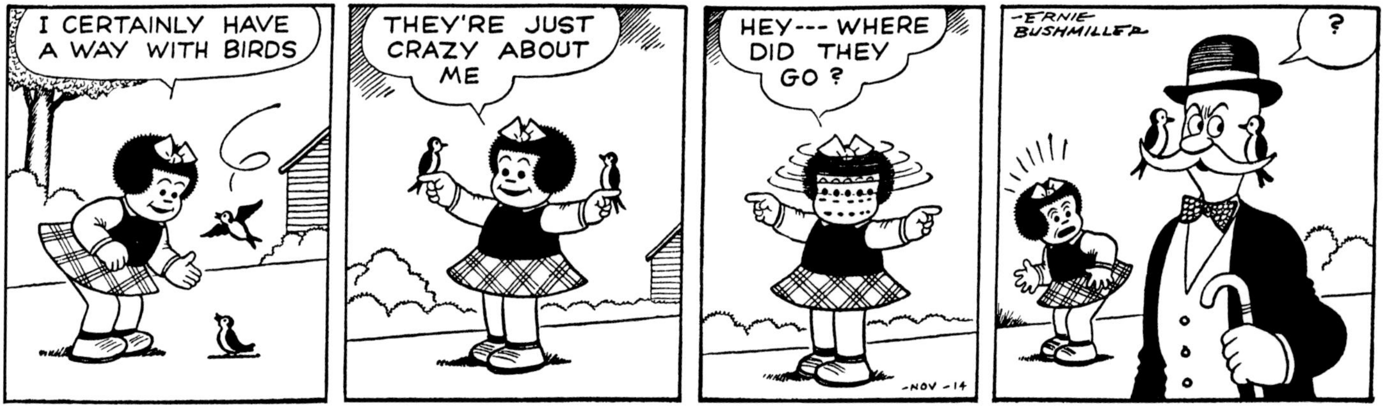
I CERTAINLY HAVE A WAY WITH BIRDS
THEY'RE JUST CRAZY ABOUT ME
HEY--- WHERE DID THEY GO ?
-NOV-14
-ERNIE BUSHMILLER
?

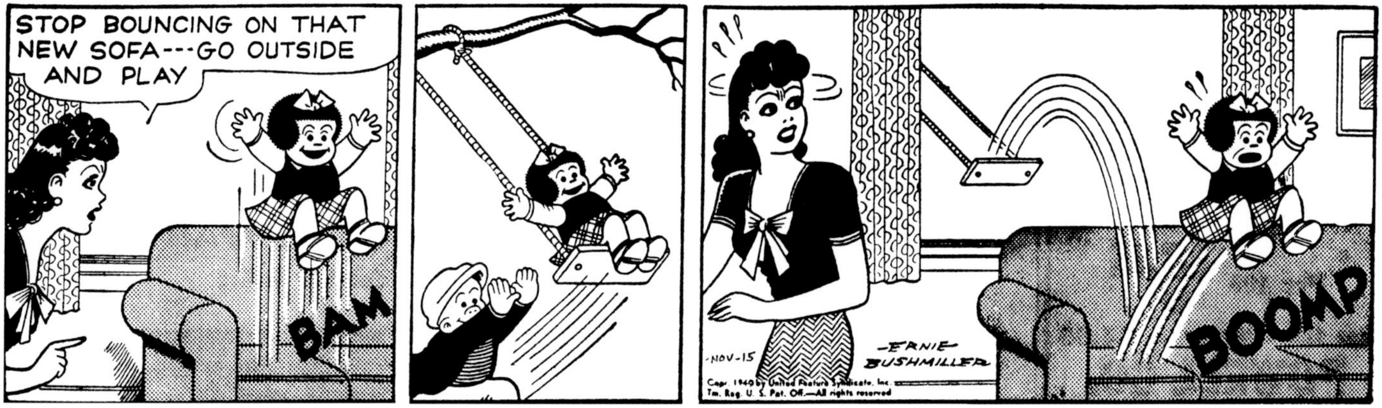
STOP BOUNCING ON THAT NEW SOFA---GO OUTSIDE AND PLAY
BAM
-NOV-15
-ERNIE BUSHMILLER
Copr. 1949 by United Feature Syndicate, Inc.
Tm. Reg. U. S. Pat. Off.—All rights reserved
BOOMP

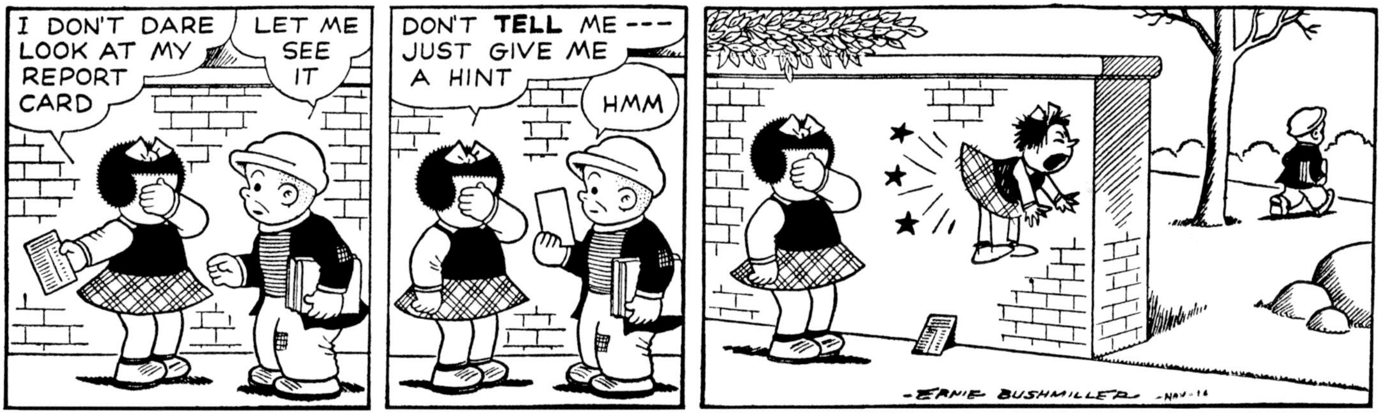
I DON'T DARE LOOK AT MY REPORT CARD
LET ME SEE IT
DON'T **TELL** ME --- JUST GIVE ME A HINT
HMM
-ERNIE BUSHMILLER
-NOV-16

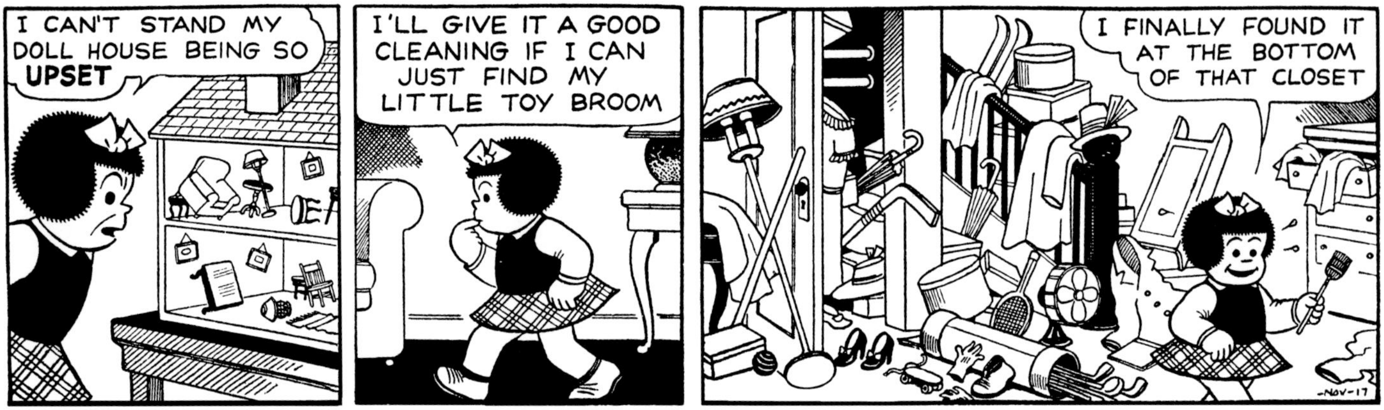
I CAN'T STAND MY DOLL HOUSE BEING SO **UPSET**
I'LL GIVE IT A GOOD CLEANING IF I CAN JUST FIND MY LITTLE TOY BROOM
I FINALLY FOUND IT AT THE BOTTOM OF THAT CLOSET
-NOV-17

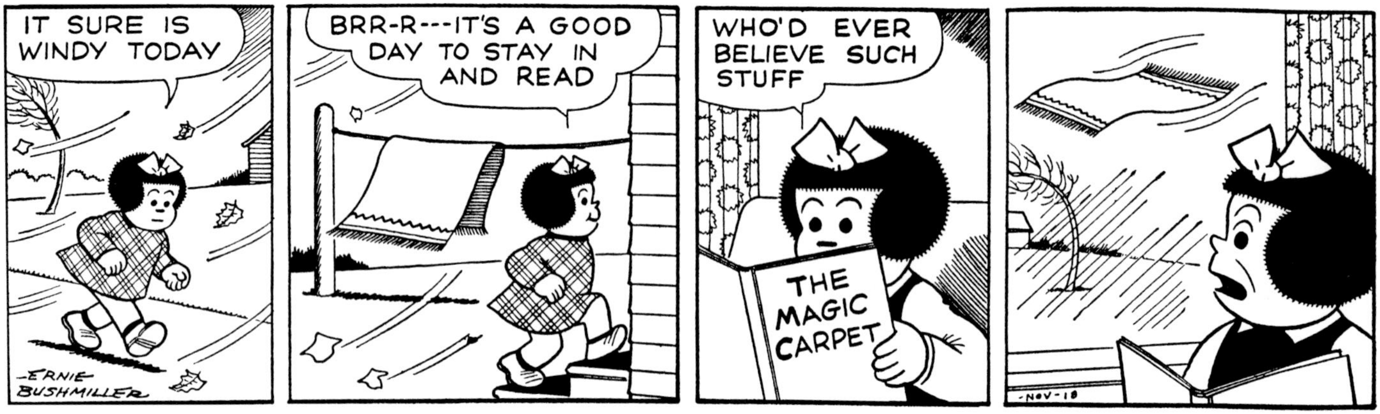
IT SURE IS WINDY TODAY
-ERNIE BUSHMILLER
BRR-R---IT'S A GOOD DAY TO STAY IN AND READ
WHO'D EVER BELIEVE SUCH STUFF
THE MAGIC CARPET
-NOV-18

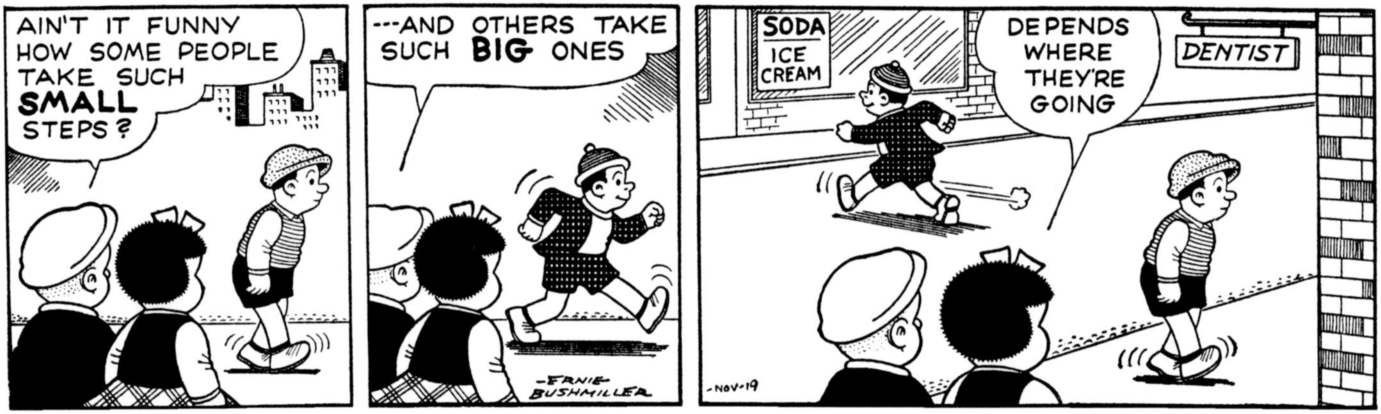
AIN'T IT FUNNY HOW SOME PEOPLE TAKE SUCH **SMALL** STEPS ?
---AND OTHERS TAKE SUCH **BIG** ONES
-ERNIE BUSHMILLER
SODA
ICE CREAM
DEPENDS WHERE THEY'RE GOING
DENTIST
-NOV-19

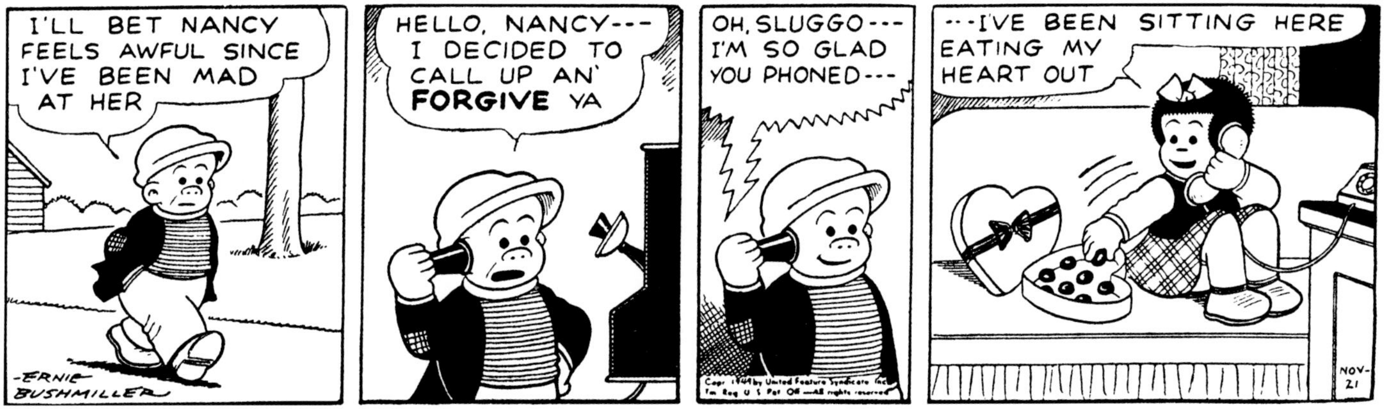

I'LL BET NANCY FEELS AWFUL SINCE I'VE BEEN MAD AT HER
-ERNIE BUSHMILLER
HELLO, NANCY--- I DECIDED TO CALL UP AN' **FORGIVE** YA
OH, SLUGGO--- I'M SO GLAD YOU PHONED---
Copr 1949 by United Feature Syndicate Inc. Tm Reg U S Pat Off—All rights reserved
---I'VE BEEN SITTING HERE EATING MY HEART OUT
NOV-21

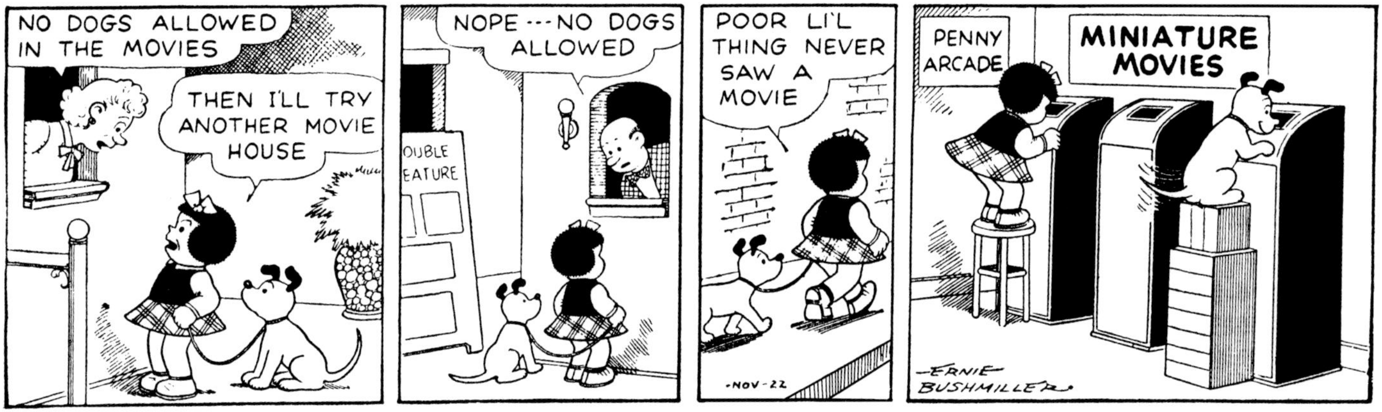

NO DOGS ALLOWED IN THE MOVIES
THEN I'LL TRY ANOTHER MOVIE HOUSE
NOPE---NO DOGS ALLOWED
OUBLE EATURE
POOR LI'L THING NEVER SAW A MOVIE
-NOV-22
PENNY ARCADE
MINIATURE MOVIES
-ERNIE BUSHMILLER

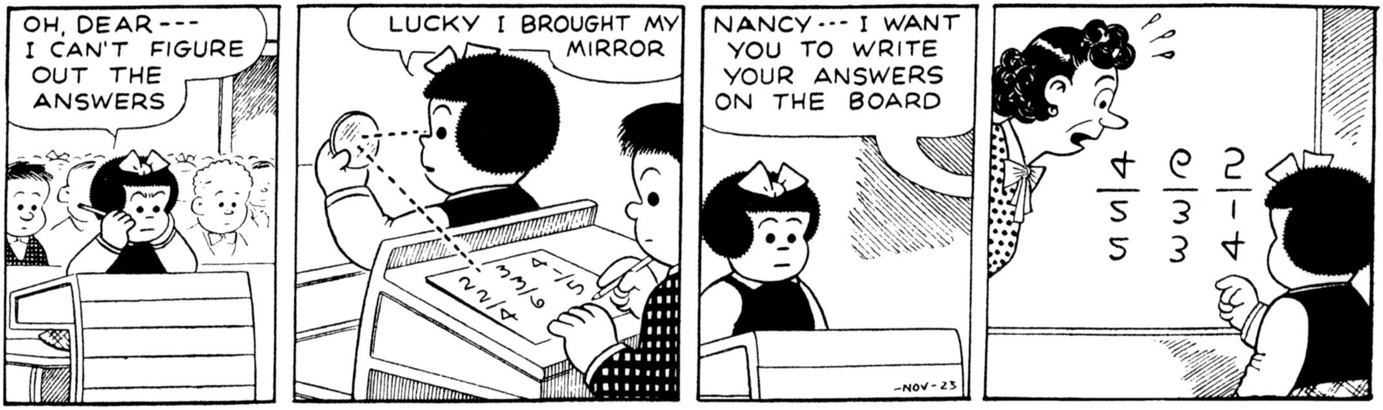

OH, DEAR--- I CAN'T FIGURE OUT THE ANSWERS
LUCKY I BROUGHT MY MIRROR
2/2/4 3/3/6 4/5
NANCY--- I WANT YOU TO WRITE YOUR ANSWERS ON THE BOARD
-NOV-23

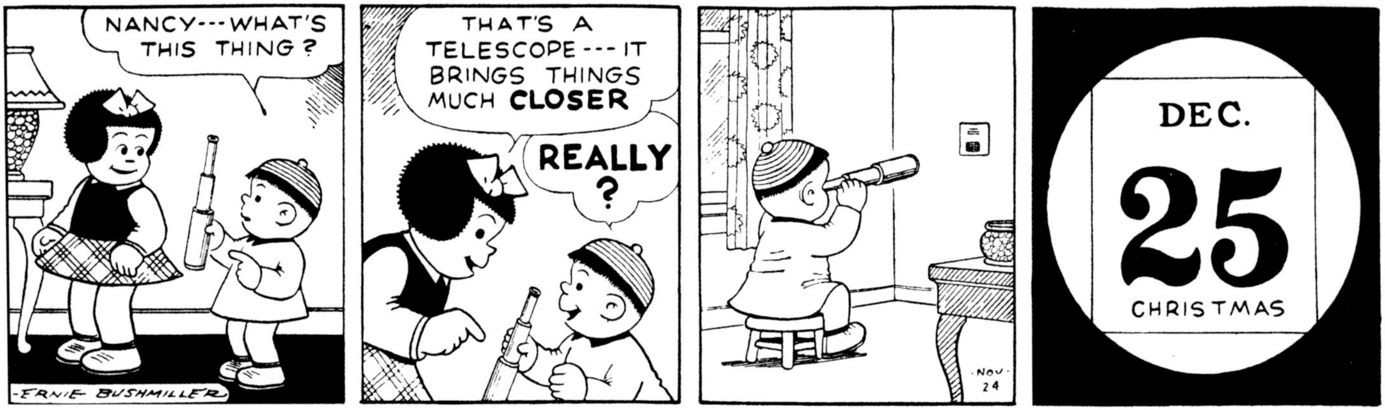
NANCY---WHAT'S THIS THING?
THAT'S A TELESCOPE---IT BRINGS THINGS MUCH **CLOSER**
REALLY ?
ERNIE BUSHMILLER
NOV-24
DEC.
25
CHRISTMAS

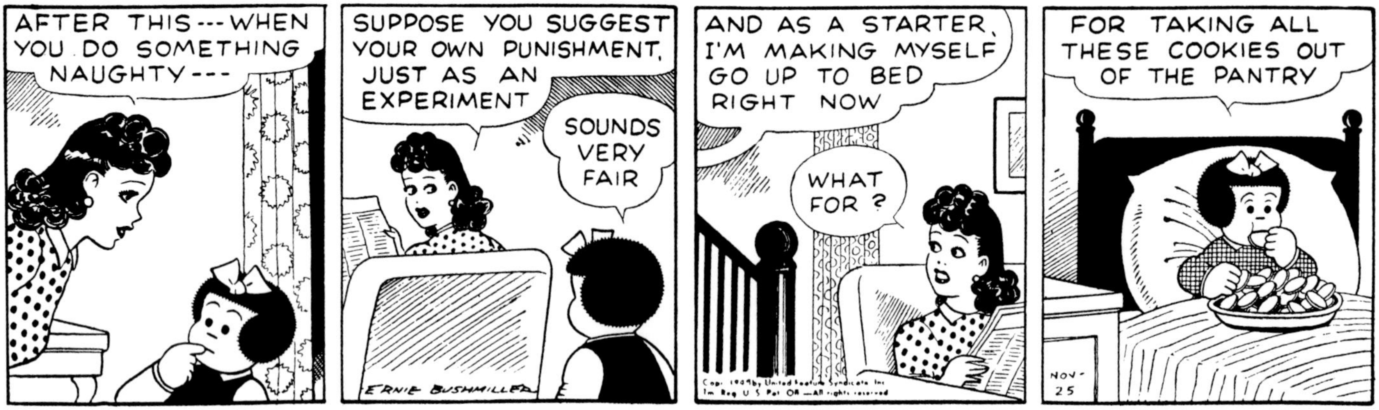
AFTER THIS---WHEN YOU DO SOMETHING NAUGHTY---
SUPPOSE YOU SUGGEST YOUR OWN PUNISHMENT, JUST AS AN EXPERIMENT
SOUNDS VERY FAIR
ERNIE BUSHMILLER
AND AS A STARTER, I'M MAKING MYSELF GO UP TO BED RIGHT NOW
WHAT FOR ?
Copr. 1949 by United Feature Syndicate Inc
Tm Reg U S Pat Off—All rights reserved
FOR TAKING ALL THESE COOKIES OUT OF THE PANTRY
NOV-25

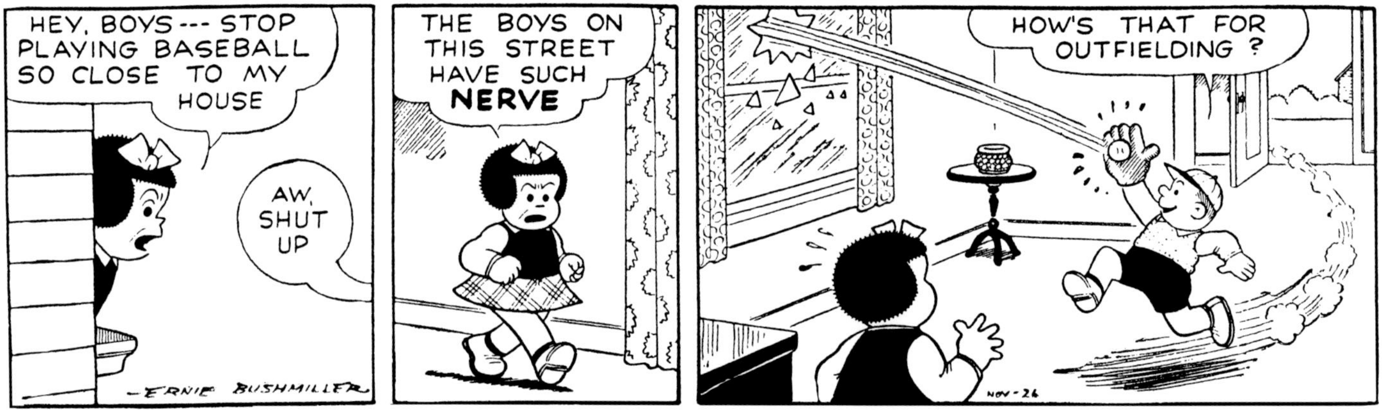
HEY, BOYS---STOP PLAYING BASEBALL SO CLOSE TO MY HOUSE
AW, SHUT UP
ERNIE BUSHMILLER
THE BOYS ON THIS STREET HAVE SUCH **NERVE**
HOW'S THAT FOR OUTFIELDING ?
NOV-26

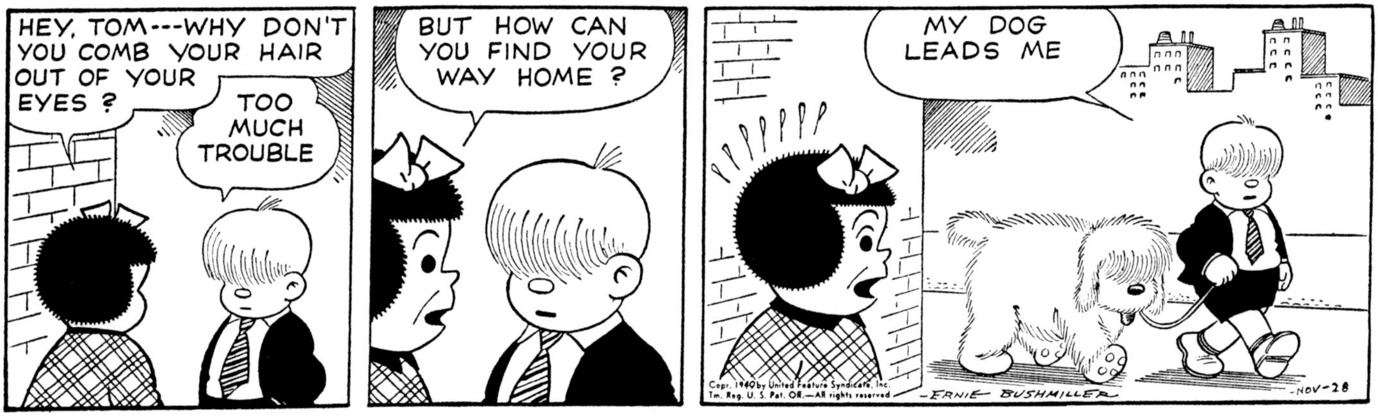
HEY, TOM---WHY DON'T YOU COMB YOUR HAIR OUT OF YOUR EYES ?
TOO MUCH TROUBLE
BUT HOW CAN YOU FIND YOUR WAY HOME ?
MY DOG LEADS ME
Copr. 1949 by United Feature Syndicate, Inc. Tm. Reg. U. S. Pat. Off.—All rights reserved
-ERNIE BUSHMILLER
-NOV-28

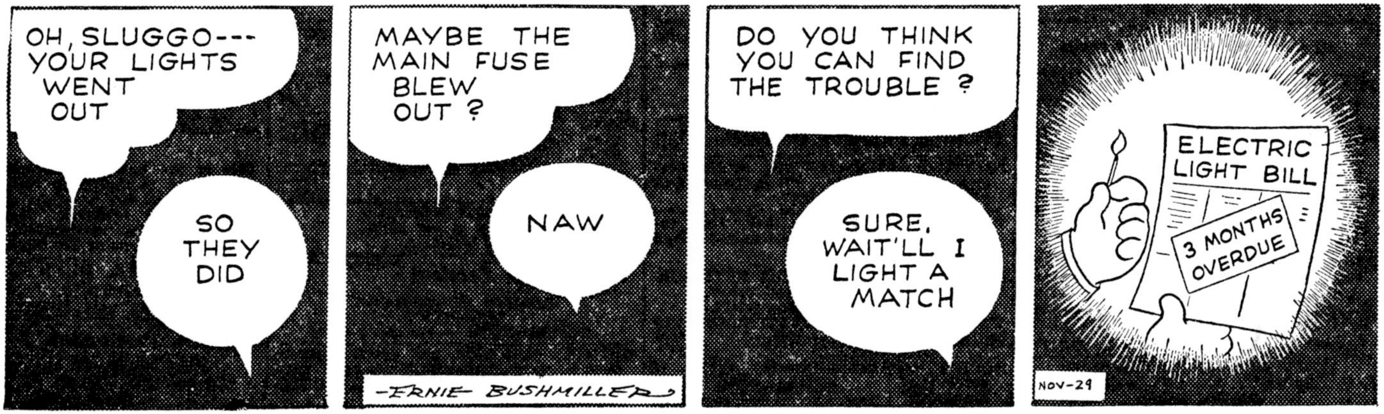
OH, SLUGGO--- YOUR LIGHTS WENT OUT
SO THEY DID
MAYBE THE MAIN FUSE BLEW OUT ?
NAW
-ERNIE BUSHMILLER
DO YOU THINK YOU CAN FIND THE TROUBLE ?
SURE, WAIT'LL I LIGHT A MATCH
ELECTRIC LIGHT BILL
3 MONTHS OVERDUE
NOV-29

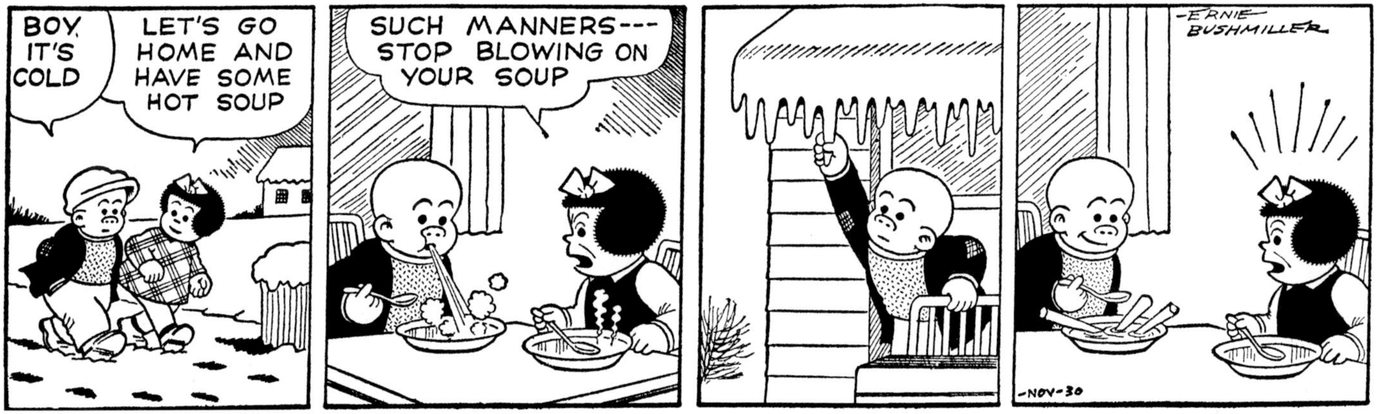
BOY, IT'S COLD
LET'S GO HOME AND HAVE SOME HOT SOUP
SUCH MANNERS--- STOP BLOWING ON YOUR SOUP
-ERNIE BUSHMILLER
-NOV-30

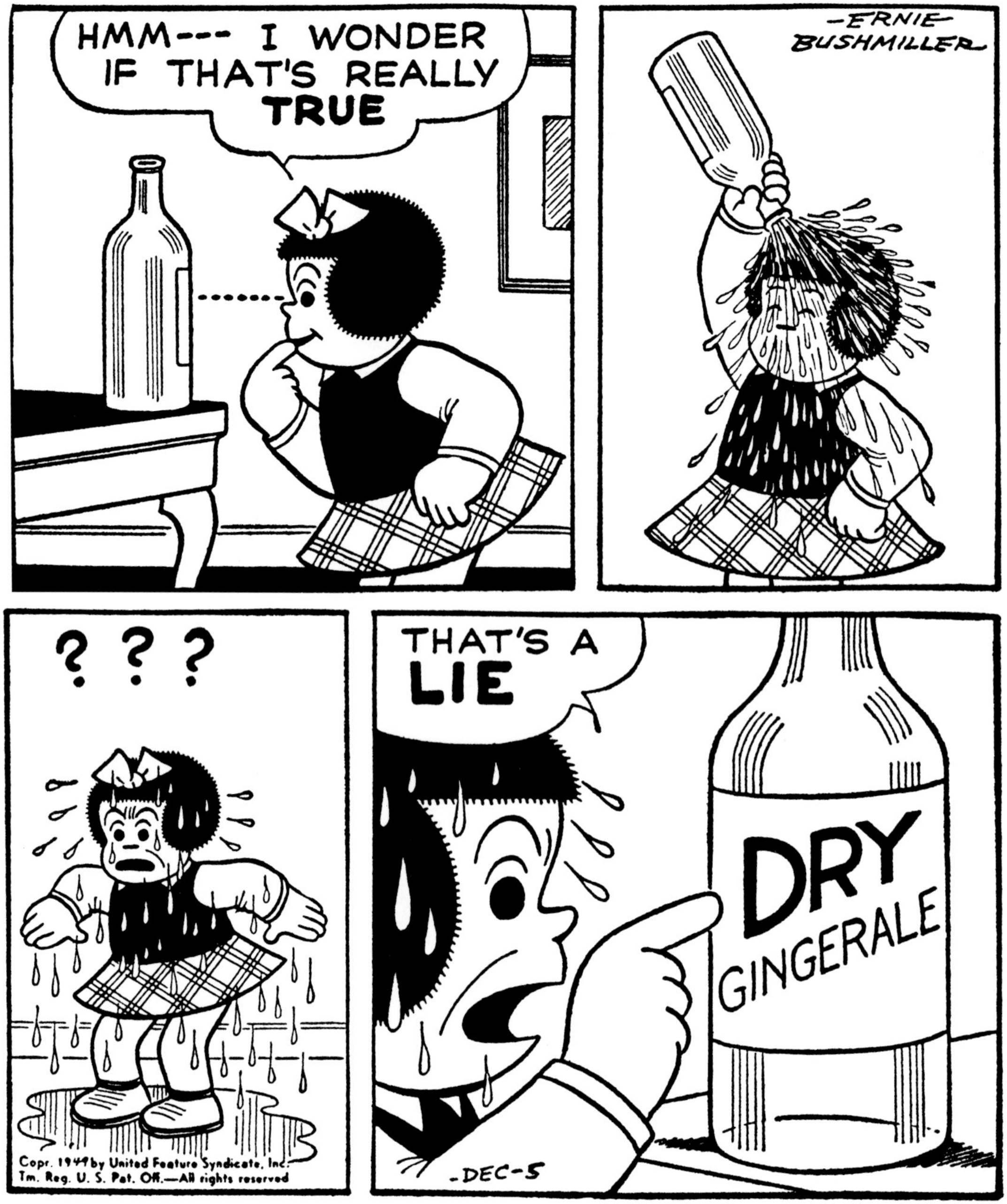
HMM--- I WONDER IF THAT'S REALLY **TRUE**
-ERNIE BUSHMILLER
? ? ?
THAT'S A **LIE**
DRY GINGERALE
-DEC-5

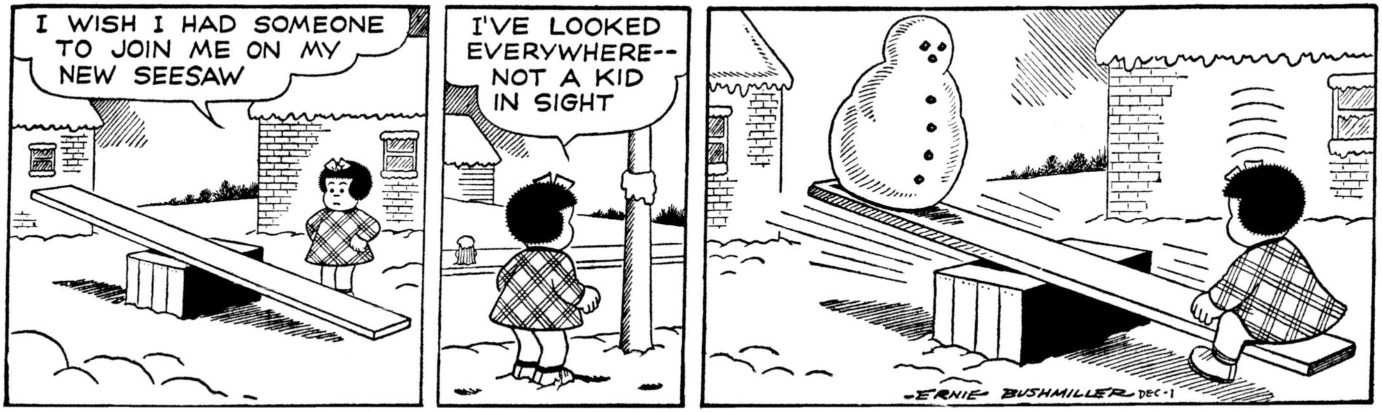
I WISH I HAD SOMEONE TO JOIN ME ON MY NEW SEESAW
I'VE LOOKED EVERYWHERE-- NOT A KID IN SIGHT
ERNIE BUSHMILLER DEC-1

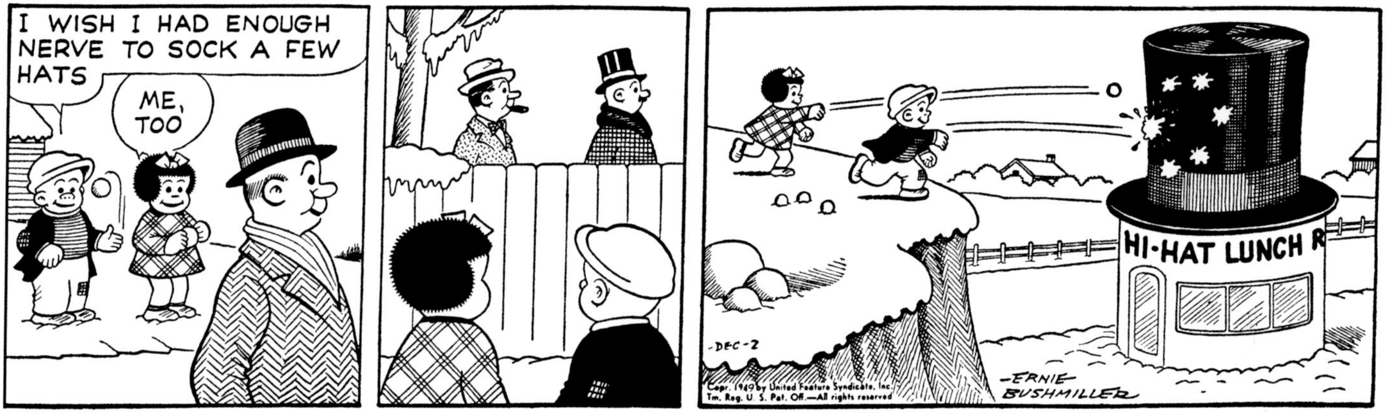
I WISH I HAD ENOUGH NERVE TO SOCK A FEW HATS
ME, TOO
HI-HAT LUNCH R
DEC-2
Copr. 1949 by United Feature Syndicate, Inc.
Tm. Reg. U. S. Pat. Off.—All rights reserved
ERNIE BUSHMILLER

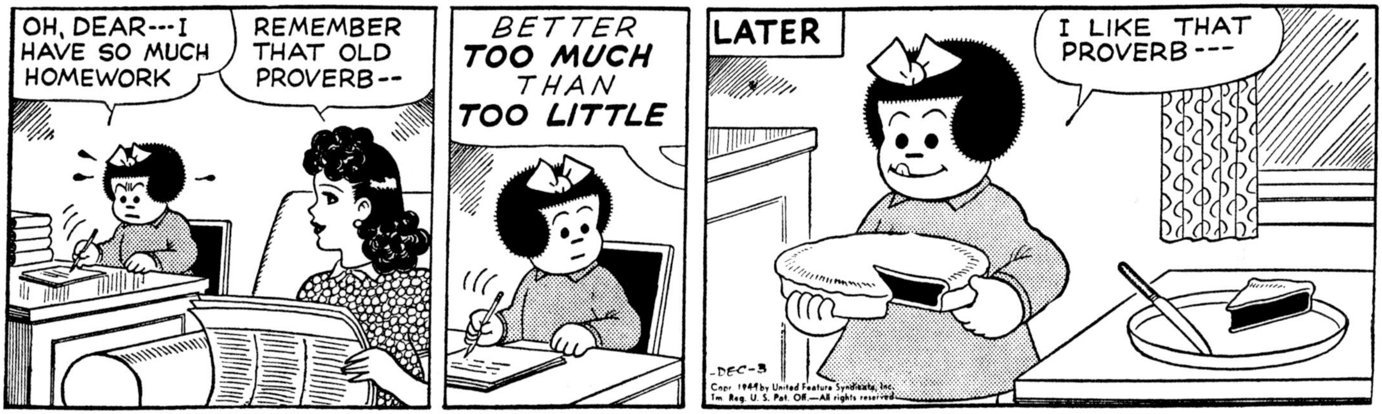
OH, DEAR---I HAVE SO MUCH HOMEWORK
REMEMBER THAT OLD PROVERB--
BETTER TOO MUCH THAN TOO LITTLE
LATER
I LIKE THAT PROVERB---
DEC-3
Copr. 1949 by United Feature Syndicate, Inc.
Tm. Reg. U. S. Pat. Off.—All rights reserved

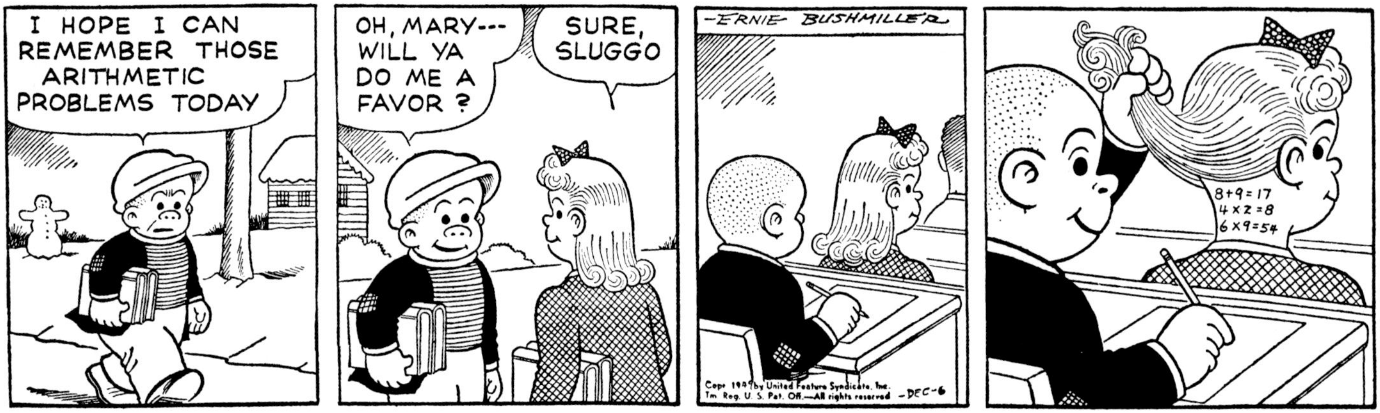
I HOPE I CAN REMEMBER THOSE ARITHMETIC PROBLEMS TODAY
OH, MARY--- WILL YA DO ME A FAVOR ?
SURE, SLUGGO
-ERNIE BUSHMILLER
Copr. 1949 by United Feature Syndicate, Inc. Tm. Reg. U. S. Pat. Off.—All rights reserved
DEC-6
8+9=17
4×2=8
6×9=54

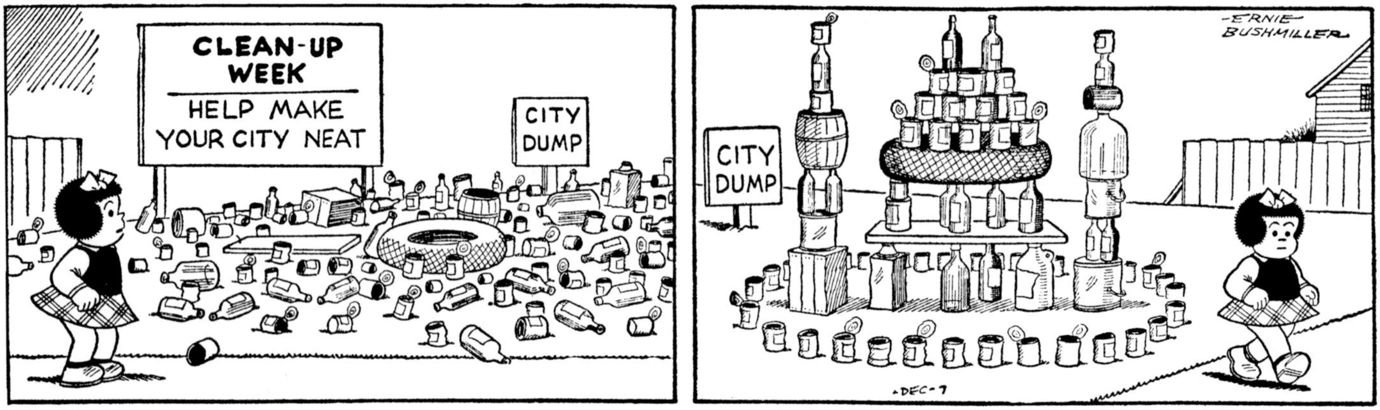
CLEAN-UP WEEK
HELP MAKE YOUR CITY NEAT
CITY DUMP
-ERNIE BUSHMILLER
CITY DUMP
DEC-7

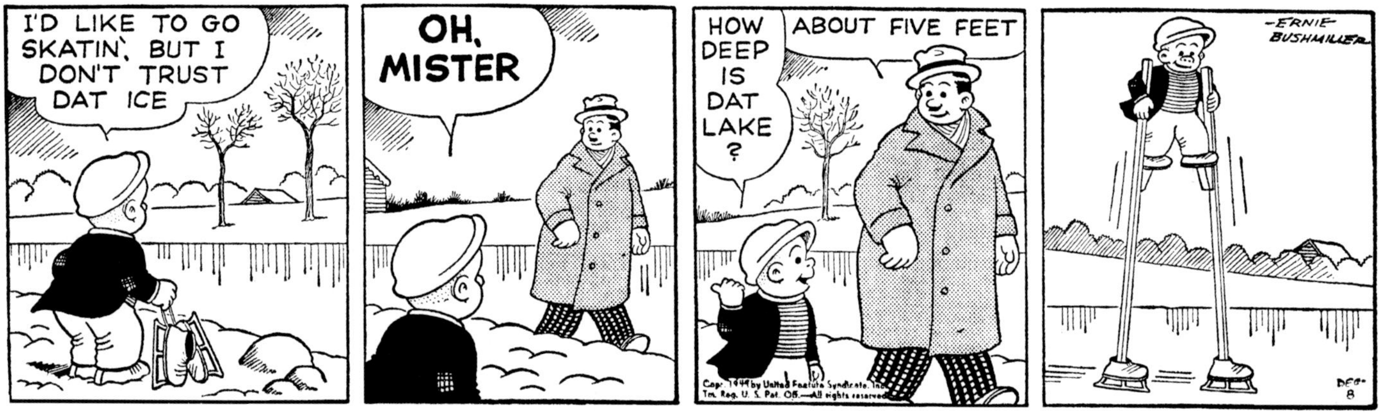
I'D LIKE TO GO SKATIN', BUT I DON'T TRUST DAT ICE
OH, MISTER
HOW DEEP IS DAT LAKE ?
ABOUT FIVE FEET
Copr. 1949 by United Feature Syndicate, Inc. Tm. Reg. U. S. Pat. Off.—All rights reserved
-ERNIE BUSHMILLER
DEC-8

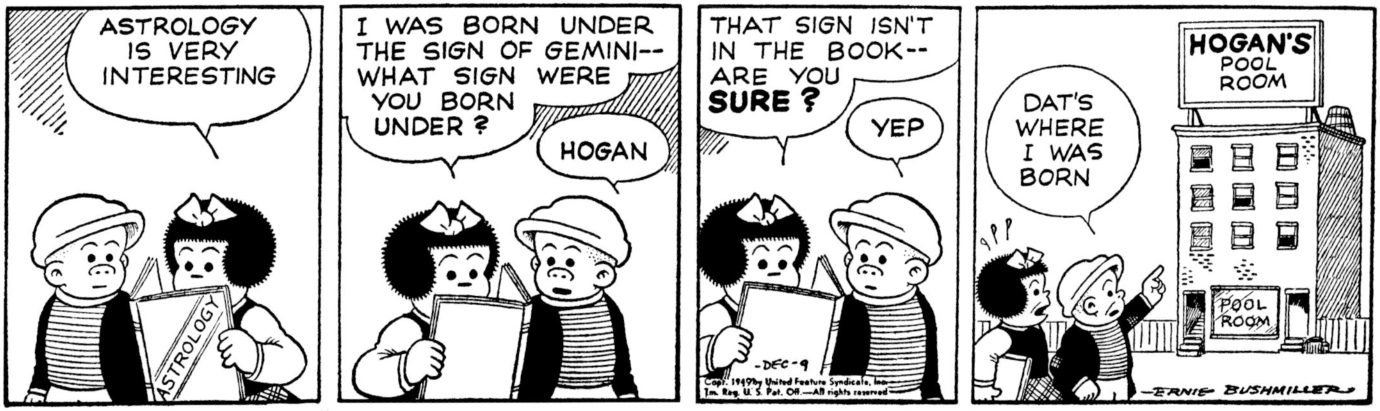
ASTROLOGY IS VERY INTERESTING
ASTROLOGY
I WAS BORN UNDER THE SIGN OF GEMINI-- WHAT SIGN WERE YOU BORN UNDER ?
HOGAN
THAT SIGN ISN'T IN THE BOOK-- ARE YOU **SURE ?**
YEP
-DEC-9
Copr. 1949 by United Feature Syndicate, Inc. Tm. Reg. U. S. Pat. Off.—All rights reserved
HOGAN'S POOL ROOM
DAT'S WHERE I WAS BORN
POOL ROOM
-ERNIE BUSHMILLER

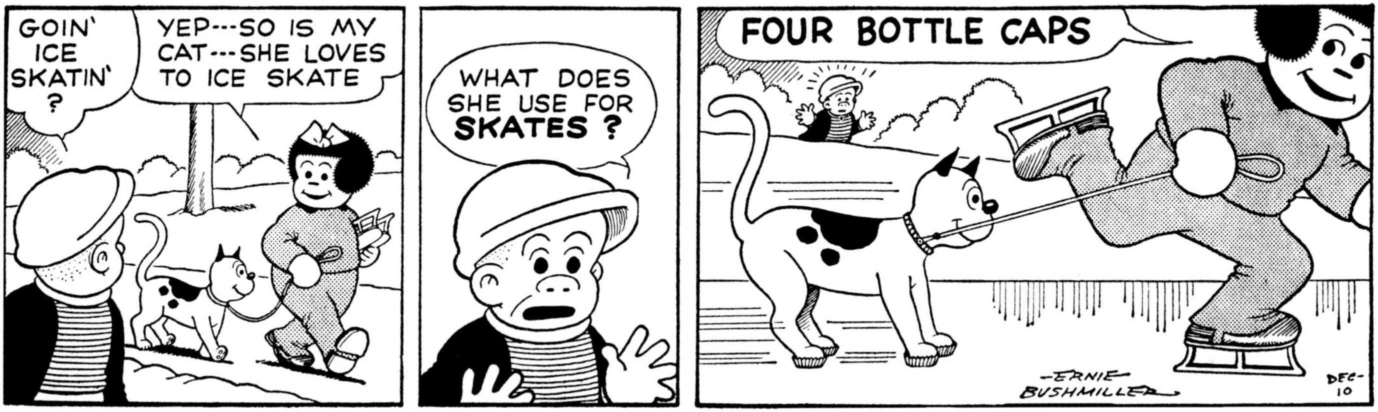
GOIN' ICE SKATIN' ?
YEP---SO IS MY CAT---SHE LOVES TO ICE SKATE
WHAT DOES SHE USE FOR **SKATES ?**
FOUR BOTTLE CAPS
-ERNIE BUSHMILLER
DEC-10

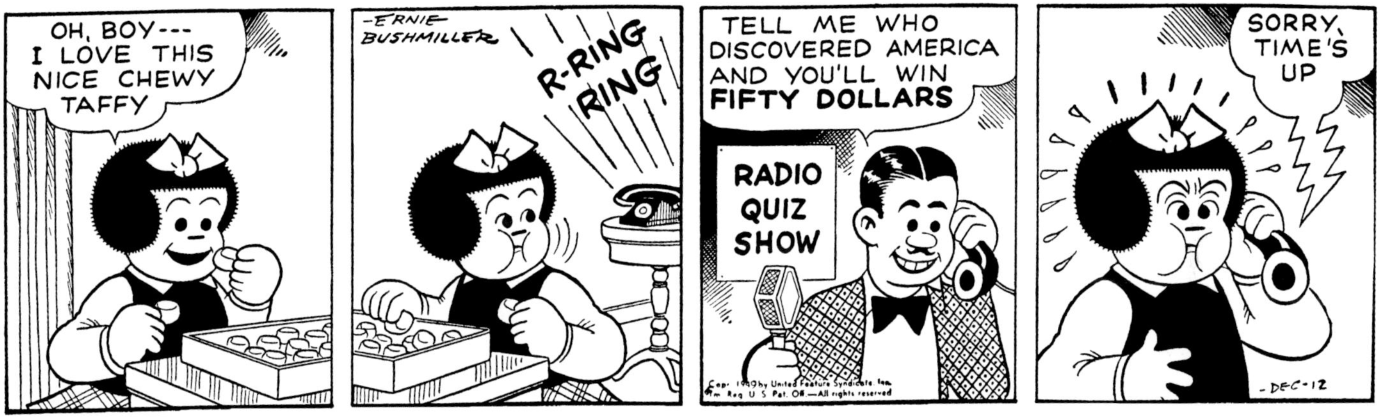
OH, BOY--- I LOVE THIS NICE CHEWY TAFFY
-ERNIE BUSHMILLER
R-RING RING
TELL ME WHO DISCOVERED AMERICA AND YOU'LL WIN **FIFTY DOLLARS**
RADIO QUIZ SHOW
Copr. 1949 by United Feature Syndicate, Inc. Tm. Reg. U. S. Pat. Off.—All rights reserved
SORRY, TIME'S UP
-DEC-12

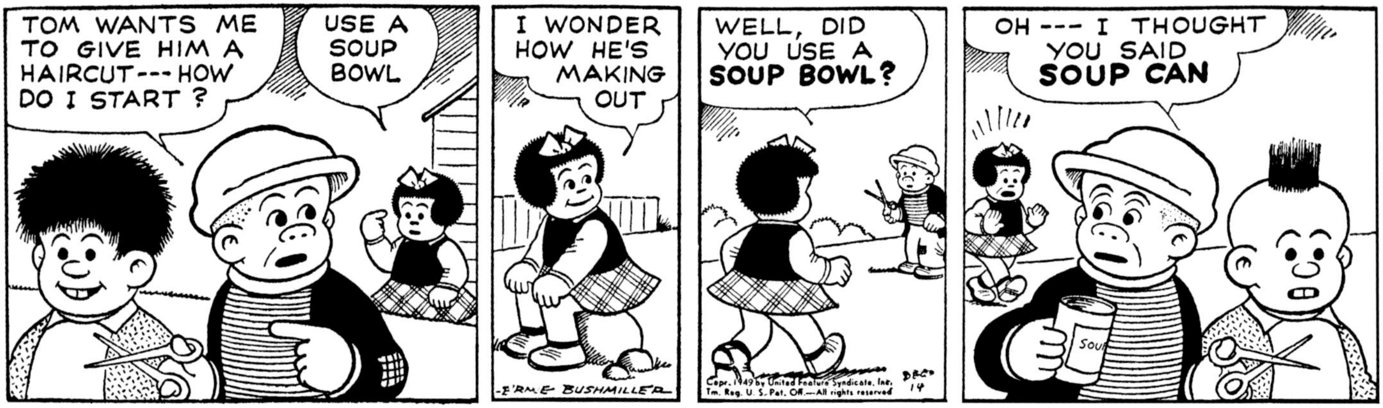
TOM WANTS ME TO GIVE HIM A HAIRCUT --- HOW DO I START ?
USE A SOUP BOWL
I WONDER HOW HE'S MAKING OUT
-ERNIE BUSHMILLER
WELL, DID YOU USE A **SOUP BOWL**?
Copr. 1949 by United Feature Syndicate, Inc. Tm. Reg. U. S. Pat. Off.—All rights reserved
DEC 14
OH --- I THOUGHT YOU SAID **SOUP CAN**
SOUP

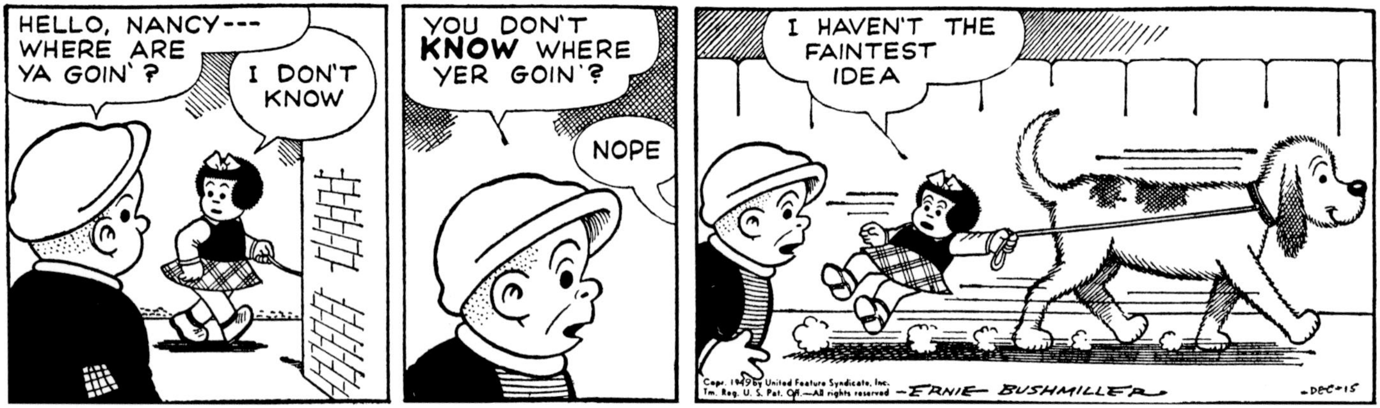
HELLO, NANCY--- WHERE ARE YA GOIN' ?
I DON'T KNOW
YOU DON'T **KNOW** WHERE YER GOIN'?
NOPE
I HAVEN'T THE FAINTEST IDEA
Copr. 1949 by United Feature Syndicate, Inc. Tm. Reg. U. S. Pat. Off.—All rights reserved
-ERNIE BUSHMILLER
DEC 15

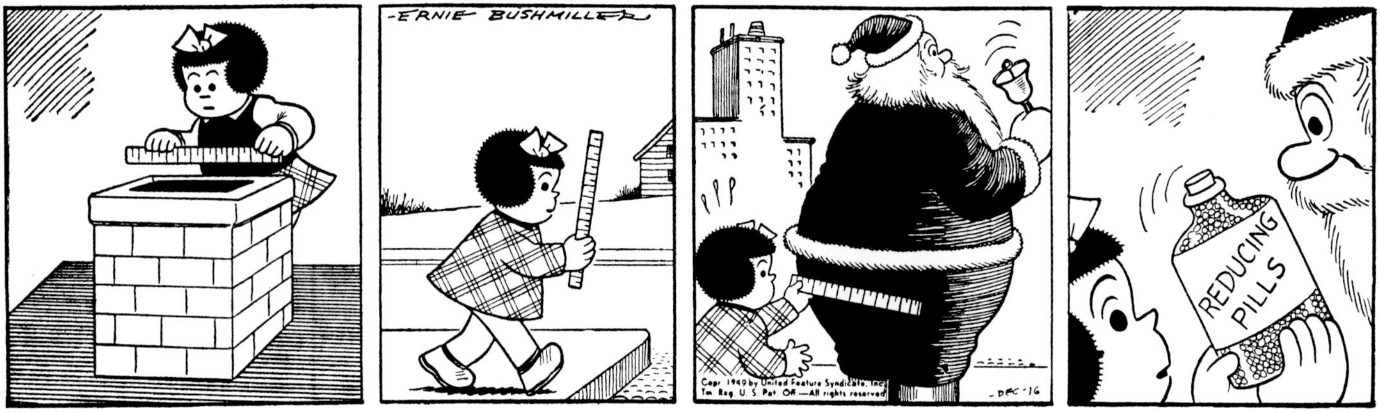
-ERNIE BUSHMILLER
Copr. 1949 by United Feature Syndicate, Inc. Tm. Reg. U. S. Pat. Off.—All rights reserved
DEC 16
REDUCING PILLS

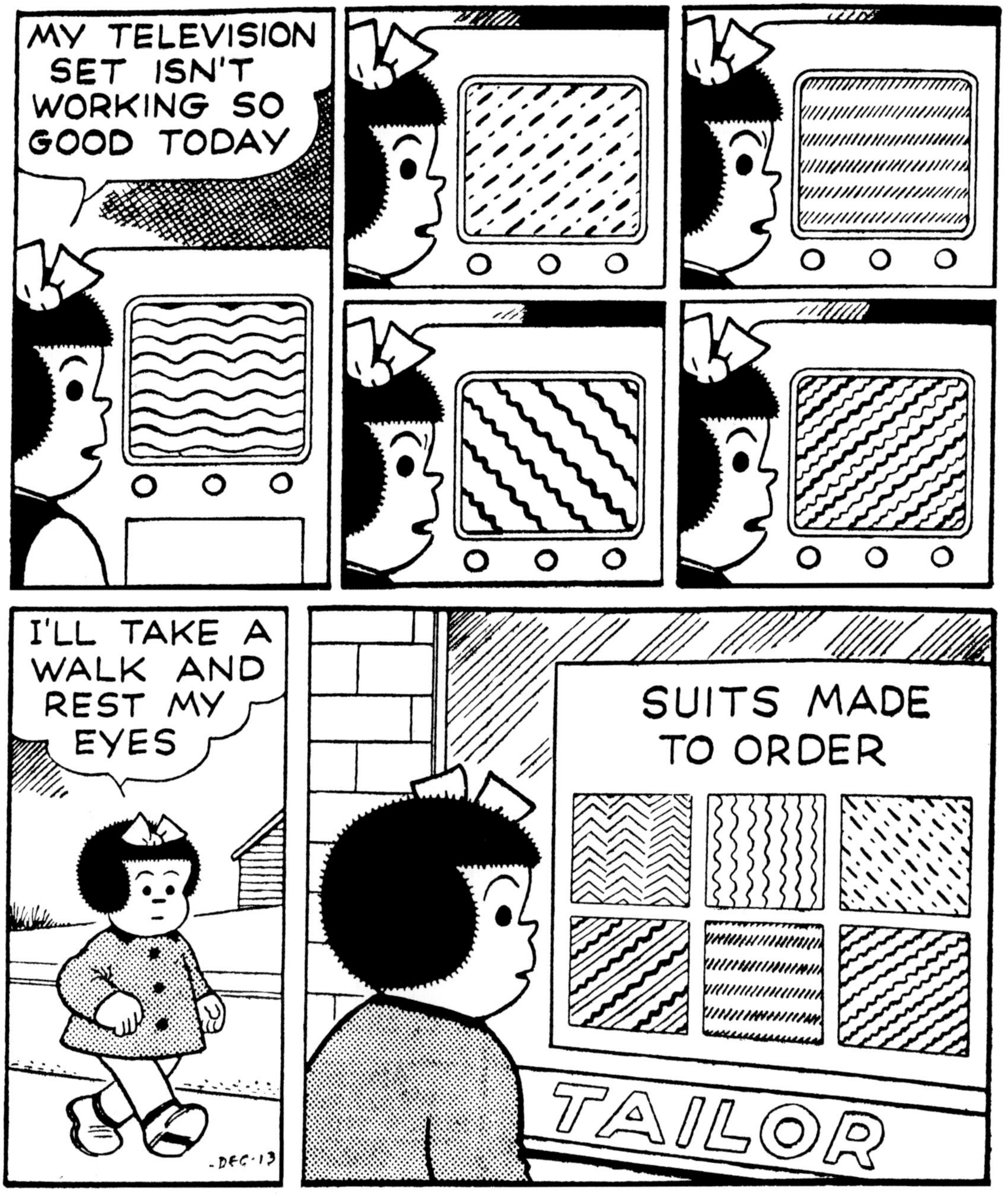
MY TELEVISION SET ISN'T WORKING SO GOOD TODAY
I'LL TAKE A WALK AND REST MY EYES
-DEC-13
SUITS MADE TO ORDER
TAILOR

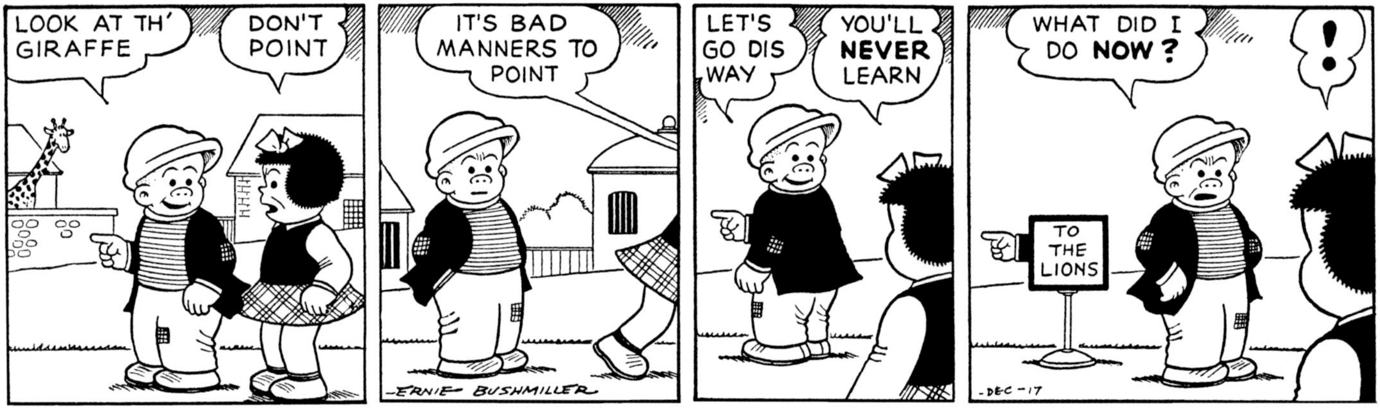
LOOK AT TH' GIRAFFE
DON'T POINT
IT'S BAD MANNERS TO POINT
ERNIE BUSHMILLER
LET'S GO DIS WAY
YOU'LL **NEVER** LEARN
WHAT DID I DO **NOW?**
!
TO THE LIONS
DEC-17

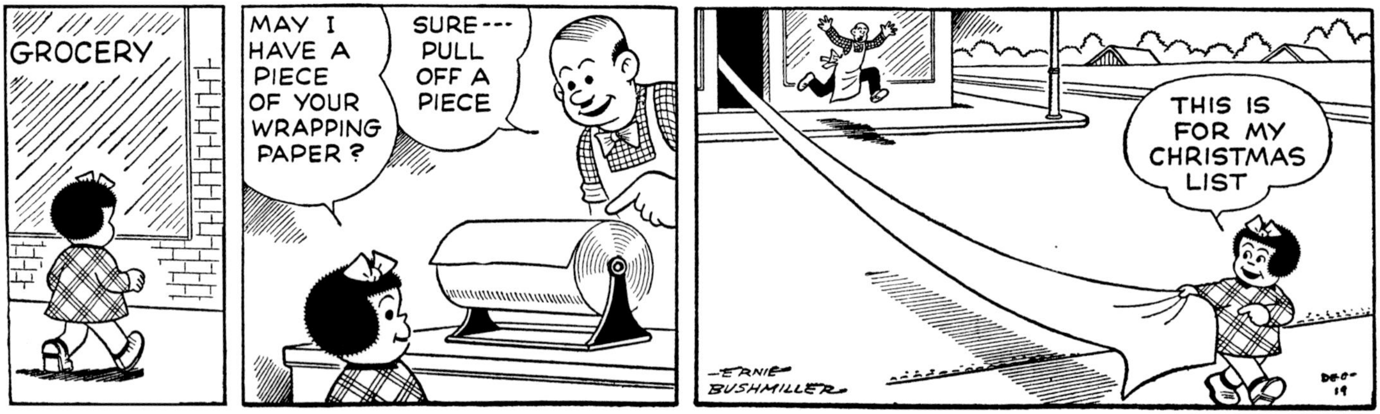
GROCERY
MAY I HAVE A PIECE OF YOUR WRAPPING PAPER?
SURE--- PULL OFF A PIECE
THIS IS FOR MY CHRISTMAS LIST
ERNIE BUSHMILLER
DEC-19

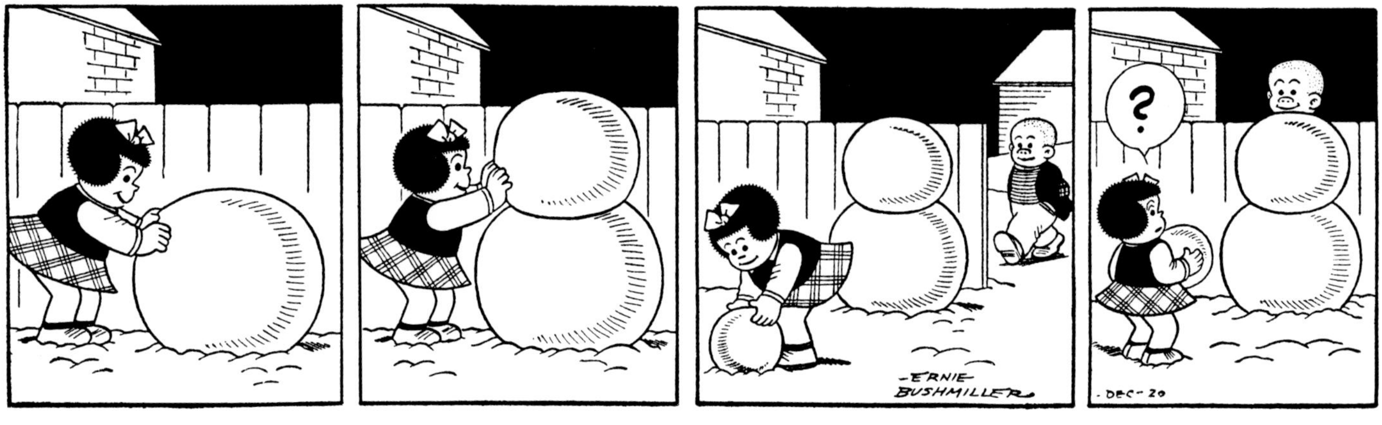
ERNIE BUSHMILLER
?
DEC-20

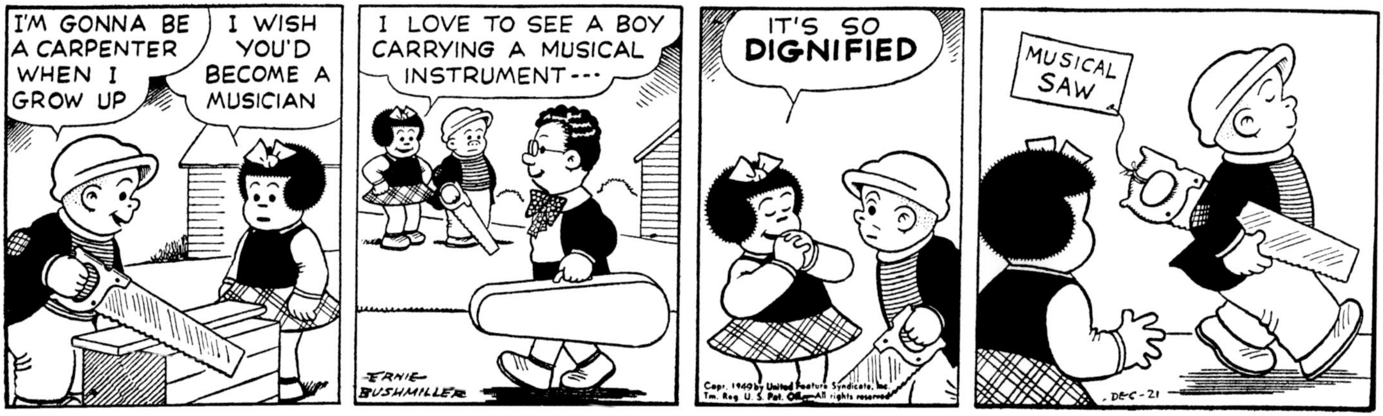
I'M GONNA BE A CARPENTER WHEN I GROW UP
I WISH YOU'D BECOME A MUSICIAN
I LOVE TO SEE A BOY CARRYING A MUSICAL INSTRUMENT---
ERNIE BUSHMILLER
IT'S SO DIGNIFIED
Copr. 1949 by United Feature Syndicate, Inc. Tm. Reg. U. S. Pat. Off.—All rights reserved
MUSICAL SAW
DEC-21

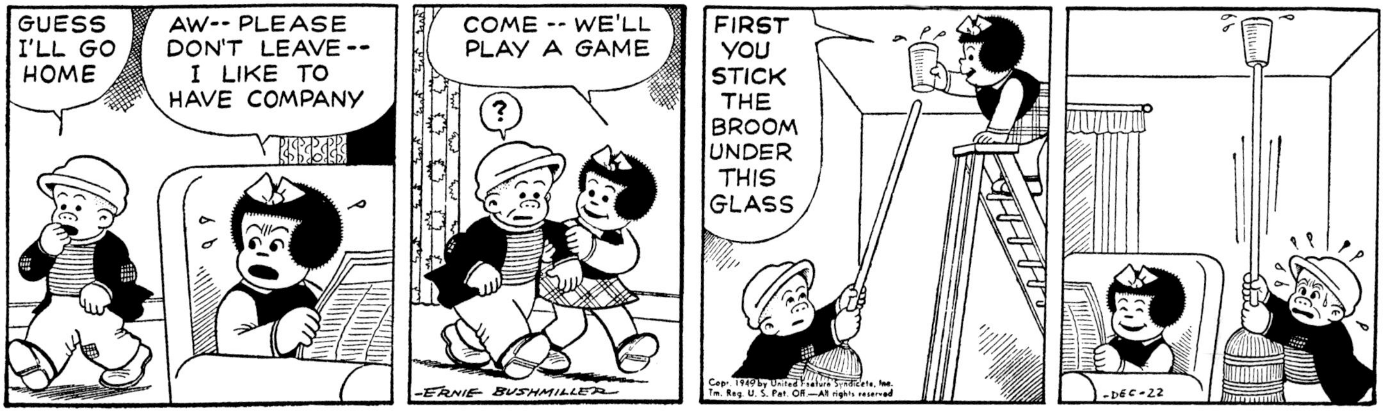
GUESS I'LL GO HOME
AW-- PLEASE DON'T LEAVE-- I LIKE TO HAVE COMPANY
COME -- WE'LL PLAY A GAME
?
ERNIE BUSHMILLER
FIRST YOU STICK THE BROOM UNDER THIS GLASS
Copr. 1949 by United Feature Syndicate, Inc. Tm. Reg. U. S. Pat. Off.—All rights reserved
DEC-22

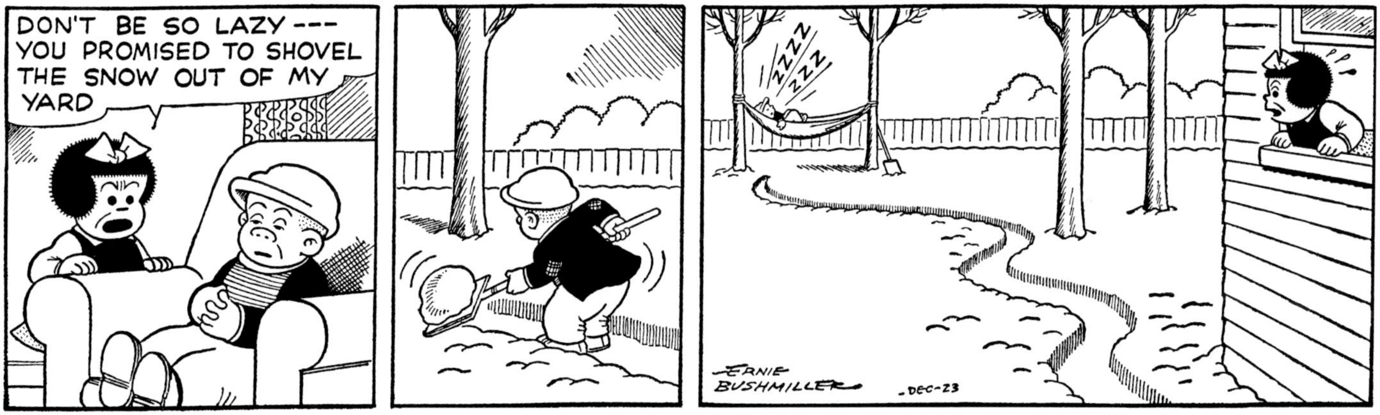
DON'T BE SO LAZY--- YOU PROMISED TO SHOVEL THE SNOW OUT OF MY YARD
ZZZZ ZZZ
ERNIE BUSHMILLER
DEC-23

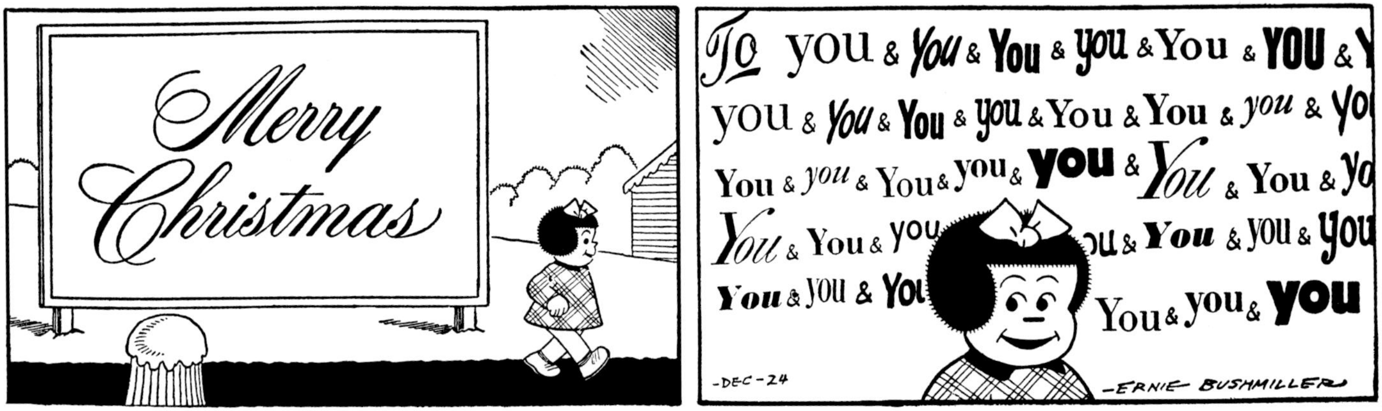
Merry Christmas
To you & You & You & you & You & YOU &
you & You & You & you & You & You & you &
You & you & You & you & you & You & You &
You & You & you
& You & you & You
You & you & You
You & you & you
-DEC-24
-ERNIE BUSHMILLER

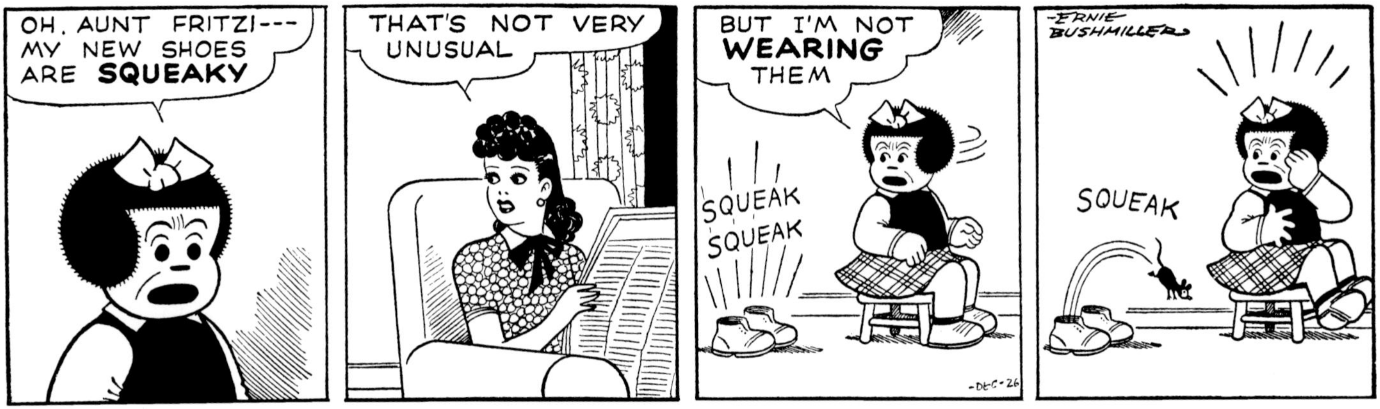
OH, AUNT FRITZI--- MY NEW SHOES ARE **SQUEAKY**
THAT'S NOT VERY UNUSUAL
BUT I'M NOT **WEARING** THEM
SQUEAK SQUEAK
-DEC-26
-ERNIE BUSHMILLER
SQUEAK

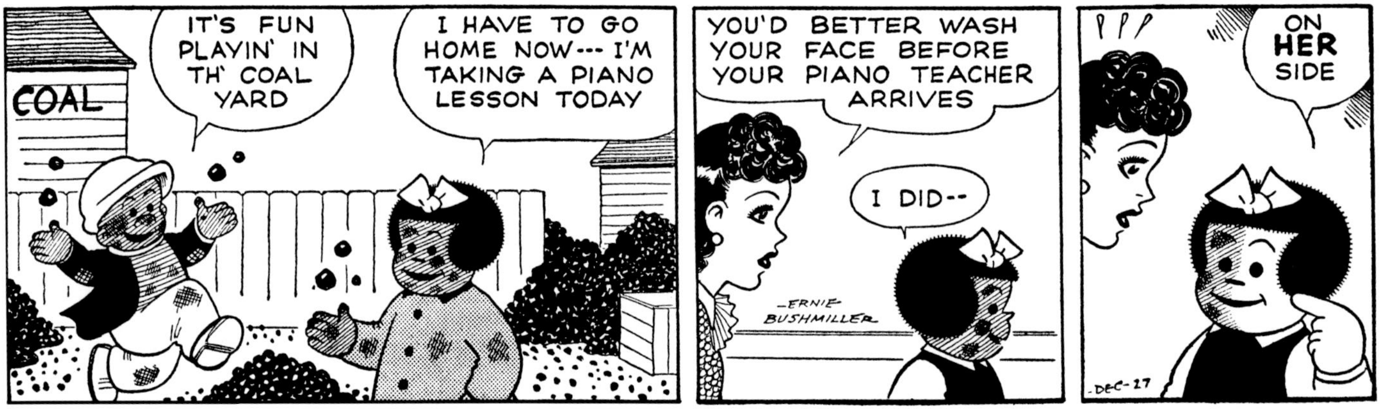
COAL
IT'S FUN PLAYIN' IN TH' COAL YARD
I HAVE TO GO HOME NOW--- I'M TAKING A PIANO LESSON TODAY
YOU'D BETTER WASH YOUR FACE BEFORE YOUR PIANO TEACHER ARRIVES
I DID--
-ERNIE BUSHMILLER
ON **HER** SIDE
-DEC-27

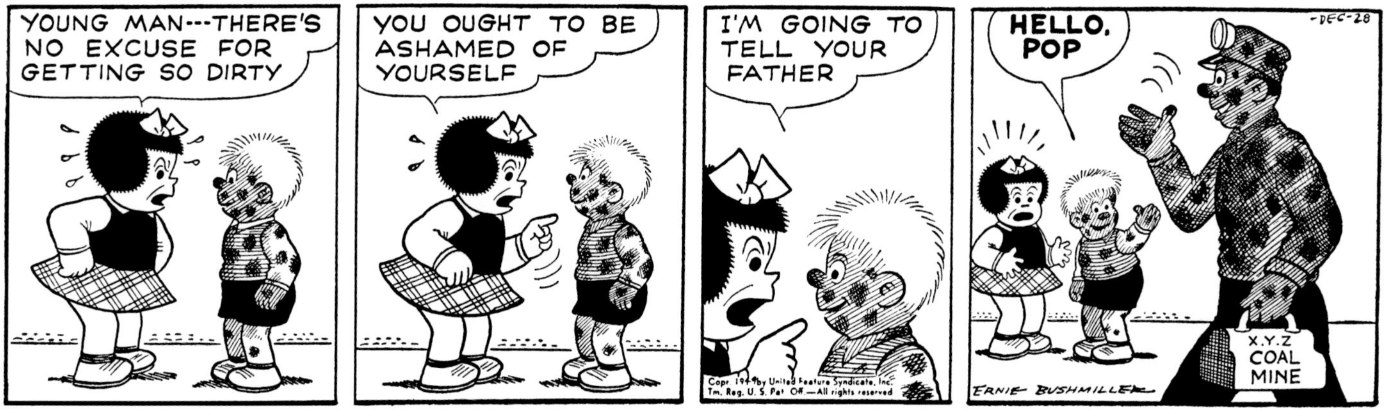
YOUNG MAN---THERE'S NO EXCUSE FOR GETTING SO DIRTY
YOU OUGHT TO BE ASHAMED OF YOURSELF
I'M GOING TO TELL YOUR FATHER
Copr. 1949 by United Feature Syndicate, Inc. Tm. Reg. U. S. Pat. Off.—All rights reserved
HELLO, POP
-DEC-28
X.Y.Z COAL MINE
ERNIE BUSHMILLER

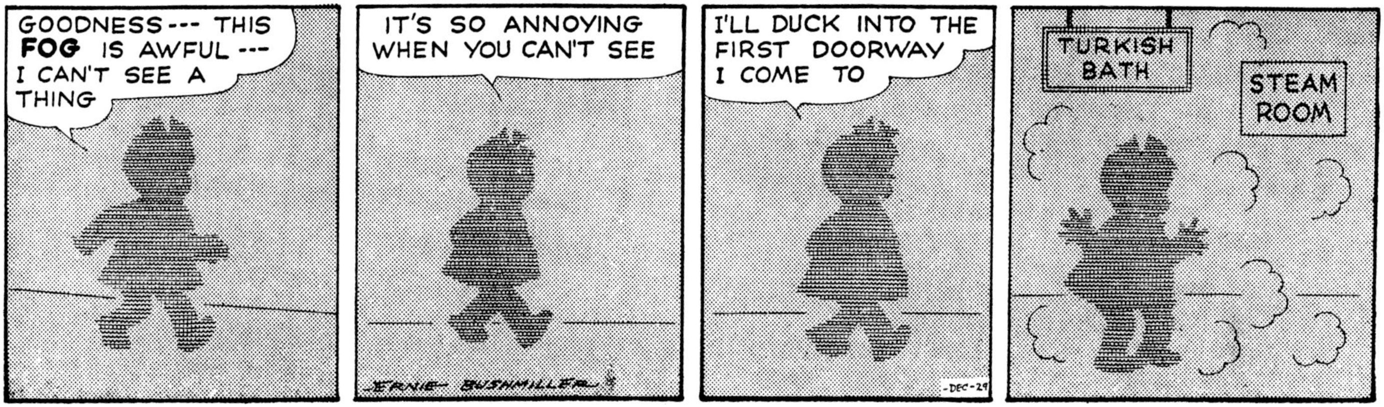
GOODNESS--- THIS **FOG** IS AWFUL--- I CAN'T SEE A THING
IT'S SO ANNOYING WHEN YOU CAN'T SEE
ERNIE BUSHMILLER
I'LL DUCK INTO THE FIRST DOORWAY I COME TO
-DEC-29
TURKISH BATH
STEAM ROOM

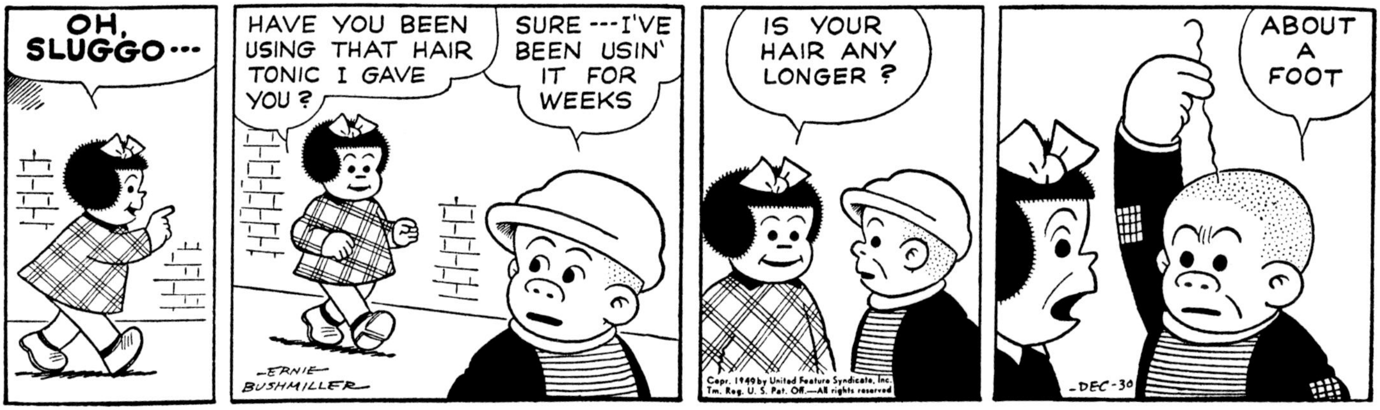
OH, SLUGGO---
HAVE YOU BEEN USING THAT HAIR TONIC I GAVE YOU?
SURE---I'VE BEEN USIN' IT FOR WEEKS
ERNIE BUSHMILLER
IS YOUR HAIR ANY LONGER?
Copr. 1949 by United Feature Syndicate, Inc. Tm. Reg. U. S. Pat. Off.—All rights reserved
ABOUT A FOOT
-DEC-30

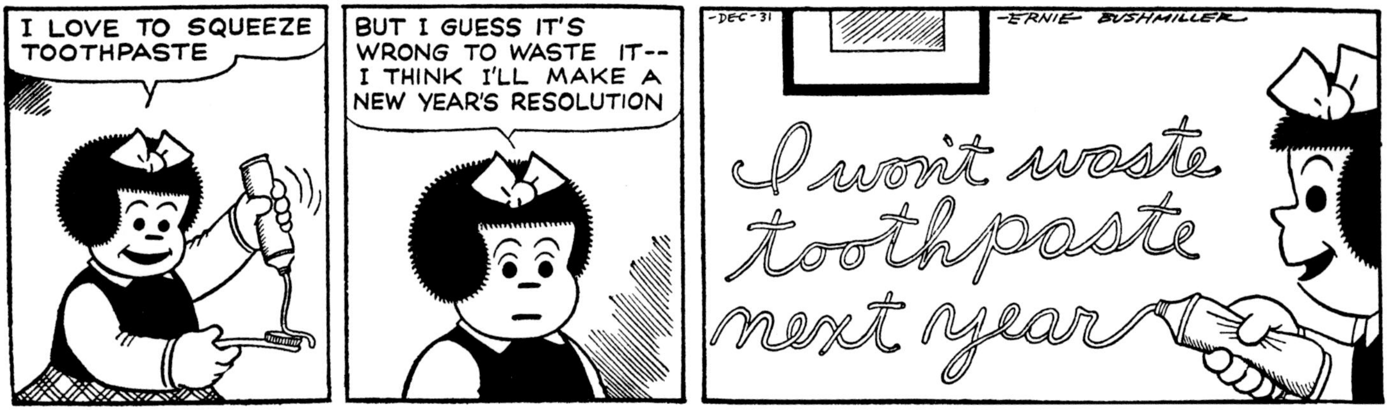
I LOVE TO SQUEEZE TOOTHPASTE
BUT I GUESS IT'S WRONG TO WASTE IT-- I THINK I'LL MAKE A NEW YEAR'S RESOLUTION
-DEC-31
-ERNIE BUSHMILLER
I won't waste toothpaste next year

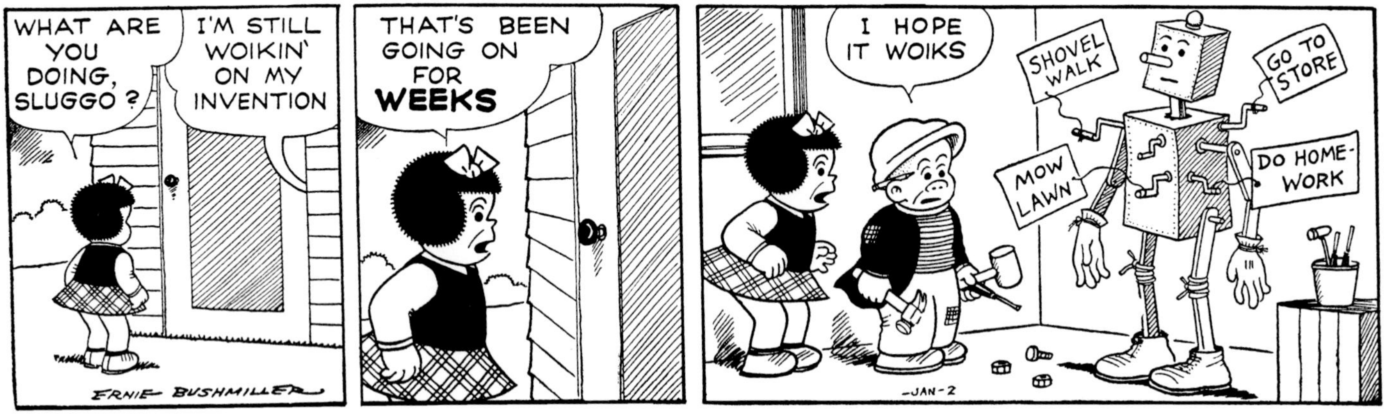
WHAT ARE YOU DOING, SLUGGO ?
I'M STILL WOIKIN' ON MY INVENTION
ERNIE BUSHMILLER
THAT'S BEEN GOING ON FOR **WEEKS**
I HOPE IT WOIKS
SHOVEL WALK
GO TO STORE
MOW LAWN
DO HOME-WORK
-JAN-2

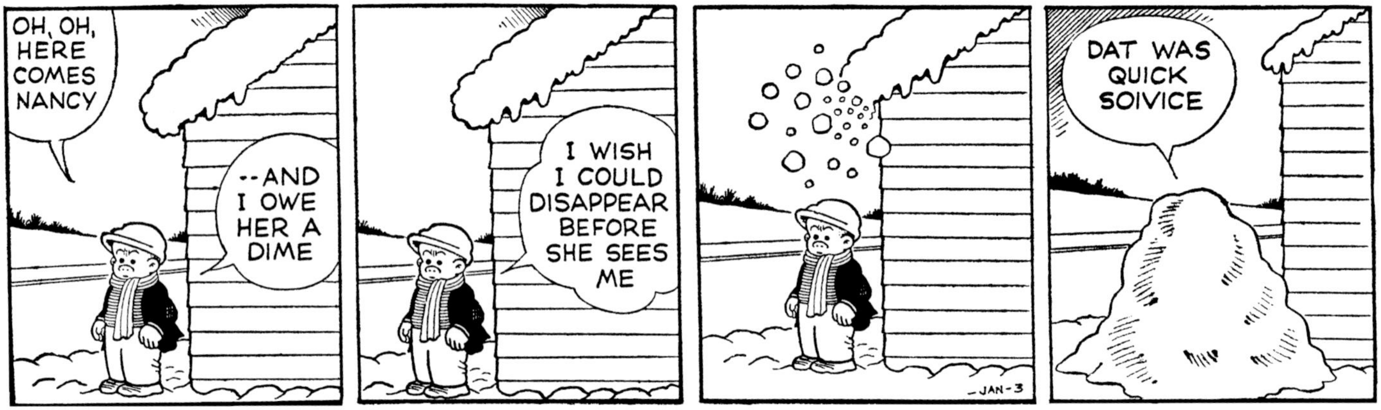
OH, OH, HERE COMES NANCY
--AND I OWE HER A DIME
I WISH I COULD DISAPPEAR BEFORE SHE SEES ME
-JAN-3
DAT WAS QUICK SOIVICE

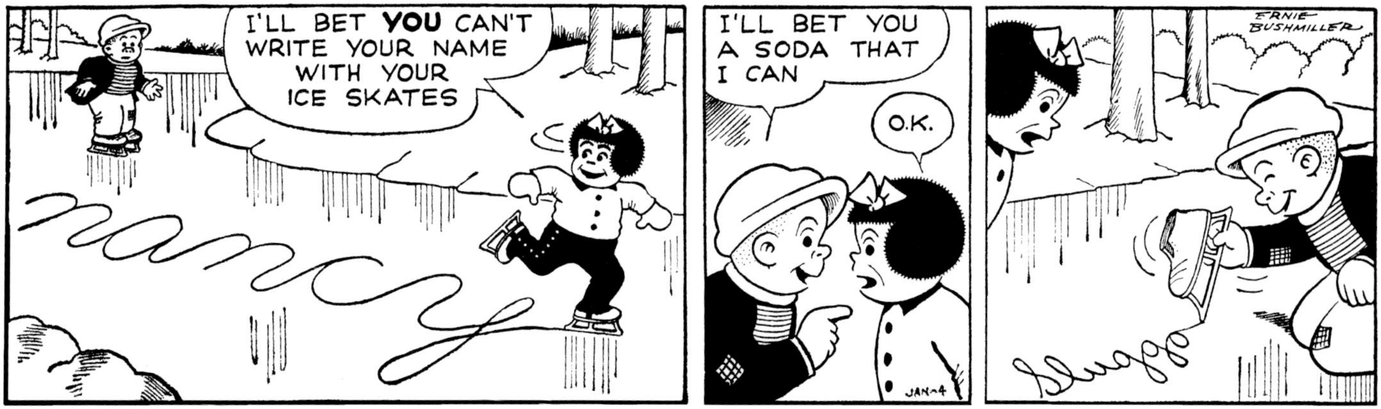
I'LL BET **YOU** CAN'T WRITE YOUR NAME WITH YOUR ICE SKATES
nancy
I'LL BET YOU A SODA THAT I CAN
O.K.
JAN-4
ERNIE BUSHMILLER

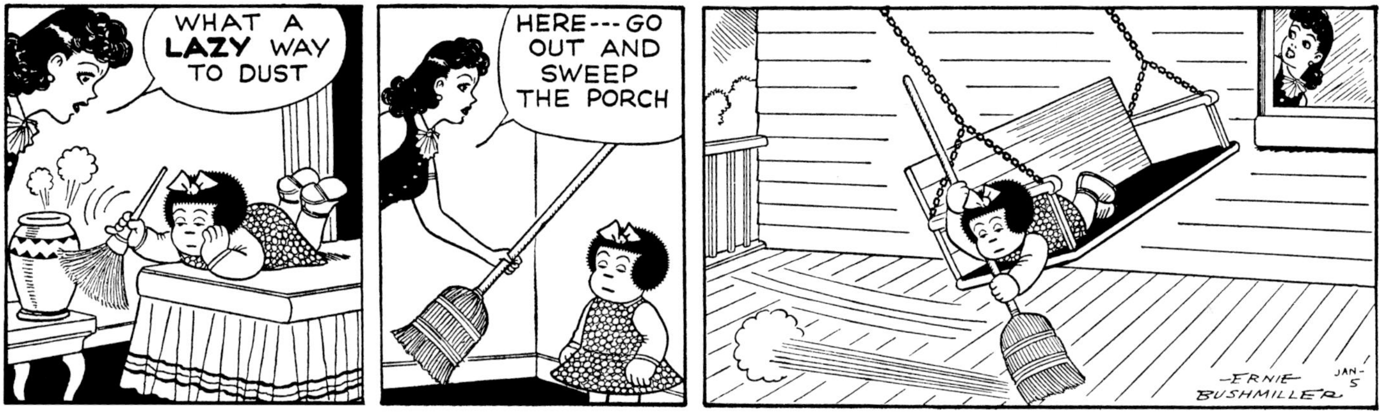
WHAT A **LAZY** WAY TO DUST
HERE---GO OUT AND SWEEP THE PORCH
JAN-5
ERNIE BUSHMILLER

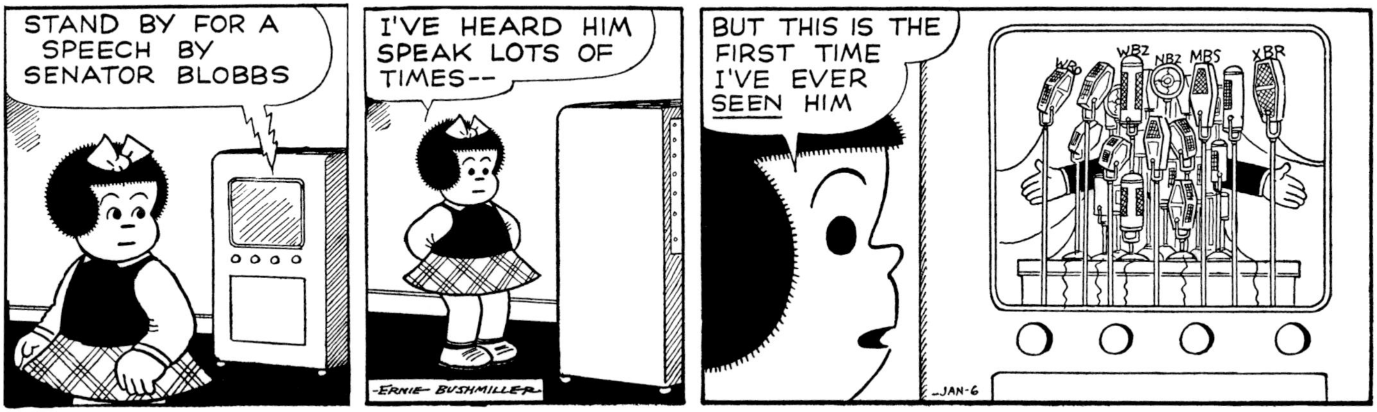
STAND BY FOR A SPEECH BY SENATOR BLOBBS
I'VE HEARD HIM SPEAK LOTS OF TIMES--
ERNIE BUSHMILLER
BUT THIS IS THE FIRST TIME I'VE EVER SEEN HIM
WBZ NBZ MBS XBR
JAN-6

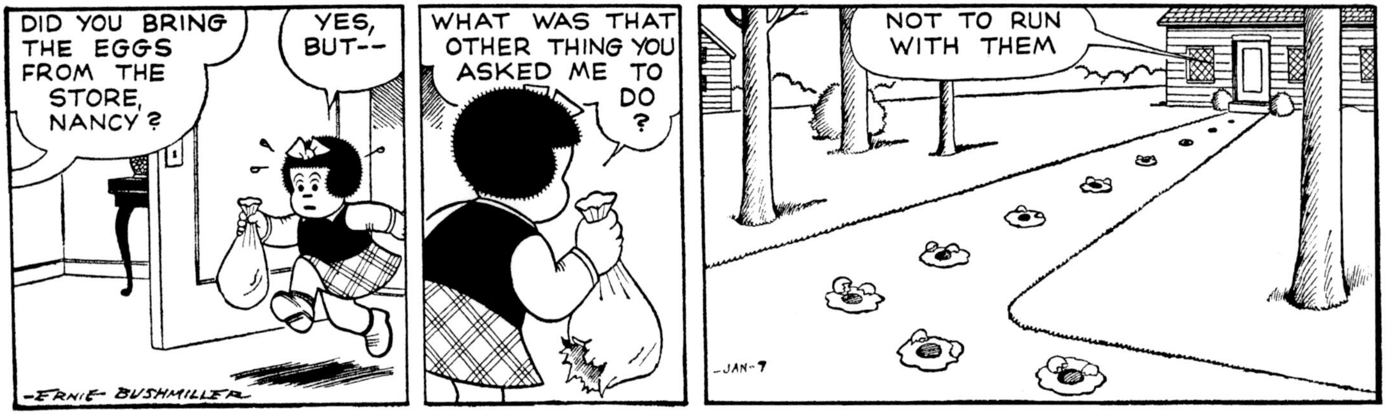
DID YOU BRING THE EGGS FROM THE STORE, NANCY?
YES, BUT--
ERNIE BUSHMILLER
WHAT WAS THAT OTHER THING YOU ASKED ME TO DO?
NOT TO RUN WITH THEM
JAN-7

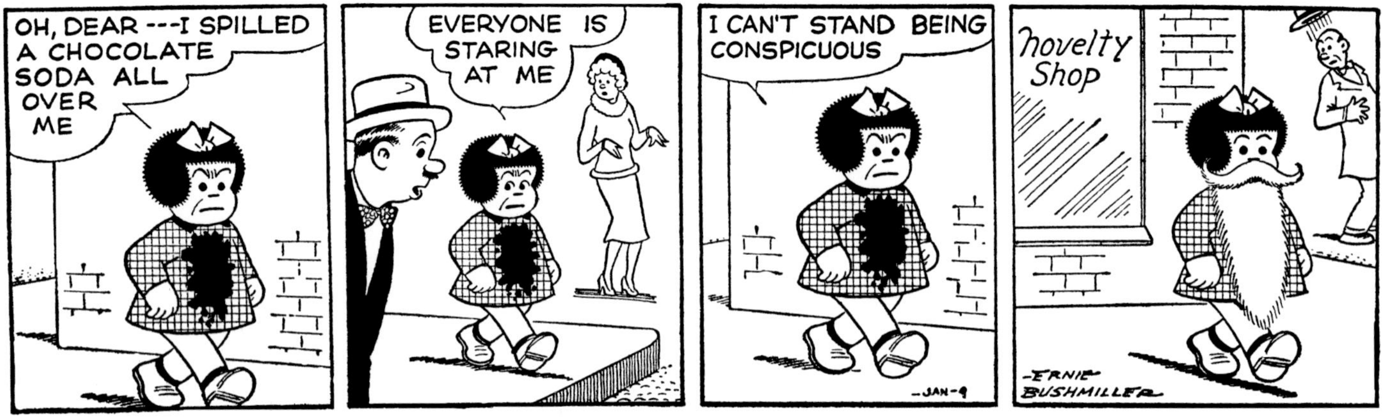
OH, DEAR---I SPILLED A CHOCOLATE SODA ALL OVER ME
EVERYONE IS STARING AT ME
I CAN'T STAND BEING CONSPICUOUS
JAN-9
Novelty Shop
ERNIE BUSHMILLER

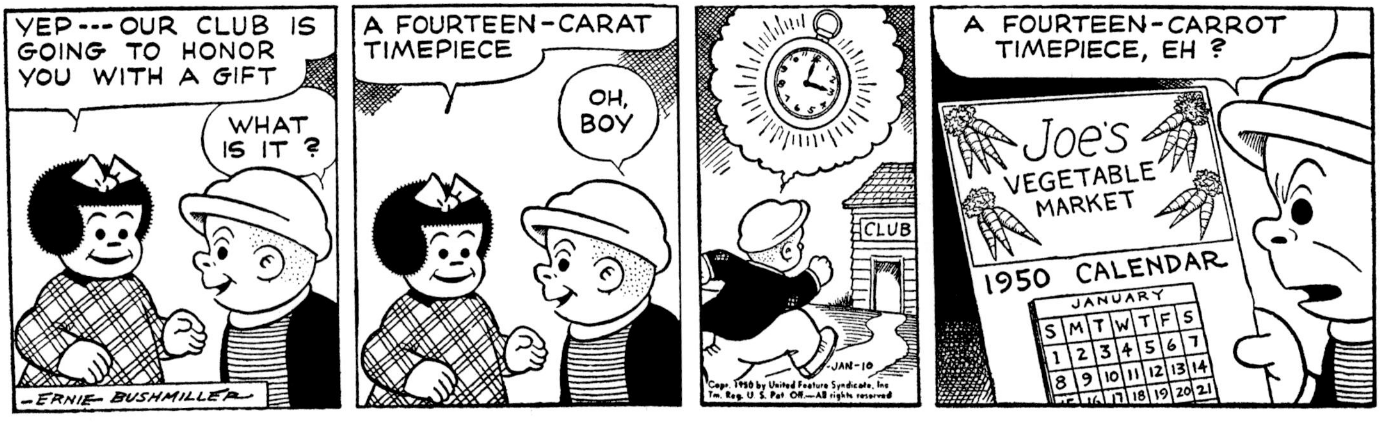
YEP---OUR CLUB IS GOING TO HONOR YOU WITH A GIFT
WHAT IS IT?
ERNIE BUSHMILLER
A FOURTEEN-CARAT TIMEPIECE
OH, BOY
CLUB
JAN-10
Copr. 1950 by United Feature Syndicate, Inc
Tm. Reg. U S. Pat Off.—All rights reserved
A FOURTEEN-CARROT TIMEPIECE, EH?
Joe's VEGETABLE MARKET
1950 CALENDAR
JANUARY

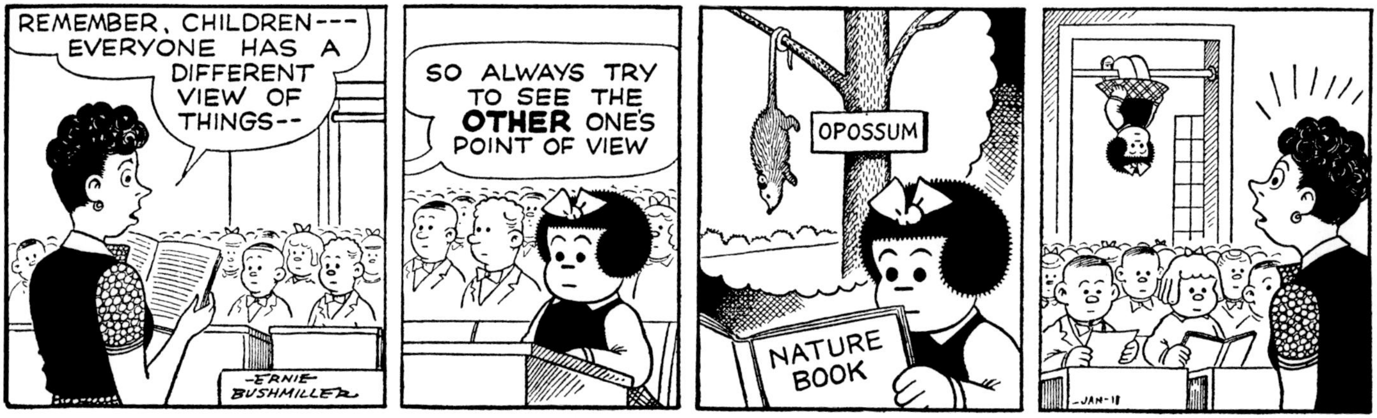
REMEMBER, CHILDREN--- EVERYONE HAS A DIFFERENT VIEW OF THINGS--
-ERNIE BUSHMILLER
SO ALWAYS TRY TO SEE THE **OTHER** ONE'S POINT OF VIEW
OPOSSUM
NATURE BOOK
-JAN-18

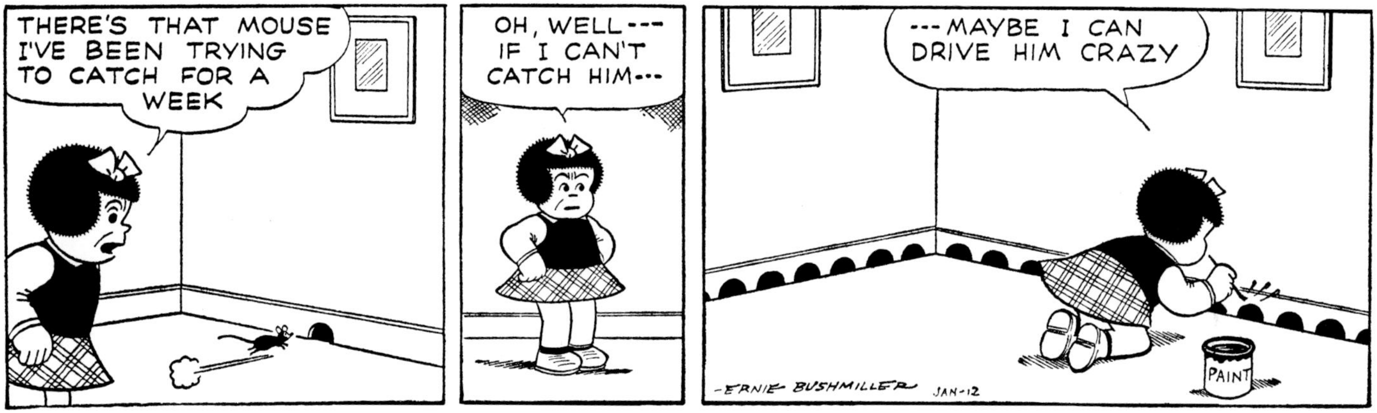
THERE'S THAT MOUSE I'VE BEEN TRYING TO CATCH FOR A WEEK
OH, WELL--- IF I CAN'T CATCH HIM---
---MAYBE I CAN DRIVE HIM CRAZY
PAINT
-ERNIE BUSHMILLER JAN-12

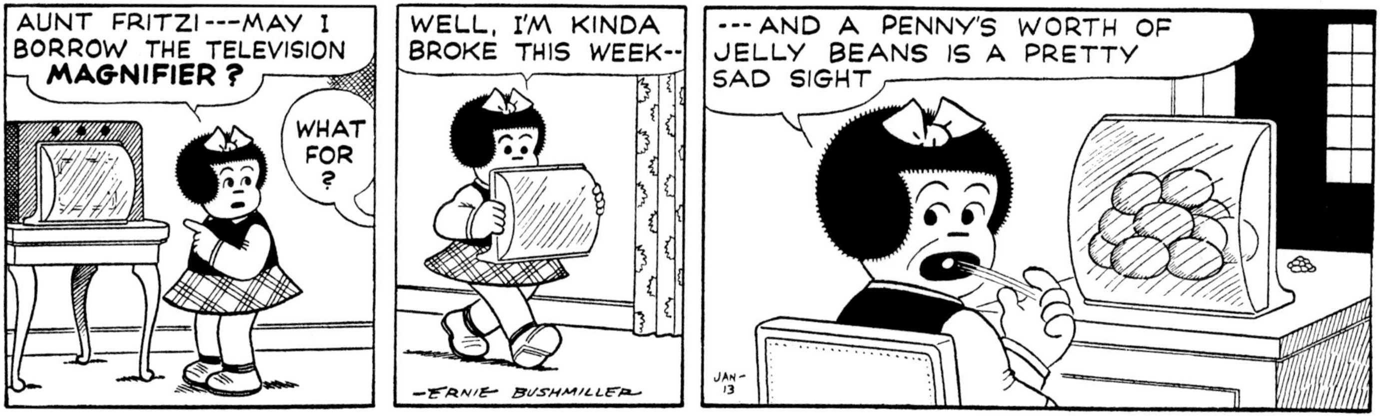
AUNT FRITZI---MAY I BORROW THE TELEVISION **MAGNIFIER ?**
WHAT FOR ?
WELL, I'M KINDA BROKE THIS WEEK--
-ERNIE BUSHMILLER
---AND A PENNY'S WORTH OF JELLY BEANS IS A PRETTY SAD SIGHT
JAN-13

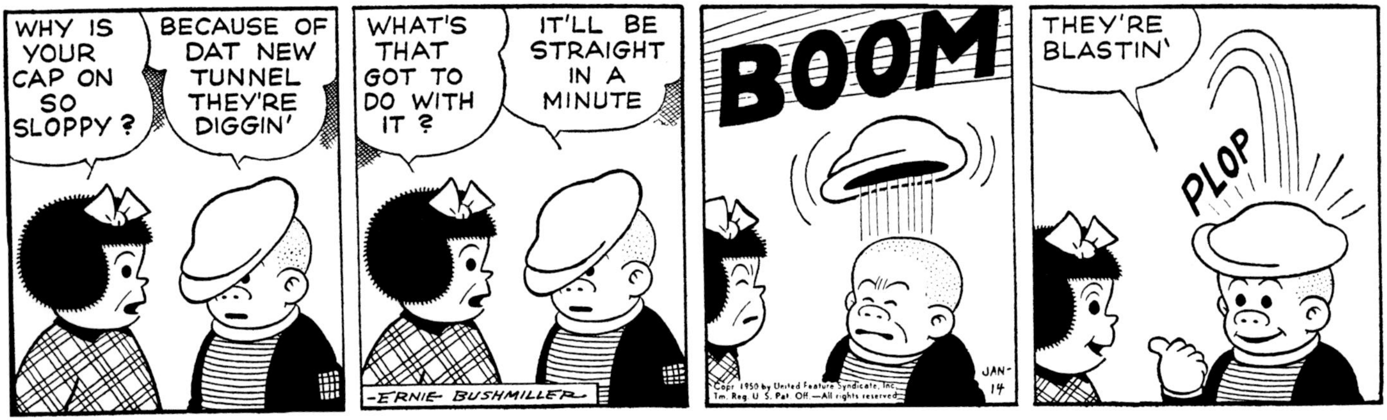
WHY IS YOUR CAP ON SO SLOPPY ?
BECAUSE OF DAT NEW TUNNEL THEY'RE DIGGIN'
WHAT'S THAT GOT TO DO WITH IT ?
IT'LL BE STRAIGHT IN A MINUTE
-ERNIE BUSHMILLER
BOOM
JAN-14
Copr. 1950 by United Feature Syndicate, Inc.
Tm. Reg. U. S. Pat. Off.—All rights reserved
THEY'RE BLASTIN'
PLOP

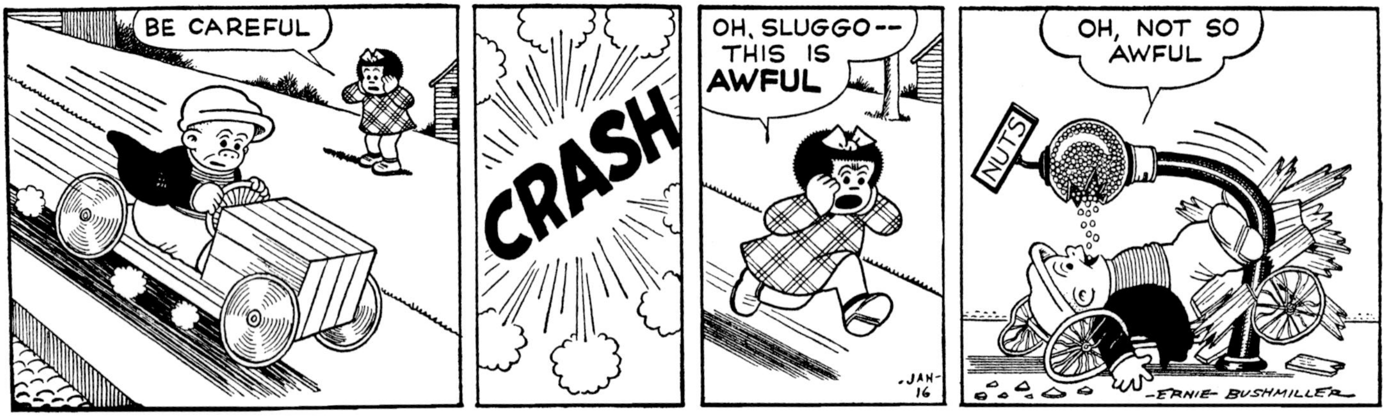
BE CAREFUL
CRASH
OH, SLUGGO-- THIS IS AWFUL
JAN-16
OH, NOT SO AWFUL
NUTS
-ERNIE BUSHMILLER

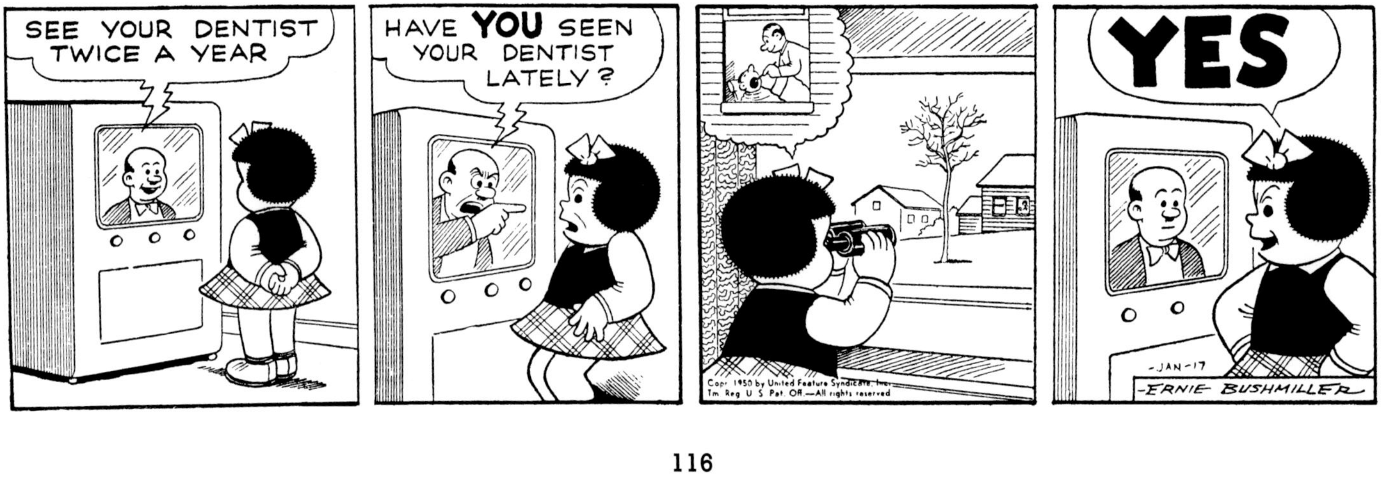
SEE YOUR DENTIST TWICE A YEAR
HAVE YOU SEEN YOUR DENTIST LATELY ?
Copr. 1950 by United Feature Syndicate, Inc.
Tm. Reg. U. S. Pat. Off.—All rights reserved
YES
JAN-17
-ERNIE BUSHMILLER

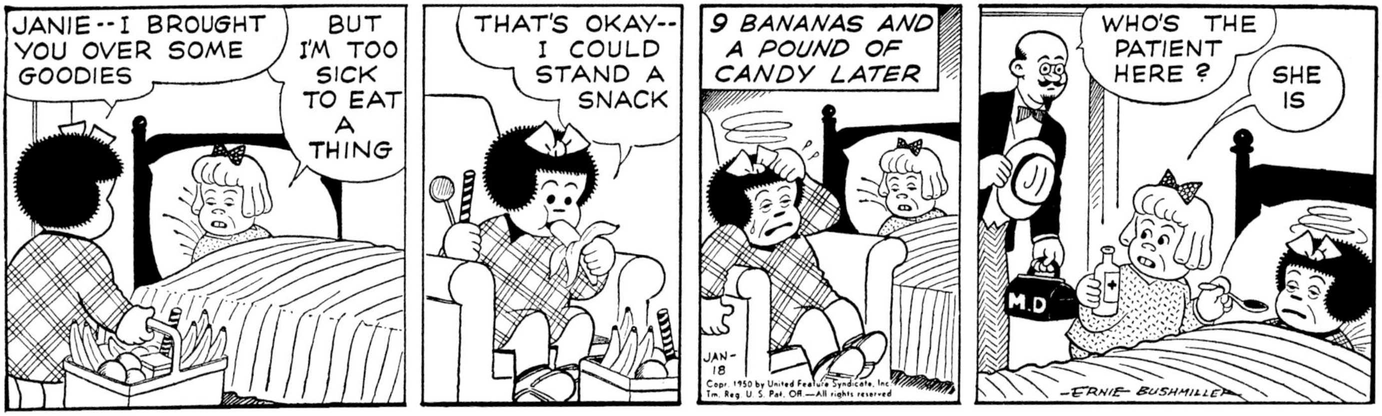
JANIE--I BROUGHT YOU OVER SOME GOODIES
BUT I'M TOO SICK TO EAT A THING
THAT'S OKAY-- I COULD STAND A SNACK
9 BANANAS AND A POUND OF CANDY LATER
JAN-18
Copr. 1950 by United Feature Syndicate, Inc. Tm. Reg. U. S. Pat. Off.—All rights reserved
WHO'S THE PATIENT HERE ?
SHE IS
M.D
-ERNIE BUSHMILLER

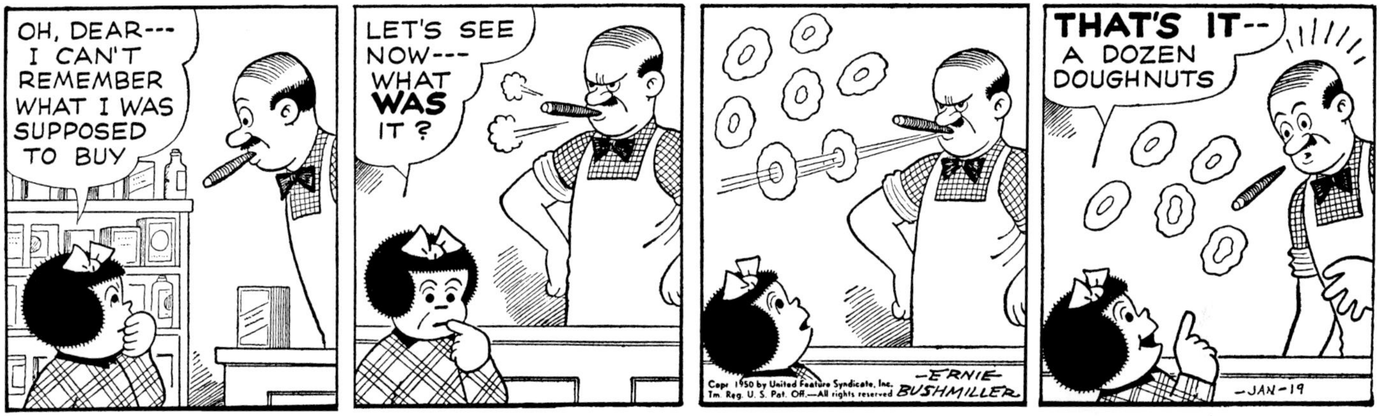
OH, DEAR--- I CAN'T REMEMBER WHAT I WAS SUPPOSED TO BUY
LET'S SEE NOW--- WHAT WAS IT ?
Copr. 1950 by United Feature Syndicate, Inc. Tm. Reg. U. S. Pat. Off.—All rights reserved
-ERNIE BUSHMILLER
THAT'S IT-- A DOZEN DOUGHNUTS
-JAN-19

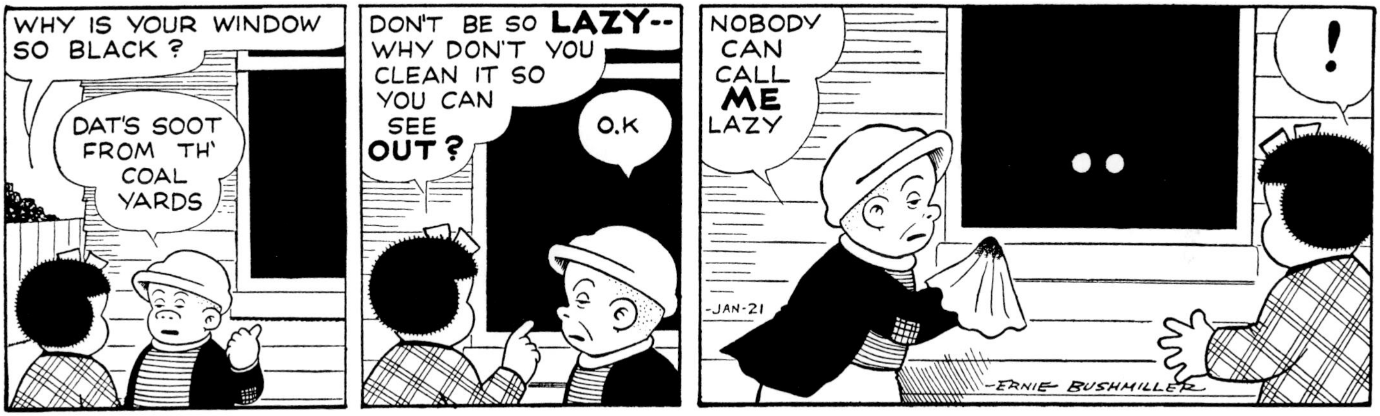
WHY IS YOUR WINDOW SO BLACK ?
DAT'S SOOT FROM TH' COAL YARDS
DON'T BE SO LAZY-- WHY DON'T YOU CLEAN IT SO YOU CAN SEE OUT ?
O.K
-JAN-21
NOBODY CAN CALL ME LAZY
!
-ERNIE BUSHMILLER

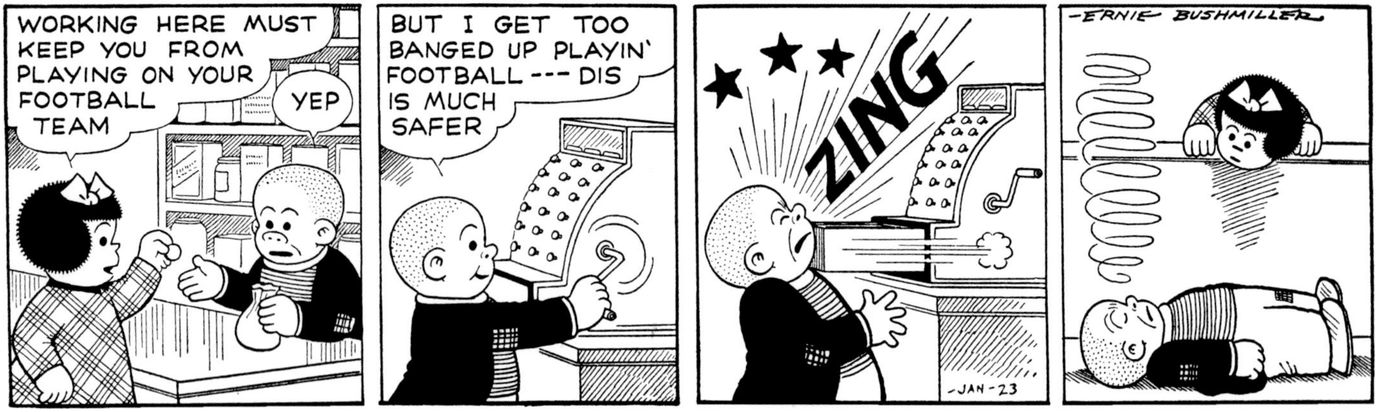
WORKING HERE MUST KEEP YOU FROM PLAYING ON YOUR FOOTBALL TEAM
YEP
BUT I GET TOO BANGED UP PLAYIN' FOOTBALL --- DIS IS MUCH SAFER
ZING
-JAN-23
-ERNIE BUSHMILLER

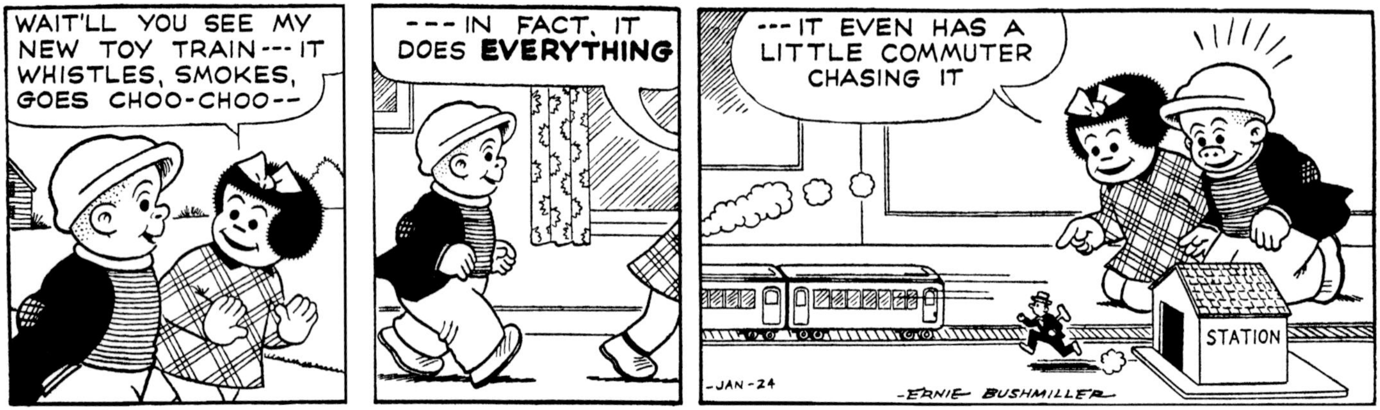
WAIT'LL YOU SEE MY NEW TOY TRAIN --- IT WHISTLES, SMOKES, GOES CHOO-CHOO--
--- IN FACT, IT DOES **EVERYTHING**
--- IT EVEN HAS A LITTLE COMMUTER CHASING IT
STATION
-JAN-24
-ERNIE BUSHMILLER

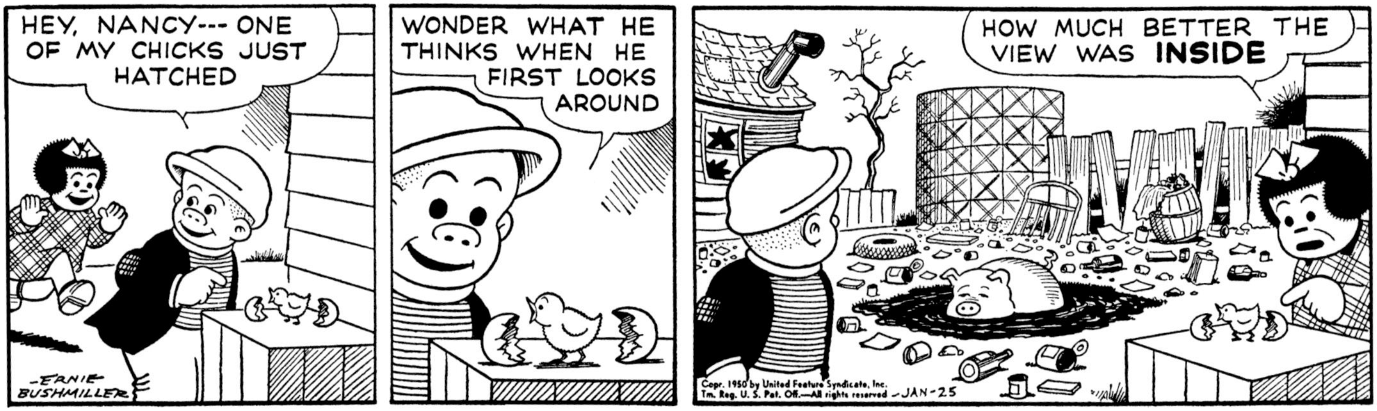
HEY, NANCY--- ONE OF MY CHICKS JUST HATCHED
-ERNIE BUSHMILLER
WONDER WHAT HE THINKS WHEN HE FIRST LOOKS AROUND
HOW MUCH BETTER THE VIEW WAS **INSIDE**
Copr. 1950 by United Feature Syndicate, Inc. Tm. Reg. U. S. Pat. Off.—All rights reserved
-JAN-25

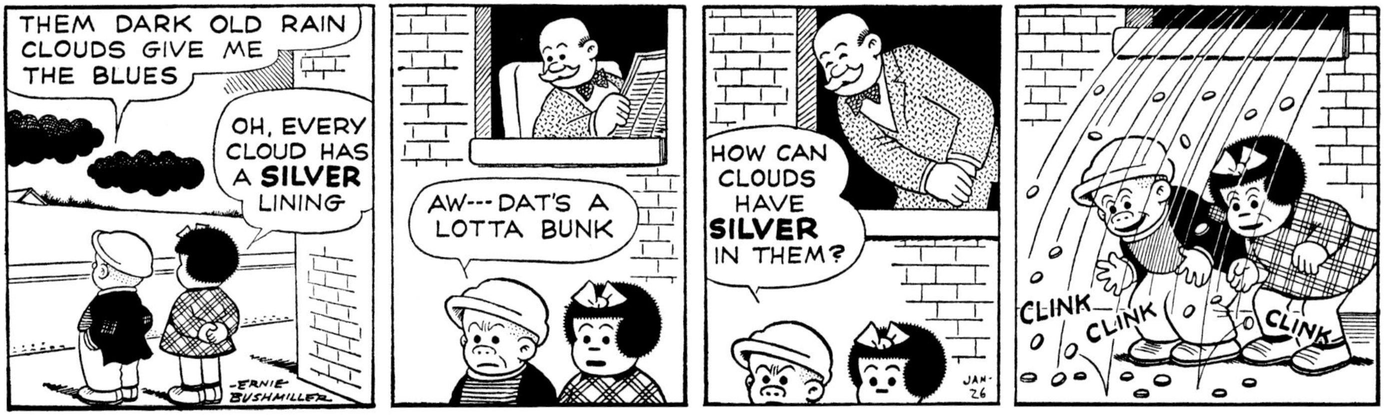
THEM DARK OLD RAIN CLOUDS GIVE ME THE BLUES
OH, EVERY CLOUD HAS A **SILVER** LINING
-ERNIE BUSHMILLER
AW---DAT'S A LOTTA BUNK
HOW CAN CLOUDS HAVE **SILVER** IN THEM?
JAN-26
CLINK
CLINK
CLINK

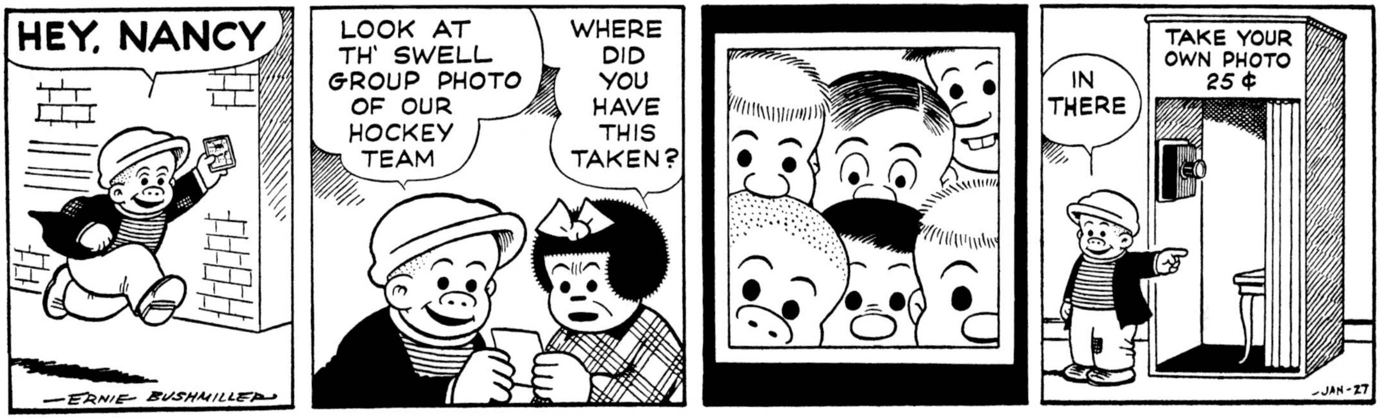
HEY, NANCY
-ERNIE BUSHMILLER
LOOK AT TH' SWELL GROUP PHOTO OF OUR HOCKEY TEAM
WHERE DID YOU HAVE THIS TAKEN?
IN THERE
TAKE YOUR OWN PHOTO 25¢
-JAN-27

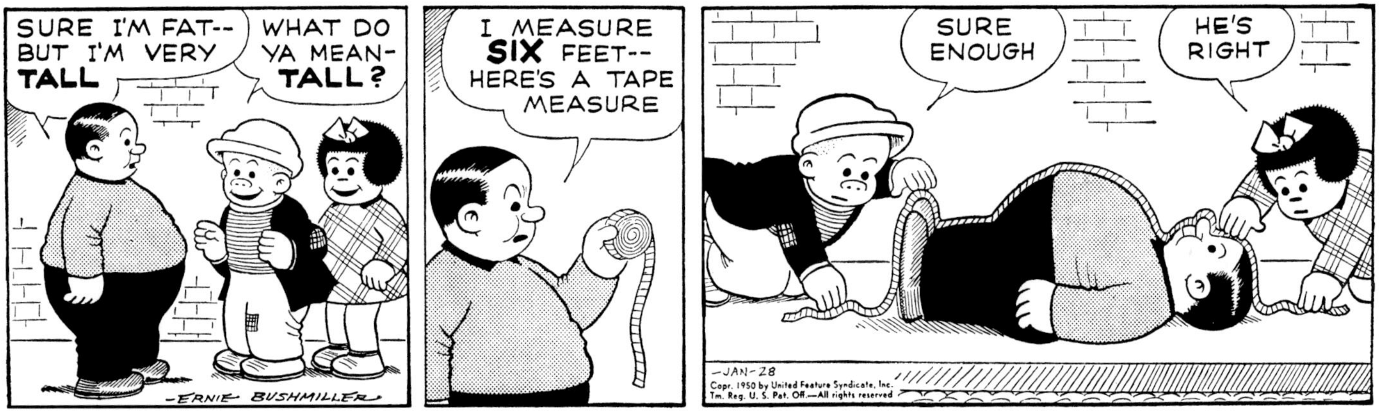
SURE I'M FAT-- BUT I'M VERY **TALL**
WHAT DO YA MEAN- **TALL**?
-ERNIE BUSHMILLER
I MEASURE **SIX** FEET-- HERE'S A TAPE MEASURE
SURE ENOUGH
HE'S RIGHT
-JAN-28
Copr. 1950 by United Feature Syndicate, Inc.
Tm. Reg. U. S. Pat. Off.—All rights reserved

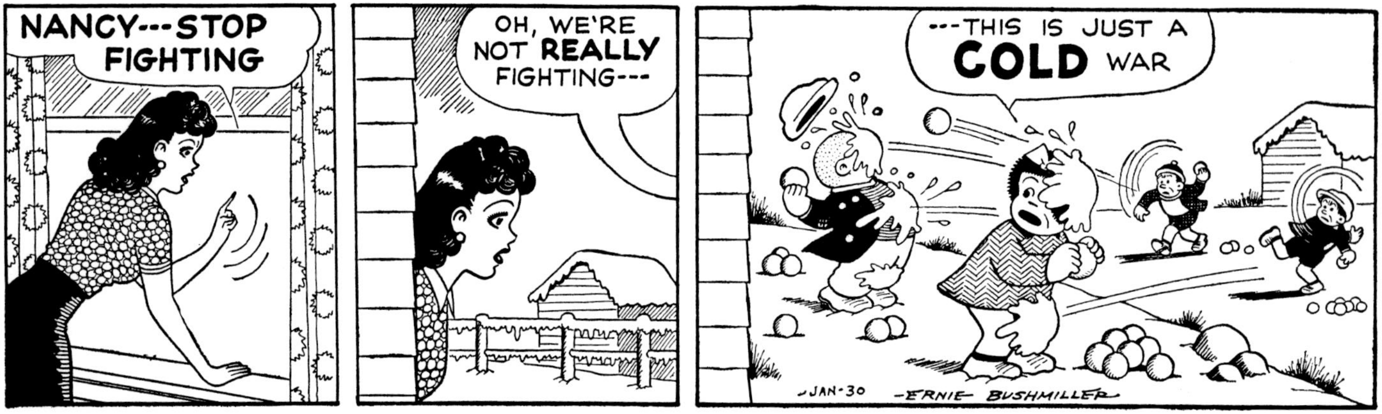
NANCY---STOP FIGHTING
OH, WE'RE NOT **REALLY** FIGHTING---
---THIS IS JUST A **COLD** WAR
JAN-30
ERNIE BUSHMILLER

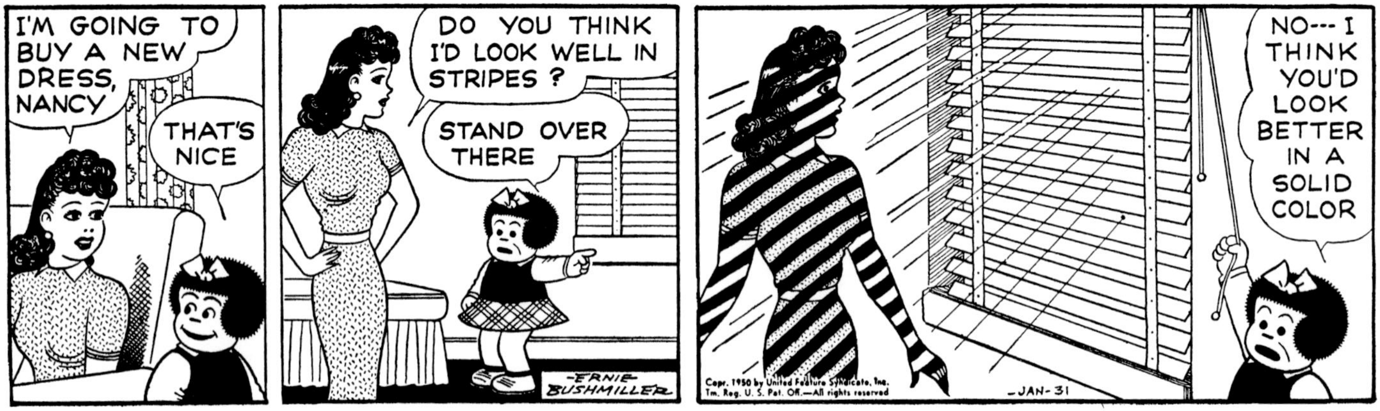
I'M GOING TO BUY A NEW DRESS, NANCY
THAT'S NICE
DO YOU THINK I'D LOOK WELL IN STRIPES ?
STAND OVER THERE
ERNIE BUSHMILLER
Copr. 1950 by United Feature Syndicate, Inc.
Tm. Reg. U. S. Pat. Off.—All rights reserved
JAN-31
NO---I THINK YOU'D LOOK BETTER IN A SOLID COLOR

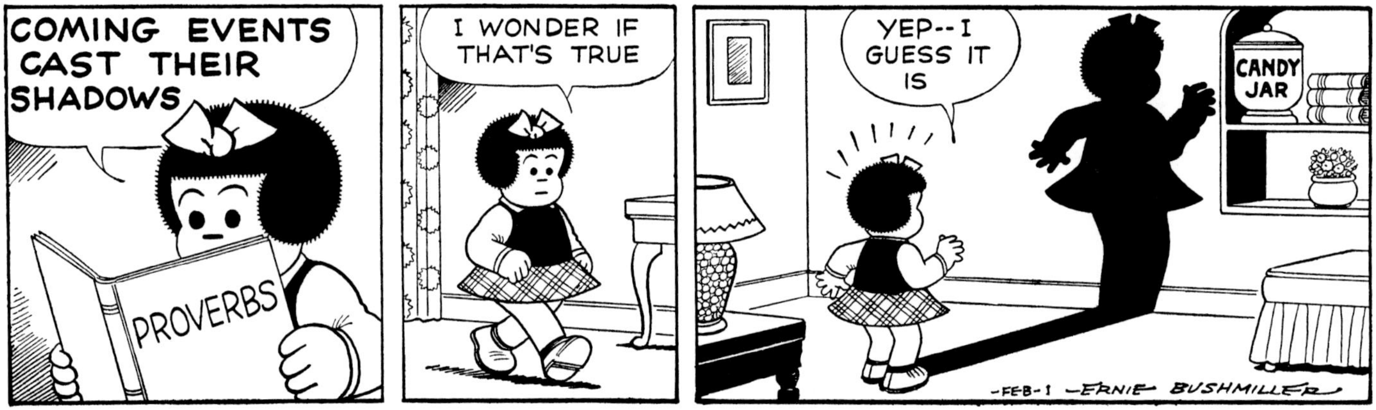
COMING EVENTS CAST THEIR SHADOWS
PROVERBS
I WONDER IF THAT'S TRUE
YEP--I GUESS IT IS
CANDY JAR
FEB-1
ERNIE BUSHMILLER

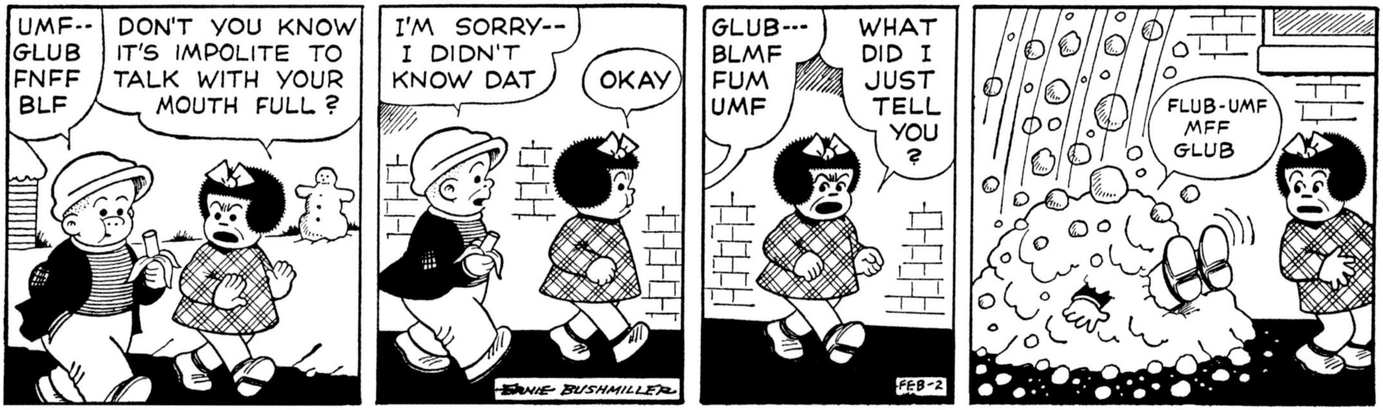
UMF-- GLUB FNFF BLF
DON'T YOU KNOW IT'S IMPOLITE TO TALK WITH YOUR MOUTH FULL ?
I'M SORRY-- I DIDN'T KNOW DAT
OKAY
ERNIE BUSHMILLER
GLUB--- BLMF FUM UMF
WHAT DID I JUST TELL YOU ?
FEB-2
FLUB-UMF MFF GLUB

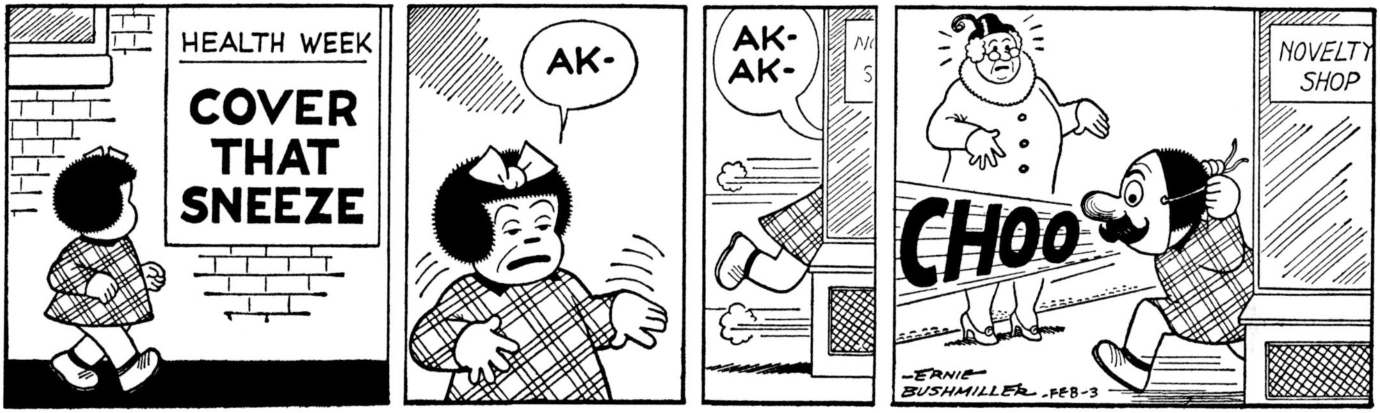
HEALTH WEEK
COVER THAT SNEEZE
AK-
AK- AK-
NOVELTY SHOP
CHOO
ERNIE BUSHMILLER FEB-3

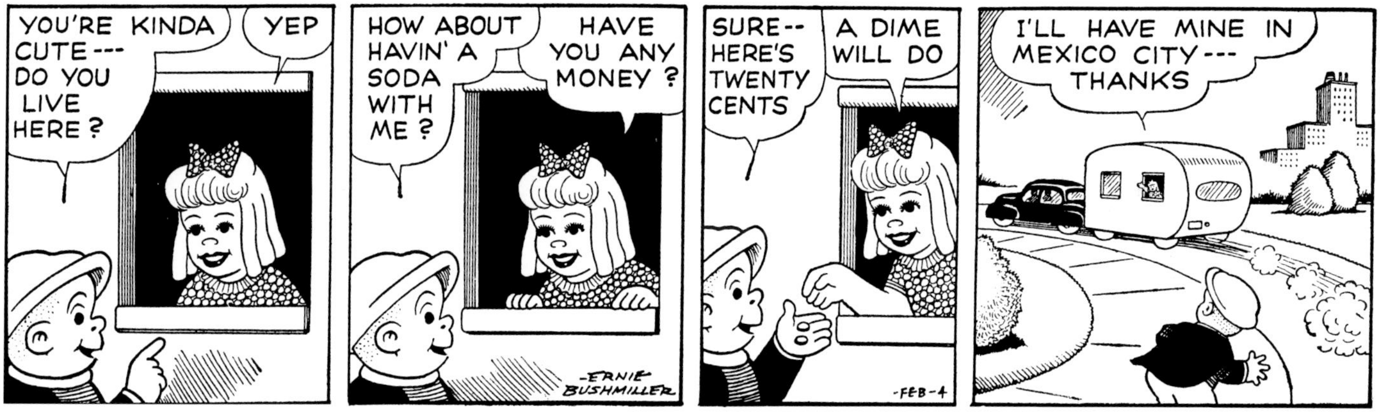
YOU'RE KINDA CUTE--- DO YOU LIVE HERE ?
YEP
HOW ABOUT HAVIN' A SODA WITH ME ?
HAVE YOU ANY MONEY ?
ERNIE BUSHMILLER
SURE-- HERE'S TWENTY CENTS
A DIME WILL DO
FEB-4
I'LL HAVE MINE IN MEXICO CITY--- THANKS

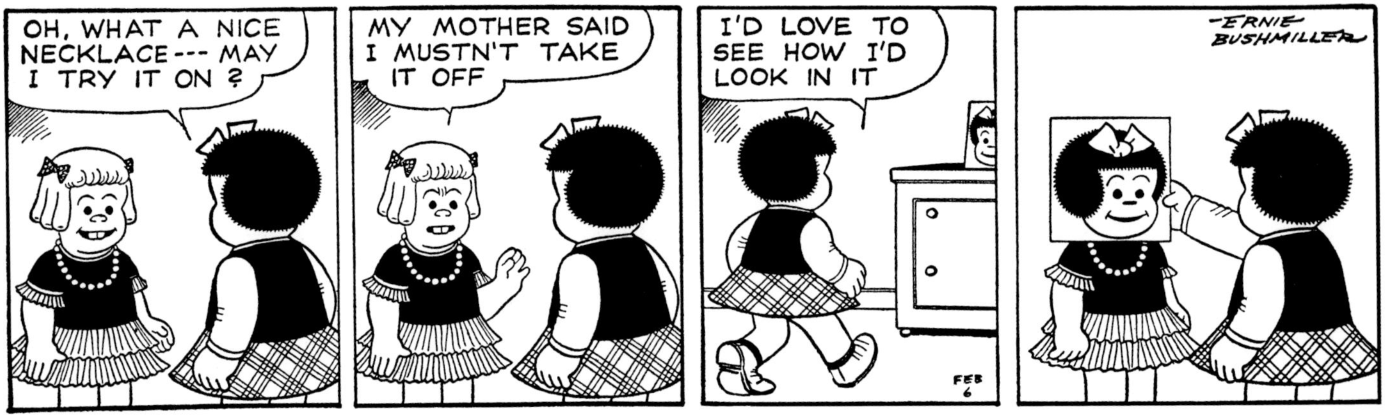
OH, WHAT A NICE NECKLACE --- MAY I TRY IT ON ?
MY MOTHER SAID I MUSTN'T TAKE IT OFF
I'D LOVE TO SEE HOW I'D LOOK IN IT
FEB 6
ERNIE BUSHMILLER

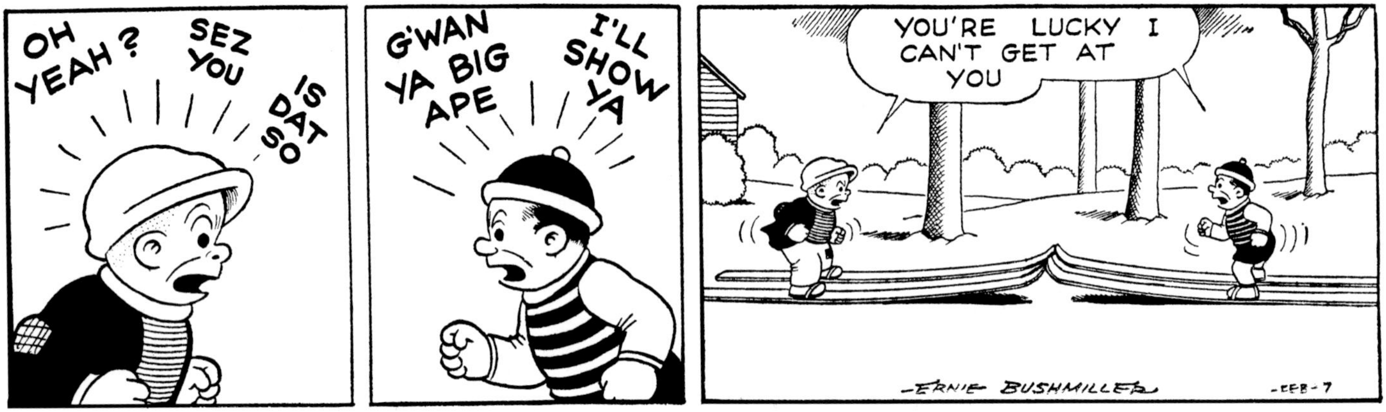
OH YEAH ?
SEZ YOU
IS DAT SO
G'WAN YA BIG APE
I'LL SHOW YA
YOU'RE LUCKY I CAN'T GET AT YOU
ERNIE BUSHMILLER
FEB-7

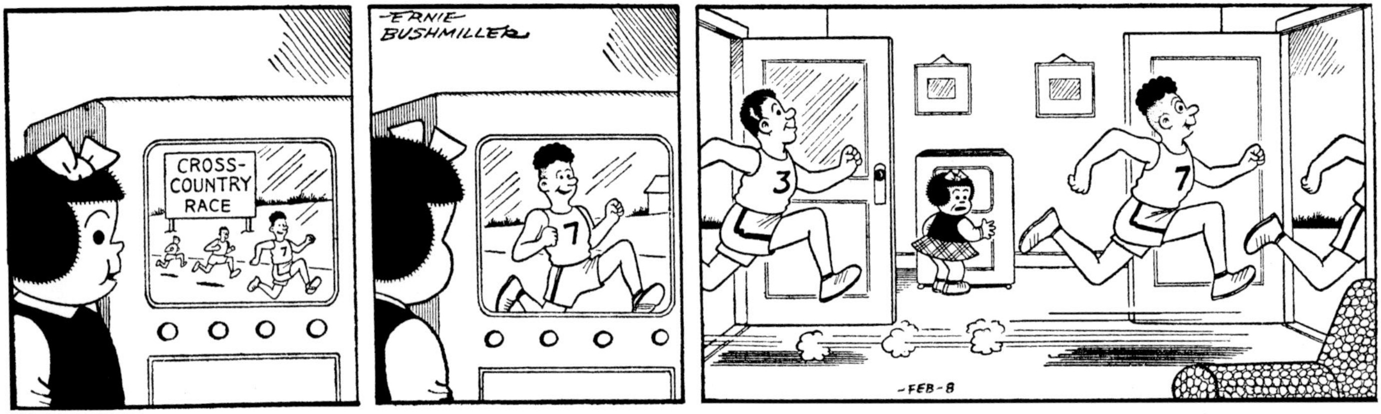
CROSS-COUNTRY RACE
7
ERNIE BUSHMILLER
7
3
7
FEB-8

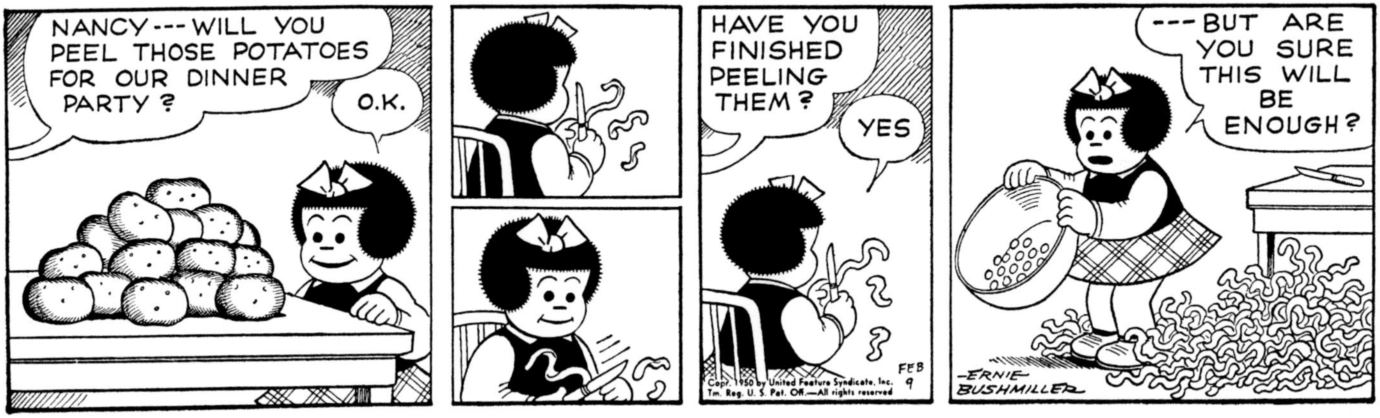
NANCY---WILL YOU PEEL THOSE POTATOES FOR OUR DINNER PARTY ?
O.K.
HAVE YOU FINISHED PEELING THEM ?
YES
FEB 9
Copr. 1950 by United Feature Syndicate, Inc. Tm. Reg. U. S. Pat. Off.—All rights reserved
---BUT ARE YOU SURE THIS WILL BE ENOUGH ?
-ERNIE BUSHMILLER

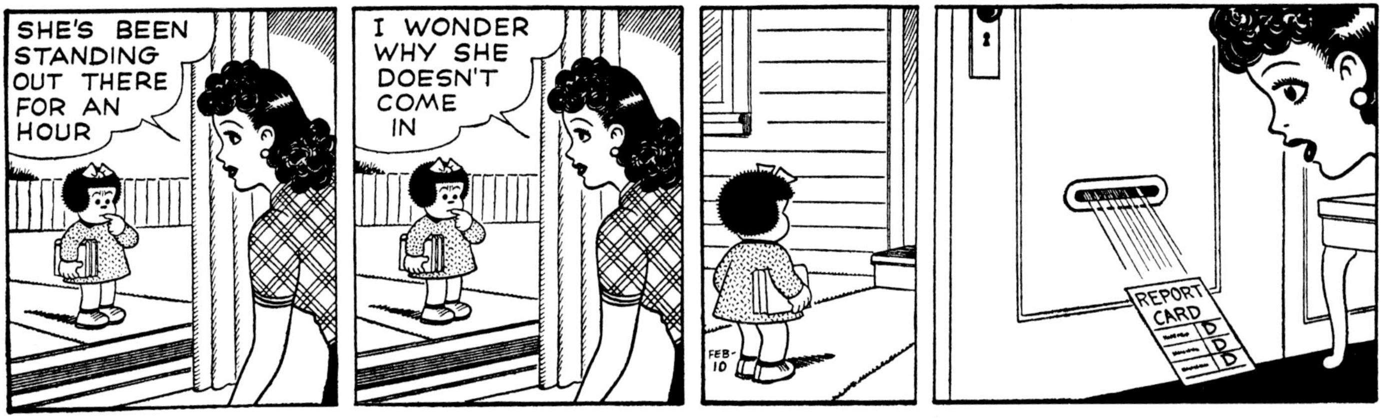
SHE'S BEEN STANDING OUT THERE FOR AN HOUR
I WONDER WHY SHE DOESN'T COME IN
FEB-10
REPORT CARD
D
D
D

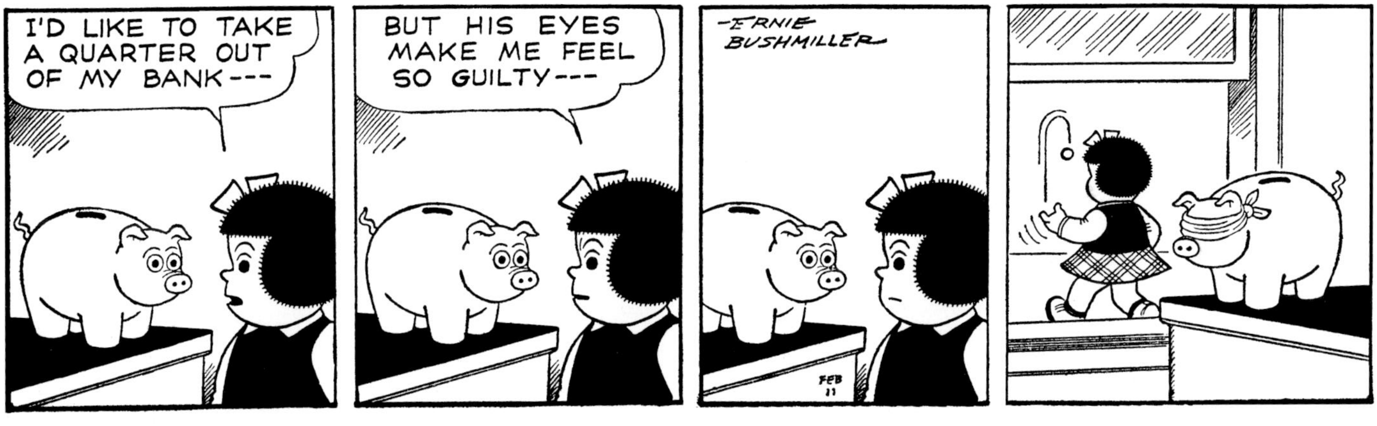
I'D LIKE TO TAKE A QUARTER OUT OF MY BANK---
BUT HIS EYES MAKE ME FEEL SO GUILTY---
-ERNIE BUSHMILLER
FEB 11

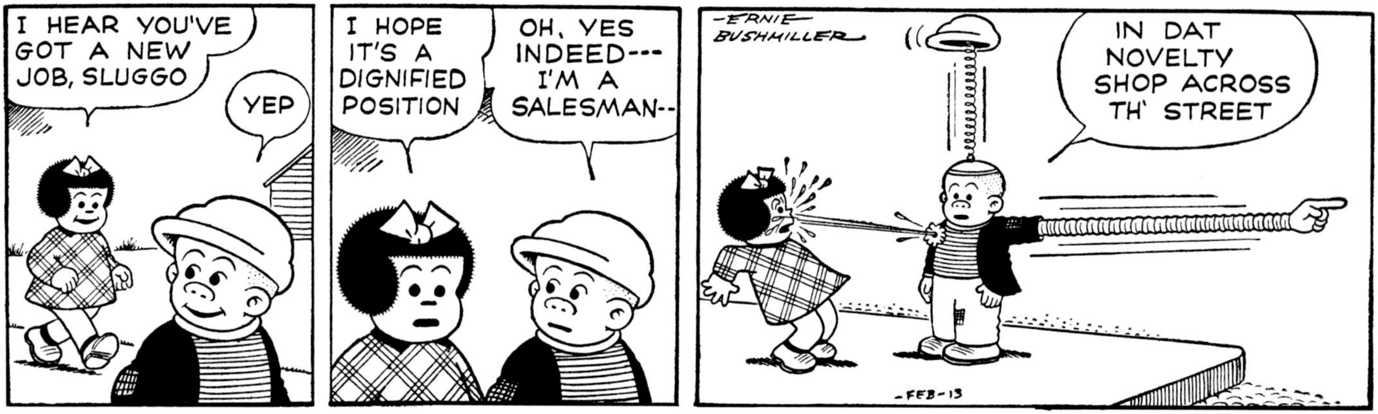
I HEAR YOU'VE GOT A NEW JOB, SLUGGO
YEP
I HOPE IT'S A DIGNIFIED POSITION
OH, YES INDEED--- I'M A SALESMAN--
-ERNIE BUSHMILLER
IN DAT NOVELTY SHOP ACROSS TH' STREET
-FEB-13

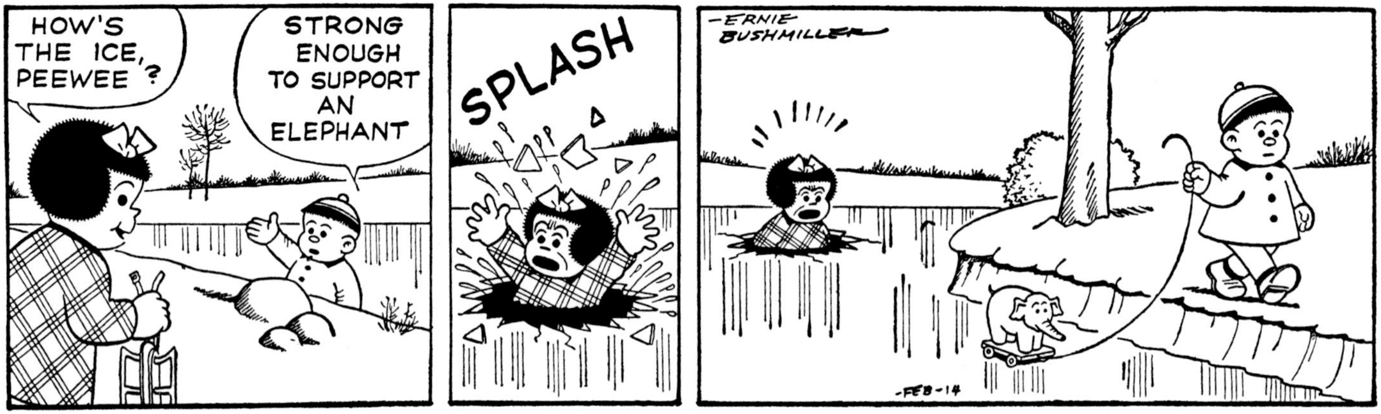
HOW'S THE ICE, PEEWEE ?
STRONG ENOUGH TO SUPPORT AN ELEPHANT
SPLASH
-ERNIE BUSHMILLER
-FEB-14

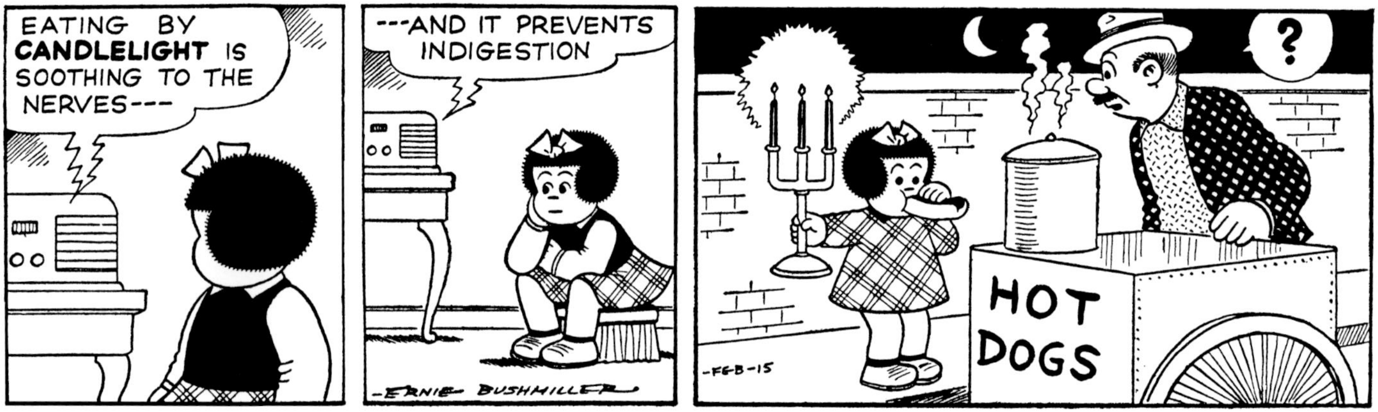
EATING BY **CANDLELIGHT** IS SOOTHING TO THE NERVES---
---AND IT PREVENTS INDIGESTION
-ERNIE BUSHMILLER
?
HOT DOGS
-FEB-15

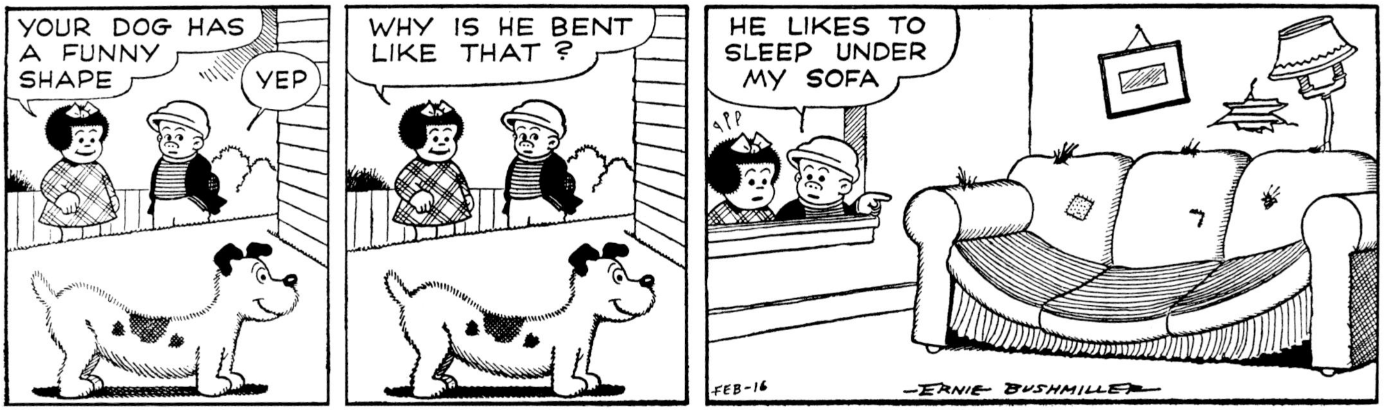
YOUR DOG HAS A FUNNY SHAPE
YEP
WHY IS HE BENT LIKE THAT ?
HE LIKES TO SLEEP UNDER MY SOFA
FEB-16
ERNIE BUSHMILLER

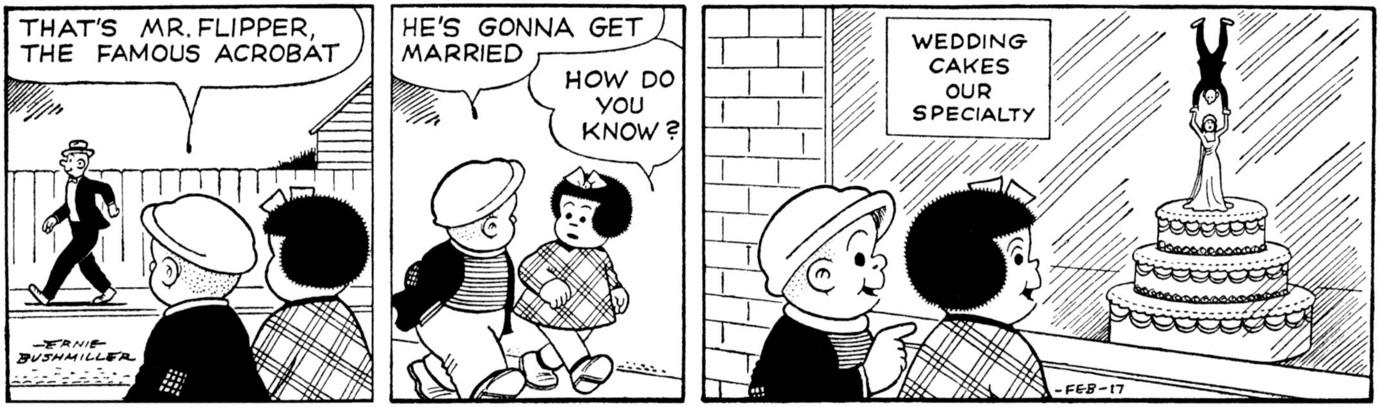
THAT'S MR. FLIPPER, THE FAMOUS ACROBAT
ERNIE BUSHMILLER
HE'S GONNA GET MARRIED
HOW DO YOU KNOW ?
WEDDING CAKES OUR SPECIALTY
FEB-17

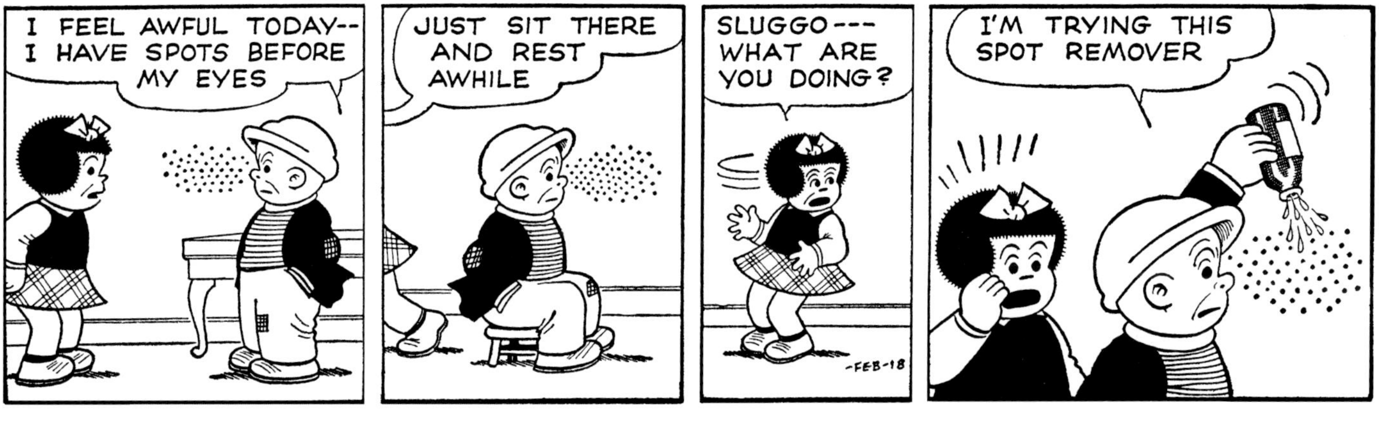
I FEEL AWFUL TODAY-- I HAVE SPOTS BEFORE MY EYES
JUST SIT THERE AND REST AWHILE
SLUGGO--- WHAT ARE YOU DOING ?
FEB-18
I'M TRYING THIS SPOT REMOVER

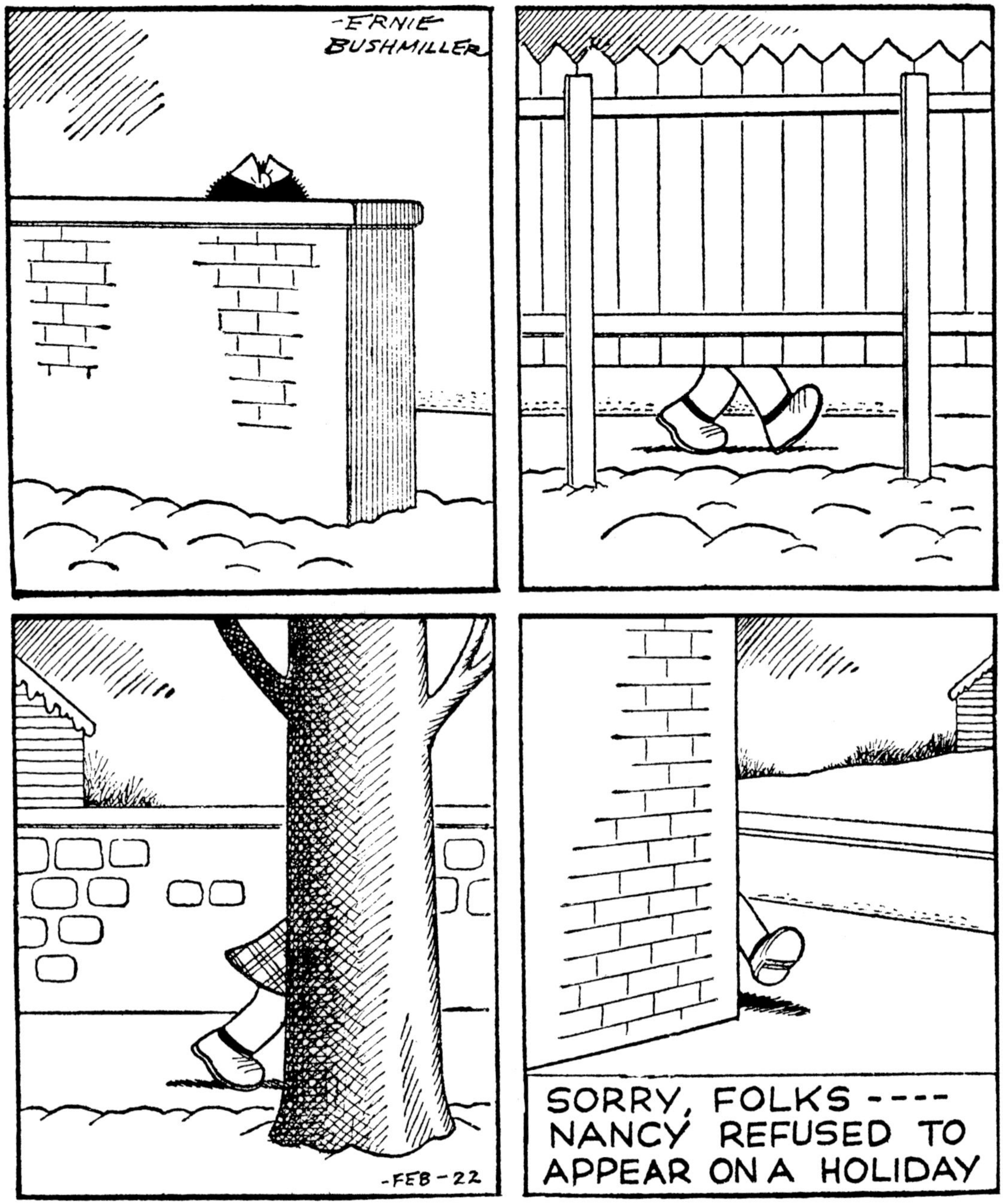
-ERNIE BUSHMILLER
-FEB-22
SORRY, FOLKS ----
NANCY REFUSED TO
APPEAR ON A HOLIDAY

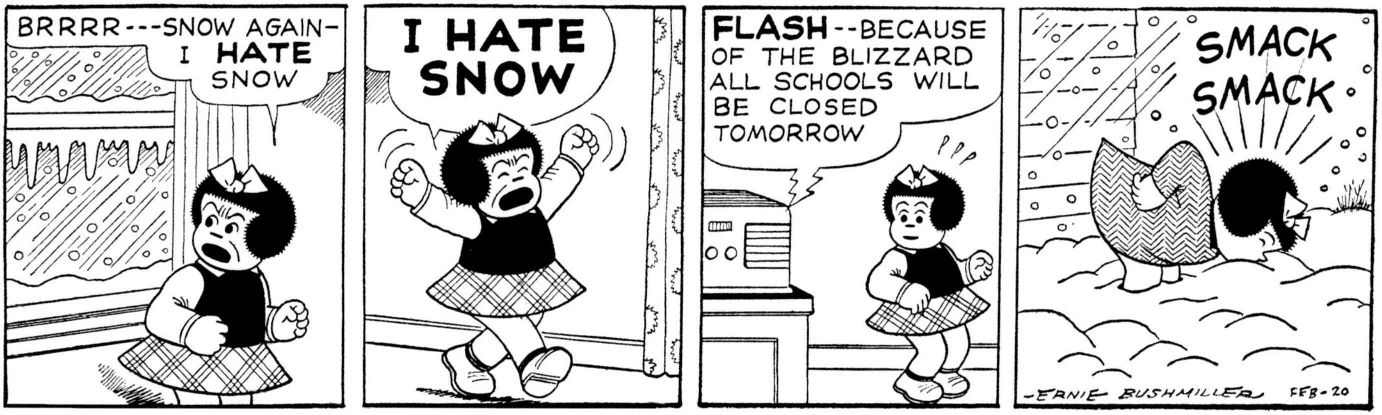
BRRRRR---SNOW AGAIN-- I HATE SNOW
I HATE SNOW
FLASH--BECAUSE OF THE BLIZZARD ALL SCHOOLS WILL BE CLOSED TOMORROW
SMACK SMACK
-ERNIE BUSHMILLER FEB-20

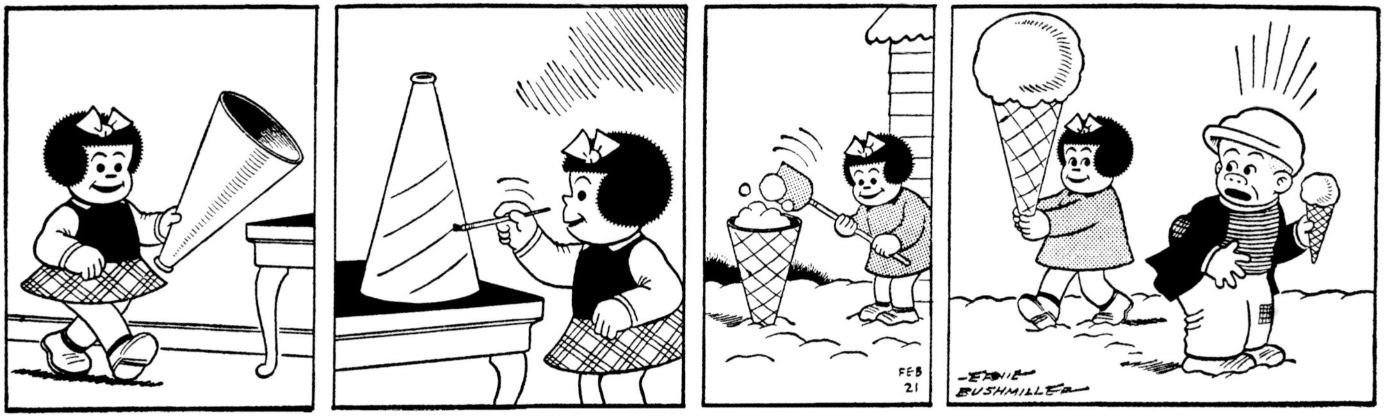
FEB 21
-ERNIE BUSHMILLER

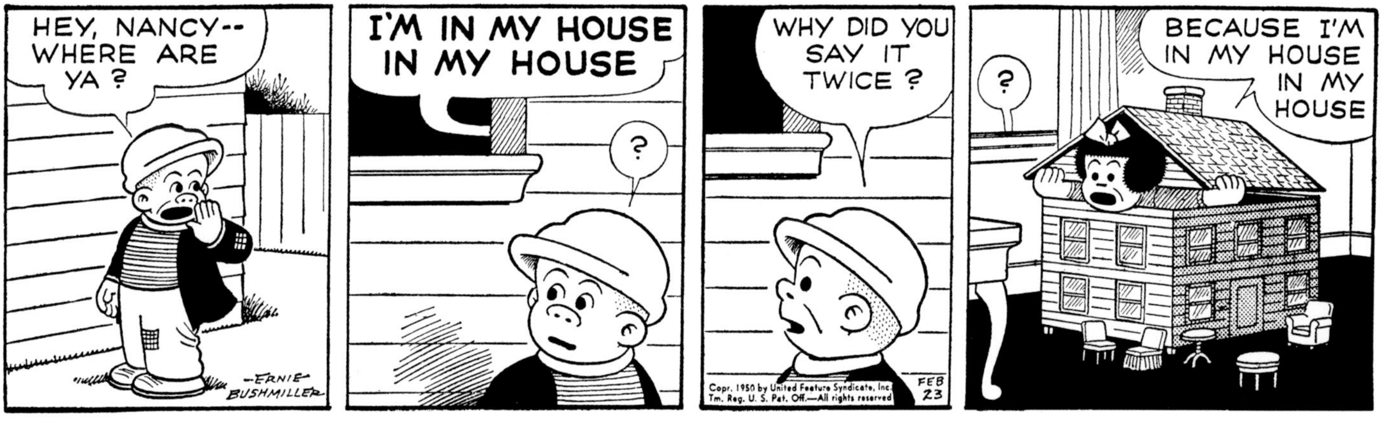
HEY, NANCY-- WHERE ARE YA ?
-ERNIE BUSHMILLER
I'M IN MY HOUSE IN MY HOUSE
?
WHY DID YOU SAY IT TWICE ?
Copr. 1950 by United Feature Syndicate, Inc. Tm. Reg. U. S. Pat. Off.—All rights reserved
FEB 23
?
BECAUSE I'M IN MY HOUSE IN MY HOUSE

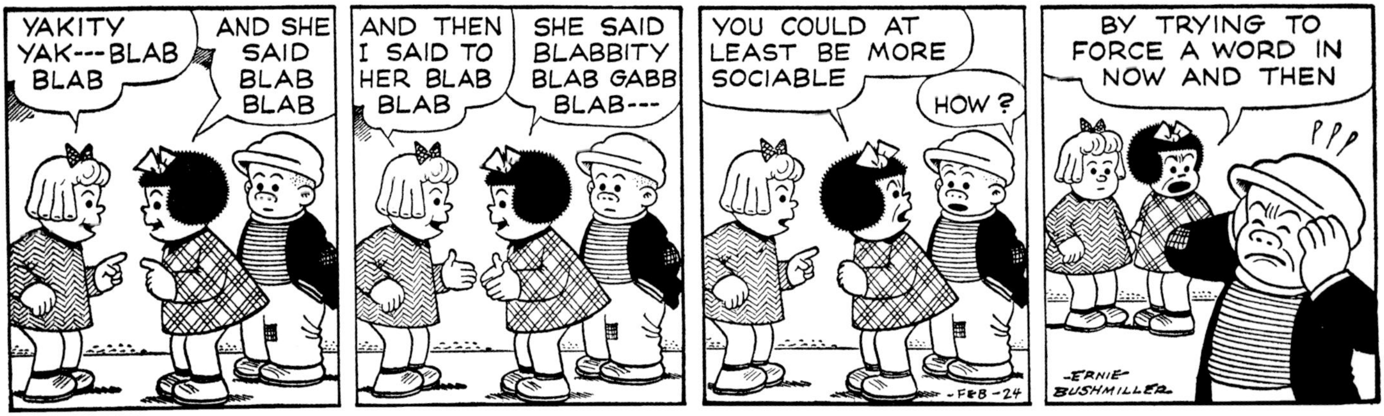
YAKITY YAK---BLAB BLAB
AND SHE SAID BLAB BLAB
AND THEN I SAID TO HER BLAB BLAB
SHE SAID BLABBITY BLAB GABB BLAB---
YOU COULD AT LEAST BE MORE SOCIABLE
HOW ?
BY TRYING TO FORCE A WORD IN NOW AND THEN
-FEB-24
-ERNIE BUSHMILLER

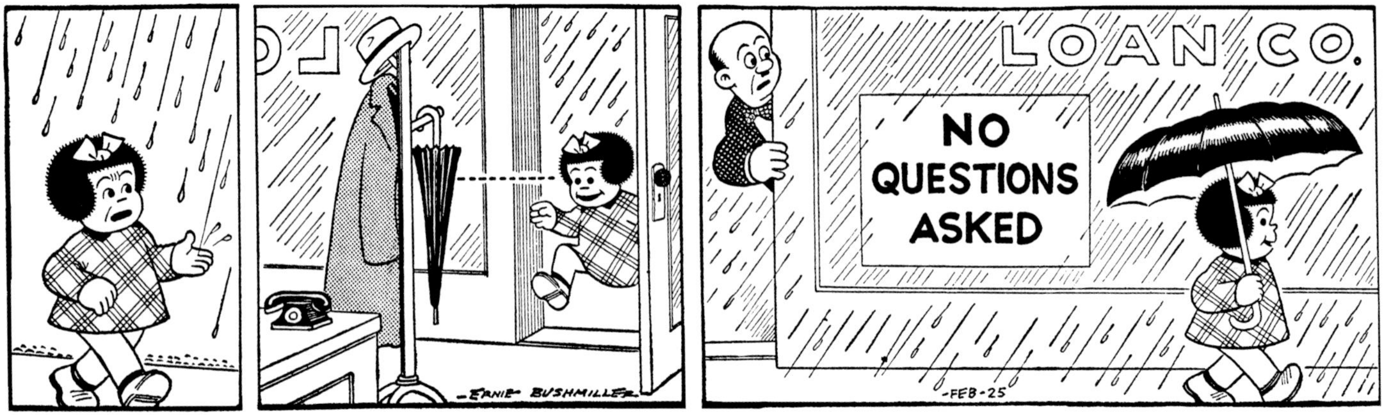
-ERNIE BUSHMILLER
LOAN CO.
NO QUESTIONS ASKED
-FEB-25

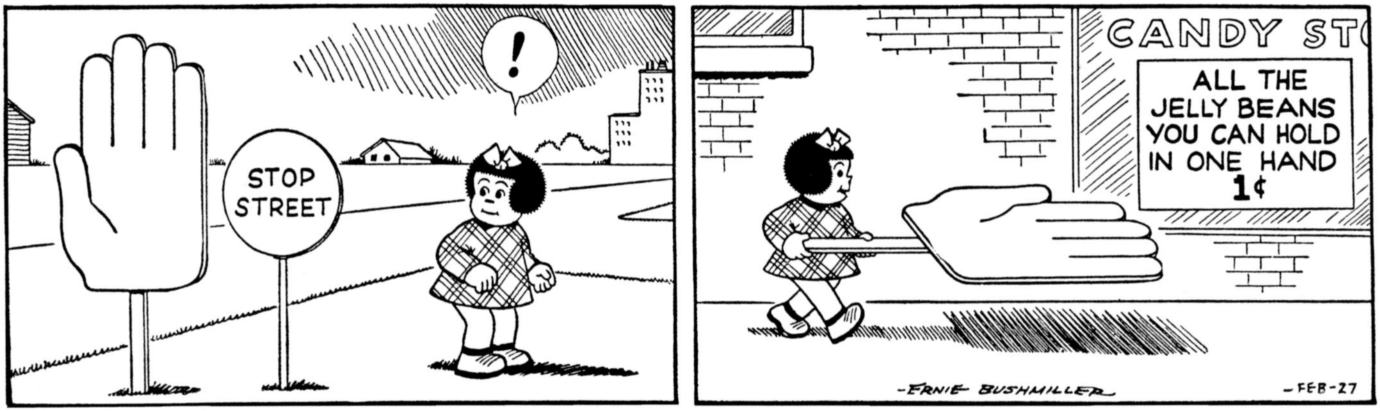
STOP STREET
!
CANDY ST
ALL THE JELLY BEANS YOU CAN HOLD IN ONE HAND 1¢
-ERNIE BUSHMILLER
-FEB-27

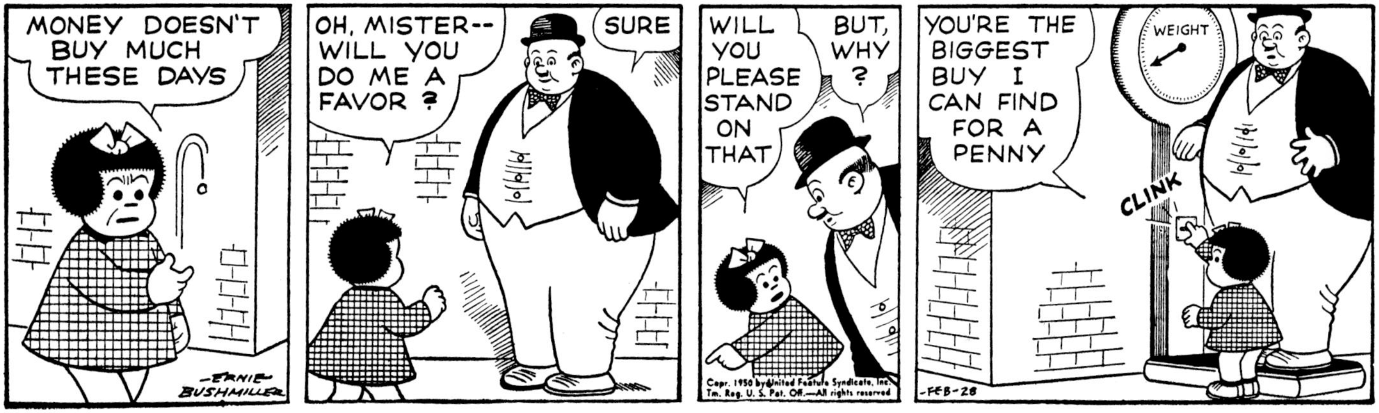
MONEY DOESN'T BUY MUCH THESE DAYS
ERNIE BUSHMILLER
OH, MISTER-- WILL YOU DO ME A FAVOR ?
SURE
WILL YOU PLEASE STAND ON THAT
BUT, WHY ?
Copr. 1950 by United Feature Syndicate, Inc. Tm. Reg. U. S. Pat. Off.—All rights reserved
YOU'RE THE BIGGEST BUY I CAN FIND FOR A PENNY
WEIGHT
CLINK
FEB-28

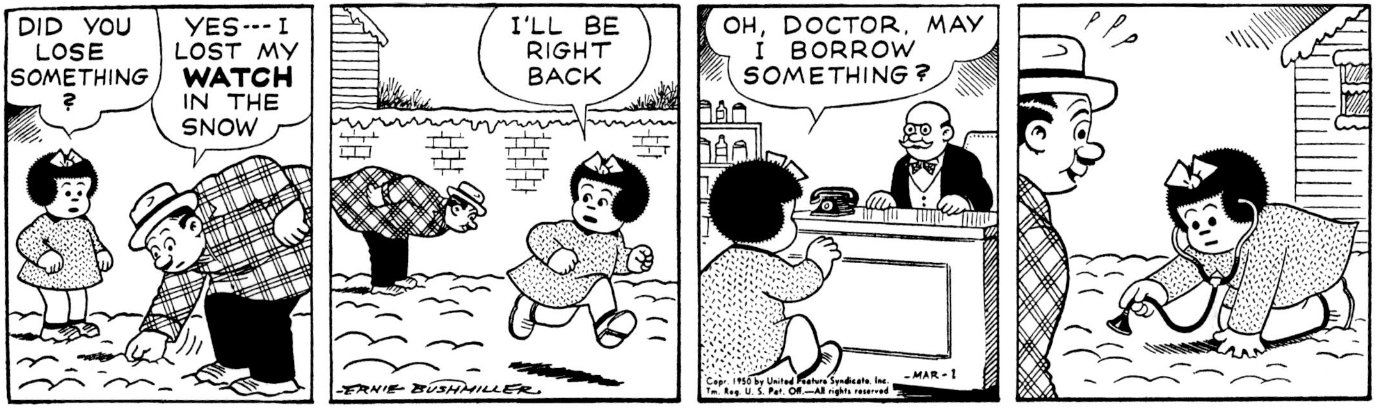
DID YOU LOSE SOMETHING ?
YES---I LOST MY WATCH IN THE SNOW
I'LL BE RIGHT BACK
ERNIE BUSHMILLER
OH, DOCTOR, MAY I BORROW SOMETHING ?
Copr. 1950 by United Feature Syndicate, Inc. Tm. Reg. U. S. Pat. Off.—All rights reserved
MAR-1

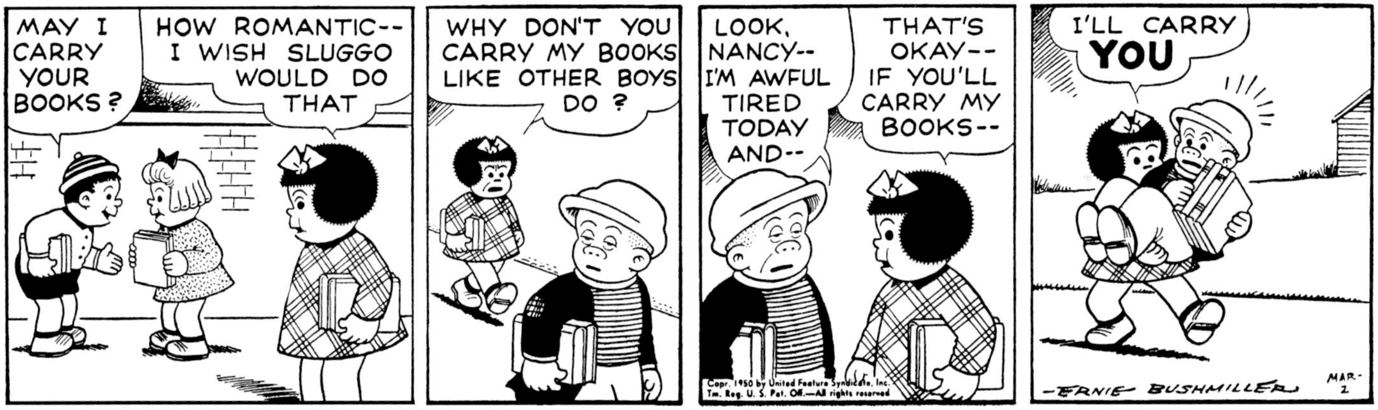
MAY I CARRY YOUR BOOKS ?
HOW ROMANTIC-- I WISH SLUGGO WOULD DO THAT
WHY DON'T YOU CARRY MY BOOKS LIKE OTHER BOYS DO ?
LOOK, NANCY-- I'M AWFUL TIRED TODAY AND--
THAT'S OKAY-- IF YOU'LL CARRY MY BOOKS--
Copr. 1950 by United Feature Syndicate, Inc. Tm. Reg. U. S. Pat. Off.—All rights reserved
I'LL CARRY YOU
ERNIE BUSHMILLER
MAR-2

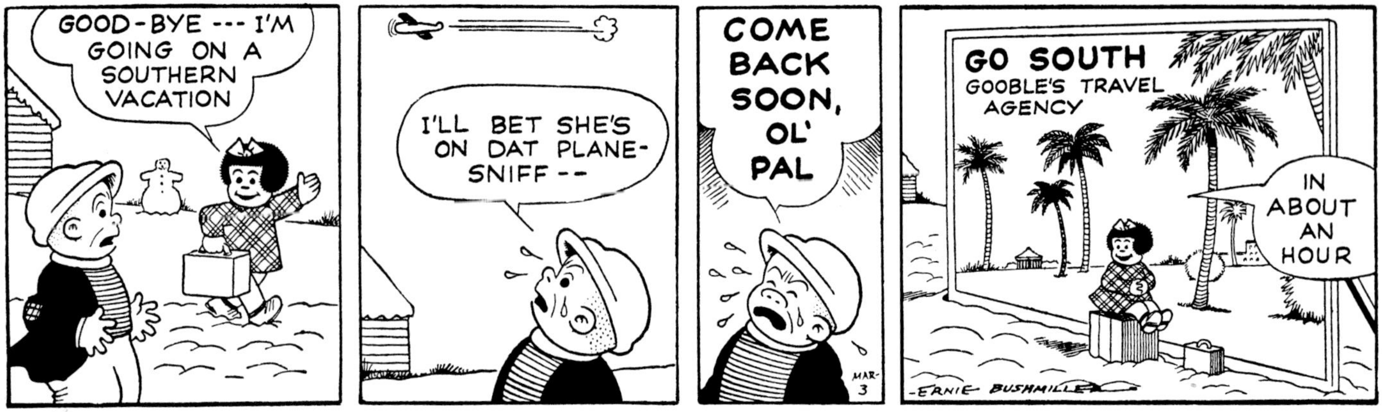
GOOD-BYE --- I'M GOING ON A SOUTHERN VACATION
I'LL BET SHE'S ON DAT PLANE-SNIFF --
COME BACK SOON, OL' PAL
MAR-3
GO SOUTH
GOOBLE'S TRAVEL AGENCY
IN ABOUT AN HOUR
ERNIE BUSHMILLER

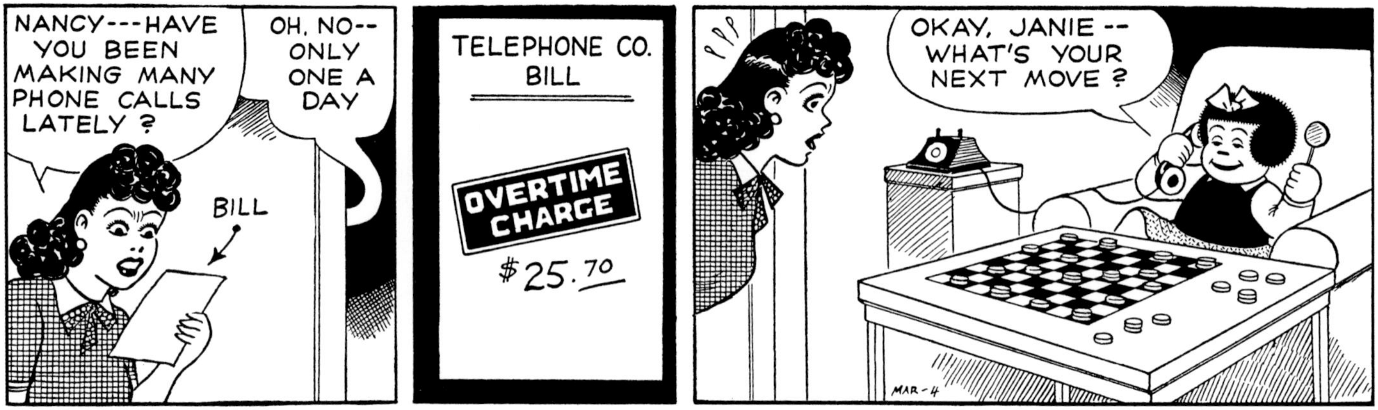
NANCY---HAVE YOU BEEN MAKING MANY PHONE CALLS LATELY ?
OH, NO-- ONLY ONE A DAY
BILL
TELEPHONE CO. BILL
OVERTIME CHARGE
$25.70
OKAY, JANIE -- WHAT'S YOUR NEXT MOVE ?
MAR-4

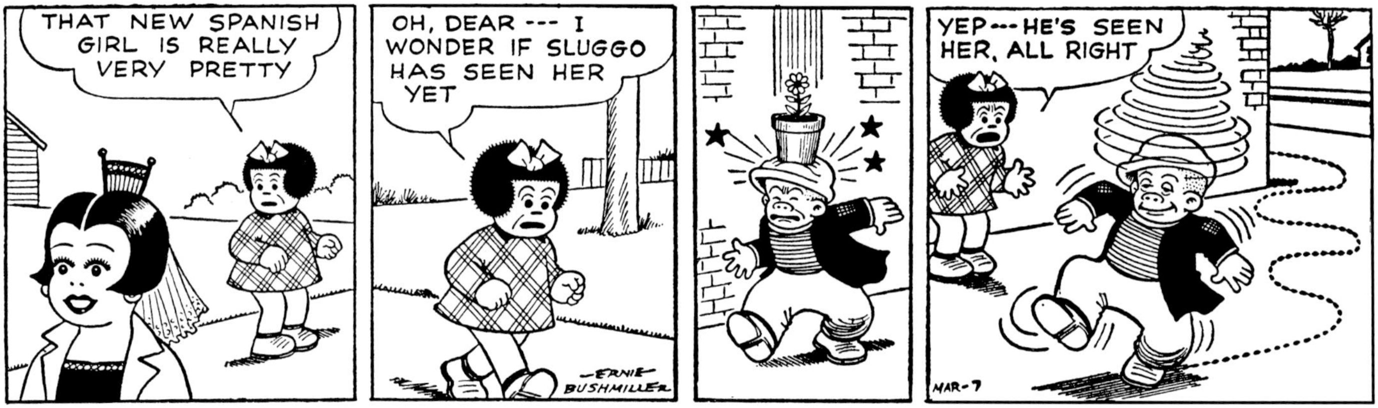
THAT NEW SPANISH GIRL IS REALLY VERY PRETTY
OH, DEAR --- I WONDER IF SLUGGO HAS SEEN HER YET
ERNIE BUSHMILLER
YEP---HE'S SEEN HER, ALL RIGHT
MAR-7

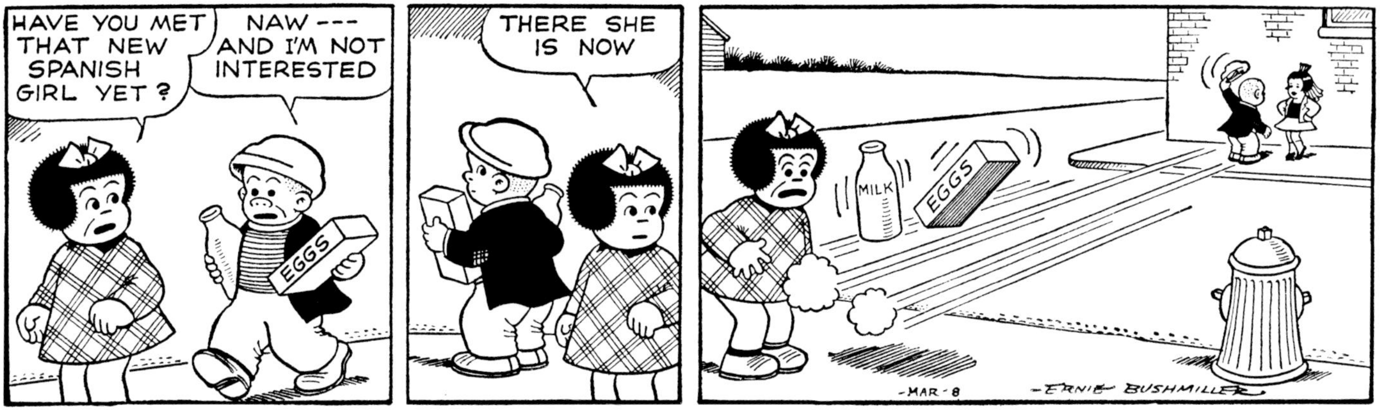
HAVE YOU MET THAT NEW SPANISH GIRL YET ?
NAW --- AND I'M NOT INTERESTED
THERE SHE IS NOW
MILK
EGGS
-MAR-8
-ERNIE BUSHMILLER

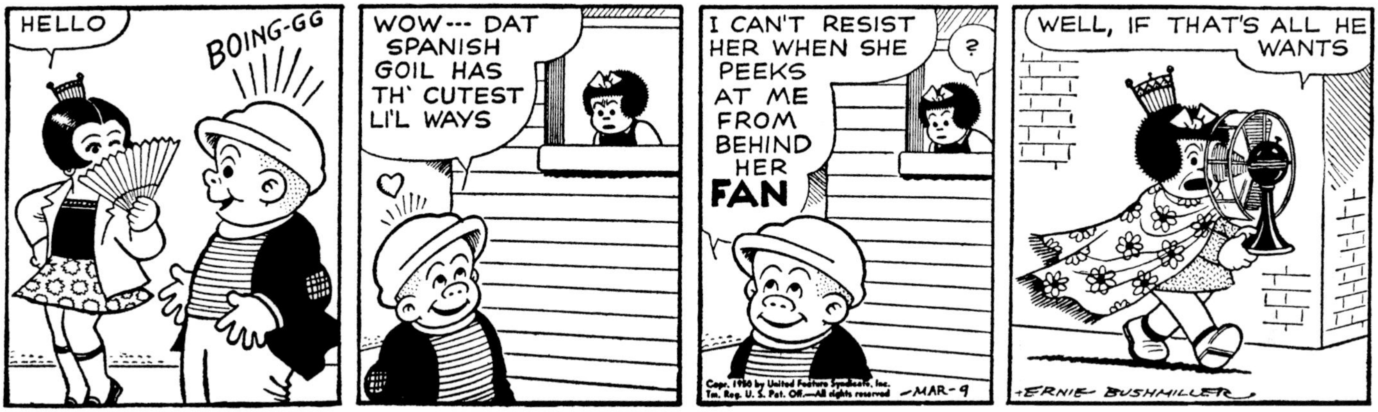
HELLO
BOING-GG
WOW--- DAT SPANISH GOIL HAS TH' CUTEST LI'L WAYS
I CAN'T RESIST HER WHEN SHE PEEKS AT ME FROM BEHIND HER FAN
?
Copr. 1950 by United Feature Syndicate, Inc. Tm. Reg. U. S. Pat. Off.—All rights reserved
-MAR-9
WELL, IF THAT'S ALL HE WANTS
-ERNIE BUSHMILLER

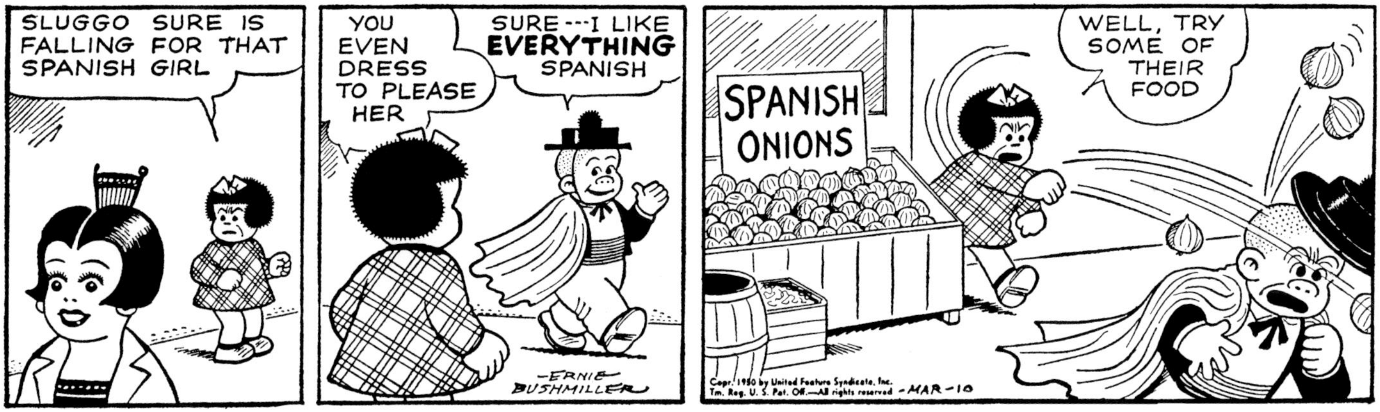
SLUGGO SURE IS FALLING FOR THAT SPANISH GIRL
YOU EVEN DRESS TO PLEASE HER
SURE---I LIKE EVERYTHING SPANISH
-ERNIE BUSHMILLER
SPANISH ONIONS
WELL, TRY SOME OF THEIR FOOD
Copr. 1950 by United Feature Syndicate, Inc. Tm. Reg. U. S. Pat. Off.—All rights reserved
-MAR-10

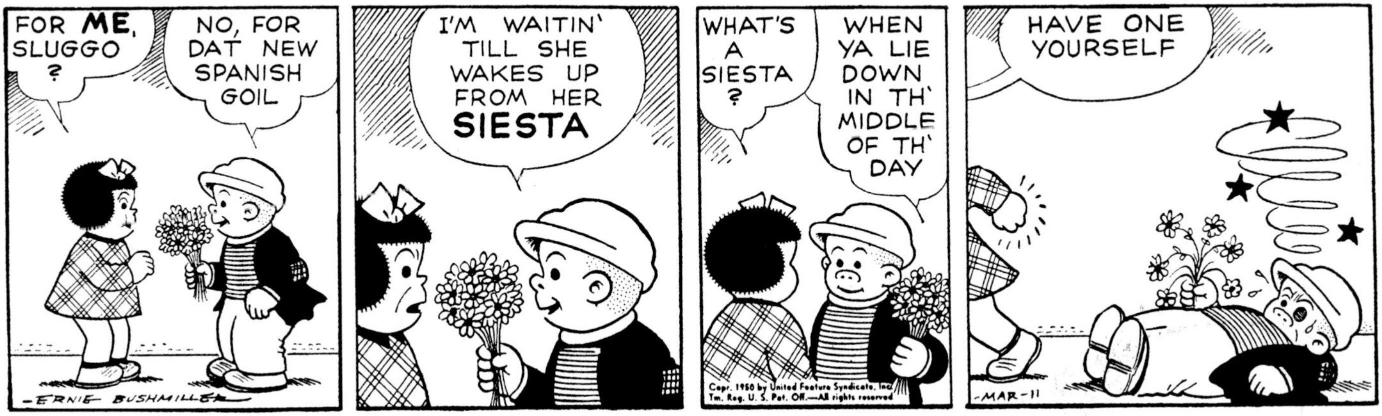

FOR ME, SLUGGO ?
NO, FOR DAT NEW SPANISH GOIL
ERNIE BUSHMILLER
I'M WAITIN' TILL SHE WAKES UP FROM HER SIESTA
WHAT'S A SIESTA ?
WHEN YA LIE DOWN IN TH' MIDDLE OF TH' DAY
Copr. 1950 by United Feature Syndicate, Inc. Tm. Reg. U. S. Pat. Off.—All rights reserved
HAVE ONE YOURSELF
MAR-11

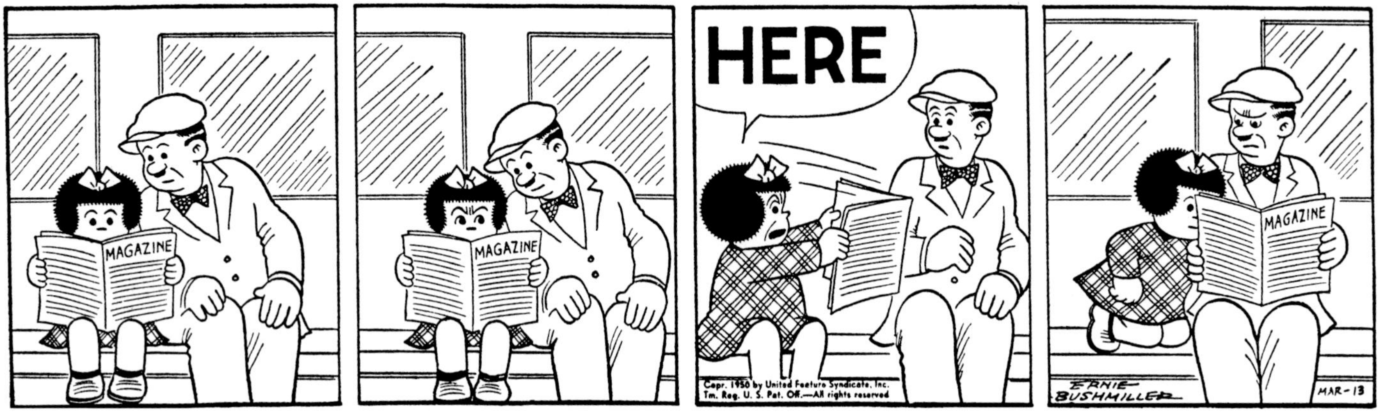

MAGAZINE
MAGAZINE
HERE
Copr. 1950 by United Feature Syndicate, Inc. Tm. Reg. U. S. Pat. Off.—All rights reserved
MAGAZINE
ERNIE BUSHMILLER
MAR-13

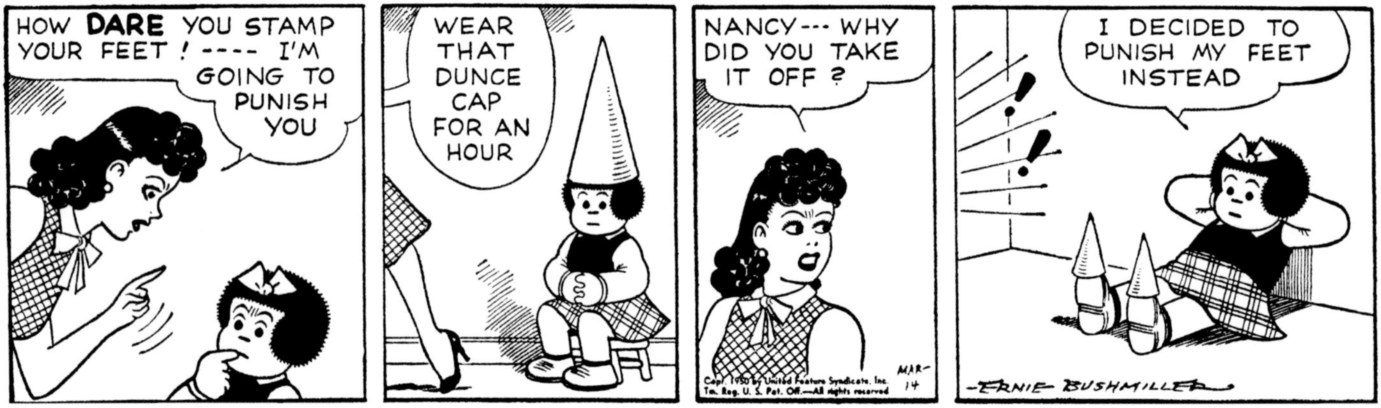

HOW DARE YOU STAMP YOUR FEET ! ---- I'M GOING TO PUNISH YOU
WEAR THAT DUNCE CAP FOR AN HOUR
NANCY--- WHY DID YOU TAKE IT OFF ?
Copr. 1950 by United Feature Syndicate, Inc. Tm. Reg. U. S. Pat. Off.—All rights reserved
MAR-14
I DECIDED TO PUNISH MY FEET INSTEAD
ERNIE BUSHMILLER

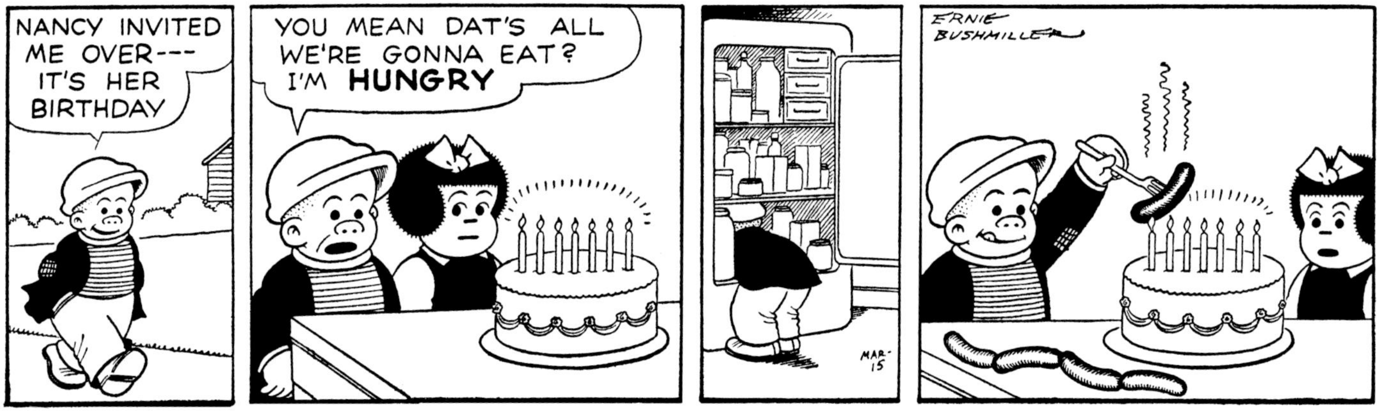
NANCY INVITED ME OVER--- IT'S HER BIRTHDAY
YOU MEAN DAT'S ALL WE'RE GONNA EAT? I'M HUNGRY
MAR-15
ERNIE BUSHMILLER

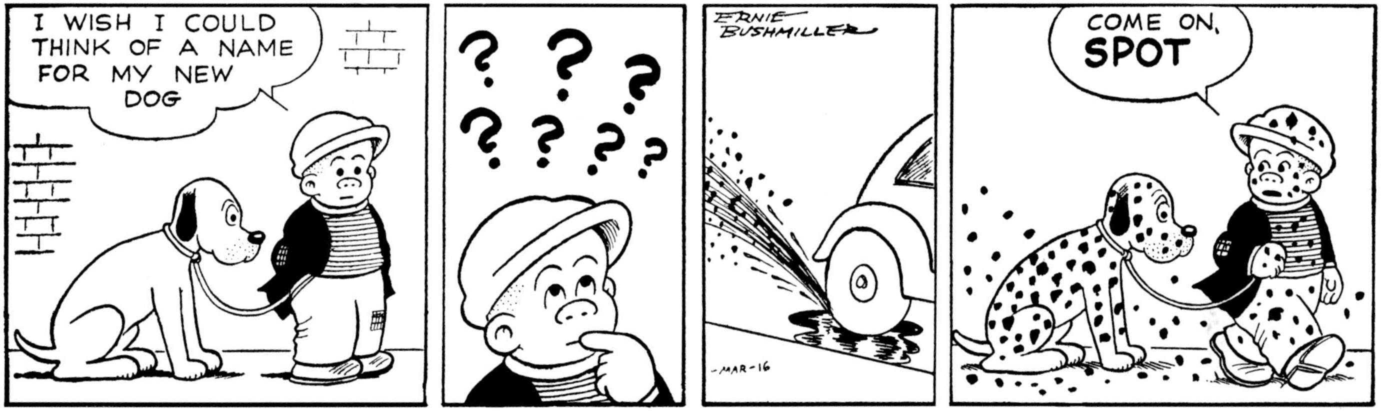
I WISH I COULD THINK OF A NAME FOR MY NEW DOG
? ? ? ? ? ? ?
ERNIE BUSHMILLER
MAR-16
COME ON, SPOT

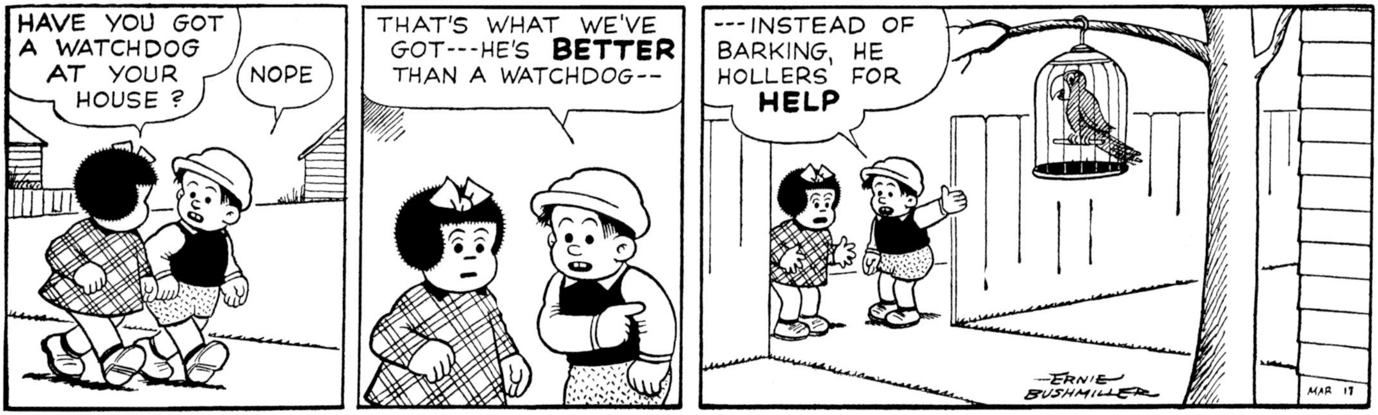
HAVE YOU GOT A WATCHDOG AT YOUR HOUSE?
NOPE
THAT'S WHAT WE'VE GOT---HE'S BETTER THAN A WATCHDOG--
---INSTEAD OF BARKING, HE HOLLERS FOR HELP
ERNIE BUSHMILLER
MAR 17

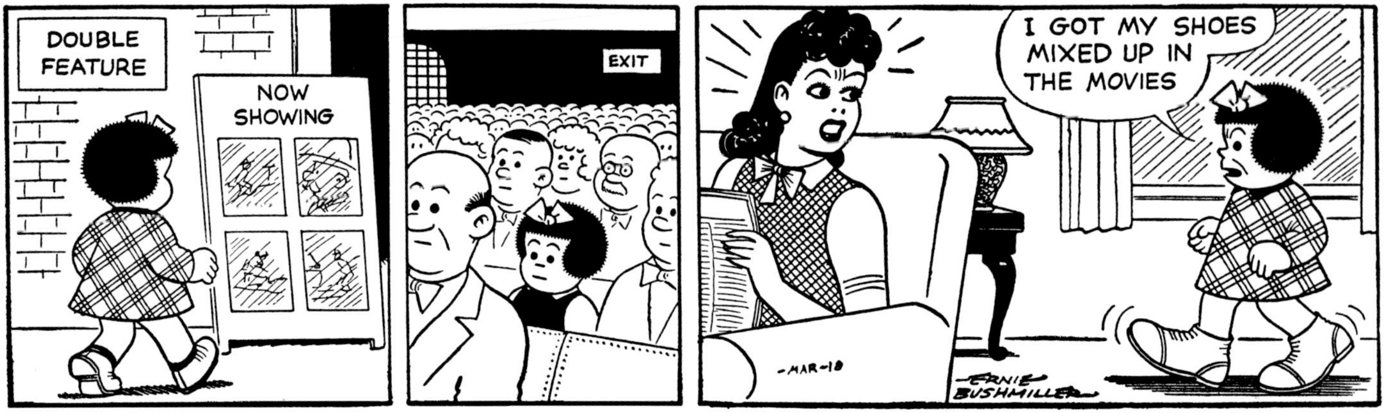
DOUBLE FEATURE
NOW SHOWING
EXIT
I GOT MY SHOES MIXED UP IN THE MOVIES
MAR-18
ERNIE BUSHMILLER

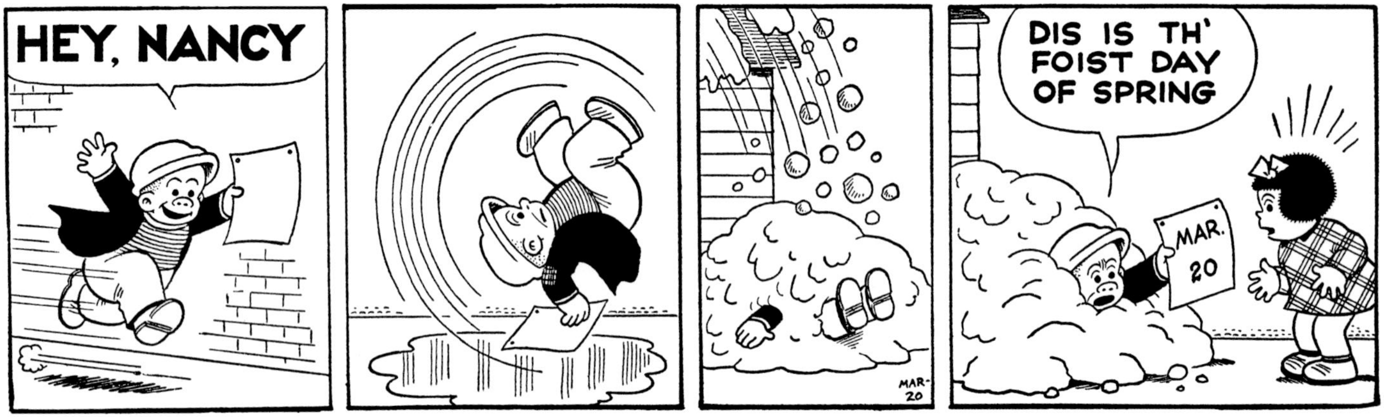
HEY, NANCY
MAR-20
DIS IS TH' FOIST DAY OF SPRING
MAR. 20

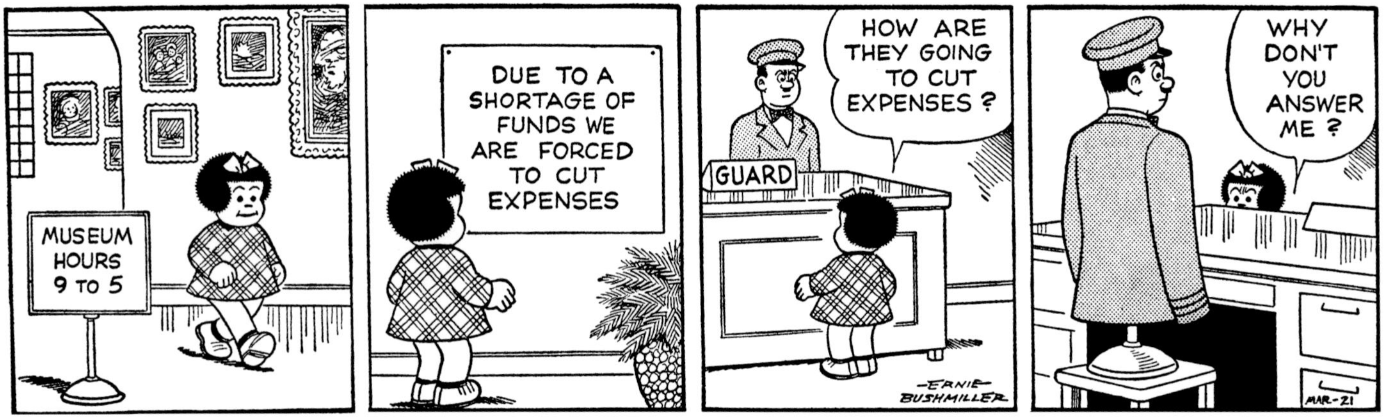
MUSEUM HOURS 9 TO 5
DUE TO A SHORTAGE OF FUNDS WE ARE FORCED TO CUT EXPENSES
GUARD
HOW ARE THEY GOING TO CUT EXPENSES ?
ERNIE BUSHMILLER
WHY DON'T YOU ANSWER ME ?
MAR-21

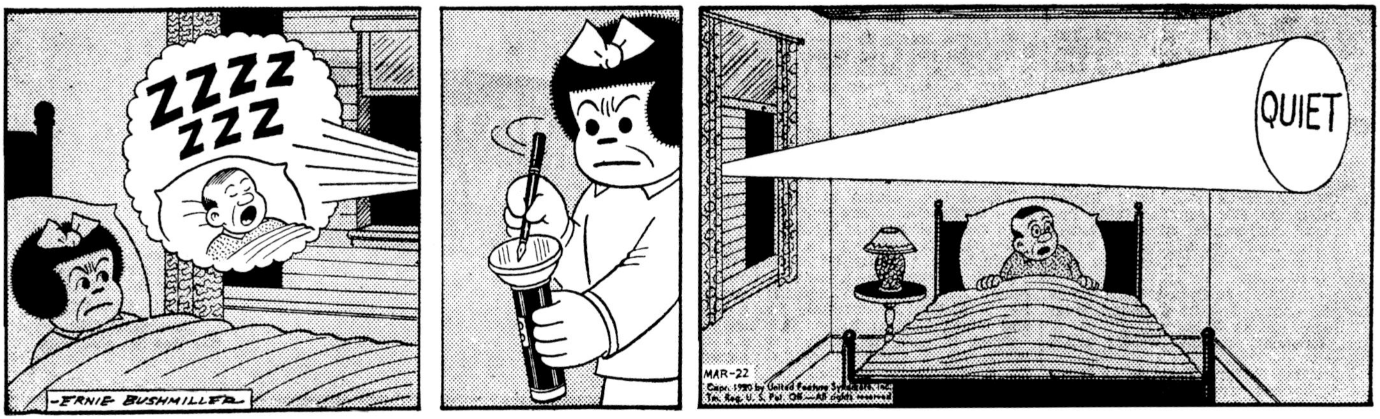
ERNIE BUSHMILLER
ZZZZ ZZZ
QUIET
MAR-22
Copr. 1950 by United Feature Syndicate, Inc.
Tm. Reg. U. S. Pat. Off.—All rights reserved

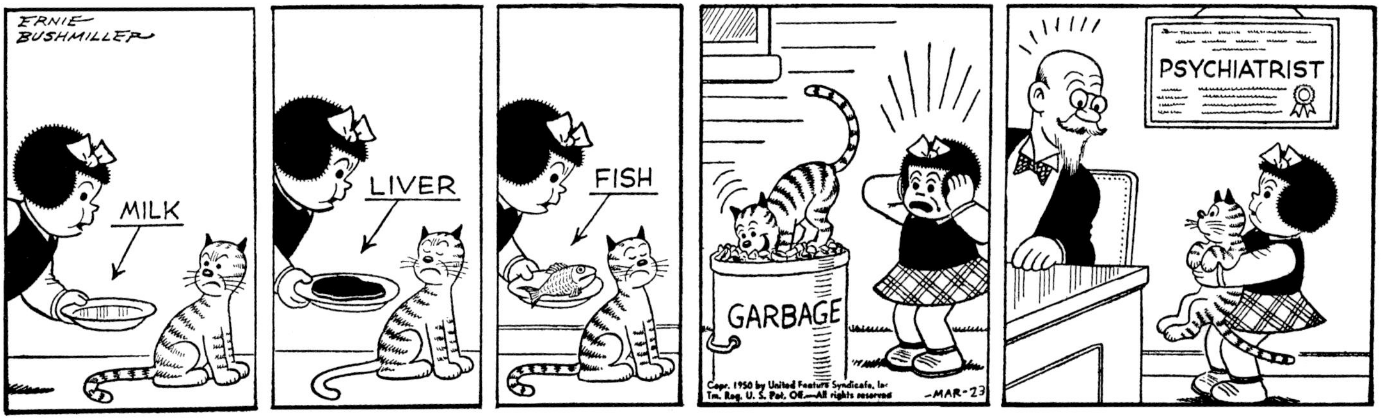
ERNIE BUSHMILLER
MILK
LIVER
FISH
GARBAGE
Copr. 1950 by United Feature Syndicate, Inc.
Tm. Reg. U. S. Pat. Off.—All rights reserved
MAR-23
PSYCHIATRIST

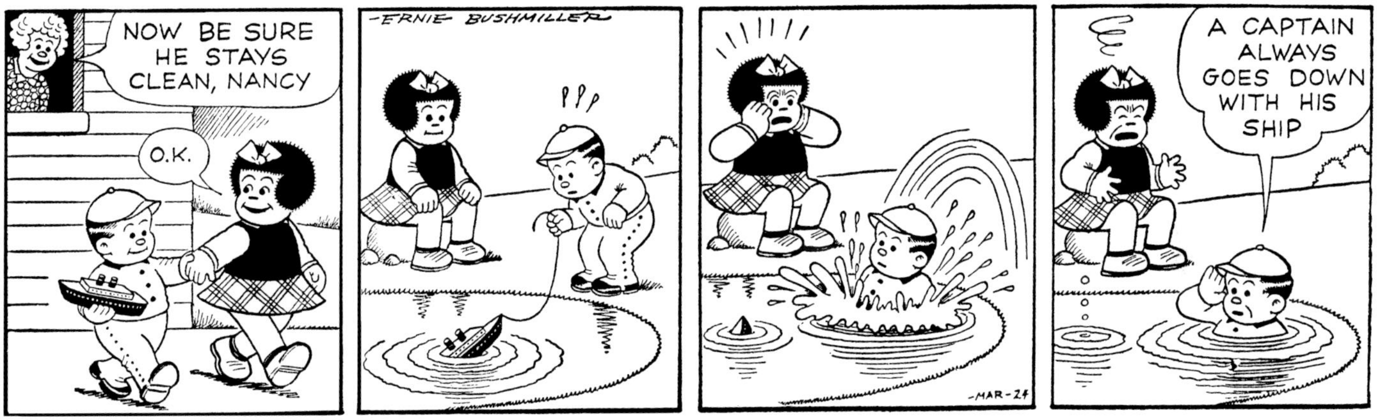
NOW BE SURE HE STAYS CLEAN, NANCY
O.K.
ERNIE BUSHMILLER
MAR-24
A CAPTAIN ALWAYS GOES DOWN WITH HIS SHIP

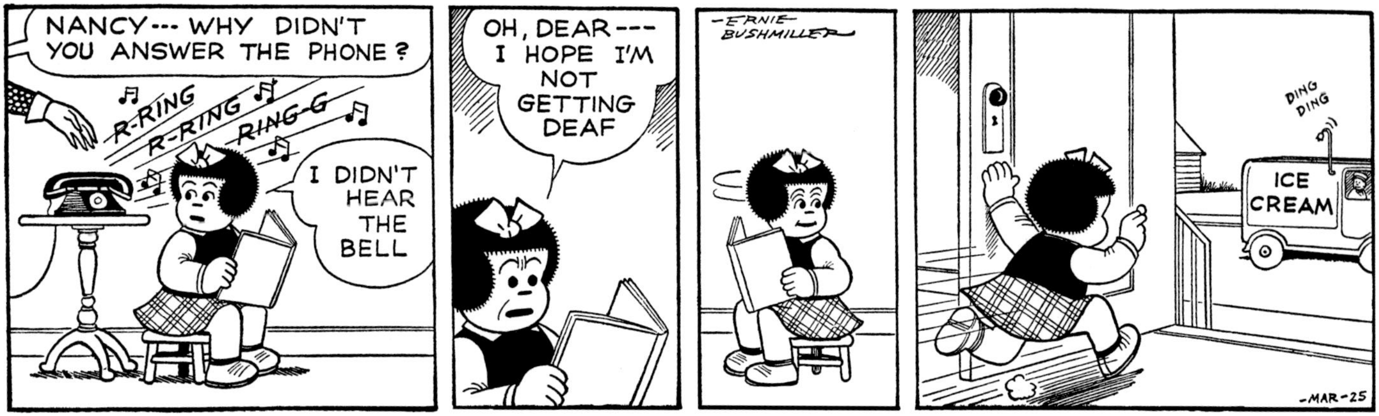
NANCY--- WHY DIDN'T YOU ANSWER THE PHONE ?
R-RING R-RING RING-G
I DIDN'T HEAR THE BELL
OH, DEAR--- I HOPE I'M NOT GETTING DEAF
-ERNIE BUSHMILLER
DING DING
ICE CREAM
-MAR-25

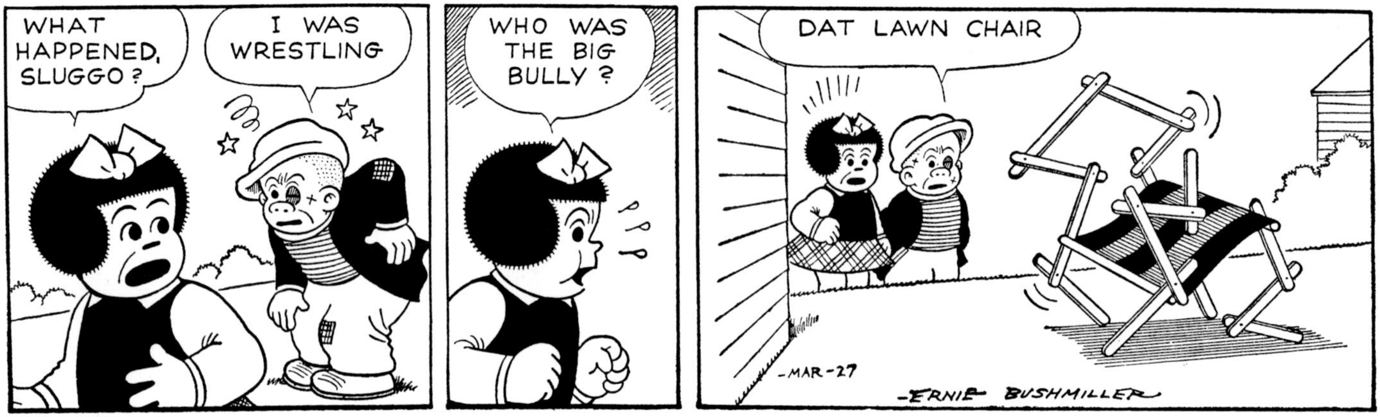
WHAT HAPPENED, SLUGGO ?
I WAS WRESTLING
WHO WAS THE BIG BULLY ?
DAT LAWN CHAIR
-MAR-27
-ERNIE BUSHMILLER

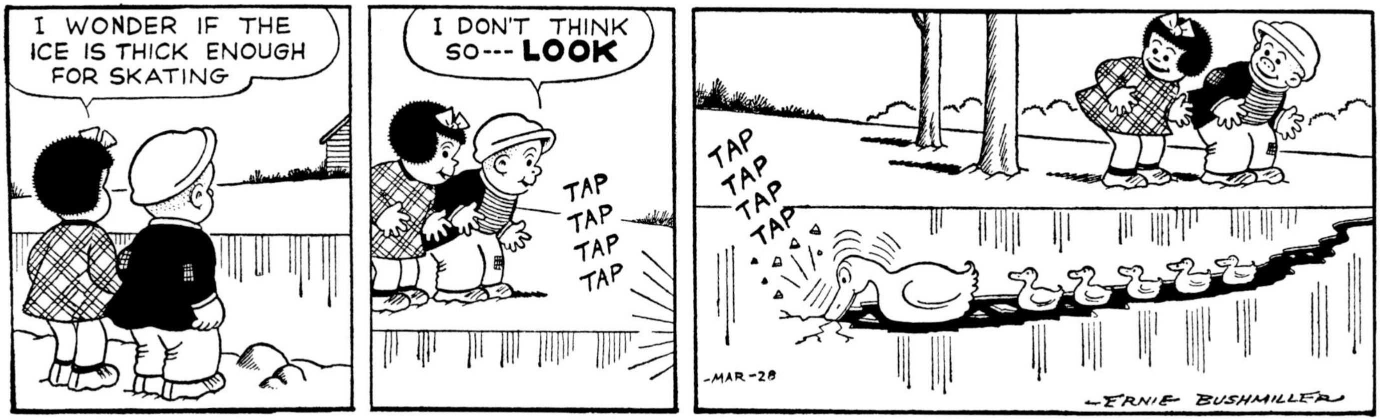
I WONDER IF THE ICE IS THICK ENOUGH FOR SKATING
I DON'T THINK SO--- LOOK
TAP TAP TAP TAP
TAP TAP TAP TAP
-MAR-28
-ERNIE BUSHMILLER

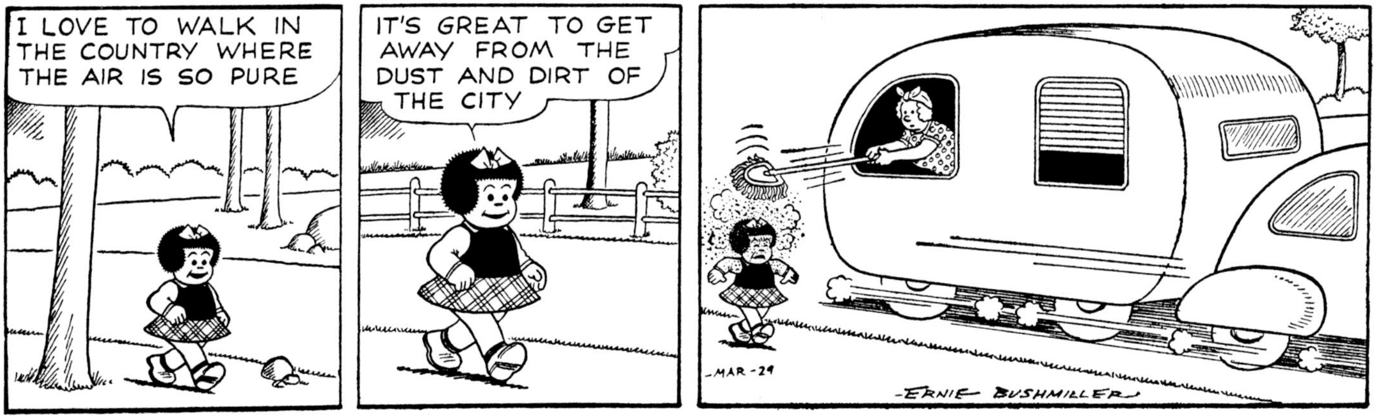
I LOVE TO WALK IN THE COUNTRY WHERE THE AIR IS SO PURE
IT'S GREAT TO GET AWAY FROM THE DUST AND DIRT OF THE CITY
MAR-29
-ERNIE BUSHMILLER

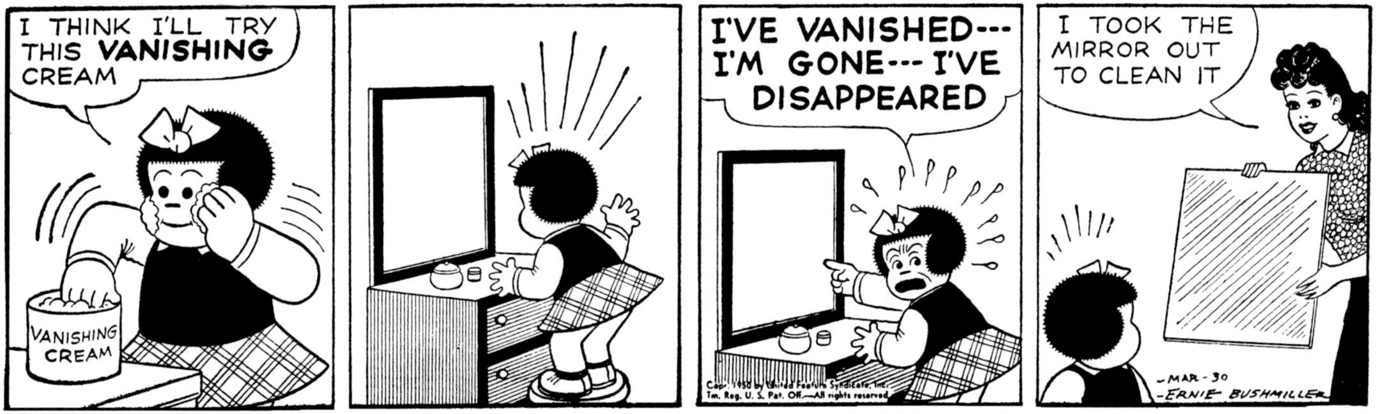
I THINK I'LL TRY THIS **VANISHING** CREAM
VANISHING CREAM
I'VE VANISHED--- I'M GONE--- I'VE DISAPPEARED
Copr. 1950 by United Feature Syndicate, Inc.
Tm. Reg. U. S. Pat. Off.—All rights reserved
I TOOK THE MIRROR OUT TO CLEAN IT
MAR-30
ERNIE BUSHMILLER

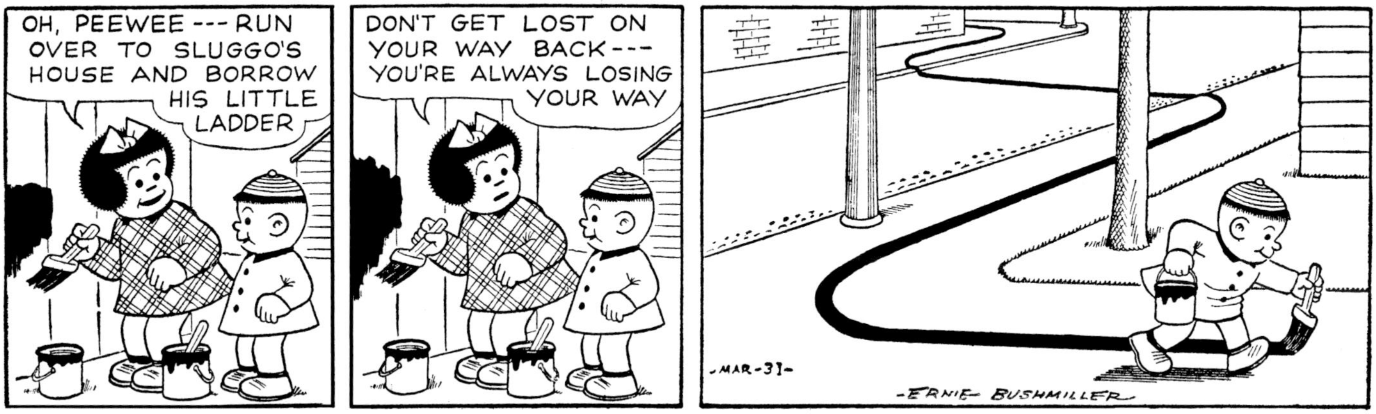
OH, PEEWEE---RUN OVER TO SLUGGO'S HOUSE AND BORROW HIS LITTLE LADDER
DON'T GET LOST ON YOUR WAY BACK--- YOU'RE ALWAYS LOSING YOUR WAY
-MAR-31-
-ERNIE BUSHMILLER

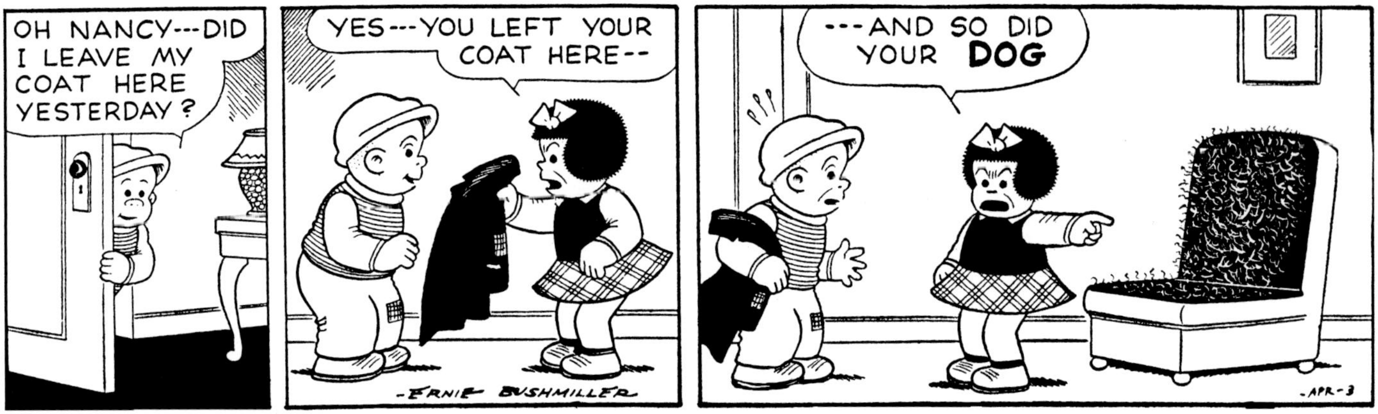
OH NANCY---DID I LEAVE MY COAT HERE YESTERDAY?
YES---YOU LEFT YOUR COAT HERE--
-ERNIE BUSHMILLER
---AND SO DID YOUR **DOG**
-APR-3

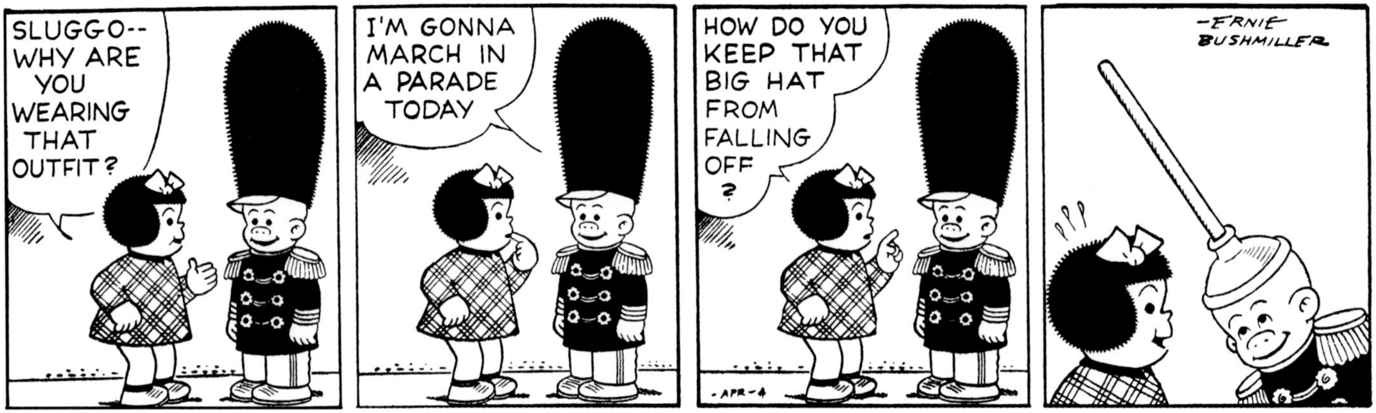
SLUGGO-- WHY ARE YOU WEARING THAT OUTFIT?
I'M GONNA MARCH IN A PARADE TODAY
HOW DO YOU KEEP THAT BIG HAT FROM FALLING OFF ?
-APR-4
-ERNIE BUSHMILLER

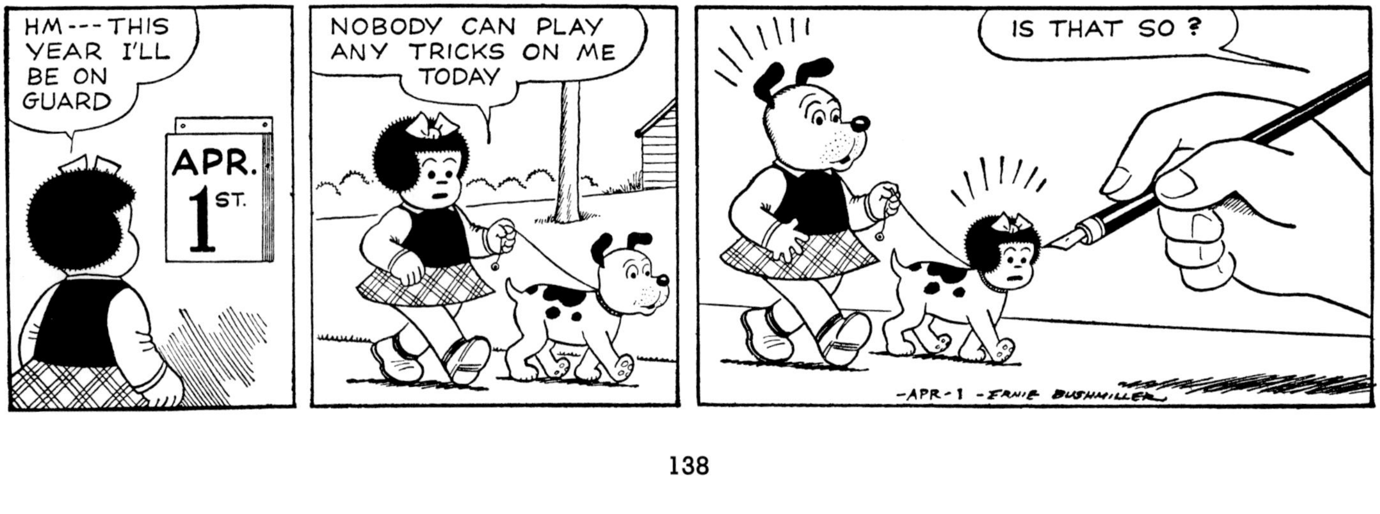
HM---THIS YEAR I'LL BE ON GUARD
APR. 1ST.
NOBODY CAN PLAY ANY TRICKS ON ME TODAY
IS THAT SO ?
-APR-1 -ERNIE BUSHMILLER

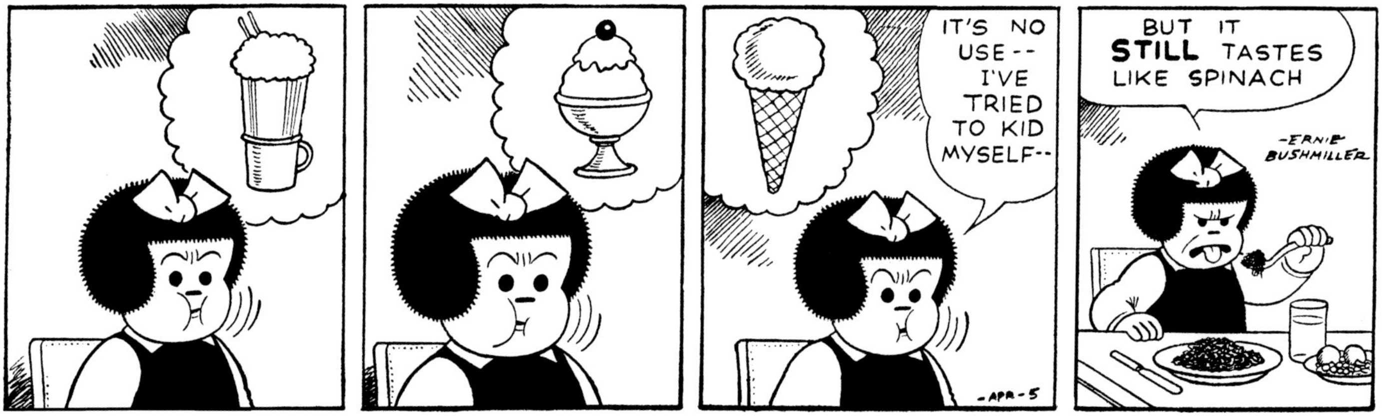
IT'S NO USE-- I'VE TRIED TO KID MYSELF--
-APR-5
BUT IT **STILL** TASTES LIKE SPINACH
-ERNIE BUSHMILLER

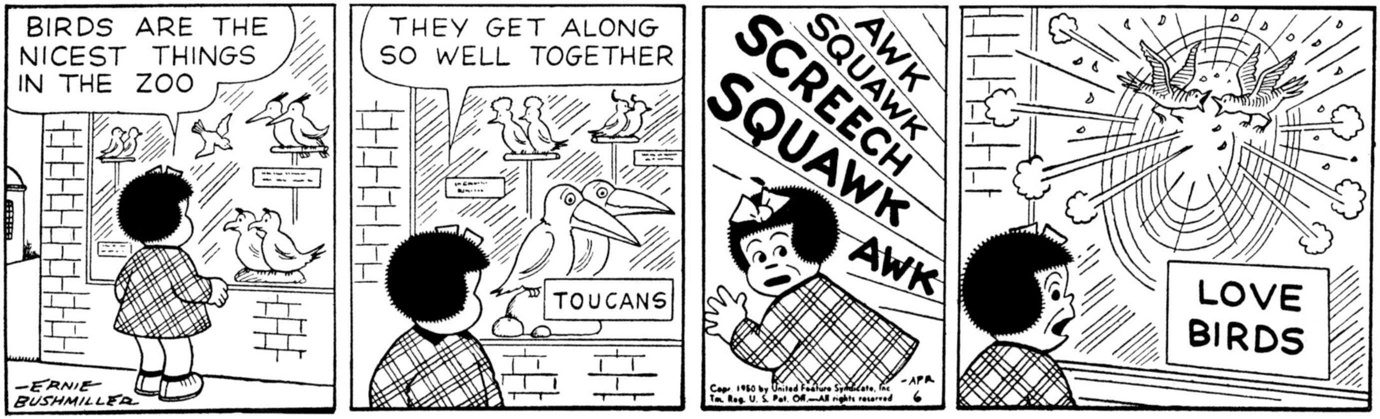
BIRDS ARE THE NICEST THINGS IN THE ZOO
-ERNIE BUSHMILLER
THEY GET ALONG SO WELL TOGETHER
TOUCANS
AWK
SQUAWK
SCREECH
SQUAWK
AWK
Copr. 1960 by United Feature Syndicate, Inc. Tm. Reg. U. S. Pat. Off.—All rights reserved
-APR 6
LOVE BIRDS

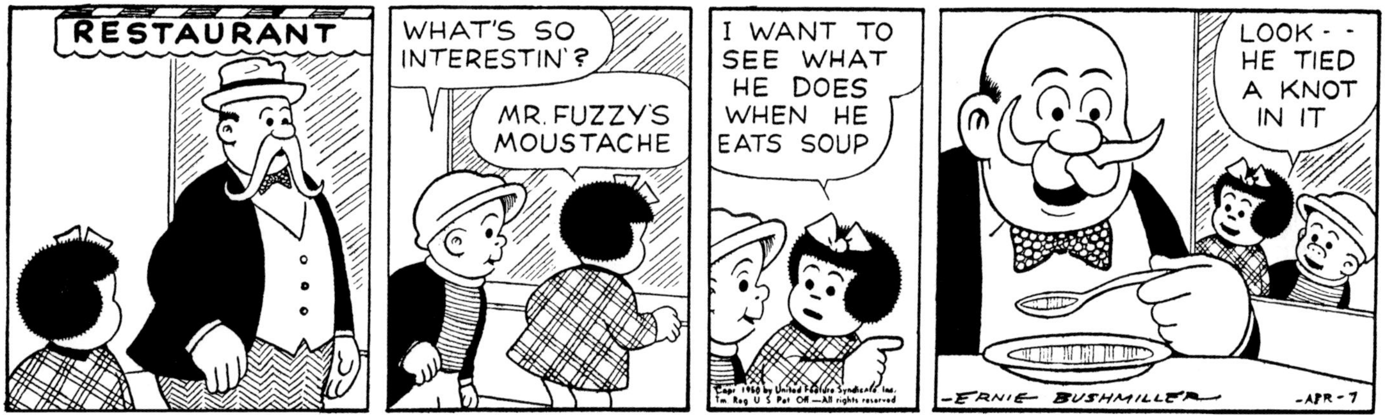
RESTAURANT
WHAT'S SO INTERESTIN'?
MR. FUZZY'S MOUSTACHE
I WANT TO SEE WHAT HE DOES WHEN HE EATS SOUP
Copr. 1960 by United Feature Syndicate, Inc. Tm. Reg. U. S. Pat. Off.—All rights reserved
LOOK-- HE TIED A KNOT IN IT
-ERNIE BUSHMILLER
-APR-7

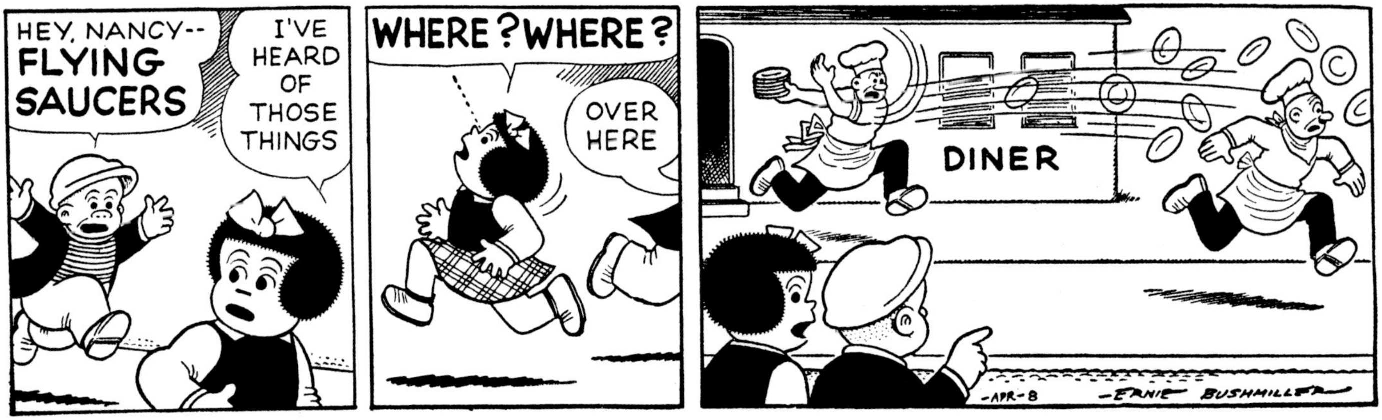
HEY, NANCY-- FLYING SAUCERS
I'VE HEARD OF THOSE THINGS
WHERE? WHERE?
OVER HERE
DINER
-APR-8
-ERNIE BUSHMILLER

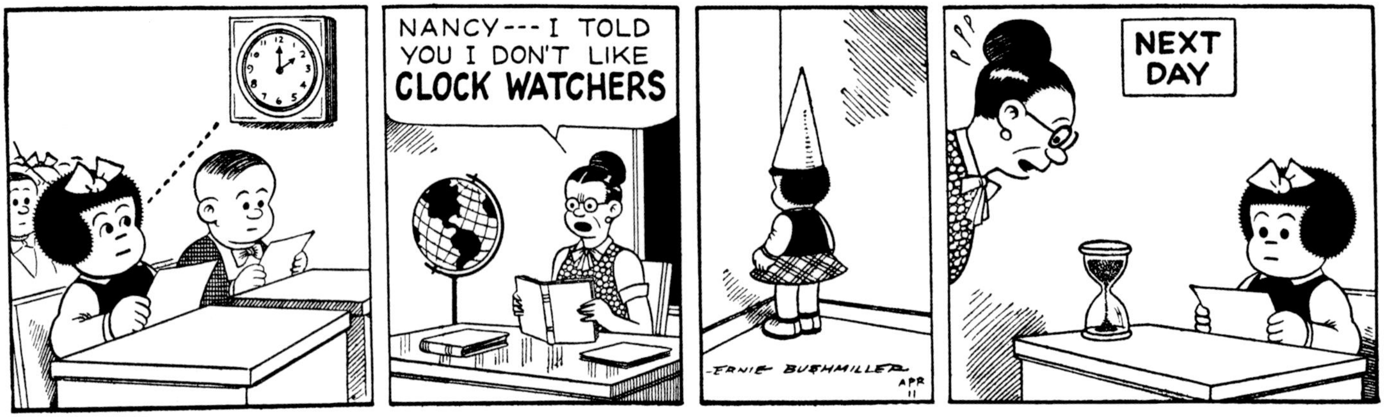
NANCY---I TOLD YOU I DON'T LIKE CLOCK WATCHERS
-ERNIE BUSHMILLER
APR 11
NEXT DAY

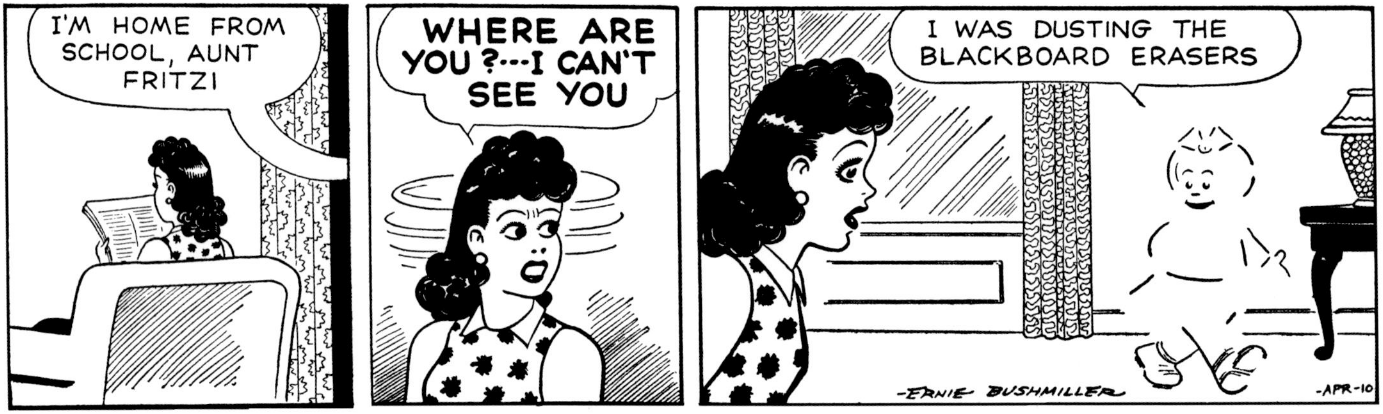
I'M HOME FROM SCHOOL, AUNT FRITZI
WHERE ARE YOU?---I CAN'T SEE YOU
I WAS DUSTING THE BLACKBOARD ERASERS
-ERNIE BUSHMILLER
-APR-10

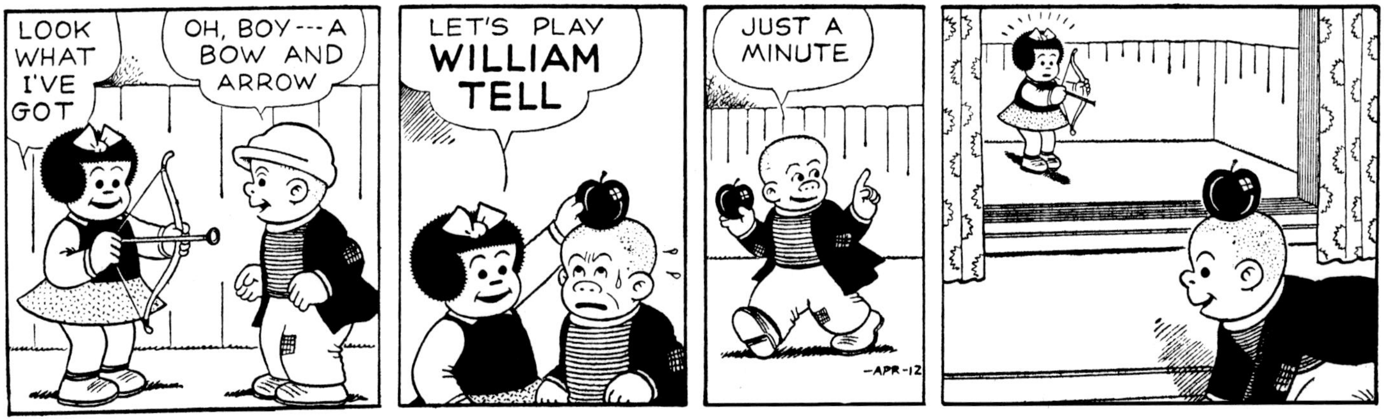
LOOK WHAT I'VE GOT
OH, BOY---A BOW AND ARROW
LET'S PLAY **WILLIAM TELL**
JUST A MINUTE
-APR-12

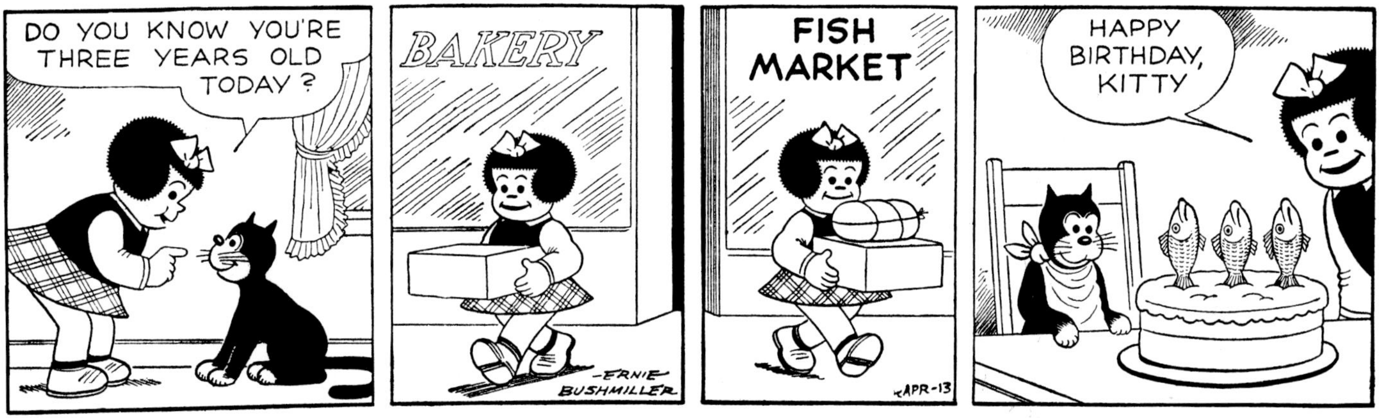
DO YOU KNOW YOU'RE THREE YEARS OLD TODAY?
BAKERY
-ERNIE BUSHMILLER
FISH MARKET
APR-13
HAPPY BIRTHDAY, KITTY

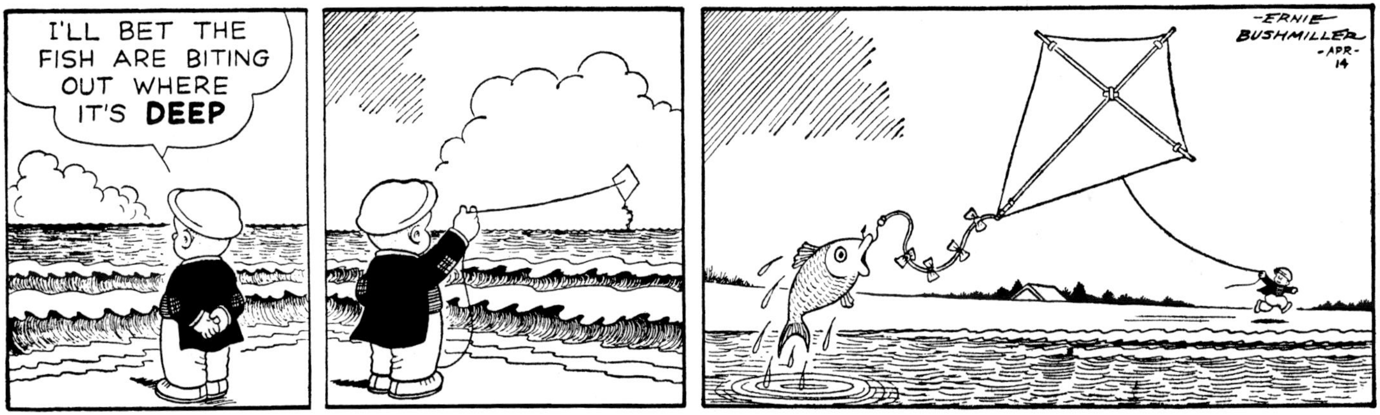
I'LL BET THE FISH ARE BITING OUT WHERE IT'S **DEEP**
-ERNIE BUSHMILLER -APR-14

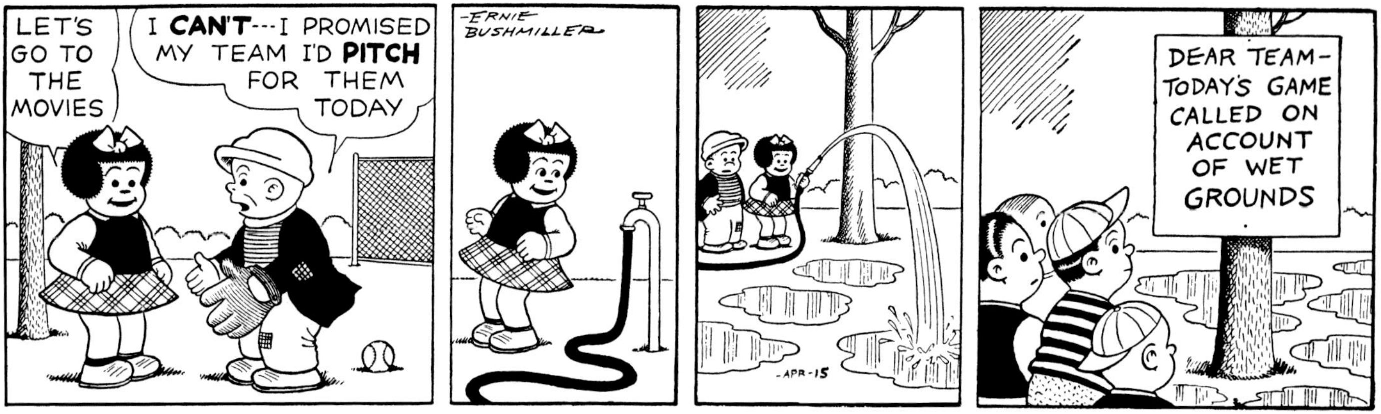
LET'S GO TO THE MOVIES
I CAN'T---I PROMISED MY TEAM I'D PITCH FOR THEM TODAY
-ERNIE BUSHMILLER
-APR-15
DEAR TEAM- TODAY'S GAME CALLED ON ACCOUNT OF WET GROUNDS

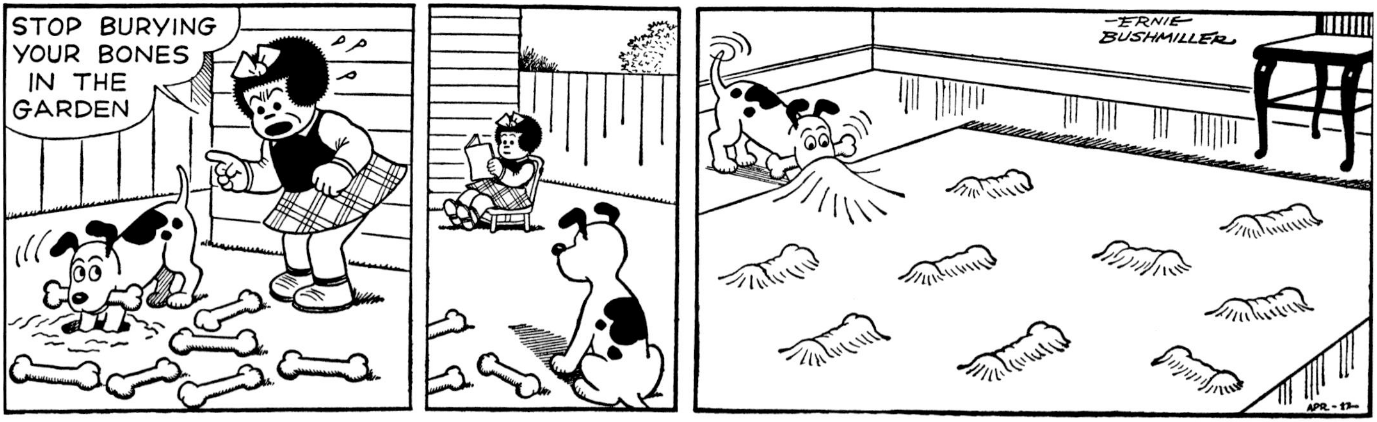
STOP BURYING YOUR BONES IN THE GARDEN
-ERNIE BUSHMILLER
APR-17

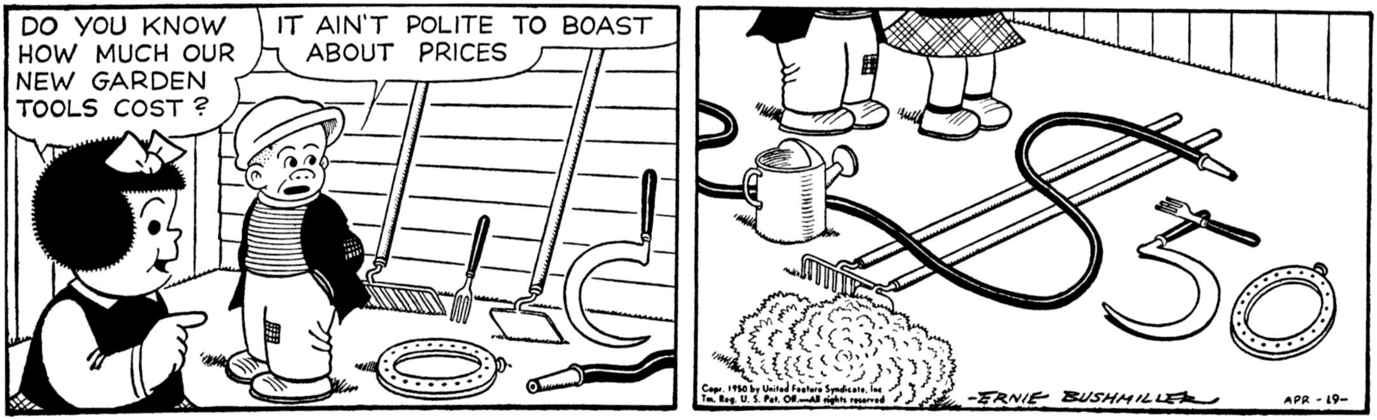
DO YOU KNOW HOW MUCH OUR NEW GARDEN TOOLS COST ?
IT AIN'T POLITE TO BOAST ABOUT PRICES
Copr. 1950 by United Feature Syndicate, Inc
Tm. Reg. U. S. Pat. Off.—All rights reserved
-ERNIE BUSHMILLER
APR-19-

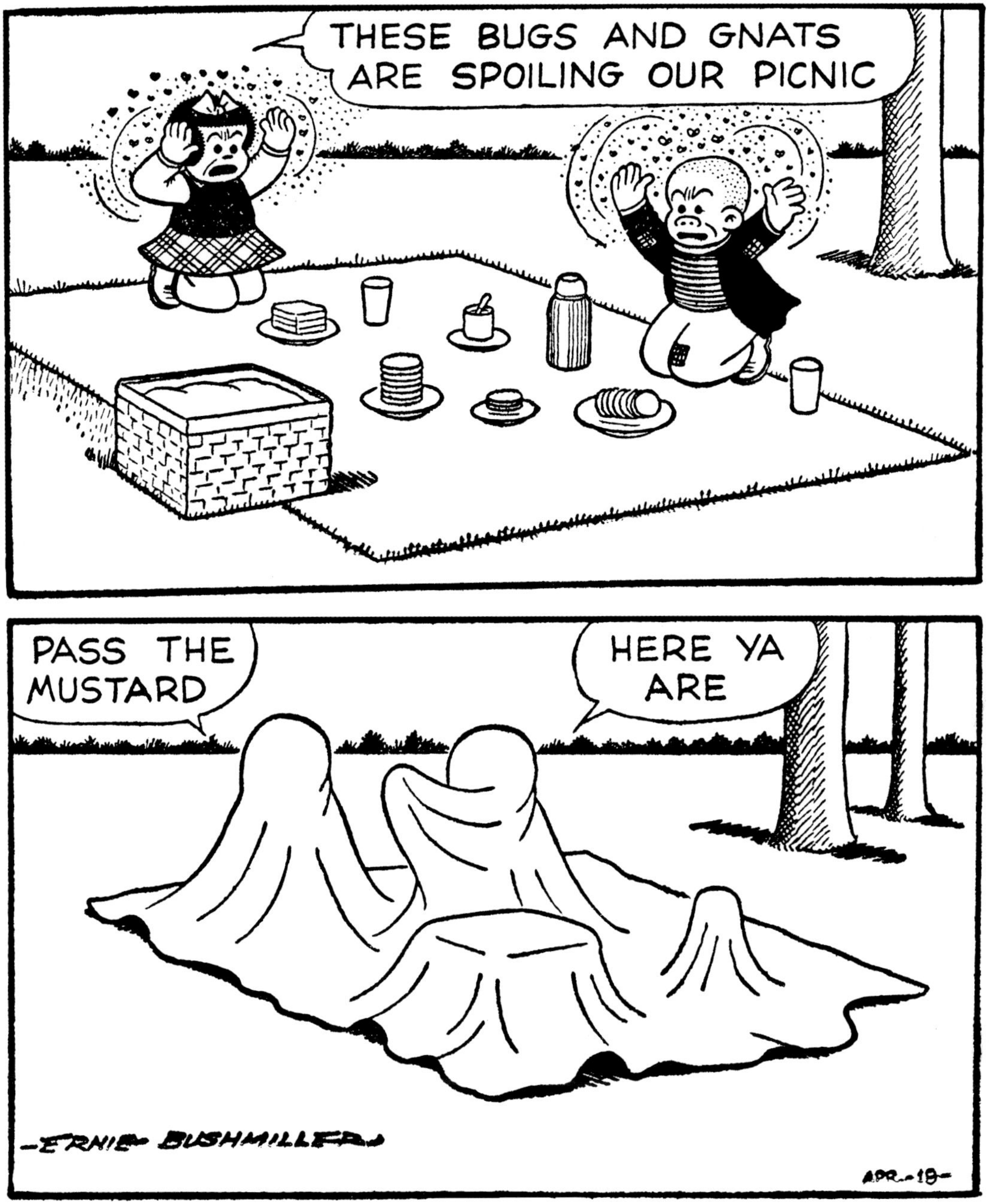
THESE BUGS AND GNATS ARE SPOILING OUR PICNIC
PASS THE MUSTARD
HERE YA ARE
ERNIE BUSHMILLER
APR-19-

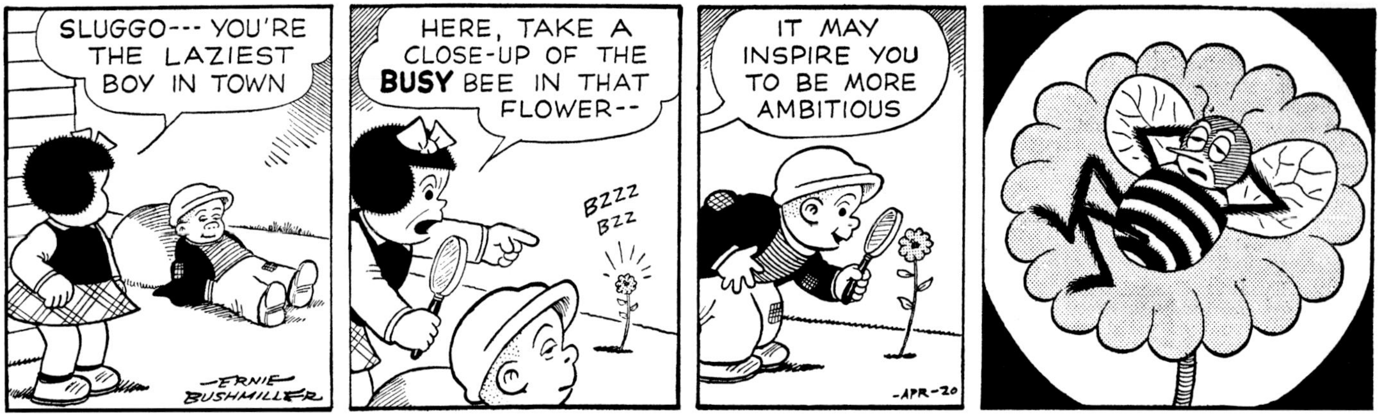
SLUGGO--- YOU'RE THE LAZIEST BOY IN TOWN
ERNIE BUSHMILLER
HERE, TAKE A CLOSE-UP OF THE **BUSY** BEE IN THAT FLOWER--
BZZZ BZZ
IT MAY INSPIRE YOU TO BE MORE AMBITIOUS
APR-20

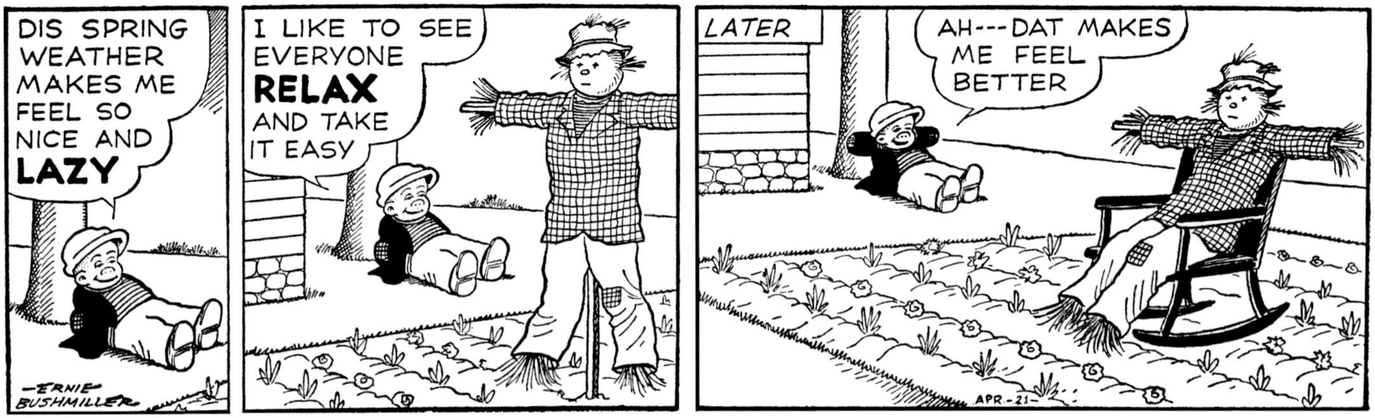
DIS SPRING WEATHER MAKES ME FEEL SO NICE AND **LAZY**
ERNIE BUSHMILLER
I LIKE TO SEE EVERYONE **RELAX** AND TAKE IT EASY
LATER
AH---DAT MAKES ME FEEL BETTER
APR-21

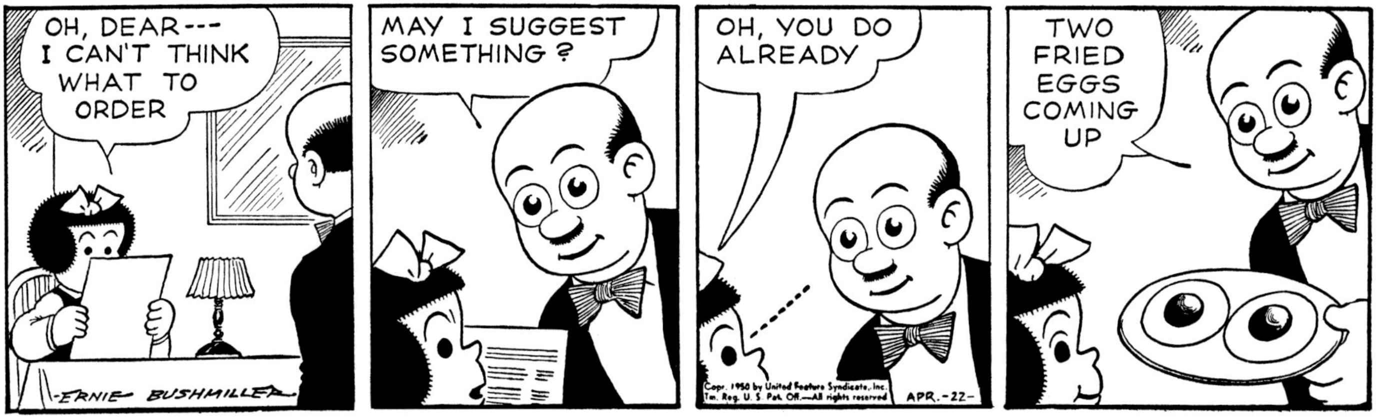
OH, DEAR--- I CAN'T THINK WHAT TO ORDER
ERNIE BUSHMILLER
MAY I SUGGEST SOMETHING?
OH, YOU DO ALREADY
Copr. 1950 by United Feature Syndicate, Inc. Tm. Reg. U. S. Pat. Off.—All rights reserved
APR.-22
TWO FRIED EGGS COMING UP

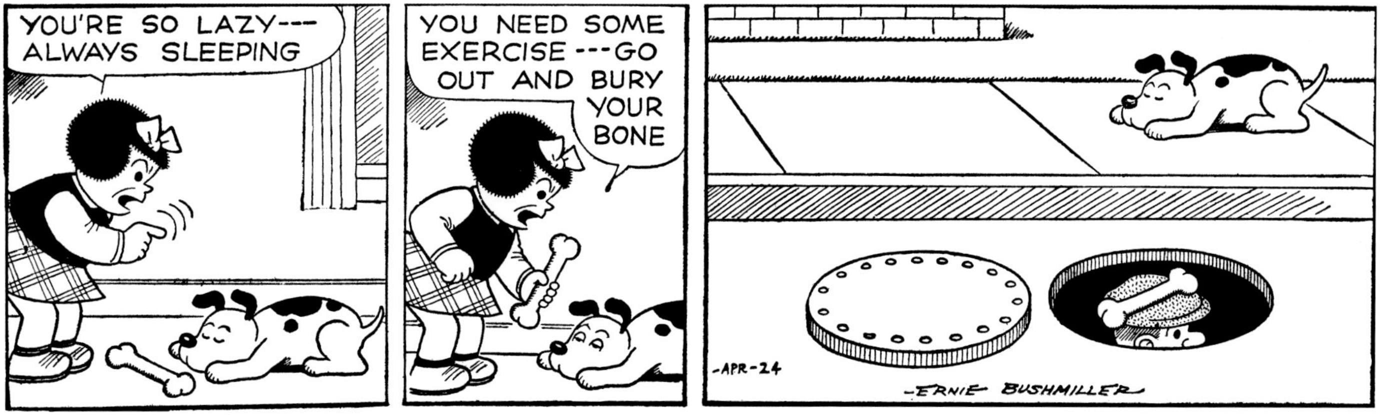
YOU'RE SO LAZY---
ALWAYS SLEEPING
YOU NEED SOME EXERCISE ---GO OUT AND BURY YOUR BONE
-APR-24
-ERNIE BUSHMILLER

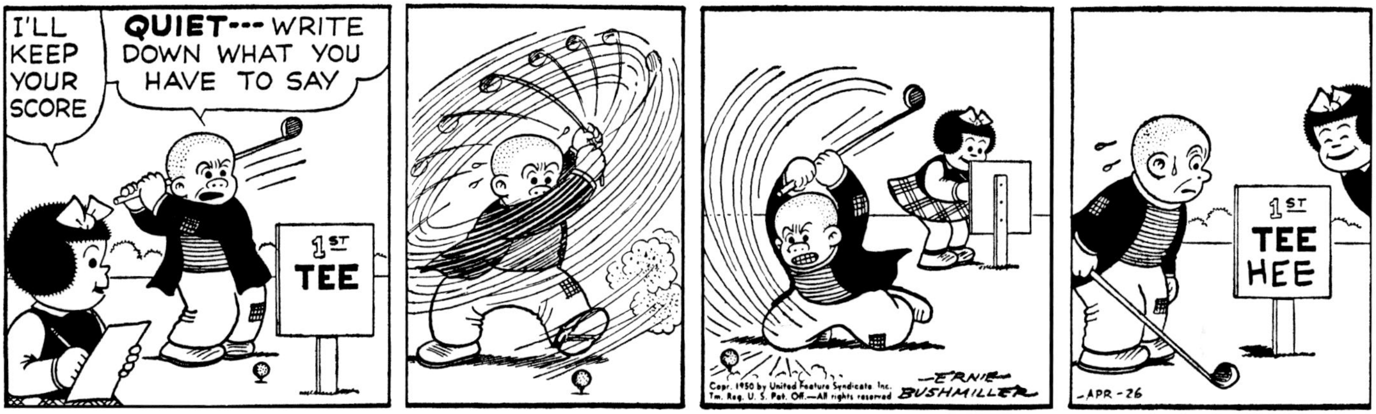
I'LL KEEP YOUR SCORE
QUIET--- WRITE DOWN WHAT YOU HAVE TO SAY
1ST TEE
Copr. 1950 by United Feature Syndicate Inc.
Tm. Reg. U. S. Pat. Off.—All rights reserved
-ERNIE BUSHMILLER
1ST TEE HEE
-APR-26

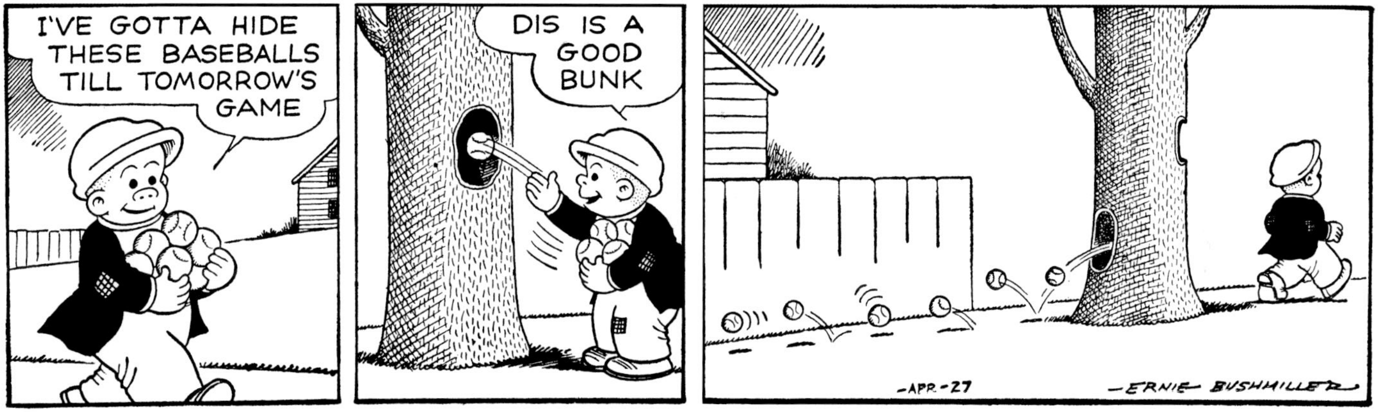
I'VE GOTTA HIDE THESE BASEBALLS TILL TOMORROW'S GAME
DIS IS A GOOD BUNK
-APR-27
-ERNIE BUSHMILLER

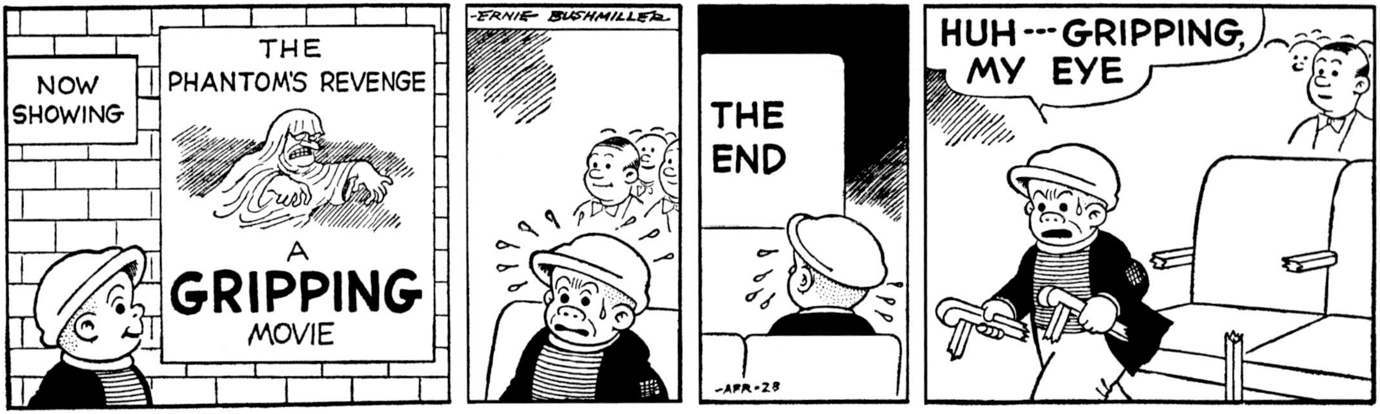
NOW SHOWING
THE PHANTOM'S REVENGE
A GRIPPING MOVIE
ERNIE BUSHMILLER
THE END
APR-28
HUH---GRIPPING, MY EYE

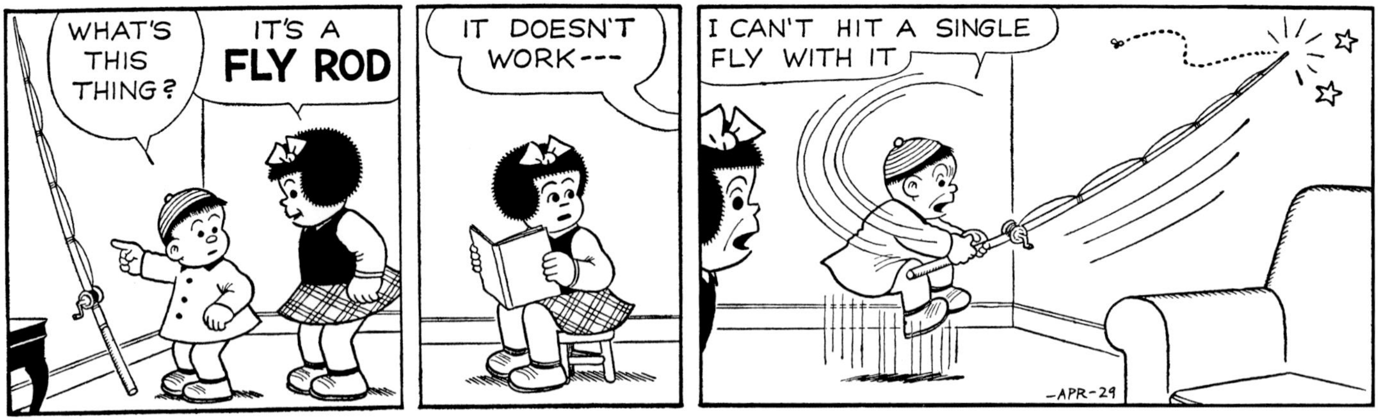
WHAT'S THIS THING?
IT'S A FLY ROD
IT DOESN'T WORK---
I CAN'T HIT A SINGLE FLY WITH IT
APR-29

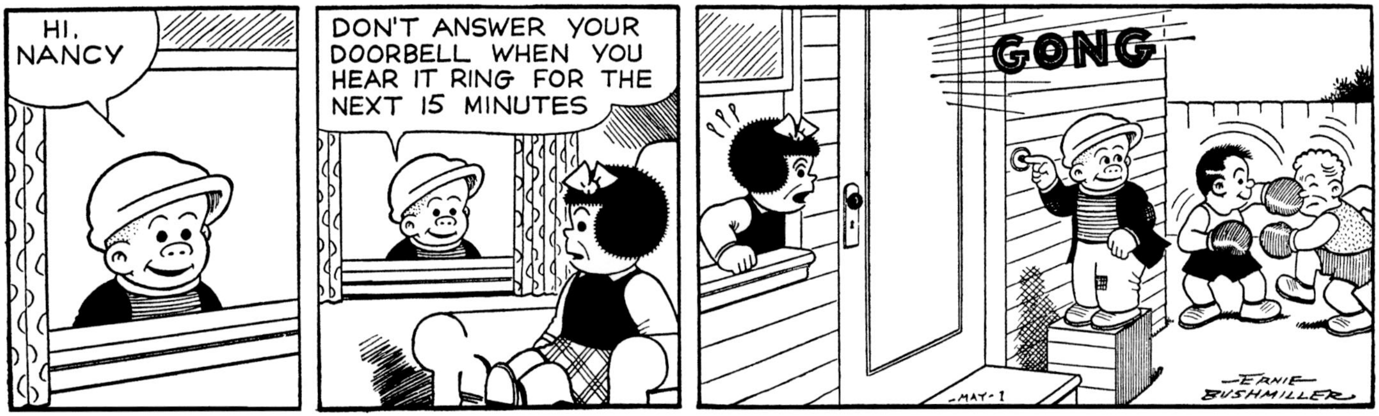
HI, NANCY
DON'T ANSWER YOUR DOORBELL WHEN YOU HEAR IT RING FOR THE NEXT 15 MINUTES
GONG
MAY-1
ERNIE BUSHMILLER

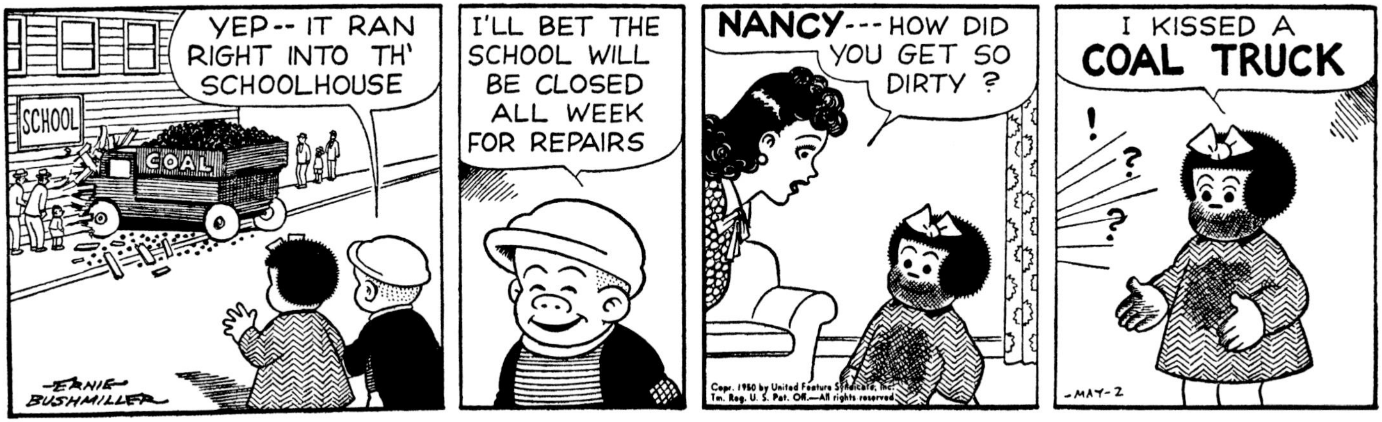
SCHOOL
COAL
YEP-- IT RAN RIGHT INTO TH' SCHOOLHOUSE
ERNIE BUSHMILLER
I'LL BET THE SCHOOL WILL BE CLOSED ALL WEEK FOR REPAIRS
NANCY--- HOW DID YOU GET SO DIRTY ?
Copr. 1950 by United Feature Syndicate, Inc. Tm. Reg. U. S. Pat. Off.—All rights reserved
I KISSED A COAL TRUCK
!
?
?
MAY-2

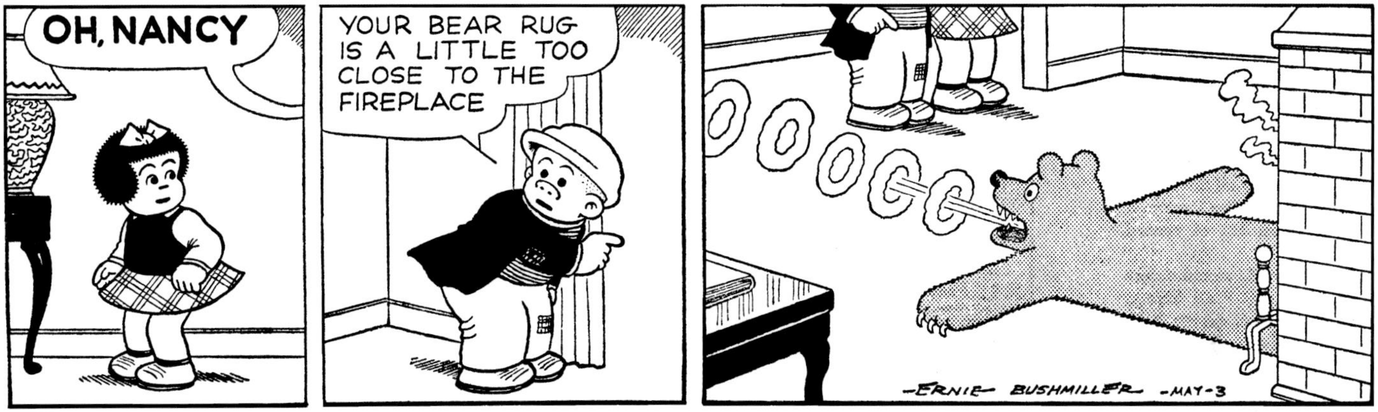
OH, NANCY
YOUR BEAR RUG IS A LITTLE TOO CLOSE TO THE FIREPLACE
ERNIE BUSHMILLER
MAY-3

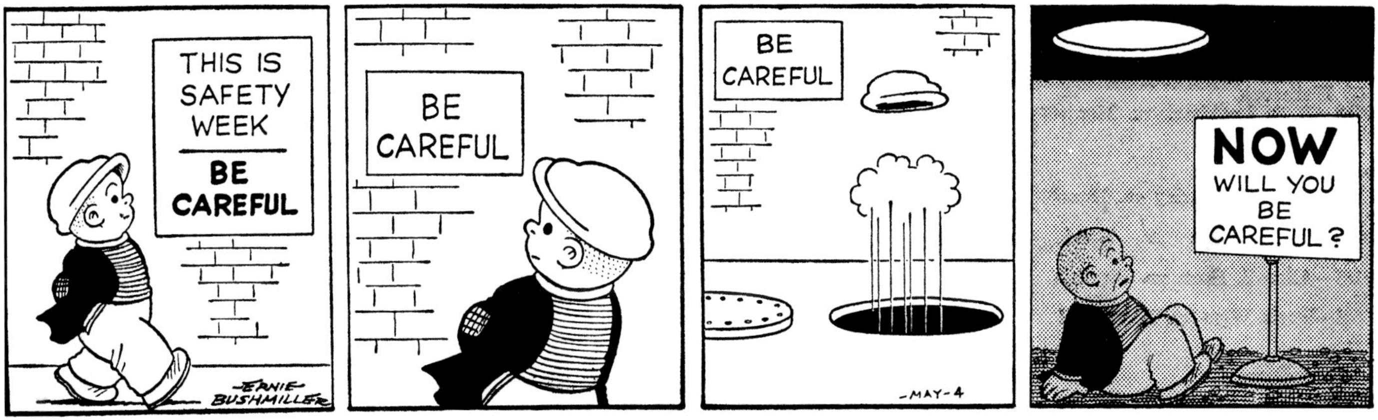
THIS IS SAFETY WEEK
BE CAREFUL
ERNIE BUSHMILLER
BE CAREFUL
BE CAREFUL
MAY-4
NOW WILL YOU BE CAREFUL ?

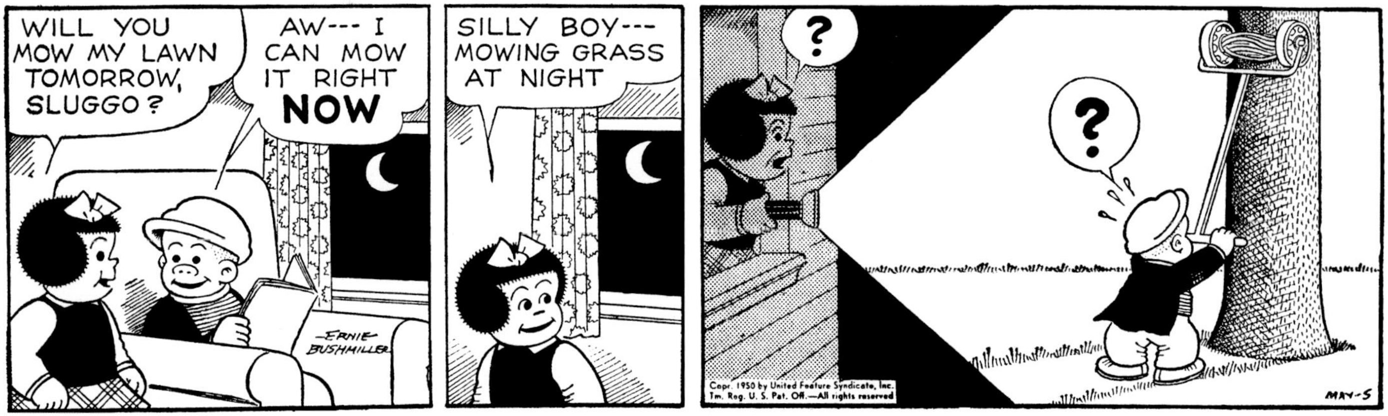
WILL YOU MOW MY LAWN TOMORROW, SLUGGO?
AW--- I CAN MOW IT RIGHT **NOW**
ERNIE BUSHMILLER
SILLY BOY--- MOWING GRASS AT NIGHT
?
?
Copr. 1950 by United Feature Syndicate, Inc. Tm. Reg. U. S. Pat. Off.—All rights reserved
MAY-5

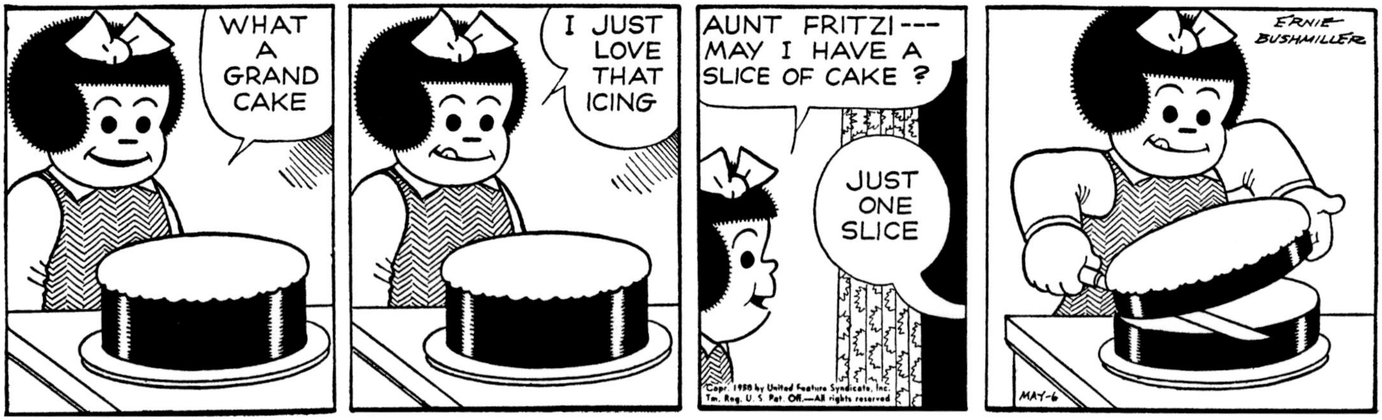
WHAT A GRAND CAKE
I JUST LOVE THAT ICING
AUNT FRITZI--- MAY I HAVE A SLICE OF CAKE?
JUST ONE SLICE
Copr. 1950 by United Feature Syndicate, Inc. Tm. Reg. U. S. Pat. Off.—All rights reserved
ERNIE BUSHMILLER
MAY-6

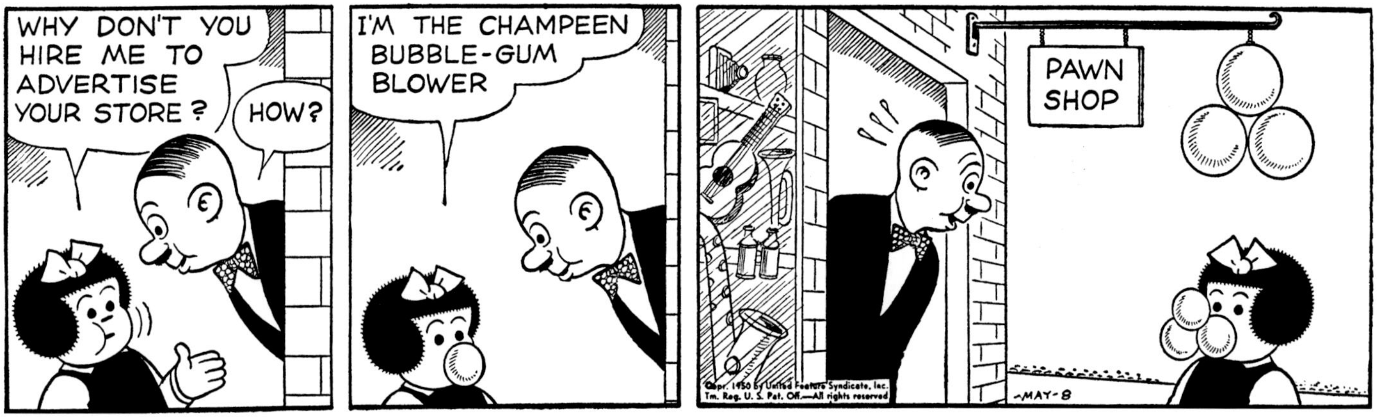
WHY DON'T YOU HIRE ME TO ADVERTISE YOUR STORE?
HOW?
I'M THE CHAMPEEN BUBBLE-GUM BLOWER
PAWN SHOP
Copr. 1950 by United Feature Syndicate, Inc. Tm. Reg. U. S. Pat. Off.—All rights reserved
MAY-8

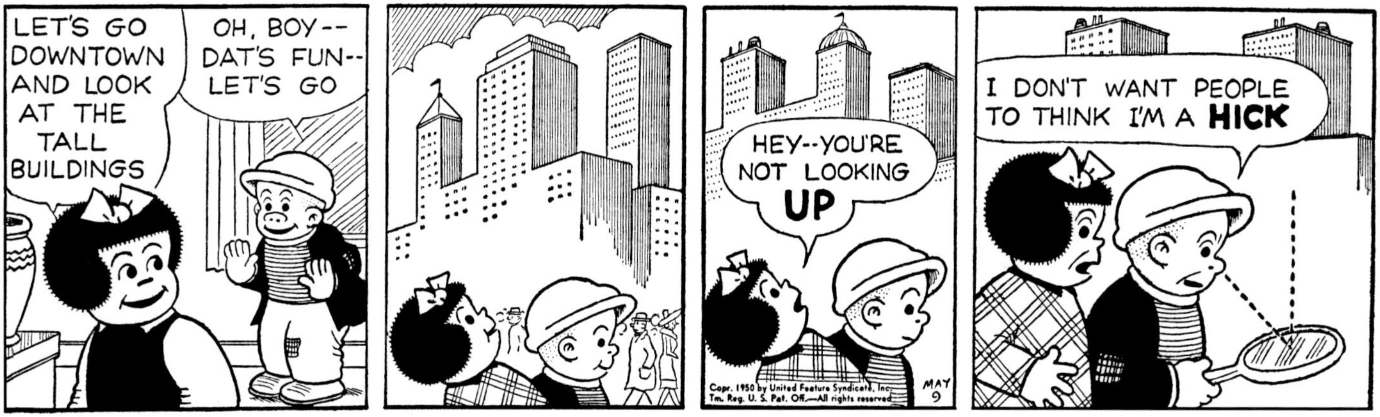
LET'S GO DOWNTOWN AND LOOK AT THE TALL BUILDINGS
OH, BOY-- DAT'S FUN-- LET'S GO
HEY--YOU'RE NOT LOOKING UP
Copr. 1950 by United Feature Syndicate, Inc. Tm. Reg. U. S. Pat. Off.—All rights reserved
MAY 9
I DON'T WANT PEOPLE TO THINK I'M A HICK

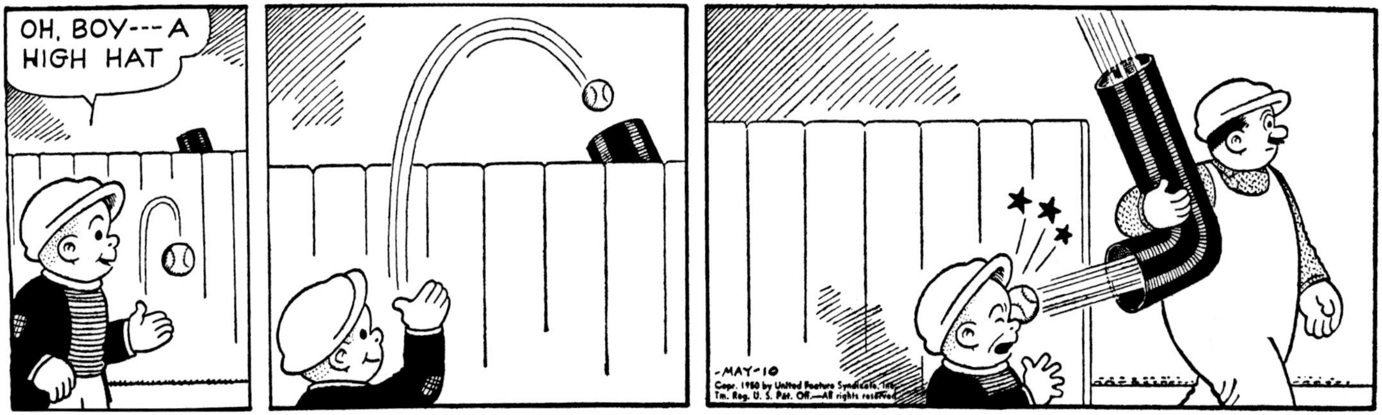
OH, BOY--- A HIGH HAT
-MAY-10
Copr. 1950 by United Feature Syndicate, Inc. Tm. Reg. U. S. Pat. Off.—All rights reserved

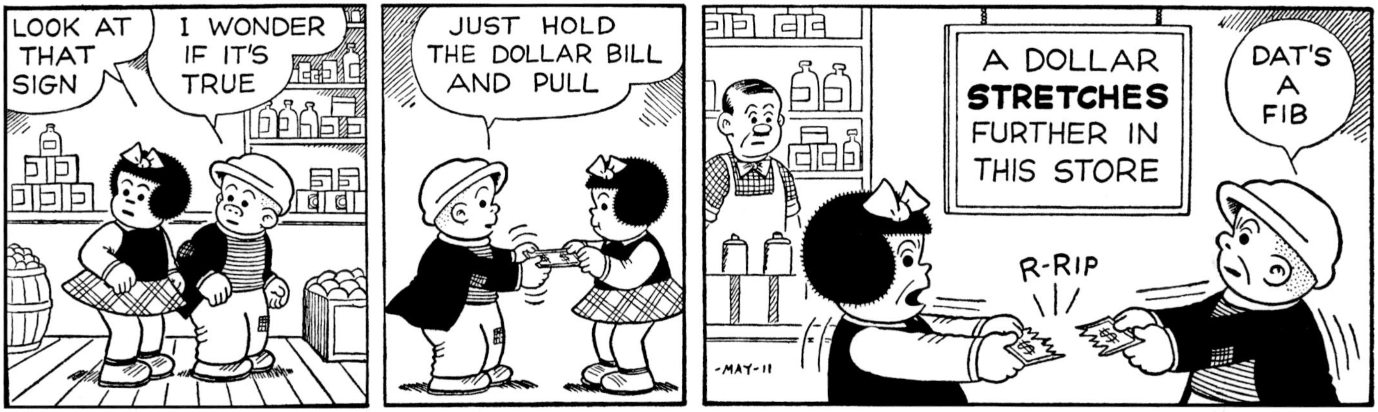
LOOK AT THAT SIGN
I WONDER IF IT'S TRUE
JUST HOLD THE DOLLAR BILL AND PULL
A DOLLAR STRETCHES FURTHER IN THIS STORE
DAT'S A FIB
R-RIP
-MAY-11

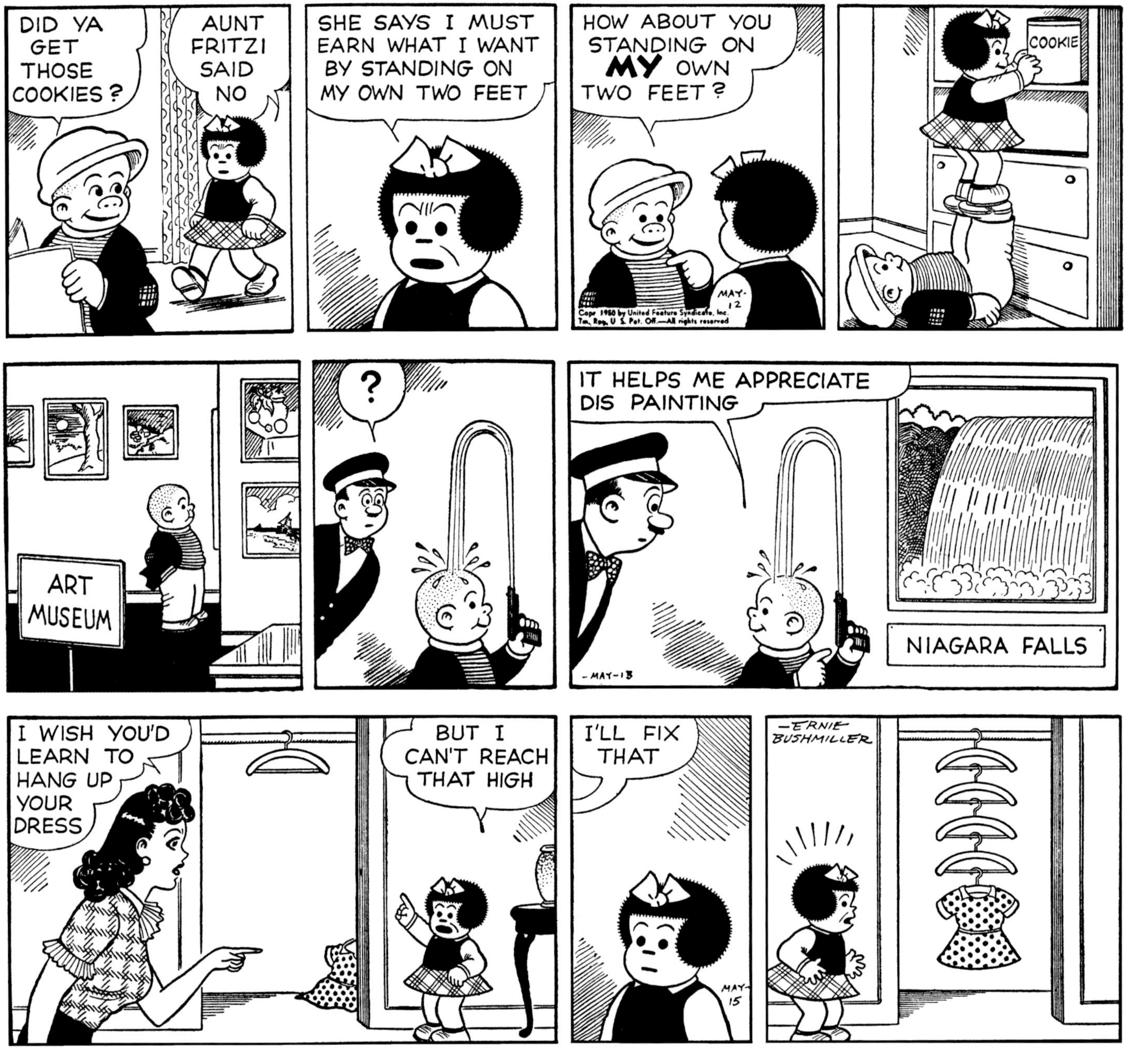
DID YA GET THOSE COOKIES?
AUNT FRITZI SAID NO
SHE SAYS I MUST EARN WHAT I WANT BY STANDING ON MY OWN TWO FEET
HOW ABOUT YOU STANDING ON MY OWN TWO FEET?
MAY-12
Copr 1950 by United Feature Syndicate, Inc. Tm. Reg. U. S. Pat. Off.—All rights reserved
COOKIE
ART MUSEUM
?
IT HELPS ME APPRECIATE DIS PAINTING
NIAGARA FALLS
MAY-13
I WISH YOU'D LEARN TO HANG UP YOUR DRESS
BUT I CAN'T REACH THAT HIGH
I'LL FIX THAT
MAY-15
ERNIE BUSHMILLER

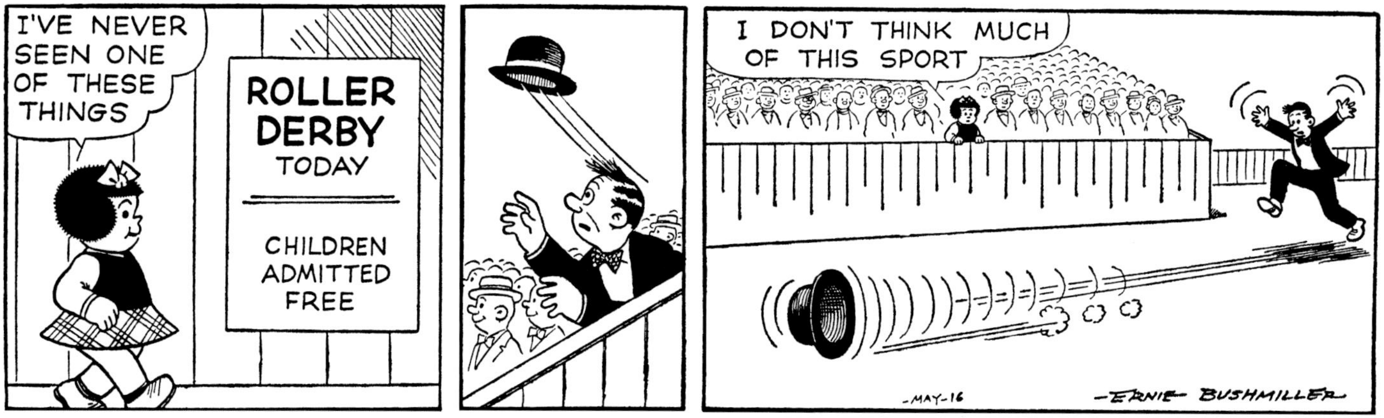
I'VE NEVER SEEN ONE OF THESE THINGS
ROLLER DERBY TODAY
CHILDREN ADMITTED FREE
I DON'T THINK MUCH OF THIS SPORT
-MAY-16
-ERNIE BUSHMILLER

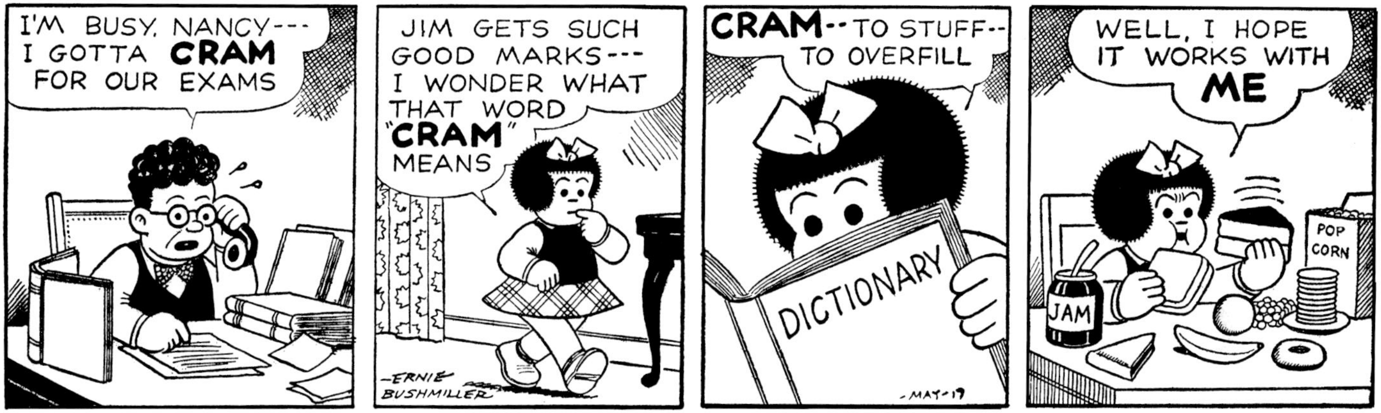
I'M BUSY, NANCY--- I GOTTA **CRAM** FOR OUR EXAMS
JIM GETS SUCH GOOD MARKS--- I WONDER WHAT THAT WORD "**CRAM**" MEANS
-ERNIE BUSHMILLER
CRAM--TO STUFF--TO OVERFILL
DICTIONARY
-MAY-17
WELL, I HOPE IT WORKS WITH **ME**
POP CORN
JAM

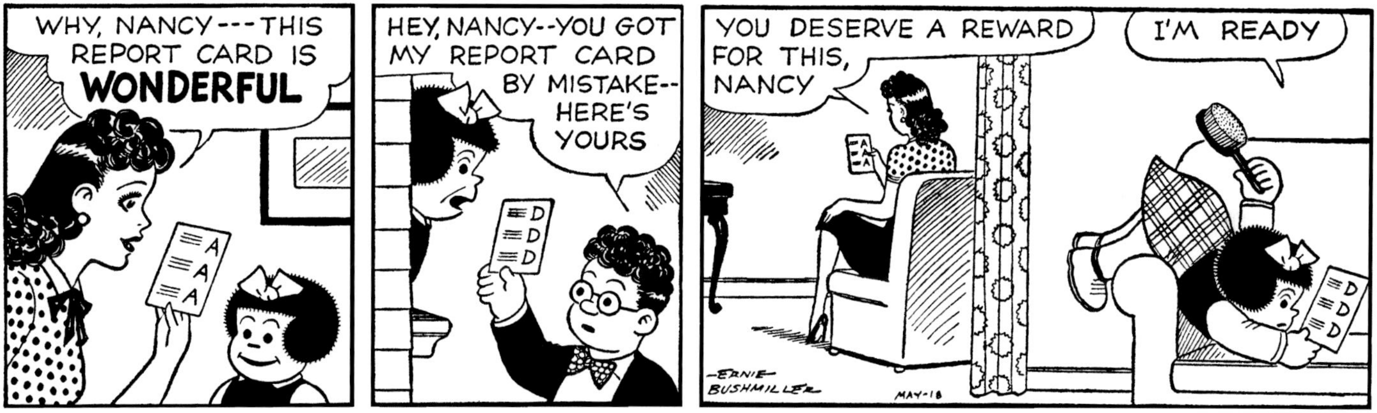
WHY, NANCY---THIS REPORT CARD IS **WONDERFUL**
A
A
A
HEY, NANCY--YOU GOT MY REPORT CARD BY MISTAKE--HERE'S YOURS
D
D
D
YOU DESERVE A REWARD FOR THIS, NANCY
I'M READY
-ERNIE BUSHMILLER
MAY-18

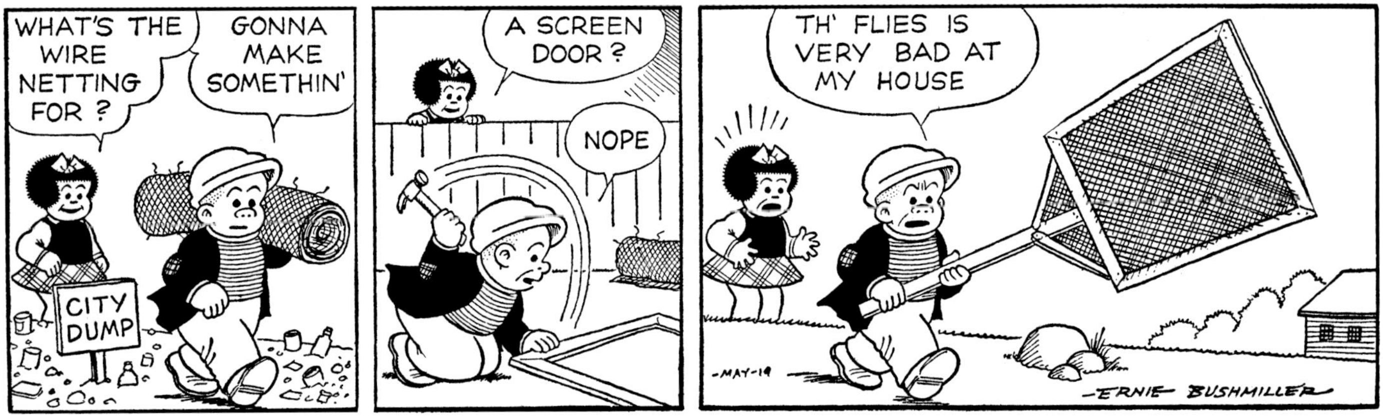
WHAT'S THE WIRE NETTING FOR ?
GONNA MAKE SOMETHIN'
CITY DUMP
A SCREEN DOOR ?
NOPE
TH' FLIES IS VERY BAD AT MY HOUSE
MAY-19
ERNIE BUSHMILLER

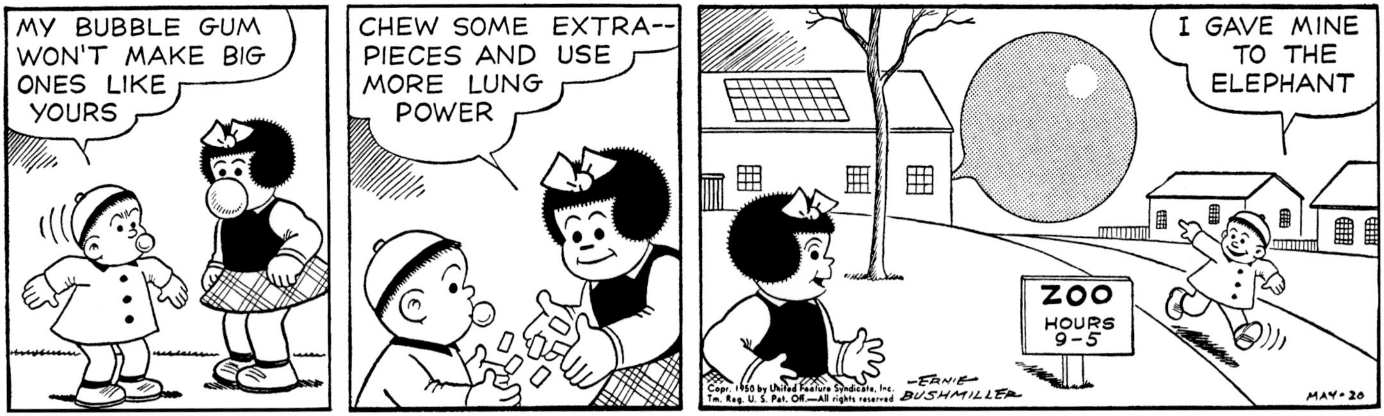
MY BUBBLE GUM WON'T MAKE BIG ONES LIKE YOURS
CHEW SOME EXTRA-- PIECES AND USE MORE LUNG POWER
I GAVE MINE TO THE ELEPHANT
ZOO
HOURS 9-5
Copr. 1950 by United Feature Syndicate, Inc.
Tm. Reg. U. S. Pat. Off.—All rights reserved
ERNIE BUSHMILLER
MAY-20

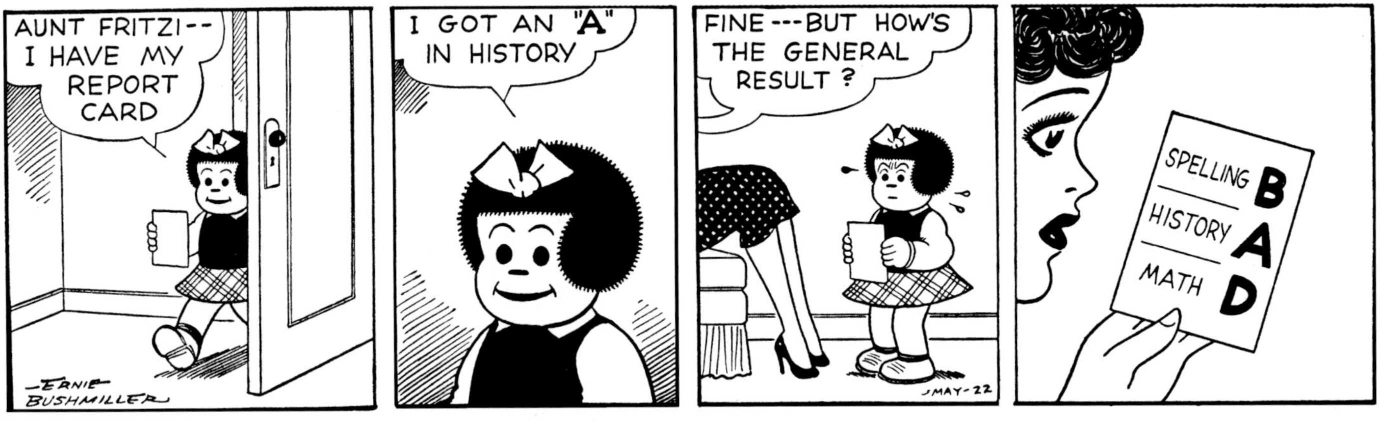
AUNT FRITZI-- I HAVE MY REPORT CARD
ERNIE BUSHMILLER
I GOT AN "A" IN HISTORY
FINE---BUT HOW'S THE GENERAL RESULT ?
MAY-22
SPELLING B
HISTORY A
MATH D

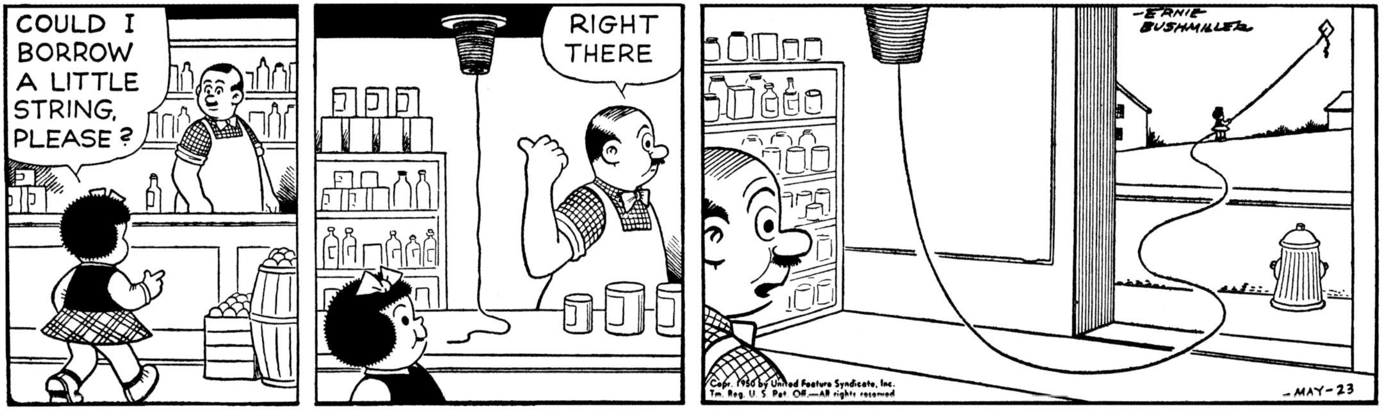
COULD I BORROW A LITTLE STRING, PLEASE?
RIGHT THERE
ERNIE BUSHMILLER
Copr. 1950 by United Feature Syndicate, Inc. Tm. Reg. U. S. Pat. Off.—All rights reserved
MAY-23

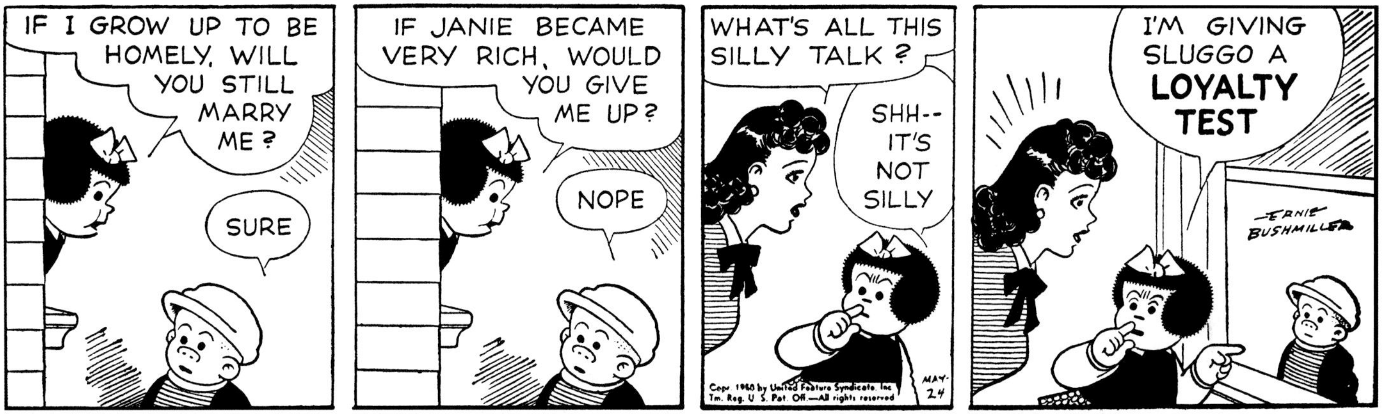
IF I GROW UP TO BE HOMELY, WILL YOU STILL MARRY ME?
SURE
IF JANIE BECAME VERY RICH, WOULD YOU GIVE ME UP?
NOPE
WHAT'S ALL THIS SILLY TALK?
SHH-- IT'S NOT SILLY
Copr. 1950 by United Feature Syndicate, Inc. Tm. Reg. U. S. Pat. Off.—All rights reserved
MAY-24
I'M GIVING SLUGGO A **LOYALTY TEST**
ERNIE BUSHMILLER

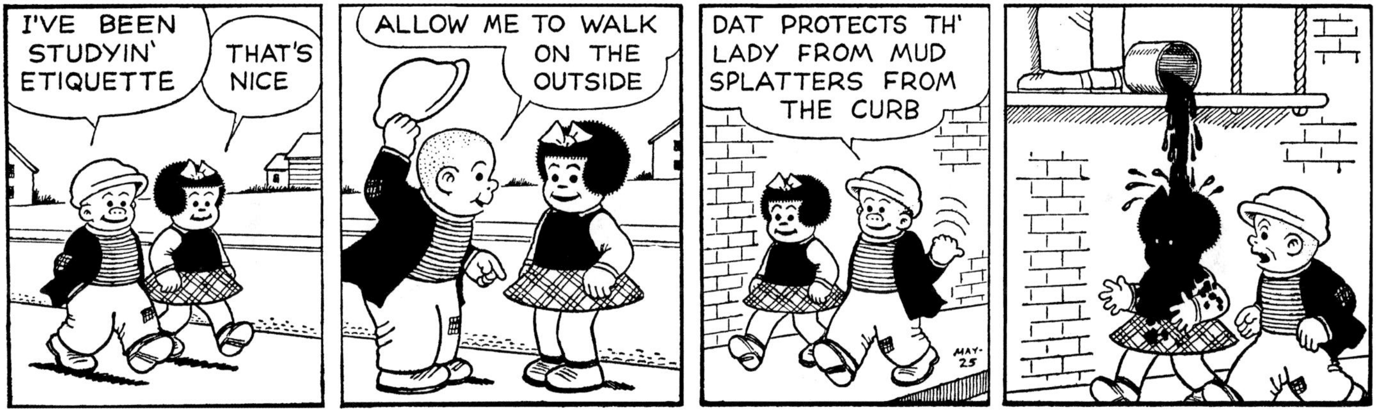
I'VE BEEN STUDYIN' ETIQUETTE
THAT'S NICE
ALLOW ME TO WALK ON THE OUTSIDE
DAT PROTECTS TH' LADY FROM MUD SPLATTERS FROM THE CURB
MAY-25

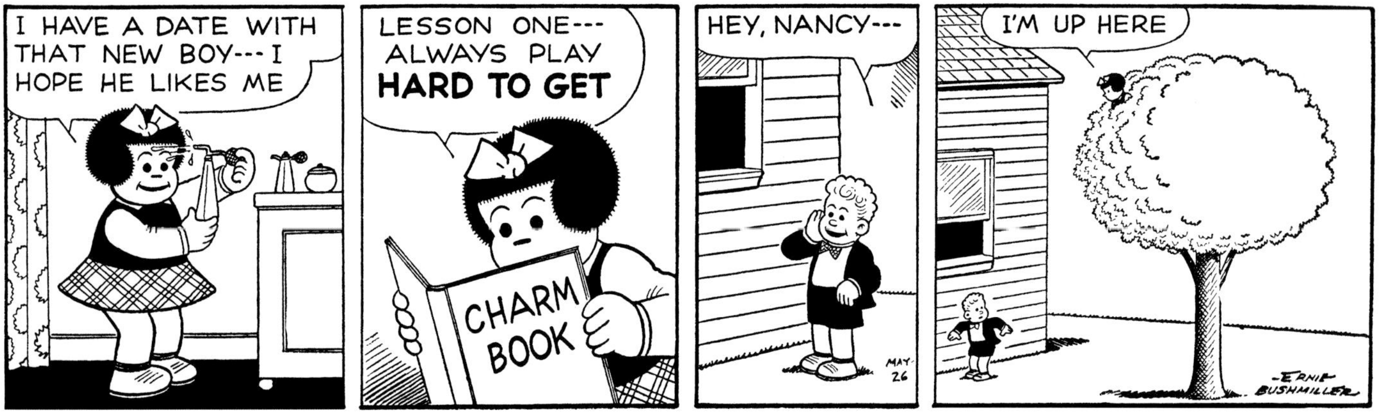
I HAVE A DATE WITH THAT NEW BOY--- I HOPE HE LIKES ME
LESSON ONE--- ALWAYS PLAY **HARD TO GET**
CHARM BOOK
HEY, NANCY---
MAY-26
I'M UP HERE
ERNIE BUSHMILLER

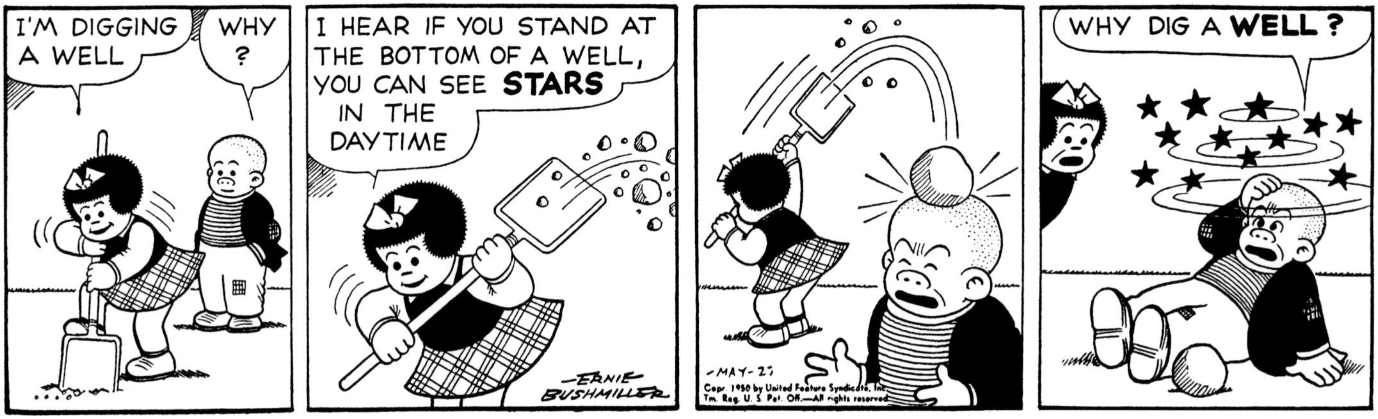
I'M DIGGING A WELL
WHY ?
I HEAR IF YOU STAND AT THE BOTTOM OF A WELL, YOU CAN SEE **STARS** IN THE DAYTIME
ERNIE BUSHMILLER
MAY-27
Copr. 1950 by United Feature Syndicate, Inc.
Tm. Reg. U. S. Pat. Off.—All rights reserved.
WHY DIG A **WELL** ?

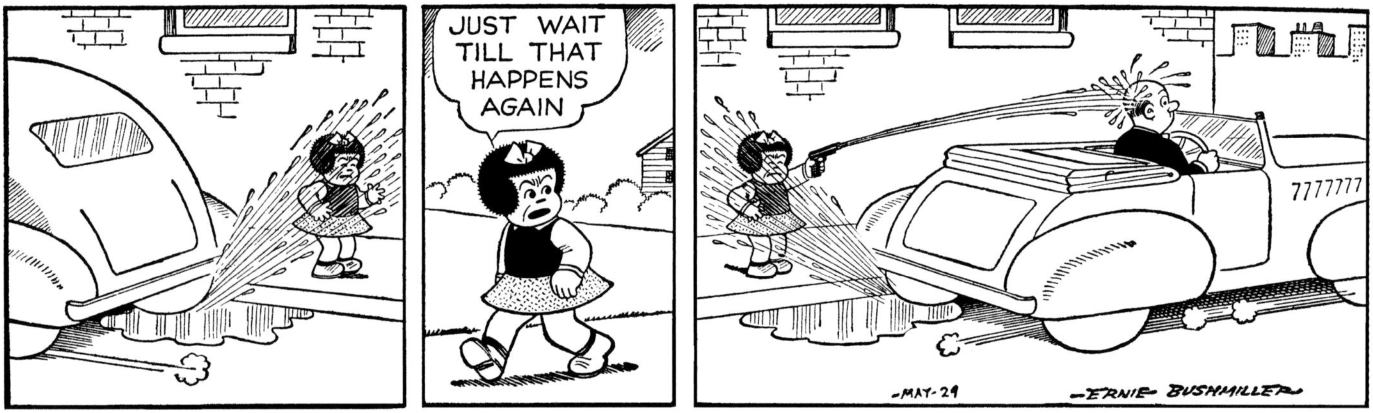
JUST WAIT TILL THAT HAPPENS AGAIN
7777777
MAY-29
ERNIE BUSHMILLER

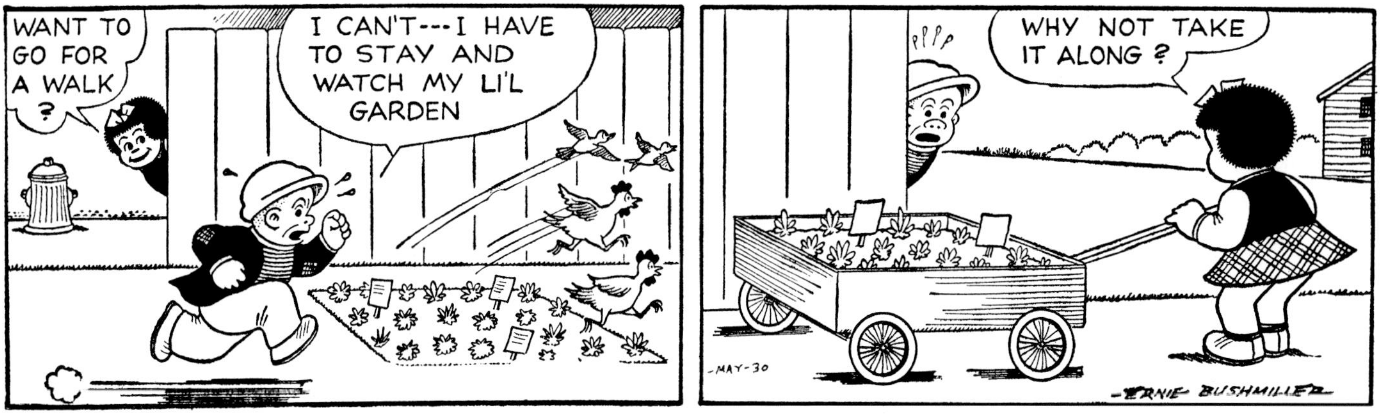
WANT TO GO FOR A WALK ?
I CAN'T---I HAVE TO STAY AND WATCH MY LI'L GARDEN
WHY NOT TAKE IT ALONG ?
MAY-30
ERNIE BUSHMILLER

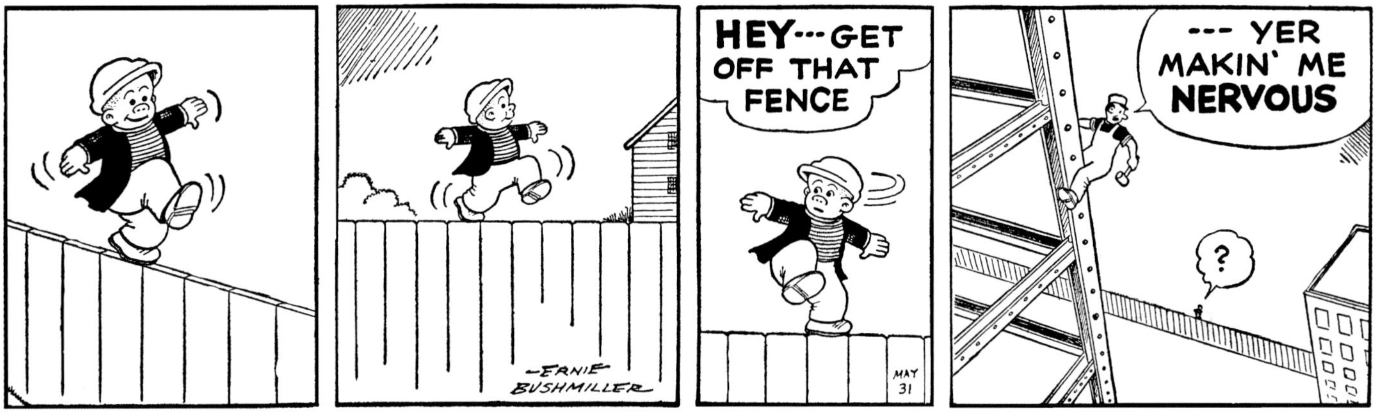
ERNIE BUSHMILLER
HEY---GET OFF THAT FENCE
MAY 31
--- YER MAKIN' ME NERVOUS
?

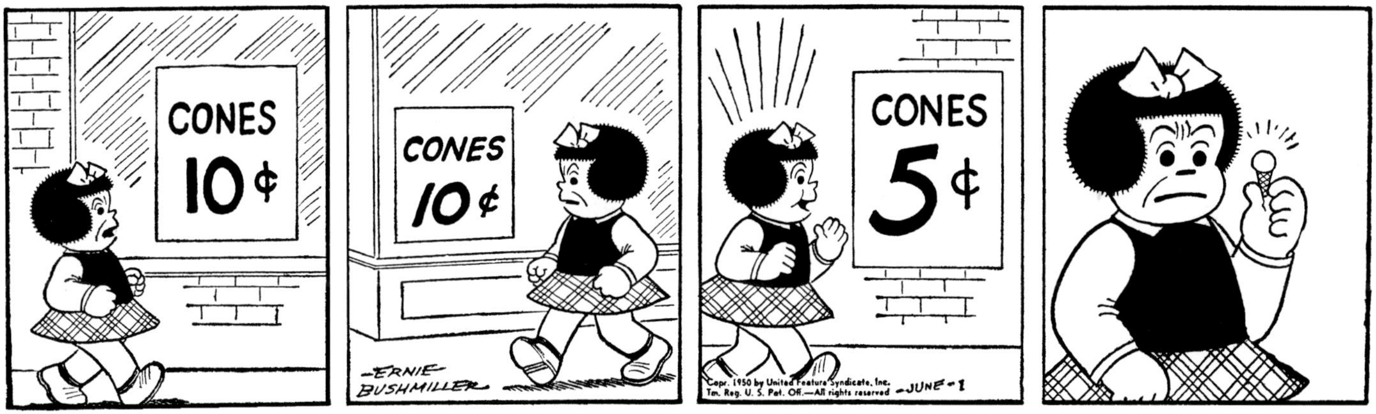
CONES 10¢
CONES 10¢
ERNIE BUSHMILLER
CONES 5¢
Copr. 1950 by United Feature Syndicate, Inc.
Tm. Reg. U. S. Pat. Off.—All rights reserved
JUNE-1

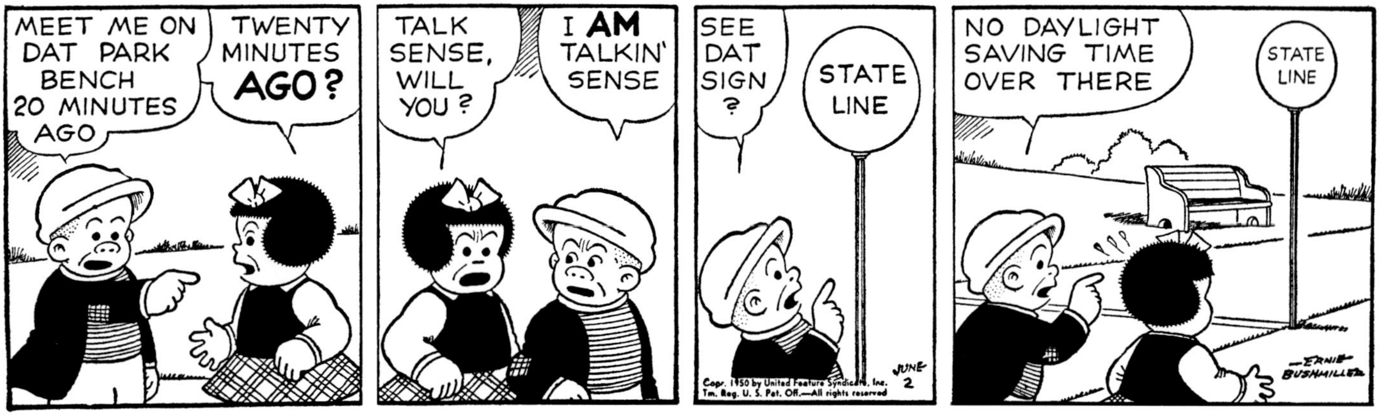
MEET ME ON DAT PARK BENCH 20 MINUTES AGO
TWENTY MINUTES AGO?
TALK SENSE, WILL YOU?
I AM TALKIN' SENSE
SEE DAT SIGN?
STATE LINE
Copr. 1950 by United Feature Syndicate, Inc. Tm. Reg. U. S. Pat. Off.—All rights reserved
JUNE 2
NO DAYLIGHT SAVING TIME OVER THERE
STATE LINE
ERNIE BUSHMILLER

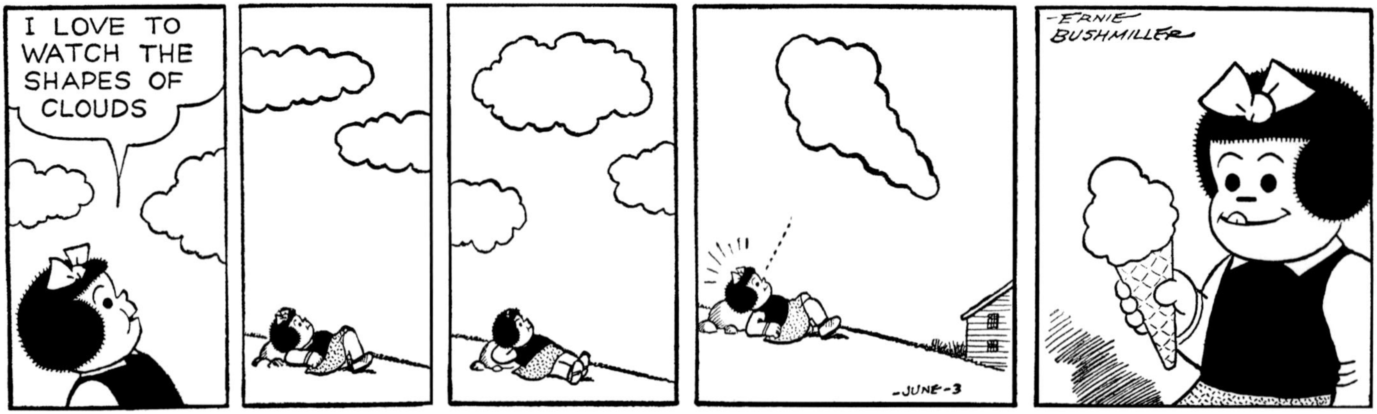
I LOVE TO WATCH THE SHAPES OF CLOUDS
JUNE-3
ERNIE BUSHMILLER

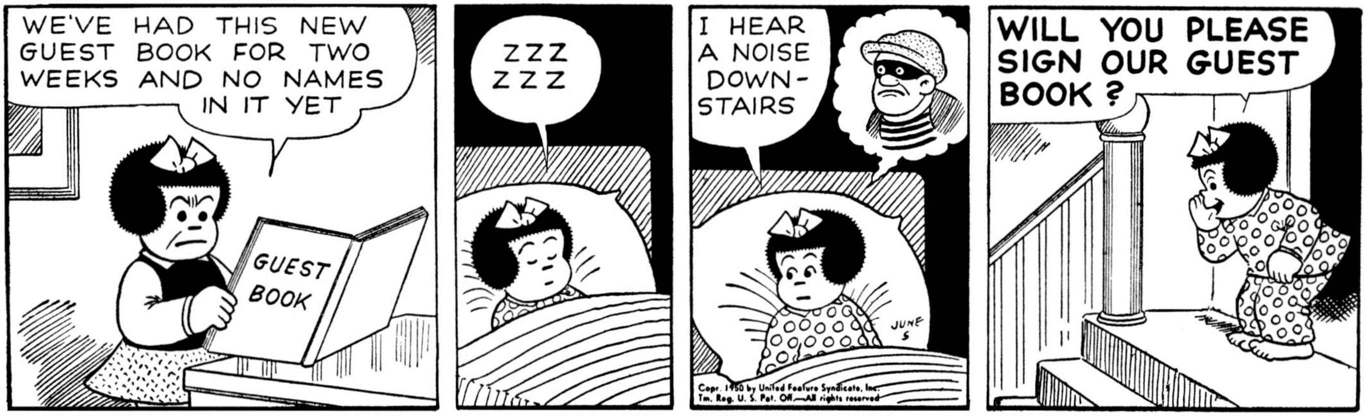
WE'VE HAD THIS NEW GUEST BOOK FOR TWO WEEKS AND NO NAMES IN IT YET
GUEST BOOK
ZZZ ZZZ
I HEAR A NOISE DOWN-STAIRS
JUNE 5
Copr. 1950 by United Feature Syndicate, Inc. Tm. Reg. U. S. Pat. Off.—All rights reserved
WILL YOU PLEASE SIGN OUR GUEST BOOK?

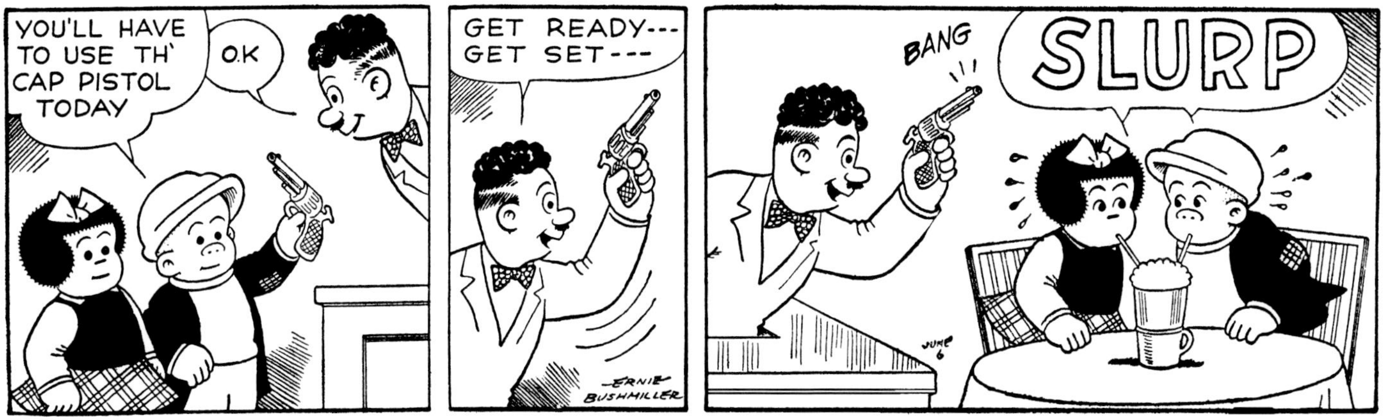
YOU'LL HAVE TO USE TH' CAP PISTOL TODAY
O.K
GET READY--- GET SET---
ERNIE BUSHMILLER
BANG
SLURP
JUNE 6

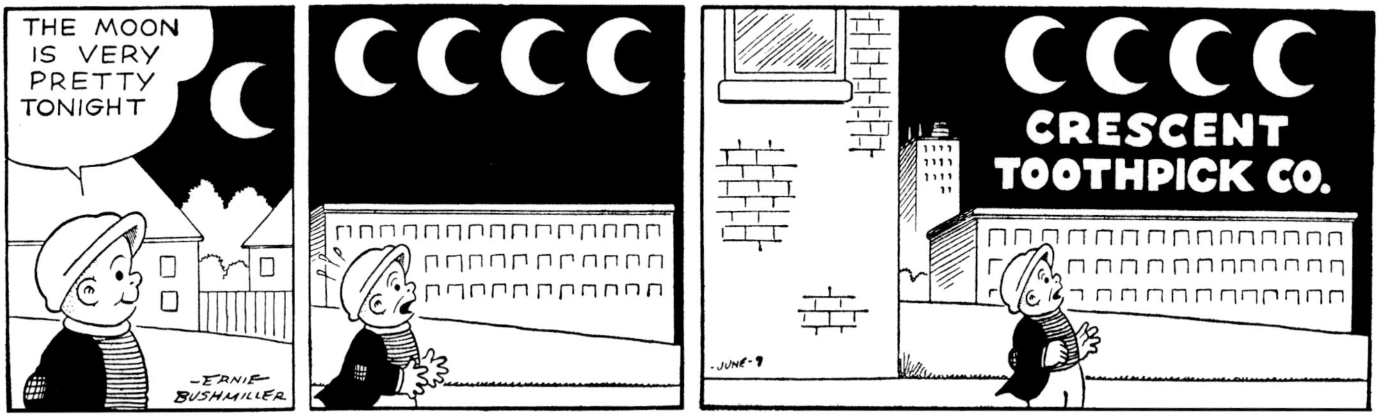
THE MOON IS VERY PRETTY TONIGHT
ERNIE BUSHMILLER
CRESCENT TOOTHPICK CO.
JUNE-7

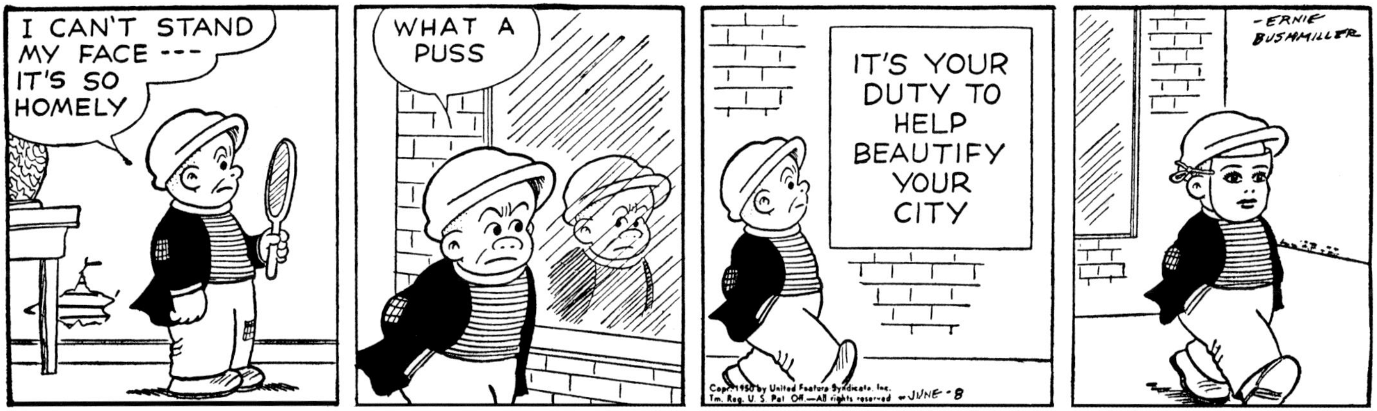
I CAN'T STAND MY FACE--- IT'S SO HOMELY
WHAT A PUSS
IT'S YOUR DUTY TO HELP BEAUTIFY YOUR CITY
Copr. 1950 by United Feature Syndicate, Inc.
Tm. Reg. U. S. Pat. Off.—All rights reserved
JUNE-8
ERNIE BUSHMILLER

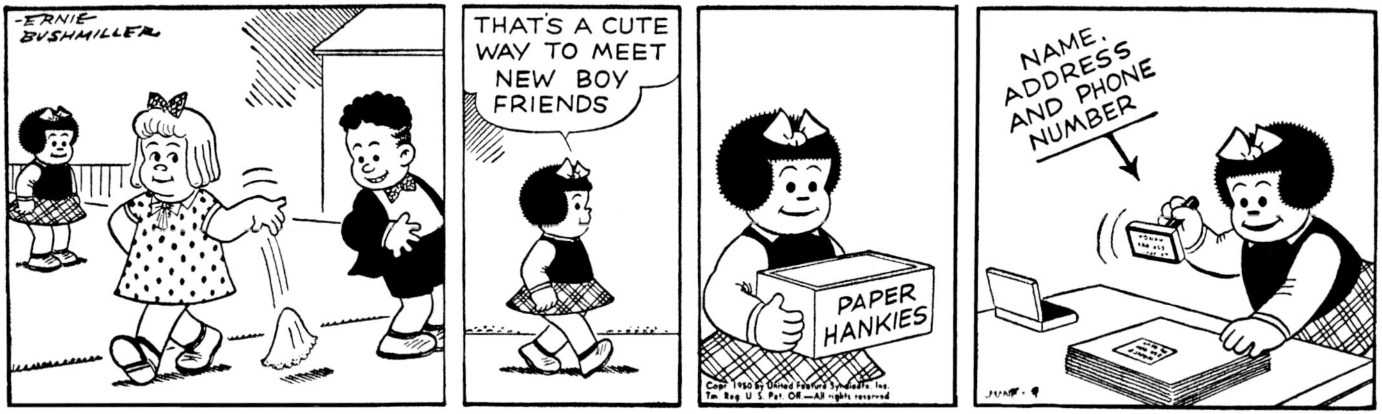

-ERNIE BUSHMILLER
THAT'S A CUTE WAY TO MEET NEW BOY FRIENDS
PAPER HANKIES
Copr. 1950 by United Feature Syndicate, Inc. Tm. Reg. U.S. Pat. Off.—All rights reserved
NAME, ADDRESS AND PHONE NUMBER
JUNE 9

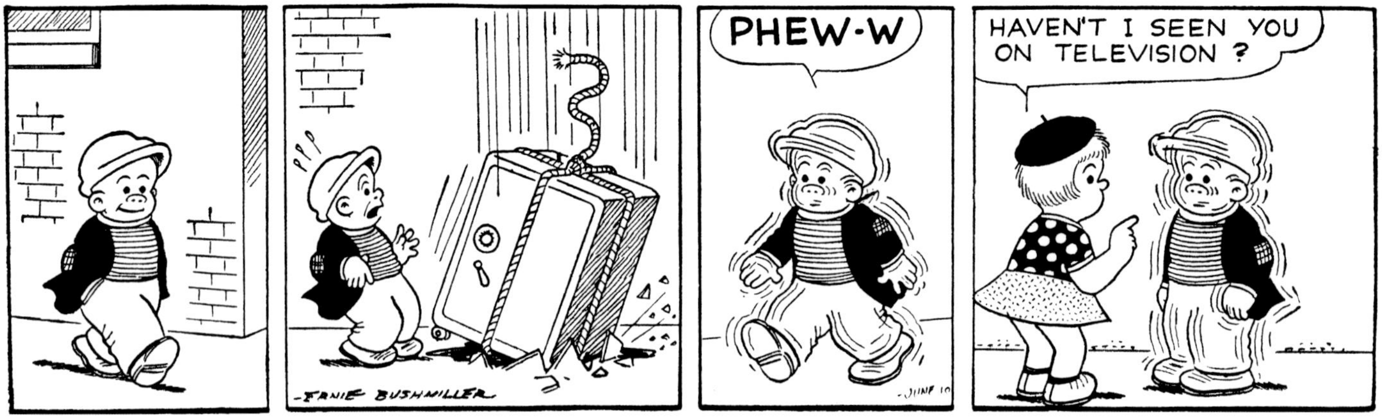

-ERNIE BUSHMILLER
PHEW-W
JUNE 10
HAVEN'T I SEEN YOU ON TELEVISION ?

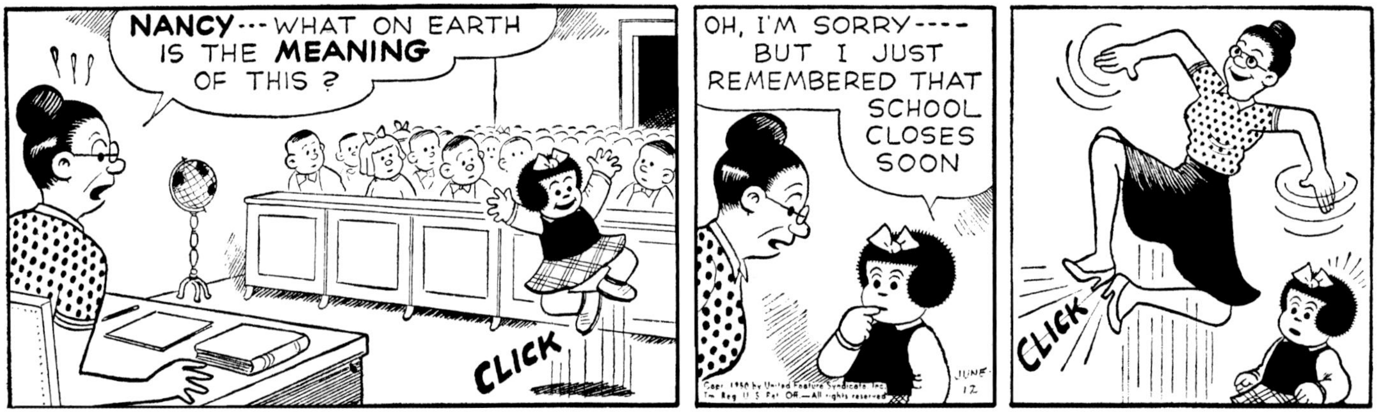

NANCY--- WHAT ON EARTH IS THE MEANING OF THIS ?
CLICK
OH, I'M SORRY---- BUT I JUST REMEMBERED THAT SCHOOL CLOSES SOON
Copr. 1950 by United Feature Syndicate, Inc. Tm. Reg. U.S. Pat. Off.—All rights reserved
JUNE 12
CLICK

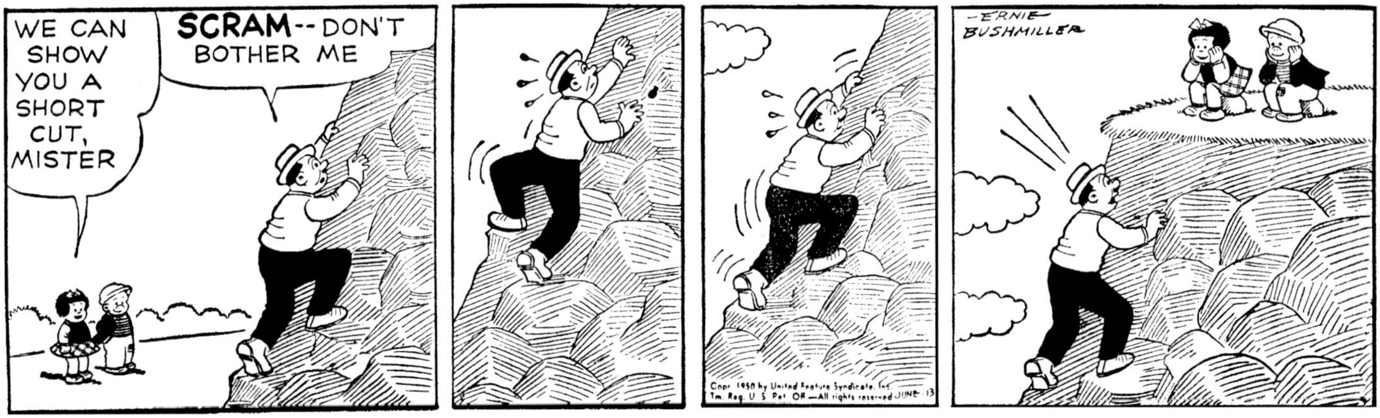
WE CAN SHOW YOU A SHORT CUT, MISTER
SCRAM-- DON'T BOTHER ME
Copr. 1950 by United Feature Syndicate, Inc. Tm. Reg. U. S. Pat. Off.—All rights reserved JUNE 13
ERNIE BUSHMILLER

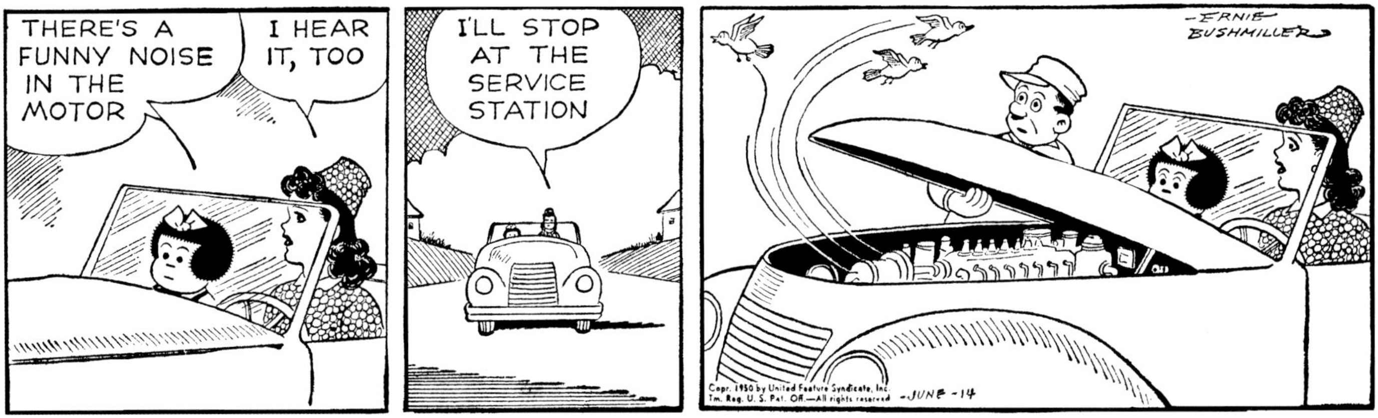
THERE'S A FUNNY NOISE IN THE MOTOR
I HEAR IT, TOO
I'LL STOP AT THE SERVICE STATION
ERNIE BUSHMILLER
Copr. 1950 by United Feature Syndicate, Inc. Tm. Reg. U. S. Pat. Off.—All rights reserved JUNE 14

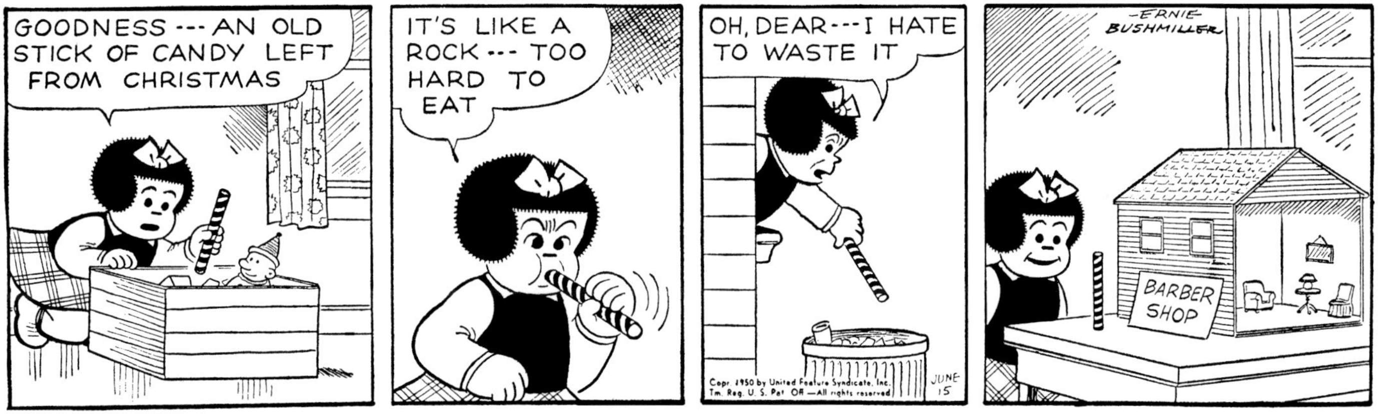
GOODNESS --- AN OLD STICK OF CANDY LEFT FROM CHRISTMAS
IT'S LIKE A ROCK --- TOO HARD TO EAT
OH, DEAR --- I HATE TO WASTE IT
Copr. 1950 by United Feature Syndicate, Inc. Tm. Reg. U. S. Pat. Off.—All rights reserved
JUNE 15
ERNIE BUSHMILLER
BARBER SHOP

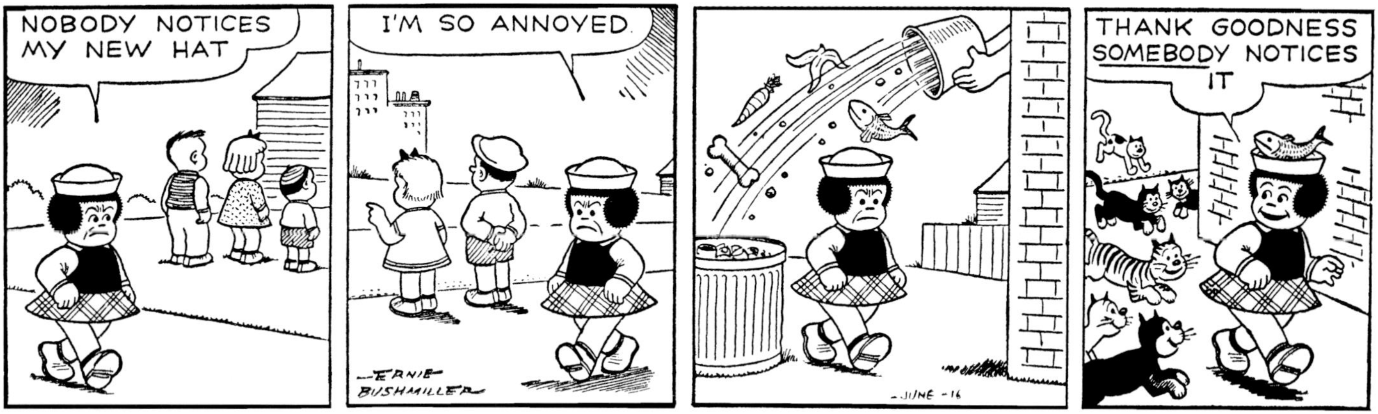
NOBODY NOTICES MY NEW HAT
I'M SO ANNOYED
ERNIE BUSHMILLER
JUNE-16
THANK GOODNESS SOMEBODY NOTICES IT

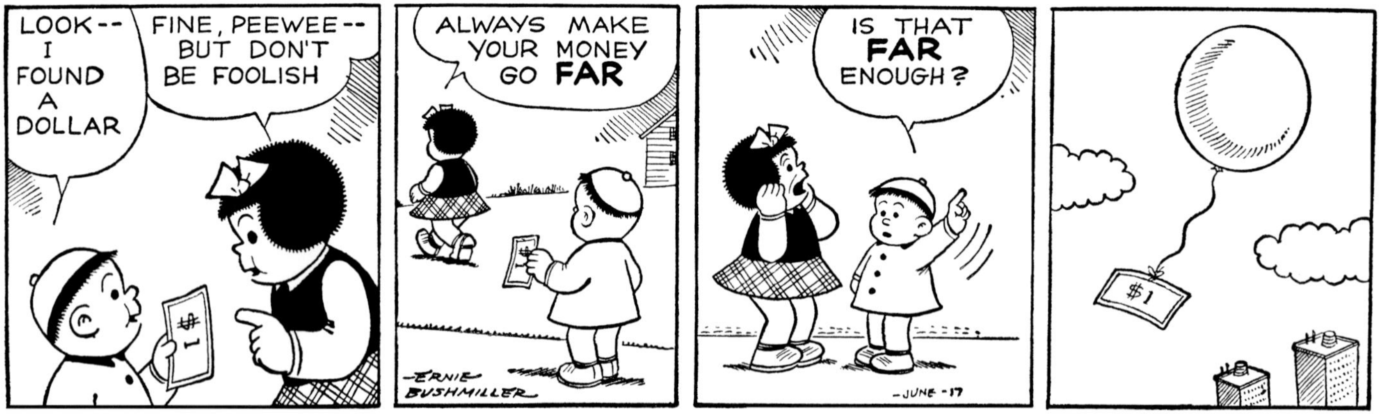
LOOK-- I FOUND A DOLLAR
FINE, PEEWEE-- BUT DON'T BE FOOLISH
ALWAYS MAKE YOUR MONEY GO FAR
ERNIE BUSHMILLER
IS THAT FAR ENOUGH?
JUNE-17
$1

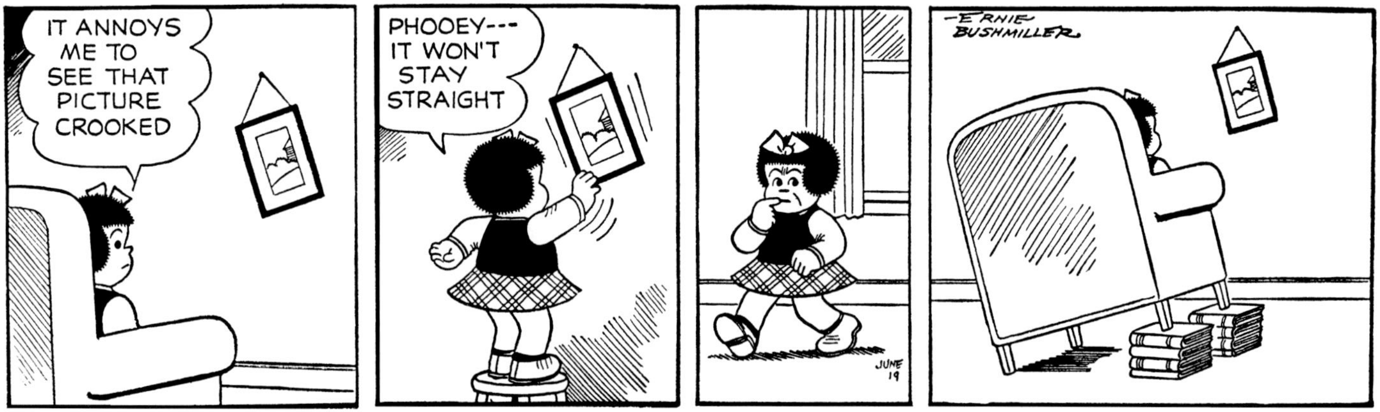
IT ANNOYS ME TO SEE THAT PICTURE CROOKED
PHOOEY--- IT WON'T STAY STRAIGHT
JUNE 19
ERNIE BUSHMILLER

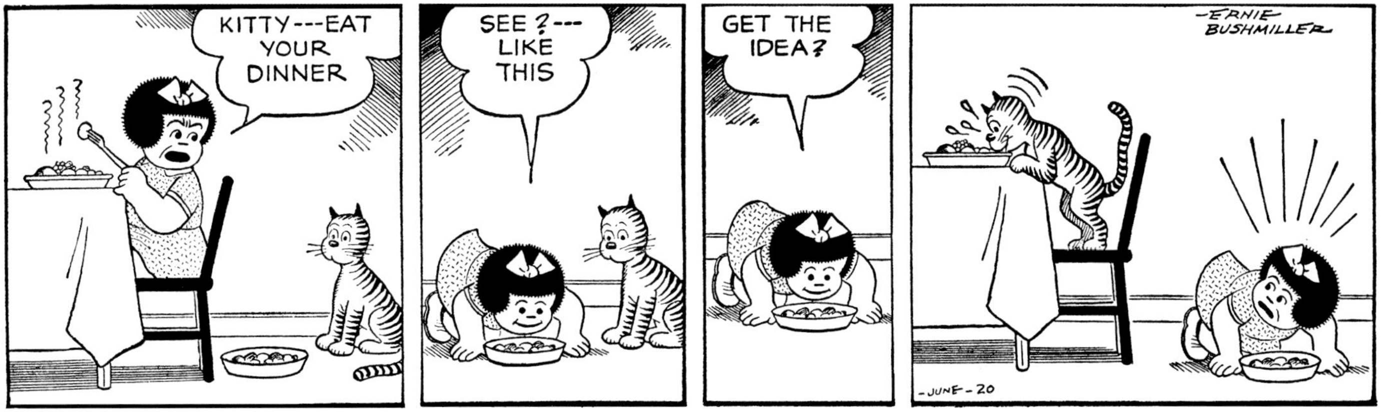
KITTY---EAT YOUR DINNER
SEE ?--- LIKE THIS
GET THE IDEA?
-ERNIE BUSHMILLER
-JUNE-20

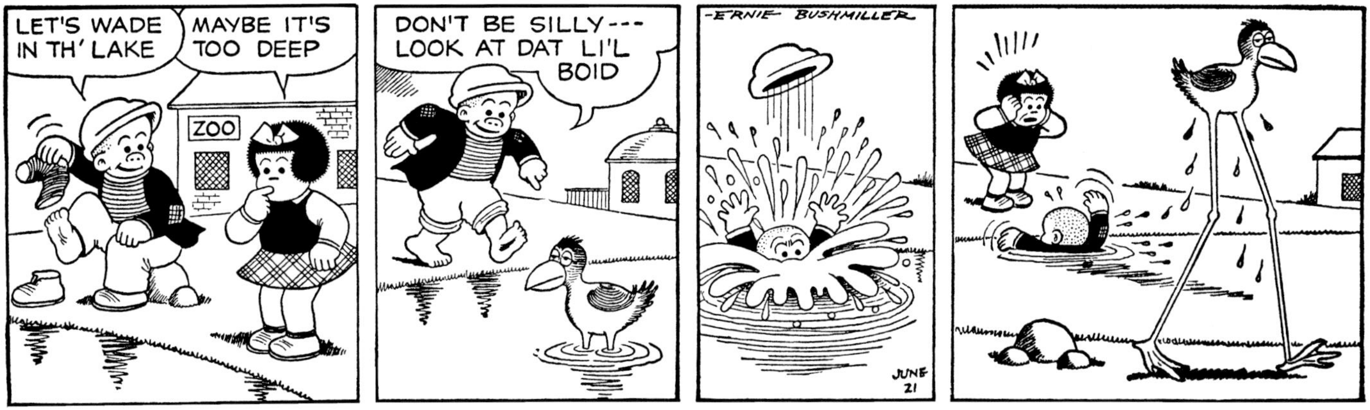
LET'S WADE IN TH' LAKE
MAYBE IT'S TOO DEEP
ZOO
DON'T BE SILLY--- LOOK AT DAT LI'L BOID
-ERNIE BUSHMILLER
JUNE 21

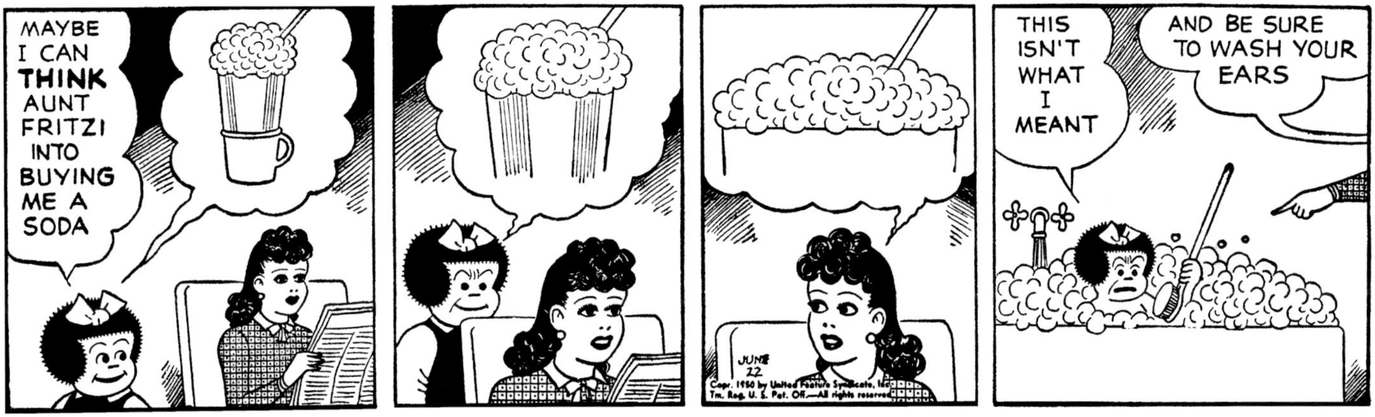
MAYBE I CAN THINK AUNT FRITZI INTO BUYING ME A SODA
JUNE 22
Copr. 1950 by United Feature Syndicate, Inc.
Tm. Reg. U. S. Pat. Off.—All rights reserved
THIS ISN'T WHAT I MEANT
AND BE SURE TO WASH YOUR EARS

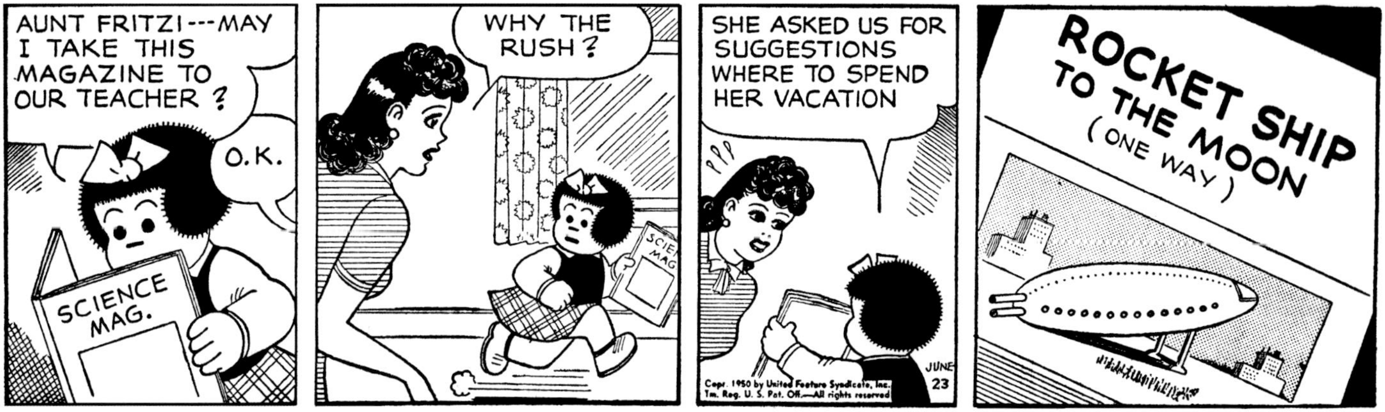
AUNT FRITZI---MAY I TAKE THIS MAGAZINE TO OUR TEACHER ?
O.K.
SCIENCE MAG.
WHY THE RUSH ?
SHE ASKED US FOR SUGGESTIONS WHERE TO SPEND HER VACATION
Copr. 1950 by United Feature Syndicate, Inc. Tm. Reg. U. S. Pat. Off.—All rights reserved
JUNE 23
ROCKET SHIP TO THE MOON
(ONE WAY)

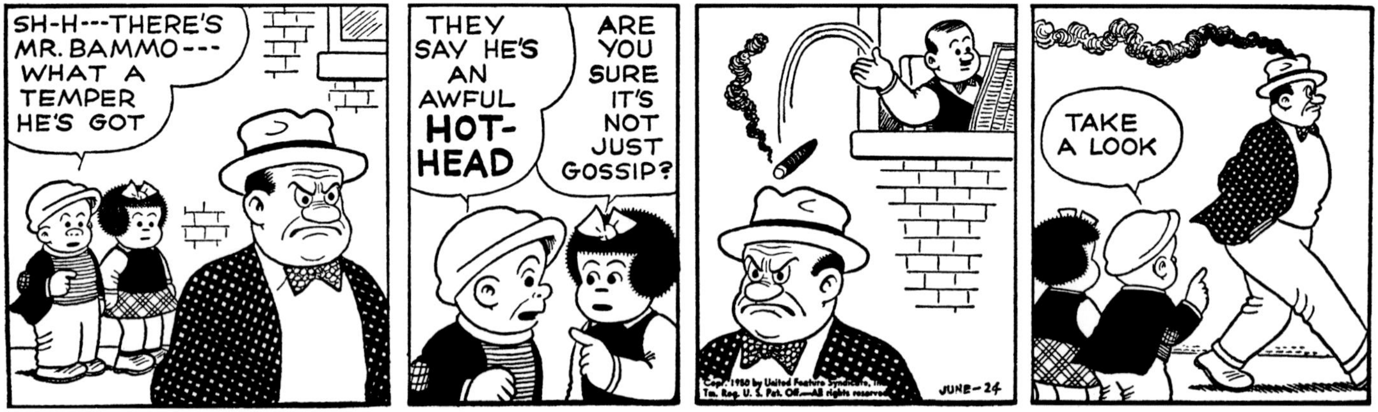
SH-H---THERE'S MR. BAMMO--- WHAT A TEMPER HE'S GOT
THEY SAY HE'S AN AWFUL HOT-HEAD
ARE YOU SURE IT'S NOT JUST GOSSIP?
Copr. 1950 by United Feature Syndicate, Inc. Tm. Reg. U. S. Pat. Off.—All rights reserved
JUNE-24
TAKE A LOOK

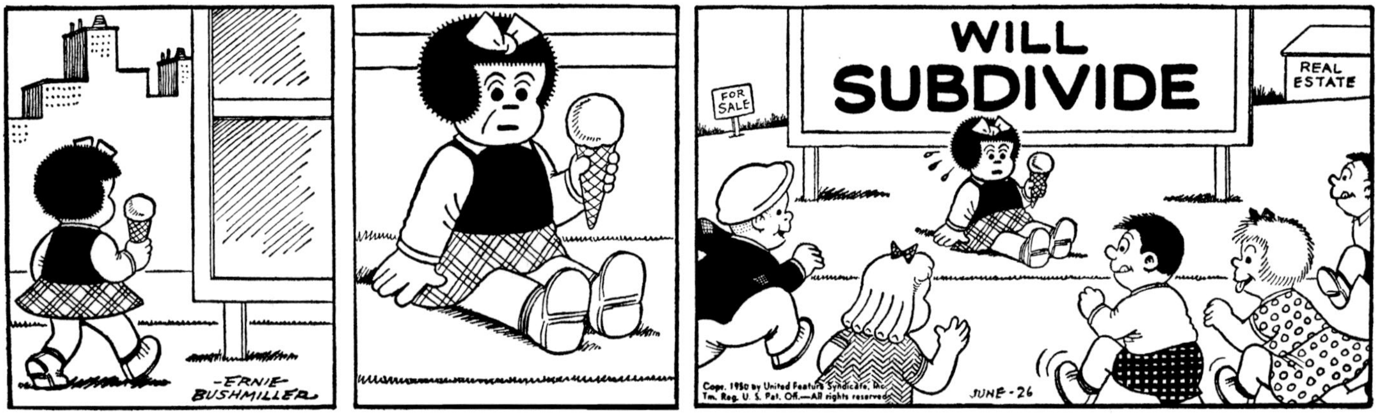
-ERNIE BUSHMILLER
FOR SALE
WILL SUBDIVIDE
REAL ESTATE
Copr. 1950 by United Feature Syndicate, Inc. Tm. Reg. U. S. Pat. Off.—All rights reserved
JUNE-26

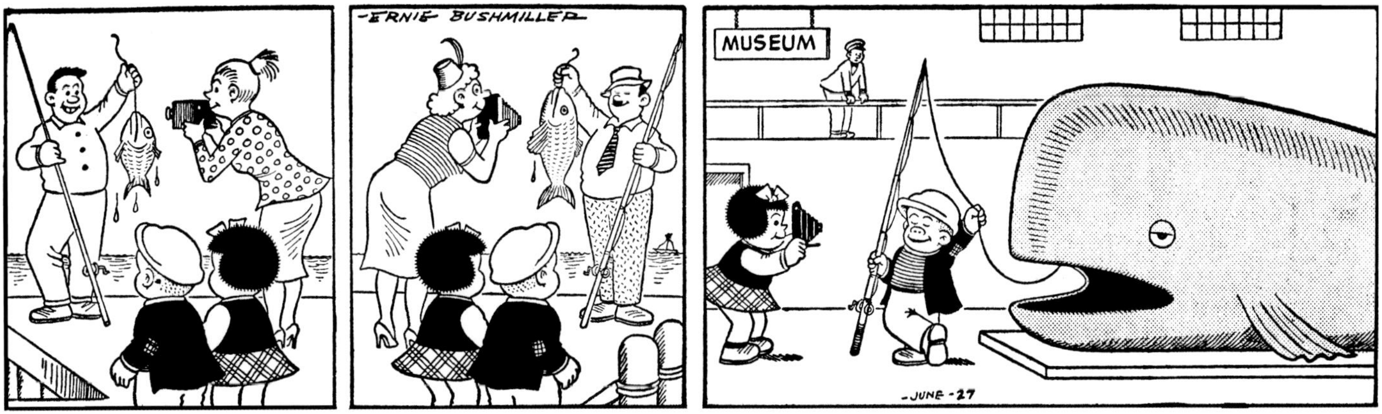

-ERNIE BUSHMILLER
MUSEUM
-JUNE-27

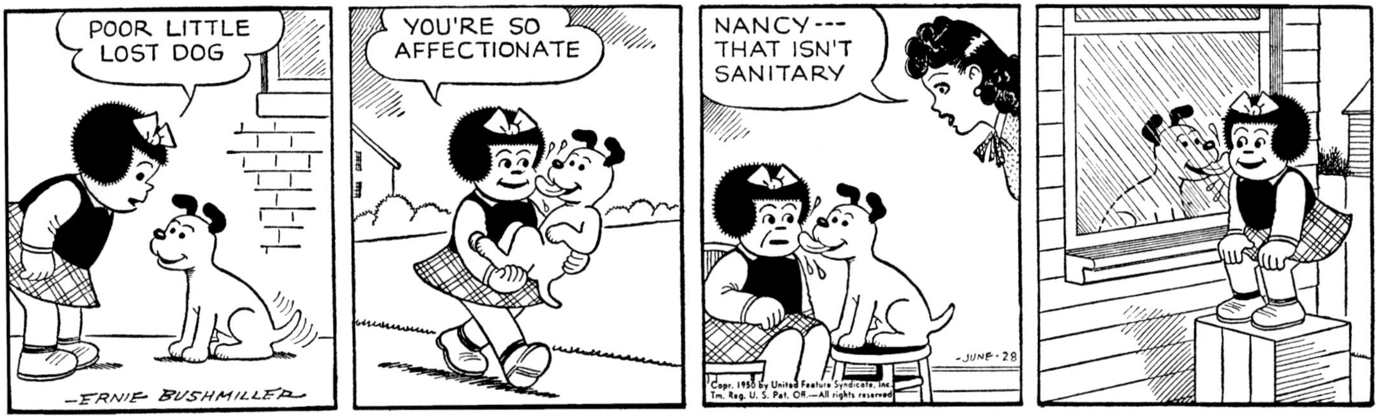

POOR LITTLE LOST DOG
-ERNIE BUSHMILLER
YOU'RE SO AFFECTIONATE
NANCY--- THAT ISN'T SANITARY
Copr. 1950 by United Feature Syndicate, Inc. Tm. Reg. U. S. Pat. Off.—All rights reserved
-JUNE-28

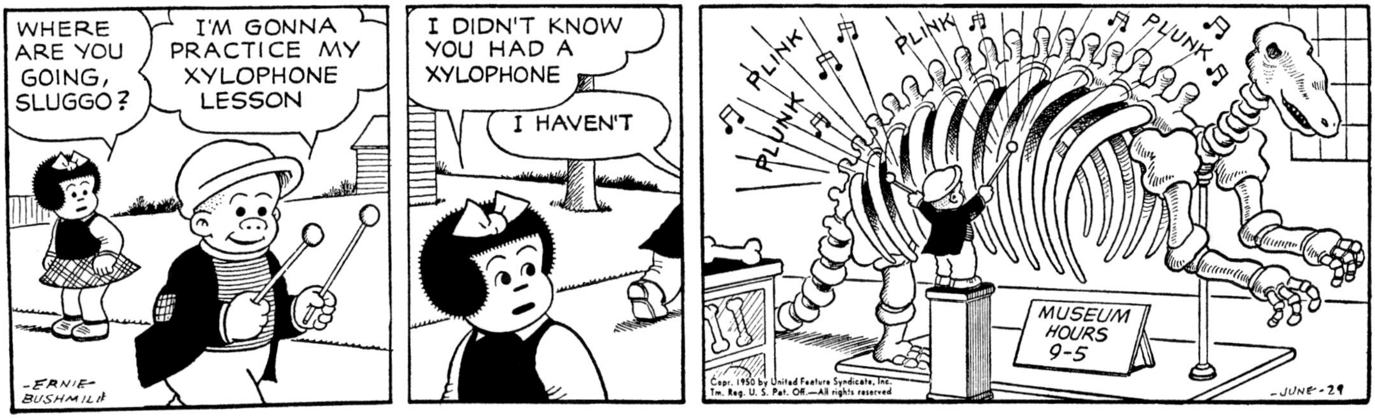

WHERE ARE YOU GOING, SLUGGO?
I'M GONNA PRACTICE MY XYLOPHONE LESSON
-ERNIE BUSHMILLER
I DIDN'T KNOW YOU HAD A XYLOPHONE
I HAVEN'T
PLUNK
PLUNK
PLUNK
PLUNK
MUSEUM HOURS 9-5
Copr. 1950 by United Feature Syndicate, Inc. Tm. Reg. U. S. Pat. Off.—All rights reserved
-JUNE-29

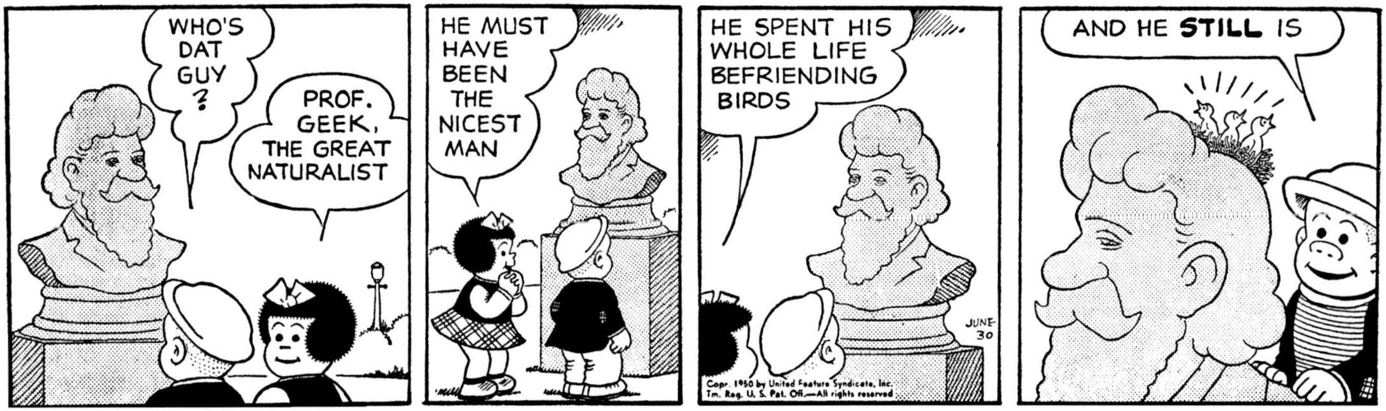
WHO'S DAT GUY ?
PROF. GEEK, THE GREAT NATURALIST
HE MUST HAVE BEEN THE NICEST MAN
HE SPENT HIS WHOLE LIFE BEFRIENDING BIRDS
JUNE 30
Copr. 1950 by United Feature Syndicate, Inc. Tm. Reg. U. S. Pat. Off.—All rights reserved
AND HE **STILL** IS

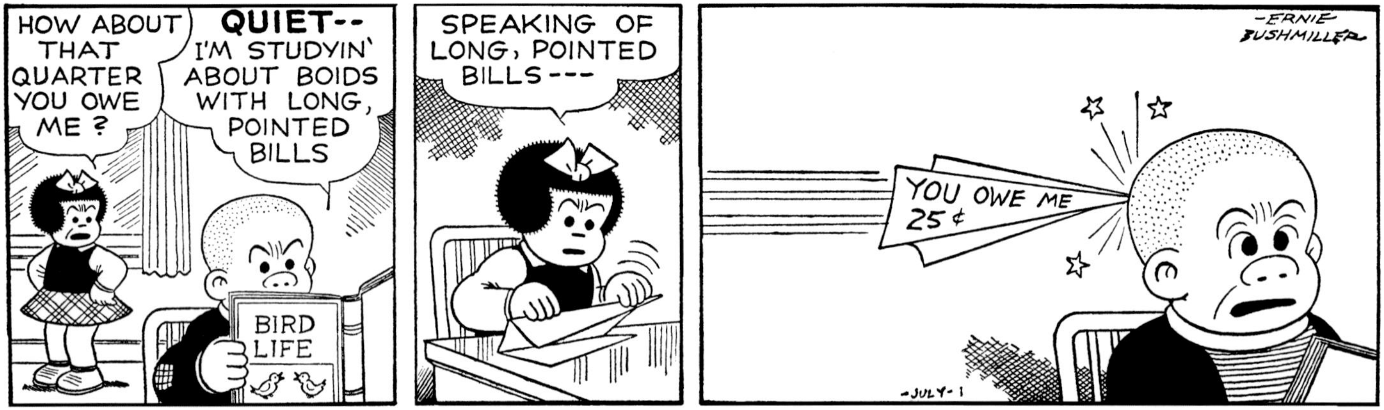
HOW ABOUT THAT QUARTER YOU OWE ME ?
QUIET-- I'M STUDYIN' ABOUT BOIDS WITH LONG, POINTED BILLS
BIRD LIFE
SPEAKING OF LONG, POINTED BILLS---
ERNIE BUSHMILLER
YOU OWE ME 25¢
JULY 1

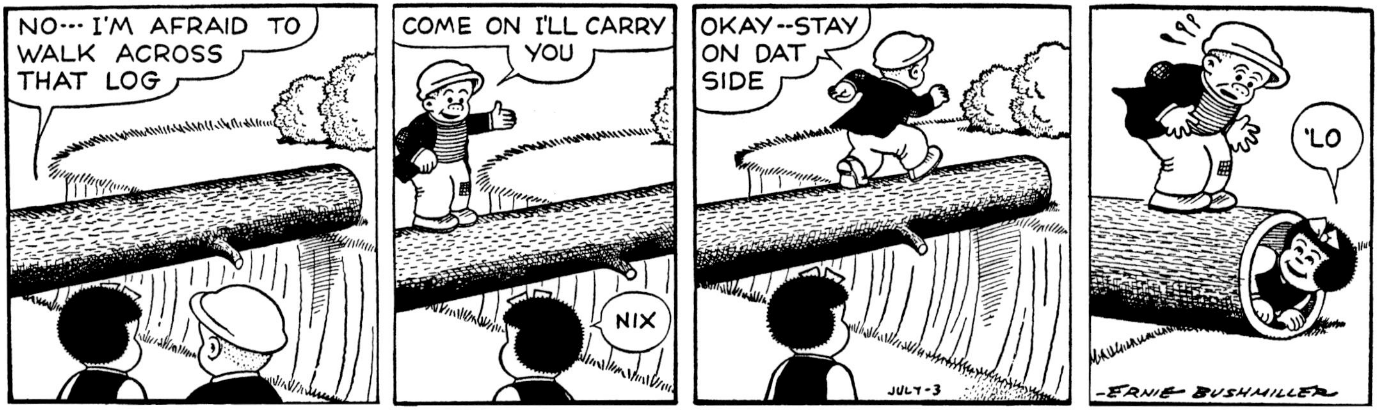
NO--- I'M AFRAID TO WALK ACROSS THAT LOG
COME ON I'LL CARRY YOU
NIX
OKAY--STAY ON DAT SIDE
JULY 3
'LO
ERNIE BUSHMILLER

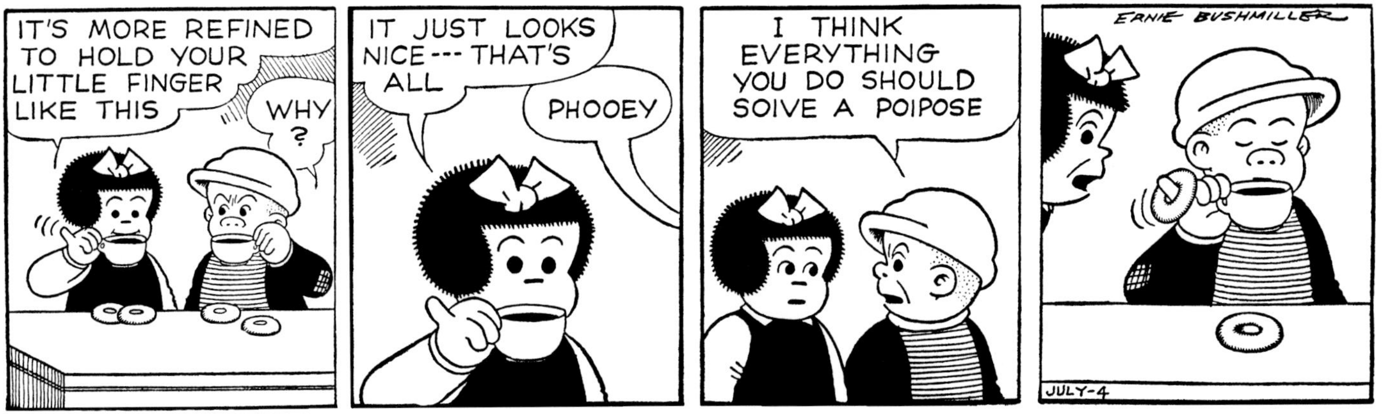
IT'S MORE REFINED TO HOLD YOUR LITTLE FINGER LIKE THIS
WHY ?
IT JUST LOOKS NICE --- THAT'S ALL
PHOOEY
I THINK EVERYTHING YOU DO SHOULD SOIVE A POIPOSE
ERNIE BUSHMILLER
JULY-4

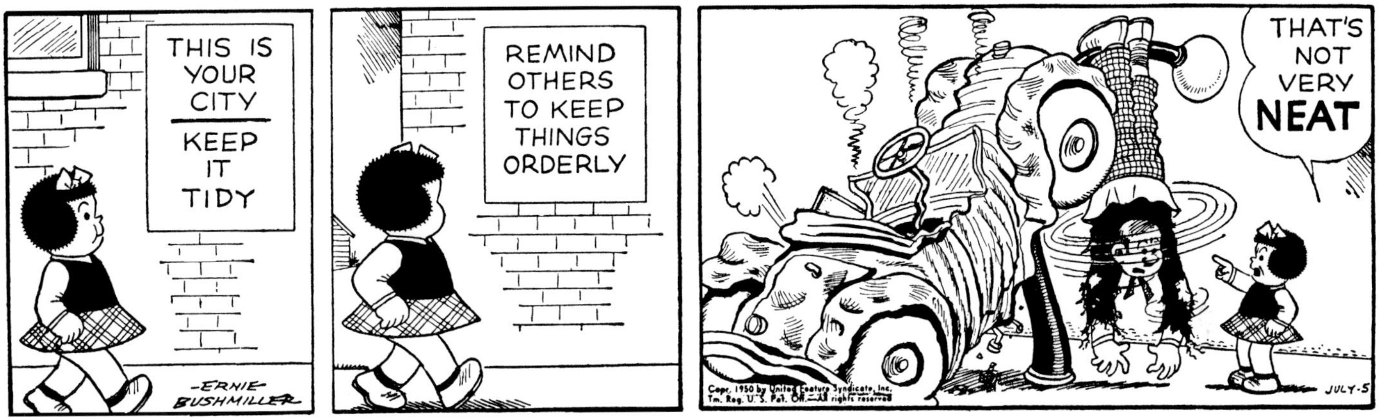
THIS IS YOUR CITY
KEEP IT TIDY
-ERNIE BUSHMILLER
REMIND OTHERS TO KEEP THINGS ORDERLY
THAT'S NOT VERY NEAT
Copr. 1950 by United Feature Syndicate, Inc.
Tm. Reg. U. S. Pat. Off.—All rights reserved
JULY-5

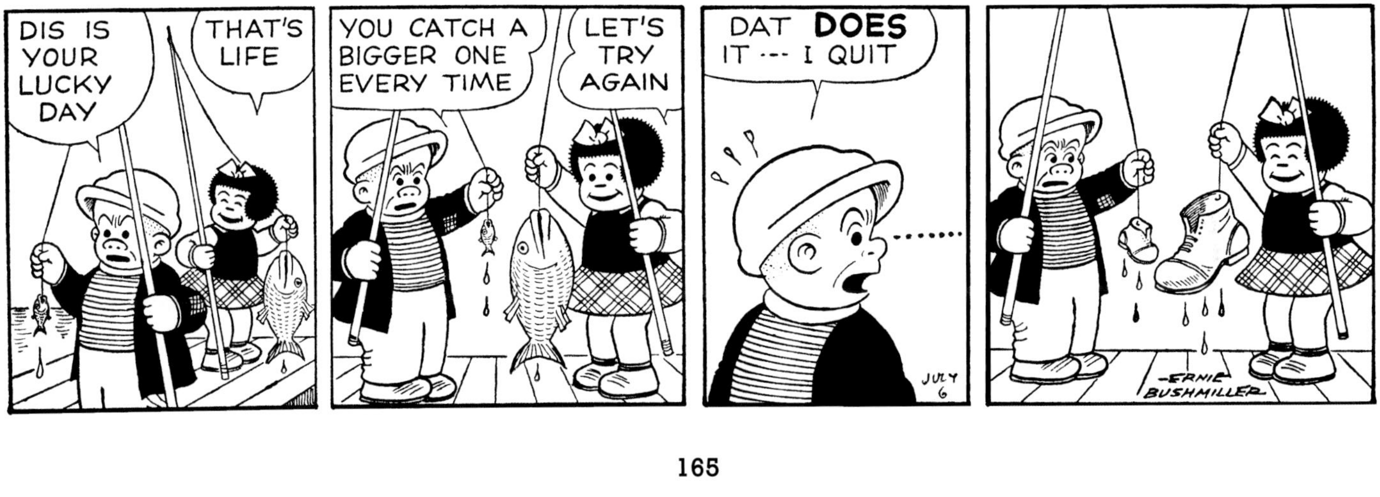
DIS IS YOUR LUCKY DAY
THAT'S LIFE
YOU CATCH A BIGGER ONE EVERY TIME
LET'S TRY AGAIN
DAT DOES IT --- I QUIT
JULY 6
-ERNIE BUSHMILLER

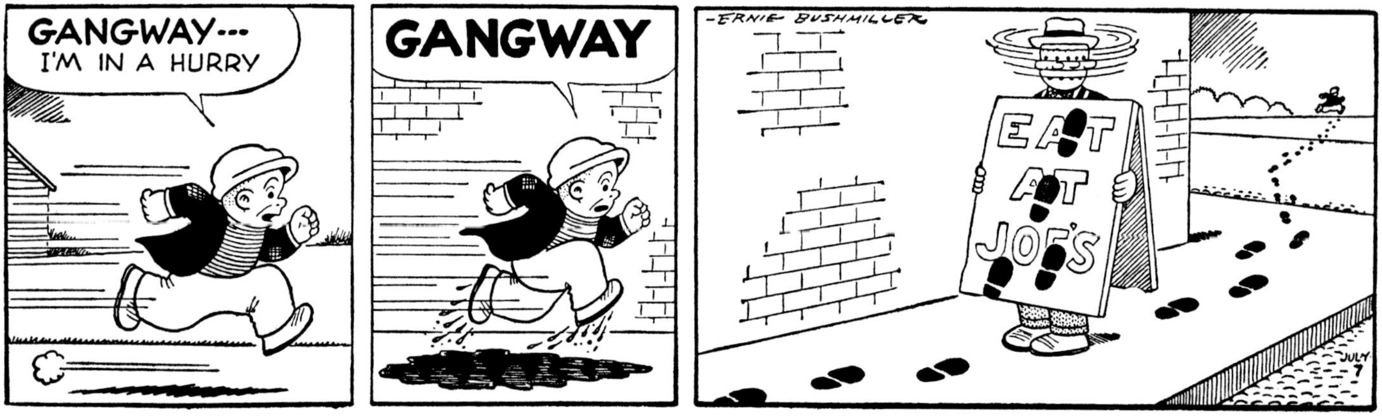
GANGWAY--- I'M IN A HURRY
GANGWAY
-ERNIE BUSHMILLER
EAT AT JOE'S
JULY 7

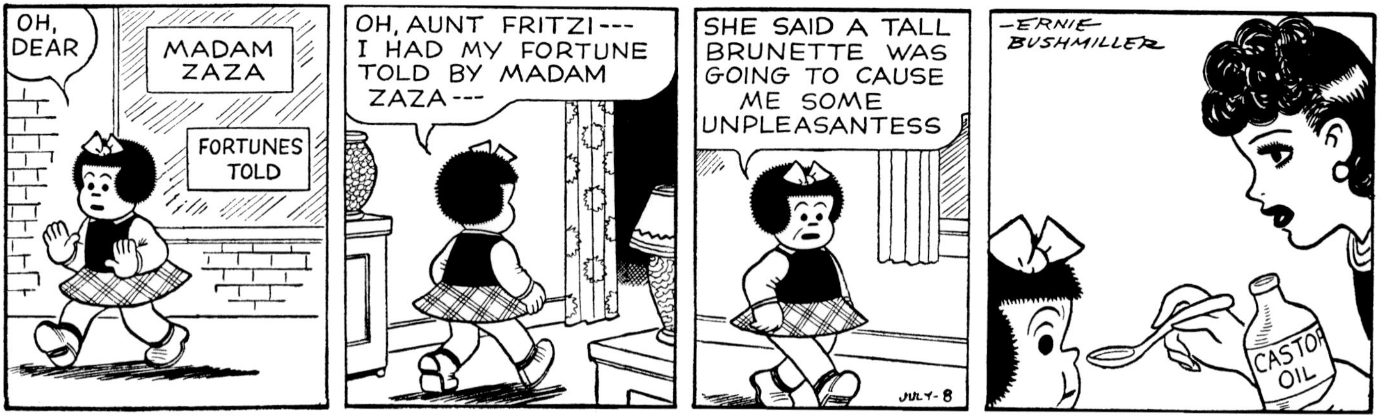
OH, DEAR
MADAM ZAZA
FORTUNES TOLD
OH, AUNT FRITZI--- I HAD MY FORTUNE TOLD BY MADAM ZAZA---
SHE SAID A TALL BRUNETTE WAS GOING TO CAUSE ME SOME UNPLEASANTESS
JULY-8
-ERNIE BUSHMILLER
CASTOR OIL

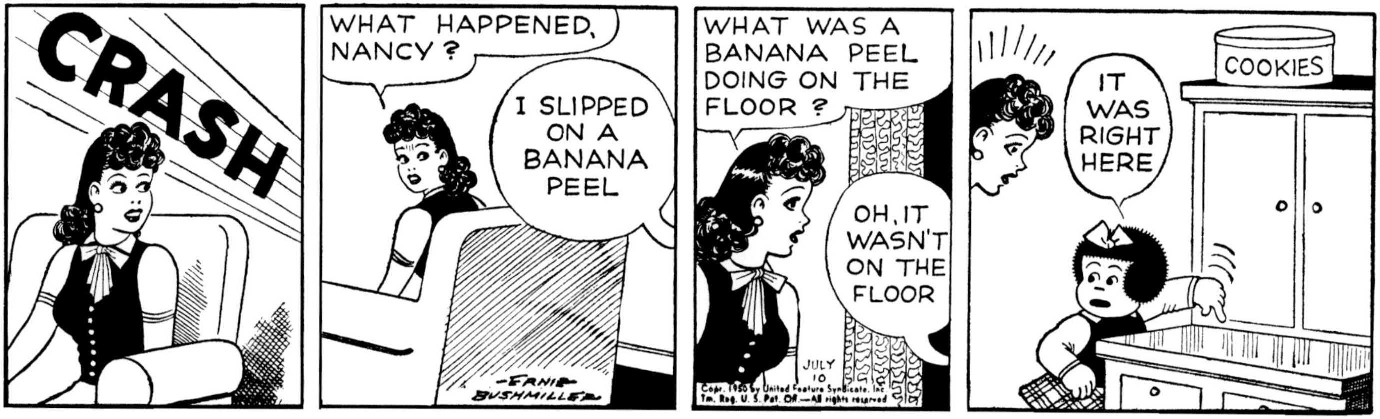
CRASH
WHAT HAPPENED, NANCY ?
I SLIPPED ON A BANANA PEEL
-ERNIE BUSHMILLER
WHAT WAS A BANANA PEEL DOING ON THE FLOOR ?
OH, IT WASN'T ON THE FLOOR
JULY 10
Copr. 1950 by United Feature Syndicate, Inc. Tm. Reg. U. S. Pat. Off.—All rights reserved
COOKIES
IT WAS RIGHT HERE

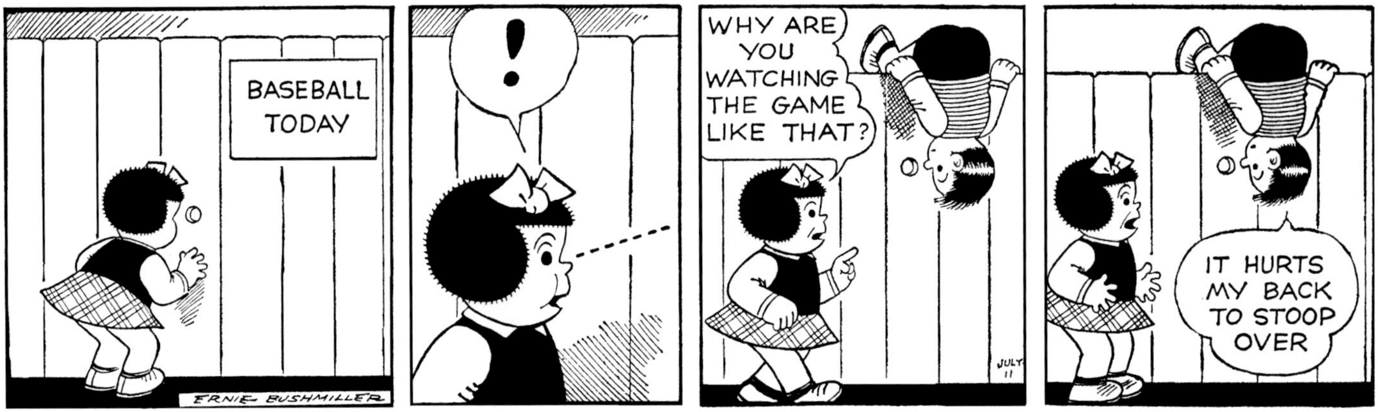
BASEBALL TODAY
ERNIE BUSHMILLER
!
WHY ARE YOU WATCHING THE GAME LIKE THAT?
JULY 11
IT HURTS MY BACK TO STOOP OVER

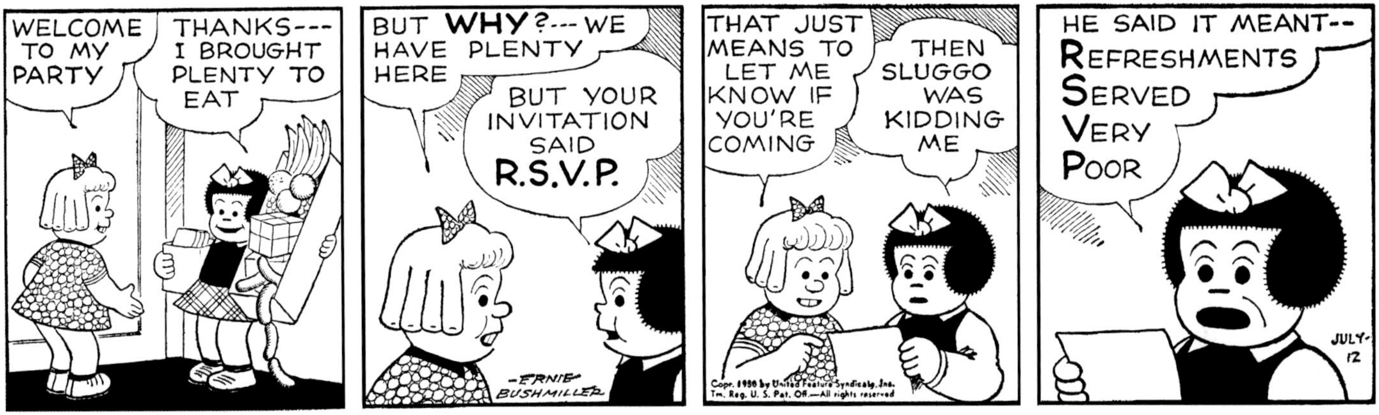
WELCOME TO MY PARTY
THANKS--- I BROUGHT PLENTY TO EAT
BUT **WHY**?--- WE HAVE PLENTY HERE
BUT YOUR INVITATION SAID **R.S.V.P.**
ERNIE BUSHMILLER
THAT JUST MEANS TO LET ME KNOW IF YOU'RE COMING
THEN SLUGGO WAS KIDDING ME
Copr. 1950 by United Feature Syndicate, Inc. Tm. Reg. U. S. Pat. Off.—All rights reserved
HE SAID IT MEANT--
REFRESHMENTS
SERVED
VERY
POOR
JULY 12

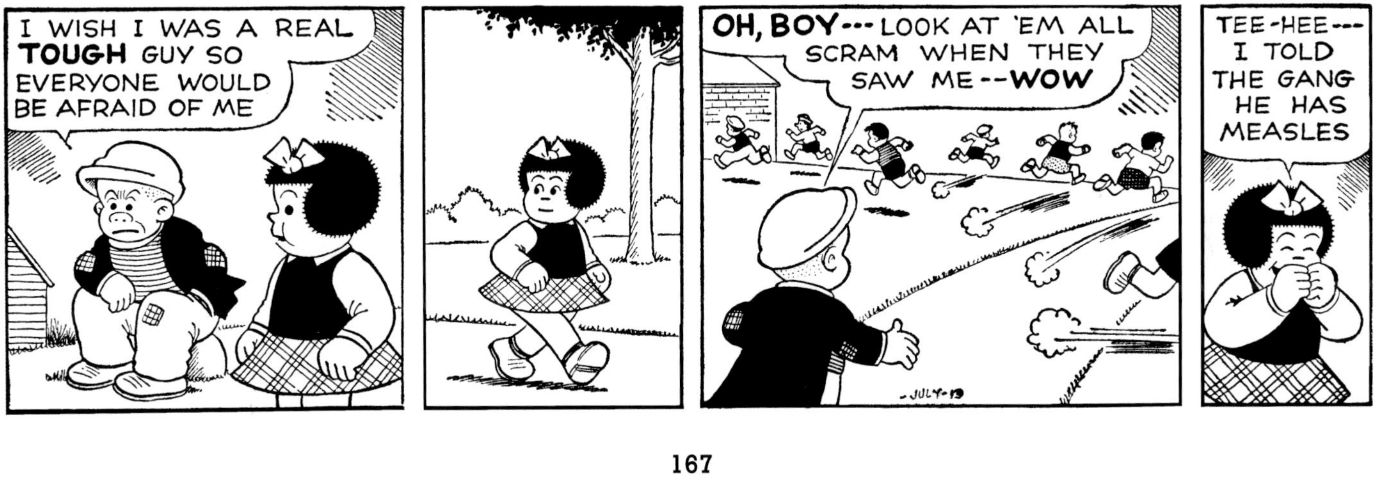
I WISH I WAS A REAL **TOUGH** GUY SO EVERYONE WOULD BE AFRAID OF ME
OH, BOY--- LOOK AT 'EM ALL SCRAM WHEN THEY SAW ME --**WOW**
JULY 13
TEE-HEE--- I TOLD THE GANG HE HAS MEASLES

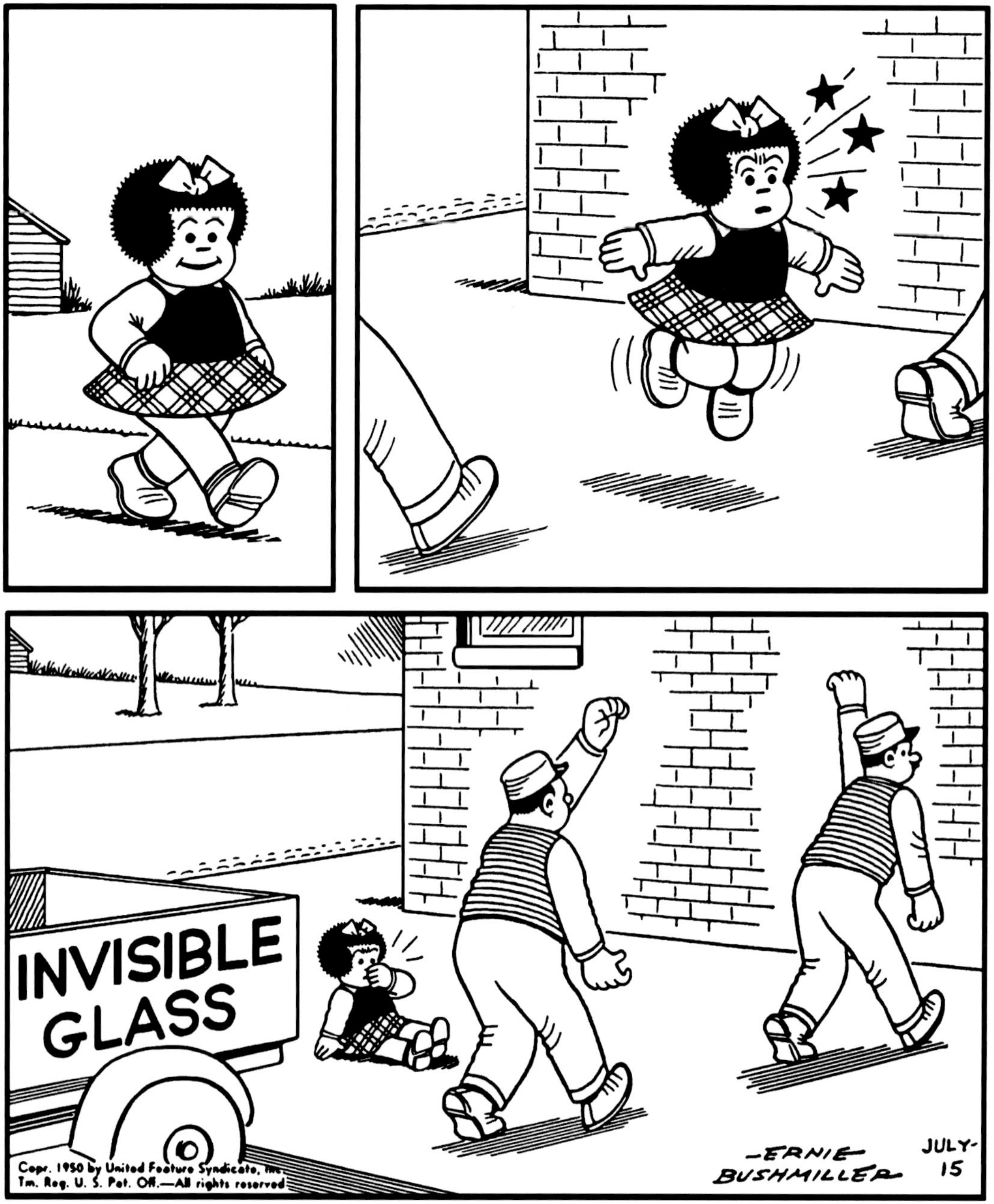
INVISIBLE
GLASS
Copr. 1950 by United Feature Syndicate, Inc.
Tm. Reg. U. S. Pat. Off.—All rights reserved
-ERNIE-
BUSHMILLER
JULY-
15

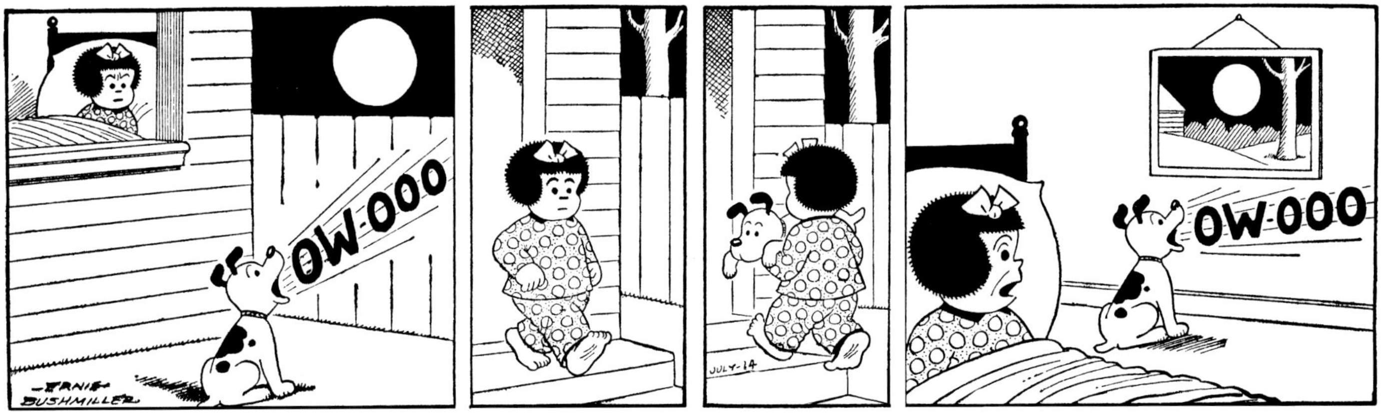
ERNIE BUSHMILLER
OW-OOO
JULY-14
OW-OOO

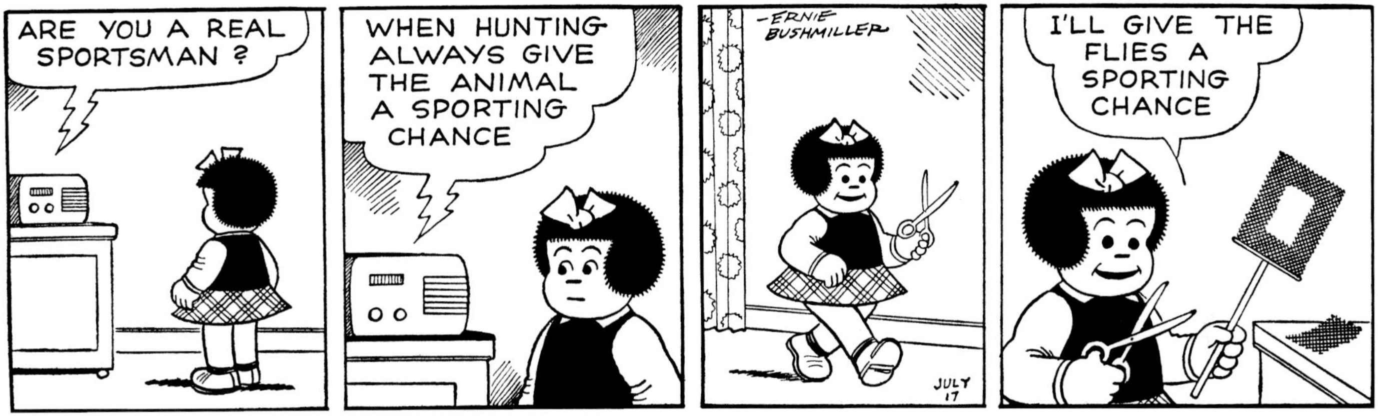
ARE YOU A REAL SPORTSMAN ?
WHEN HUNTING ALWAYS GIVE THE ANIMAL A SPORTING CHANCE
ERNIE BUSHMILLER
JULY 17
I'LL GIVE THE FLIES A SPORTING CHANCE

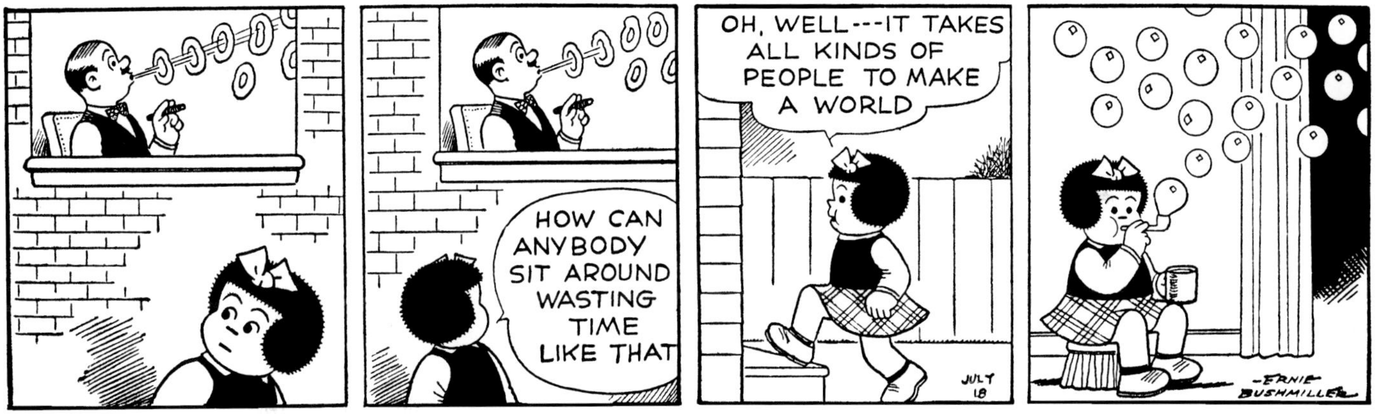
HOW CAN ANYBODY SIT AROUND WASTING TIME LIKE THAT
OH, WELL---IT TAKES ALL KINDS OF PEOPLE TO MAKE A WORLD
JULY 18
ERNIE BUSHMILLER

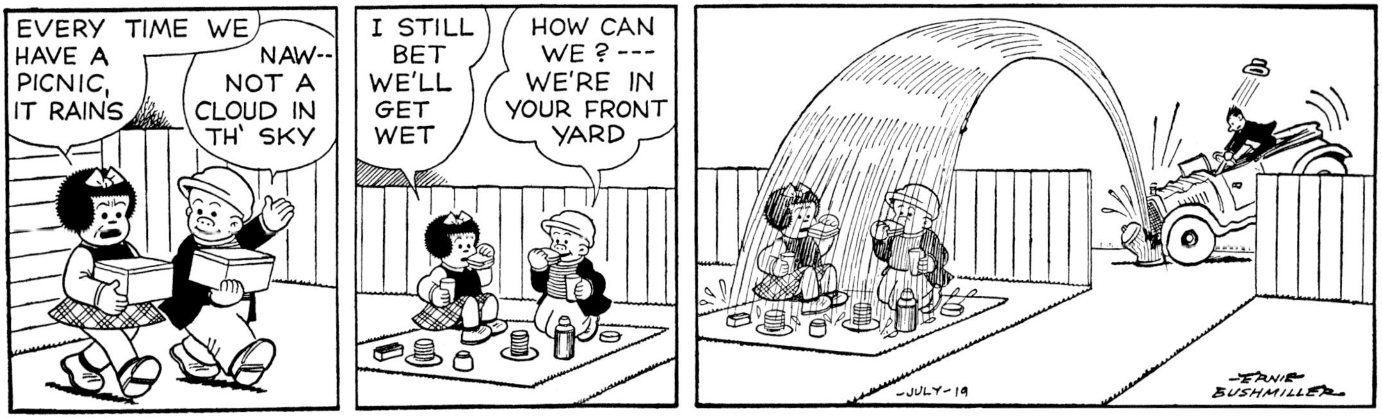
EVERY TIME WE HAVE A PICNIC, IT RAINS
NAW-- NOT A CLOUD IN TH' SKY
I STILL BET WE'LL GET WET
HOW CAN WE? --- WE'RE IN YOUR FRONT YARD
-JULY-19
-ERNIE BUSHMILLER

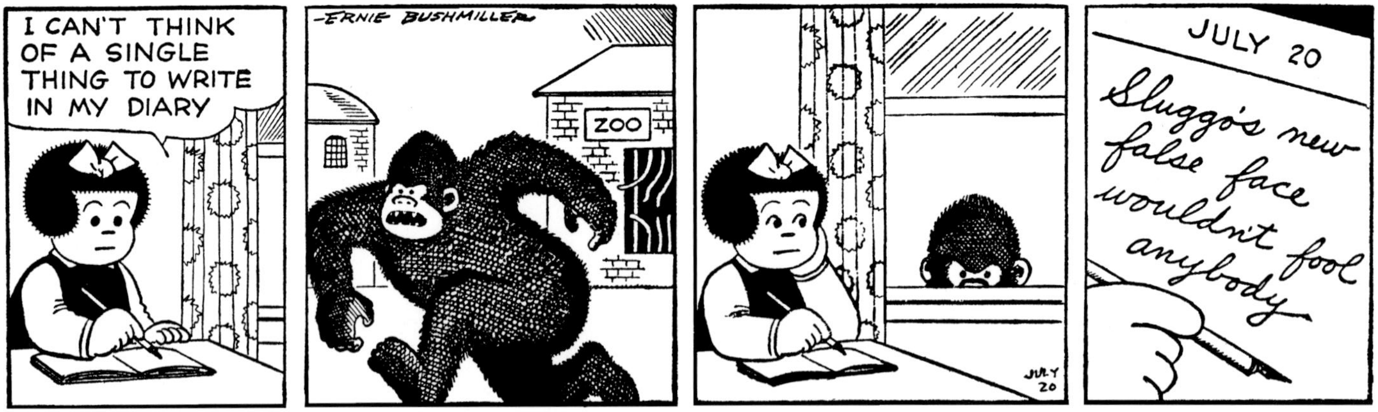
I CAN'T THINK OF A SINGLE THING TO WRITE IN MY DIARY
-ERNIE BUSHMILLER
ZOO
JULY 20
JULY 20
Sluggo's new false face wouldn't fool anybody

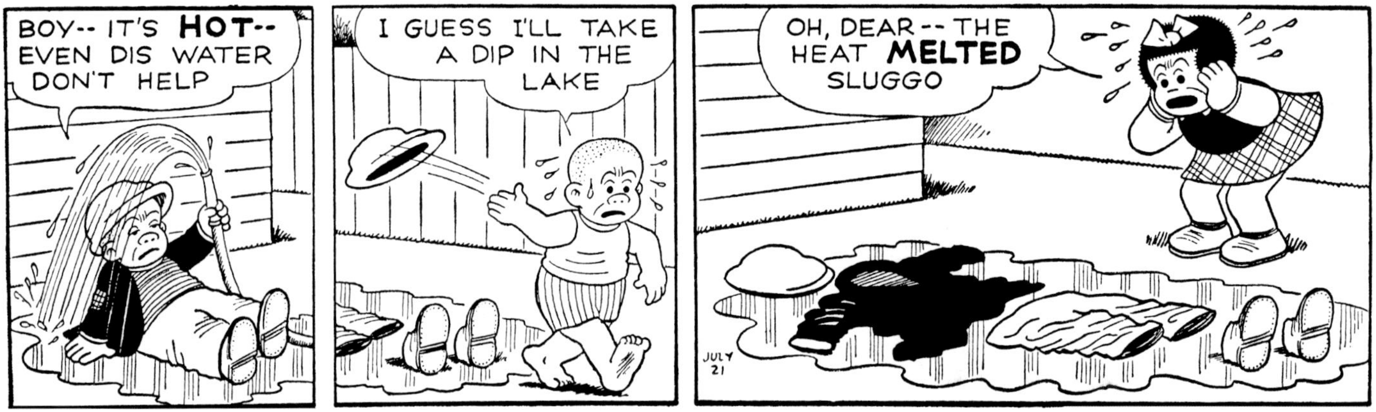
BOY-- IT'S **HOT**-- EVEN DIS WATER DON'T HELP
I GUESS I'LL TAKE A DIP IN THE LAKE
OH, DEAR -- THE HEAT **MELTED** SLUGGO
JULY 21

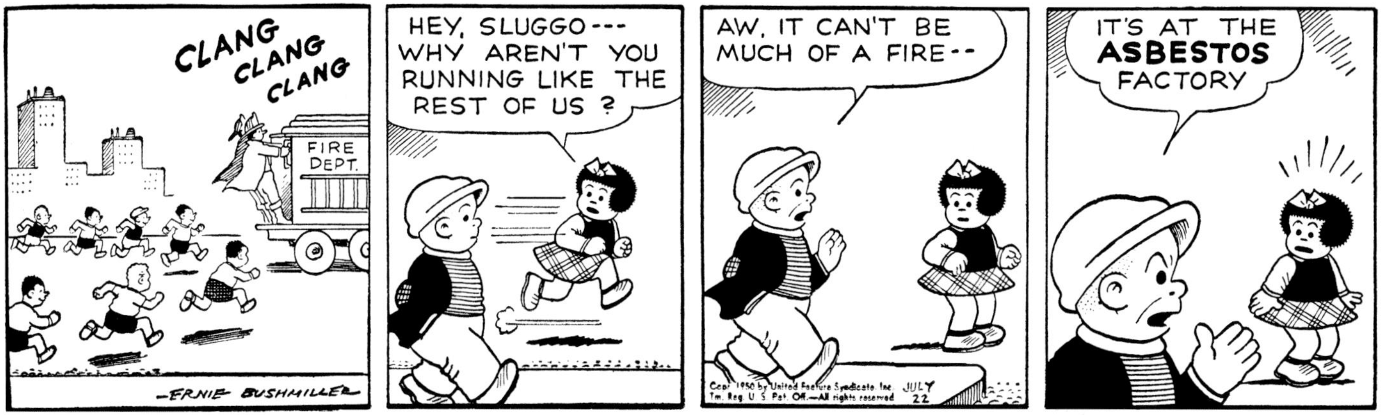
CLANG CLANG CLANG
FIRE DEPT.
-ERNIE BUSHMILLER
HEY, SLUGGO--- WHY AREN'T YOU RUNNING LIKE THE REST OF US ?
AW, IT CAN'T BE MUCH OF A FIRE--
Copr. 1950 by United Feature Syndicate, Inc. Tm. Reg. U. S. Pat. Off.—All rights reserved
JULY 22
IT'S AT THE **ASBESTOS** FACTORY

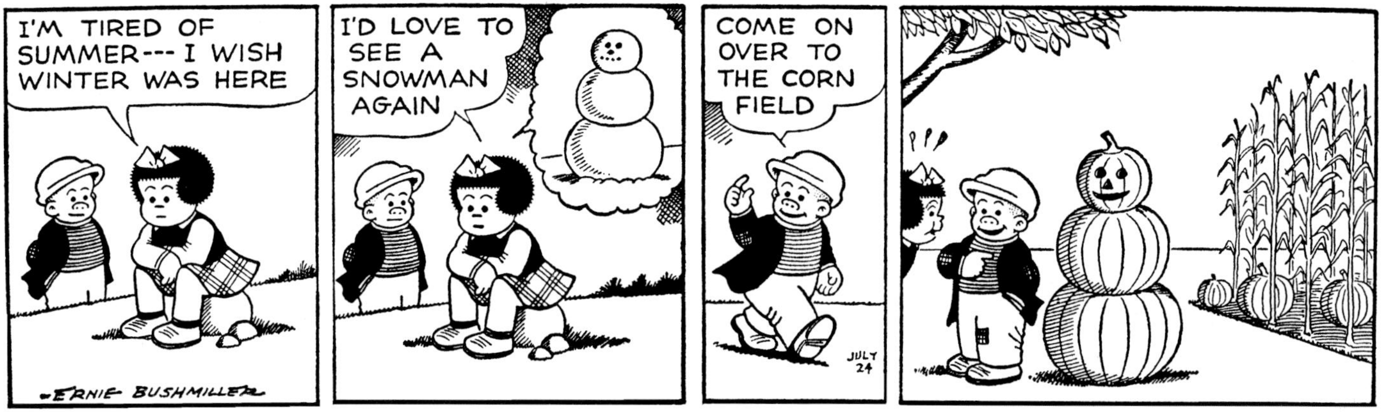
I'M TIRED OF SUMMER--- I WISH WINTER WAS HERE
-ERNIE BUSHMILLER
I'D LOVE TO SEE A SNOWMAN AGAIN
COME ON OVER TO THE CORN FIELD
JULY 24

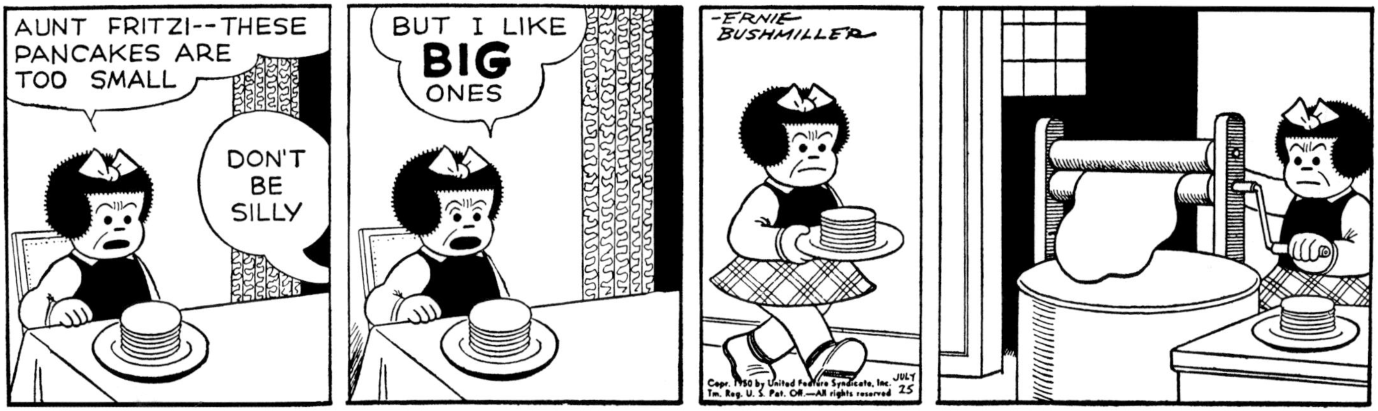
AUNT FRITZI--THESE PANCAKES ARE TOO SMALL
DON'T BE SILLY
BUT I LIKE **BIG** ONES
-ERNIE BUSHMILLER
Copr. 1950 by United Feature Syndicate, Inc. Tm. Reg. U. S. Pat. Off.—All rights reserved
JULY 25

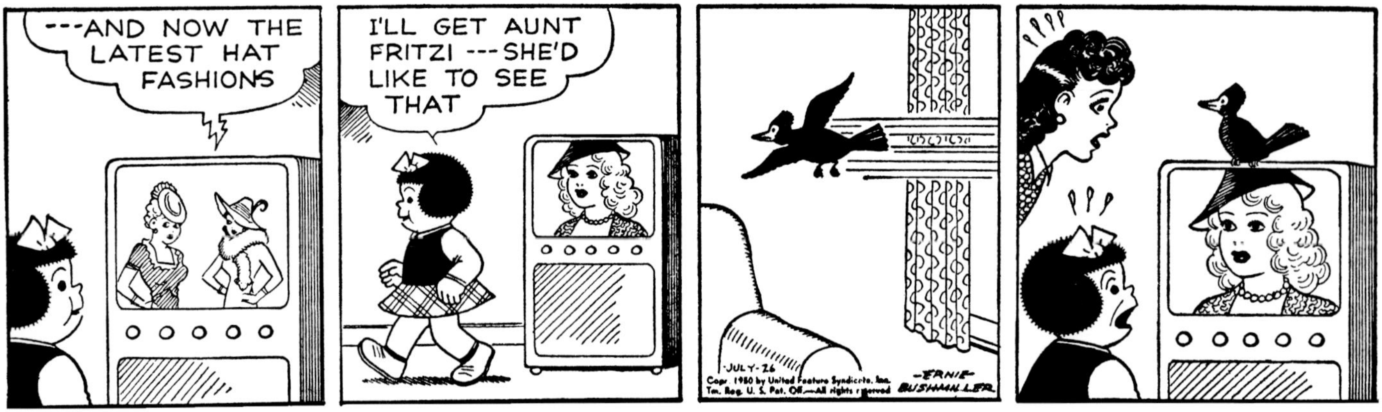
---AND NOW THE LATEST HAT FASHIONS
I'LL GET AUNT FRITZI ---SHE'D LIKE TO SEE THAT
JULY-26
Copr. 1950 by United Feature Syndicate, Inc. Tm. Reg. U. S. Pat. Off.—All rights reserved
ERNIE BUSHMILLER

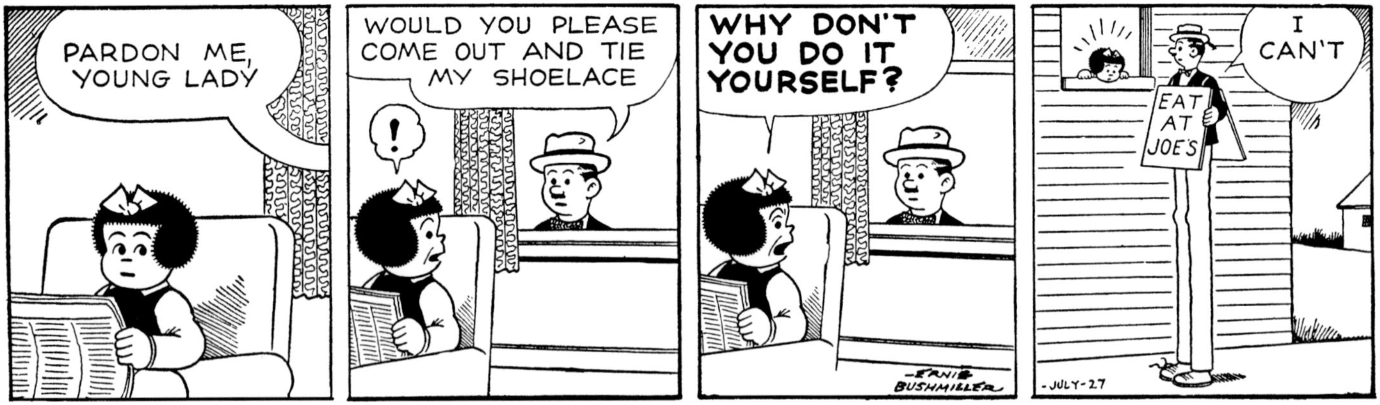
PARDON ME, YOUNG LADY
WOULD YOU PLEASE COME OUT AND TIE MY SHOELACE
!
WHY DON'T YOU DO IT YOURSELF?
ERNIE BUSHMILLER
I CAN'T
EAT AT JOE'S
JULY-27

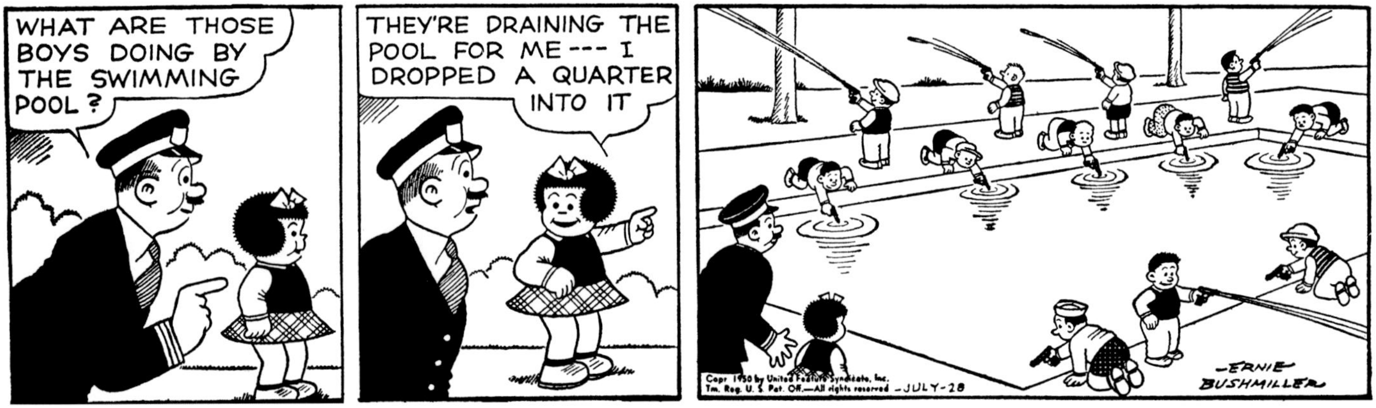
WHAT ARE THOSE BOYS DOING BY THE SWIMMING POOL?
THEY'RE DRAINING THE POOL FOR ME --- I DROPPED A QUARTER INTO IT
Copr. 1950 by United Feature Syndicate, Inc. Tm. Reg. U. S. Pat. Off.—All rights reserved
JULY-28
ERNIE BUSHMILLER

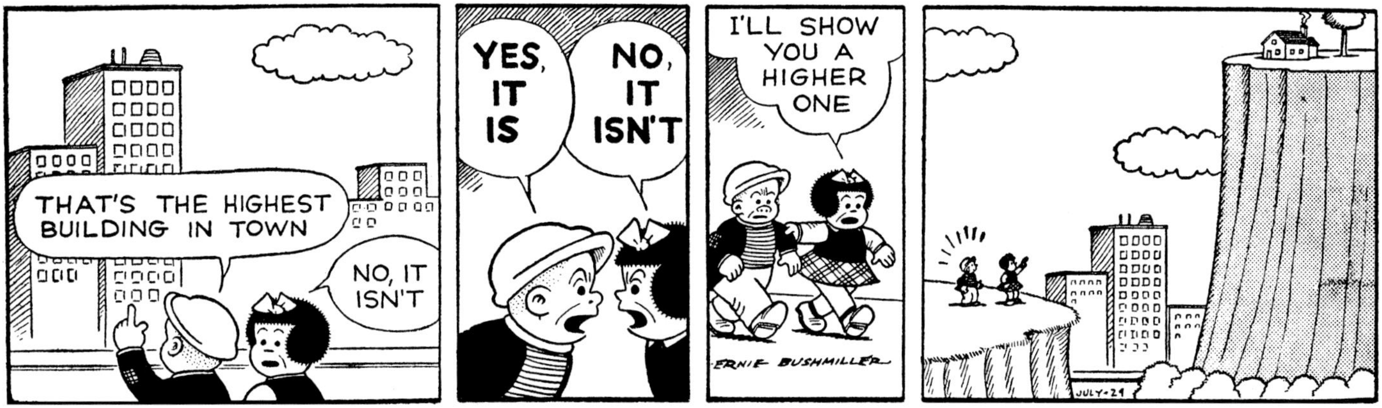
THAT'S THE HIGHEST BUILDING IN TOWN
NO, IT ISN'T
YES, IT IS
NO, IT ISN'T
I'LL SHOW YOU A HIGHER ONE
ERNIE BUSHMILLER
JULY-29

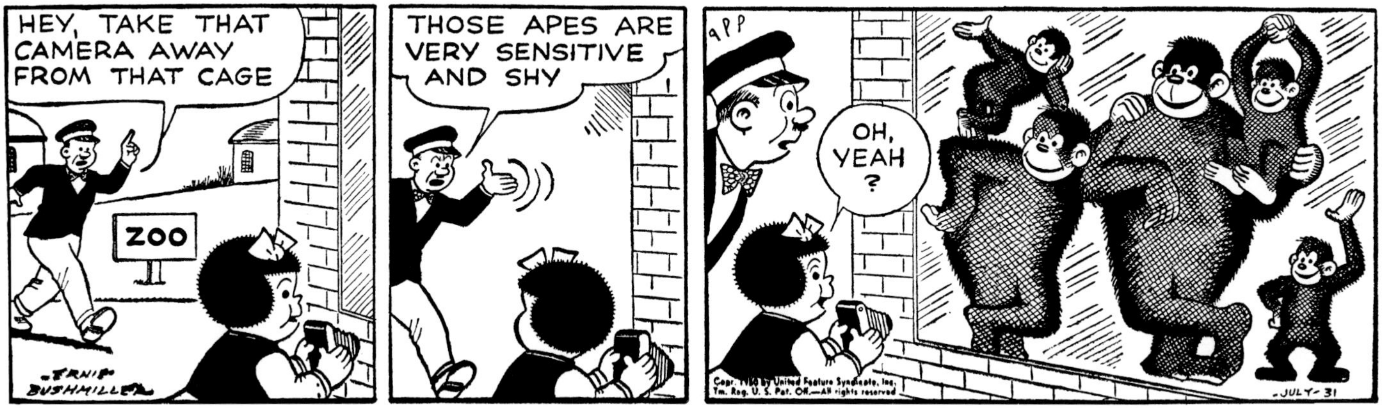
HEY, TAKE THAT CAMERA AWAY FROM THAT CAGE
ZOO
ERNIE BUSHMILLER
THOSE APES ARE VERY SENSITIVE AND SHY
OH, YEAH ?
Copr. 1950 by United Feature Syndicate, Inc.
Tm. Reg. U. S. Pat. Off.—All rights reserved
JULY-31

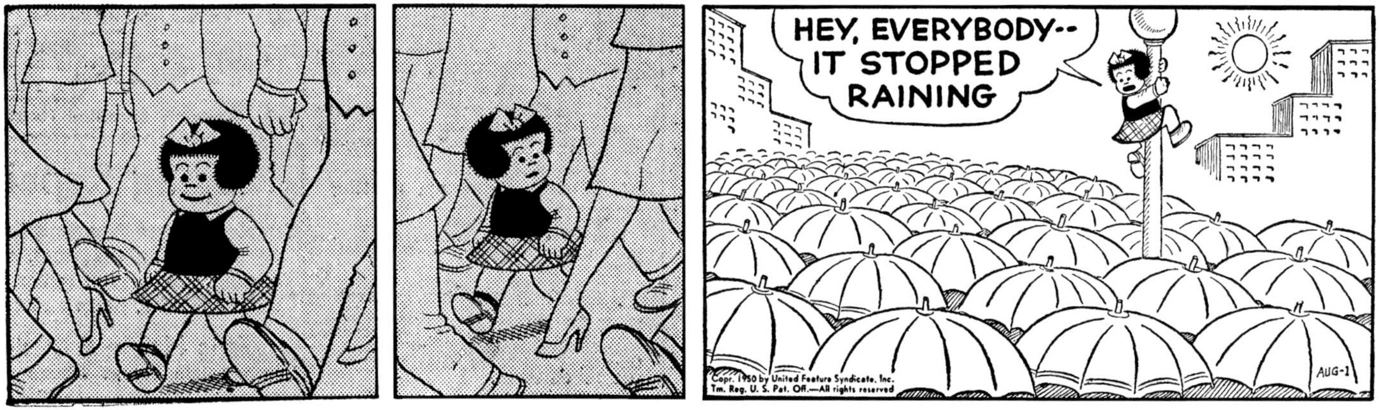
HEY, EVERYBODY-- IT STOPPED RAINING
Copr. 1950 by United Feature Syndicate, Inc.
Tm. Reg. U. S. Pat. Off.—All rights reserved
AUG-1

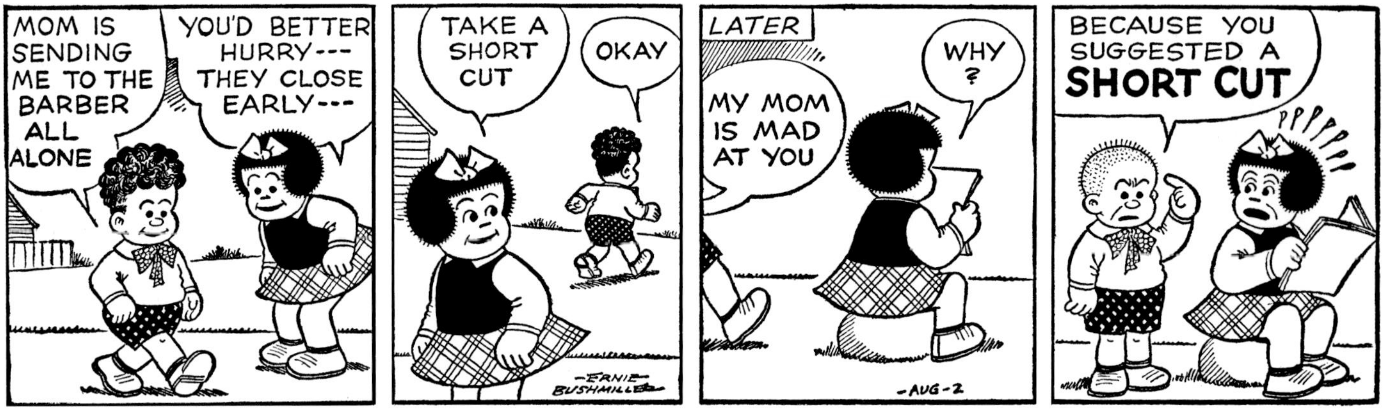
MOM IS SENDING ME TO THE BARBER ALL ALONE
YOU'D BETTER HURRY--- THEY CLOSE EARLY---
TAKE A SHORT CUT
OKAY
ERNIE BUSHMILLER
LATER
MY MOM IS MAD AT YOU
WHY ?
AUG-2
BECAUSE YOU SUGGESTED A SHORT CUT

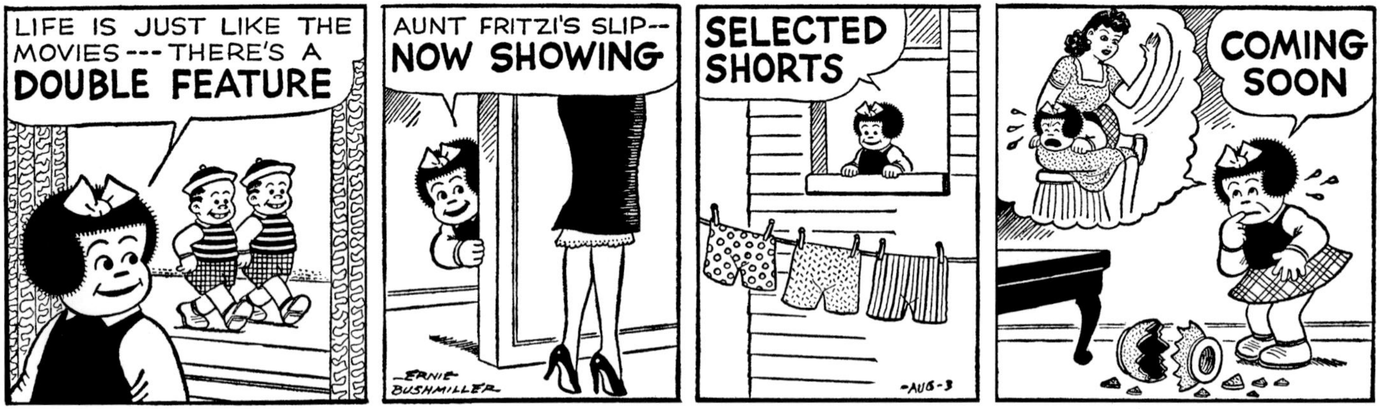
LIFE IS JUST LIKE THE MOVIES --- THERE'S A DOUBLE FEATURE
AUNT FRITZI'S SLIP-- NOW SHOWING
ERNIE BUSHMILLER
SELECTED SHORTS
AUG-3
COMING SOON

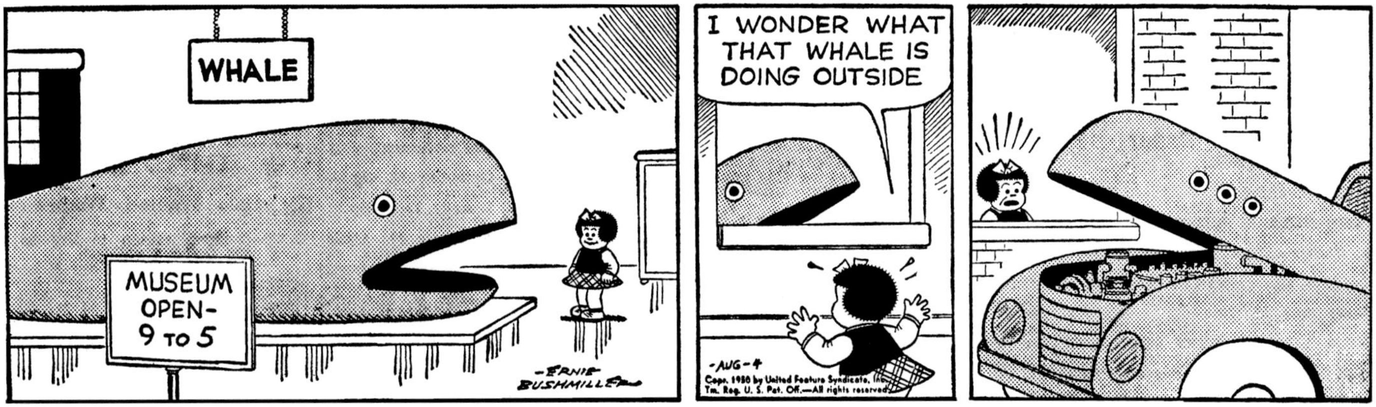
WHALE
MUSEUM OPEN- 9 TO 5
ERNIE BUSHMILLER
I WONDER WHAT THAT WHALE IS DOING OUTSIDE
AUG-4
Copr. 1950 by United Feature Syndicate, Inc.
Tm. Reg. U. S. Pat. Off.—All rights reserved

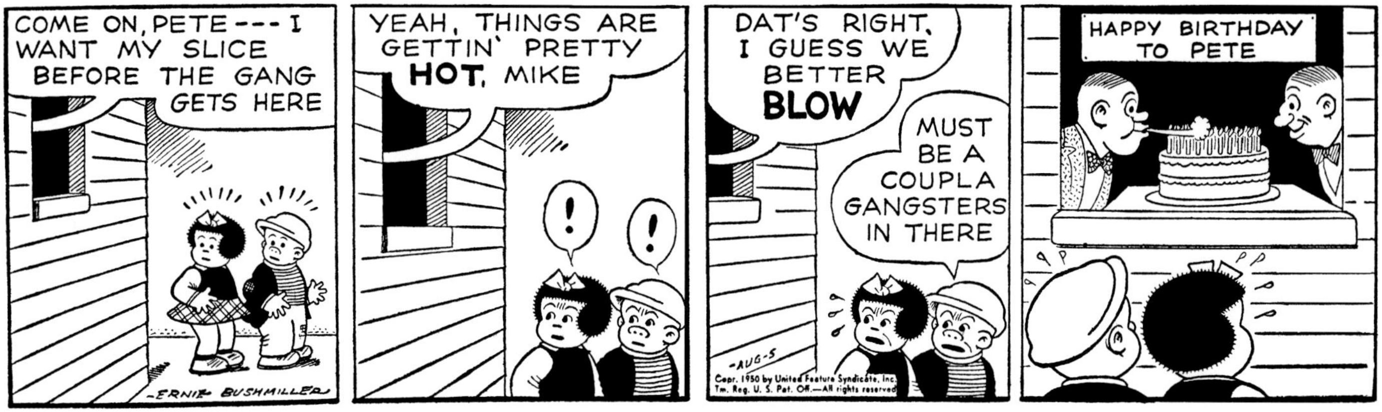
COME ON, PETE --- I WANT MY SLICE BEFORE THE GANG GETS HERE
ERNIE BUSHMILLER
YEAH, THINGS ARE GETTIN' PRETTY **HOT**, MIKE
!
!
DAT'S RIGHT, I GUESS WE BETTER **BLOW**
MUST BE A COUPLA GANGSTERS IN THERE
AUG-5
Copr. 1950 by United Feature Syndicate, Inc. Tm. Reg. U. S. Pat. Off.—All rights reserved
HAPPY BIRTHDAY TO PETE

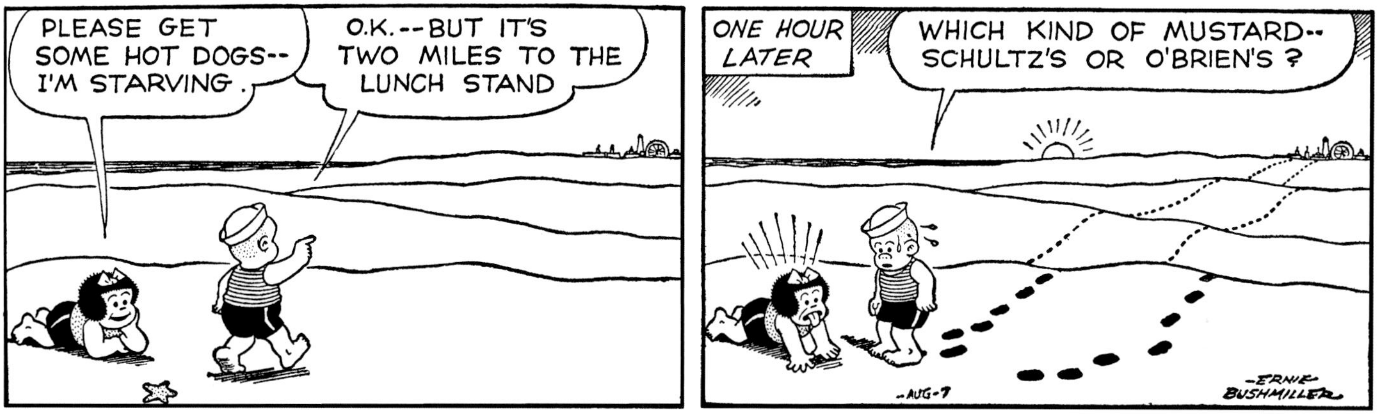
PLEASE GET SOME HOT DOGS-- I'M STARVING.
O.K.--BUT IT'S TWO MILES TO THE LUNCH STAND
ONE HOUR LATER
WHICH KIND OF MUSTARD-- SCHULTZ'S OR O'BRIEN'S?
AUG-7
ERNIE BUSHMILLER

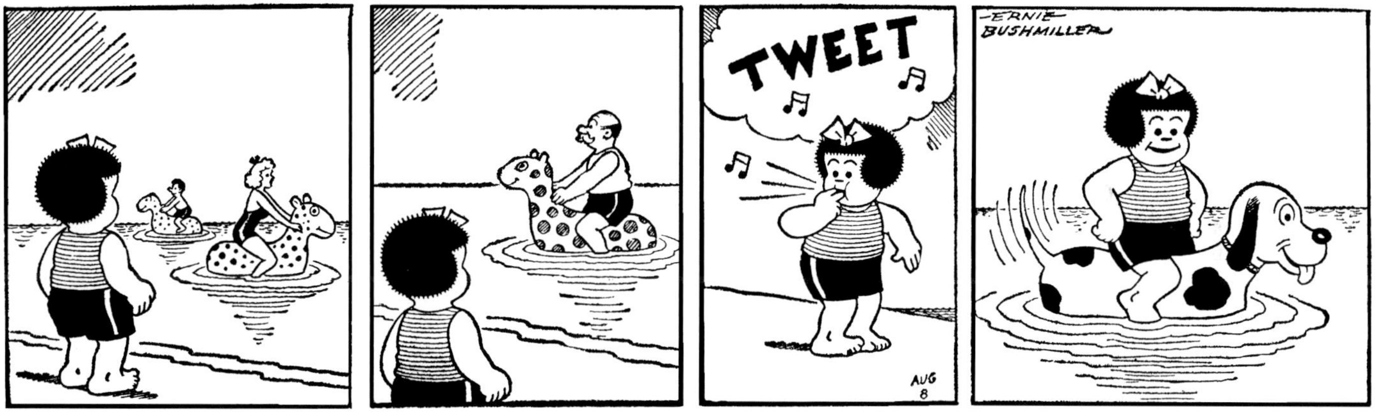
TWEET
AUG 8
ERNIE BUSHMILLER

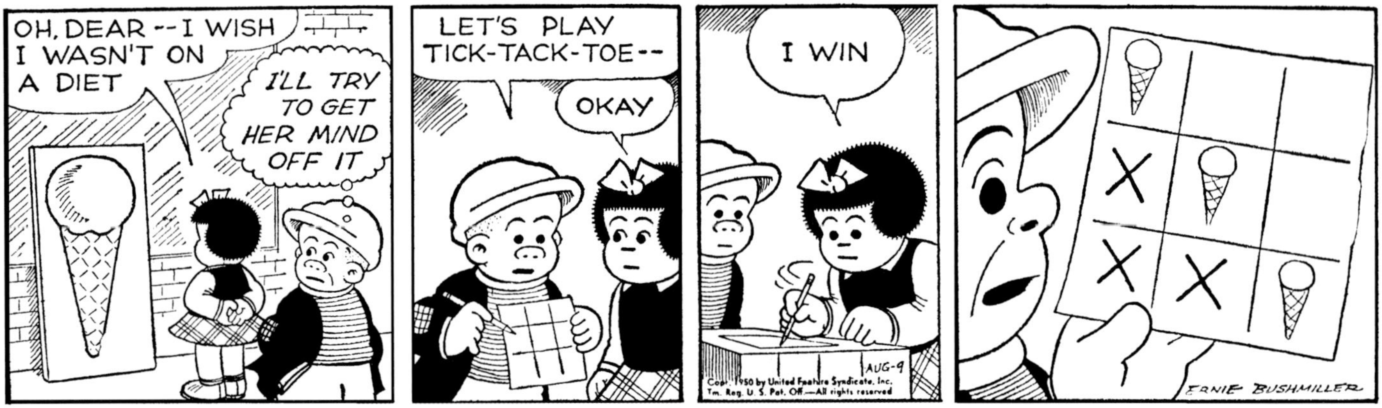
OH, DEAR --I WISH I WASN'T ON A DIET
I'LL TRY TO GET HER MIND OFF IT
LET'S PLAY TICK-TACK-TOE--
OKAY
I WIN
AUG-9
Copr. 1950 by United Feature Syndicate, Inc. Tm. Reg. U. S. Pat. Off.—All rights reserved
ERNIE BUSHMILLER

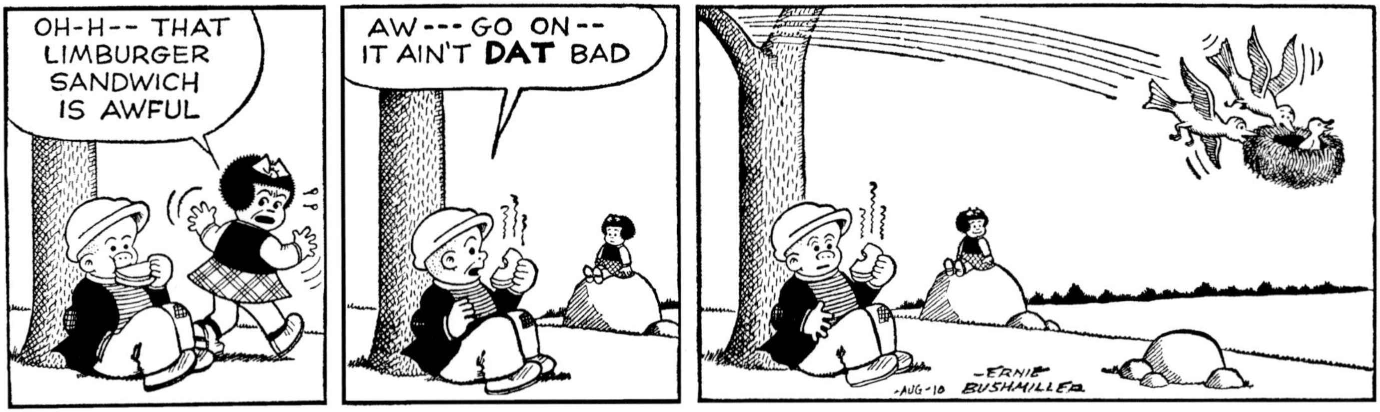
OH-H-- THAT LIMBURGER SANDWICH IS AWFUL
AW --- GO ON -- IT AIN'T **DAT** BAD
AUG-10
ERNIE BUSHMILLER

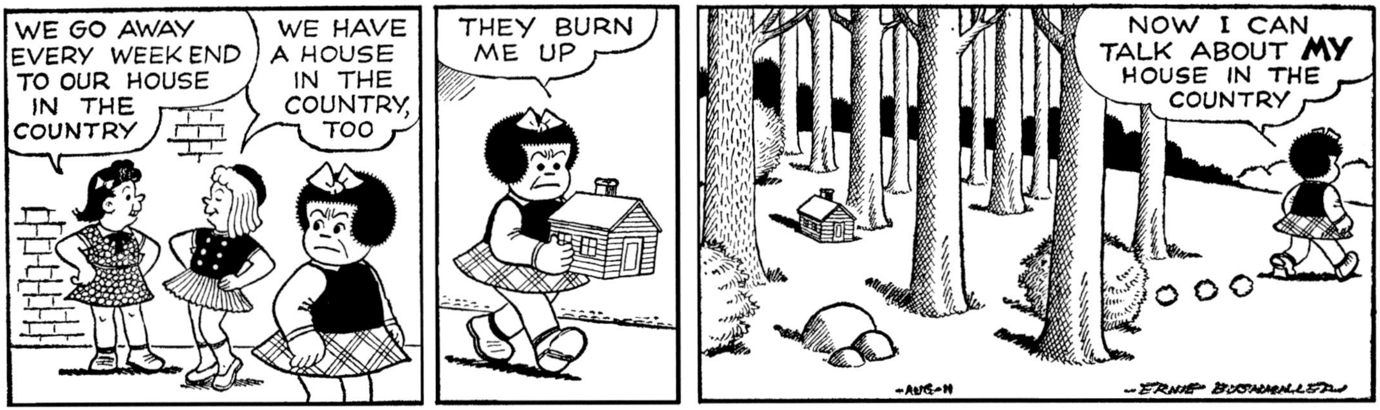
WE GO AWAY EVERY WEEK END TO OUR HOUSE IN THE COUNTRY
WE HAVE A HOUSE IN THE COUNTRY, TOO
THEY BURN ME UP
NOW I CAN TALK ABOUT **MY** HOUSE IN THE COUNTRY
AUG-11
ERNIE BUSHMILLER

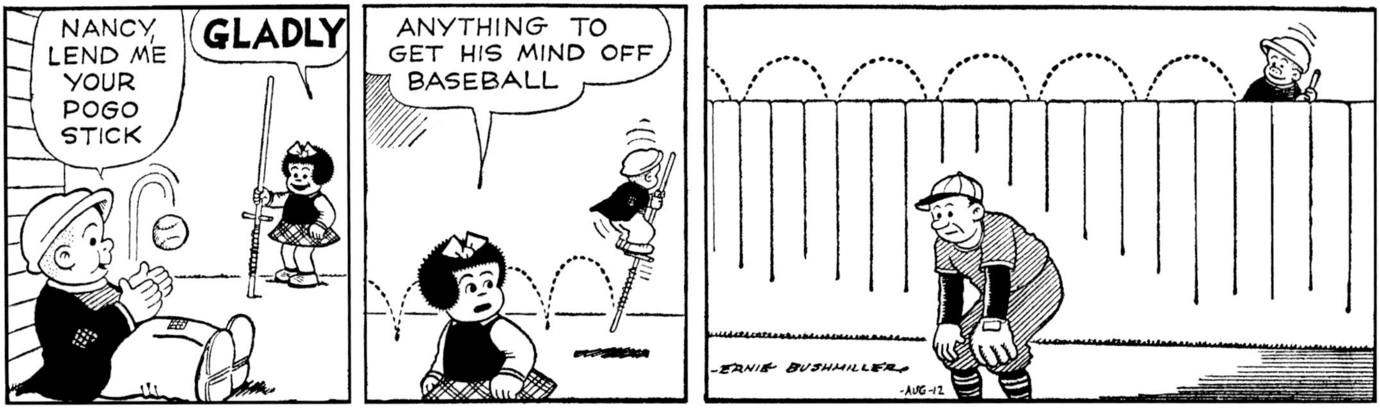
NANCY, LEND ME YOUR POGO STICK
GLADLY
ANYTHING TO GET HIS MIND OFF BASEBALL
-ERNIE BUSHMILLER
-AUG-12

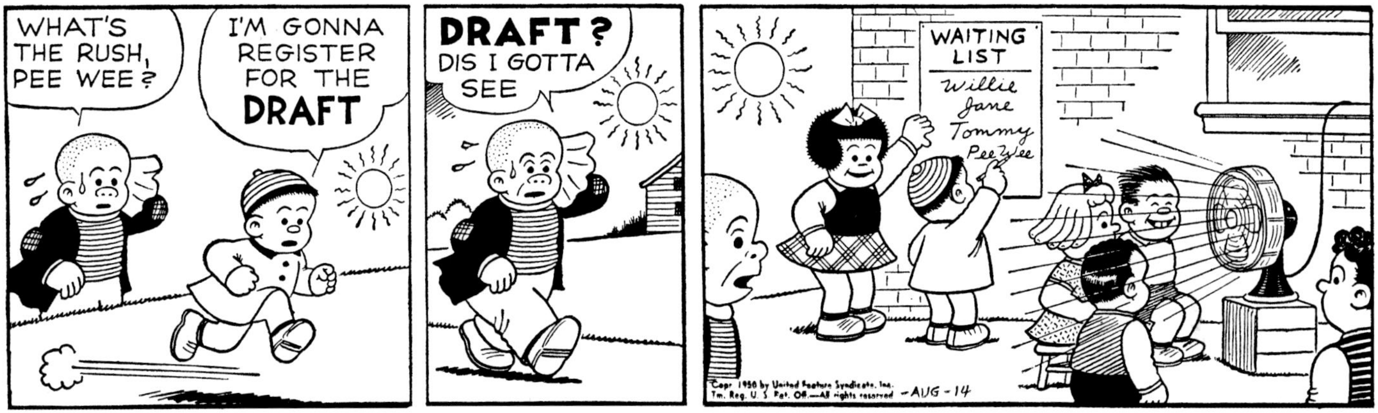
WHAT'S THE RUSH, PEE WEE?
I'M GONNA REGISTER FOR THE DRAFT
DRAFT? DIS I GOTTA SEE
WAITING LIST
Willie
Jane
Tommy
PeeWee
Copr. 1950 by United Feature Syndicate, Inc. Tm. Reg. U. S. Pat. Off.—All rights reserved
-AUG-14

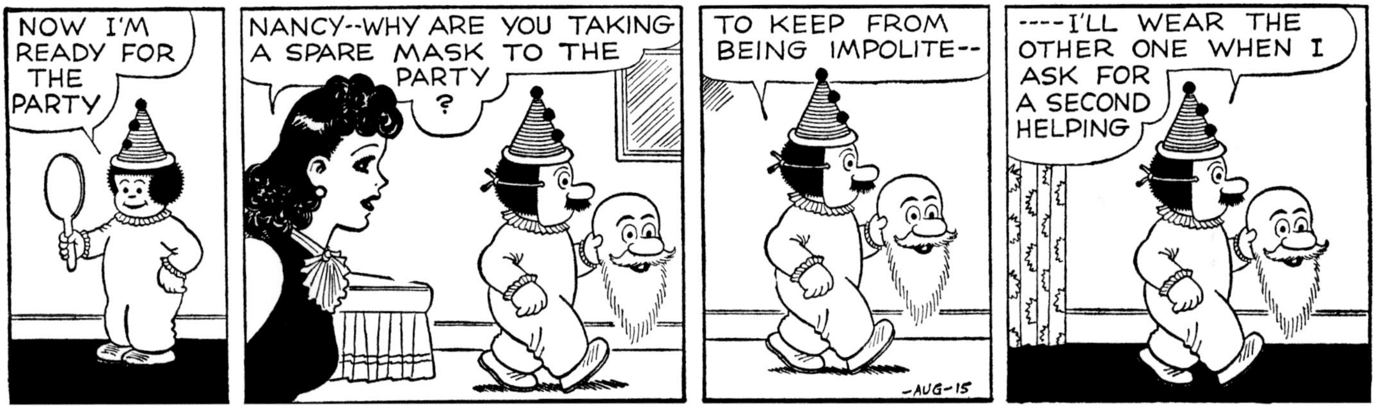
NOW I'M READY FOR THE PARTY
NANCY--WHY ARE YOU TAKING A SPARE MASK TO THE PARTY?
TO KEEP FROM BEING IMPOLITE--
----I'LL WEAR THE OTHER ONE WHEN I ASK FOR A SECOND HELPING
-AUG-15

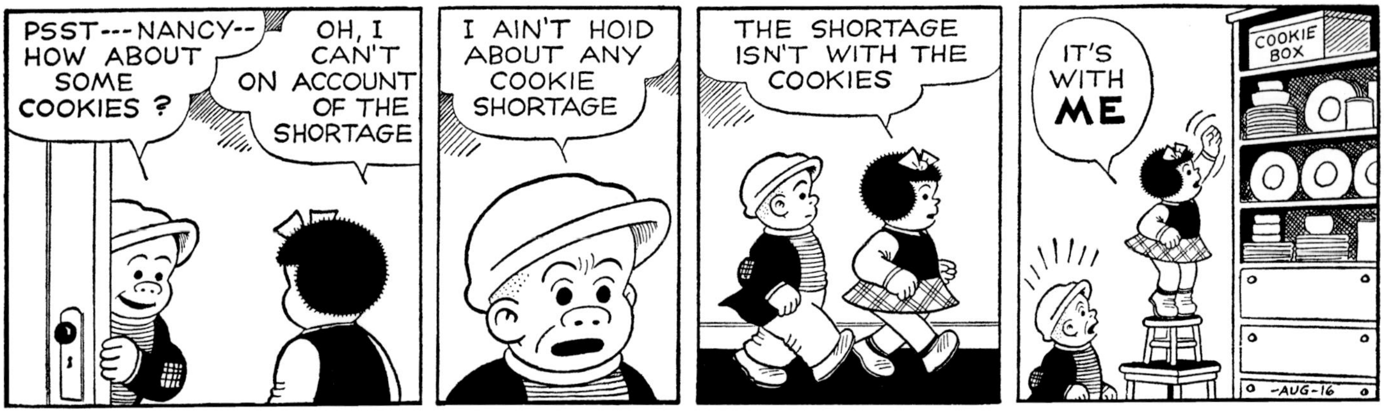
PSST---NANCY-- HOW ABOUT SOME COOKIES ?
OH, I CAN'T ON ACCOUNT OF THE SHORTAGE
I AIN'T HOID ABOUT ANY COOKIE SHORTAGE
THE SHORTAGE ISN'T WITH THE COOKIES
IT'S WITH **ME**
COOKIE BOX
-AUG-16

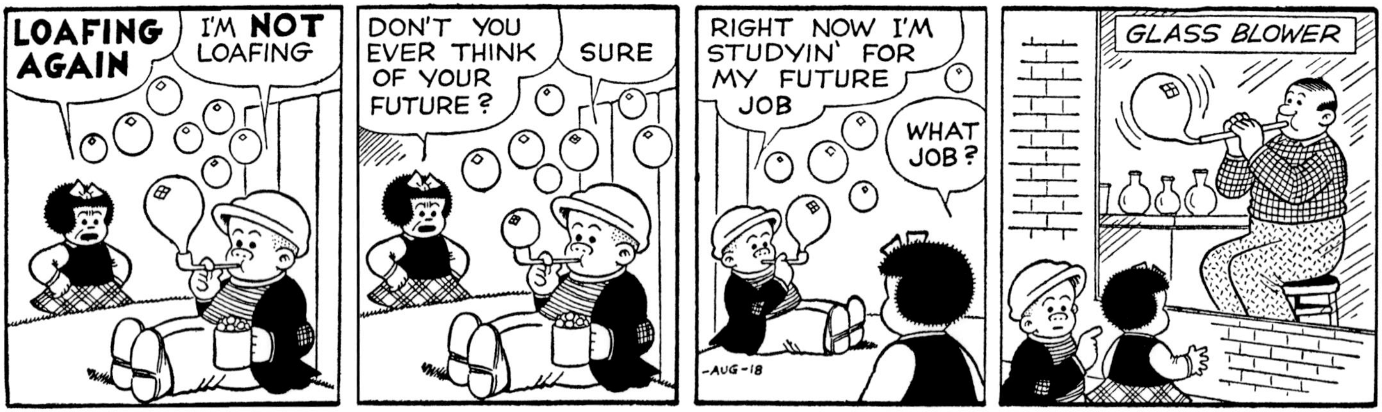
LOAFING AGAIN
I'M **NOT** LOAFING
DON'T YOU EVER THINK OF YOUR FUTURE ?
SURE
RIGHT NOW I'M STUDYIN' FOR MY FUTURE JOB
WHAT JOB ?
-AUG-18
GLASS BLOWER

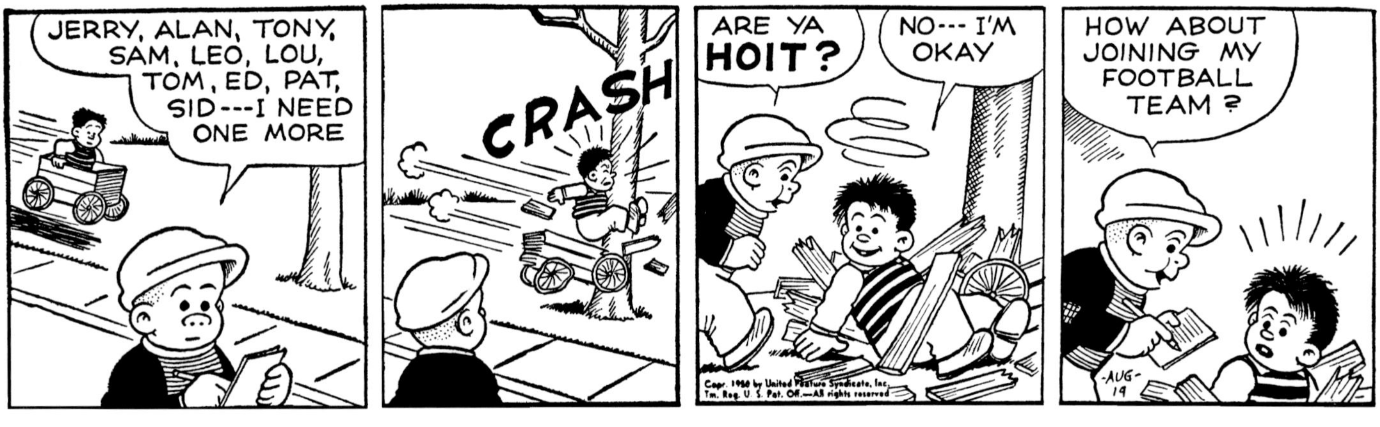
JERRY, ALAN, TONY, SAM, LEO, LOU, TOM, ED, PAT, SID---I NEED ONE MORE
CRASH
ARE YA **HOIT ?**
NO--- I'M OKAY
Copr. 1950 by United Feature Syndicate, Inc. Tm. Reg. U. S. Pat. Off.—All rights reserved
HOW ABOUT JOINING MY FOOTBALL TEAM ?
-AUG-19

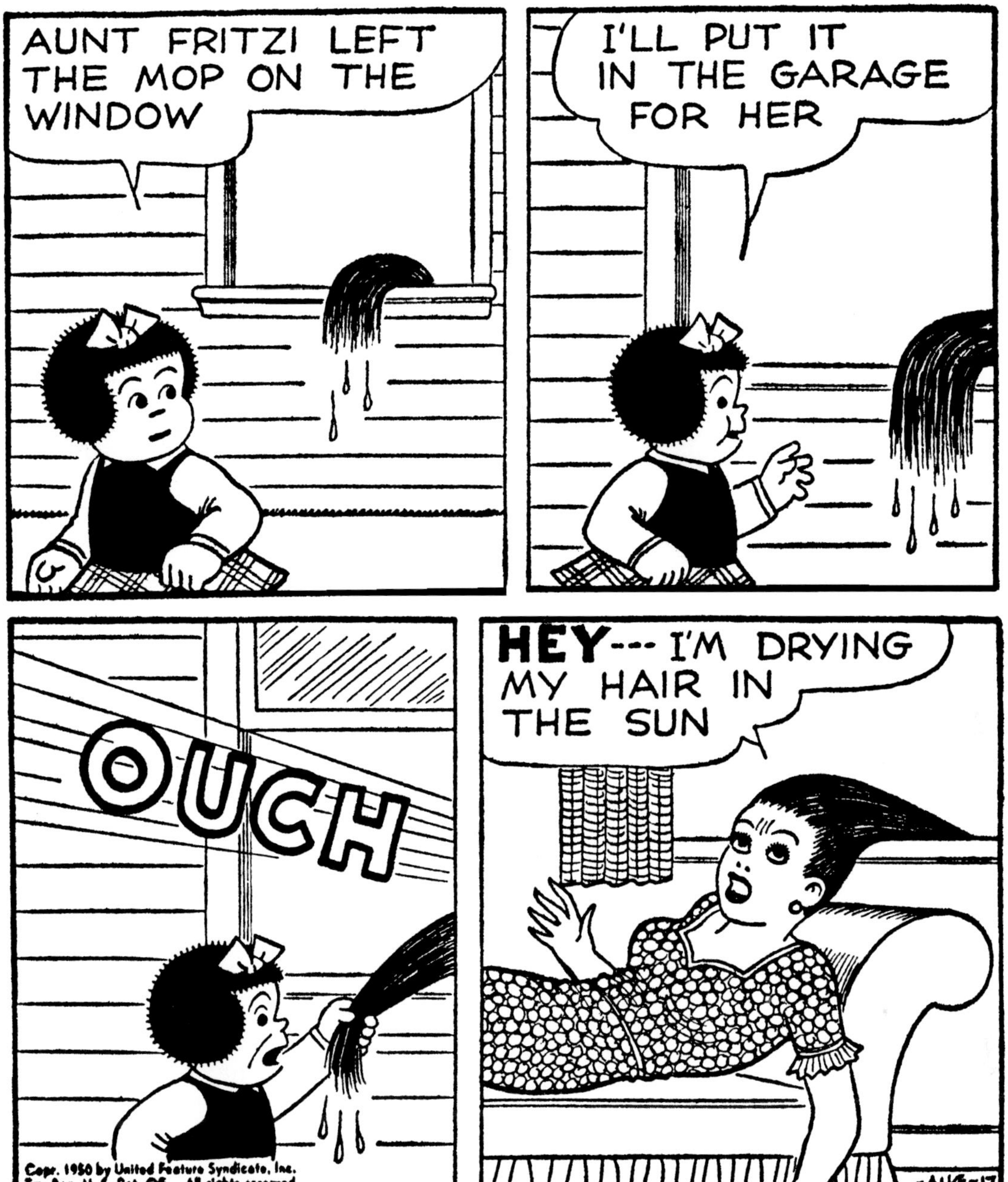
AUNT FRITZI LEFT THE MOP ON THE WINDOW
I'LL PUT IT IN THE GARAGE FOR HER
OUCH
Copr. 1950 by United Feature Syndicate, Inc.
Tm. Reg. U. S. Pat. Off.—All rights reserved
HEY--- I'M DRYING MY HAIR IN THE SUN
AUG-17

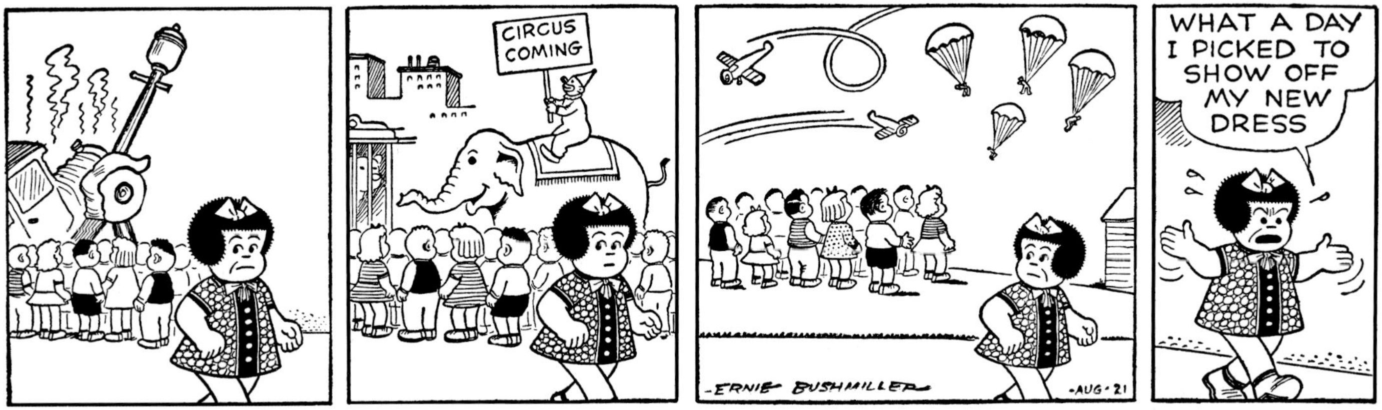
CIRCUS COMING
-ERNIE BUSHMILLER
-AUG-21
WHAT A DAY I PICKED TO SHOW OFF MY NEW DRESS

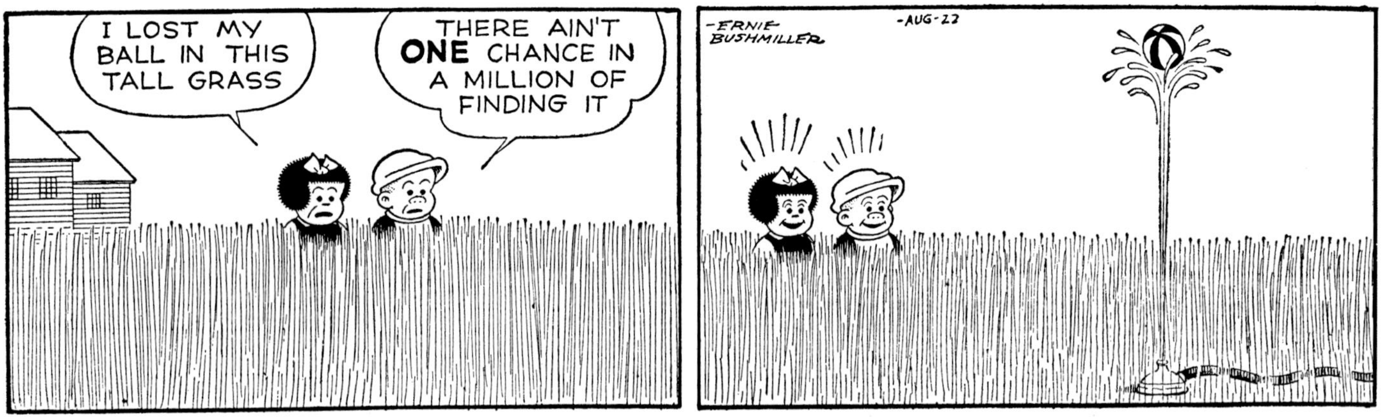
I LOST MY BALL IN THIS TALL GRASS
THERE AIN'T **ONE** CHANCE IN A MILLION OF FINDING IT
-ERNIE BUSHMILLER
-AUG-22

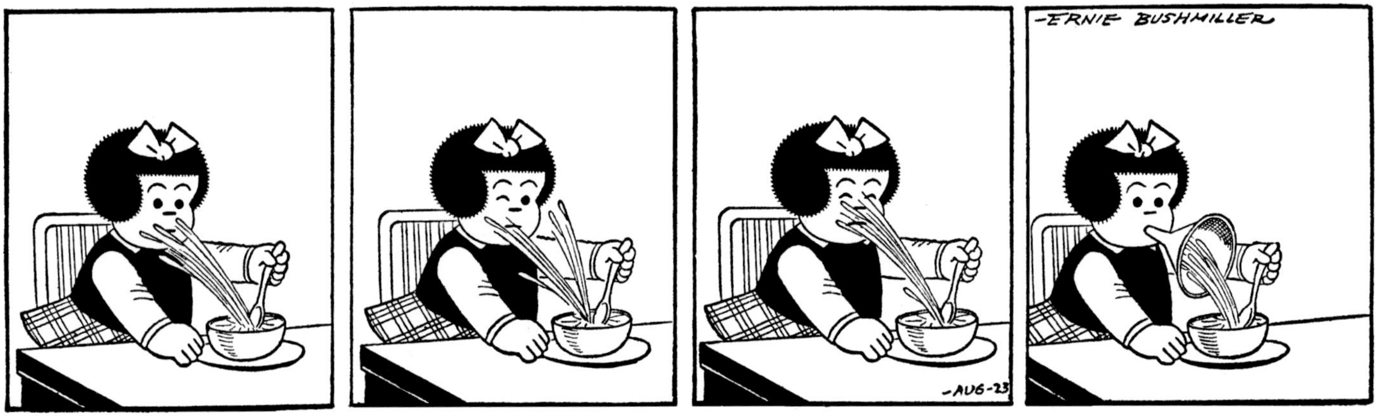
-AUG-23
-ERNIE BUSHMILLER

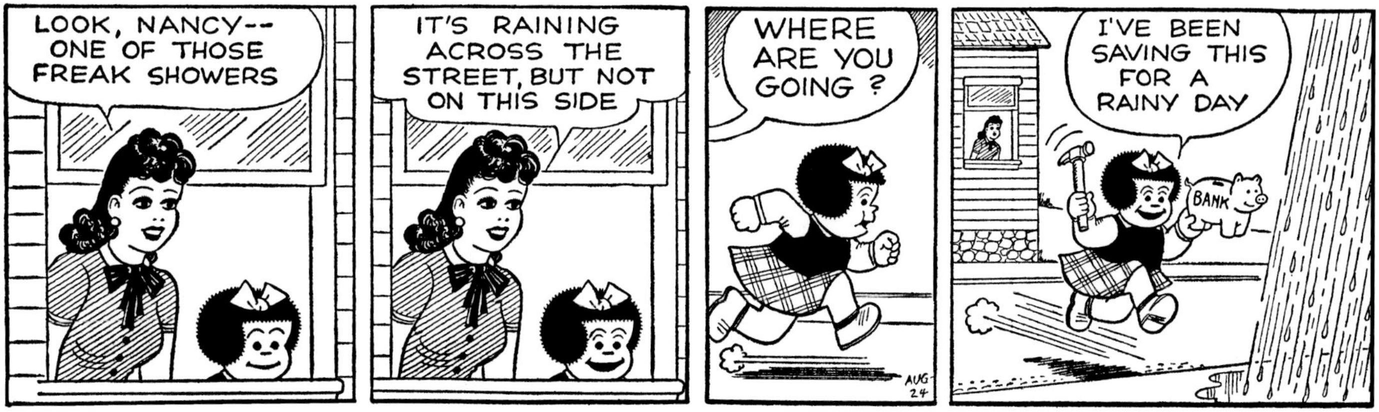

LOOK, NANCY-- ONE OF THOSE FREAK SHOWERS
IT'S RAINING ACROSS THE STREET, BUT NOT ON THIS SIDE
WHERE ARE YOU GOING ?
AUG 24
I'VE BEEN SAVING THIS FOR A RAINY DAY
BANK

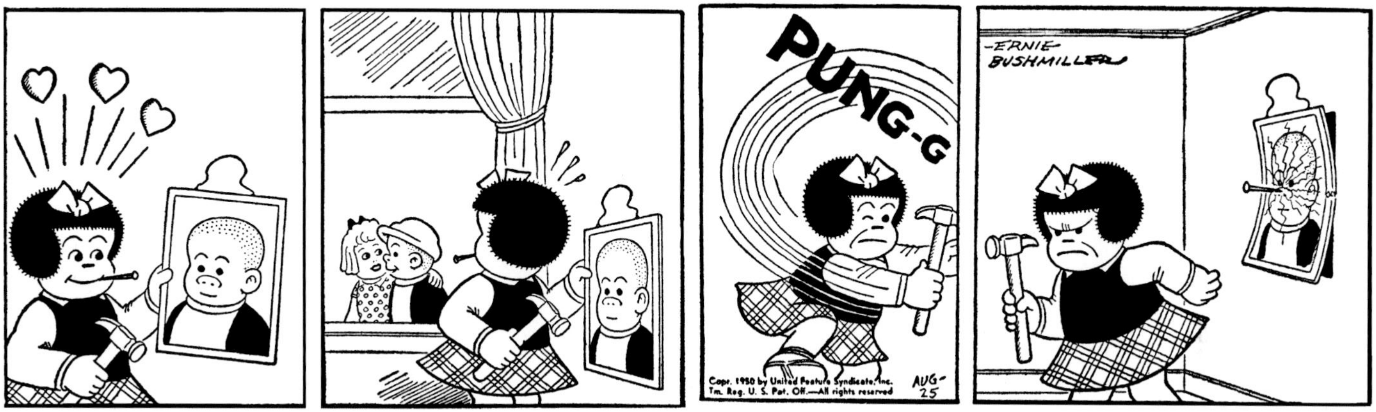

PUNG-G
Copr. 1950 by United Feature Syndicate, Inc. Tm. Reg. U. S. Pat. Off.—All rights reserved
AUG-25
-ERNIE BUSHMILLER

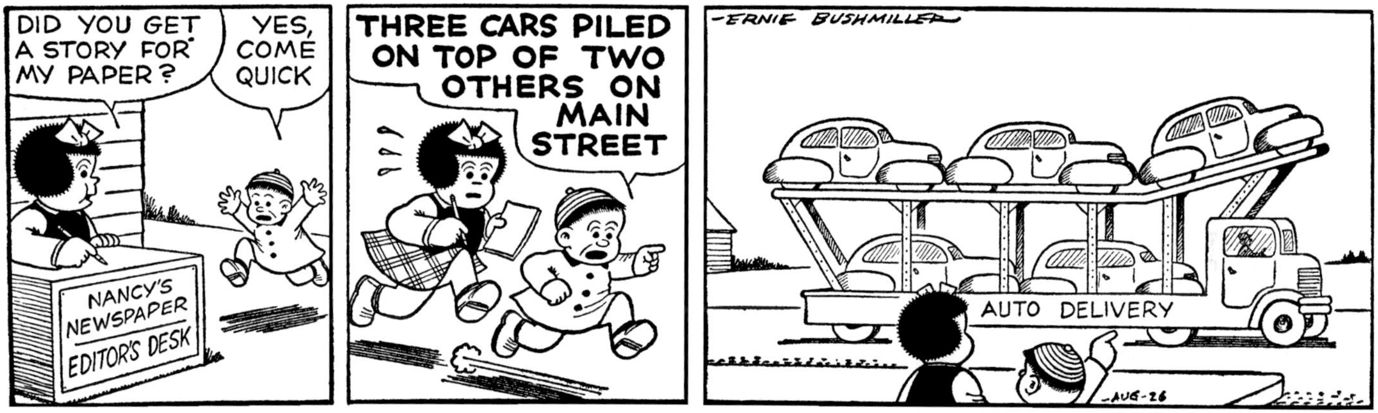

DID YOU GET A STORY FOR MY PAPER ?
YES, COME QUICK
NANCY'S NEWSPAPER
EDITOR'S DESK
THREE CARS PILED ON TOP OF TWO OTHERS ON MAIN STREET
-ERNIE BUSHMILLER
AUTO DELIVERY
AUG-26

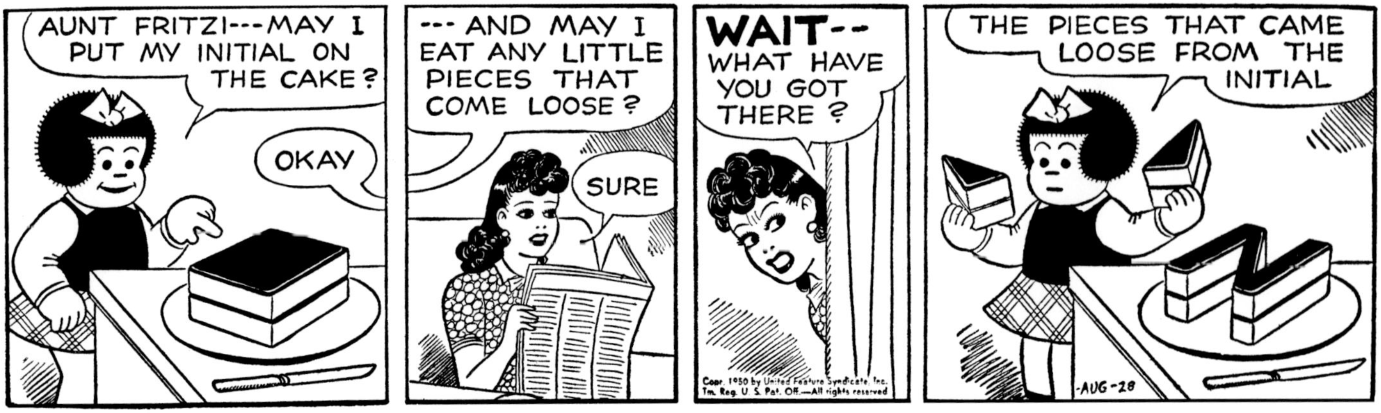
AUNT FRITZI---MAY I PUT MY INITIAL ON THE CAKE?
OKAY
--- AND MAY I EAT ANY LITTLE PIECES THAT COME LOOSE?
SURE
WAIT-- WHAT HAVE YOU GOT THERE?
Copr. 1950 by United Feature Syndicate, Inc. Tm. Reg. U. S. Pat. Off.—All rights reserved
THE PIECES THAT CAME LOOSE FROM THE INITIAL
AUG-28

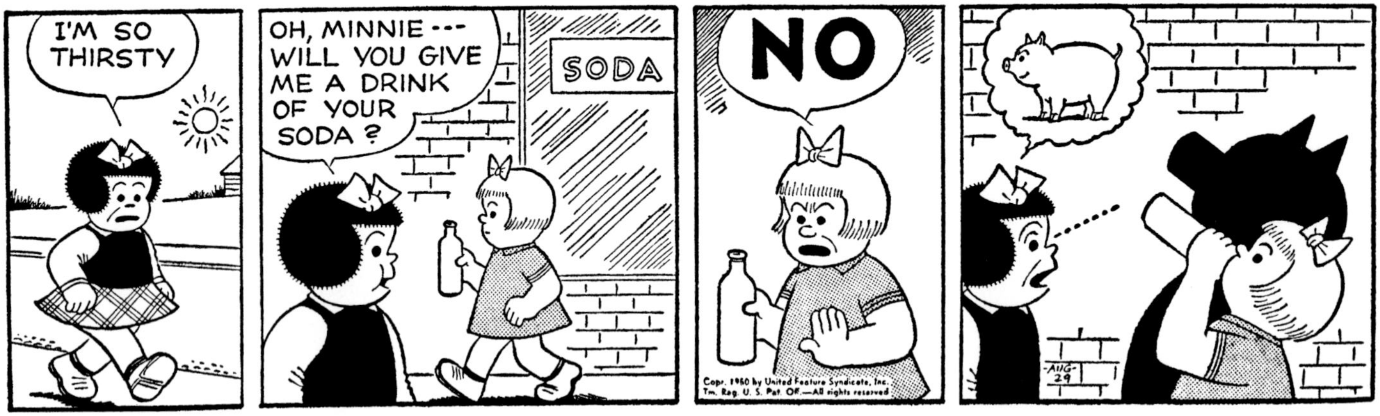
I'M SO THIRSTY
OH, MINNIE --- WILL YOU GIVE ME A DRINK OF YOUR SODA?
SODA
NO
Copr. 1950 by United Feature Syndicate, Inc. Tm. Reg. U. S. Pat. Off.—All rights reserved
AUG-29

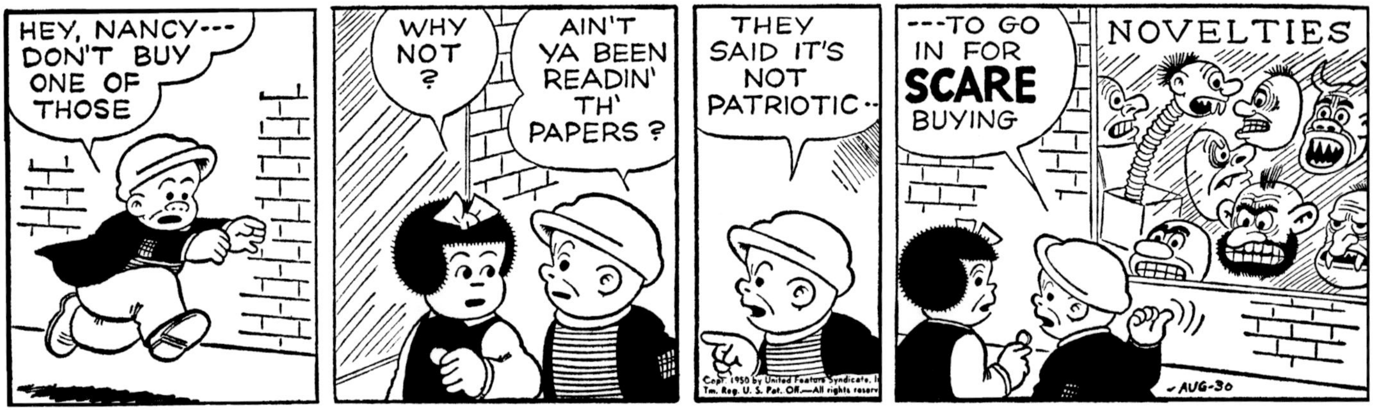
HEY, NANCY--- DON'T BUY ONE OF THOSE
WHY NOT?
AIN'T YA BEEN READIN' TH' PAPERS?
THEY SAID IT'S NOT PATRIOTIC--
---TO GO IN FOR SCARE BUYING
NOVELTIES
AUG-30

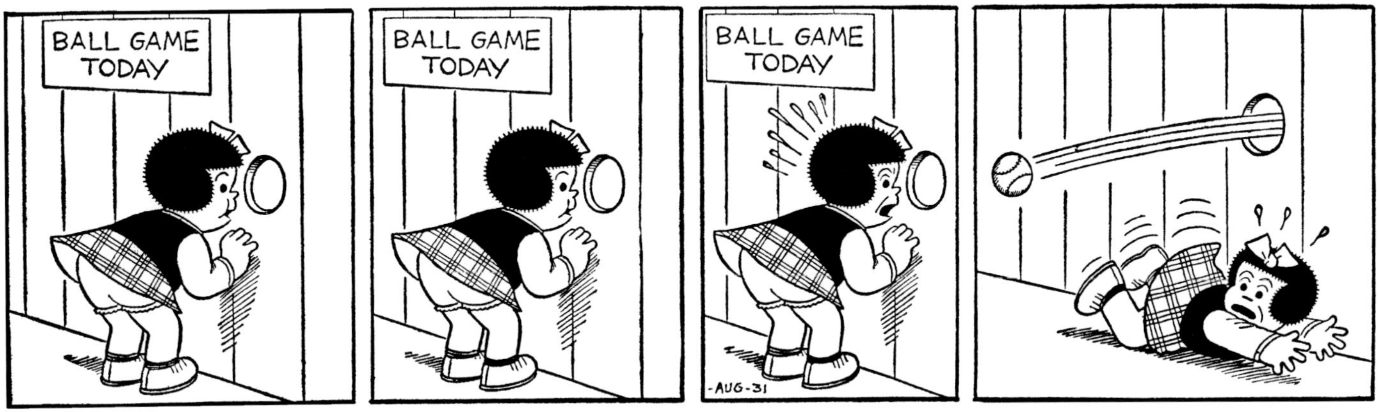
BALL GAME TODAY
BALL GAME TODAY
BALL GAME TODAY
AUG-31

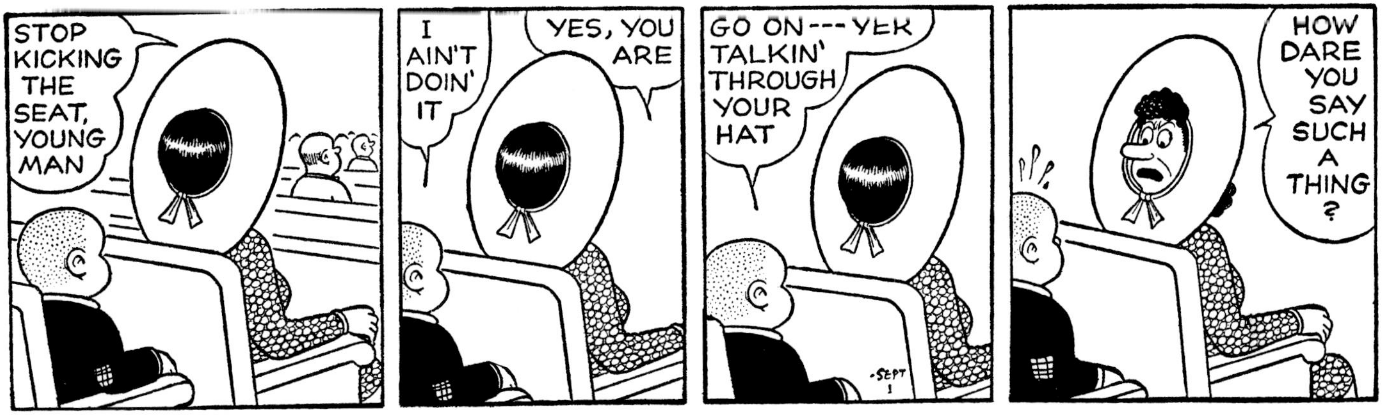
STOP KICKING THE SEAT, YOUNG MAN
I AIN'T DOIN' IT
YES, YOU ARE
GO ON---YER TALKIN' THROUGH YOUR HAT
SEPT 1
HOW DARE YOU SAY SUCH A THING?

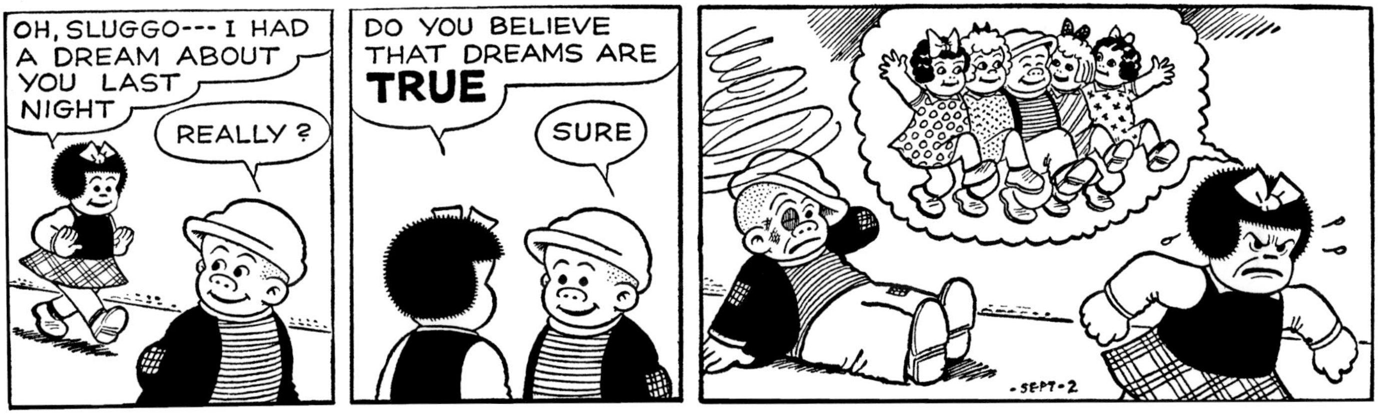
OH, SLUGGO--- I HAD A DREAM ABOUT YOU LAST NIGHT
REALLY?
DO YOU BELIEVE THAT DREAMS ARE **TRUE**
SURE
SEPT-2

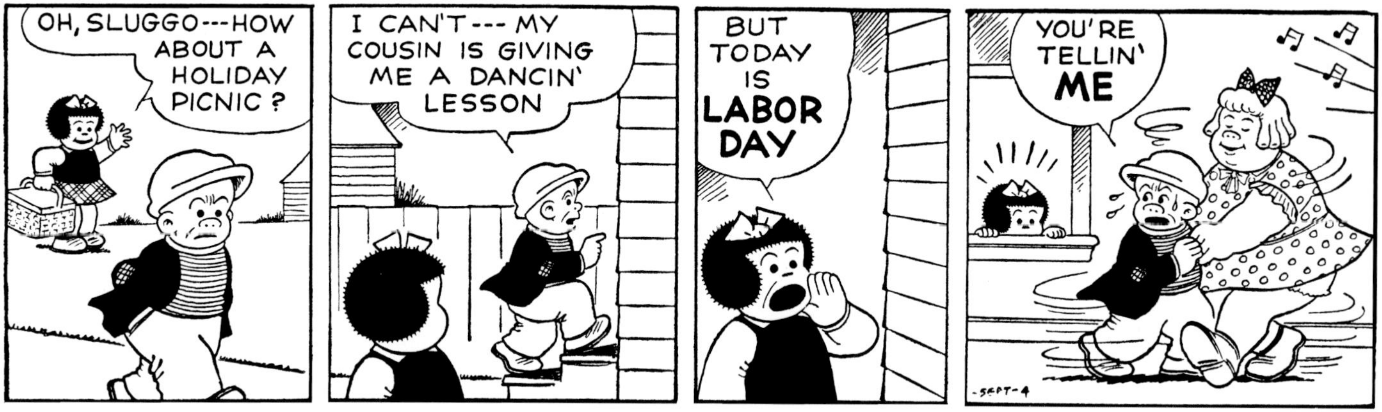
OH, SLUGGO---HOW ABOUT A HOLIDAY PICNIC?
I CAN'T---MY COUSIN IS GIVING ME A DANCIN' LESSON
BUT TODAY IS LABOR DAY
YOU'RE TELLIN' ME
SEPT-4

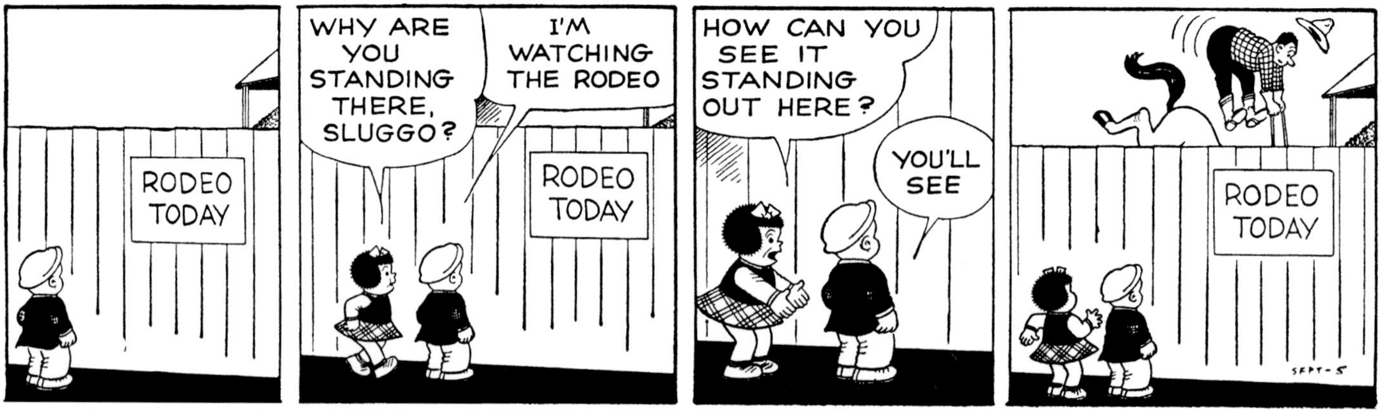
RODEO TODAY
WHY ARE YOU STANDING THERE, SLUGGO?
I'M WATCHING THE RODEO
RODEO TODAY
HOW CAN YOU SEE IT STANDING OUT HERE?
YOU'LL SEE
RODEO TODAY
SEPT-5

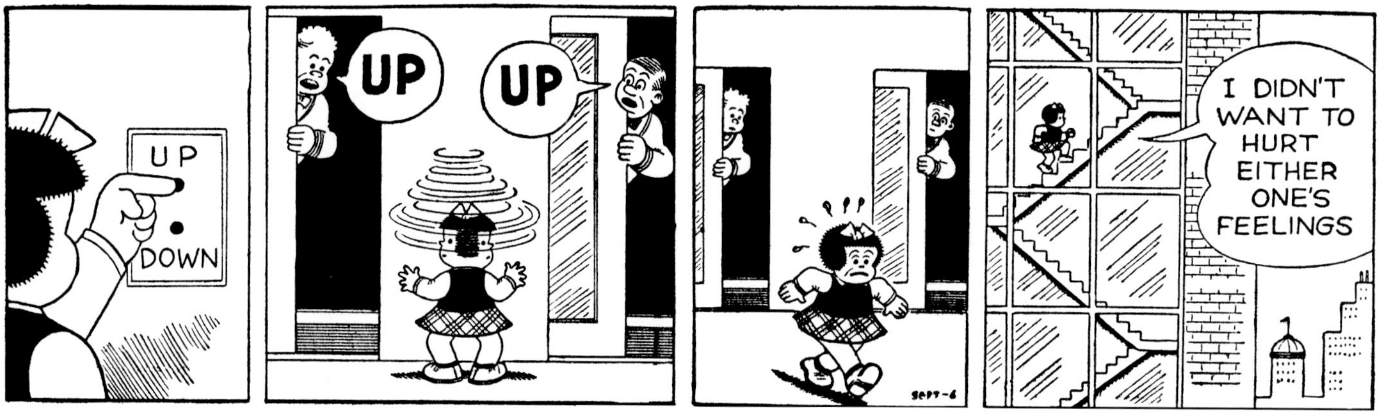
UP
DOWN
UP
UP
SEPT-6
I DIDN'T WANT TO HURT EITHER ONE'S FEELINGS

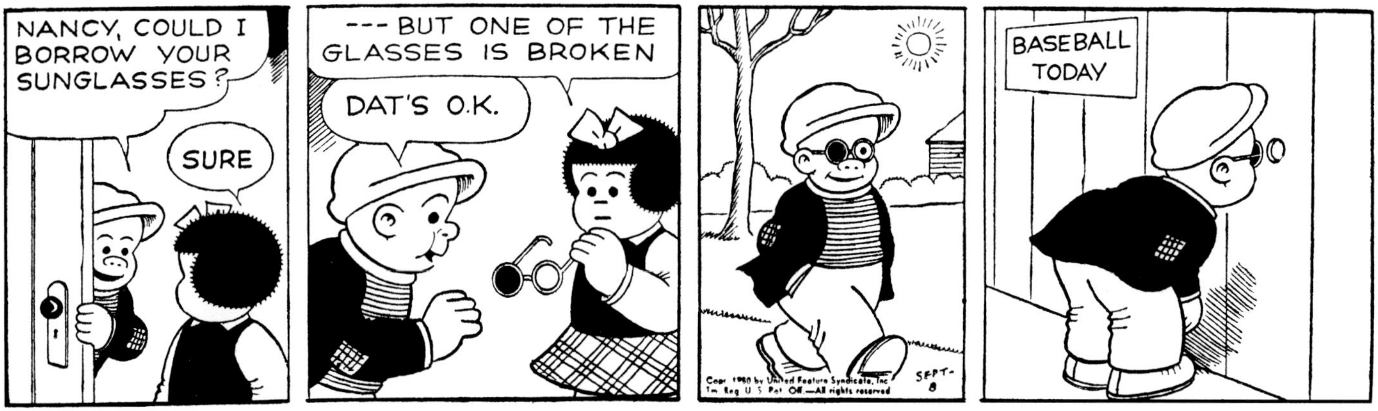
NANCY, COULD I BORROW YOUR SUNGLASSES?
SURE
---BUT ONE OF THE GLASSES IS BROKEN
DAT'S O.K.
Copr. 1960 by United Feature Syndicate, Inc. Tm. Reg. U.S. Pat. Off.—All rights reserved
SEPT-8
BASEBALL TODAY

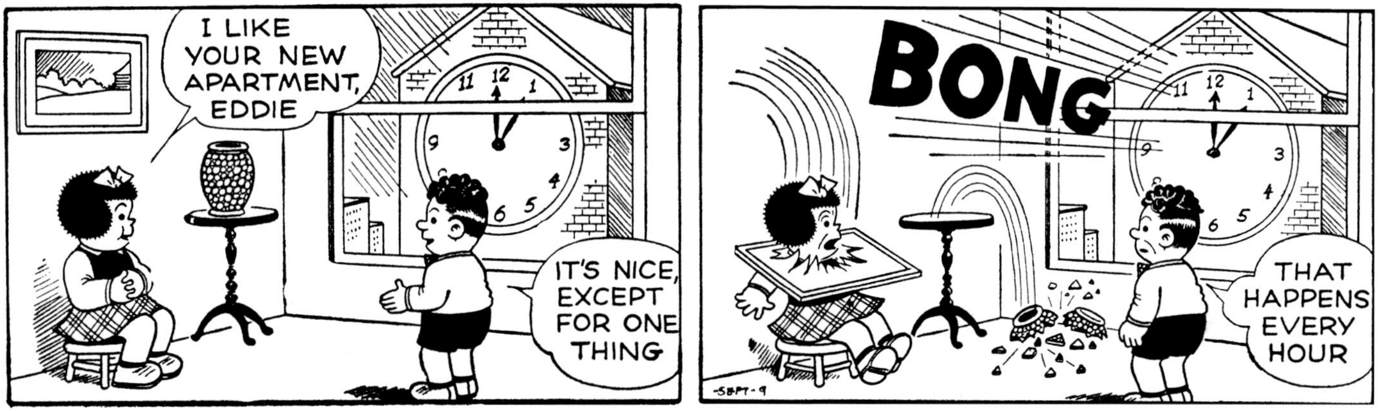
I LIKE YOUR NEW APARTMENT, EDDIE
IT'S NICE, EXCEPT FOR ONE THING
BONG
THAT HAPPENS EVERY HOUR
SEPT-9

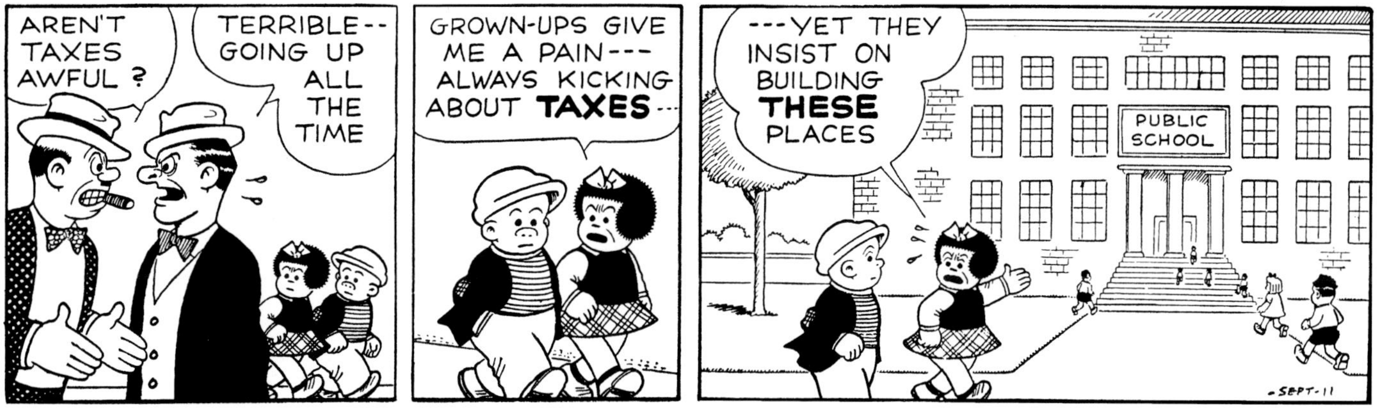
AREN'T TAXES AWFUL?
TERRIBLE-- GOING UP ALL THE TIME
GROWN-UPS GIVE ME A PAIN--- ALWAYS KICKING ABOUT TAXES---
---YET THEY INSIST ON BUILDING THESE PLACES
PUBLIC SCHOOL
SEPT-11

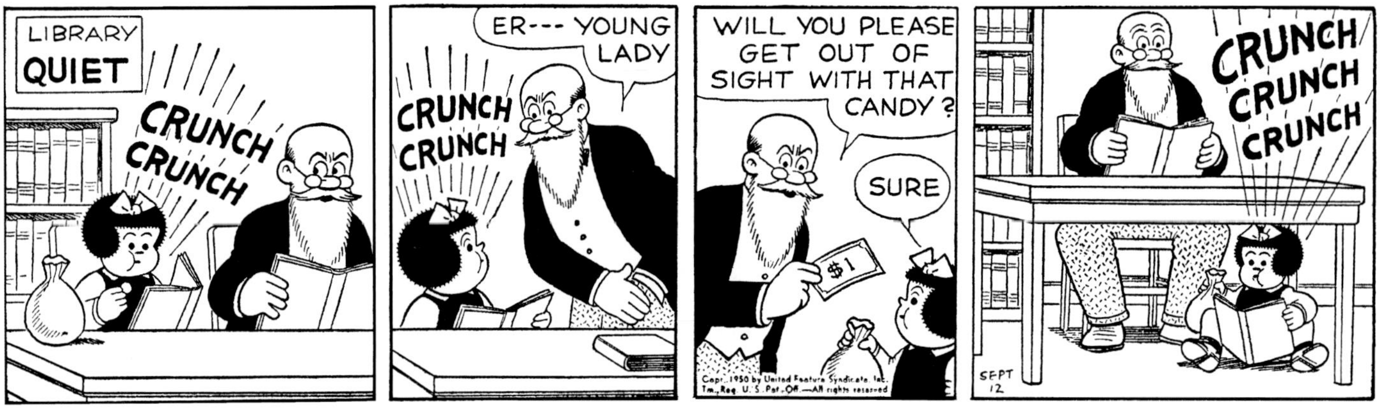
LIBRARY
QUIET
CRUNCH CRUNCH
ER--- YOUNG LADY
CRUNCH CRUNCH
WILL YOU PLEASE GET OUT OF SIGHT WITH THAT CANDY?
SURE
$1
Copr. 1950 by United Feature Syndicate, Inc. Tm. Reg. U. S. Pat. Off.—All rights reserved
CRUNCH CRUNCH CRUNCH
SEPT 12

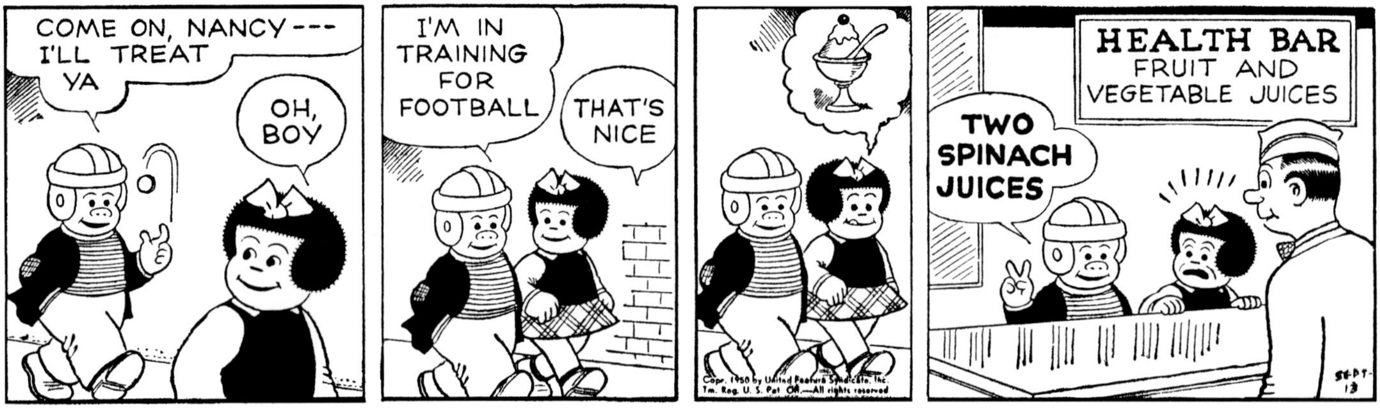
COME ON, NANCY--- I'LL TREAT YA
OH, BOY
I'M IN TRAINING FOR FOOTBALL
THAT'S NICE
Copr. 1950 by United Feature Syndicate, Inc. Tm. Reg. U. S. Pat. Off.—All rights reserved
HEALTH BAR
FRUIT AND VEGETABLE JUICES
TWO SPINACH JUICES
SEPT-13

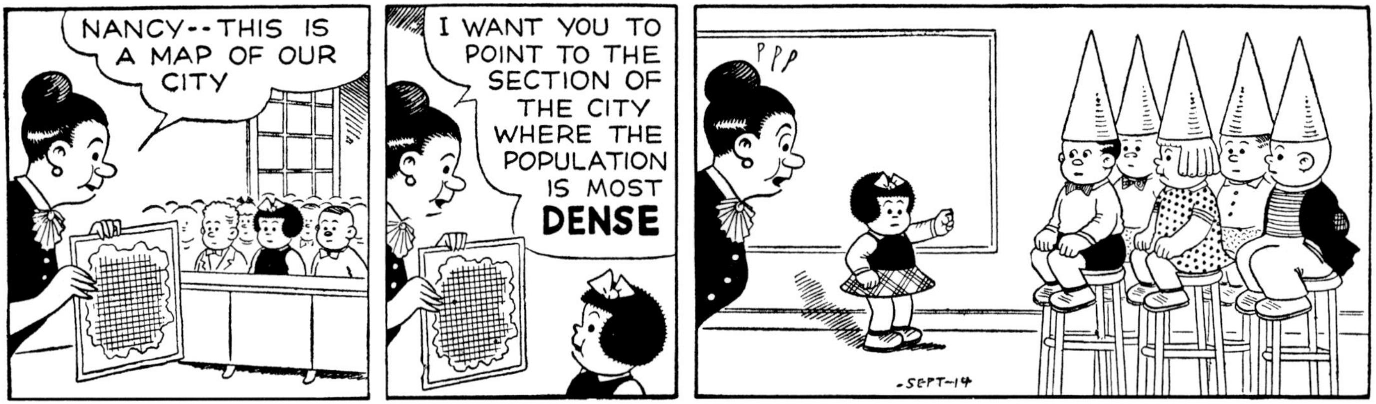
NANCY--THIS IS A MAP OF OUR CITY
I WANT YOU TO POINT TO THE SECTION OF THE CITY WHERE THE POPULATION IS MOST DENSE
SEPT-14

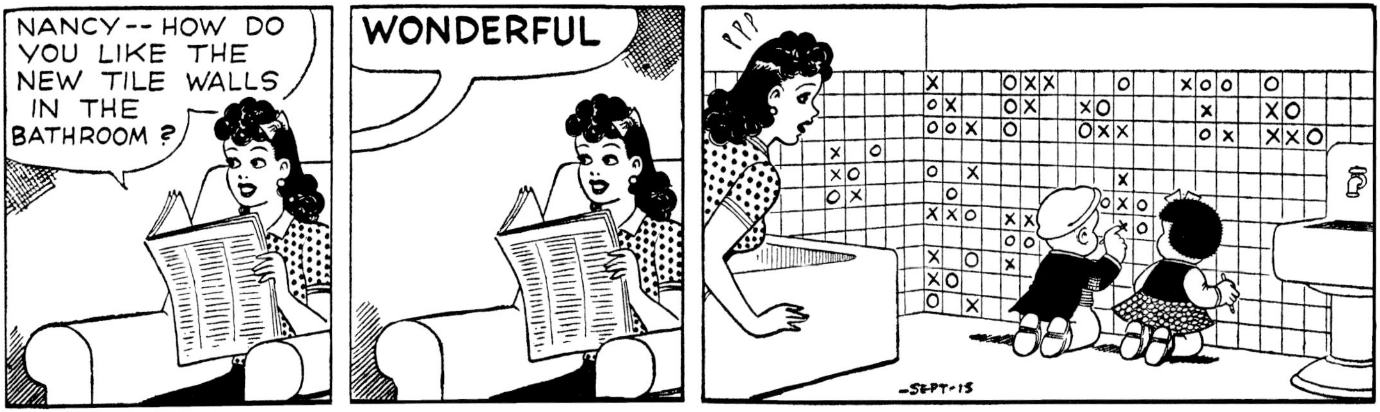
NANCY--HOW DO YOU LIKE THE NEW TILE WALLS IN THE BATHROOM ?
WONDERFUL
SEPT-15

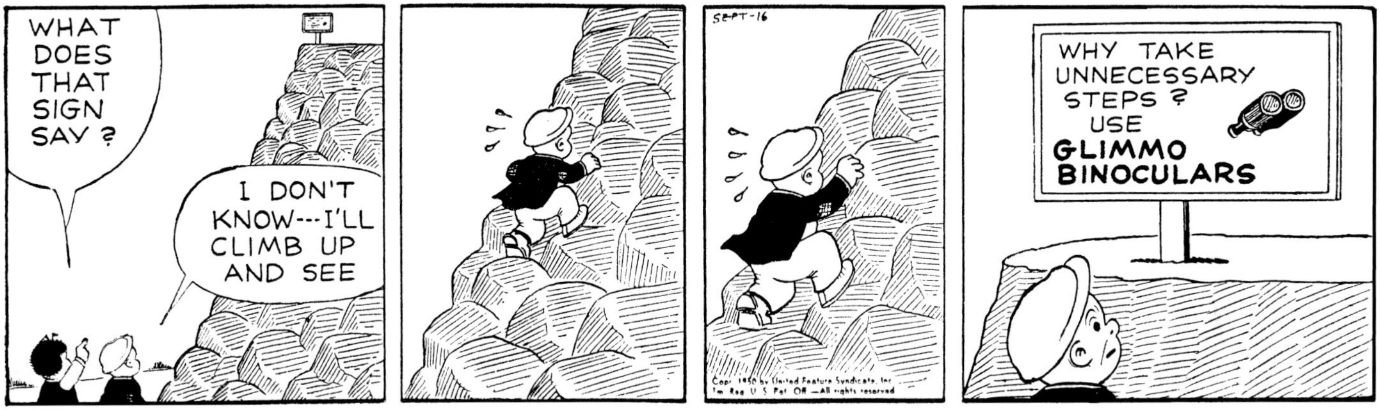
WHAT DOES THAT SIGN SAY ?
I DON'T KNOW---I'LL CLIMB UP AND SEE
SEPT-16
Copr. 1950 by United Feature Syndicate, Inc. Tm. Reg. U. S. Pat. Off.—All rights reserved
WHY TAKE UNNECESSARY STEPS ? USE
GLIMMO BINOCULARS

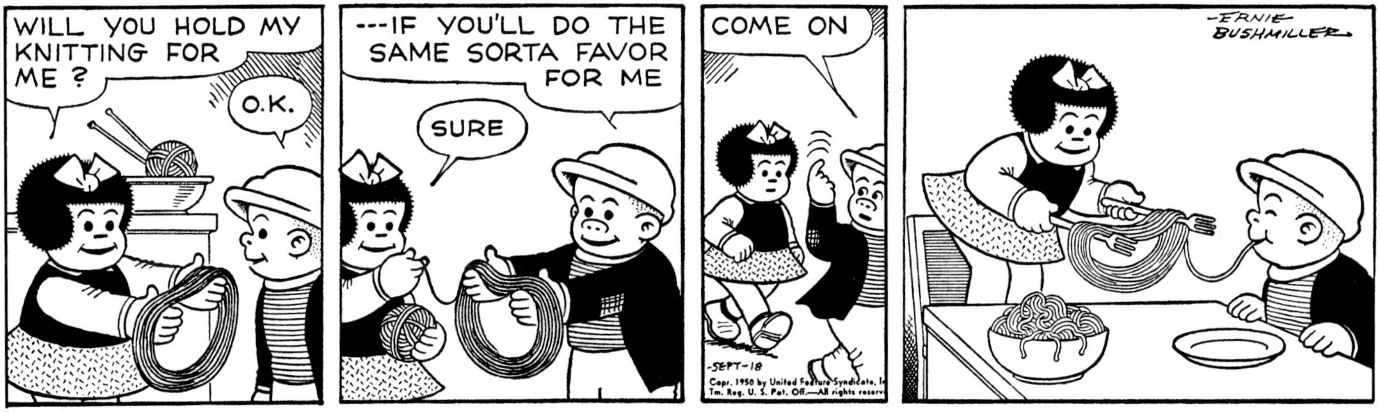
WILL YOU HOLD MY KNITTING FOR ME ?
O.K.
---IF YOU'LL DO THE SAME SORTA FAVOR FOR ME
SURE
COME ON
SEPT-18
Copr. 1950 by United Feature Syndicate, Inc. Tm. Reg. U. S. Pat. Off.—All rights reserved
ERNIE BUSHMILLER

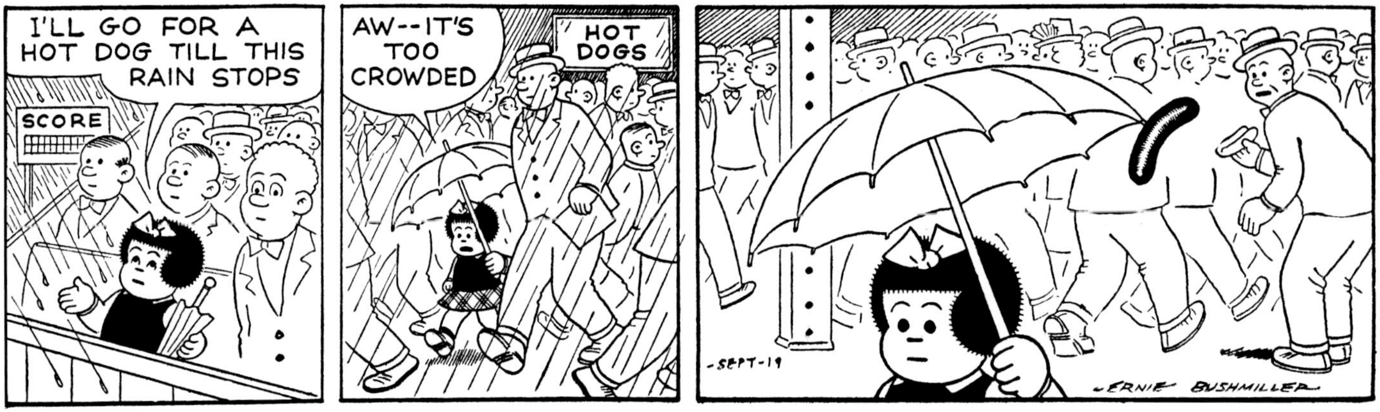
I'LL GO FOR A HOT DOG TILL THIS RAIN STOPS
SCORE
AW--IT'S TOO CROWDED
HOT DOGS
-SEPT-19
ERNIE BUSHMILLER

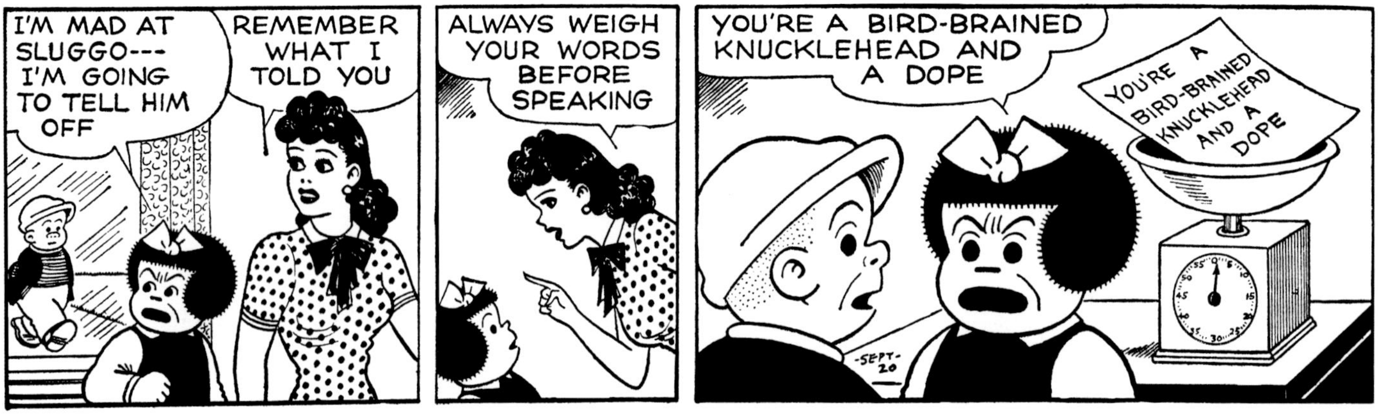
I'M MAD AT SLUGGO--- I'M GOING TO TELL HIM OFF
REMEMBER WHAT I TOLD YOU
ALWAYS WEIGH YOUR WORDS BEFORE SPEAKING
YOU'RE A BIRD-BRAINED KNUCKLEHEAD AND A DOPE
YOU'RE A BIRD-BRAINED KNUCKLEHEAD AND A DOPE
-SEPT-20

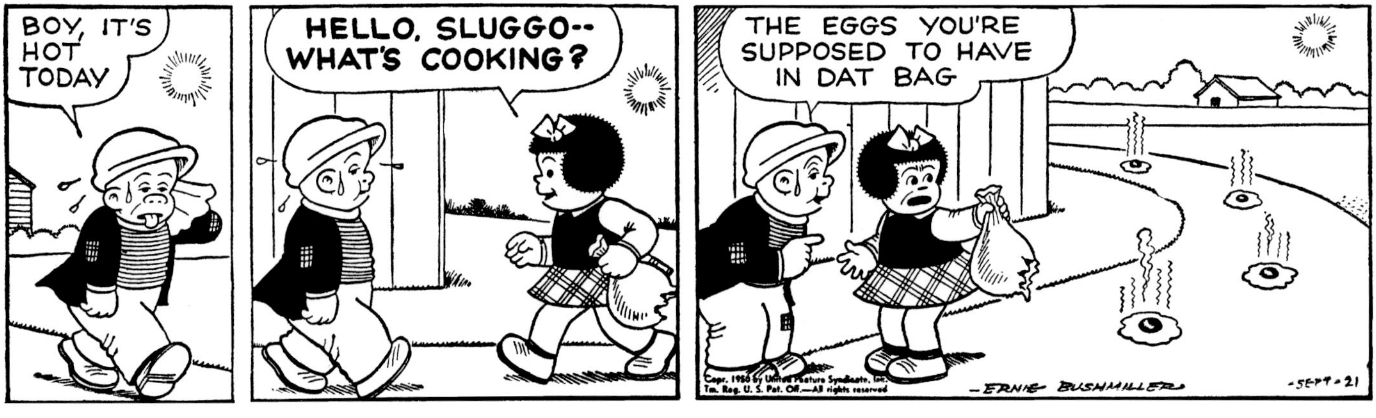
BOY, IT'S HOT TODAY
HELLO, SLUGGO-- WHAT'S COOKING?
THE EGGS YOU'RE SUPPOSED TO HAVE IN DAT BAG
Copr. 1950 by United Feature Syndicate, Inc.
Tm. Reg. U. S. Pat. Off.—All rights reserved
-ERNIE BUSHMILLER
-SEPT-21

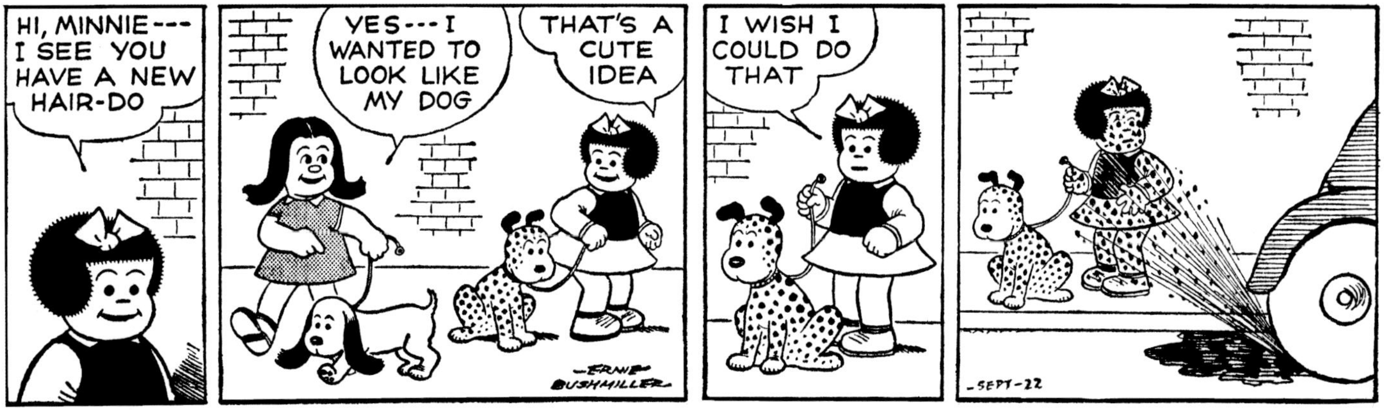
HI, MINNIE--- I SEE YOU HAVE A NEW HAIR-DO
YES---I WANTED TO LOOK LIKE MY DOG
THAT'S A CUTE IDEA
-ERNIE BUSHMILLER
I WISH I COULD DO THAT
-SEPT-22

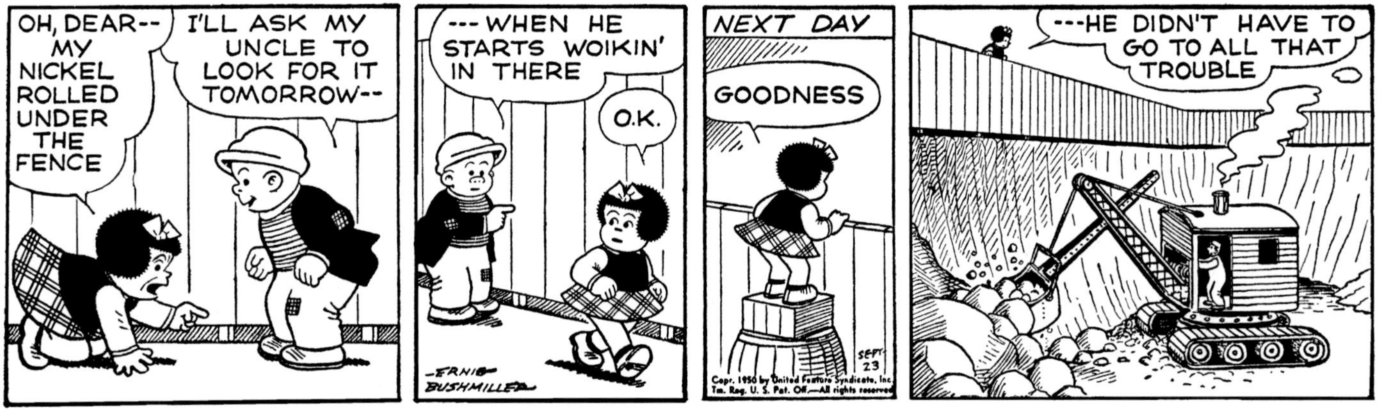
OH, DEAR-- MY NICKEL ROLLED UNDER THE FENCE
I'LL ASK MY UNCLE TO LOOK FOR IT TOMORROW--
---WHEN HE STARTS WOIKIN' IN THERE
O.K.
-ERNIE BUSHMILLER
NEXT DAY
GOODNESS
SEPT 23
Copr. 1950 by United Feature Syndicate, Inc. Tm. Reg. U. S. Pat. Off.—All rights reserved
---HE DIDN'T HAVE TO GO TO ALL THAT TROUBLE

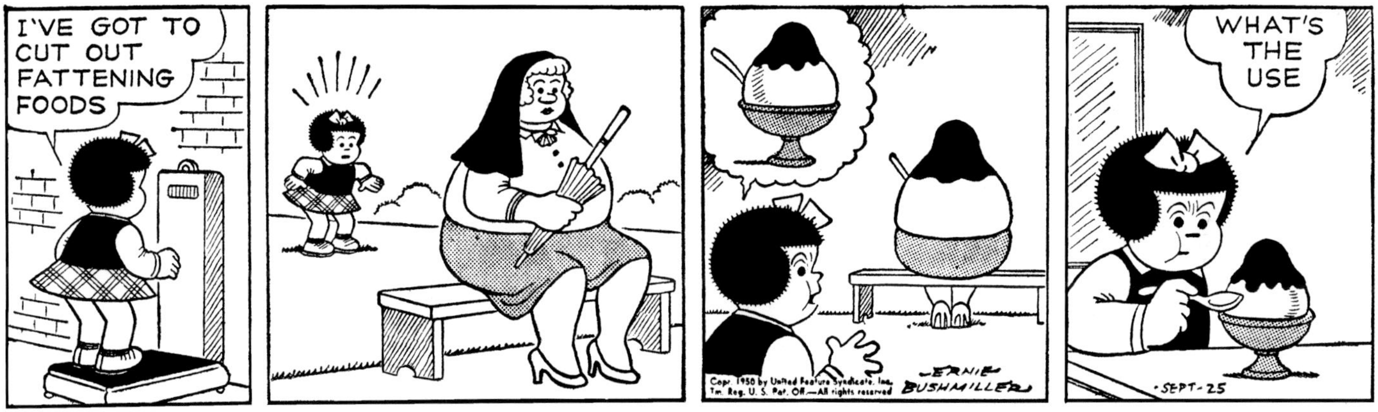
I'VE GOT TO CUT OUT FATTENING FOODS
Copr. 1950 by United Feature Syndicate, Inc. Tm. Reg. U. S. Pat. Off.—All rights reserved
-ERNIE BUSHMILLER
WHAT'S THE USE
-SEPT-25

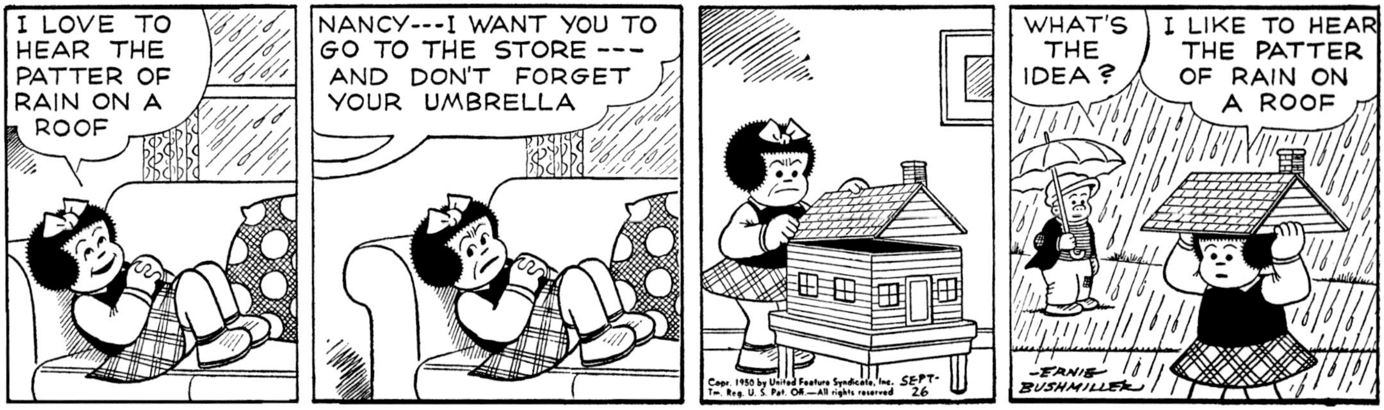
I LOVE TO HEAR THE PATTER OF RAIN ON A ROOF
NANCY---I WANT YOU TO GO TO THE STORE --- AND DON'T FORGET YOUR UMBRELLA
Copr. 1950 by United Feature Syndicate, Inc. Tm. Reg. U. S. Pat. Off.—All rights reserved
SEPT-26
WHAT'S THE IDEA?
I LIKE TO HEAR THE PATTER OF RAIN ON A ROOF
-ERNIE BUSHMILLER

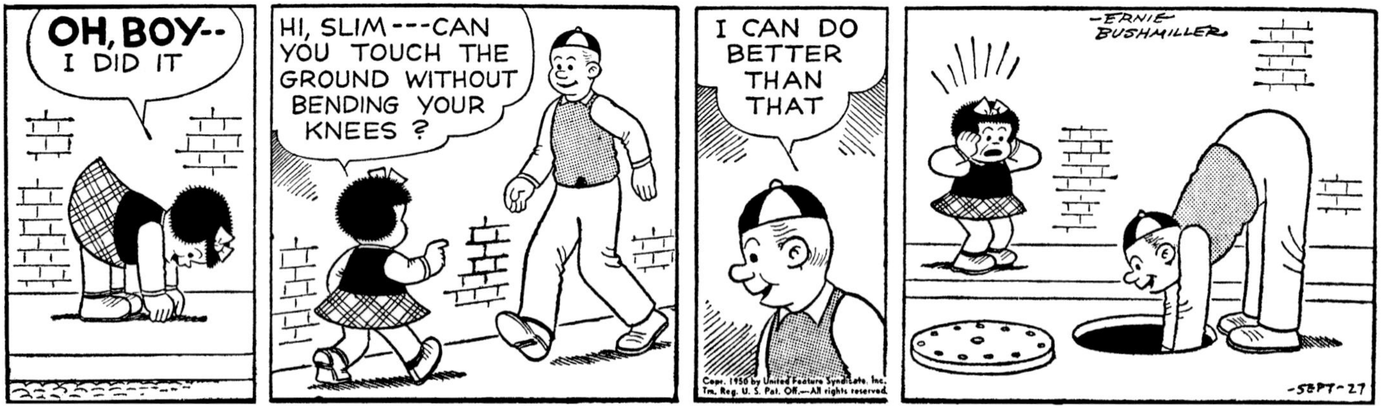
OH, BOY-- I DID IT
HI, SLIM---CAN YOU TOUCH THE GROUND WITHOUT BENDING YOUR KNEES ?
I CAN DO BETTER THAN THAT
Copr. 1950 by United Feature Syndicate, Inc. Tm. Reg. U. S. Pat. Off.—All rights reserved
-ERNIE BUSHMILLER
-SEPT-27

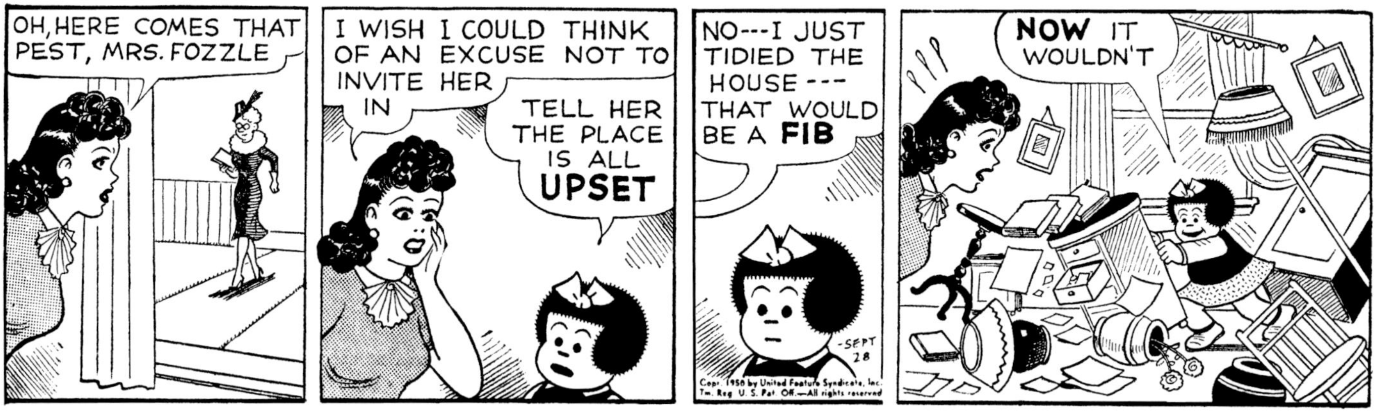
OH, HERE COMES THAT PEST, MRS. FOZZLE
I WISH I COULD THINK OF AN EXCUSE NOT TO INVITE HER IN
TELL HER THE PLACE IS ALL UPSET
NO---I JUST TIDIED THE HOUSE--- THAT WOULD BE A FIB
-SEPT 28
Copr. 1950 by United Feature Syndicate, Inc. Tm. Reg. U. S. Pat. Off.—All rights reserved
NOW IT WOULDN'T

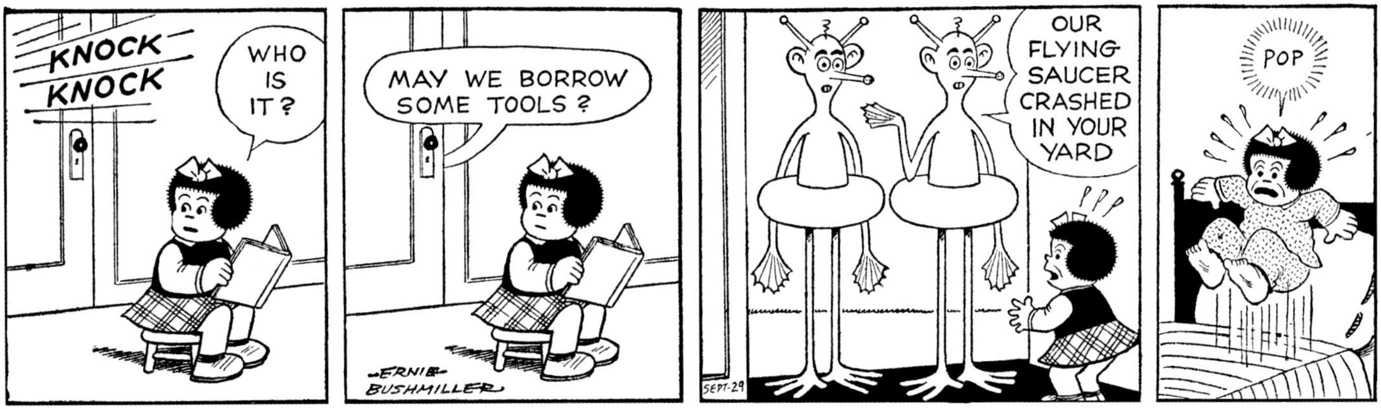
KNOCK
KNOCK
WHO IS IT?
MAY WE BORROW SOME TOOLS?
-ERNIE- BUSHMILLER
SEPT-29
OUR FLYING SAUCER CRASHED IN YOUR YARD
POP

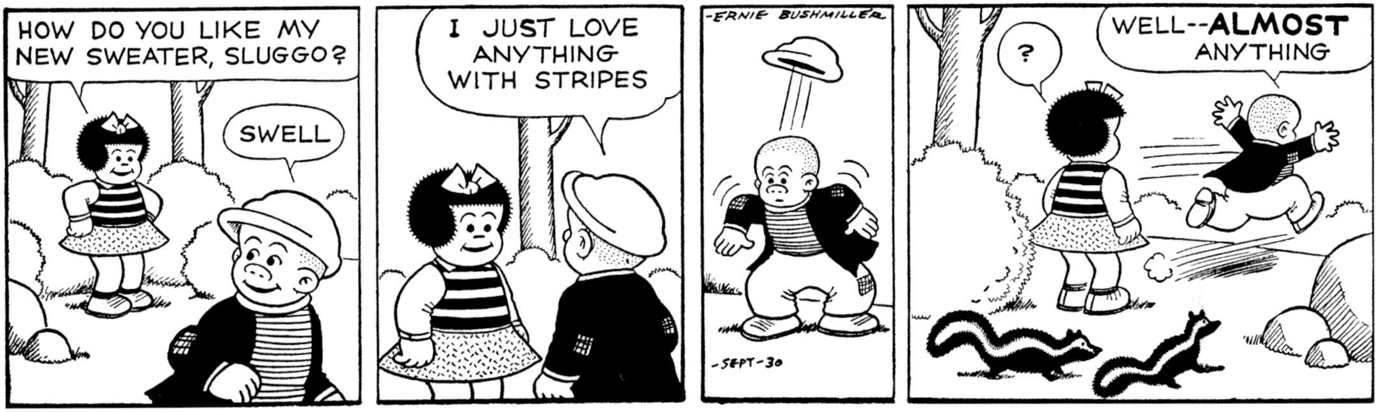
HOW DO YOU LIKE MY NEW SWEATER, SLUGGO?
SWELL
I JUST LOVE ANYTHING WITH STRIPES
-ERNIE BUSHMILLER
-SEPT-30
?
WELL--**ALMOST** ANYTHING

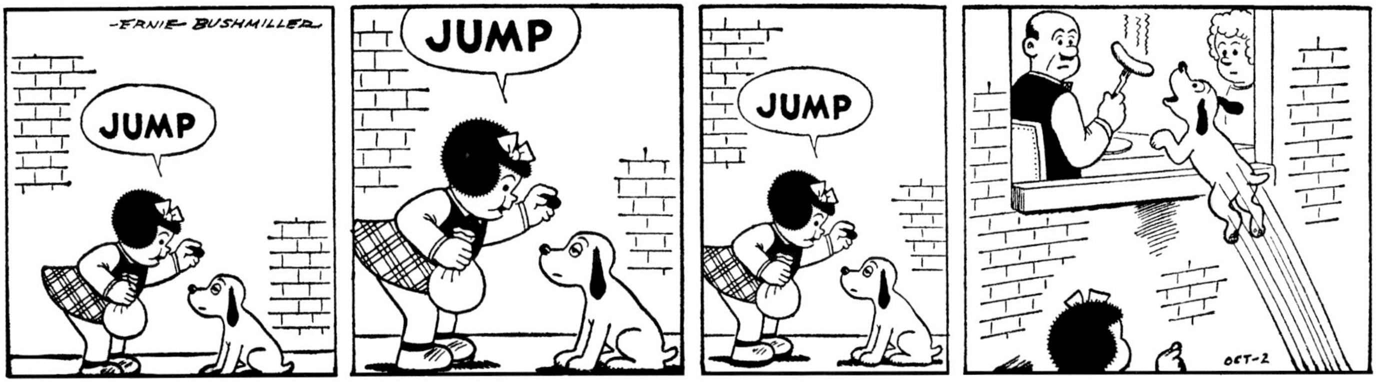
-ERNIE- BUSHMILLER
JUMP
JUMP
JUMP
OCT-2

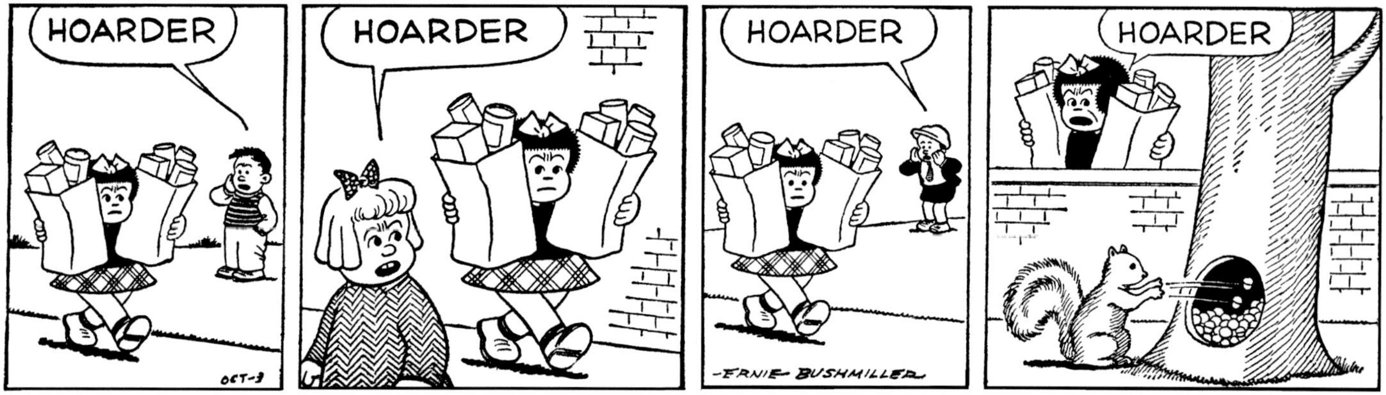
HOARDER
OCT-3
HOARDER
HOARDER
-ERNIE BUSHMILLER
HOARDER

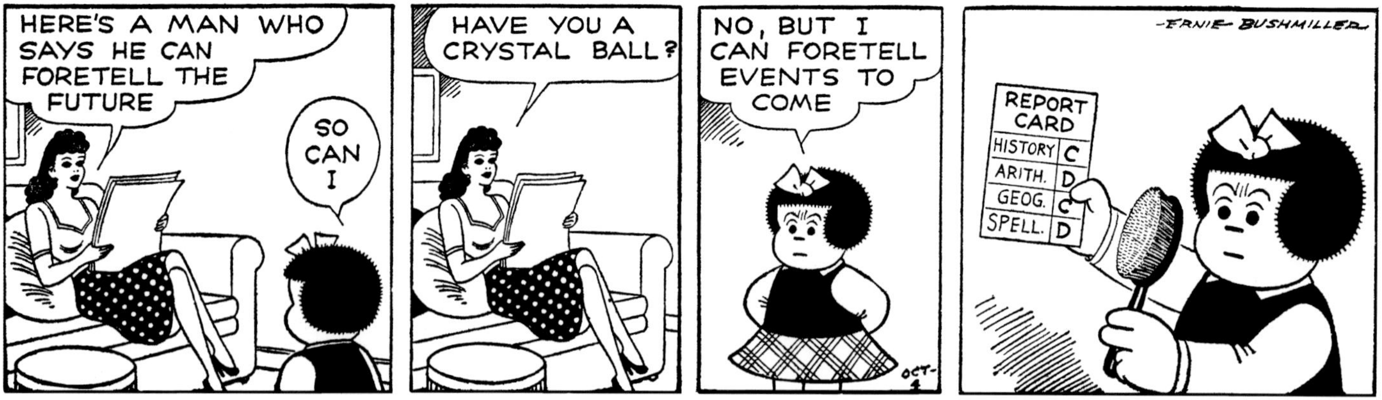
HERE'S A MAN WHO SAYS HE CAN FORETELL THE FUTURE
SO CAN I
HAVE YOU A CRYSTAL BALL?
NO, BUT I CAN FORETELL EVENTS TO COME
OCT-4
-ERNIE BUSHMILLER
REPORT CARD
HISTORY C
ARITH. D
GEOG. C
SPELL. D

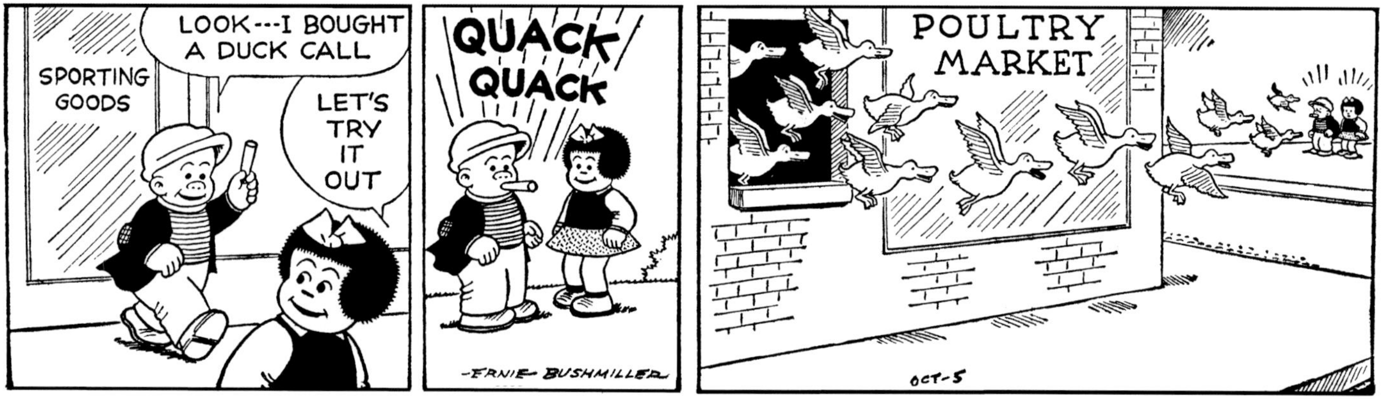
SPORTING GOODS
LOOK---I BOUGHT A DUCK CALL
LET'S TRY IT OUT
QUACK
QUACK
-ERNIE BUSHMILLER
POULTRY MARKET
OCT-5

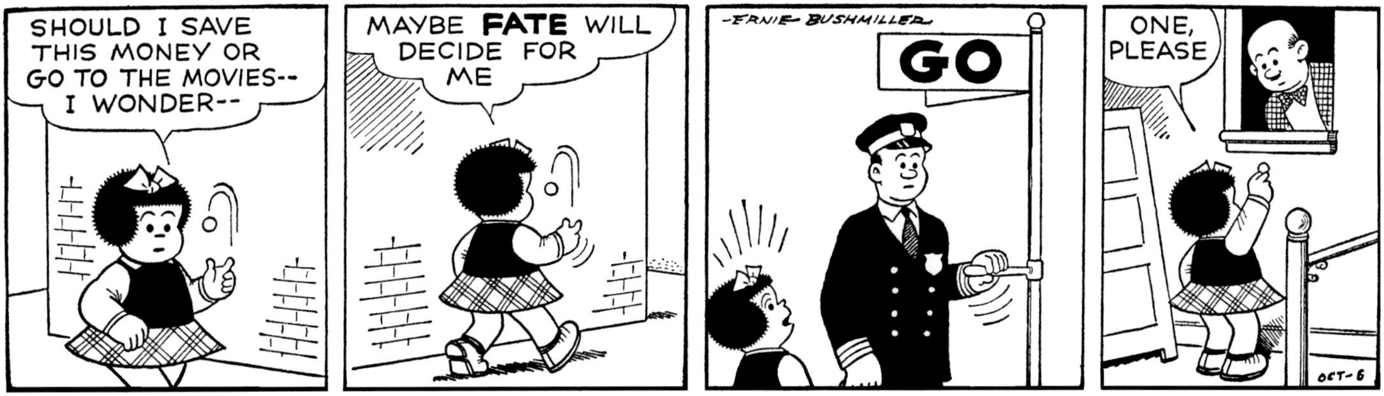
SHOULD I SAVE THIS MONEY OR GO TO THE MOVIES-- I WONDER--
MAYBE **FATE** WILL DECIDE FOR ME
-ERNIE BUSHMILLER-
GO
ONE, PLEASE
OCT-6

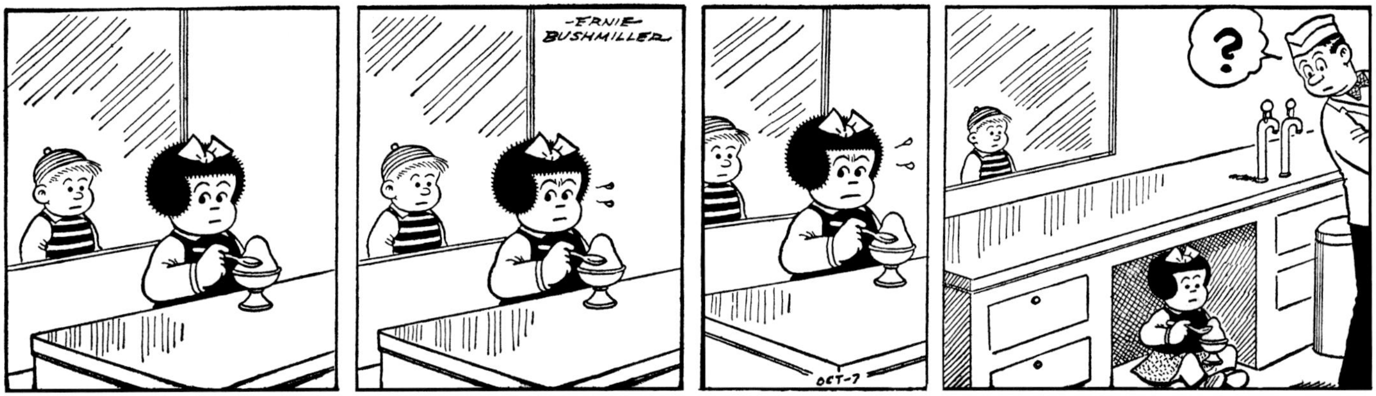
-ERNIE BUSHMILLER-
OCT-7
?

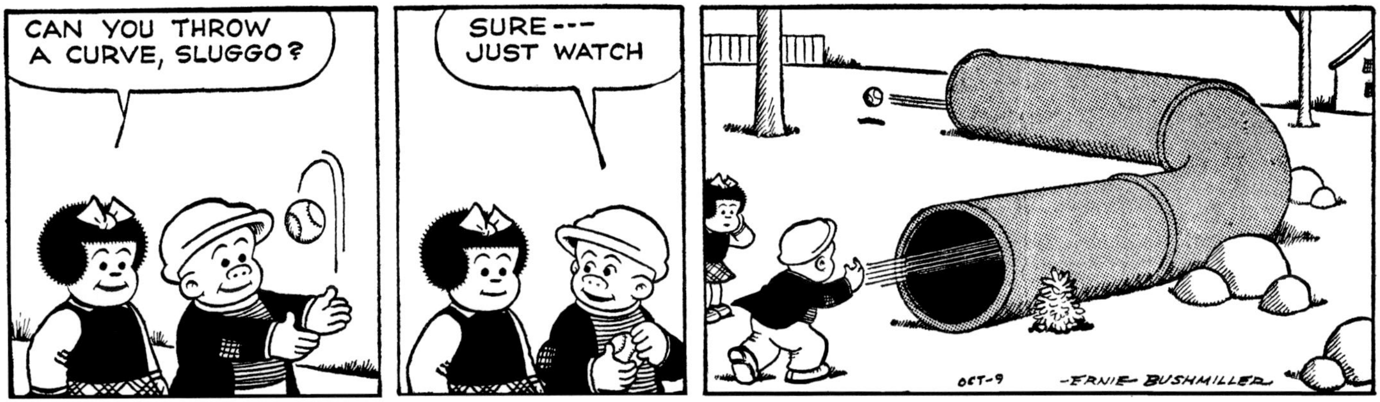
CAN YOU THROW A CURVE, SLUGGO?
SURE--- JUST WATCH
OCT-9
-ERNIE BUSHMILLER-

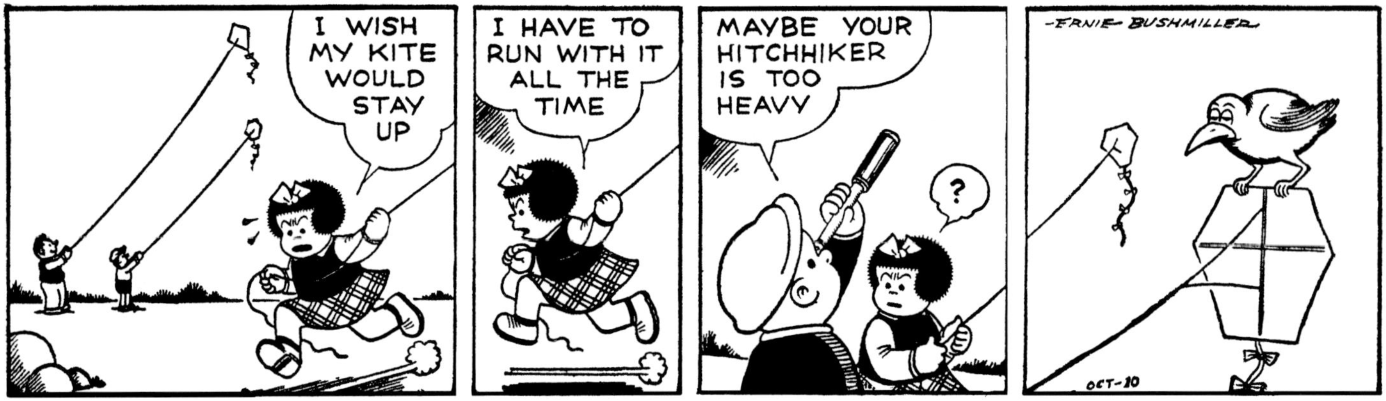
I WISH MY KITE WOULD STAY UP
I HAVE TO RUN WITH IT ALL THE TIME
MAYBE YOUR HITCHHIKER IS TOO HEAVY
?
ERNIE BUSHMILLER
OCT-10

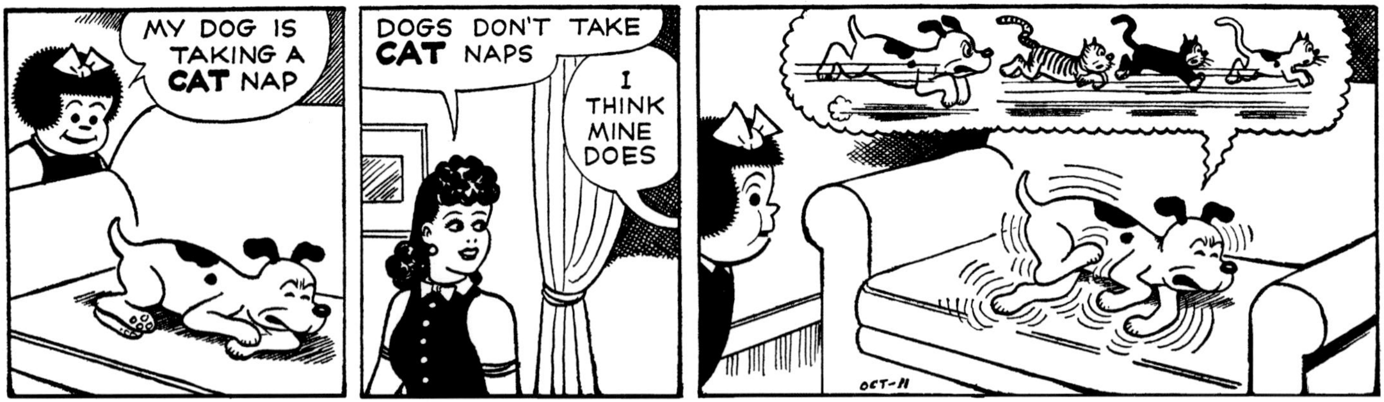
MY DOG IS TAKING A **CAT** NAP
DOGS DON'T TAKE **CAT** NAPS
I THINK MINE DOES
OCT-11

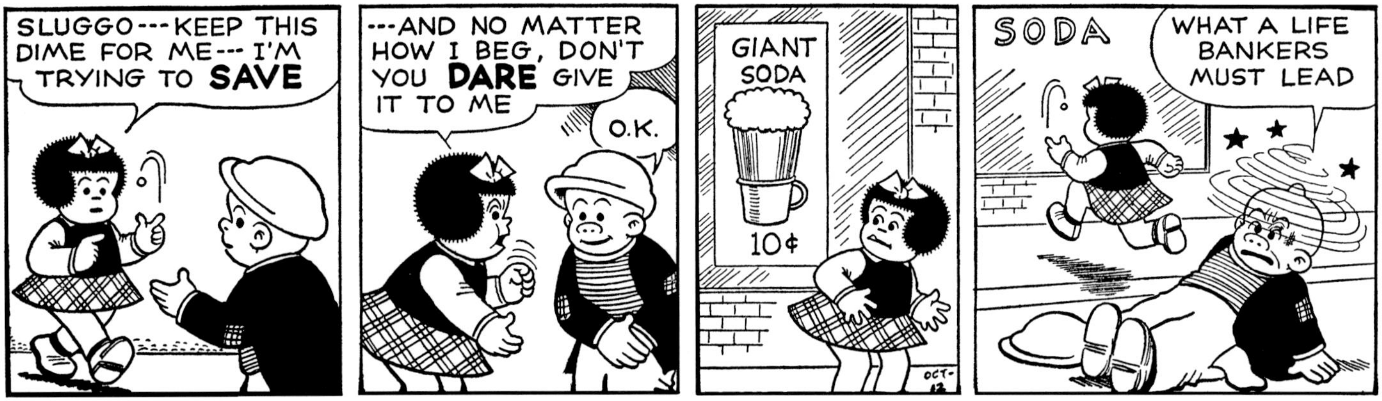
SLUGGO---KEEP THIS DIME FOR ME--- I'M TRYING TO **SAVE**
---AND NO MATTER HOW I BEG, DON'T YOU **DARE** GIVE IT TO ME
O.K.
GIANT SODA
10¢
OCT-12
SODA
WHAT A LIFE BANKERS MUST LEAD

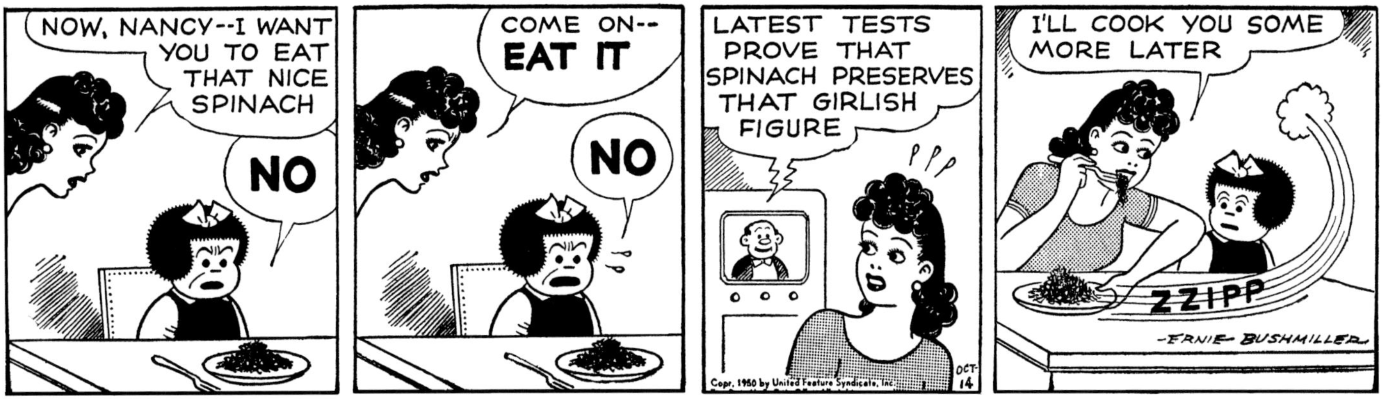
NOW, NANCY--I WANT YOU TO EAT THAT NICE SPINACH
NO
COME ON-- EAT IT
NO
LATEST TESTS PROVE THAT SPINACH PRESERVES THAT GIRLISH FIGURE
Copr. 1950 by United Feature Syndicate, Inc.
OCT-14
I'LL COOK YOU SOME MORE LATER
ZZIPP
-ERNIE BUSHMILLER-

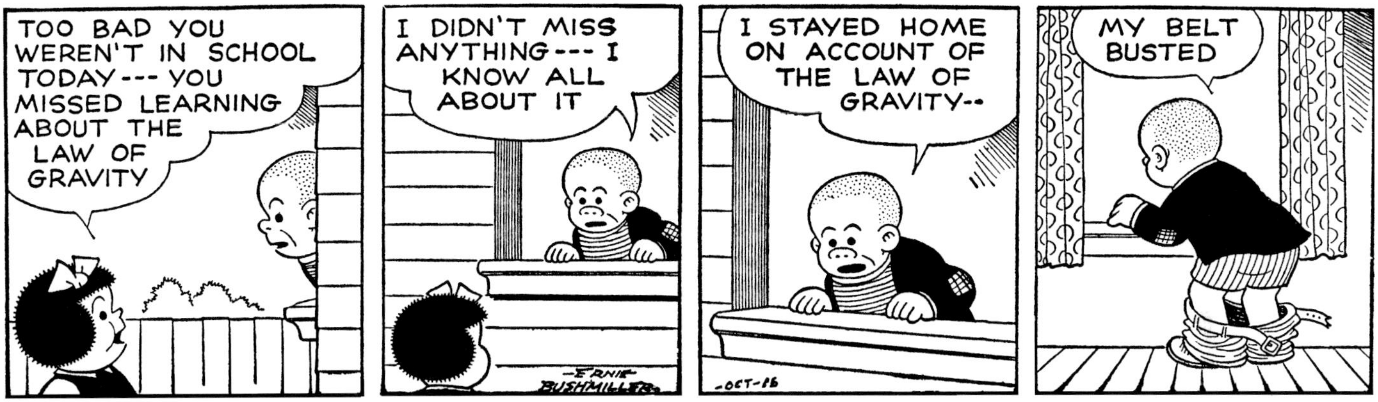
TOO BAD YOU WEREN'T IN SCHOOL TODAY--- YOU MISSED LEARNING ABOUT THE LAW OF GRAVITY
I DIDN'T MISS ANYTHING--- I KNOW ALL ABOUT IT
-ERNIE BUSHMILLER-
I STAYED HOME ON ACCOUNT OF THE LAW OF GRAVITY--
-OCT-16
MY BELT BUSTED

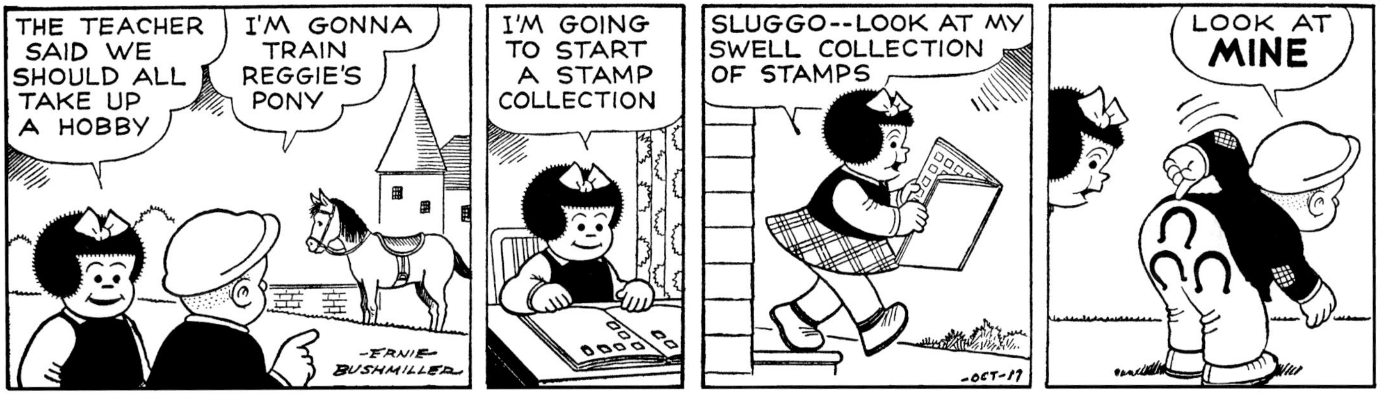
THE TEACHER SAID WE SHOULD ALL TAKE UP A HOBBY
I'M GONNA TRAIN REGGIE'S PONY
-ERNIE BUSHMILLER-
I'M GOING TO START A STAMP COLLECTION
SLUGGO--LOOK AT MY SWELL COLLECTION OF STAMPS
-OCT-17
LOOK AT MINE

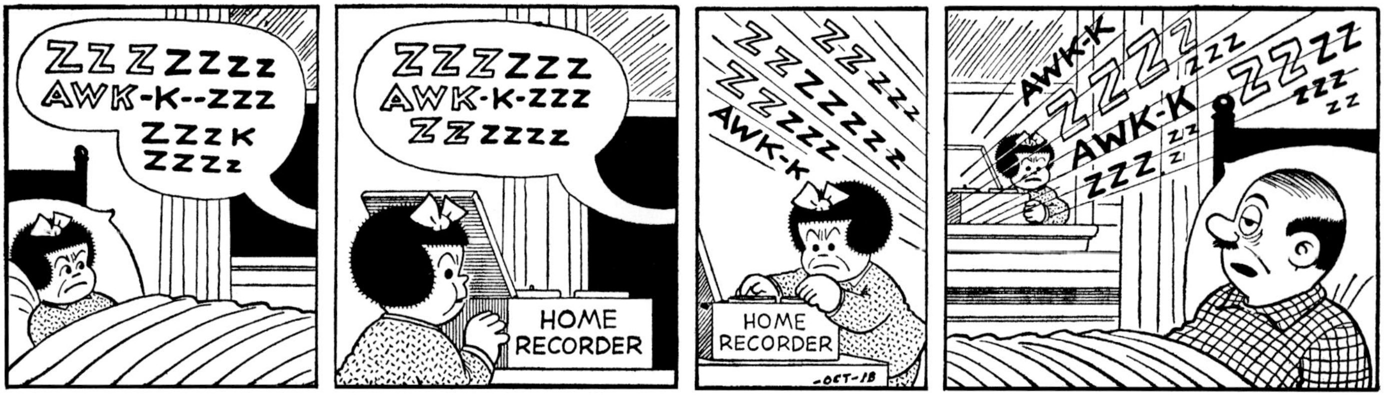
ZZZZZZZ
AWK-K--ZZZ
ZZZK
ZZZZ
ZZZZZZZ
AWK-K-ZZZ
ZZZZZZ
HOME RECORDER
ZZZZZ
ZZZZZZZZ
AWK-K
HOME RECORDER
OCT-18
AWK-K
ZZZZ
AWK-K
ZZZ

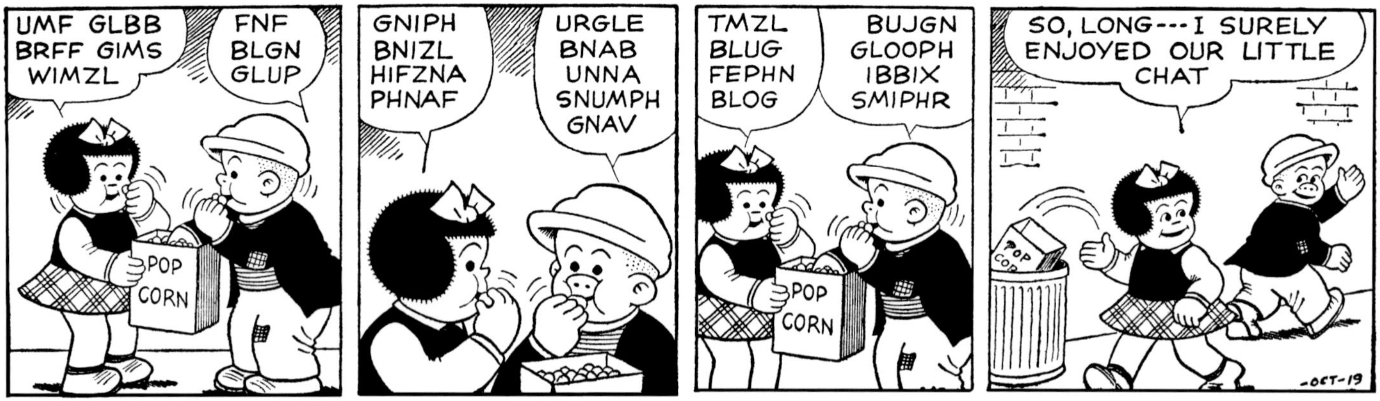
UMF GLBB BRFF GIMS WIMZL
FNF BLGN GLUP
POP CORN
GNIPH BNIZL HIFZNA PHNAF
URGLE BNAB UNNA SNUMPH GNAV
TMZL BLUG FEPHN BLOG
BUJGN GLOOPH IBBIX SMIPHR
POP CORN
SO, LONG---I SURELY ENJOYED OUR LITTLE CHAT
OCT-19

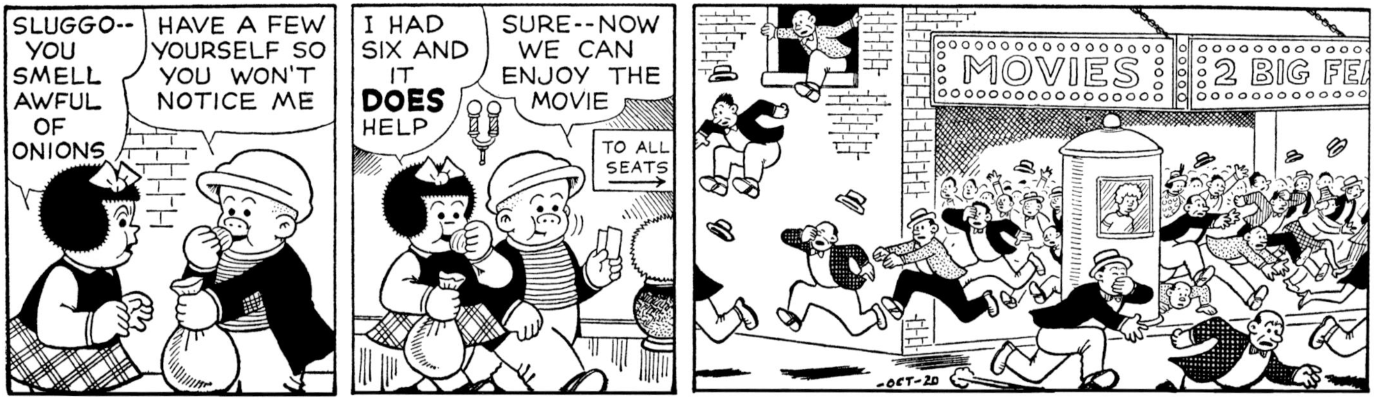
SLUGGO-- YOU SMELL AWFUL OF ONIONS
HAVE A FEW YOURSELF SO YOU WON'T NOTICE ME
I HAD SIX AND IT **DOES** HELP
SURE--NOW WE CAN ENJOY THE MOVIE
TO ALL SEATS
MOVIES
2 BIG FE
OCT-20

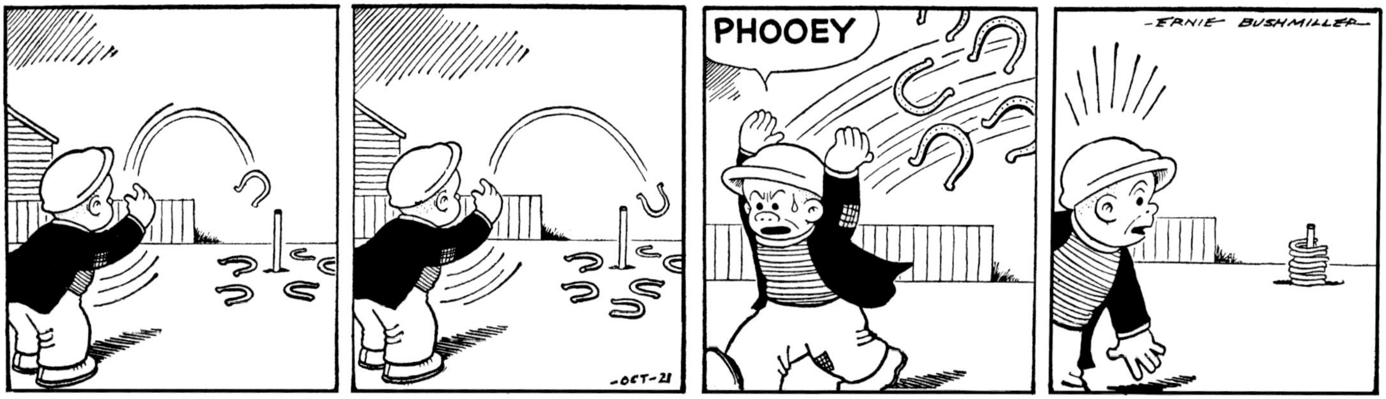
PHOOEY
-ERNIE BUSHMILLER-
-OCT-21

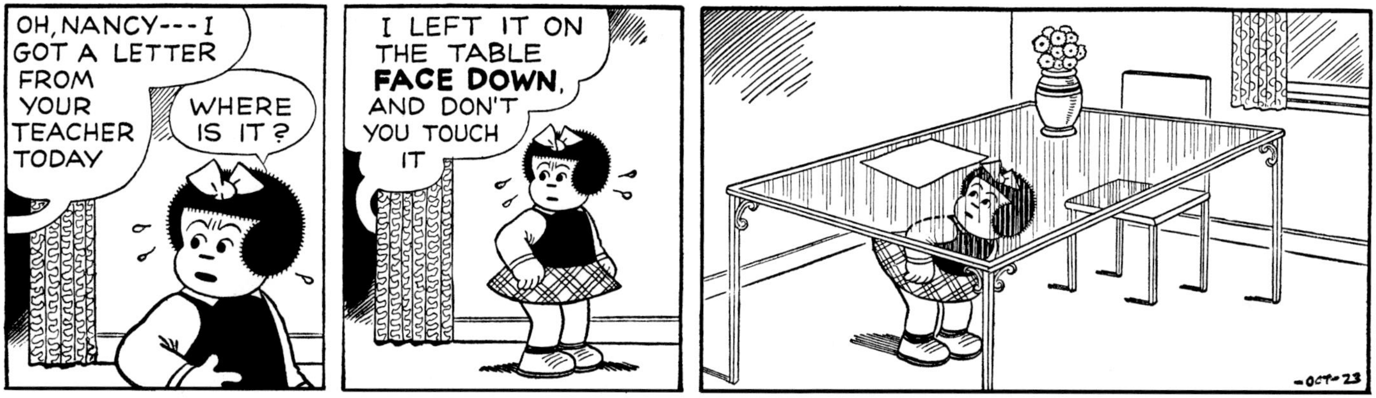
OH, NANCY--- I GOT A LETTER FROM YOUR TEACHER TODAY
WHERE IS IT?
I LEFT IT ON THE TABLE FACE DOWN, AND DON'T YOU TOUCH IT
-OCT-23

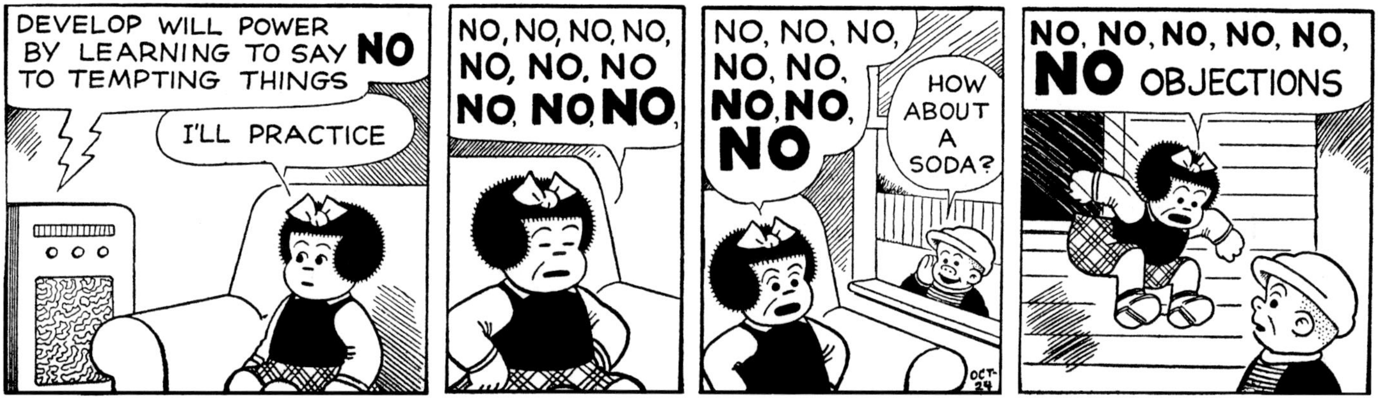
DEVELOP WILL POWER BY LEARNING TO SAY NO TO TEMPTING THINGS
I'LL PRACTICE
NO, NO, NO, NO, NO, NO, NO NO, NO, NO,
NO, NO, NO, NO, NO, NO, NO, NO
HOW ABOUT A SODA?
OCT-24
NO, NO, NO, NO, NO, NO OBJECTIONS

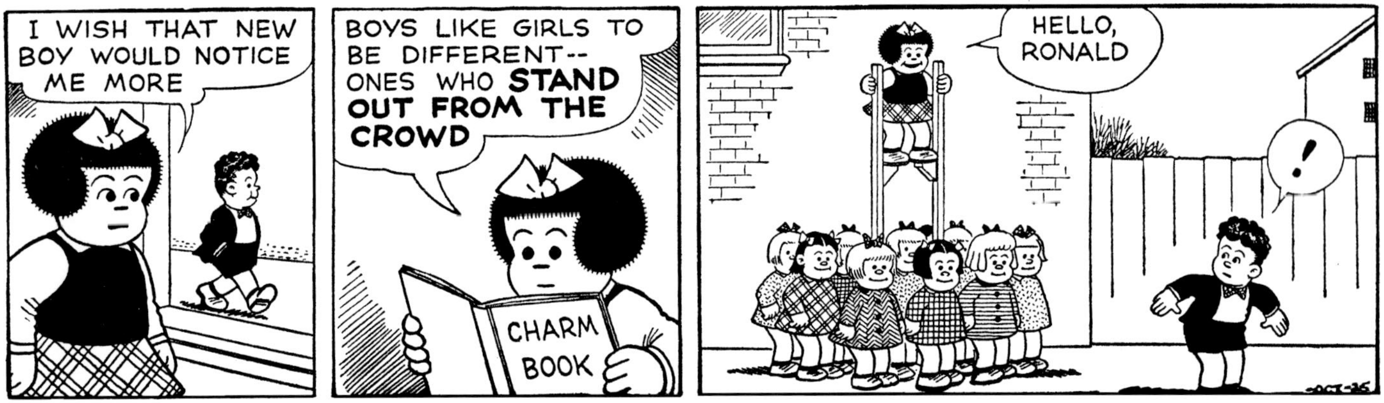
I WISH THAT NEW BOY WOULD NOTICE ME MORE
BOYS LIKE GIRLS TO BE DIFFERENT-- ONES WHO **STAND OUT FROM THE CROWD**
CHARM BOOK
HELLO, RONALD
!
OCT-25

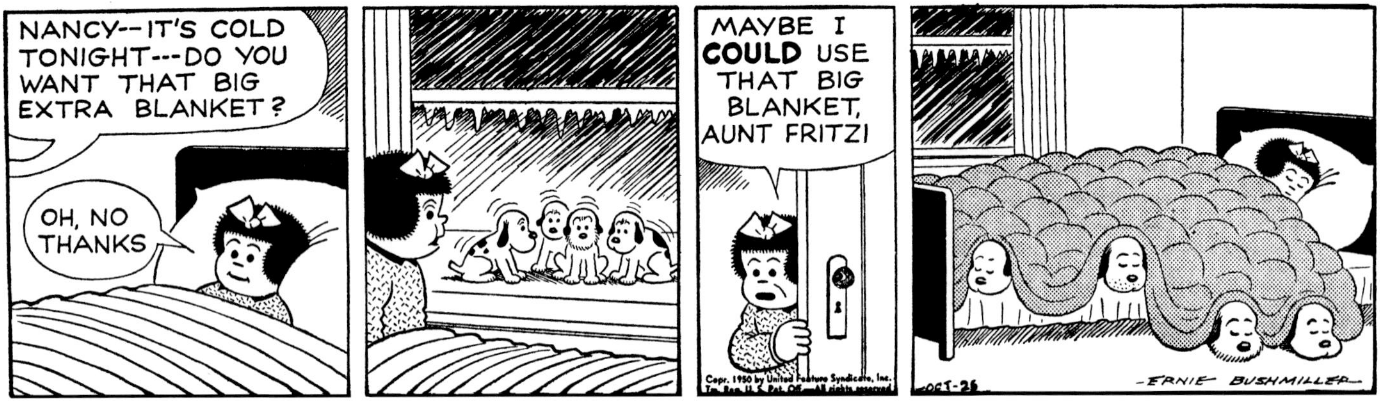
NANCY--IT'S COLD TONIGHT---DO YOU WANT THAT BIG EXTRA BLANKET?
OH, NO THANKS
MAYBE I **COULD** USE THAT BIG BLANKET, AUNT FRITZI
Copr. 1950 by United Feature Syndicate, Inc. Tm. Reg. U. S. Pat. Off.—All rights reserved
OCT-26
ERNIE BUSHMILLER

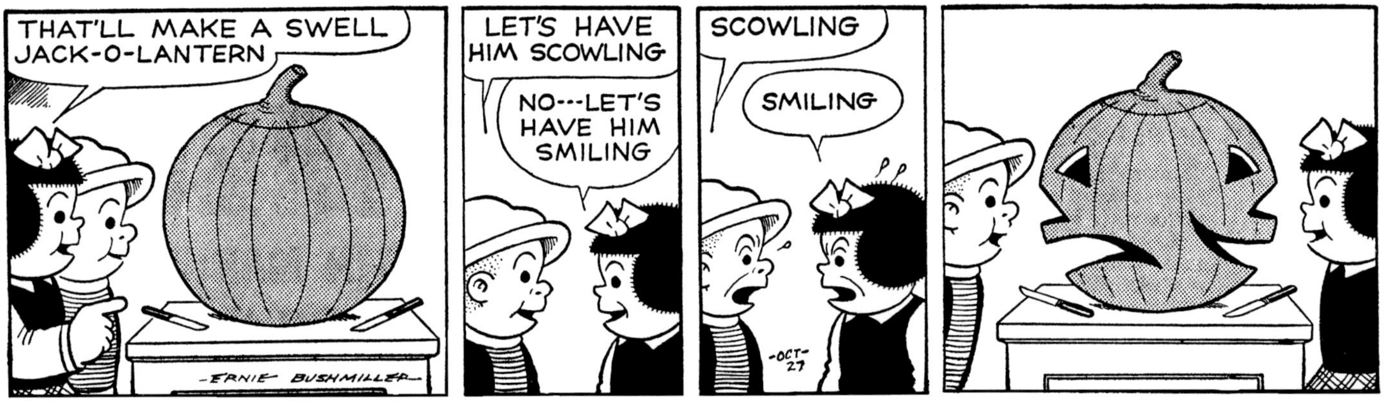
THAT'LL MAKE A SWELL JACK-O-LANTERN
ERNIE BUSHMILLER
LET'S HAVE HIM SCOWLING
NO---LET'S HAVE HIM SMILING
SCOWLING
SMILING
OCT-27

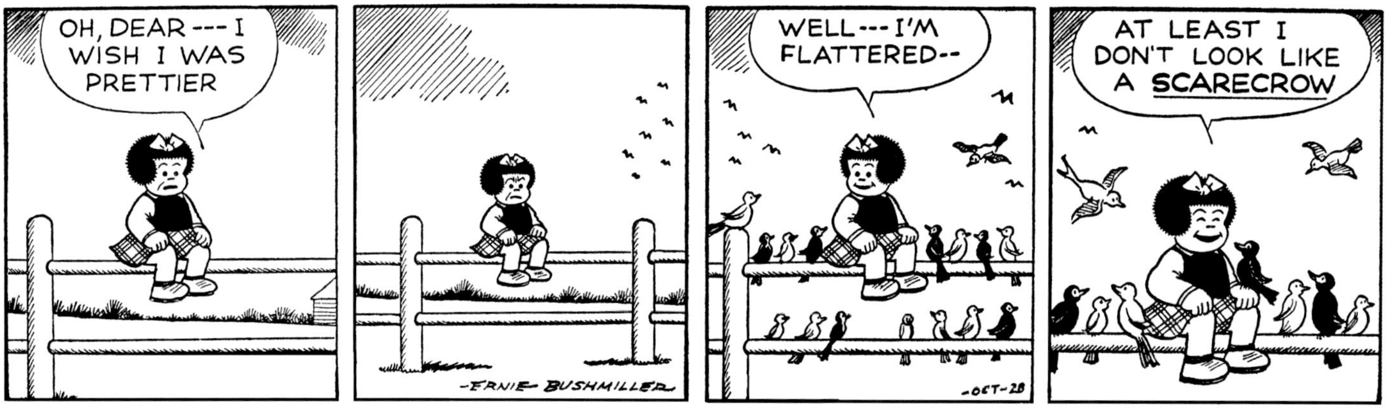
OH, DEAR --- I WISH I WAS PRETTIER
-ERNIE BUSHMILLER
WELL --- I'M FLATTERED--
-OCT-28
AT LEAST I DON'T LOOK LIKE A SCARECROW

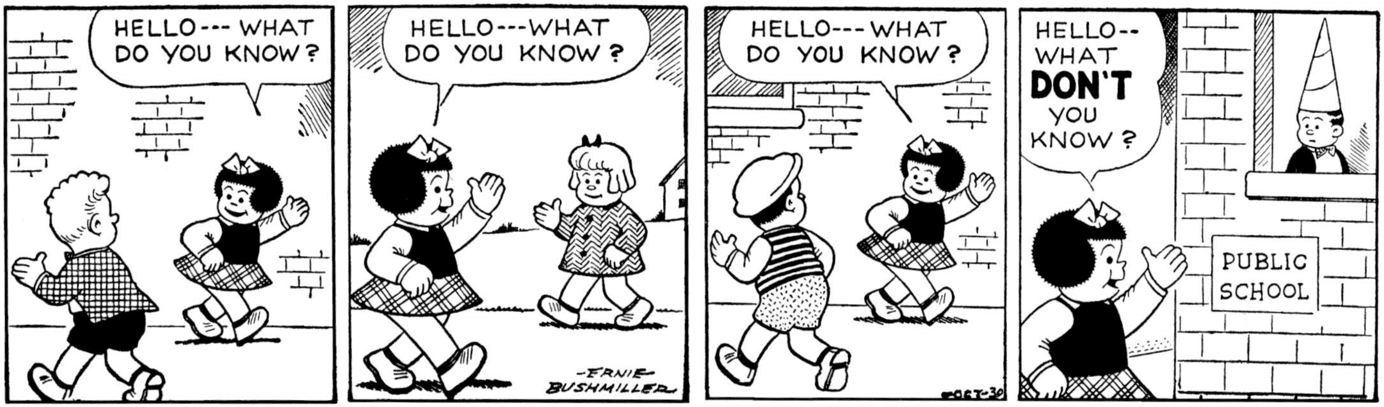
HELLO --- WHAT DO YOU KNOW?
HELLO---WHAT DO YOU KNOW?
-ERNIE BUSHMILLER
HELLO--- WHAT DO YOU KNOW?
-OCT-30
HELLO-- WHAT DON'T YOU KNOW?
PUBLIC SCHOOL

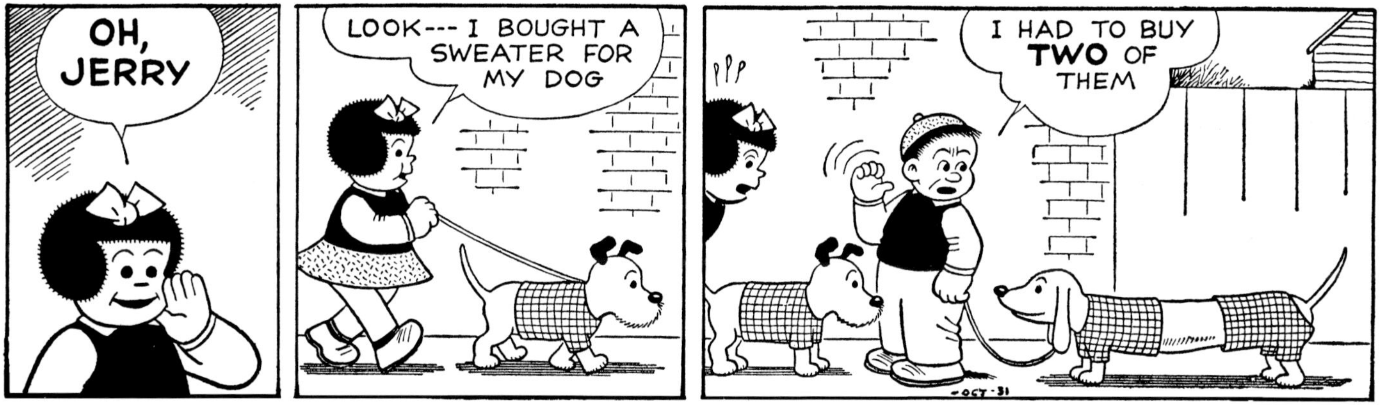
OH, JERRY
LOOK--- I BOUGHT A SWEATER FOR MY DOG
I HAD TO BUY TWO OF THEM
-OCT-31

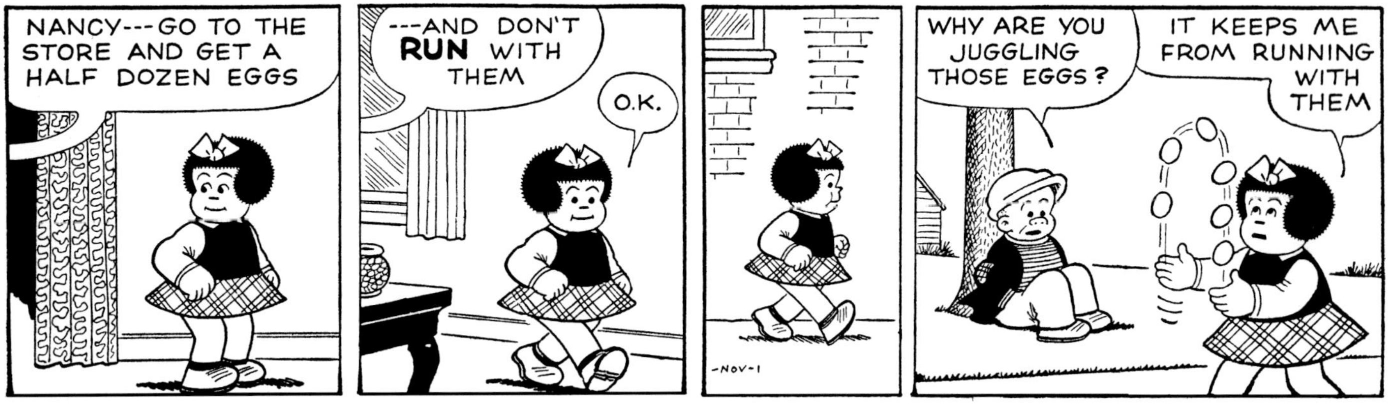

NANCY---GO TO THE STORE AND GET A HALF DOZEN EGGS
---AND DON'T **RUN** WITH THEM
O.K.
-NOV-1
WHY ARE YOU JUGGLING THOSE EGGS?
IT KEEPS ME FROM RUNNING WITH THEM

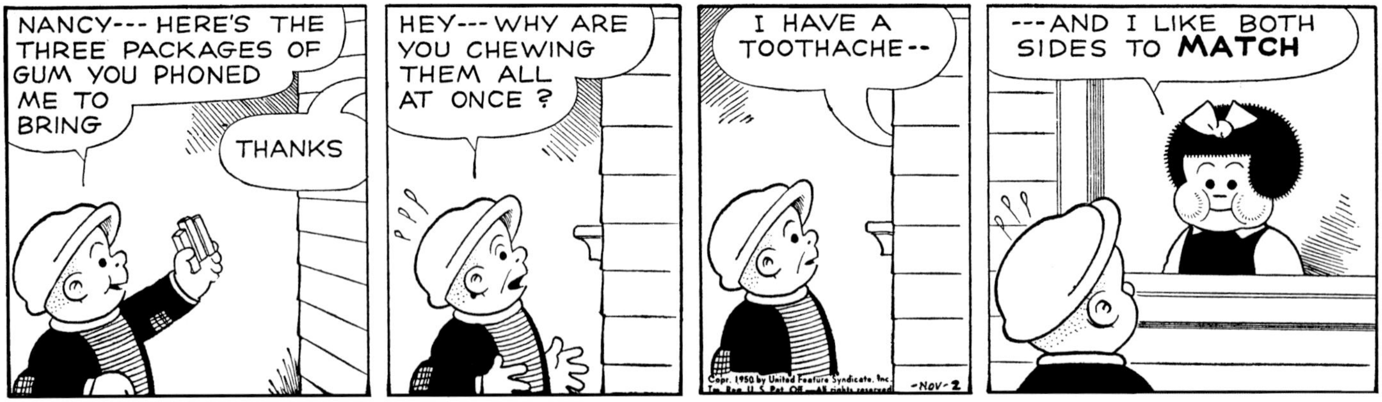

NANCY--- HERE'S THE THREE PACKAGES OF GUM YOU PHONED ME TO BRING
THANKS
HEY---WHY ARE YOU CHEWING THEM ALL AT ONCE?
I HAVE A TOOTHACHE--
Copr. 1950 by United Feature Syndicate, Inc.
-NOV-2
---AND I LIKE BOTH SIDES TO **MATCH**

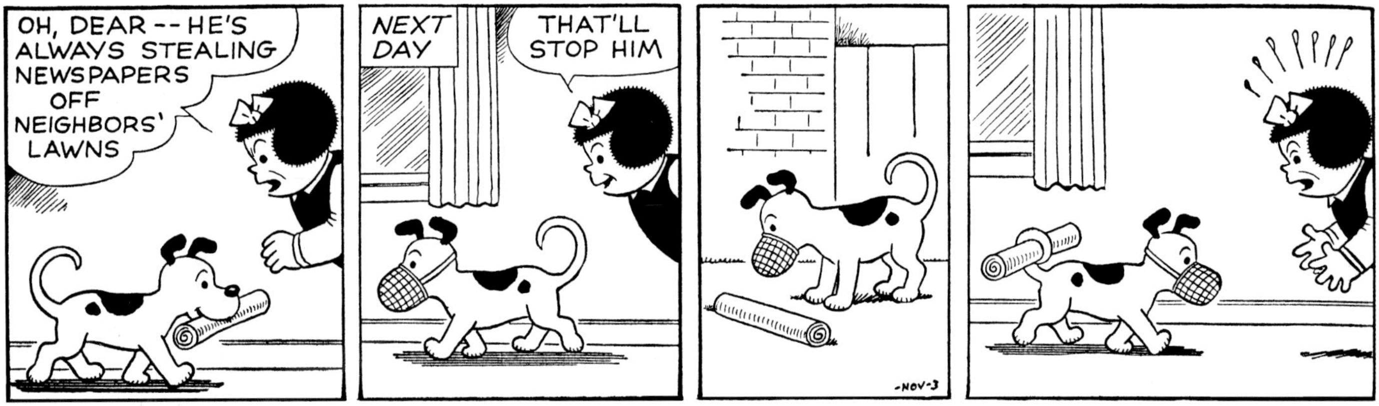

OH, DEAR--HE'S ALWAYS STEALING NEWSPAPERS OFF NEIGHBORS' LAWNS
NEXT DAY
THAT'LL STOP HIM
-NOV-3

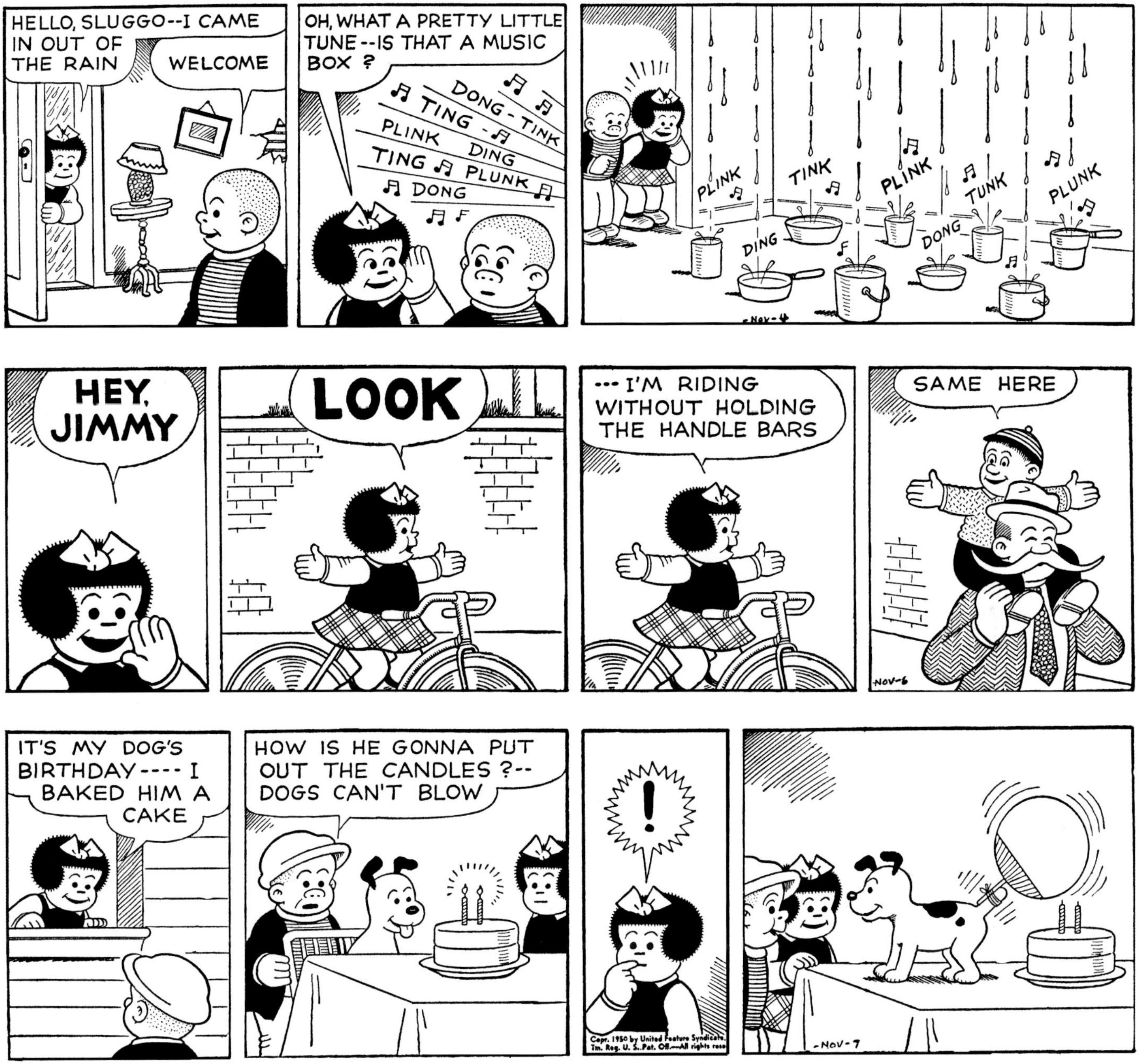

HELLO, SLUGGO--I CAME IN OUT OF THE RAIN
WELCOME
OH, WHAT A PRETTY LITTLE TUNE--IS THAT A MUSIC BOX ?
DONG-TINK
TING-
PLINK DING
TING PLUNK
DONG
PLINK
TINK
PLINK
PLUNK
TUNK
DING
DONG
NOV-4
HEY, JIMMY
LOOK
---I'M RIDING WITHOUT HOLDING THE HANDLE BARS
SAME HERE
NOV-6
IT'S MY DOG'S BIRTHDAY---- I BAKED HIM A CAKE
HOW IS HE GONNA PUT OUT THE CANDLES ?-- DOGS CAN'T BLOW
!
Copr. 1950 by United Feature Syndicate, Tm. Reg. U. S. Pat. Off.—All rights rese
NOV-7

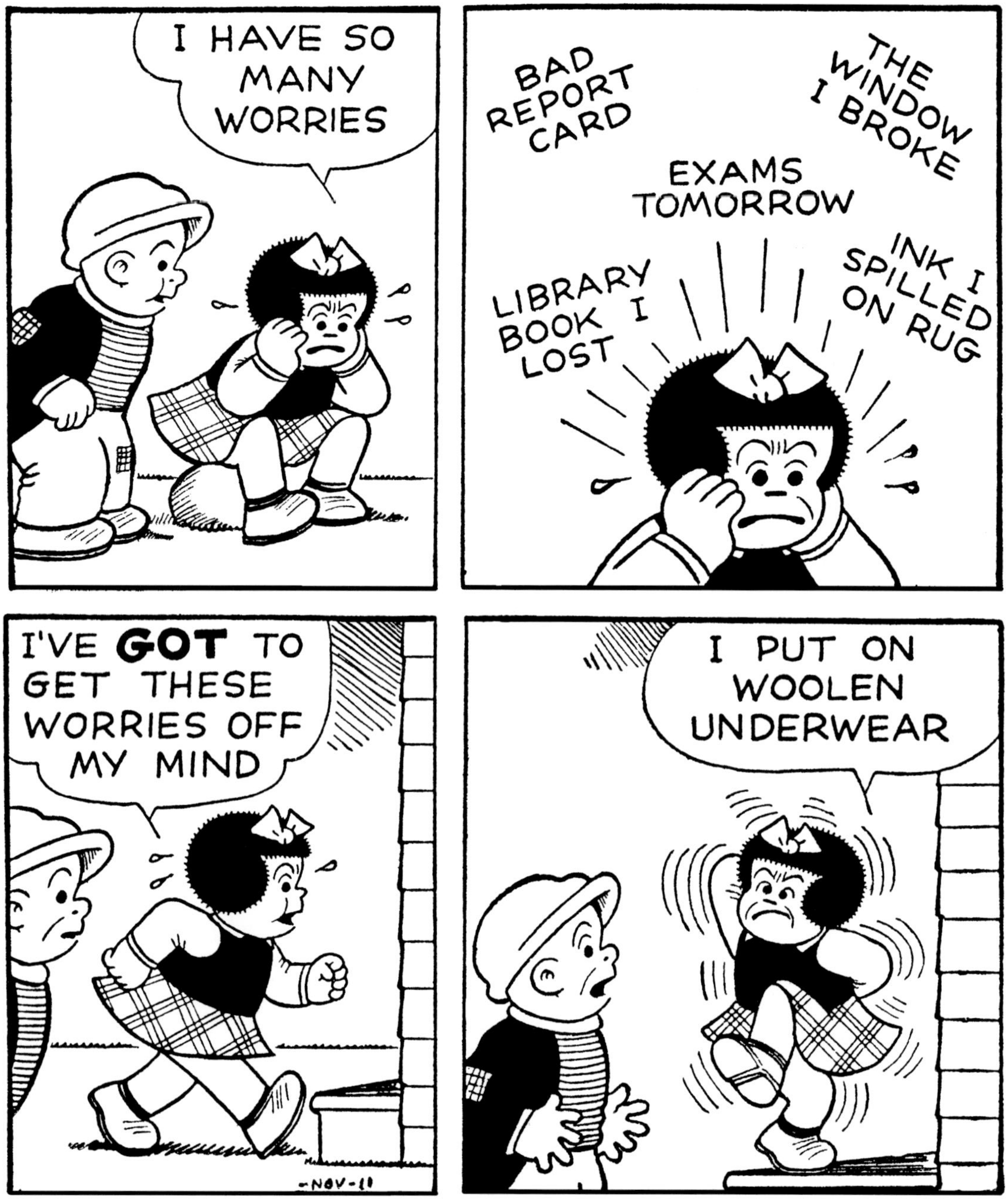
I HAVE SO MANY WORRIES
BAD REPORT CARD
THE WINDOW I BROKE
EXAMS TOMORROW
LIBRARY BOOK I LOST
INK I SPILLED ON RUG
I'VE **GOT** TO GET THESE WORRIES OFF MY MIND
I PUT ON WOOLEN UNDERWEAR

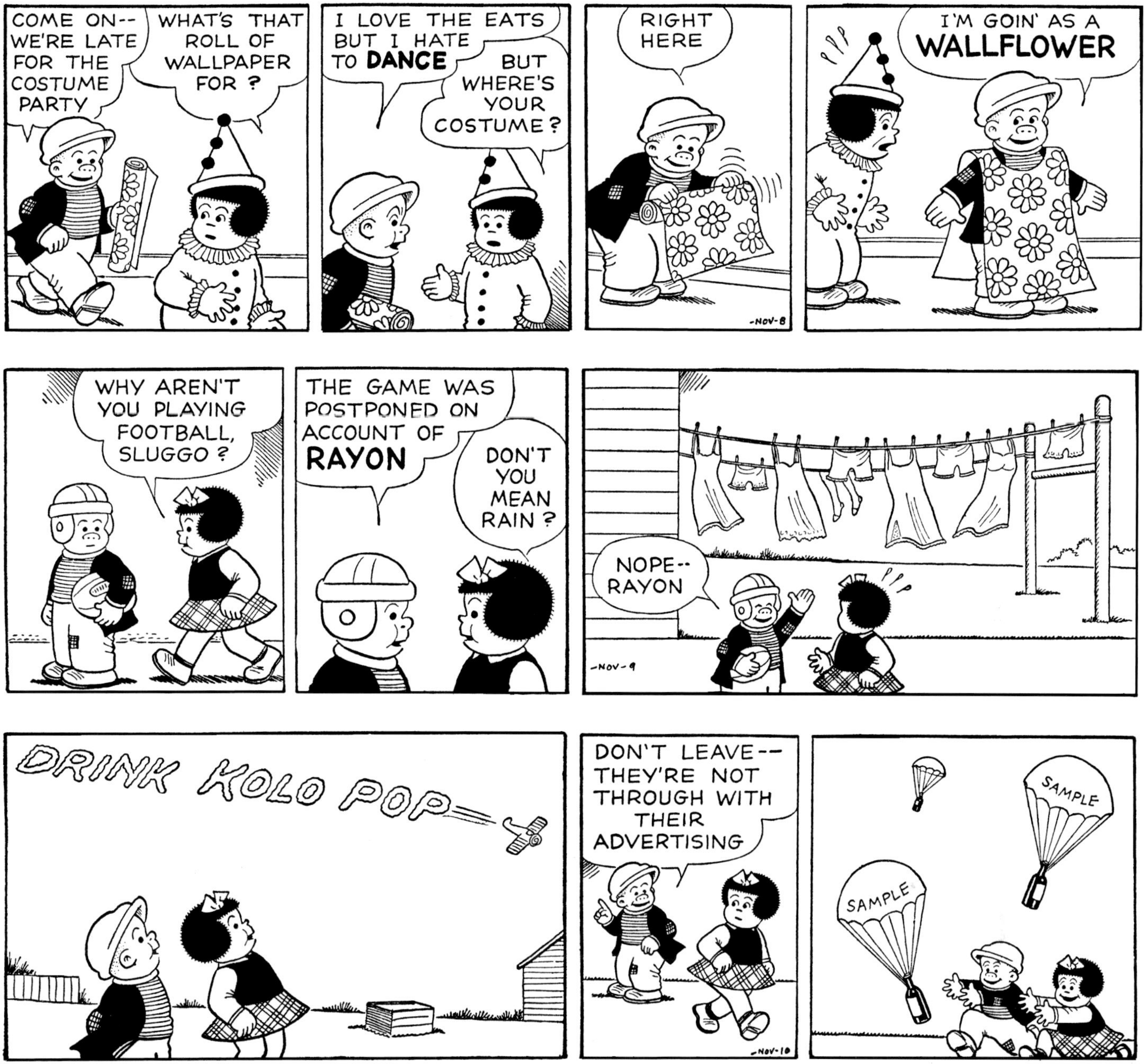
COME ON-- WE'RE LATE FOR THE COSTUME PARTY
WHAT'S THAT ROLL OF WALLPAPER FOR ?
I LOVE THE EATS BUT I HATE TO DANCE
BUT WHERE'S YOUR COSTUME ?
RIGHT HERE
I'M GOIN' AS A WALLFLOWER
NOV-8
WHY AREN'T YOU PLAYING FOOTBALL, SLUGGO ?
THE GAME WAS POSTPONED ON ACCOUNT OF RAYON
DON'T YOU MEAN RAIN ?
NOPE-- RAYON
NOV-9
DRINK KOLO POP
DON'T LEAVE-- THEY'RE NOT THROUGH WITH THEIR ADVERTISING
NOV-10
SAMPLE
SAMPLE

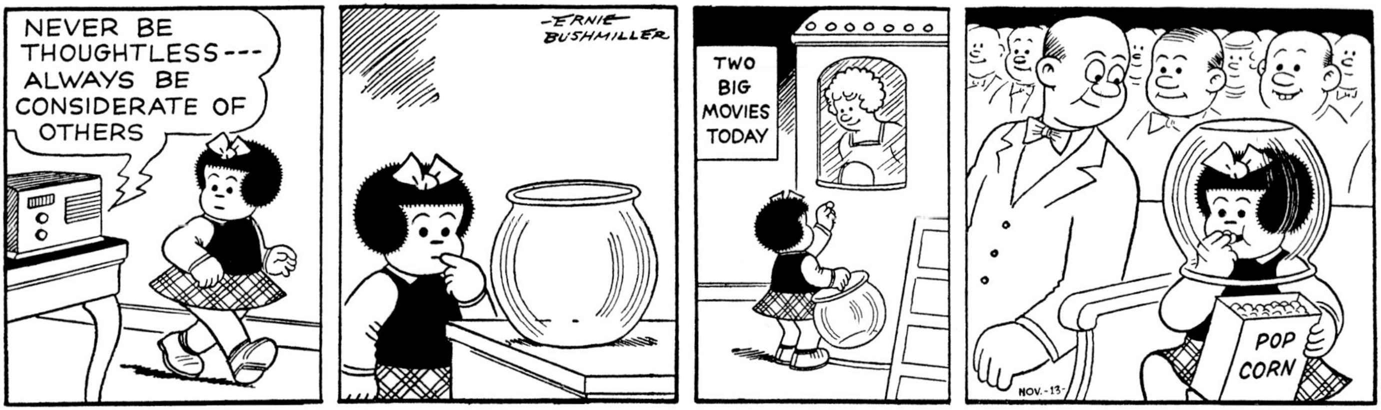
NEVER BE THOUGHTLESS--- ALWAYS BE CONSIDERATE OF OTHERS
-ERNIE- BUSHMILLER
TWO BIG MOVIES TODAY
POP CORN
NOV.-13-

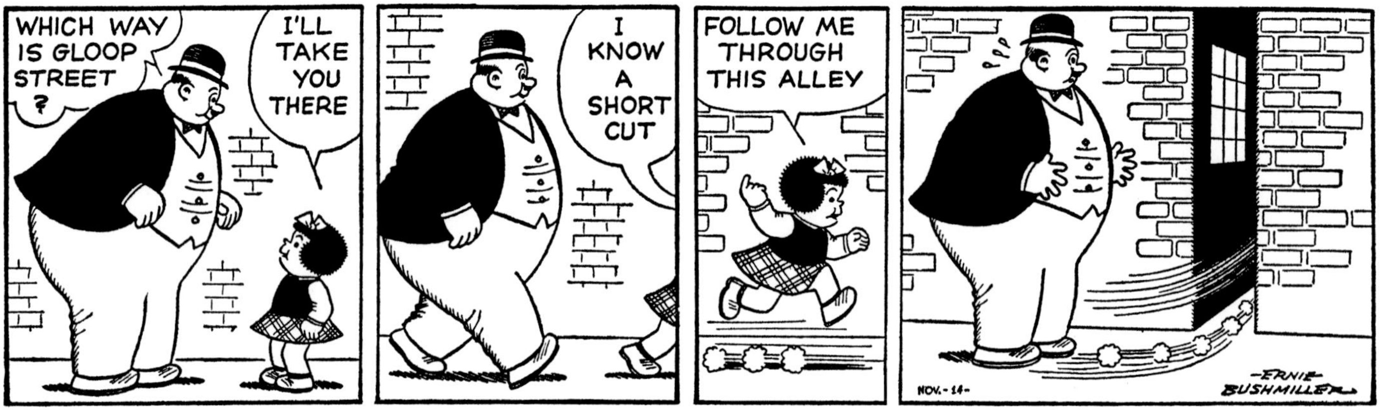
WHICH WAY IS GLOOP STREET ?
I'LL TAKE YOU THERE
I KNOW A SHORT CUT
FOLLOW ME THROUGH THIS ALLEY
NOV.-14-
-ERNIE- BUSHMILLER

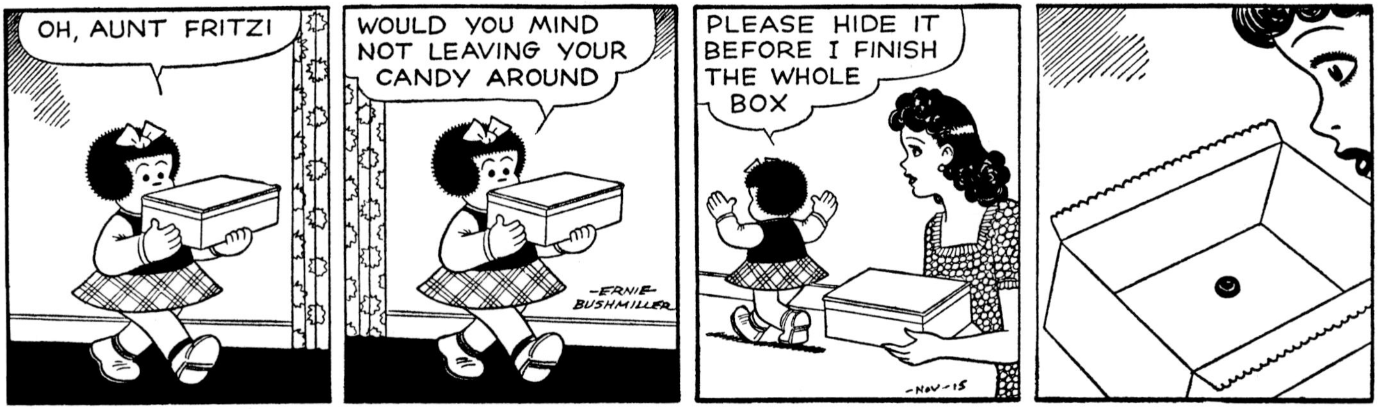
OH, AUNT FRITZI
WOULD YOU MIND NOT LEAVING YOUR CANDY AROUND
-ERNIE- BUSHMILLER
PLEASE HIDE IT BEFORE I FINISH THE WHOLE BOX
-NOV-15

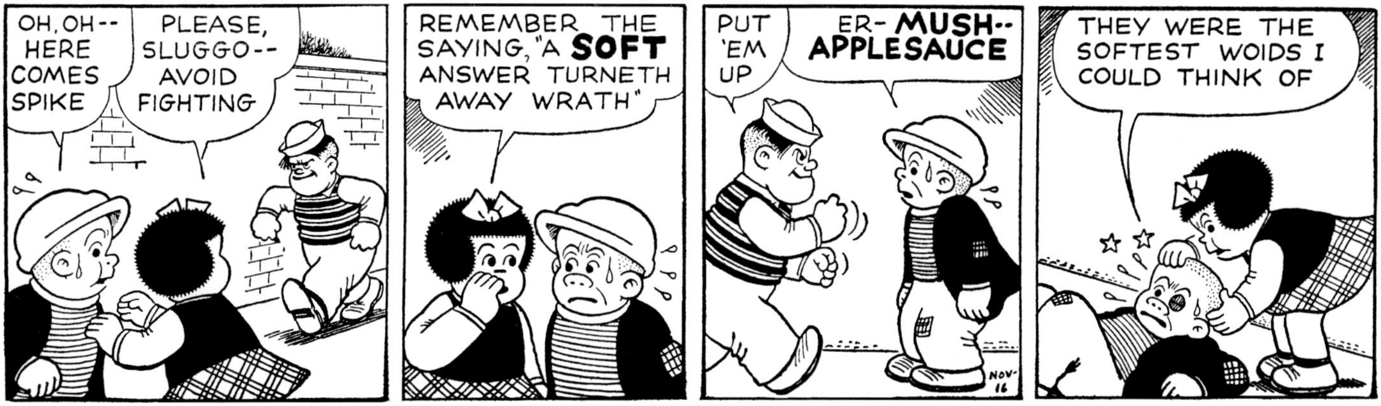
OH, OH-- HERE COMES SPIKE
PLEASE, SLUGGO-- AVOID FIGHTING
REMEMBER THE SAYING, "A **SOFT** ANSWER TURNETH AWAY WRATH"
PUT 'EM UP
ER- **MUSH-- APPLESAUCE**
NOV-16
THEY WERE THE SOFTEST WOIDS I COULD THINK OF

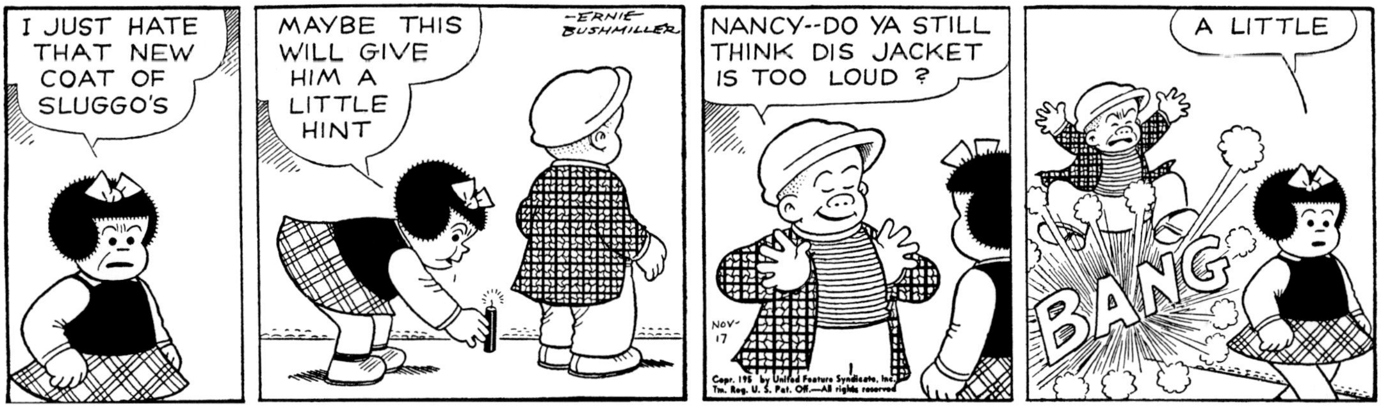
I JUST HATE THAT NEW COAT OF SLUGGO'S
-ERNIE BUSHMILLER
MAYBE THIS WILL GIVE HIM A LITTLE HINT
NANCY--DO YA STILL THINK DIS JACKET IS TOO LOUD ?
NOV-17
Copr. 195 by United Feature Syndicate, Inc.
Tm. Reg. U. S. Pat. Off.—All rights reserved
A LITTLE
BANG

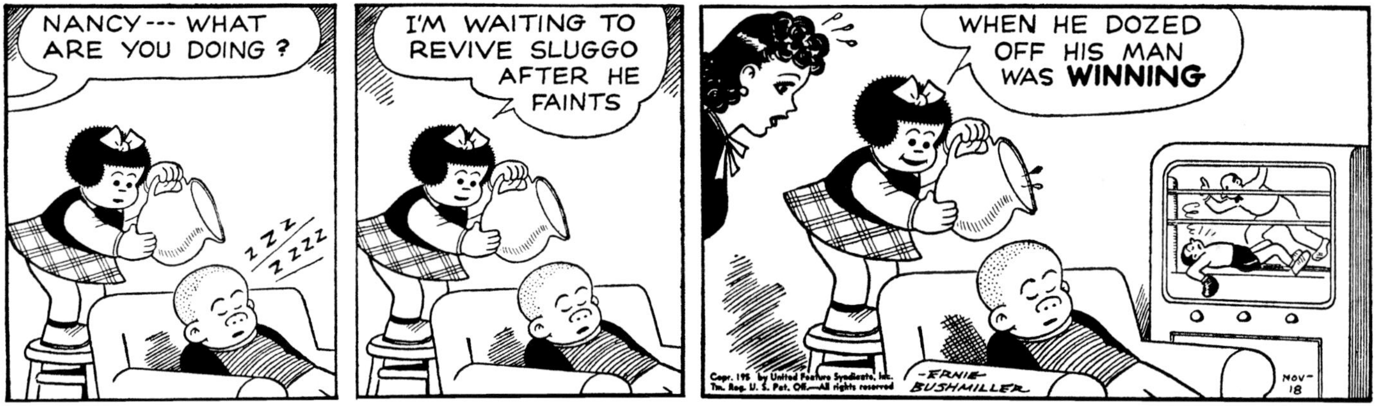
NANCY--- WHAT ARE YOU DOING ?
Z Z Z Z Z Z Z
I'M WAITING TO REVIVE SLUGGO AFTER HE FAINTS
WHEN HE DOZED OFF HIS MAN WAS **WINNING**
Copr. 195 by United Feature Syndicate, Inc.
Tm. Reg. U. S. Pat. Off.—All rights reserved
-ERNIE BUSHMILLER
NOV-18

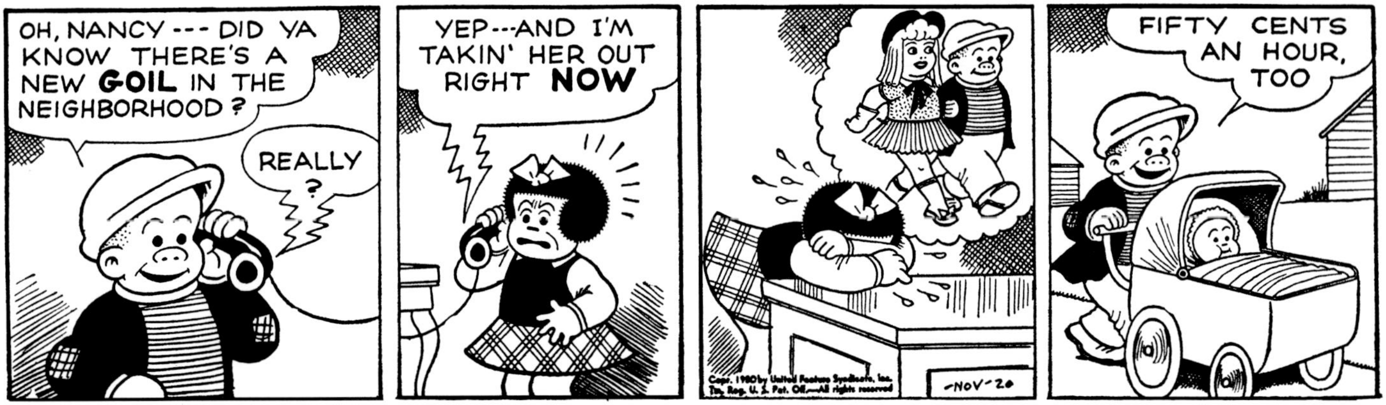

OH, NANCY --- DID YA KNOW THERE'S A NEW **GOIL** IN THE NEIGHBORHOOD?
REALLY?
YEP--AND I'M TAKIN' HER OUT RIGHT **NOW**
Copr. 1950 by United Feature Syndicate, Inc. Tm. Reg. U. S. Pat. Off.—All rights reserved
NOV-20
FIFTY CENTS AN HOUR, TOO

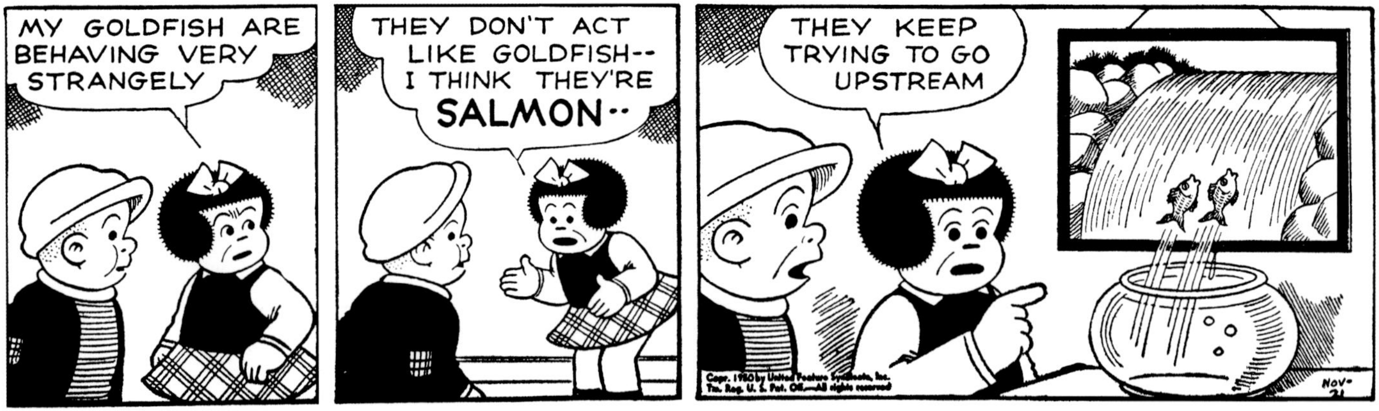

MY GOLDFISH ARE BEHAVING VERY STRANGELY
THEY DON'T ACT LIKE GOLDFISH-- I THINK THEY'RE **SALMON**--
THEY KEEP TRYING TO GO UPSTREAM
Copr. 1950 by United Feature Syndicate, Inc. Tm. Reg. U. S. Pat. Off.—All rights reserved
NOV-21

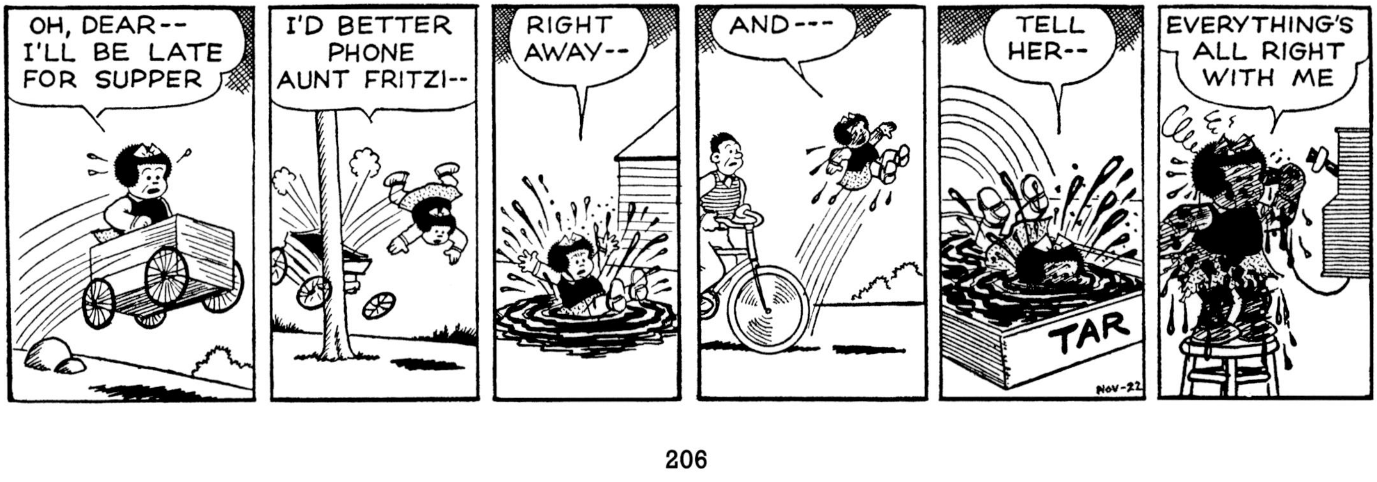

OH, DEAR-- I'LL BE LATE FOR SUPPER
I'D BETTER PHONE AUNT FRITZI--
RIGHT AWAY--
AND---
TELL HER--
TAR
NOV-22
EVERYTHING'S ALL RIGHT WITH ME

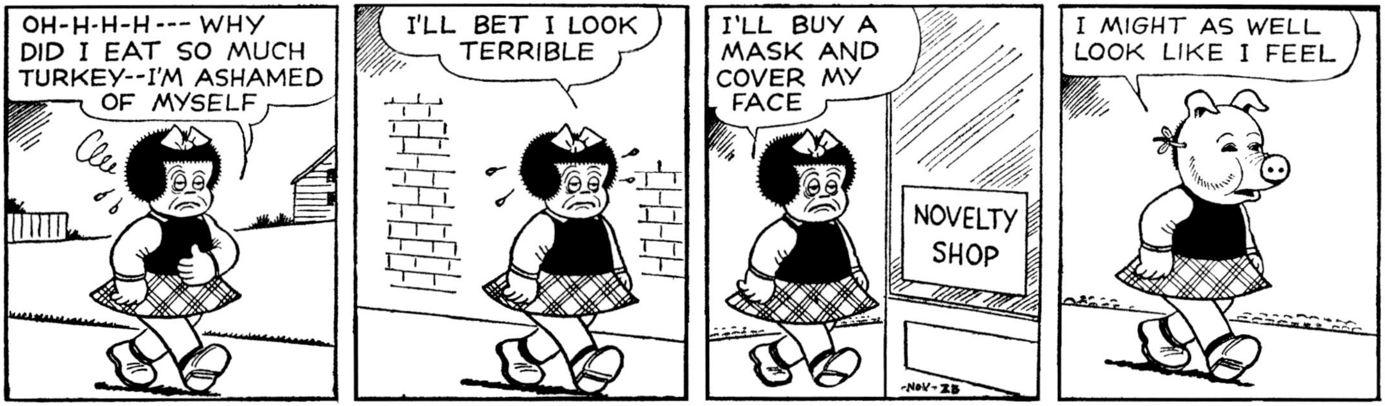
OH-H-H-H --- WHY DID I EAT SO MUCH TURKEY--I'M ASHAMED OF MYSELF
I'LL BET I LOOK TERRIBLE
I'LL BUY A MASK AND COVER MY FACE
NOVELTY SHOP
NOV-23
I MIGHT AS WELL LOOK LIKE I FEEL

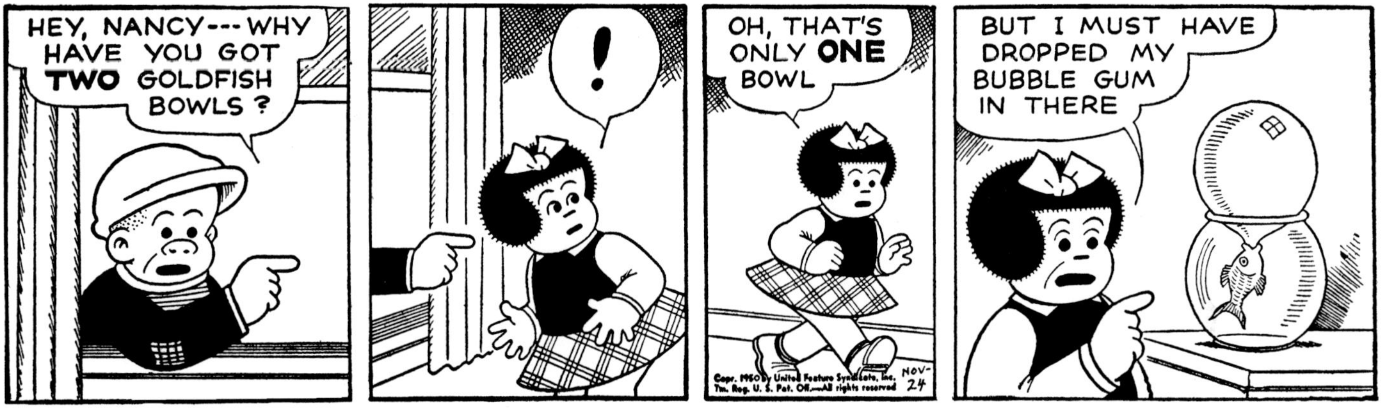
HEY, NANCY--- WHY HAVE YOU GOT TWO GOLDFISH BOWLS ?
!
OH, THAT'S ONLY ONE BOWL
Copr. 1950 by United Feature Syndicate, Inc. Tm. Reg. U. S. Pat. Off.—All rights reserved
NOV-24
BUT I MUST HAVE DROPPED MY BUBBLE GUM IN THERE

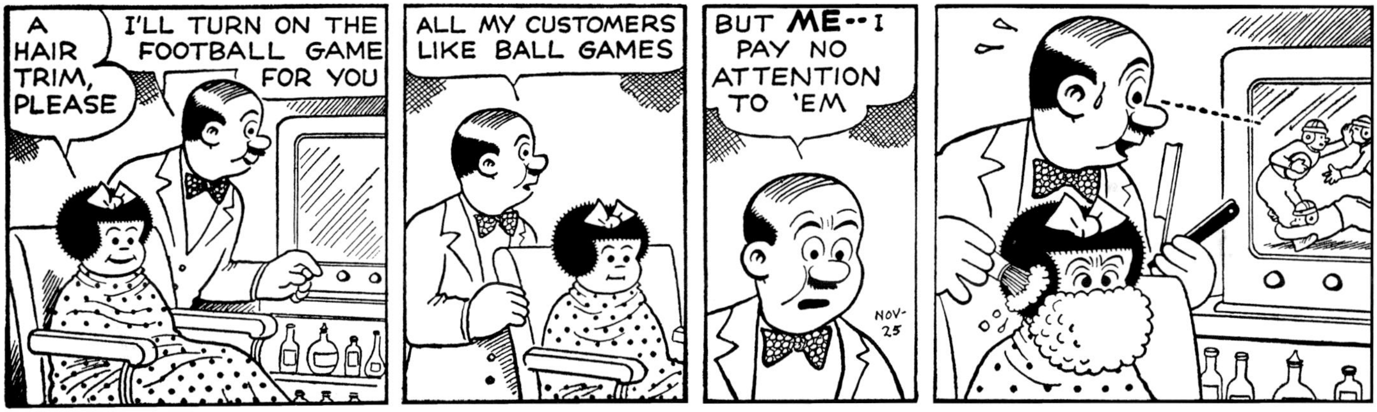
A HAIR TRIM, PLEASE
I'LL TURN ON THE FOOTBALL GAME FOR YOU
ALL MY CUSTOMERS LIKE BALL GAMES
BUT ME-- I PAY NO ATTENTION TO 'EM
NOV-25

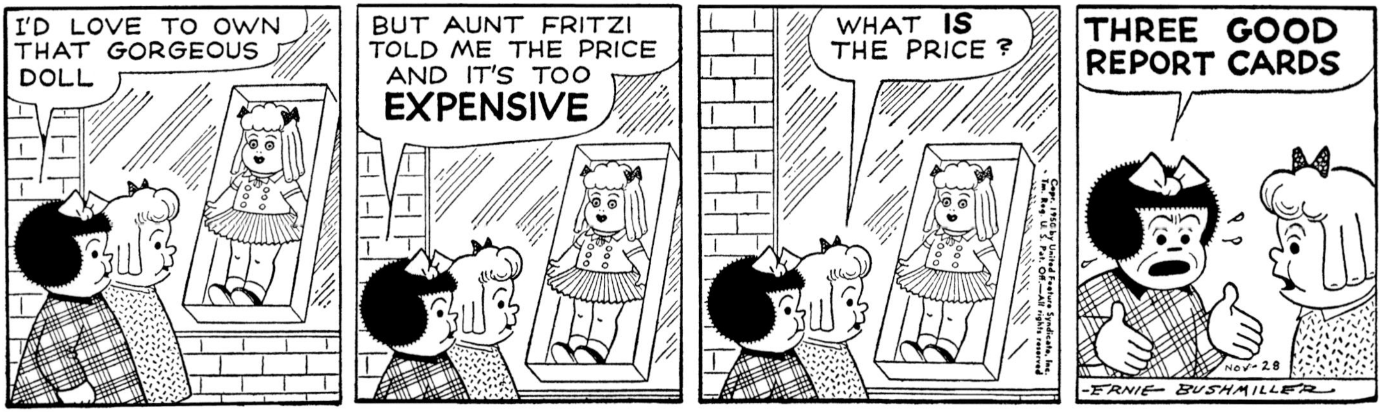
I'D LOVE TO OWN THAT GORGEOUS DOLL
BUT AUNT FRITZI TOLD ME THE PRICE AND IT'S TOO **EXPENSIVE**
WHAT **IS** THE PRICE ?
Copr. 1950 by United Feature Syndicate, Inc. Tm. Reg. U. S. Pat. Off.—All rights reserved
THREE GOOD REPORT CARDS
NOV-28
-ERNIE BUSHMILLER

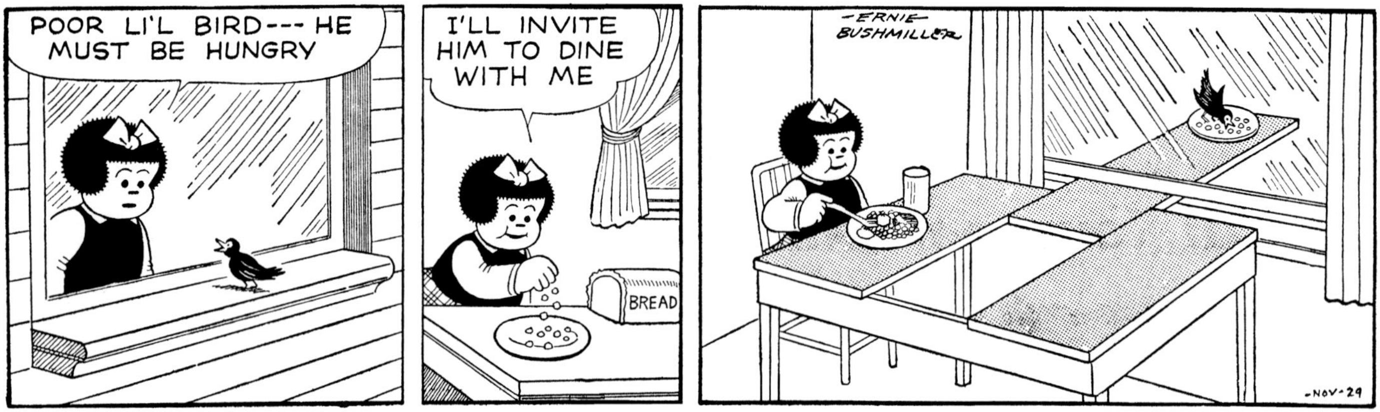
POOR LI'L BIRD--- HE MUST BE HUNGRY
I'LL INVITE HIM TO DINE WITH ME
BREAD
-ERNIE BUSHMILLER
-NOV-29

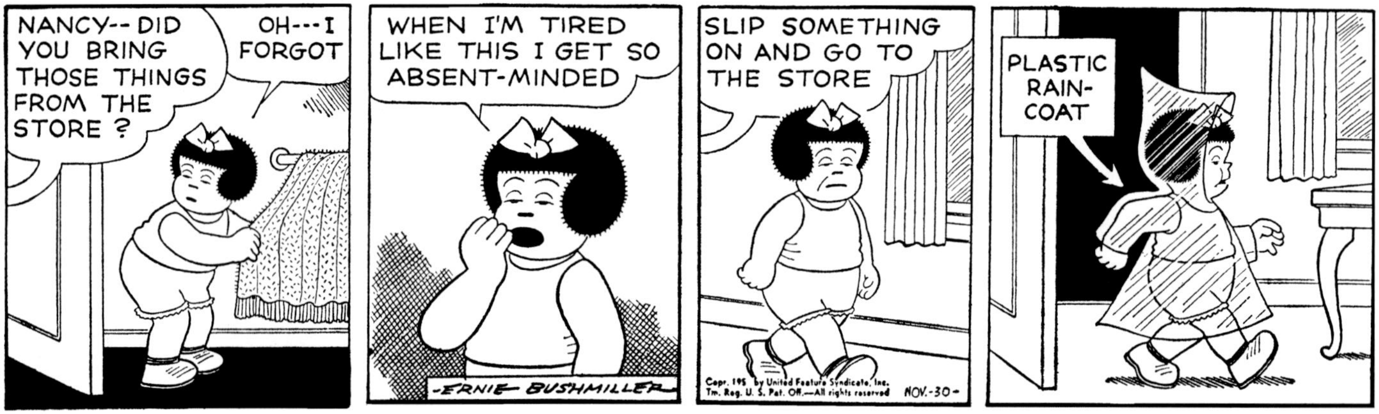
NANCY-- DID YOU BRING THOSE THINGS FROM THE STORE ?
OH---I FORGOT
WHEN I'M TIRED LIKE THIS I GET SO ABSENT-MINDED
-ERNIE BUSHMILLER
SLIP SOMETHING ON AND GO TO THE STORE
Copr. 195 by United Feature Syndicate, Inc. Tm. Reg. U. S. Pat. Off.—All rights reserved
NOV.-30-
PLASTIC RAIN-COAT

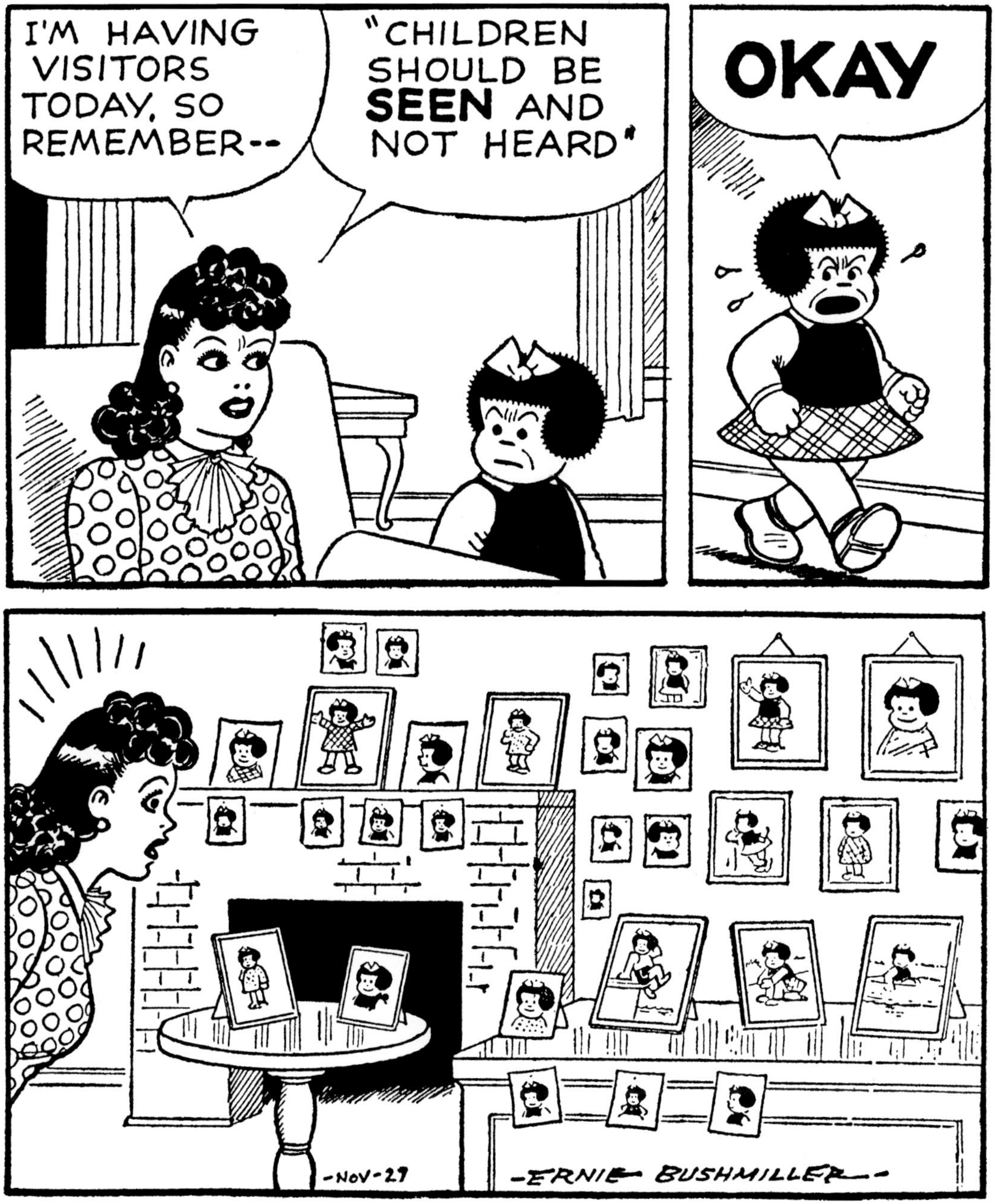
I'M HAVING VISITORS TODAY, SO REMEMBER--
"CHILDREN SHOULD BE **SEEN** AND NOT HEARD"
OKAY
-NOV-29
-ERNIE BUSHMILLER-

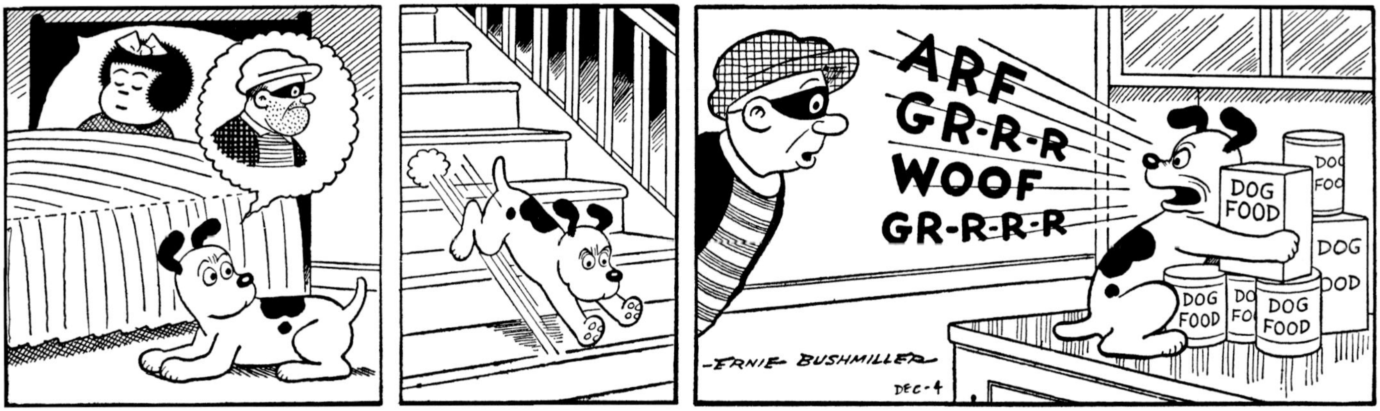
ARF
GR-R-R
WOOF
GR-R-R-R
DOG FOOD
DOG FOOD
DOG FOOD
-ERNIE BUSHMILLER
DEC-4

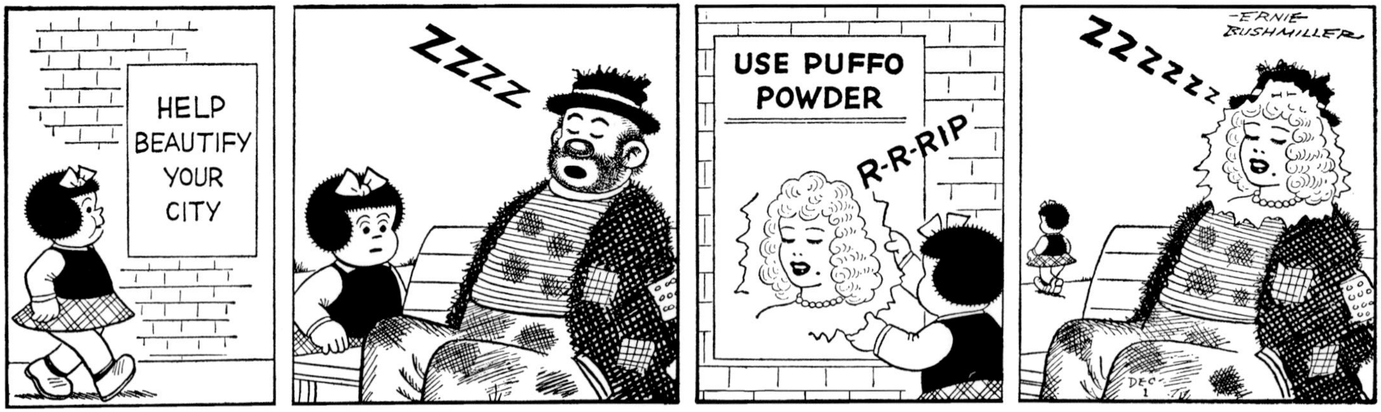
HELP BEAUTIFY YOUR CITY
ZZZZ
USE PUFFO POWDER
R-R-RIP
-ERNIE BUSHMILLER
ZZZZZZZ
DEC-1

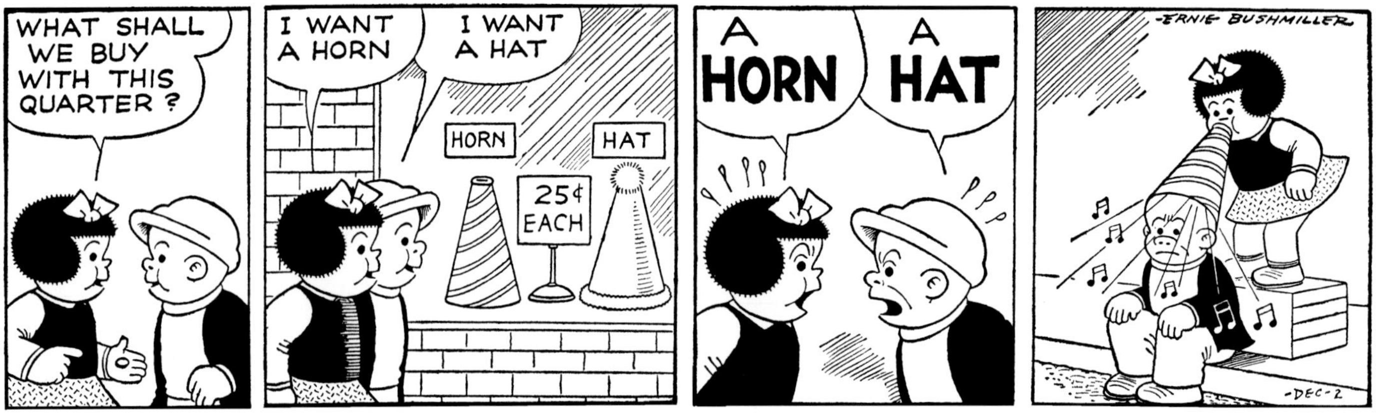
WHAT SHALL WE BUY WITH THIS QUARTER ?
I WANT A HORN
I WANT A HAT
HORN
HAT
25¢ EACH
A HORN
A HAT
-ERNIE BUSHMILLER
-DEC-2

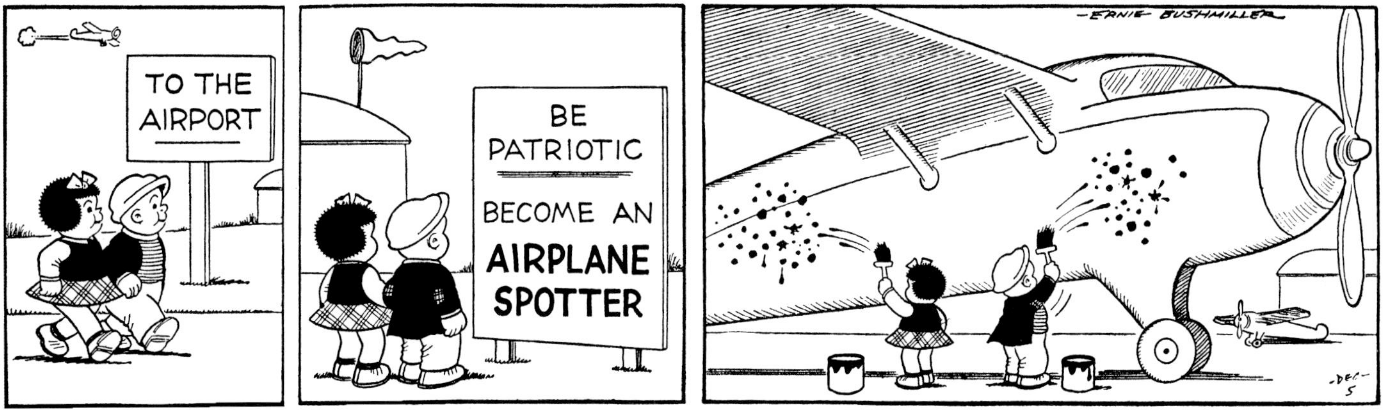
-ERNIE BUSHMILLER
TO THE AIRPORT
BE PATRIOTIC
BECOME AN AIRPLANE SPOTTER
-DEC-5

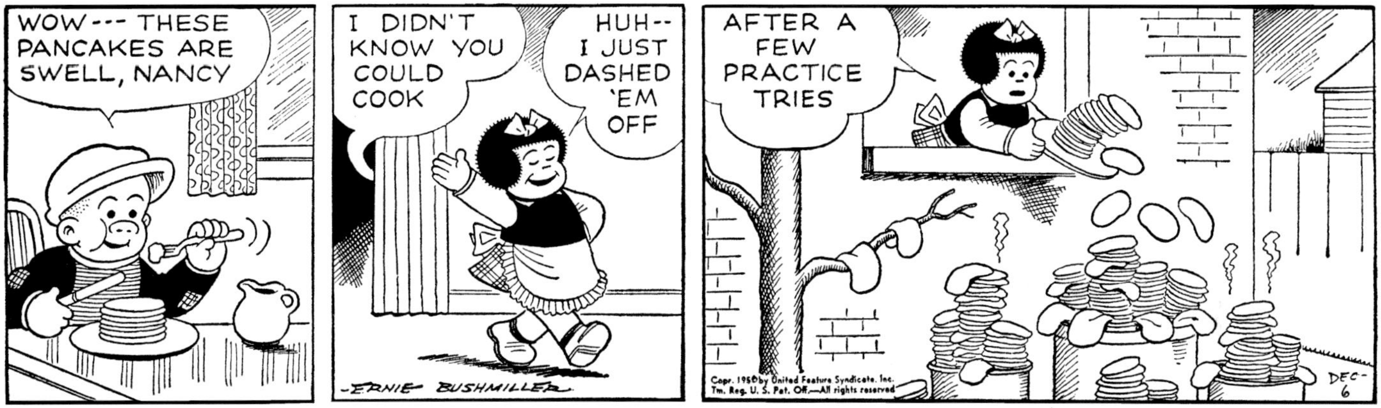
WOW--- THESE PANCAKES ARE SWELL, NANCY
I DIDN'T KNOW YOU COULD COOK
HUH-- I JUST DASHED 'EM OFF
-ERNIE BUSHMILLER
AFTER A FEW PRACTICE TRIES
Copr. 1950 by United Feature Syndicate, Inc.
Tm. Reg. U. S. Pat. Off.—All rights reserved
DEC-6

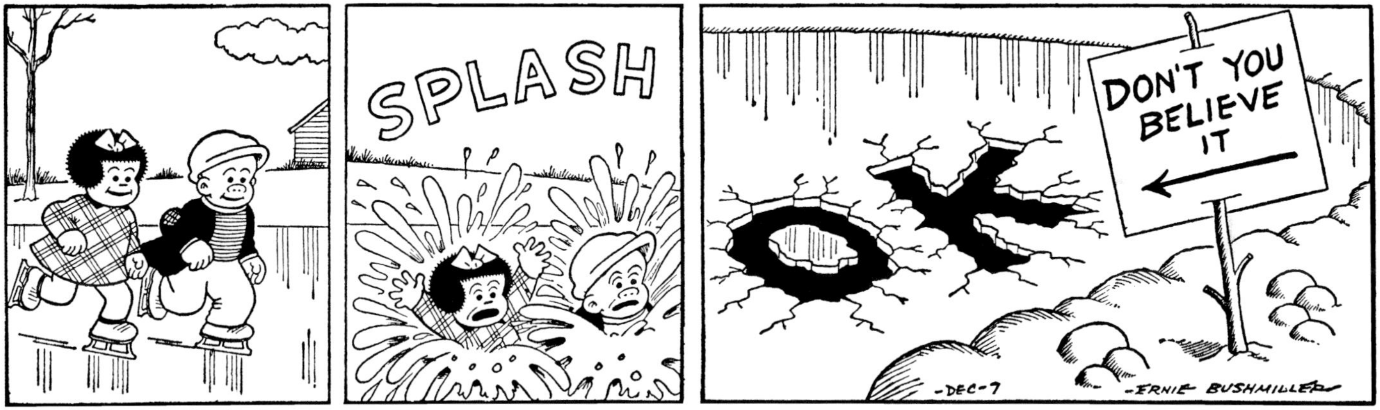
SPLASH
DON'T YOU BELIEVE IT
-DEC-7
-ERNIE BUSHMILLER

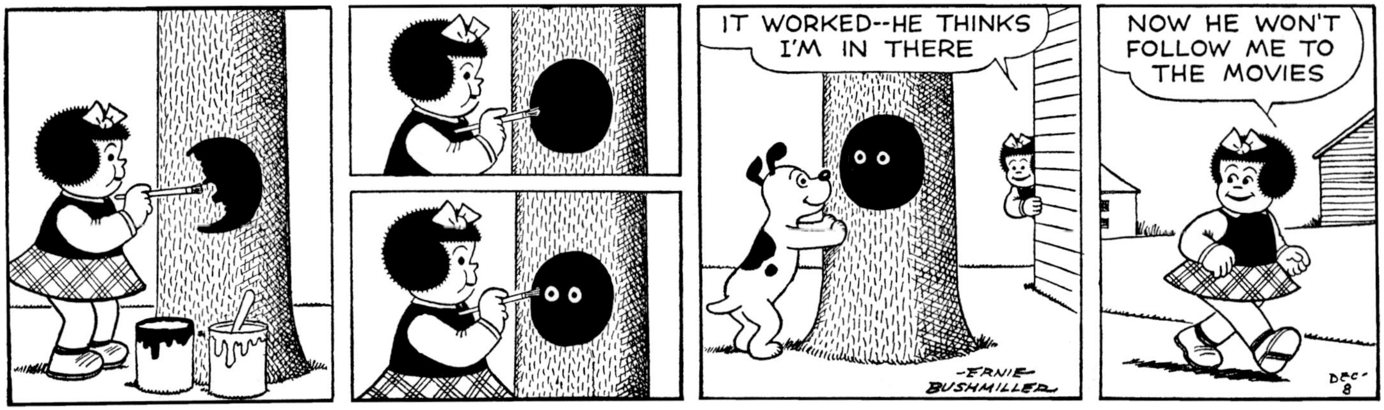
IT WORKED--HE THINKS I'M IN THERE
NOW HE WON'T FOLLOW ME TO THE MOVIES
-ERNIE BUSHMILLER
DEC-8

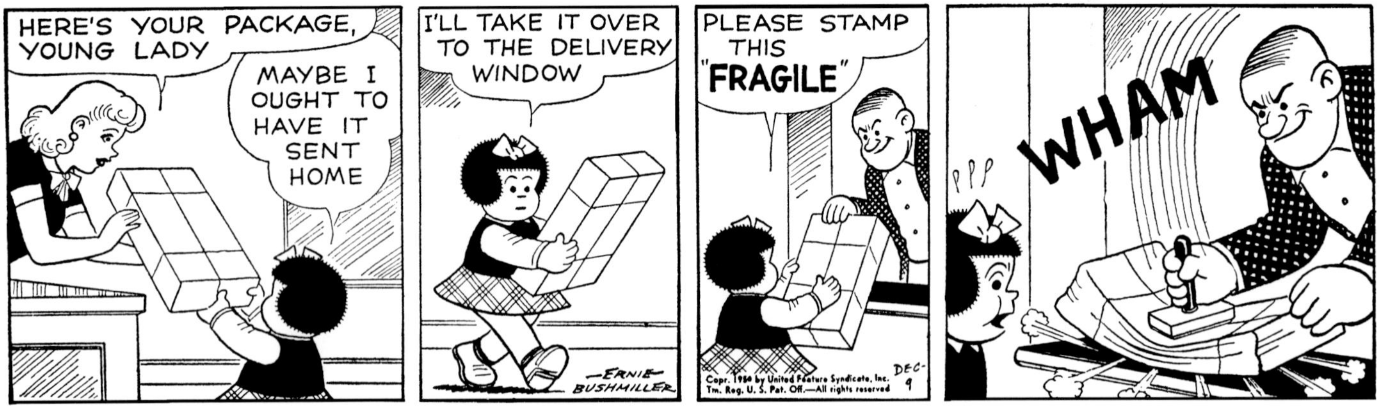
HERE'S YOUR PACKAGE, YOUNG LADY
MAYBE I OUGHT TO HAVE IT SENT HOME
I'LL TAKE IT OVER TO THE DELIVERY WINDOW
-ERNIE BUSHMILLER
PLEASE STAMP THIS "FRAGILE"
Copr. 1950 by United Feature Syndicate, Inc. Tm. Reg. U. S. Pat. Off.—All rights reserved
DEC-9
WHAM

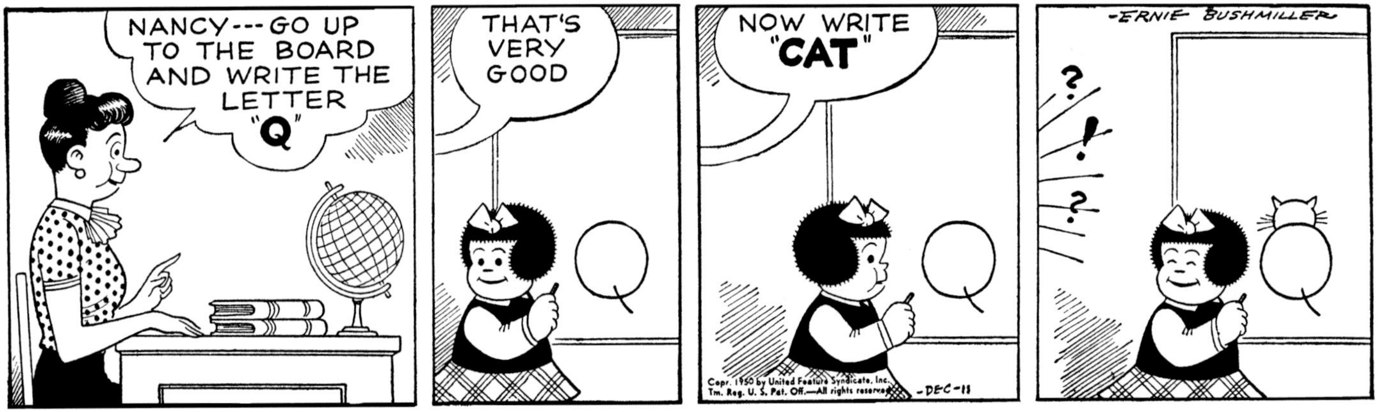
NANCY---GO UP TO THE BOARD AND WRITE THE LETTER "Q"
THAT'S VERY GOOD
NOW WRITE "CAT"
Copr. 1950 by United Feature Syndicate, Inc. Tm. Reg. U. S. Pat. Off.—All rights reserved
-DEC-11
-ERNIE BUSHMILLER
?
!
?

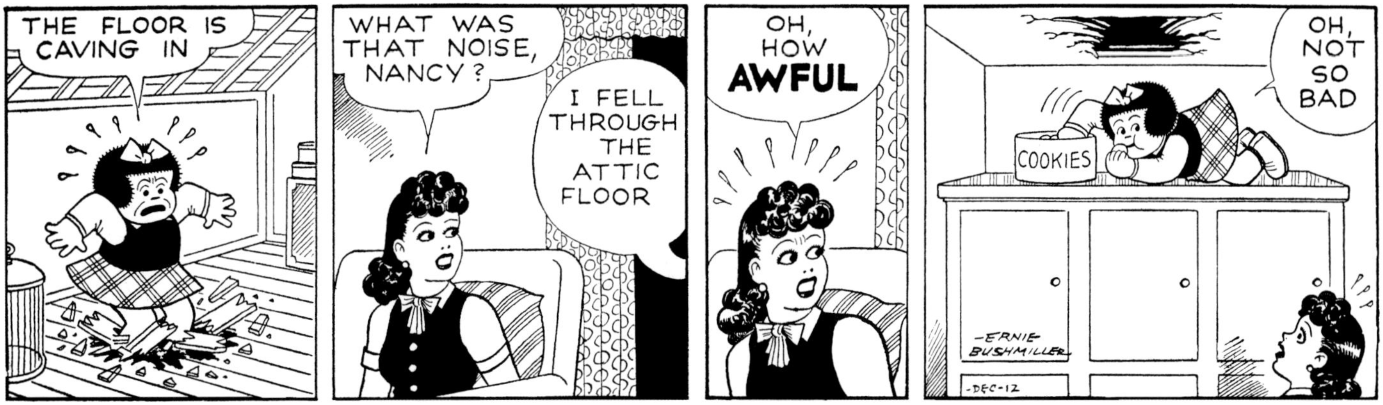
THE FLOOR IS CAVING IN
WHAT WAS THAT NOISE, NANCY?
I FELL THROUGH THE ATTIC FLOOR
OH, HOW **AWFUL**
OH, NOT SO BAD
COOKIES
-ERNIE BUSHMILLER
-DEC-12

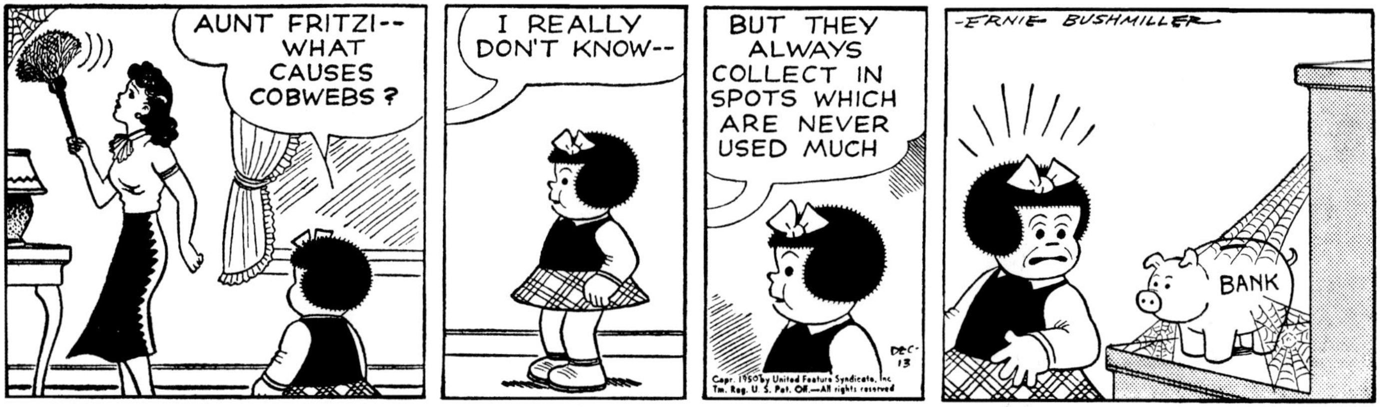
AUNT FRITZI-- WHAT CAUSES COBWEBS?
I REALLY DON'T KNOW--
BUT THEY ALWAYS COLLECT IN SPOTS WHICH ARE NEVER USED MUCH
DEC-13
Copr. 1950 by United Feature Syndicate, Inc. Tm. Reg. U. S. Pat. Off.—All rights reserved
-ERNIE BUSHMILLER
BANK

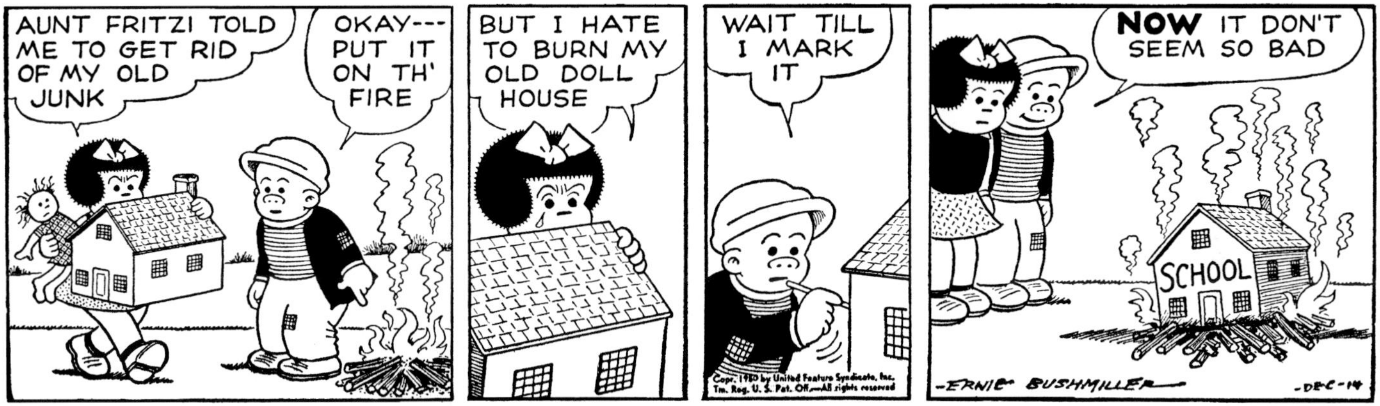
AUNT FRITZI TOLD ME TO GET RID OF MY OLD JUNK
OKAY--- PUT IT ON TH' FIRE
BUT I HATE TO BURN MY OLD DOLL HOUSE
WAIT TILL I MARK IT
Copr. 1950 by United Feature Syndicate, Inc. Tm. Reg. U. S. Pat. Off.—All rights reserved
NOW IT DON'T SEEM SO BAD
SCHOOL
-ERNIE BUSHMILLER
-DEC-14

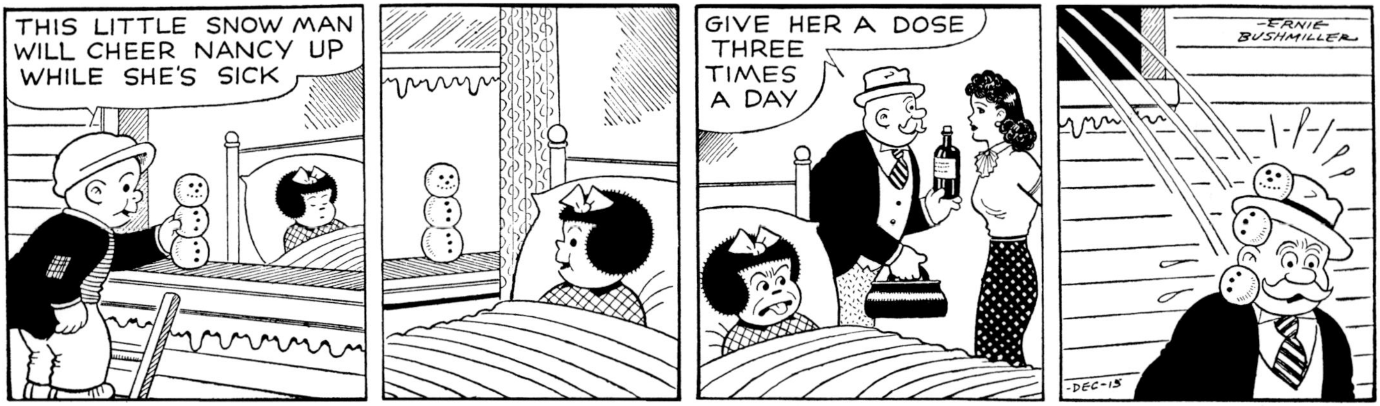
THIS LITTLE SNOW MAN WILL CHEER NANCY UP WHILE SHE'S SICK
GIVE HER A DOSE THREE TIMES A DAY
-ERNIE BUSHMILLER
-DEC-15

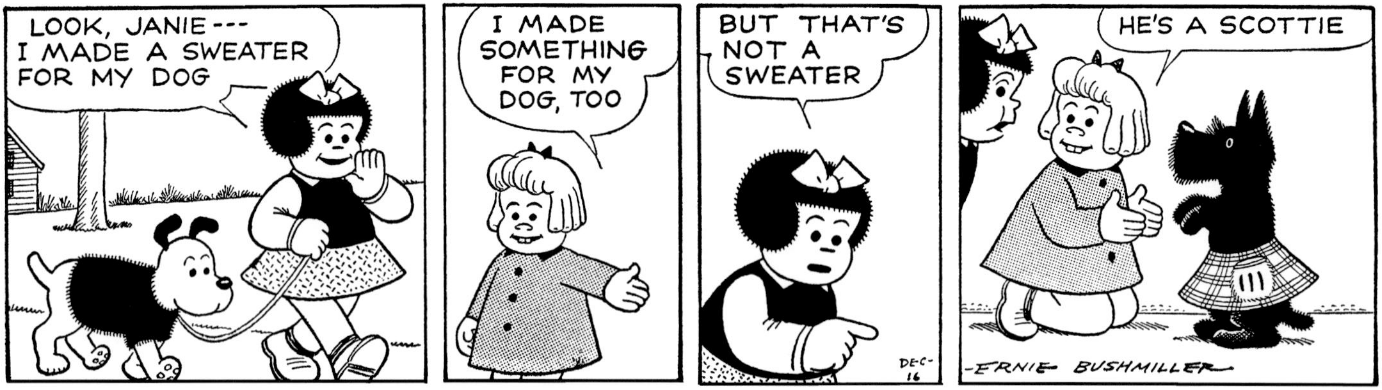
LOOK, JANIE--- I MADE A SWEATER FOR MY DOG
I MADE SOMETHING FOR MY DOG, TOO
BUT THAT'S NOT A SWEATER
DEC-16
HE'S A SCOTTIE
-ERNIE BUSHMILLER

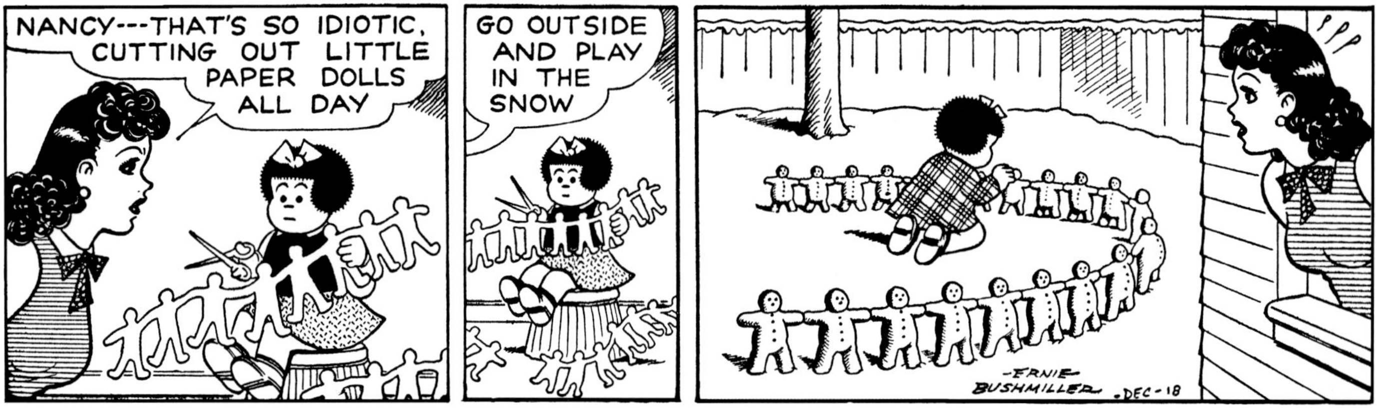
NANCY---THAT'S SO IDIOTIC, CUTTING OUT LITTLE PAPER DOLLS ALL DAY
GO OUTSIDE AND PLAY IN THE SNOW
-ERNIE BUSHMILLER
DEC-18

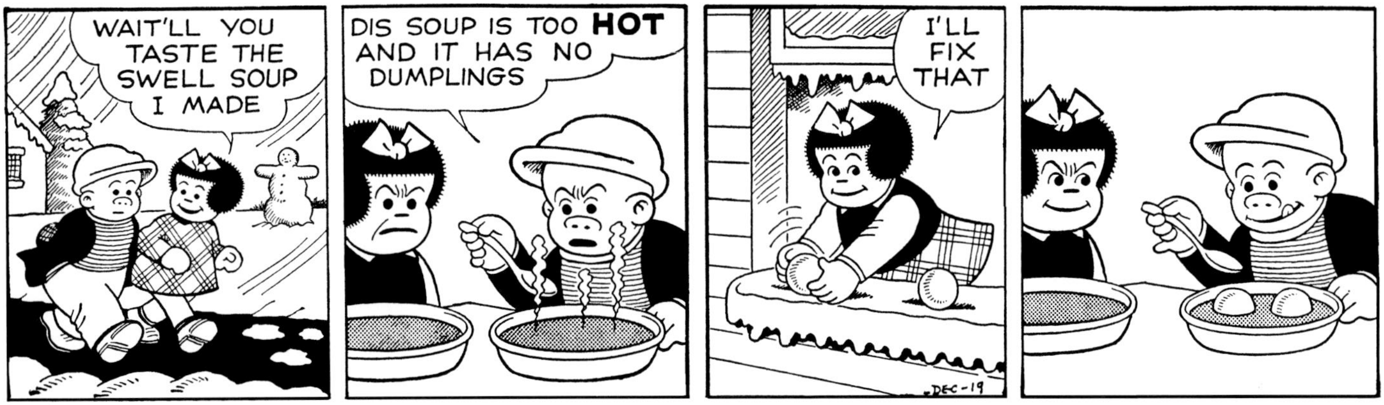
WAIT'LL YOU TASTE THE SWELL SOUP I MADE
DIS SOUP IS TOO **HOT** AND IT HAS NO DUMPLINGS
I'LL FIX THAT
DEC-19

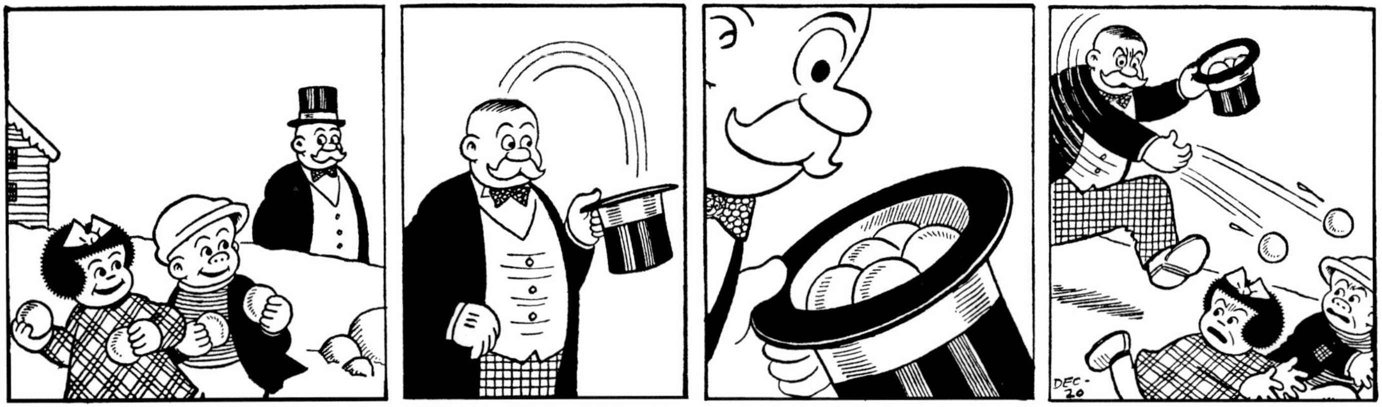
DEC-20

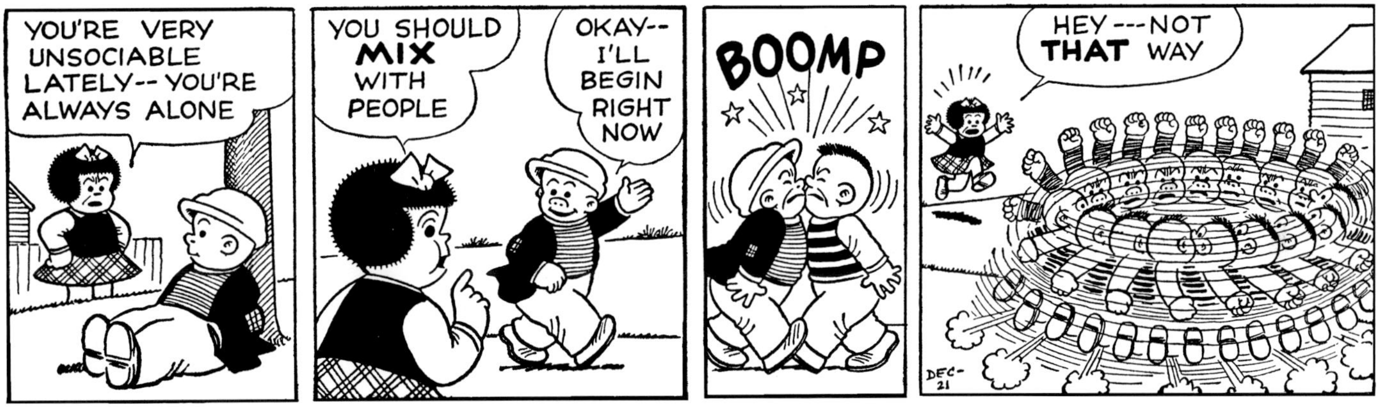
YOU'RE VERY UNSOCIABLE LATELY-- YOU'RE ALWAYS ALONE
YOU SHOULD **MIX** WITH PEOPLE
OKAY-- I'LL BEGIN RIGHT NOW
BOOMP
HEY---NOT **THAT** WAY
DEC-21

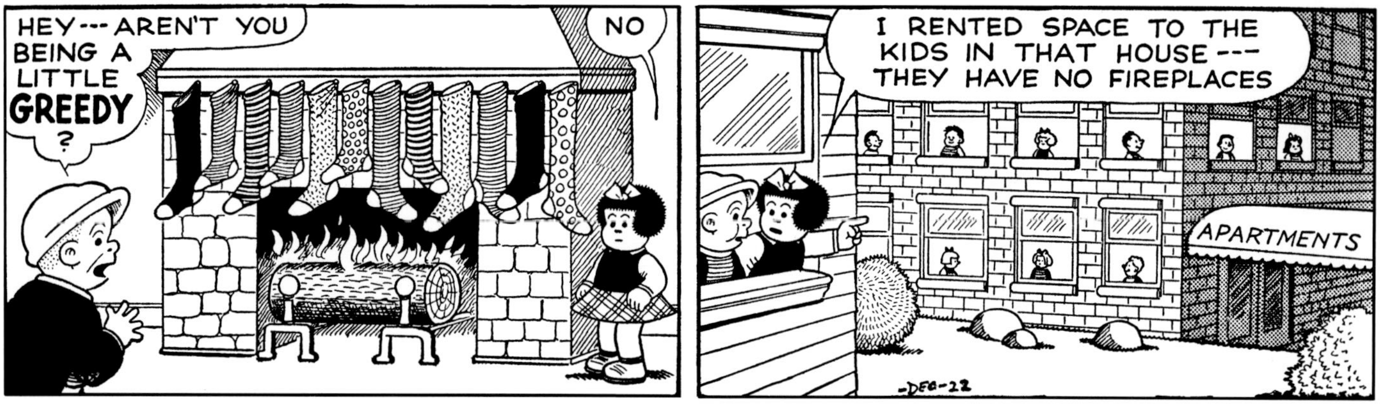
HEY--- AREN'T YOU BEING A LITTLE GREEDY ?
NO
I RENTED SPACE TO THE KIDS IN THAT HOUSE --- THEY HAVE NO FIREPLACES
APARTMENTS
DEC-22

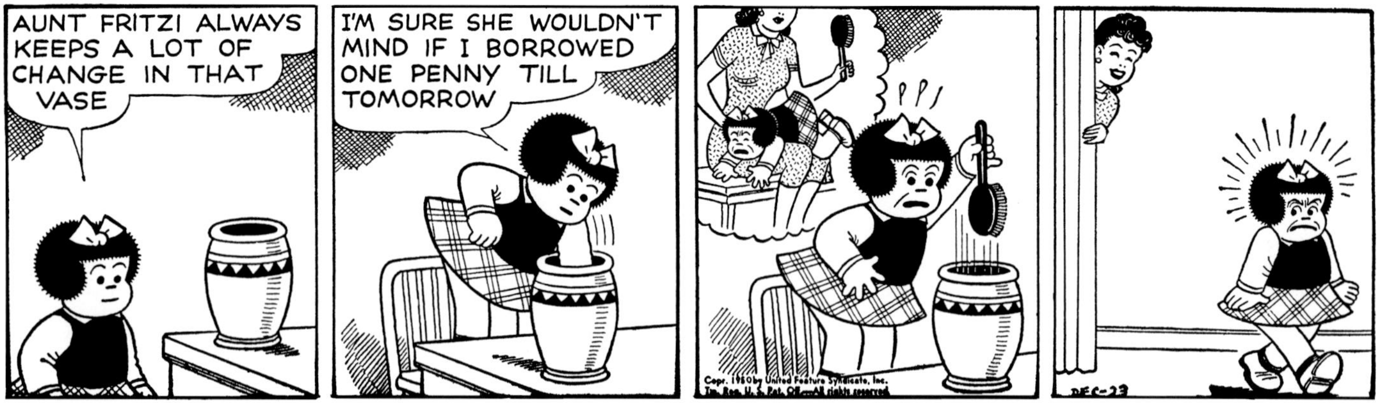
AUNT FRITZI ALWAYS KEEPS A LOT OF CHANGE IN THAT VASE
I'M SURE SHE WOULDN'T MIND IF I BORROWED ONE PENNY TILL TOMORROW
Copr. 1950 by United Feature Syndicate, Inc. Tm. Reg. U. S. Pat. Off.—All rights reserved
DEC-23

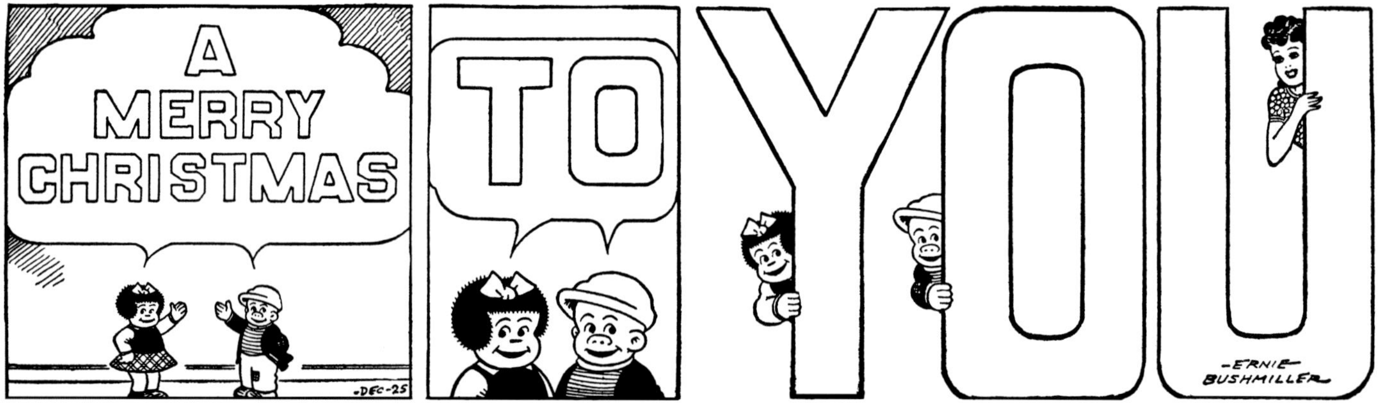
A MERRY CHRISTMAS
TO
YOU
DEC-25
ERNIE BUSHMILLER

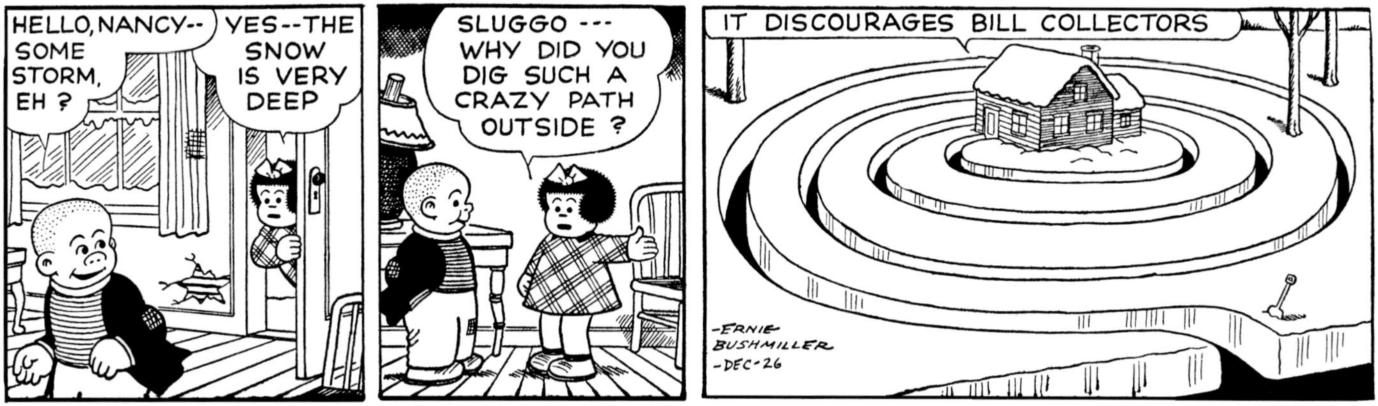
HELLO, NANCY-- SOME STORM, EH ?
YES--THE SNOW IS VERY DEEP
SLUGGO --- WHY DID YOU DIG SUCH A CRAZY PATH OUTSIDE ?
IT DISCOURAGES BILL COLLECTORS
-ERNIE BUSHMILLER
-DEC-26

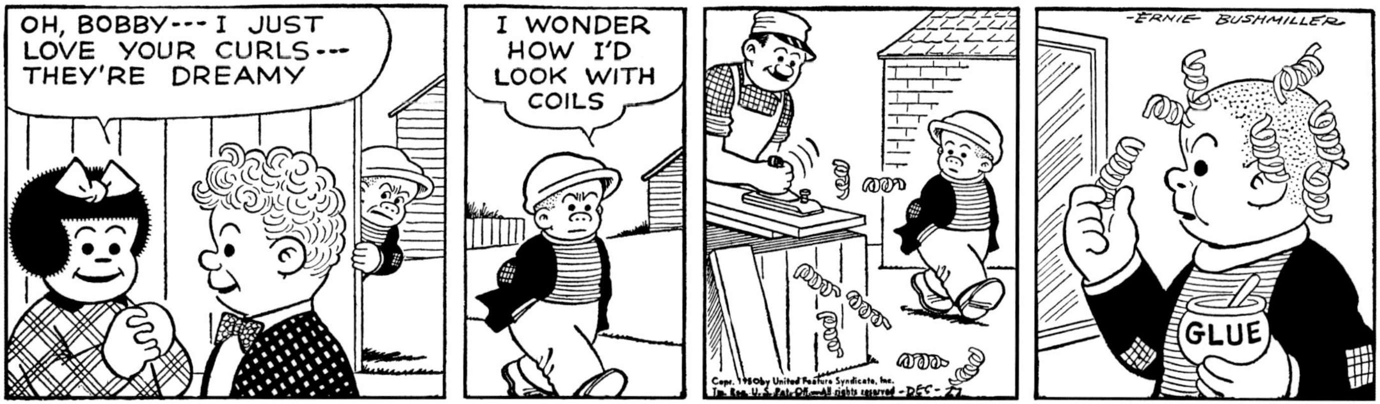
OH, BOBBY--- I JUST LOVE YOUR CURLS--- THEY'RE DREAMY
I WONDER HOW I'D LOOK WITH COILS
Copr. 1950 by United Feature Syndicate, Inc.
Tm. Reg. U.S. Pat. Off.—All rights reserved -DEC-27
-ERNIE BUSHMILLER
GLUE

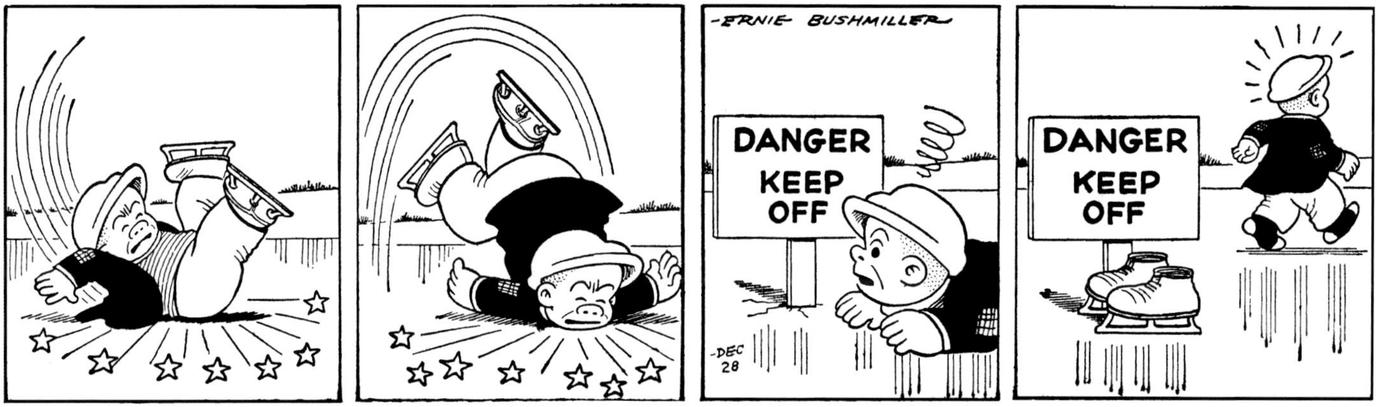
-ERNIE BUSHMILLER
DANGER KEEP OFF
-DEC 28
DANGER KEEP OFF

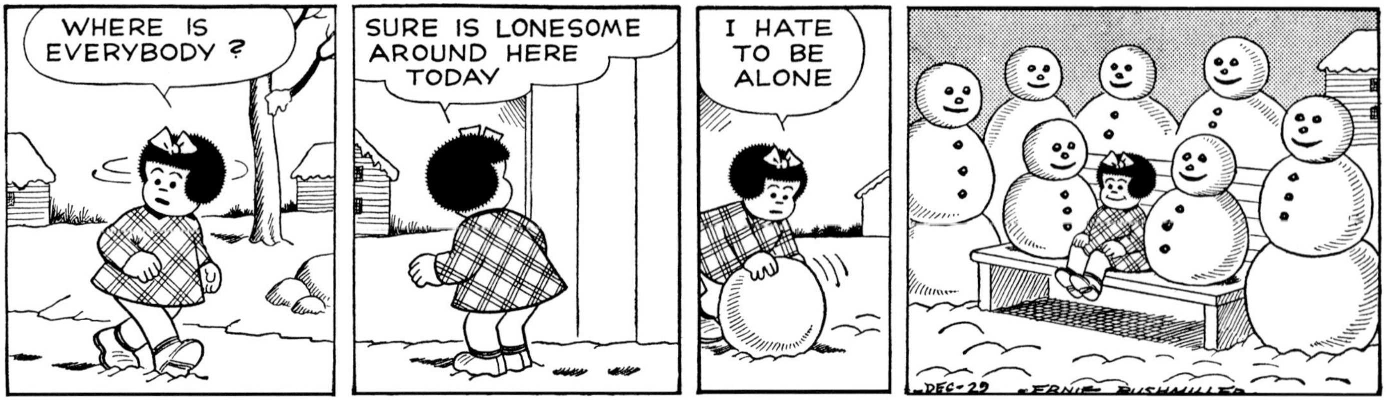
WHERE IS EVERYBODY ?
SURE IS LONESOME AROUND HERE TODAY
I HATE TO BE ALONE
DEC-29

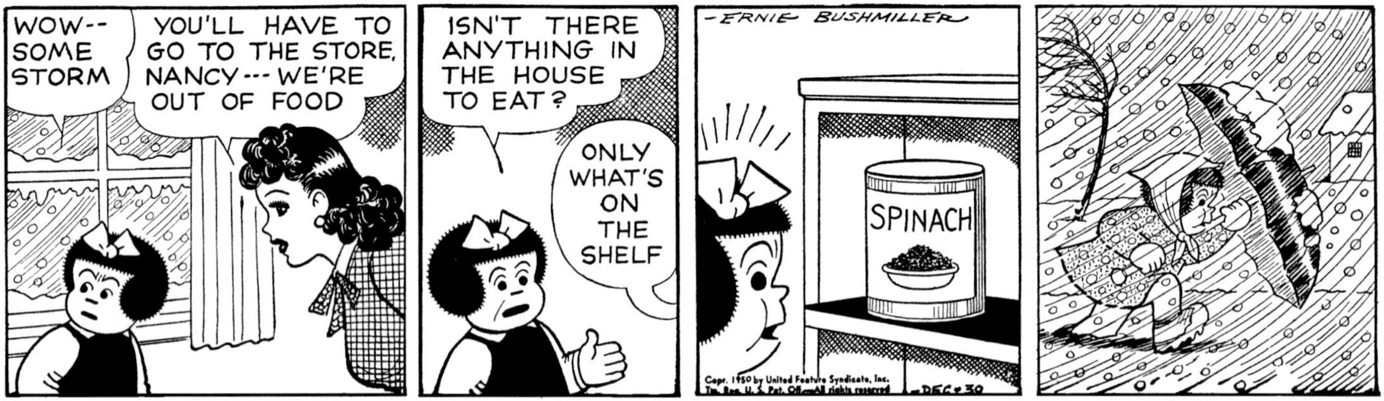
WOW-- SOME STORM
YOU'LL HAVE TO GO TO THE STORE, NANCY--- WE'RE OUT OF FOOD
ISN'T THERE ANYTHING IN THE HOUSE TO EAT ?
ONLY WHAT'S ON THE SHELF
ERNIE BUSHMILLER
SPINACH
Copr. 1950 by United Feature Syndicate, Inc.
DEC 30

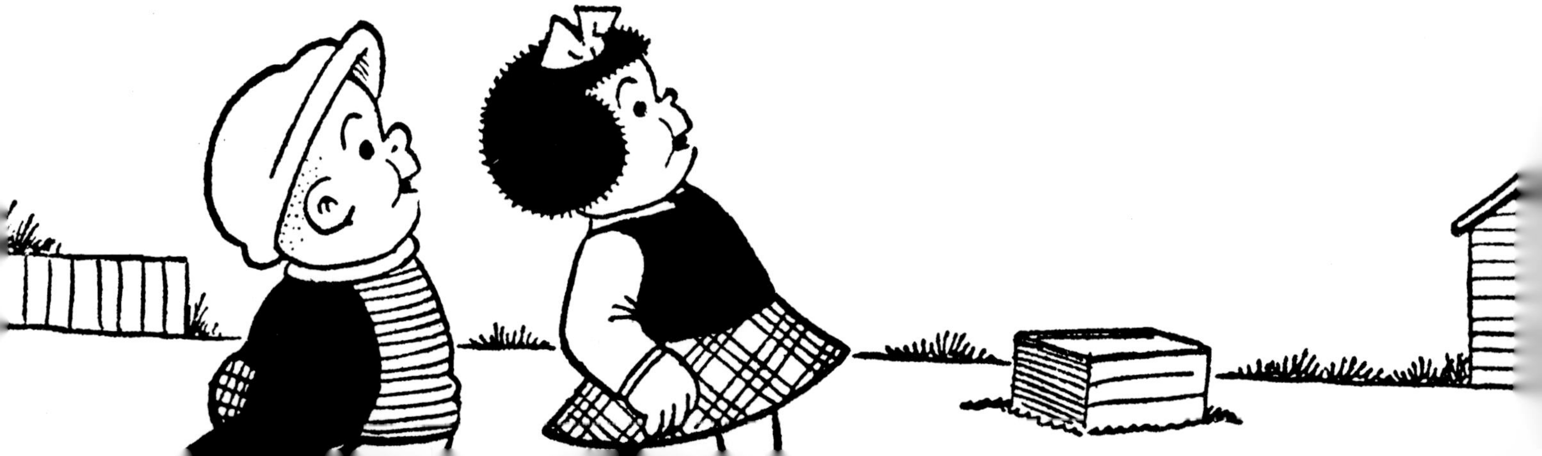

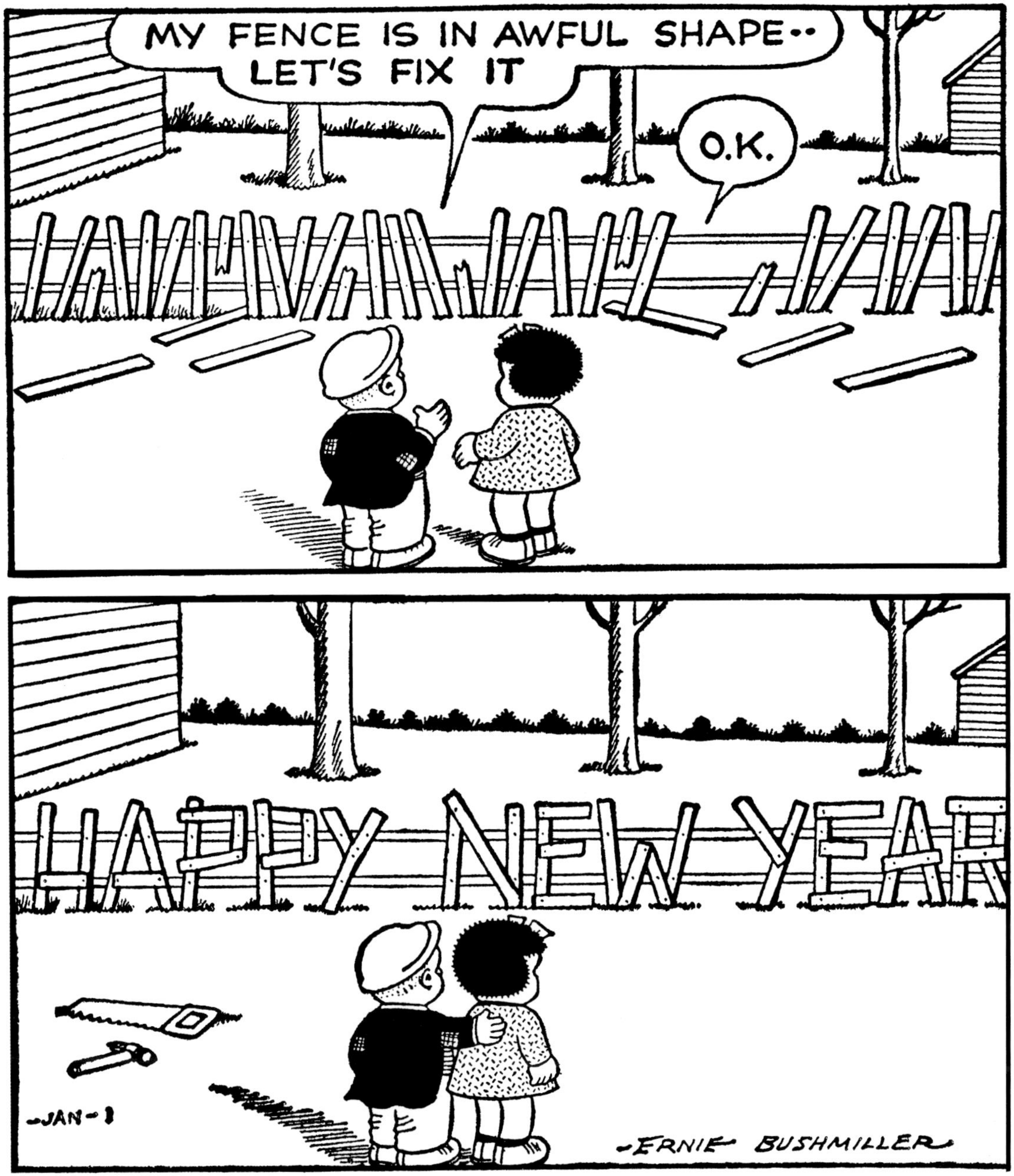
MY FENCE IS IN AWFUL SHAPE--
LET'S FIX IT
O.K.
HAPPY NEW YEAR
-JAN-1
-ERNIE BUSHMILLER

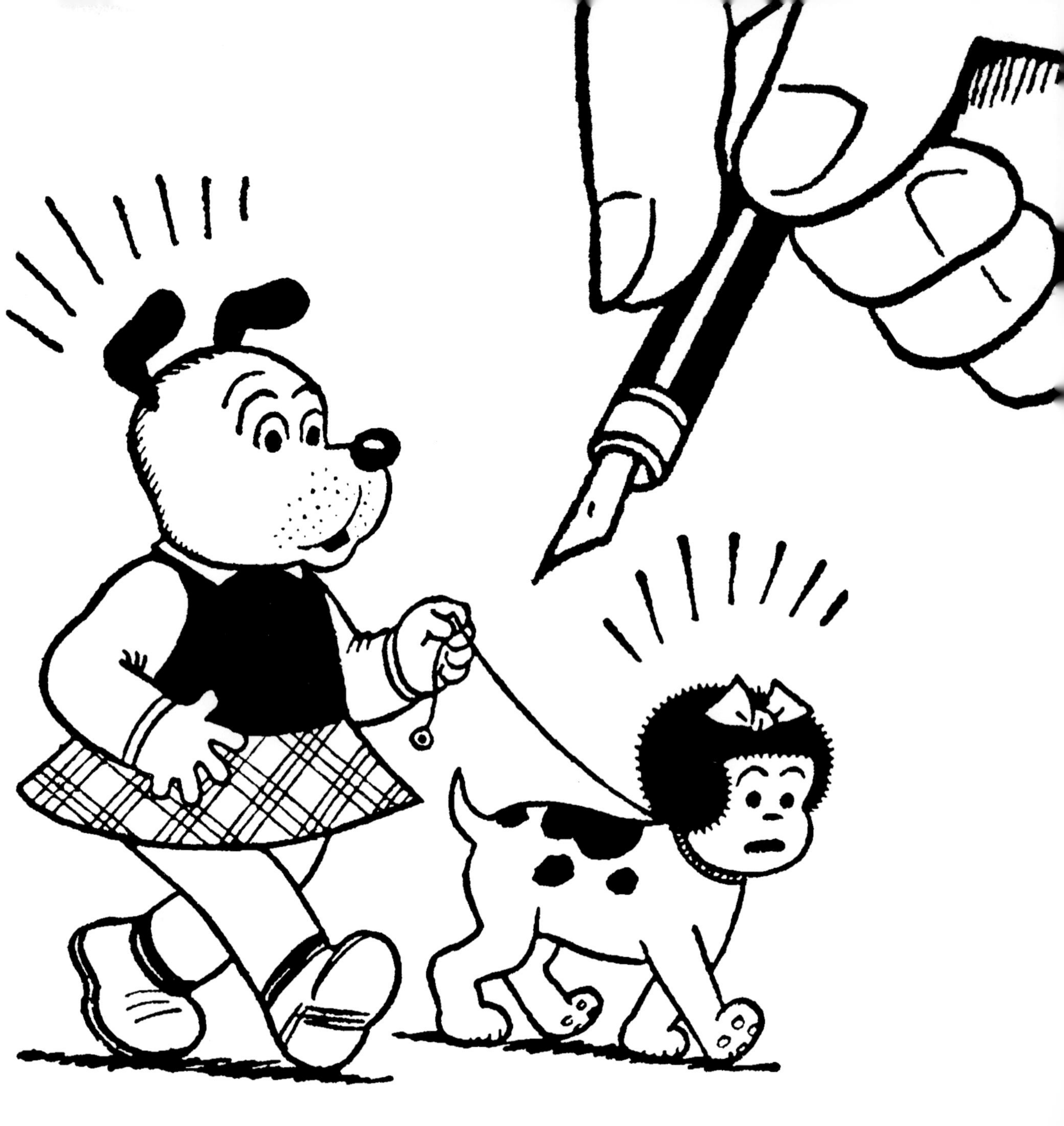

ERNIE & NANCY

Although Nancy's creator Ernie Bushmiller passed away at age 76, Nancy has been 8 years old for more than 90 years! Imagine that! When he created her in 1933, Ernie never figured he'd be drawing her every day for the next 50 years. "I planned to keep her for about a week and then dump her," he once said. "But the little dickens was soon stealing the show!"

And while Nancy continues to live on in the hands of other cartoonists, many years after Ernie's death in 1982, it is her creator's work that is still most closely identified with her strip and enjoyed by generations of readers, of all ages, and studied by historians and scholars despite Ernie's belief that his comics were for "the gum chewers" and not the "caviar eaters." Nancy the kid is wonderfully imperfect, but *Nancy* the comic strip is perfection in Ernie's hands. Every gag, every line, every patch of black ink makes for a chiseled diamond—one that'll make readers spit their gum or caviar out.

Nancy is an American icon. She's timeless. She's a meme. The world-famous artist Andy Warhol once painted her portrait. She's been on a postage stamp. To this day, when you look up "comic strip" in *The American Heritage Dictionary of the English Language*, it shows a *Nancy* comic by Bushmiller! As another famous cartoonist once put it, "It's easier to read a *Nancy* comic than it is to not read one." Who's lit now, Sluggo? ✳

FANTAGRAPHICS
www.fantagraphics.com
7563 Lake City Way NE
Seattle, Washington, 98115

Design: Kayla E.
Production: Paul Baresh & Ben Horak
VP / Associate Publisher / Editor: Eric Reynolds
President / Publisher: Gary Groth

Nancy is copyright © 2025 Scripps Licensing, Inc.
This edition of *Nancy Wears Hats* is copyright © 2025
Fantagraphics. All rights reserved. Fantagraphics and
the Fantagraphics logo are trademarks of Fantagraphics
Books Inc. This volume collects Ernie Bushmiller daily
Nancy newspaper comic strips from 1949–1950.

ISBN 979-8-8750-0101-7
Library of Congress Control No. 2024949615
First edition: June 2025
Printed in China

TO LEARN MORE ABOUT NANCY AND ERNIE BUSHMILLER, SLUGGO RECOMMENDS:

How To Read Nancy: The Elements of Comics in Three Easy Panels

By Paul Karasik & Mark Newgarden

The Nancy Show: Celebrating the Art of Ernie Bushmiller

Edited by Peter Maresca & Brian Walker